D-DR

D0472366

History (General)
History of Europe

Library of Congress Classification
2007

Prepared by the Cataloging Policy and Support Office
Library Services

LIBRARY OF CONGRESS
Cataloging Distribution Service
Washington, D.C.

This edition cumulates all additions and changes to Classes D-DR through Weekly List 2007/30, dated July 25, 2007. Additions and changes made subsequent to that date are published in weekly lists posted on the World Wide Web at

<http://www.loc.gov/aba/cataloging/classification/weeklylists/>

and are also available in *Classification Web*, the online Web-based edition of the Library of Congress Classification.

Library of Congress Cataloging-in-Publication Data

Library of Congress.
    Library of Congress classification. D-DR. History (general). History of Europe / prepared by the Cataloging Policy and Support Office, Library Services. — 2007 ed.
        p. cm.
    Rev. ed. of: Library of Congress classification. D-DR. History (general) and history of Europe. 2001 ed.
    "This edition cumulates all additions and changes to Classes D-DR through Weekly list 2007/30, dated July 25, 2007. Additions and changes made subsequent to that date are published in weekly lists posted on the World Wide Web ... and are also available in Classification Web, the online Web-based edition of the Library of Congress Classification"—T.p. verso.
    Includes index.
    ISBN-13: 978-0-8444-1178-1
    ISBN-10: 0-8444-1178-7
    1. Classification—Books—History. 2. Classification—Books—Europe. 3. Classification, Library of Congress. I. Library of Congress. Cataloging Policy and Support Office. II. Library of Congress. Library of Congress classification. D-DR. History (general) and history of Europe. III. Title. IV. Title: History (general). V. Title: History of Europe.
    Z696.U5D25 2007   025.4'69—dc22   2007039934

For sale by the Library of Congress Cataloging Distribution Service,
101 Independence Avenue, S.E., Washington, DC 20541-4912.
Product catalog available on the Web at **www.loc.gov/cds**.

PREFACE

Class D, *History*, was first drafted in 1901 and after undergoing revision was published in 1916. Two supplements were published: *European War* (first edition, 1921; second edition, 1933; reprinted in 1954 with additions and changes) and *Second World War* (1947). The second edition of class D was published in 1959, containing additions and changes through June 1957. A reprint edition was published in 1966, containing a supplementary section of additions and changes through July 1965. The third edition was published in five parts between 1987 and 1990: D-DJ, DJK-DK, DL-DR, DS, and DT-DX. Subclasses D-DR, *History (General) and History of Europe*, were published in a single edition in 2001, complementing a 1998 edition of DS-DX. This 2007 edition of D-DR cumulates all additions and changes that have been made since the publication of the 2001 edition.

Access to the online version of the full Library of Congress Classification is available on the World Wide Web by subscription to *Classification Web*. Details about ordering and pricing may be obtained from the Cataloging Distribution Service at

<http://www.loc.gov/cds/>

New or revised numbers and captions are added to the L.C. Classification schedules as a result of development proposals made by the cataloging staff of the Library of Congress and cooperating institutions. Upon approval of these proposals by the weekly editorial meeting of the Cataloging Policy and Support Office, new classification records are created or existing records are revised in the master classification database. Weekly lists of newly approved or revised classification numbers and captions are posted on the World Wide Web at

<http://www.loc.gov/aba/cataloging/classification/weeklylists/>

Lynn El-Hoshy, senior cataloging policy specialist in the Cataloging Policy and Support Office, is responsible for coordinating the overall intellectual and editorial content of class D and its various subclasses. Kent Griffiths, assistant editor, creates new classification records and their associated index terms, and maintains the master database.

Barbara B. Tillett, Chief
Cataloging Policy and Support Office

August 2007

OUTLINE

OUTLINE

OUTLINE

History of France
History
By period
Modern, 1515- - Continued
20th century

OUTLINE

OUTLINE

OUTLINE

OUTLINE

History of Balkan Peninsula
Turkey
History - Continued

	History (General)
	Including Europe (General)
	For individual counties, see the country
1	Periodicals. Societies. Serials
2	Yearbooks. Registers
	Museums, exhibitions, etc.
2.5	General
2.514.A-Z	Individual. By place, A-Z
	Congresses, conferences, etc.
	International Congress of Historical Sciences
3.A15-.A19	Serials
3.A2	Reports. By date
3.A22	Works about the I.C.H.S.
3.A3A-.A3Z	Other international, A-Z
3.A4-Z	By region or country, A-Z
5	Sources and documents
5.5	Minor. Source books
	Collected works (Monographs, essays, etc.). Festschriften
6	Several authors
7	Individual authors
8	Pamphlets, etc.
9	Dictionaries
10	Minor reference books (Anecdotes, curiosa, allusions, etc.)
11	Chronological tables, etc.
11.5	Special
	Including books of days, dates, etc., famous events throughout the calendar year, etc.
	Historical atlases
	General see G1030+
12	Pictorial atlases
	Historiography
	For historiography of the history of individual countries, see DA-DU
13	General works
13.2	Criticism and reviews
13.5.A-Z	By region or country, A-Z
	Biography of historians
14	Collective
15.A-Z	Individual, A-Z
	e.g.
15.A25	Acton, John Emerich E.D.A., Baron
15.B8	Burckhardt, Jakob Christoph
15.R3	Ranke, Leopold von
15.R6	Roscoe, William
15.R7	Rotteck, Karl Wenzeslaus R., von
	Methodology. Relation to other sciences
	Cf. D56+ Methodology in ancient history

World histories -- Continued

21.1	Pictorial works
21.3	General special
21.5	Historical geography
22	History of several countries treated together
23	General popular works
23.5	Comic and satirical works
24	Historical events not restricted to one country or period

          Including disasters as historic events
          For specific disasters treated as historic events in individual
             countries, see the country in DA-F

24.5	Other

          For great cities of the world see G140
          For folklore and history see GR41

Military history
     Including Europe
     For individual countries, see DA-DU

25.A2	Dictionaries. Chronological tables, etc.
25.A3-Z	General works
25.5	General special
25.9	Pamphlets, etc.
27	Naval history

     Including Europe
     For individual countries, see DA-DU

Political and diplomatic history
     Including Europe

31	General works

        Including Europe

32	General special
33	Pamphlets, etc.
34.A-Z	Relations between Europe and individual countries, A-Z

        For relations between Europe and individual countries
           limited to 1945- see D1065.A+

Biography (Collective)
     General works
        see CT
     Rulers, kings see D107

Ancient history
     Including Europe
     For individual countries, see DA-DU

51	Periodicals. Societies. Serials
52	Sources and documents

Collected works

53.A2	Several authors
53.A3-Z	Individual authors
54	Dictionaries
54.5	Chronological tables, etc.

Ancient history -- Continued
55   Biography (Collective)
                               Cf. D107 Rulers, kings, etc.
                               Cf. DE7 Classical antiquity
                          Historiography. Methodology
56   General works
                          Biography of historians
56.5   Collective
56.52.A-Z   Individual, A-Z
                               e.g.
56.52.H45   Herodotus
                          General works
                               Cf. DS62.2+ Ancient Orient
                               To 1525 see D17
57   1525-
58   Works by classical historians
                               e.g., Diodorus, Herodotus, Polybius
                               At the Library of Congress the distinction in use between
                                  Classes D and PA in classifying works by ancient Greek
                                  and Roman historians, as well as criticism and
                                  commentaries on such works, is as follows: In Class D: (1)
                                  Translations with or without original text, except translations
                                  into Latin (PA) (2) Criticism and commentaries (with or
                                  without the original text), if substantive in nature, i.e.,
                                  dealing primarily with the historical events discussed by the
                                  original author. In Class PA: (1) Original Greek and Latin
                                  texts (except as noted above) (2) Latin translations (3)
                                  Philological or textual criticism and commentaries (with or
                                  without the original text) (4) Commentaries specifically
                                  designed for use in conjunction with the original text
59   Compends. Textbooks. Outlines. Syllabi. Questions
60   Addresses, essays, lectures
62   General special
                          Earliest history. Dawn of history
                               Cf. DS62.2+ Ancient history
                               Cf. GN803+ Prehistoric antiquities in western Europe
65   General works
70   Celts. Celtic antiquities
                               For Celts in the Balkan Peninsula see DR39.3
                               Cf. CB206 Celtic culture
                               Cf. GN549.C3 Celtic race (Anthropology
                          General classical antiquity. Ancient nations
                               Including manners and customs, etc.
                               For archaeology see CC1+
                               For Greek and Roman antiquities see DE46
78   Early works through 1700
80   1701-

Ancient history

    Earliest history. Dawn of history -- Continued

85.A-Z	Special topics, A-Z
85.B7	Bow and arrow
90.A-Z	Ancient peoples not limited to one country, A-Z

        Cf. D135+ Migrations of peoples

        Dacians see DR239.2

        Illyrians see DR39.5

        Saka see DS328.4.S35

95	Naval history

Medieval and modern history, 476-

    Including Europe

    For individual countries, see DA-DU

    Periodicals. Societies. Serials see D1

    Yearbooks. Registers see D2

101	Sources and documents

        For collections of treaties of peace, alliance, and confederation see KZ184+

        For individual treaties and related legal materials of war, peace, and alliance to ca. 1900 see KZ1328+

101.2	Minor collections
101.5	Dictionaries. Albums
101.7	Chronological tables, etc.
102	General works

    Early see D17

103	Compends. Textbooks. Outlines. Syllabi. Questions
104	General special
104.5	Military history
105	Political and diplomatic history

    Pamphlets see D8

Biography and memoirs

106	Collective
107	Rulers, kings, etc.

      Including works covering ancient and modern rulers

107.3	Queens. Women rulers. Women heads of state

      Including female consorts

107.5	Princes and princesses
107.6	Claimants to royalty. Pretenders
107.7	Favorites
107.9	Houses, noble families, etc.
108	Public men
109	Women
110	Other special classes
110.5	Other

Medieval history

    Including Europe

    For individual countries, see DA-DU

	Medieval history -- Continued
111	Periodicals. Societies. Serials
113	Sources and documents. Collections. Chronicles
113.5	Minor collections
114	Dictionaries
115	Biography (Collective)
	Historiography
116	General works
	Biography of historians
116.5	Collective
116.7.A-Z	Individual, A-Z
	General works
117.A2	Early
	For chronicles see D113
117.A3-Z	Modern
118	Compends. Textbooks. Outlines. Syllabi. Questions
119	Addresses, essays, lectures
	By period
121-123	Early to 10th century
121	General works
123	9th-10th centuries
	Later see D135+
125	Antiquities
(127)	Social life and customs
	see GT120
	Civilization see CB351+
128	Military and naval history
	Political history and institutions
	Including feudalism
	For theory see JC109+
131	General works
(133)	Church and state
	see BV629+
134	The medieval city
	Cf. HT115 Urban communities
	Cf. JS61 Local government
	Migrations
135	General works
137	Goths (General). Visigoths
	Cf. DG506+ Gothic Kingdom in Italy, 489-553
	Cf. DP96 Visigoths in Spain, 414-711
138	Ostrogoths
139	Vandals
	Cf. DT171 Vandals in North Africa, 439-534
	Huns. Attila
	Cf. DB927+ History of Hungary to 1301
141	General works

Medieval history
Crusades
Third crusade, 1189-1193 -- Continued
163.5.A-Z   Part taken by individual countries, A-Z
Fourth crusade, 1196-1198; 1204-1219
Including the siege of Constantinople, 1203-1204
164.A2   Sources
164.A3   Memoirs and contemporary accounts
Class here text of Villehardouin's Conquête de
Constantinople
For biography and criticism see PQ1545.V475
164.A4-Z   General works
164.3   Pamphlets, etc.
164.5.A-Z   Part taken by individual countries, A-Z
165   Fifth crusade, 1217-1221
Including the siege of Damietta, 1218-1219
166   Sixth crusade, 1228-1229
166.5   Crusade, 1239-1241. Baron's Crusade, 1239-1241
167   Seventh crusade, 1248-1250
168   Eighth crusade, 1270
169   Children's crusade, 1212
Later crusades in the 13th, 14th, and 15th centuries.
Crusades in the east
171   General works
172   General special
173   Crusades in the west
Latin Kingdom of Jerusalem. Latin Orient. 1099-1291
Cf. DF610+ Latin Empire, 1204-1261 (Greece)
175   Periodicals. Societies. Serials
176   Sources and documents
177   Chronicles
Collected works
178   Several authors
179   Individual authors
Biography, memoirs, journals
Cf. D156 Memoirs of the crusades
180   Collective
181.A-Z   Individual, A-Z
e.g.
181.P5   Philippe, of Novara
General works
Chronicles see D177
182.A2   Early through 1800
182.A3-Z   1801-
183   General special
Individual rulers
183.3   Godfrey of Bouillon, 1099

	Medieval history
	Latin Kingdom of Jerusalem. Latin Orient. 1099-1291
	Individual rulers -- Continued
183.5	Baldwin I, 1100-1118
183.7	Baldwin II, 1118-1131
183.9	Foulque, 1131-1143
184	Baldwin III, 1143-1162
184.3	Amalric I, 1162-1174
184.4	Baldwin IV, 1174-1183
184.5	Baldwin V, 1183-1192
184.7	Guy of Lusignan, 1186-1192
184.75	Sibyl, Queen of Jerusalem, 1186-1190
184.8	Conquest of Jerusalem by Saladin, 1187
184.9	Conrad of Montferrat, 1192
185	Henry I (II of Champagne), 1192-1197
185.3	Amalric II, 1197-1205
185.5	Mary, 1205-1210
185.7	John of Brienne, 1210-1225
186	Frederick II, 1225-1250
186.3	Conrad IV, 1250-1254
186.5	Conradin, 1254-1268
	Cf. DD147.5.C64 Biography
	Cf. DG847.166 Kingdom of the two Sicilies
187	Hugh I (III of Cyprus), 1269-1284
187.3	John, 1284-1285
187.5	Henry II, 1285-1291
	Local
190	Edessa
192	Antioch
194	Tripoli
195.A-Z	Other, A-Z
	e.g.
195.S9	Syria
	Cf. DS97+ Medieval Syria, 638-1517
(198-199.7)	Arab (Islamic) Empire
	see DS36.85+, DS38.14+
	Later medieval. 11th-15th centuries
200	General works
	11th-12th centuries
201	General works
	11th century
201.3	Sources and documents. Contemporary works
201.4	General works
	12th century
201.7	Sources and documents. Contemporary works
201.8	General works
	13th-15th centuries

	Medieval history
	Later medieval. 11th-15th centuries
	13th-15th centuries -- Continued
202	General works
	13th century
202.3	Sources and documents. Contemporary works
202.4	General works
	14th century
202.7	Sources and documents. Contemporary works
202.8	General works
203	15th century
	Modern history, 1453-
	Including Europe
	For individual countries, see DA+
	Periodicals. Societies. Serials see D1
	Yearbooks. Registers see D2
	Sources and documents see D5
(204)	Collected works
	see D6+
205	Dictionaries
	Biography see D106
206	Historiography
208	General works
209	Compends. Textbooks. Outlines
210	General special. Addresses, essays, lectures
(211)	Social life and customs
	see GT129
213	Pamphlets, etc.
214	Military history
215	Naval history
217	Political and diplomatic history. European concert. Balance of power
	1453-1648
	Including 16th century
	Cf. BR300+ Reformation
	Cf. CB361+ Renaissance
219	Periodicals. Serials
220	Sources and documents
221.A-Z	Reports and communications of ambassadors, etc.
	By accrediting country, A-Z
	Collected works
223	Several authors
224	Individual authors
	Biography and memoirs
226	Collective
226.3	Women
226.6	Military and naval

Modern history, 1453-
1601-1715. 17th century
Thirty Years' War, 1618-1648 -- Continued

267.A-Z	Special events, battles, etc., A-Z
	e.g.
267.B3	Bergen op Zoom, Siege of, 1622
267.B8	Brünn, Siege of, 1645
(267.E3)	Edict of Restitution, 1629
	see KZ1330.7.E3
267.F85	Freiburg i. B., Battle of, 1644
267.H2	Hameln, Siege of, 1633
267.H3	Heilbronn, Union of, 1633
267.J3	Jankau, Battle of, 1645
267.L3	Leipzig, Battle of, 1631
267.M2	Magdeburg, Siege and sack of, 1631
267.N7	Nördlingen, Battle of, 1634
267.N8	Nördlingen, Battle of, 1645
267.O6	Oldendorf, Battle of, 1633
267.R3	Ratisbon, Electoral Assembly of, 1630
267.R6	Rocroi, Battle of, 1643
267.S8	Stralsund, Siege of, 1628
267.U6	Ulm, Truce of, 1647
	For legal works, including texts of the treaty and
	related documents see KZ1330.9
267.W4	Weisser Berg, Battle of, 1620
267.W6	Wittstock, Battle of, 1636
269	Peace of Westphalia, 1648
	Cf. KZ1331+ Treaties of Münster and Osnabrück,
	1648
	Biography of participants
270.A2	Collective
270.A3-Z	Individual, A-Z
270.A7	Arnim, Hans Georg von
	Gustaf II, Adolf, King of Sweden see DL706
270.M3	Mansfeld, Ernst, graf von
270.T5	Tilly, Jean t'Serclaes, comte de
270.T8	Torstenson, Lennart, greve af Ortala
270.W19	Wallenstein, Albrecht Wenzel E. von
271.A-Z	Relations of individual countries, A-Z
	1648-1715
273.A2	Sources and documents
273.A3-Z	General works
273.5	General special
273.7	Diplomatic history
	Biography and memoirs
	Collective see D244

	Modern history, 1453-
	1601-1715. 17th century
	1648-1715
	Biography and memoirs -- Continued
274.A-Z	Individual, A-Z
	e.g.
274.E8	Eugène, Prince of Savoie-Carignan
274.5	Anglo-French War, 1666-1667
274.6	Peace of Breda, 1667
	Cf. DA448 England, 1660-1685
	Cf. DJ180+ Netherlands, 1652-1702
	Cf. KZ1333.3 Treaty of Breda, 1667
	War of Devolution, 1667-1668
275	General works
275.5	Pamphlets, etc.
276.A-Z	Special events, battles, etc., A-Z
	e.g.
276.A3	Aix-la-Chapelle, Peace of, 1668
	Cf. KZ1333.32 Treaty of Aix-la-Chapelle, 1668
	Dutch War, 1672-1678
	Cf. DJ190+ Netherlands during war with France
277	General works
277.5	General special
278.A-Z	Special events, battles, etc., A-Z
278.C37	Cassell, Battle of, 1677
278.C37	Schooneveld, Battle of, 1673
278.E6	Enzheim, Battle of, 1674
278.M3	Masstricht, Siege of, 1673
278.S4	Seneffe, Battle of, 1674
278.S7	Southwold Bay, Battle of, 1672
278.T4	Texel, Battle of the, 1673
278.T6	Tobago, Battle of, 1677
278.5	Peace of Nijmegen, 1678-1679
	Cf. KZ1333.4 Treaty of Nijmegen, 1678-1679
	War of the Grand Alliance, 1688-1697
279	General works
279.5	General special
280.A-Z	Special events, battles, etc., A-Z
	e.g.
280.A8	Ath, Siege of, 1697
280.F6	Fleurus, Battle of, 1690
280.H6	Hogue, La, Battle of, 1692
280.N2	Namur, Siege of, 1692
280.5	Peace of Ryswick, 1697
	Cf. KZ1333.5 Treaty of Ryswick, 1697
	War of Spanish Succession, 1701-1714
281.A2	Sources and documents

Modern history, 1453-
1601-1715. 17th century
1648-1715
War of Spanish Succession, 1701-1714 -- Continued

281.A3-Z	Memoirs and early works
281.5	General works
282	General special
282.5	Pamphlets, etc.
283.A-Z	Special events, battles, etc., A-Z
	e.g.
283.B3	Barcelona, Siege of, 1713-1714
283.B6	Blenheim, Battle of, 1704
283.L5	Lille, Siege of, 1707
283.T7	Toulon, Siege of, 1707
283.T8	Turin, Siege of, 1706
283.5	Congress of Utrecht, 1713

For the Treaty of Rastatt and Baden, 1714 see
KZ1335.5
Cf. KZ1334+ Treaty of Utrecht, 1713
1715-1789. 18th century

284	Sources and documents
284.5	Historiography
	Biography and memoirs
	Collective
285	General works
285.1	Minor
285.3	Women
285.5	Public men
285.7	Rulers, kings, queens, etc.
285.8.A-Z	Individual, A-Z
	e.g.
	Ahmet, Paşa, Kumbaracibaşi, 1675-1747 see D285.8.B6
285.8.B6	Bonneval, Claude Alexandre, comte de, 1675-1747
285.8.C4	Casanova, Giacomo, 1725-1798

For literary works (French) see PQ1959.C6
For literary works (Italian) see PQ4687.C274

285.8.H7	Hordt, Johann Ludwig, graf von
285.8.L5	Ligne, Charles Joseph, prince de
285.8.P7	Pöllnitz, Karl Ludwig, freiherr von
285.8.T65	Trenck, Franz
285.8.T7	Trenck, Friedrich
286	General works
	Diplomatic history. Foreign relations
287	General works
287.5	Quadruple Alliance, 1718

Cf. KZ1339.Q83 Quadruple Alliance Treaty, 1718

Modern history, 1453-
    1715-1789. 18th century
       Diplomatic history. Foreign relations -- Continued

287.7	Alliance of Hanover, 1725
	Cf. KZ1339.H36 Treaty of Hanover, 1725
287.8	Negotiation of Seville, 1729
	Cf. KZ1339.S48 Treaty of Seville, 1729
288	Other special
	1740-1789
	Cf. D295 Political and military history, 1750-1789
289	General works
289.4	Family Pact, Fontainebleau, 1743
	For legal works, including texts of the treaty and
	related documents see KZ1339.F66
289.5	Family Pact, Paris, 1761
	For legal works, including texts of the treaty and
	related documents see KZ1339.P37
290	18th century minor works. Pamphlets, etc.
	War of Austrian Succession, 1740-1748
	Cf. DB72 Austria during the period of the war
291	Sources and documents
292	General works
292.8	Pamphlets, etc.
293	Silesian campaigns. International relations
	For military history see DD406+
	Rhine and Danube, 1741-1744
293.2	General works
293.3.A-Z	Special events, battles, etc., A-Z
	Italy, 1741-1748
293.4	General works
293.5.A-Z	Special events, battles, etc., A-Z
	e.g.
293.5.A8	Assietta, Battle of, 1747
293.5.V4	Velletri, Battle of, 1744
293.55	Other
	Netherlands, 1743-1748
293.6	General works
293.7.A-Z	Special events, battles, etc., A-Z
	e.g.
293.7.F6	Fontenoy, Battle of, 1745
	Colonial, 1739-1748. Naval operations
293.8	General works
	Cf. E198 King George's War, 1744-1748
293.9.A-Z	Special events, battles, etc., A-Z
294	Peace of Aix-la-Chapelle, 1748
	Cf. KZ1339.A59 Treaty of Aix-la-Chapelle, 1748
	1750-1789

Modern history, 1453-
1715-1789. 18th century
1750-1789 -- Continued
295   Political and military history
Including history of the armed neutrality of 1780
For the Treaty of Versailles, 1783 see KZ1339.V47
Cf. E208 American Revolution, 1775-1783
Cf. JZ6422+ Neutrality
Seven Years' War, 1756-1763
297   General international aspects, results, etc. Peace of
Paris, 1763
For the war between Friedrich II and Maria
Theresia see DD409+
For French and Indian War, 1756-1763 see E199
Cf. DS462+ French (1664-1761) and English
(1761-1798) in India
Cf. KZ1336+ Treaty of Paris, 1763
1789-
Including 18th and 19th centuries together
299   General works
1789-1815. Period of the French Revolution
301   Periodicals. Sources and documents. Collections
304.A-Z   Biography and memoirs, A-Z
e.g.
Cf. DC145+ Biography, memoirs, etc. of French
contemporaries of the French Revolution
304.J7   Jomini, Henri, baron
304.M15   Maistre, Joseph Marie, comte de
308   General works
309   Other
Revolutionary and Napoleonic wars see DC220+
19th century. 1801-1914/1920
351   Sources and documents
Biography and memoirs
352   Collective
352.1   Rulers, kings, princes, etc.
352.3   Queens, princesses
352.5   Public men
352.7   Women
352.8.A-Z   Individual, A-Z
e.g.
352.8.L6-.L7   Lieven, Darʹia Khristoforovna (Benckendorff),
kniaginia
352.8.M4   Metternich-Winneburg, Pauline Clementine M.W.
(Sándor von Szlavnicza), fürst von
352.8.P3   Pückler-Muskau, Hermann, fürst von
352.8.S7   Stockmar, Ernst Alfred C., freiherr von

	Modern history, 1453-
	1789-
	19th century. 1801-1914/1920 -- Continued
352.9	Historiography
	Collected works
353	Several authors
354	Individual authors
355	Addresses, essays, lectures
356	Dictionaries, etc.
358	19th century (General)
358.5	Popular works
359	Europe in the 19th century, 1801-1914
	For sources, biography, etc., see D351+, D359.2+
359.2	Syllabi, outlines, tables, etc.
359.7	General special
(360)	Social life and customs
	see GT146
	Civilization see CB415+
361	Military history
362	Naval history
363	Political and diplomatic history
	Eastern question
371	General works
372	General special
373	Early history to 1800
374	19th century
	For the Congress of Paris, 1856, see DK215
	For legal works on the Treaty of Paris, 1856, see KZ1369
	Cf. DR475 Turkey, 1812-1918
375	General special
375.3	Conference of Berlin, 1878
	For legal works on the Treaty of Berlin, 1878, see KZ1383
	Cf. DR573.7 San Stefano, 1878
	20th century see D461+
376.A-Z	Relations of individual countries, A-Z
	Slavs
377.A1	Periodicals. Societies. Serials
377.A2-Z	General works
	Panslavism
	Cf. D449 Panslavism, 20th century
377.3	General works, especially political
377.5.A-Z	By region or country, A-Z
	Central Asian question
	Cf. DK750 Soviet Asia
378	General works

Modern history, 1453-
1789-
19th century. 1801-1914/1920
Eastern question
Central Asian question -- Continued

378.5.A-Z	By region or country, A-Z
(379)	Far East
	see DS515+
383	1815-1830. Congress of Vienna, 1814-1815. Holy Alliance. Quadruple Alliance, 1815
	For legal works on the Holy Alliance Treaty, 1815, see KZ1358+
	1830-1848
385	General works
387	1848
	1848-1859
388	Sources and documents
389	General works
	1860-1870
391	Sources and documents
392	General works
393	Pamphlets, etc.
	1871- . Later 19th century
394	Sources and documents
395	General works
395.2	Syllabi, outlines, tables, questions, etc.
396	Military history
397	Political and diplomatic history
	Including Franco-Russian alliance, Triple Alliance, 1882
	For legal works on the Triple Alliance Treaty, 1882, see KZ1384
398	Other
	Biography and memoirs
399	Collective
399.5	Women
399.6	Public men
399.7	Rulers, kings, etc.
399.8	Queens, princesses, etc.
400.A-Z	Individual, A-Z
	e.g.
400.B6	Blount, Sir Edward Charles
400.B85	Bunsen, Marie von
400.P3	Paget, Walpurga Ehrengarde H. (von Hohenthal), lady
400.R33	Redesdale, Algernon Bertram Freeman-Mitford, Baron
400.R5	Rennell, James Rennell Rodd, Baron

	Modern history, 1453-
	1789-
	19th century. 1801-1914/1920
	1871- . Later 19th century
	Biography and memoirs
	Individual, A-Z -- Continued
400.R7	Rumbold, Sir Horace, bart.
400.S2	Salm-Salm, Agnes (Joy), prinzessin zu
400.Z3	Zaharoff, Sir Basil
	20th century
410	Periodicals. Societies. Serials
410.5	Yearbooks of current events (nonserial)
	Arrange chronologically by year; subarrange by author
	Including pictorial works
411	Sources and documents
	Biography and memoirs
412	Collective
412.5	Women
412.6	Public men
412.7	Rulers, kings, etc.
412.8	Queens, princesses, etc.
413.A-Z	Individual, A-Z
413.5	Historiography
	Collected works
414	Several authors
415	Individual authors
416	Pamphlets, etc.
419	Dictionaries
421	20th century (General)
422	Popular works
	Europe in the 20th century
	For periodicals, etc. see D410
	For sources, etc. see D426
424	General works
	Europe, 1945- see D1050+
425	Popular works
426	Pictorial history
427	Syllabi, outlines, tables, etc.
(429)	Social life and customs
	see GT150
	Civilization see CB425+
431	Military history
436	Naval history
437	Air warfare

Modern history, 1453-
   1789-
      20th century -- Continued
         Political and diplomatic history
            Including world politics, Triple Entente, 1907
            Cf. D397 Political and diplomatic history of the later
               19th century
            Cf. D511+ Causes and origins of World War I, 1914-
               1918

440	Annual registers
	Cf. D2 Annual registers (General history)
441	Sources and documents
442	Collected works
443	General works
445	General special
	e.g. Imaginary wars and future world politics
446	Anglo-Saxon supremacy
	Cf. CB216 Anglo-Saxon civilization
	Cf. DA118 National characteristics of the English
447	Pangermanism (International)
	Cf. DD118.5+ German imperialism
	Panislamism
	see DR476; DS35.7
448	Panlatinism
448.5	Panceltism
449	Panslavism
	Cf. D377.A+ Panslavism in the 19th century
450	Pamphlets, etc.
	Diplomatic history. Foreign relations
451	Sources and documents
453	General works
455	General special
457	Pamphlets, etc.
(458)	Triple Alliance, 1882
	see D397, KZ1384
(459)	Triple Entente, 1907-
	see D443, D511, JZ1391.2
460	Little Entente, 1920-1939
	Eastern question
	Cf. D371+ Eastern question in the 19th century
	Cf. DR475 Political and diplomatic history of Turkey
461	Sources and documents
462	Conferences, etc. By date
	e.g.
462 1922	Lausanne
463	General works
465	General special

Modern history, 1453-
  1789-
    20th century
      Eastern question -- Continued
468   Pamphlets, etc.
469.A-Z   By region or country, A-Z
           Central Asian question
            1901-1914 see D378+
471   1914-
472.A-Z   By region or country, A-Z
         Macedonian question see DR2152+
(475)   Moroccan question
            see DT317
         Far East see DS515
World War I (1914-1918)
501   Periodicals. Serials
502   Societies
        Cf. D570.A1+ American Legion, Disabled American
          Veterans of the World War, etc.
503   Museums. Exhibitions, etc.
        Cf. CJ5780 Medals of the 20th century
        Cf. N9152.A+ Art exhibitions of World War I
504   Congresses, conferences, etc.
505   Sources and documents
        Biography
507   Collective
         Individual
         For individual biography of prominent military leaders see the
          country of the individual in DA-DU, E-F, or other
          appropriate class, e. g. DD231.H5, Paul von Hindenburg;
          DA68.32.K6, Horatio Herbert Kitchener
         For all other biography chiefly describing the subject's
          participation in the war see the topic, troops, campaign,
          or battle, e. g. D602, English aerial operations; D570.32,
          United States field artillery; D545.M3, Battle of the Marne
         For individual biography not limited to the war see the country
          of the individual in DA-DU, E-F, or other appropriate class
509   Collected works
510   Dictionaries
        Causes. Origins. Aims
511   General works. Triple Entente, 1907
         Cf. JZ1391.2 International relations
512   Austria
513   Serbia
514   Soviet Union. Panslavism
515   Germany
        Cf. DD119 Pangermanism

World War I (1914-1918)
    Causes. Origins. Aims -- Continued

516	France
517	Great Britain
	Including colonies (General)
518	Belgium
519	Japan
520.A-Z	Other regions or countries, A-Z
	e.g.
520.A8	Arabia
	Armenia see DS195+
520.B6	Bohemia
520.I65	Ireland
	Cf. DA962 Ireland, 1914-1921
520.I7	Italy
	Cf. D617 Neutrality of Italy
	Latin America see D520.S8
520.O8	Orient. Far East
	Poland see DK4390+
520.S8	South America. Latin America
520.T8	Turkey. Islam
521	General works
522	Pictorial works
	For art and the war see N9150+
522.22	Films, slides, etc. Catalogs
522.23	Motion pictures about the war
522.25	Posters
522.27	Collectibles
(522.3)	Maps and atlases
	see G1037, etc.
522.4	Study and teaching
522.42	Historiography
522.5	Outlines, syllabi, tables, etc.
522.6	Examinations, questions, etc.
522.7	Juvenile works. Elementary textbooks
523	General special
524	Ethical and religious aspects. Prophecy
	Cf. D639.R4 Religion and Christianity in the war
524.5	Psychological aspects
	Social aspects
524.6	General works
524.7.A-Z	By region or country, A-Z
525	Pamphlets, addresses, sermons, etc.
	War poetry
	see class P
526	Satire, caricature, etc.
526.2	English

World War I (1914-1918)

    Satire, caricature, etc. -- Continued

526.3	French
526.5	German
526.7.A-Z	Other languages, A-Z
	e.g.
526.7.I8	Italian
526.7.R8	Russian
(527-527.5)	Pictorial works
	see D522+
527.8	Commemorative ribbons, etc.
528	Guides to the battlefields
	For guides to special battlefields, see the battle
528.5	Beginnings of the war. Mobilization, etc.
	Military operations
529	Collections of official reports
	General works see D521
	Special arms
529.3	Infantry
529.4	Cavalry
529.5	Artillery
529.7	Engineers
529.9.A-Z	Other special, A-Z
	For individual countries see D570+
	Cf. D600+ Aerial operations, tank operations
	Western
530	General works
	German
	Including memoirs by Falkenhayn, Hindenburg, and Ludendorff
531	General works
	Prussian
532	General works
532.1	Army
532.2	Corps
532.3	Infantry
532.4	Cavalry
532.47	Uhlans
532.5	Artillery
532.6	Machine gun regiments
532.7	Gas regiments
532.8	Engineers
532.9	Other
	Baden
533	General works
533.1	Army
533.2	Corps

World War I (1914-1918)
Military operations
Western
German
Baden -- Continued

533.3	Infantry
533.4	Cavalry
533.47	Uhlans
533.5	Artillery
533.6	Machine gun regiments
533.7	Gas regiments
533.8	Engineers
533.9	Other

Bavaria

534	General works
534.1	Army
534.2	Corps
534.3	Infantry
534.4	Cavalry
534.47	Uhlans
534.5	Artillery
534.6	Machine gun regiments
534.7	Gas regiments
534.8	Engineers
534.9	Other

Hessian

535	General works
535.1	Army
535.2	Corps
535.3	Infantry
535.4	Cavalry
535.47	Uhlans
535.5	Artillery
535.6	Machine gun regiments
535.7	Gas regiments
535.8	Engineers
535.9	Other

Saxon

536	General works
536.1	Army
536.2	Corps
536.3	Infantry
536.4	Cavalry
536.47	Uhlans
536.5	Artillery
536.6	Machine gun regiments
536.7	Gas regiments

World War I (1914-1918)
　　Military operations
　　　Western
　　　　Belgian and operations in Belgium
　　　　　Individual campaigns, sieges, battles, etc., A-Z --
　　　　　　Continued

542.Y7	Ypres, 2d battle of, 1915
542.Y72	Ypres, 3d battle of, 1917
542.Y8	Yser, Battle of the, 1914

　　　　Anglo-French. Allies

544	General works
545.A-Z	Individual campaigns, sieges, battles, etc., A-Z
	e.g.
545.A5	Aisne
(545.A55)	Alsace
	see DC647+
545.A6	Argonne, Battle of the, 1915
545.A63	Argonne, Battle of the, 1918
545.A7	Arras
545.B4	Belleau Wood
545.C37	Champagne
545.C4	Château-Thierry, Battle of, 1918
545.C45	Chemin des dames
545.C7	Compiègne
545.L5	Lille
545.L7	Lorraine, Battle of, 1914
545.M3	Marne, Battle of the, 1914
545.N7	Noyon
545.P5	Picardy
545.R4	Reims
545.S35	Seicheprey
545.S4	Senlis
545.S7	Somme, Battle of the, 1916
545.S75	Somme, 2d battle of the, 1918
545.V25	Verdun, Battle of, 1914
545.V3	Verdun, Battle of, 1916

　　　　English

546.A1-.A19	Societies
	e.g.
546.A12	Comrades of the Great War
546.A2-Z	General works
546.3	Officers Training Corps
546.5	Individual divisions, etc. By number
	Cf. D547.A+ Individual divisions by region or name
546.5 5th	The Fifth Army
546.52	Artillery
546.53	Infantry

World War I (1914-1918)
Military operations
Western
English
Individual divisions, etc. By number -- Continued

546.54	Cavalry
546.55	Engineers
547.A-Z	Individual. By region or name, A-Z
	e.g.
547.A1	Colonies (General)
547.A4	Africa, South
547.A5	Africa, West
547.A8	Australia. The Anzacs
547.B6	Black Watch
547.C2	Canada
547.C6	Coldstream Guards
547.G5	Glasgow Highlanders
547.G6	Gordon Highlanders
547.G7	Grenadier Guards
547.G8	Guards Division
547.I5	India
547.I6	Ireland
547.J3	Jamaica
547.K4	Kent
547.K43	King's (Liverpool Regiment)
547.K45	King's Overseas Dominions Regiment
547.K47	King's Own Scottish Borderers
547.K5	King's Own Rifle Corps
547.L2	Labour Corps
547.L6	London regiments
547.M3	Manchester Regiment
547.M8	Munster
547.N4	Negroes
547.N5	New Zealand
547.N55	Newfoundland
547.N58	Niue
547.N6	North Midland Division
547.N7	Northumberland Fusiliers
547.O7	Oxford University
547.Q18	Queen's Own Oxfordshire Hussars
547.Q2	Queen's Own Royal West Kent Regiment
547.Q3	Queen's Westminster and Civil Service Rifles
547.R4	Remount Service
547.R5	Royal Artillery Regiment
547.R6	Royal Fusiliers
547.R63	Royal Highlanders of Canada
547.R7	Royal Naval Division

World War I (1914-1918)
  Military operations
    Western
      English
        Individual. By region or name, A-Z -- Continued

547.R8	Royal Scots
547.S4	Scots Guard
547.S5	Sherwood Foresters
547.S6	South Staffordshire Regiment
547.T3	Tasmania
547.W4	Wales
547.W5	West Riding Territorials
547.8.A-Z	English local history, A-Z
	e.g.
547.8.E3	East Anglia
547.8.H6	Hornchurch
547.8.L7	London
547.8.P7	Preston
	French
548	General works
	Societies
548.03	General works
548.033.A-Z	Special, A-Z
	Special
548.1	Army corps
548.2	Divisions
548.3	Infantry
548.35	Foreign Legion
548.4	Cavalry
548.5	Chasseurs. "Blue devils." Chasseurs à pied.
	Chasseurs alpine
548.6	Artillery
548.7	Machine gun regiments
548.75	Gas regiments
548.8	Engineers
548.9.A-Z	Other, A-Z
	Including colonial
549.A-Z	Other special, A-Z
549.C4	Czechoslovakian troops
549.C5	Chinese troops
549.C7	Colored troops
549.P6	Polish troops
549.5.A-Z	Other countries, A-Z
	Portugal
	Including colonial history
549.5.P8	General works
549.5.P82A-.P82Z	Local history, A-Z

	World War I (1914-1918)
	Military operations
	Eastern
	Turkey and the Near East -- Continued
568.7	Palestine
568.8	Persia. Iran
568.9	West Turkestan and Khurasan
	Italian
569.A2	General works
569.A25	Divisions, regiments, etc. By author, A-Z
569.A3-Z	Individual campaigns, sieges, battles, etc., A-Z
	e.g.
569.G7	Gorizia
569.P4	Piave, 1st battle of the, 1917
569.P5	Piave, 2nd battle of the, 1918
569.V4	Venice (Italy), Defense of
569.V5	Vittorio Veneto, Battle of, 1918
	Greece. Salonica (Thessalonike). Macedonian
	campaign
569.2	General works
569.3.A-Z	Individual campaigns, sieges, battles, etc., A-Z
569.5	Albania
	United States
	For internal history of the United States, 1914-1918 see
	E780
	Societies
	American Legion
570.A1	General works
570.A12A-.A12W	By state, A-W
570.A13A-.A13Z	By city, A-Z
570.A135	American Legion, France
	Auxiliary
570.A14A1-.A14A4	Official publications
570.A14A5	Nonofficial publications
570.A14A6-.A14W	By state, A-W
570.A14Z9	Pamphlets, etc.
570.A15A-.A15Z	Other societies, A-Z
	e.g.
570.A15D5	Disabled American Veterans of the World War
570.A15M5	Military Order of the World War
570.A2	Collections. Serials. Official bulletins, etc.
	Special documents of a general nature
	Prefer the special topic
(570.A3)	Legislative acts
	see KF5951+
570.A35	Other special
	General works on participation in the war

World War I (1914-1918)
  Military operations
    United States
      General works on participation in the war -- Continued

570.A4	Official
570.A5-Z	Nonofficial
570.1	General special
570.15	Pamphlets, etc.
	Causes and antecedent history see D619
	Military operations
	General works see D570.A4+
570.2	General special
	Individual expeditions, battles, etc. see D545.A+
	Special divisions, regiments, etc.
570.25	Headquarters. General Staff
570.27	Army corps

        Subarrange: General works, .A1; individual units by
          number and author, e.g. 1st, 2nd, 51st, etc.

570.3	Divisions

        Subarrange: General works, .A1; individual units by
          number and author, e.g. 1st, 2nd, 51st, etc.

570.309	Engineers
570.31	Special units. By number and author
570.315	Air Defense Artillery

        Subarrange: General works, .A1; individual units by
          number and author, e.g. 1st, 2nd, 51st, etc.

570.32	Field artillery

        Subarrange: General works, .A1; individual units by
          number and author, e.g. 1st, 2nd, 51st, etc.

570.325	Coast artillery

        Subarrange: General works, .A1; individual units by
          number and author, e.g. 1st, 2nd, 51st, etc.

570.327	Trench artillery

        Subarrange: General works, .A1; individual units by
          number and author, e.g. 1st, 2nd, 51st, etc.

570.33	Infantry

        Subarrange: General works, .A1; individual units by
          number and author, e.g. 1st, 2nd, 51st, etc.

570.34	Machine gun battalions

        Subarrange: General works, .A1; individual units by
          number and author, e.g. 1st, 2nd, 51st, etc.

570.345	Gas regiments

        Subarrange: General works, .A1; individual units by
          number and author, e.g. 1st, 2nd, 51st, etc.

570.346	Signal Corps

        Subarrange: General works, .A1; individual units by
          number and author, e.g. 1st, 2nd, 51st, etc.

	World War I (1914-1918)
	Military operations
	United States
	Military operations
	Special divisions, regiments, etc. -- Continued
570.348	Marine Corps (Land operations only)
	Subarrange: General works, .A1; individual units by number and author, e.g. 1st, 2nd, 51st, etc.
	Cf. D570.45 Marine Corps
570.35	Military police
	Subarrange: General works, .A1; individual units by number and author, e.g. 1st, 2nd, 51st, etc.
570.352	Ammunition trains
	Subarrange: General works, .A1; individual units by number and author, e.g. 1st, 2nd, 51st, etc.
570.354	Field hospital companies
	Subarrange: General works, .A1; individual units by number and author, e.g. 1st, 2nd, 51st, etc.
570.355	Ambulance companies
	Subarrange: General works, .A1; individual units by number and author, e.g. 1st, 2nd, 51st, etc.
570.358	Other
570.36	Training camps
	Individual camps
570.37.A-Z	In Europe. A-Z
	e.g.
570.37.B7	Brest
	In United States see U294.5.A+
	Naval operations
(570.4)	General works
	see D589.U5+
570.45	General special
	e.g. Defensive areas; land batteries, Marine Corps
	Cf. D570.348 Marine Corps (Land operations)
(570.5.A-Z)	Individual engagements, A-Z
	see D589.U6+
	Aerial operations
(570.6)	General works
	see D606
570.65	General special
570.7	Individual squadrons
570.72	Transportation service
	Including transports
570.73.A-Z	Special, A-Z
	e.g.
570.73.H7	Hoboken
570.73.L4	Le Mans

World War I (1914-1918)
  Military operations
    United States -- Continued

570.75	Services of supply. Quartermaster Corps
570.8.A-Z	Special topics, A-Z
570.8.A6	Alien enemies

        Cf. KF4850+ Law
      Alien property custodian see K728+
      Americanization see JK1758
      Bolshevism (Russian Revolution) see DK265+
      Bolshevism (Socialism) see HX1+

(570.8.C4)	Civil liberty. Freedom of speech

        see KF4741+

570.8.C5	Commissions of foreign nations, A-Z

        e.g.

570.8.C5F8	Haut Commissariat de la République Française

      Conscientious objectors (Law) see KF7266.C6
      Conscientious objectors (Military administration) see
        UB341+

570.8.C7	Council of National Defense
570.8.C8A-.C8Z	Councils of defense, committees of public safety. By state, A-W

      Economic aspects see D635
      Economic history of the war see HC106.2
      Education and the war see D639.E3+
      Espionage see D619.3

570.8.E8	Executions

      Food control see HD9000.9.A+
      German-Americans and the war see D620

570.8.I6	Indian soldiers

        Cf. E98.M5 Military capacity of Indians (General)
      Medals, etc.
        see UB433; UC533; VB333; VC345
      Missions to the United States

570.8.M5	General works
570.8.M6A-.M6Z	Individual missions, A-Z
570.8.M6B3	Belgian
570.8.M6B5	British
570.8.M6F4	French
570.8.M6G8	Guatemalan
570.8.M6I8	Italian
570.8.M6J4	Japanese
570.8.M6R7	Russian
570.8.M6S4	Serbian
570.8.N3	National Research Council
570.8.P7	Political prisoners

      Prisons and prisoners see D627.A+

	World War I (1914-1918)
	Military operations
	United States
	Special topics, A-Z -- Continued
	Red Cross and hospital service see D629.U6+
570.8.R4	Registration
	Relief, charities, etc. see D637+
570.8.S4	Seizure and disposition of German ships
570.8.S5	Service flags
570.85.A-Z	By region or state, A-Z
	Alabama
570.85.A2	General works
570.85.A21A-.A21Z	Local, A-Z
	Arizona
570.85.A7	General works
570.85.A71A-.A71Z	Local, A-Z
	Arkansas
570.85.A8	General works
570.85.A81A-.A81Z	Local, A-Z
	California
570.85.C2	General works
570.85.C21A-.C21Z	Local, A-Z
	Colorado
570.85.C6	General works
570.85.C61A-.C61Z	Local, A-Z
	Connecticut
570.85.C8	General works
570.85.C81A-.C81Z	Local, A-Z
	Delaware
570.85.D4	General works
570.85.D41A-.D41Z	Local, A-Z
570.85.D6	District of Columbia
	Florida
570.85.F5	General works
570.85.F51A-.F51Z	Local, A-Z
	Georgia
570.85.G4	General works
570.85.G41A-.G41Z	Local, A-Z
	Idaho
570.85.I2	General works
570.85.I21A-.I21Z	Local, A-Z
	Illinois
570.85.I3	General works
570.85.I31A-.I31Z	Local, A-Z
	Indiana
570.85.I6	General works
570.85.I7A-.I7Z	Local, A-Z

World War I (1914-1918)
Military operations
United States
By region or state, A-Z -- Continued
Iowa

570.85.I8	General works
570.85.I9A-.I9Z	Local, A-Z
	Kansas
570.85.K2	General works
570.85.K21A-.K21Z	Local, A-Z
	Kentucky
570.85.K4	General works
570.85.K41A-.K41Z	Local, A-Z
	Louisiana
570.85.L6	General works
570.85.L61A-.L61Z	Local, A-Z
	Maine
570.85.M2	General works
570.85.M21A-.M21Z	Local, A-Z
	Maryland
570.85.M3	General works
570.85.M31A-.M31Z	Local, A-Z
	Massachusetts
570.85.M4	General works
570.85.M41A-.M41Z	Local, A-Z
	Michigan
570.85.M5	General works
570.85.M51A-.M51Z	Local, A-Z
	Minnesota
570.85.M6	General works
570.85.M61A-.M61Z	Local, A-Z
	Mississippi
570.85.M7	General works
570.85.M71A-.M71Z	Local, A-Z
	Missouri
570.85.M8	General works
570.85.M81A-.M81Z	Local, A-Z
	Montana
570.85.M9	General works
570.85.M91A-.M91Z	Local, A-Z
	Nebraska
570.85.N19	General works
570.85.N2A-.N2Z	Local, A-Z
	Nevada
570.85.N22	General works
570.85.N23A-.N23Z	Local, A-Z
570.85.N24	New England

World War I (1914-1918)
Military operations
United States
By region or state, A-Z -- Continued
New Hampshire

570.85.N25	General works
570.85.N26A-.N26Z	Local, A-Z
	New Jersey
570.85.N3	General works
570.85.N31A-.N31Z	Local, A-Z
	New Mexico
570.85.N33	General works
570.85.N34A-.N34Z	Local, A-Z
	New York
570.85.N4	General works
570.85.N5A-.N5Z	Local, A-Z
	North Carolina
570.85.N8	General works
570.85.N81A-.N81Z	Local, A-Z
	North Dakota
570.85.N9	General works
570.85.N91A-.N91Z	Local, A-Z
	Ohio
570.85.O3	General works
570.85.O31A-.O31Z	Local, A-Z
	Oklahoma
570.85.O5	General works
570.85.O51A-.O51Z	Local, A-Z
	Oregon
570.85.O8	General works
570.85.O81A-.O81Z	Local, A-Z
	Pennsylvania
570.85.P4	General works
570.85.P41A-.P41Z	Local, A-Z
	Rhode Island
570.85.R4	General works
570.85.R41A-.R41Z	Local, A-Z
	South Carolina
570.85.S6	General works
570.85.S61A-.S61Z	Local, A-Z
	South Dakota
570.85.S7	General works
570.85.S71A-.S71Z	Local, A-Z
	Tennessee
570.85.T2	General works
570.85.T21A-.T21Z	Local, A-Z
	Texas

World War I (1914-1918)
  Military operations
    United States
      By region or state, A-Z
        Texas -- Continued

570.85.T4	General works
570.85.T41A-.T41Z	Local, A-Z
	Utah
570.85.U8	General works
570.85.U81A-.U81Z	Local, A-Z
	Vermont
570.85.V5	General works
570.85.V51A-.V51Z	Local, A-Z
	Virginia
570.85.V8	General works
570.85.V81A-.V81Z	Local, A-Z
	Washington
570.85.W3	General works
570.85.W31A-.W31Z	Local, A-Z
	West Virginia
570.85.W4	General works
570.85.W41A-.W41Z	Local, A-Z
	Wisconsin
570.85.W6	General works
570.85.W61A-.W61Z	Local, A-Z
	Wyoming
570.85.W8	General works
570.85.W81A-.W81Z	Local, A-Z
570.87.A-Z	Outlying states, possessions, etc., A-Z
	e.g.
570.87.H3	Hawaii
570.87.P7	Puerto Rico
570.88.A-Z	Individual nationalities, A-Z
	e.g.
570.88.B6	Bohemians in United States Army
570.9.A-Z	Personal narratives and other accounts of American expeditions after declaration of war by the United States, A-Z

          For military biography see E745
          Cf. D640.A+ Personal narratives (General)
    Japanese

571	General works
572.A-Z	Individual campaigns, sieges, battles, etc., A-Z
572.5	Thailand
	Colonial
573	General works
	German

	World War I (1914-1918)
	Military operations
	Colonial
	German -- Continued
574	General works
	African
575	General works
576.A-Z	Individual colonies, A-Z
	e.g.
576.C3	Cameroons
576.G3	German East Africa
576.G5	German Southwest Africa
576.G7	Gold Coast (Ghana)
(576.K3)	Kameruns (German West Africa)
	see D576.C3
576.T7	Togoland
	Pacific, Asiatic, etc.
577	General works
578.A-Z	Individual colonies, A-Z
	e.g.
578.N4	New Guinea
578.S2	Samoa
	Naval operations
580	General works. Freedom of the seas
	Anglo-German
581	General works. Blockade
582.A-Z	By engagement, ship, etc., A-Z
	e.g.
582.A8	Ayesha (Schooner)
582.B3	Baralong (Cruiser)
582.D8	Dresden (Cruiser)
582.E6	Emden (Cruiser)
582.F2	Falkland Islands, Battle of, 1914
582.G7	Goeben and Breslau (Cruisers)
582.J8	Jutland, Battle of, 1916
582.K3	Karlsruhe (Cruiser)
582.K6	Königsberg (Cruiser)
582.K7	Kronprinz Wilhelm (Cruiser)
582.M6	Möwe (Steamship)
	Franco-Austrian. French
583	General works
584.A-Z	By engagement, ship, etc., A-Z
	e.g.
584.O8	Otranto Straits, Battle of the, 1917
	Japanese see D571+
585	Russian
586	Egyptian

	World War I (1914-1918)
	Naval operations -- Continued
587	Turkish
588	Italian
589.A-Z	Other, A-Z
	e.g.
	United States
589.U5	Documents
589.U6	General works
589.U7A-.U7Z	By engagement, ship, etc., A-Z
589.U8	Awarding of medals
	Submarine operations
	Including operations of submarine chasers
590	General works
	German
591	General works
592.A-Z	By engagement, ship, etc., A-Z
	e.g.
592.D4	Deutschland (Submarine)
592.L8	Lusitania (Steamship)
592.S8	Sussex (Steamship)
	English
593	General works
594.A-Z	By engagement, ship, etc., A-Z
	e.g.
594.Z4	Zeebrugge-Ostend raids, 1918
595.A-Z	Other, A-Z
	Aerial operations
600	General works
602	English
603	French
604	German
605	Russian
606	United States
607.A-Z	Other, A-Z
607.3	Engineering operations
(607.5)	Gas warfare
	see UG447
608	Tank operations
	Cf. UG446.5 Military engineering
	Medals, badges, decorations of honor
	Including lists of recipients of medals
608.5	General works
608.6.A-Z	By region or country, A-Z
	Including individual recipients of medals
	Registers, lists of dead and wounded, etc.
609.A2	General

World War I (1914-1918)
Registers, lists of dead and wounded, etc. -- Continued

609.A3-Z	By region or country, A-Z
	e.g.
	Austria-Hungary
609.A6	General
609.A7	Slavic
609.A8	Hungarian
	France
609.F8	General works
609.F82	French colonies
	United States
609.U6	General
609.U7	Special
	Diplomatic history
610	General works
611	General special
	Including neutrality, etc.
	Peace efforts during the war
	Cf. D642+ Peace at close of the war
613	General works
613.5	Ford Peace Expedition
(614.A-Z)	Treaties
	see KZ185.5-KZ186.5
	Individual regions or countries
615	Belgian neutrality. Case of Belgium
616	Greece and the war
	Cf. DF837+ Greece under Constantine I
617	Italy and the war. Neutrality
	Cf. D520.I7 Origins of the war in Italy
618	South America and the war
	For individual countries see D621.A+
619	United States and the war. Neutrality
	Including reasons for American participation
619.3	German conspiracies. Propaganda. Espionage, etc.
619.5.A-Z	Individual cases, A-Z
	e.g.
619.5.A7	Archibald, James Francis J.
619.5.G7	Goltz, Horst von der
619.5.M3	Martens, Ludwig Christian A.K.
619.5.O4	O'Leary, Jeremiah A.
619.5.P2	Papen, Franz von
620	German-Americans and the war
621.A-Z	Other regions or countries, A-Z
	e.g.
621.A8	Argentina
621.S3	Scandinavia

World War I (1914-1918)
  Diplomatic history
    Individual regions or countries
      Other regions or countries, A-Z -- Continued

621.S4	Denmark
621.S45	Norway
621.S5	Sweden

Special topics
622	Catholic Church and the war

Occupied territory
  Including underground movements
623.A2	General works
623.A3-Z	By region or country, A-Z
	e.g.
623.B4	Belgium

Atrocities. War crimes
  For trials see KZ1170+
625	General works
626.A-Z	By region or country committing atrocity, A-Z

Prisoners and prisons
627.A1	Periodicals and societies
627.A2	General works
627.A3-Z	In individual countries, A-Z
	Under each country, use .A1-.A19 for Periodicals

Medical and sanitary services. Hospitals. Red Cross
628	General works
629.A-Z	By region or country
629.B4	Belgium
629.G7	Great Britain
	Including Voluntary Aid Detachments work

United States
629.U6	General works
629.U62A-.U62W	By state, A-W

Hospitals and rest camps
629.U7A-.U7Z	In United States, by place, A-Z
629.U8A-.U8Z	In other countries, A-Z
	Subarrange alphabetically by place, e.g. .F5-9, France; .F7, Langres
630.A-Z	Biography, A-Z
	e.g.
630.C3	Cavell, Edith

Press. Censorship. Publicity
631	General works
632	The American press. Committee on public information
632.5.A-Z	Other regions or countries, A-Z
633	Other special

World War I (1914-1918)

     Special topics -- Continued

635	Economic aspects. Commerce, finance, etc. (General)
	For specific topics or for individual countries, see HC, HF, HJ
	Alien enemies
	Cf. K7205 Law
636.A2	General works
636.A3-Z	By region or country, A-Z
	e.g.
636.F8	France
	United States see D570.8.A6
	Relief work. Charities. Protection. Refugees
637	General works
638.A-Z	By region or country, A-Z
	e.g.
638.A7	Armenia
638.E2	East, Near
638.U5	United States
639.A-Z	Other special topics, A-Z
	For topics applicable only to the United States see D570.8.A+
	African Americans see D639.N4
(639.A6)	Amnesty
	see class K
639.A64	Anarchism. Anarchists
639.A65	Animals, War use of
639.A7	Anthropology and ethnology. Race problems
639.A73	Art and the war
639.A75	Astrology
639.A8	Automobiles
	Blacks see D639.N4
639.B6	Boy Scouts
	Cemeteries see D639.D4
639.C38	Chaplains
639.C39	Chemical warfare
639.C4	Children. Orphans
639.C5	Christian Science
639.C54	Church of England
639.C75	Cryptography
639.D4	Dead, Care of. Burial. Cemeteries
	Cf. D675.A+ Tomb of the Unknown Soldier
639.D45	Democracy and the war
639.D5	Deportation of Belgians, French, etc.
639.D53	Desertions
639.D6	Dogs
639.D7	Dreams
639.D87	Dutch

World War I (1914-1918)
Special topics
Other special topics, A-Z -- Continued
Education and the war
639.E2   General works
United States
639.E3   General works. Student Army Training Corps
639.E35   A.E.F. University
639.E37   A.E.F. in Great Britain
639.E4A-.E4Z   By college, school, etc., A-Z
e.g.
639.E4H3   Harvard University
639.E4S3   St. Louis public schools
639.E42A-.E42Z   By fraternity, A-Z
e.g.
639.E42S5   Sigma Alpha Epsilon
639.E45   France
639.E47   Germany
Great Britain
639.E5   General works
639.E52A-.E52Z   Colonies, A-Z
e.g.
639.E52C3   Canada
639.E53A-.E53Z   By university, A-Z
639.E6A-.E6Z   Other regions or countries, A-Z
639.E8   Entertainment and recreation for soldiers
Including liberty theaters
639.E94   Executions
639.F3   Fashion
639.F8   Freemasons
639.F9   Friends, Society of
639.G8   Gynecology
639.H5   Historic monuments
639.I2   Idealism
639.I5   Illegitimacy. War babies
639.I56   Indians
639.J4   Jews
Including the Jewish pogroms in Ukraine
For the "Protocols of the wise men of Zion" see
DS145.P49+
639.L2   Labor
For the labor situation in individual countries, see HD
639.L4   Lawyers
(639.L5)   Library service to military personnel
see Z675.W2
639.M37   Mennonites
Merchant marine

World War I (1914-1918)
 Special topics
  Other special topics, A-Z
   Merchant marine -- Continued

639.M4	General works
639.M5A-.M5Z	By region or country, A-Z
639.M56	Missing in action
	Mutinies
639.M8	General works
639.M82A-.M82Z	By region or country, A-Z
	Naturalized subjects in belligerent countries
639.N2	General works
639.N3A-.N3Z	By region or country, A-Z

      For alien enemies in the United States see
       D570.8.A6
      For German-Americans in the United States see
       D620

639.N4	Negroes. African Americans. Blacks
639.P39	Photography
639.P45	Pigeons
639.P5	Population and the war
	Propaganda
639.P6	General works
639.P7A-.P7Z	By region or country, A-Z

     e.g.

639.P7F7	France
639.P7G3	Germany

      For German propaganda in the United States see
       D619.3

639.P75	Prophecies
639.P77	Protest movements
639.P78	Protestant churches
639.P8	Psychic phenomena
	Public opinion
639.P87	General works
639.P88A-.P88Z	By region or country, A-Z
	Race problems see D639.A7
639.R4	Religious aspects
639.S15	Salvation Army
639.S2	Science and technology

     Cf. UG447+ Chemical warfare

639.S3	Sex
639.S4	Slavs
639.S5	Snowshoes and snowshoeing
639.S6	Socialism

     For Bolshevism (Russian Revolution) see DK265+
     For Bolshevism (Socialism) see HX1+

World War I (1914-1918)
   Special topics
      Other special topics, A-Z -- Continued
         Spies. Secret service

639.S7	General works
639.S8A-.S8Z	Individual, A-Z
	e.g.
	Mata Hari see D639.S8Z4
639.S8Z4	Zelle (Mata Hari)
639.S9	Supplies
	Talbot House (Poperinghe, Belgium) see D639.T6
639.T35	Telegraph. Radio
639.T4	Telephone
639.T6	Toc H. Talbot House (Poperinghe, Belgium)
639.T8	Transportation
	Cf. D570.72 Transportation service (United States)
	War babies see D639.I5
639.W7	Women
639.Y7	Young Men's Christian Association. Young Women's Christian Association

   Personal narratives and other accounts
      Cf. D570.9.A+ Personal narratives of United States
         soldiers, etc.

640.A2	Collective
640.A22-Z	Individual, A-Z
641	Armistice of Compiègne, 1918

   Peace
      Cf. D613+ Peace efforts during the war

642	Sources and documents
	For legal works on treaties and surrender documents of Allied and Associated Powers, 1914-1920 see KZ185+
644	General works
645	General special
646	Pamphlets, etc.

      Peace commissions (Personnel)

647.A2	General works
647.A3-Z	Special. By region or country
	e.g.
647.U6	United States

      Special topics
         Indemnity and reparation
            Class here non-official works
            Cf. KK7558.R46, Reparations and demontage
            For texts of treaties and related legal materials see
               KZ186.2

648	General works

World War I (1914-1918)
  Peace
    Special topics
      Indemnity and reparation -- Continued

649.A-Z	By region or country, A-Z
649.G3	Germany
	Dawes plan
	see KZ186+
(649.G3A4)	Texts. By date
(649.G3A45)	Documents of the different countries. By date
649.G3A5-.G3A59	Works on the Dawes plan. Alphabetically by author
649.G3A6-.G3A7	Young plan
	Subarrange like .G3A5-59
649.G3A6	Text. By date
649.G3A65	Documents of the different countries. By date
649.G3A7-.G3A79	Works on the Young plan. Alphabetically by author
649.G3A8-.G3Z	General works
650.A-Z	Other special, A-Z
	e.g.
650.B7	Bridges of the Rhine
650.D5	Disarmament (German)
	Eastern question see D461+
	Fiume (Rijeka) see D651.I6+
650.I6	Inter-allied Military Commission of Control in Germany
650.J4	Jews
650.M5	Military occupation of the Rhine
650.R8	Ruhr River and Valley
	Shantung see D651.C4+
650.T4	Territorial questions
	For special see D651.A+
	Cf. KZ186+ Peace treaties
651.A-Z	Individual regions or countries, A-Z
	Class here works on the beginnings of organization of new countries where territorial questions are concerned
	For treaties of the Allied and Associated Powers with the Central Powers, 1914-1920 see KZ186+
651.A42	Africa, German Southwest
651.A5	Albania and Epirus
651.A7	Armenia
651.A95	Austria
651.A98	Azerbaijan
651.B2	Baltic provinces
651.B25	Banat
651.B3	Belgium
651.B4	Bessarabia

World War I (1914-1918)
  Peace
    Individual regions or countries, A-Z -- Continued

651.B8	Bulgaria
651.C3	Cameroons
	Carinthia see DB281+
	China
651.C4	General works
651.C5	Relations of America to Shantung
651.C6	Relations of Japan to Shantung
651.C7A-.C7Z	Relations of other countries, A-Z
651.C75	Circassia
651.C78	Croatia
651.C8	Cuba
651.C9	Czechoslovakia
651.D3	Dalmatia
	Dobruja see DR281.D5
651.E3	Egypt
651.E8	Estonia
	France
	General works
651.F5A1-.F5A29	Collections
(651.F5A3)	Comprehensive treaty texts
	see KZ186.2+
651.F5A4-.F5Z	Other
	Relations of United States to France
	Including Defensive alliance between France, United
	States, and Great Britain
(651.F6A2)	Treaty texts and related legal materials
	see KZ186.2+
651.F6A6-.F6Z	Nonofficial works
651.F7	Relations of other countries to France
651.G18	Galicia
651.G2	Georgia (Transcaucasia)
	Germany
651.G3A2	Collections
	Treaty text see KZ186.5.A+
651.G4	Görz
651.G5-.G7	Great Britain
	General works
651.G5A1-.G5A29	Collections
(651.G5A3)	Comprehensive treaty texts
	see KZ186.2+
651.G5A4-.G5Z	Other
	Relations of United States to Great Britain
	Including Defensive alliance between France, United
	States, and Great Britain

World War I (1914-1918)
    Peace
        Individual regions or countries, A-Z
            Great Britain
                Relations of United States to Great Britain -- Continued

(651.G6A2)	Treaty texts and related legal materials
	see KZ186.2+
651.G6A6-.G6Z	Nonofficial works
651.G7	Relations of other countries to Great Britain
651.G8	Greece. Unredeemed Greeks
651.H7	Hungary
651.I5	Istria
651.I6-.I8	Italy
	Including Fiume (Rijeka)

                      General works

651.I6A1-.I6A29	Collections
(651.I6A3)	Comprehensive treaty texts
	see KZ186.2+
651.I6A4-.I6Z	Other

                Relations of United States to Italy

(651.I7A2)	Treaty texts and related legal materials
	see KZ186.2+
651.I7A6-.I7Z	Nonofficial works
651.I8	Relations of other countries to Italy
651.J3-.J5	Japan
	For Relation to Shantung see D651.C6

                General works

651.J3A1-.J3A29	Collections
(651.J3A3)	Comprehensive treaty texts
	see KZ186.2+
651.J3A4-.J3Z	Other

                Relations of United States to Japan

(651.J4A2)	Treaty texts and related legal materials
	see KZ186.2+
651.J4A6-.J4Z	Nonofficial works
651.J5	Relations of other countries to Japan
	Kamerun see D651.C3
651.K87	Kurdistan
651.L4	Latvia. Letts
651.L45	Lebanon
651.L5	Lithuania
651.L8	Luxemburg
651.M3	Macedonia
	Cf. DR2152+ Modern of history of Macedonia
651.M4	Mesopotamia
651.M7	Montenegro
651.N3	Nauru

World War I (1914-1918)
    Peace
       Individual regions or countries, A-Z -- Continued

651.N5	Nicaragua
651.P2	Pacific Islands, German
651.P3	Palestine
651.P4	Persia
651.P7	Poland
651.P75	Portugal
651.P8	Posen
651.P89	Prussia, East
651.P9	Prussia, West
651.R6	Romania
651.R8	Russia
651.R9	Ruthenia
651.S13	Saar Valley
651.S3	Samoa
651.S4	Schleswig
	Serbia see D651.Y8+
651.S5	Silesia (Upper)
651.S53	Slovenia
	Soviet Union see D651.R8
	Spalato see D651.D3
651.S7	Styria
651.S9	Syria
651.T5	Thrace
651.T7	Togoland
651.T8	Transylvania
651.T85	Trieste
651.T9	Turkey
651.T95	Tyrol
651.U6	Ukraine
	Cf. DK508+ History of the Ukraine
	Yugoslavia
651.Y8	General works
651.Y9A-.Y9Z	Relations of other countries to Yugoslavia, A-Z
	For Fiume see D651.I6+
	Cf. D465 Eastern question

    Reconstruction. Post-war period

652	Sources and documents
653	General works
655	Other
	Individual countries
	United States
657	General works
658.A-.W	By state, A-W
	e.g.

World War I (1914-1918)
    Reconstruction. Post-war period
      Individual countries
        United States
          By state, A-W -- Continued

658.C2	California
658.I6	Indiana
658.M4	Massachusetts
658.M5	Michigan
658.N6	North Carolina
659.A-Z	Other regions or countries, A-Z

    Celebrations. Memorials. Monuments
        Including memorials to special regiments, etc., with their history
        Cf. D503 Museums
        Cf. NA9325+ Fine arts

663	General works
665	Other

      United States

670	General works
671	Veterans Day (Armistice Day) services and addresses
673.A-.W	States, A-W
675.A-Z	Cities, A-Z
	e.g.
675.W2	Washington, D.C. Tomb of the Unknown Soldier
	Including addresses
680.A-Z	Other regions or countries, A-Z

    Period between world wars (1919-1939)

720	General works
723	General special
725	Essays, etc.

      European social life and customs. Civilization

726	General works
726.5	Fascism
727	Political and diplomatic history
728	Rome-Berlin axis

    World War II (1939-1945)

731	Periodicals. Serials. Collections
732	Societies

      Museums, exhibitions, etc.

733.A1	General works	
733.A2-Z	By region or country, A-Z	
	Under each country:	
	.x	*General works*
	.x2A-.x2Z	*Special, by city, A-Z*
	Denmark	
733.D39	General works	

World War II (1939-1945)
Museums, exhibitions, etc.
By region or country, A-Z
Denmark -- Continued

733.D4C65   Copenhagen. Museet for Danmarks frihedskamp
1940-1945
Congresses, conferences, etc.

734.A1   General works
Including works on two or more conferences

734.A2-Z   Individual congresses, conferences, etc.
Sources and documents

735.A1   Collection and preservation of war records

735.A7   Atlantic Declaration, August 14, 1941
Biography
For personal narratives see D811+

736   Collective
Class here collective military biography
For collective military biography limited to a country see the
military operations of the country, e.g. D764, Soviet
Union
For collective biography limited to a campaign, battle, etc.,
special troops, or topic, see the campaign, battle, etc.,
troops, or topic e. g. D756.5.D8, Dunkirk, Battle of;
D757.6, German airborne troops; D769.8.A6, Japanese
Americans
Individual
For individual biography of prominent military leaders see the
country of the individual in DA-DU, E-F, or other
appropriate class, e. g. E745, George S. Patton;
DA69.3.H3, Douglas Haig
For all other biography chiefly describing the subject's
participation in the war see the topic, troops, campaign or
battle, e. g. D761, general works on French participation;
D756.5.D8, Dunkirk, Battle of; D757.6, German airborne
troops, D769.8.A6, Japanese Americans
For individual biography not limited to the war see the country
of the individual in DA-DU, E-F, or other appropriate class

739   Collected works

740   Dictionaries
Causes. Origins. Aims

741   General works

742.A-Z   By region or country, A-Z

743   General works

743.2   Pictorial works
For art and the war see N9160+

743.22   Films, slides, etc. Catalogs

743.23   Motion pictures about the war

World War II (1939-1945) -- Continued

743.25	Posters
743.27	Collectibles
(743.3)	Maps and atlases
	see G1038, etc.
743.4	Study and teaching
743.42	Historiography
	Including criticism of books on the war
743.5	Outlines, syllabi, tables, etc.
	Including chronology of the war
743.6	Examinations, questions, etc.
743.7	Juvenile works. Elementary textbooks
743.9	Pamphlets, addresses, sermons, etc.
744	General special
	Ethical and religious aspects
	Cf. D810.C5+ Churches
744.4	General works
744.5.A-Z	By region or country, A-Z
744.55	Psychological aspects
	Social aspects
744.6	General works
744.7.A-Z	By region or country, A-Z
	War poetry
	see class P
745	Satire, caricature, etc.
745.2	English
745.3	French
745.5	German
745.7.A-Z	Other languages, A-Z
	e.g.
745.7.I8	Italian
745.7.P6	Polish
745.7.R9	Russian
(746-746.5)	Views, films, posters, etc.
	see D743.2+
747	Guides to the battlefields
	For guides to special battlefields, see the individual battle
	Diplomatic history. General relations (towards war)
748	General works
749	General special. Neutrality
749.5.A-Z	Separate treaties during the war, A-Z
749.5.A5	Anglo-Soviet treaty, May 26, 1942
749.5.A55	Anti-Comintern pact
749.5.G7	Great Britain-Poland mutual assistance treaty, August 25, 1939
	Hitler-Stalin pact see D749.5.R8
749.5.R8	Russo-German treaty, August 23, 1939

World War II (1939-1945)
   Diplomatic history. General relations (towards war)
     Separate treaties during the war, A-Z -- Continued

749.5.U6	United States-Iraq mutual aid treaty, July 31, 1945
	By region or country
750	Great Britain
751	Germany
752	France
752.8	The Americas. Neutrality
	United States and the war. Neutrality
	For reasons for American participation, see D742.U5
753	General works
753.2.A-Z	Mutual aid (Lend-lease) agreements. By region or country, A-Z
753.3	Enemy conspiracies, propaganda, espionage, etc.
753.7	Asian Americans and the war
753.8	Japanese Americans and the war
	Cf. D769.8.A6 Japanese American participation in the war and evacuation, relocation, and internment of Japanese Americans
754.A-Z	Other regions, countries, or groups of countries, A-Z
	e.g.
754.A34	Africa
754.A46	Alps, Western
754.B36	Balkan Peninsula
	Ireland
754.I5	General works
754.I6	Irish Free State
754.I7	Northern Ireland
	Levant see D754.N34
754.N34	Near East
754.S29	Scandinavia
754.Y9	Yugoslavia
	Military operations. The war effort
	General works see D743
	By period
	September 1939-December 1941
755	General works
755.1	September 1939-May 1940
755.2	1940
755.3	1941
755.4	1942
755.5	1943
755.6	1944
	1945
755.7	General works
755.8	VE Day to VJ Day

World War II (1939-1945)
Military operations. The war effort
By region
Western

756	General works
756.3	General special
756.5.A-Z	Individual campaigns, battles, etc., A-Z
	e.g.
756.5.A7	Ardennes, Battle of the, 1944-1945
756.5.A78	Arras, Battle of, 1940
756.5.C2	Calais, Battle of, 1940
756.5.D5	Dieppe raid, 1942
756.5.D8	Dunkirk, France, Battle of, 1940
756.5.M4	Meuse, Battle of the, 1940-
756.5.V3	Verdun, Battle of, 1940
	Germany
757	General works
757.1	Armies
757.2	Army Corps
	Infantry
757.3	General works
757.32.A-Z	Divisions, regiments, etc. By author, A-Z
	Mountain troops
757.39	General works
757.4.A-Z	Divisions, regiments, etc. By author, A-Z
757.5	Artillery
757.53	Anti-aircraft artillery
	Panzer troops
757.54	General works
757.55.A-Z	Divisions, regiments, etc. By name, A-Z
	e.g.
757.55.R6	"Die roten Teufel"
757.56	Individual divisions. By number
757.565	Individual corps. By number
757.57	Individual regiments. By number
757.6	Airborne troops
757.63	Parachute troops
757.64	Motorcycle troops
757.65	Signal Corps (Nachrichten truppen)
757.66	Reconnaissance troops
757.8	Engineers
757.83	Nebeltruppe
757.85	Waffenschutzstaffel of the Nazi Party (Waffen SS)
757.855	Technische Truppen
757.9.A-Z	Local, A-Z
	e.g.
757.9.H3	Hamburg

World War II (1939-1945)
Military operations. The war effort
By region
Western -- Continued
Great Britain

759	General works
759.5	Divisions, regiments, etc. By number
	e.g.
759.5 51st	The Fifty-first (Highland) Division
759.52	Artillery
	Cf. D760.A+ By region or name
759.523	Anti-Aircraft Command
759.527	Light Anti-Aircraft Artillery regiments
759.528	Armored divisions, regiments, etc.
759.53	Infantry
	Cf. D760.A+ By region or name
759.54	Cavalry
	Cf. D760.A+ By region or name
759.55	Engineers
	Airborne troops
759.6	General works
759.63	Parachute troops
760.A-Z	Special, by region or name, A-Z
	e.g.
760.A1	Colonies (General)
760.A8	Auxiliary territorial service
760.D4	Devonshire Regiment
760.I7	Irish Guards
760.P5	Pioneer Corps
760.R7	Royal Armoured Corps
760.8.A-Z	Local history, A-Z
	e.g.
760.8.B3	Bath
760.8.B4	Belfast
760.8.B7	Bristol
760.8.C6	Coventry
760.8.D6	Dover
760.8.E3	East Downing
760.8.E7	Essex
760.8.E88	Exeter
760.8.K4	Kent
760.8.L6	Liverpool
760.8.L7	London
760.8.M3	Manchester
760.8.S75	Stepney (Middlesex)
	France
761	General works

World War II (1939-1945)
Military operations. The war effort
By region
Western
France -- Continued

761.1	Armies
761.15	Army Corps
761.2	Divisions
	Infantry
761.3	General works
761.38	Zouaves
761.5	Chasseurs. Chasseurs alpins
761.6	Artillery
761.7	Parachute troops
761.9.A-Z	Other, A-Z
	e.g.
761.9.A1	Colonies (General)
761.9.F7	France combattante. French volunteer force. Free French forces
761.9.P6	Polish forces
762.A-Z	Local history, A-Z
	e.g.
762.P3	Paris
763.A-Z	Other regions or countries, A-Z
	e.g.
	Belgium
763.B4	General works
	Divisions, regiments, etc.
763.B41	By number
763.B415	By name
763.B42A-.B42Z	Local history, A-Z
	Denmark
763.D4	General works
763.D413-.D42	Divisions, regiments, etc. By author, A-Z
763.D42A-.D42Z	Local history, A-Z
763.I2	Iceland
	Italy
763.I8	General works
763.I813A-.I813Z	Divisions, regiments, etc. By author, A-Z
	Corpo volontari della libertà
763.I815	General works
763.I817A-.I817Z	Divisions, brigades, A-Z
763.I82A-.I82Z	Local history, A-Z
763.L9	Luxembourg
763.M3	Malta
	Netherlands
763.N4	General works

World War II (1939-1945)
 Military operations. The war effort
  By region
   Western
    Other regions or countries, A-Z
     Netherlands -- Continued

763.N41	Divisions, regiments, etc. (not A-Z)
763.N42A-.N42Z	Local history, A-Z
	Norway
763.N6	General works
763.N613A-.N613Z	Divisions, regiments, etc. By author, A-Z
763.N62A-.N62Z	Local history, A-Z
763.S5	Sicily
763.5	Arctic regions
	Including Greenland
	Eastern
764	General works. Soviet Union (General)
764.3.A-Z	Individual campaigns, battles, etc., A-Z
	e.g.
764.3.L4	Leningrad, Siege of, 1941-1944
	Saint Petersburg, Siege of, 1941-1944 see D764.3.L4
764.3.S7	Stalingrad, Battle of, 1942-1943
764.6	Divisions, regiments, etc. (not A-Z)
764.7.A-Z	Local history, A-Z
	e.g.
764.7.K5	Klintsy
	Poland
765	General works
765.13	Divisions, regiments, etc. (not A-Z)
765.2.A-Z	Local history, A-Z
	e.g.
765.2.W3	Warsaw
	Including Warsaw Ghetto Uprising, 1943, and Warsaw Uprising, 1944
765.2.W7	Wrocław (Breslau)
	Finland
	Including Continuation War, 1941-1944
765.3	General works
765.32	Divisions, regiments, etc. (not A-Z)
765.35.A-Z	Local history, A-Z
	Austria
765.4	General works
765.45.A-Z	Local history, A-Z
	e.g.
765.45.V6	Vorarlberg
	Czechoslovakia

World War II (1939-1945)
Military operations. The war effort
By region
Eastern
Czechoslovakia -- Continued

765.5	General works
765.53	Divisions, regiments, etc. (not A-Z)
765.55.A-Z	Local history, A-Z
	e.g.
765.55.P7	Prague

Hungary

765.56	General works
765.562.A-Z	Local, A-Z
	e.g.
765.562.B8	Budapest

Balkans and the Near East. Eastern Mediterranean

766	General works

By country

766.3	Greece
766.32.A-Z	Local history, A-Z
	e.g.
766.32.C4	Cephalonia

Romania

766.4.A1-.A15	Societies
766.4.A2	Collections
766.4.A3-Z	General works
766.413	Divisions, regiments, etc. (not A-Z)
766.42.A-Z	Local history, A-Z

Yugoslavia

766.6.A1-.A15	Societies
766.6.A2	Collections
766.6.A3-Z	General works
766.613	Divisions, regiments, etc. (not A-Z)
766.62.A-Z	Local history, A-Z
	e.g.
766.62.Z3	Zagreb
766.7.A-Z	Other regions or countries, A-Z
	e.g.
766.7.A4	Albania
766.7.C7	Crete
766.7.S9	Syria

Africa

766.8	General works
766.82	North Africa
766.83	Northeast Africa
766.84	East Africa
766.9	Egypt

                              World War II (1939-1945)
                                Military operations. The war effort
                                  By region
                                    Africa -- Continued
766.92   Ethiopia
766.93   Libya
766.95   Zaire
766.96   French Equatorial Africa
766.97   South Africa
766.99.A-Z   Other regions or countries, A-Z
                                          e.g.
766.99.A4   Algeria
766.99.M3   Madagascar
766.99.T8   Tunisia
                                    Far East. Battle of the Pacific
                                        Including military and naval operations
767   General works
                                      Japan
767.2   General works
767.23   Divisions, regiments, etc. (not A-Z)
767.25.A-Z   Local history, A-Z
                                            e.g.
767.25.H6   Hiroshima
767.25.N3   Nagasaki
                                          Okinawa Island see D767.99.O45
                                          Ryukyu Islands see D767.99.O45
767.255   Korea
767.3   China
                                      Cochin China
767.35   General works
767.352.A-Z   Local history, A-Z
                                            e.g.
767.352.S3   Saigon
767.4   Philippines
767.45   French Indochina
767.47   Thailand
767.5   Malay Peninsula
767.55   Singapore
                                      India. Burma
767.6   General works
767.63   Free India (Azad Hind), 1943-1945
                                          Including Indian National Army, 1942-1945
767.7   Indonesia
                                      Australia
767.8   General works
767.813.A-Z   Divisions, regiments, etc. By author, A-Z
767.82.A-Z   Local history, A-Z

	World War II (1939-1945)
	Military operations. The war effort
	By region
	Far East. Battle of the Pacific
	Australia
767.83.A-Z	Special topics, A-Z
767.83.A98	Australians of Italian descent. Italian Australians. Italians
	Italian Australians see D767.83.A98
	Italians see D767.83.A98
	New Zealand
767.85	General works
767.851.A-Z	Divisions, regiments, etc. By author, A-Z
767.852.A-Z	Local history, A-Z
	Pacific islands
767.9	General works
(767.913)	Aleutian Islands
	see D769.87.A4
767.917	Gilbert Islands
767.92	Hawaiian Islands
767.94	Midway Islands
	Cf. D774.M5 Battle of Midway, 1942
767.95	New Guinea
767.98	Solomon Islands
767.99.A-Z	Other islands, A-Z
	e.g.
767.99.I9	Iwo Jima
767.99.M3	Marshall Islands
767.99.N4	New Britain (Island)
767.99.O45	Okinawa Island. Ryukyu Islands
767.99.P4	Pelew Islands
767.99.S3	Saipan
	The Americas
768	General works
	Canada
768.15	General works
768.153.A-Z	Divisions, regiments, etc. By author, A-Z
768.154.A-Z	Local history, A-Z
768.155.A-Z	Special topics, A-Z
768.155.C34	Canadians of German descent. German Canadians. Germans
	Including evacuation, relocation, and internment
768.155.C35	Canadians of Japanese descent. Japanese Canadians. Japanese
	Including evacuation, relocation, and internment
	Latin America
768.18	General works

World War II (1939-1945)
  Military operations. The war effort
    By region
      The Americas
        Latin America -- Continued
768.2   Mexico
768.3   Brazil
768.7   Suriname
              United States
                  For the internal history of the United States see
                      E806+
769.A1-.A15   Societies
769.A2   Collections
(769.A3)   Compendium of legislative acts
                      see KF
769.A5-Z   General works on participation in the war
769.1   General special
                      For reasons for American participation, see D742.U5
769.15   Pamphlets, etc.
                  Military operations
                    General works see D769.A5+
769.2   General special
                    Individual expeditions, battles, etc.
                        see D756.5, D767, etc.
                    Armies, divisions, regiments, etc.
                        For Army Air Forces see D790.2+
769.25   Headquarters, general staff, etc.
769.255   Army Groups. By number
769.26   Armies. By number
769.27   Army Corps
                    Divisions, regiments, etc.
769.29   General works
                      Individual divisions
769.295.A-Z   By name, A-Z
                            Subarrange by author
769.295.A5   Americal
769.3   By number
                            Subarrange by author
                      Armored divisions
769.305   General works
769.3053   By number
                            Subarrange by author
769.3055   Armored regiments. By name
                            Subarrange by author
769.3058   Reconnaissance battalions. By number
                            Subarrange by author

World War II (1939-1945)
Military operations. The war effort
By region
The Americas
United States
Military operations
Armies, divisions, regiments, etc.
Divisions, regiments, etc.
Armored divisions -- Continued

769.306	Tank battalions. By number
	Subarrange by author
769.307	Tank destroyer battalions. By name
	Subarrange by author
769.308	First Cavalry Division
769.309	Civil Affairs Division
	Infantry
769.31	Regiments, combat teams, etc. By number
	Subarrange by author
	Cavalry
769.32	General works
769.325	Individual groups, squadrons, etc. By number
	Subarrange by author
	Engineers
769.33	General works
	Individual battalions, brigades, etc.
769.335	By number
	Subarrange by author
769.337.A-Z	By name, A-Z
	Subarrange by author
	Field artillery
769.34	Individual groups, battalions, etc. By number
	Subarrange by author
	Anti-aircraft artillery
769.342	General works
769.343	Individual battalions, etc. By number
	Airborne troops
769.345	General works
769.346	Individual battalions, etc. By number
	Parachute troops
769.347	General works
769.348	Individual battalions, etc. By number
	Subarrange by author
	Chemical Corps
769.35	General works
769.353	Individual battalions, companies, etc. By type
	Subarrange by number
	Signal Corps

World War II (1939-1945)
  Military operations. The war effort
    By region
      The Americas
        United States
          Military operations
            Armies, divisions, regiments, etc.
              Signal Corps -- Continued

769.36	General works
769.363	Individual battalions, etc. By number

             Marine Corps
              Class here land operations only
              For Marine aerial operations see D790.4+
              Cf. D769.45 Naval operations

769.369	General works
769.37	Individual divisions. By number
769.372	Individual regiments. By number
769.375	Chaplain Corps

              Cf. D810.C35+ Chaplain service in the war

769.39	Women's Army Corps
769.4	Other

           Naval operations
            For Naval aerial operations see D790.3+
            General works see D773+

769.45	General special

              Including defensive areas, land batteries, Marine
                Corps
              Cf. D769.369+ Land operations of Marine
                Corps
             Individual engagements
              see D767, D774
             Fleets, squadrons, etc.

769.5	Individual fleets. By number
769.52.A-Z	Forces, divisions. By name, A-Z
769.53	Task forces. By number

              For individual ships see D774.A+
             Service squadrons

769.535	General works
769.537	Individual squadrons. By number

            Naval operating bases

769.54	General works
769.542.A-Z	Individual bases. By place, A-Z

              e.g.

769.542.G5	Guam

              Established by Lion Six
           Construction battalions

769.55	General works

World War II (1939-1945)
Military operations. The war effort
By region
The Americas
United States
Naval operations
Construction battalions -- Continued
769.552	Individual battalions. By number
	Construction battalion maintenance units
769.554	General works
769.555	Individual units. By number
769.585	Coast Guard Reserve (Temporary Reserve)
	Including U.S. Volunteer Port Security Force
769.59	Chaplain Corps
	Cf. D810.C35+ Chaplains (General)
769.597	Naval Reserve. Women's Reserve (WAVES)
769.598	Coast Guard Reserve. Women's Reserve (SPARS)
769.64	Sino-American Cooperative Organization
	Transportation service
(769.72)	General works
	see D810.T8
	Transportation Corps
769.73	General works
769.733	Individual battalions, etc. By number
	Ordnance
769.74	General works
769.743	Individual battalions, etc. By number
	Services of supply. Army service forces
769.75	General works
769.753	Quartermaster base depots. By number
769.76	Technical intelligence service
	Provost-Marshal-General's Bureau
769.77	General works
769.775	Military Police
769.8.A-Z	Special topics, A-Z
	African Americans see D810.N4
769.8.A5	Alien enemies
769.8.A6	Americans of Japanese descent. Japanese Americans. Japanese
	Including participation in the war and evacuation, relocation, and internment of Japanese Americans
	Cf. D753.8 Japanese Americans and the war
	Cf. KF7224.5 Legal aspects
(769.8.C4)	Civil liberty. Freedom of speech
	see KF4741+

World War II (1939-1945)
  Military operations. The war effort
    By region
      The Americas
        United States
          Special topics, A-Z -- Continued
            Conscientious objectors see UB342.A+
            Economic aspects see HC106.4
            Espionage see D753.3
            Food control see HD9000.9.A+
769.8.F6   Foreign population
                     Including contribution to the war effort
                     Cf. D769.8.A5 Alien enemies
769.8.F7A-.F7Z   Special nationalities, A-Z
769.8.F7G4   German Americans
                         Including evacuation, relocation, and internment
769.8.F7I8   Italian Americans
                         Including evacuation, relocation, and internment
                       Japanese Americans see D769.8.A6
769.8.F7K67   Korean Americans
769.8.F7M45   Mexican Americans
769.8.F7Y84   Yugoslav Americans
769.8.H58   Hispanic Americans
                    Indians see D810.I5
769.8.L6   Local government and the war
769.8.P6   Political prisoners
                    Red Cross and hospital service see D807.U6+
                    Relief, charities, etc. see D809.U5
769.8.S5   Service flags
769.8.T8   Trophies, Military
769.85.A-Z   By region or state, A-Z
                    Alabama
769.85.A2   General works
769.85.A21A-.A21Z   Local, A-Z
                    Arizona
769.85.A7   General works
769.85.A71A-.A71Z   Local, A-Z
                    Arkansas
769.85.A8   General works
769.85.A81A-.A81Z   Local, A-Z
                    California
769.85.C2   General works
769.85.C21A-.C21Z   Local, A-Z
                    Colorado
769.85.C6   General works
769.85.C61A-.C61Z   Local, A-Z
                    Connecticut

World War II (1939-1945)
   Military operations. The war effort
     By region
       The Americas
         United States
           By region or state, A-Z
             Connecticut -- Continued

769.85.C8	General works
769.85.C81A-.C81Z	Local, A-Z
	Delaware
769.85.D4	General works
769.85.D41A-.D41Z	Local, A-Z
769.85.D6	District of Columbia
	Florida
769.85.F5	General works
769.85.F51A-.F51Z	Local, A-Z
	Georgia
769.85.G4	General works
769.85.G41A-.G41Z	Local, A-Z
	Idaho
769.85.I2	General works
769.85.I21A-.I21Z	Local, A-Z
	Illinois
769.85.I3	General works
769.85.I31A-.I31Z	Local, A-Z
	Indiana
769.85.I6	General works
769.85.I7A-.I7Z	Local, A-Z
	Iowa
769.85.I8	General works
769.85.I9A-.I9Z	Local, A-Z
	Kansas
769.85.K2	General works
769.85.K21A-.K21Z	Local, A-Z
	Kentucky
769.85.K4	General works
769.85.K41A-.K41Z	Local, A-Z
	Louisiana
769.85.L6	General works
769.85.L61A-.L61Z	Local, A-Z
	Maine
769.85.M2	General works
769.85.M21A-.M21Z	Local, A-Z
	Maryland
769.85.M3	General works
769.85.M31A-.M31Z	Local, A-Z
	Massachusetts

World War II (1939-1945)
>
> Military operations. The war effort
>
>> By region
>>
>>> The Americas
>>>
>>>> United States
>>>>
>>>>> By region or state, A-Z
>>>>>
>>>>>> Massachusetts -- Continued

769.85.M4	General works
769.85.M41A-.M41Z	Local, A-Z
	Michigan
769.85.M5	General works
769.85.M51A-.M51Z	Local, A-Z
	Minnesota
769.85.M6	General works
769.85.M61A-.M61Z	Local, A-Z
	Mississippi
769.85.M7	General works
769.85.M71A-.M71Z	Local, A-Z
	Missouri
769.85.M8	General works
769.85.M81A-.M81Z	Local, A-Z
	Montana
769.85.M9	General works
769.85.M91A-.M91Z	Local, A-Z
	Nebraska
769.85.N19	General works
769.85.N2A-.N2Z	Local, A-Z
	Nevada
769.85.N22	General works
769.85.N23A-.N23Z	Local, A-Z
	New Hampshire
769.85.N25	General works
769.85.N26A-.N26Z	Local, A-Z
	New Jersey
769.85.N3	General works
769.85.N31A-.N31Z	Local, A-Z
	New Mexico
769.85.N33	General works
769.85.N34A-.N34Z	Local, A-Z
	New York
769.85.N4	General works
769.85.N5A-.N5Z	Local, A-Z
	North Carolina
769.85.N8	General works
769.85.N81A-.N81Z	Local, A-Z
	North Dakota
769.85.N9	General works

World War II (1939-1945)
Military operations. The war effort
By region
The Americas
United States
By region or state, A-Z
North Dakota -- Continued

769.85.N91A-.N91Z	Local, A-Z
	Ohio
769.85.O3	General works
769.85.O31A-.O31Z	Local, A-Z
	Oklahoma
769.85.O5	General works
769.85.O51A-.O51Z	Local, A-Z
	Oregon
769.85.O8	General works
769.85.O81A-.O81Z	Local, A-Z
	Pennsylvania
769.85.P4	General works
769.85.P41A-.P41Z	Local, A-Z
	Rhode Island
769.85.R4	General works
769.85.R41A-.R41Z	Local, A-Z
	South Carolina
769.85.S6	General works
769.85.S61A-.S61Z	Local, A-Z
	South Dakota
769.85.S7	General works
769.85.S71A-.S71Z	Local, A-Z
	Tennessee
769.85.T2	General works
769.85.T21A-.T21Z	Local, A-Z
	Texas
769.85.T4	General works
769.85.T41A-.T41Z	Local, A-Z
	Utah
769.85.U8	General works
769.85.U81A-.U81Z	Local, A-Z
	Vermont
769.85.V5	General works
769.85.V51A-.V51Z	Local, A-Z
	Virginia
769.85.V8	General works
769.85.V81A-.V81Z	Local, A-Z
	Washington
769.85.W3	General works
769.85.W31A-.W31Z	Local, A-Z

World War II (1939-1945)
  Military operations. The war effort
    By region
      The Americas
        United States
          By region or state, A-Z -- Continued
            West Virginia

769.85.W4	General works
769.85.W41A-.W41Z	Local, A-Z
	Wisconsin
769.85.W6	General works
769.85.W61A-.W61Z	Local, A-Z
	Wyoming
769.85.W8	General works
769.85.W81A-.W81Z	Local, A-Z
769.87.A-Z	Outlying possessions, A-Z
769.87.A4	Aleutian Islands
(769.87.H3)	Hawaii
	see D767.92
769.88.A-Z	Special nationalities, A-Z
	e.g.
769.88.A7	Armenian
(769.9)	Personal narratives and other accounts
	see D811

Naval operations
  For freedom of the seas see KZA1348+

770	General works. Battle of the Atlantic
	Anglo-German
771	General works. Blockade
772.A-Z	By engagement, ship, etc., A-Z
	e.g.
772.A4	Altmark (Ship)
772.A5	Anglo-Saxon (Steamship)
772.A66	Ark Royal (Aircraft carrier)
772.A7	Athenia (Steamship)
772.B5	Bismarck (Battleship)
772.D7	Dragon (Cruiser)
772.F5	Firedrake (Destroyer)
772.G7	Admiral Graf Spee (Battleship)
772.H6	Hood (Battle cruiser)
772.P4	Penelope (Cruiser)
772.S25	San Demetrio (Tanker)
772.3	Russo-German
	Including Arctic Ocean and Baltic Sea only
	United States
773	General works. Blockade. Patrol

World War II (1939-1945)
  Naval operations
    United States -- Continued

774.A-Z	By engagement, ship, etc., A-Z
	e.g.
774.A7	Arkansas (Battleship)
774.B57	Bismarck Sea, Battle of the, 1943
774.B6	Boise (Cruiser)
774.D3	Dashiell (Destroyer)
774.E5	Enterprise (Aircraft carrier)
774.E7	Essex (Aircraft carrier)
774.G3	General W.H. Gordon (Transport)
774.H3	Hancock (Aircraft carrier)
774.H4	Helena (Cruiser)
774.H6	Hornet (Aircraft carrier)
774.L4	Lexington (Aircraft carrier, 1st of the name)
774.M3	Marblehead (Cruiser)
774.M35	Maryland (Battleship)
774.M5	Midway, Battle of, 1942
774.N4	New Orleans (Cruiser)
774.O3	O'Bannon (Destroyer)
774.P7	Princess (Aircraft carrier)
774.S3	Saratoga (Aircraft carrier)
774.S318	Savo Island, Battle of, 1942
774.S32	Savo Island (Aircraft carrier)
774.S6	South Dakota (Battleship)

    Anglo-Italian

775	General works
775.5.A-Z	By engagement, ship, etc., A-Z
	e.g.
775.5.S8	Sydney (Cruiser)

    Japan

777	General works
777.5.A-Z	By engagement, ship, etc., A-Z
	Bismarck Sea, Battle of the, 1943 see D774.B57
	Midway, Battle of, 1942 see D774.M5
	Savo Island, Battle of, 1942 see D774.S318
779.A-Z	Other regions or countries, A-Z

  Submarine operations
    Including operations of submarine chasers

780	General works

    Germany

781	General works
782.A-Z	By engagement, ship, etc., A-Z
	e.g.
782.C6	City of Benares (Steamship)
782.M6	Montevideo (Steamship)

	World War II (1939-1945)
	Submarine operations
	Germany
	By engagement, ship, etc., A-Z -- Continued
782.R6	Robin Moor (Steamship)
	United States
783	General works
783.5.A-Z	By engagement, ship, etc., A-Z
	e.g.
783.5.C6	Coast guard reserve boat 3070
783.5.S4	Seawolf (Submarine)
783.5.S5	Silversides (Submarine)
783.5.S8	Sturgeon (Submarine)
	Japan
783.6	General works
783.7	By engagement, ship, etc. (not A-Z)
784.A-Z	Other regions or countries, A-Z
	Amphibious operations
784.5	General works
784.52.A-Z	By region or country, A-Z
	Aerial operations
785	General works
	U.S. Strategic Bombing Survey reports
785.U57	General works
785.U58A-.U58Z	By industry, A-Z
785.U6	European War
785.U63	Pacific War
786	Great Britain
787	Germany
788	France
	United States
790	General works
	Class works on individual campaigns or battles with the campaign or battle
	Army Air Forces
790.2	General works
790.22	Individual air forces. By number. Subarrange by author
790.23	Individual divisions. By number. Subarrange by author
790.24	Individual wings. By number. Subarrange by author
	Commands
790.244	General works
790.2442	Individual bomber commands. By number. Subarrange by author
790.2443	Individual fighter commands. By number. Subarrange by author
	Groups

World War II (1939-1945)
Aerial operations
United States
Army Air Forces
Groups -- Continued

790.25	General works
790.252	Individual fighter groups. By number. Subarrange by author
790.253	Individual bomber groups. By number. Subarrange by author
790.254	Other. Subarrange by author
	Squadrons
790.26	General works
790.262	Individual fighter squadrons. By number. Subarrange by author
790.263	Individual bomber squadrons. By number. Subarrange by author
790.264	Other. Subarrange by author
	Navy
790.3	General works
790.33	Air groups (General)
790.35	Individual air groups. By number. Subarrange by author
	Squadrons
790.37	General works
790.373	Individual attack squadrons. By number. Subarrange by author
790.375	Individual fighter squadrons. By number. Subarrange by author
790.376	Individual patrol squadrons. By number. Subarrange by author
790.378	Individual torpedo squadrons. By number. Subarrange by author
	Marine Corps
790.4	General works
	Air wings
790.43	General works
790.433	Individual wings. By number. Subarrange by author
	Air groups
790.45	General works
790.453	Individual groups. By number. Subarrange by author
	Squadrons
790.47	General works
790.473	Individual squadrons. Subarrange by author
790.5	Women's Air Force Service Pilots (WASPs)
792.A-Z	Other regions or countries, A-Z

	World War II (1939-1945) -- Continued
793	Tank operations
	Cf. UE159 Tactics
	Cf. UG446.5 Military engineering
794	Cavalry operations
	Cf. D769.32+ United States
794.5	Commando operations
	Engineering operations
795.A2	General works
795.A3-Z	By region or country, A-Z
	Medals, badges, decorations of honor
	Including lists of recipients and individual recipients of medals
796	General works
796.5.A-Z	By region or country, A-Z
	Registers, lists of dead and wounded, etc.
797.A2	General
797.A3-Z	By region or country, A-Z

Under each country:

| .x | General works |
| .x2A-.x2Z | Local, A-Z |

	Press. Censorship. Publicity. Radio
798	General works
799.A-Z	By region or country, A-Z
800	Economic aspects. Commerce, finance, etc. (General)
	For special topics or individual countries, see HC, HF, HJ
	Alien enemies
801.A2	General works
801.A3-Z	By region or country, A-Z
	e.g.
801.F8	France
	United States see D769.8.A6
	Occupied territory
	Including underground movements
802.A2	General works
802.A3-Z	By region or country, A-Z

Under each country:

| .x | General works |
| .x2A-.x2Z | Local, A-Z |

	e.g.
802.C7-.C72	Croatia
802.M3-.M32	Marshall Islands
802.N7-.N72	Norway
802.R95-.R952	Ruthenia
802.S55-.S552	Sicily
802.S67-.S672	Slovenia
802.T7-.T72	Tripolitania

World War II (1939-1945) -- Continued
    Atrocities. War crimes.
        For war crimes trials, see KZ1174+

803	General works
804.A-Z	By region or country committing atrocity, A-Z

        For works on atrocities in a particular locality see D756+
        Holocaust
            For works on the Holocaust in a particular locality see
                DS135.A+
            Cf. BM645.H6 Holocaust in Jewish theology
            Cf. D810.J4 Jewish military participation in World War II

804.15	Periodicals. Societies. Serials

        Museums. Exhibitions, etc.
            Cf. D805.5.A+ Individual concentration camp
                memorials

804.17	General works
804.175.A-Z	Individual. By city, A-Z
804.177	Holocaust Remembrance Day. Days of Remembrance of the Victims of the Shoah
804.18	Congresses
804.19	Sources and documents

        Biography and memoirs (General and Jewish)
            For history and criticism of biography and memoirs
                see D804.348

804.195	Collective

        Individual by place see DS135.A+

804.196	Individual not limited by place, A-Z
804.25	Dictionaries. Chronological tables, outlines, etc.
804.3	General works
804.32	Pictorial works
804.33	Study and teaching
804.34	Juvenile literature
804.348	Historiography

            Including history and criticism of biography and memoirs

804.35	Holocaust denial literature
804.355	Holocaust denial. Criticism of Holocaust denial literature

        Public opinion

804.44	General works
804.45.A-Z	By region or country, A-Z

        Special groups of Jewish victims

804.47	Women
804.48	Children
804.5.A-Z	Other victim groups, A-Z

            Including biography (Individual and collective)

804.5.B55	Blacks
804.5.C37	Catholics

                                 World War II (1939-1945)
                                   Atrocities. War crimes
                                     Holocaust
                                       Other victim groups, A-Z -- Continued
804.5.C45   Children (General)
                                             Cf. D804.48 Jewish children
804.5.C47   Christians (General)
                                             Cf. D804.5.C37 Catholics
                                             Cf. D804.5.J44 Jehovah's Witnesses
                                             Cf. D804.5.J48 Jewish Christians
804.5.G38   Gays
                                             Cf. D810.G39 Gays in World War II
804.5.G85   Gypsies. Romanies
                                             Cf. D810.G9 Gypsies in World War II. Romanies in
                                                 World War II
804.5.H35   Handicapped. People with disabilities
                                             Including people with mental disabilities
804.5.J44   Jehovah's Witnesses
804.5.J46   Jesuits
804.5.J48   Jewish Christians
                                         People with disabilities see D804.5.H35
                                         People with mental disabilities see D804.5.H35
                                         Romanies see D804.5.G85
804.5.W65   Women (General)
                                             Cf. D804.47 Jewish women
                                     Rescue efforts
804.6   General works
                                       Righteous Gentiles
804.65   General works
804.66.A-Z   Individual, A-Z
804.7.A-Z   Other topics, A-Z
804.7.D43   Death marches
804.7.E26   Economic aspects
804.7.M67   Moral and ethical aspects
804.7.P73   Press coverage
                                 Prisoners and prisons
                                     Including internment camps, concentration camps, death
                                         camps, etc.
805.A1   Periodicals and societies
805.A2   General works
805.A3-Z   By individual regions or countries, A-Z
                                         Under each country:
                                         .A1-.A19   *Periodicals*
                                         .A2-.Z7   *General works*
                                         (.xZ8-9)   *Individual prisons, camps, etc., see*
                                                                     D805.5

	World War II (1939-1945)
	Prisoners and prisons -- Continued
805.5.A-Z	Individual prisons, camps, etc. By name, A-Z
	Including individual concentration camp memorials
	e. g.
805.5.A96	Auschwitz
805.6.A-Z	Special topics, A-Z
805.6.L35	Language
805.6.T44	Theater
	Medical and sanitary services. Hospitals. Red Cross
806	General works
807.A-Z	By region or country, A-Z
	e.g.
807.A8	Australia
807.H3	Hawaii
	United States
807.U6	General works
807.U62A-.U62W	By state, A-W
	Hawaii see D807.H3
(807.U72-.U74)	Army hospitals
(807.U85-.U87)	Navy hospitals
	Relief work. Charities. Protection. Refugees. Displaced persons
	Cf. D804.6+ Rescue efforts in the Holocaust
808	General works
809.A-Z	By region or country, A-Z
	e. g.
809.B4	Belgium
809.U5	United States
	Including American relief in other countries
810.A-Z	Other special topics, A-Z
	Adventists see D810.C53
	African Americans see D810.N4
810.A53	Aleuts
810.A6	Anarchism. Anarchists
810.A65	Animals in the war
	Including war use of dogs
	Cf. D810.V45 Veterinary service
810.A67	Antiquities
810.A7	Art and the war
810.A75	Astrology
810.A79	Athletes
810.B3	Bacterial warfare
	Baptists see D810.C56
810.B37	Basques
	Blacks see D810.N4
810.B55	Blind

World War II (1939-1945)
>> Other special topics, A-Z -- Continued

810.B66	Bomb reconnaissance
810.B7	Boy Scouts
	Buddhism
810.B83	General works
	By sect
810.B839	Zen Buddhism
	Burials see D810.D4
810.C2	Camouflage
	Carrier pigeons see D810.P53
810.C26	Cartography
810.C27	Catalans
	Catholic Church see D810.C6
	Chaplains (General)
810.C35	General works
810.C36A-.C36Z	By region or country, A-Z
	e.g.
810.C36U6	United States
	Cf. D769.375 Army Chaplain Corps (U.S.)
	Cf. D769.59 Navy Chaplain Corps (U.S.)
810.C38	Chemical warfare
810.C4	Children. Orphans
	Church of Christ, Scientist see D810.C62
	Church of the Brethren see D810.C63
	Churches
810.C5	General works
	By denomination
810.C53	Adventists
810.C56	Baptists
810.C6	Catholic Church
810.C62	Church of Christ, Scientist
810.C63	Church of the Brethren
810.C64	Evangelical and Reformed Church
810.C65	Friends, Society of
810.C66	Lutheran Church
810.C665	Mennonites
810.C67	Methodist Church
810.C674	Nihon Kirisuto Kyōdan
810.C6745	Orthodox Eastern Church
810.C68	Presbyterian Church
810.C69	Civil defense
	For technical works see UA926+
810.C698	Comfort women
810.C7	Communications
810.C8	Confiscation
810.C82	Conscientious objectors. War resisters. Draft resisters

World War II (1939-1945)
Other special topics, A-Z -- Continued

810.C83	Cossacks
810.C85	Counterfeiting
810.C88	Cryptography
810.D4	Dead, Care of. Repatriation of dead. Burial. Cemeteries
810.D5	Deportation
810.D57	Desertions
810.D6	Destruction and pillage

        Cf. D785.U57+ United States Strategic Bombing
           Survey reports

Draft resisters see D810.C82

Education and the war

810.E2	General works
	United States
810.E3	General works
810.E4A-.E4W	By state, A-W
810.E45A-.E45Z	By college, school, etc., A-Z
810.E46A-.E46Z	By fraternity, A-Z
810.E5A-.E5Z	Other regions or countries, A-Z
810.E6	Elks, Benevolent and Protective Order of
810.E8	Entertainment and recreation for soldiers

Evangelical and Reformed Church see D810.C64

Friends, Society of see D810.C65

810.F83	Fuel supplies
810.G39	Gays. Gay military participation

        Cf. D804.5.G38 Gay Holocaust victims

810.G57	Girl Scouts
810.G6	Governments in exile
810.G9	Gypsies. Romanies. Romani military participation

Homing pigeons see D810.P53

810.I5	Indians

Jewish military participation see D810.J4

810.J4	Jews. Jewish military participation

        Cf. D804.15+ Holocaust

810.L4	Lawyers and the war
810.L53	Libraries

        Class here works on the condition of libraries during the war,
           the effect of the war on libraries, etc.
        For works on library service to military personnel see
           Z675.W2

Logistics

810.L64	General works
810.L642A-.L642Z	By region or country, A-Z

Lutherans see D810.C66

Mennonites see D810.C665

Merchant marine see D810.T8

	World War II (1939-1945)
	Other special topics, A-Z -- Continued
810.M42	Meteorology
	Methodists see D810.C67
	Military intelligence see D810.S7+
810.M8	Muslims
	Naturalized subjects in belligerent countries
810.N2	General works
810.N3A-.N3Z	By region or country, A-Z
	For Japanese Americans in the United States see D753.8
	For alien enemies in the United States see D769.8.A5
810.N4	Negroes. African Americans. Blacks
	Nihon Kirisuto Kyōdan see D810.C674
	Orthodox Eastern Church see D810.C6745
810.P4	Photography
810.P53	Pigeons
	Presbyterians see D810.C68
	Propaganda
810.P6	General works
810.P7A-.P7Z	By region or country, A-Z
	Property damage see D810.D6
810.P75	Prophecies
810.P76	Protest movements
	Public opinion
810.P8	General works
810.P85A-.P85Z	By region or country, A-Z
810.R3	Race problems
810.R33	Radio, radar, etc.
	Romanies see D810.G9
810.R6	Rotary International
810.S2	Science and technology
	Search and rescue operations
810.S42	General works
810.S45A-.S45Z	By region or country, A-Z
	Seventh-Day Adventists see D810.C53
810.S46	Sex
	Cf. D810.C698 Comfort women
810.S47	Shinto
810.S5	Slavs
810.S6	Socialism
810.S65	Spaniards
	Spies. Secret service. Military intelligence
810.S7	General works
810.S8A-.S8Z	Individual spies, A-Z
	Technology see D810.S2

World War II (1939-1945)

Other special topics, A-Z -- Continued

810.T37	Tatars
810.T4	Temperance
810.T8	Transportation
	Including merchant marine
810.T95	Tyroleans
	Veterans
810.V4	General works
810.V42A-.V42Z	By region or country, A-Z
810.V45	Veterinary service
	War resisters see D810.C82
	Weather see D810.M42
810.W7	Women
810.Y7	Young Men's Christian Association. Young Women's Christian Association
810.Y74	Youth
	Zen Buddhism see D810.B839

Personal narratives and other accounts

For individual biography, see country of the individual in DA-F

For collective military biography of World War II see D736

811.A2	Collections

For collected personal narratives limited to military combatants of a country see the military operations of the country, e. g. D764, Soviet Union

For collected personal narratives limited to a campaign, battle, etc., special troops, or topics see the campaign, battle, etc., troops or topics, e. g. D756.D8, Dunkirk, Battle of; D757.6, German airborne troops; D769.8, Japanese Americans

811.A3-Z	Individual, A-Z

For personal narratives limited to a campaign, battle, etc., special troops, or topic see the campaign, battle, etc., troops or topic, e. g. D756.5.D8, Dunkirk, Battle of; D757.6, German airborne troops, D769.8.A6, Japanese Americans

811.5	Narratives by noncombatants
	Including collective and individual
	Armistice
812	General works
813.A-Z	By region or country, A-Z
	Peace
814	Sources and documents
	Surrender documents. By country
814.1	Germany
814.2	Italy

World War II (1939-1945)
 Peace
  Sources and documents
   Surrender documents. By country -- Continued

814.3	Japan
814.4	Council of Foreign Ministers (General)
814.413	Meeting in London, September 11-October 2, 1945
814.415	Meeting in Moscow, December 16-26, 1945
814.42	Meeting in Paris, April, 1946
814.425	Meeting in Paris, June 15-July 1946
814.43	Meeting in New York, November-December, 1946
814.44	Meeting in Moscow, March 10-April 24, 1947
814.45	Meeting in London, November 25-December 16, 1947
814.46	Meeting in Paris, May 23-June 20, 1949
814.47	Meeting in Berlin, January 25-February 18, 1954
	Treaties with Axis powers
814.55	Collections
814.56	Peace conferences (General)
814.565	Paris Conference, July 29-October 15, 1946
814.6	Germany
814.7	Italy
814.8	Japan
814.9.A-Z	Other countries, A-Z
815	General works
816	General special
816.5	Pamphlets, etc.
818	Indemnity and reparation
819.A-Z	By region or country, A-Z
820.A-Z	Other special topics, A-Z
820.D5	Disarmament
	Population transfers
820.P7	General works
820.P72A-.P72Z	By nationality, A-Z
820.T4	Territorial questions
	Special see D821.A+
821.A-Z	By country, groups of countries, etc., A-Z
	Class here beginnings of organization of new countries where territorial questions are concerned
	e.g.
	For annual reports, etc., of areas under international trusteeship, see JN and JQ
821.L4	Levant
821.L5	Lithuania
821.P3	Palestine
821.T8	Transylvania
821.Y8	Yugoslavia
	Including Trieste

World War II (1939-1945) -- Continued
Reconstruction

824	Sources and documents
825	General works
826	Pamphlets, etc.

By region or country
United States

827	General works
828.A-.W	By state, A-W
829.A-Z	Other countries or groups of countries, nationalities, etc., A-Z

e.g.

829.A33	Africa, South
829.D8	Dutch East Indies
829.E2	East Asia
829.J4	Jews

Cf. D829.P3 Palestine

829.L5	Lithuania
829.P3	Palestine

Cf. D829.J4 Jews

Celebrations. Memorials. Monuments
For memorials to special divisions, etc., see the history of the division

830	General works
831	Other

By region or country
United States

833	General works
835.A-.W	By state, A-W
836.A-Z	By city, A-Z
838.A-Z	Other regions or countries, A-Z

Under each country (except Great Britain):
.x   General works
.x2A-.x2Z   Local, A-Z
Great Britain

838.G6	General works
838.G7A-.G7Z	Local, A-Z

Post-war history (1945-   )
For Europe, 1945- see D1050+

839	Periodicals. Societies. Serials
839.2	Congresses. Conferences, etc.
839.3	Sources and documents

Biography
Collective

839.5	General works
839.66	Queens, princesses, etc.
839.7.A-Z	Individual, A-Z

Post-war history (1945-   ) -- Continued

840	General works
842	General special
	Including refugees
842.2	Military history
842.3	Naval history
	Ethnography of Western countries
842.4	General works
842.42.A-Z	Individual elements in the population not limited to special territorial divisions, A-Z
842.42.M87	Muslims
	1945-1965
	Periodicals see D839
842.5	General works
	Political and diplomatic history
843	General works
844	Pamphlets, etc.
845	North Atlantic Treaty, 1949
845.2	North Atlantic Treaty Council
847	Soviet bloc. Communist countries
847.2	Warsaw pact, 1955
	1965-1989
	Periodicals see D839
848	General works
	Political and diplomatic history
849	General works
849.5	Pamphlets, etc.
850	Soviet bloc. Communist countries
	1989-
856	General works
857	Social life and customs. Civilization. Intellectual life
858	Military history
860	Political and diplomatic history
	21st century
861	Periodicals. Societies. Serials
861.3	Congresses
861.4	Sources and documents
861.5	Dictionaries
861.6	Historiography
862	General works
862.3	Social life and customs. Civilization. Intellectual life
862.5	Military history
862.7	Naval history
863	Political history
863.3	Foreign and general relations
863.5-.7	Biography and memoirs
863.5	Collective

	21st century
	Biography and memoirs -- Continued
863.7.A-Z	Individual, A-Z
	Developing countries
880	Periodicals. Societies. Serials
881	Congresses
882	Sources and documents
883	General works
	Foreign and general relations
887	General works
888.A-Z	Relations with individual countries, A-Z
	Eastern hemisphere
890	Periodicals. Societies. Serials
891	General works
892	Description
	For voyages and travels see G490
893	History
	Europe (General)
	For individual countries, see DA-DR
900	Geography
	Description and travel
901	Periodicals. Collections
904	Gazetteers
905	Place names (General)
907	General works
908	Directories
909	Guidebooks
910	Pamphlets, etc.
	Including minor cruises, itineraries, etc.
910.5	Monumental and picturesque. Castles, halls, cathedrals, etc. Views
	By period
911	Through 1450
913	1451-1600
915	1601-1700
917	1701-1800
919	1801-1900
921	1901-1950
922	1951-1970
923	1971-
	By region
	Black Sea see DJK63
965	Northern Europe
965.5	North Sea
967	Western Europe
	Central Europe see DAW1014+
	Eastern Europe see DJK13+

	Europe (General)
	Description and travel
	By region -- Continued
	Balkan Peninsula see DR11.5+
971	Adriatic Sea
972	East-northern Mediterranean. Adriatic and Aegean
	Cf. DF895+ Islands of the Aegean
	Cf. DF901.C9 Cyclades
	Cf. DF901.I695 Ionian Sea
	Cf. DS51.A+ Turkish Islands in the Aegean Sea
973	General Mediterranean
	Including modern geography
974	Southern Europe
	Including general western Mediterranean
975	Old World (Europe, including Egypt and Palestine)
	Eastern Mediterranean (Bible lands, Orient) see DS41+
980	Juvenile travel
	Antiquities see CC160+
	Antiquities, Prehistoric see GN803+
990	Ethnography
	History
	For history of Europe to 1945, see D1+
	1945-
1050	Periodicals. Sources and documents. Collections
1050.5	Congresses. Conferences, etc.
	Study and teaching
1050.8	General works
1050.82.A-Z	By region or country, A-Z

Under each country:

.x	General works
.x2A-.x2Z	Schools. By place, A-Z

1051	General works
1053	General special
1055	Social life and customs. Civilization. Intellectual life
	Ethnography
1056	General works
1056.2.A-Z	Individual elements in the population not limited to special territorial divisions, A-Z
1056.2.A38	Africans
1056.2.A43	Algerians
1056.2.A7	Arabs
1056.2.B55	Blacks
1056.2.C55	Chinese
1056.2.F75	Frisians
1056.2.G35	Galicians (Spain)
1056.2.G45	Germans
1056.2.G73	Greeks

Europe (General)
History
1945-
Ethnography
Individual elements in the population not limited to
special territorial divisions, A-Z -- Continued

1056.2.I73	Iranians
1056.2.I75	Irish
1056.2.I82	Italians
1056.2.K87	Kurds
1056.2.L38	Latin Americans
1056.2.M87	Muslims
1056.2.P64	Poles
1056.2.S47	Serbs
1056.2.T87	Turks
1056.2.W34	Walsers
1056.2.Y83	Yugoslavs

Political and diplomatic history

1058	General works
1060	European federation
	Cf. JN15 Constitutional history
1065.A-Z	Relations with region and countries, A-Z
	For relations with individual countries prior to 1945
	see D34.A+
1065.U5	United States

Biography
Collective

1070	General works
1071	Women
1072	Public men
1073	Rulers, kings, etc.
1074	Queens, princesses, etc.
1075.A-Z	Individual, A-Z

1989-

2001	Congresses
2003	General works
2009	Political history

2001-

2015	Periodicals. Societies. Serials
2016	Congresses
2017	Sources and documents
2018	Dictionaries
2019	Historiography
2020	General works
2021	Social life and customs. Civilization. Intellectual life
2022	Military history
2023	Naval history

Europe (General)
  History
    2001- -- Continued

2024	Political history
	Foreign and general relations
2025	General works
2025.5.A-Z	Relations with individual regions or countries, A-Z
	e. g.
2025.5.U64	United States
	Biography and memoirs
2026	Collective
2027.A-Z	Individual, A-Z

History of Great Britain
  Historiography

1	General works
	Biography of historians
3.A1	Collective
3.A2-Z	Individual, A-Z
	e.g.
3.F9	Froude, James Anthony
3.M3	Macaulay, Thomas Babington Macaulay, baron
	For collected works and works about Macaulay as a literary author see PR4963
4	Study and teaching

British Empire. Commonwealth of Nations. The Commonwealth
      Including Great Britain, the dominions, and the colonies.
      For individual dominions and colonies, see DS-DU, F, etc.
      For administration of the British Colonies collectively and colonial policy see JV1000+

10	Periodicals. Societies. Collections
10.5	General works
11	Description and travel
13	Historical geography
16	History
	Biography and memoirs
16.8	Collective
17.A-Z	Individual, A-Z
	e.g.
17.D9	Dufferin and Ava, Frederick Temple Hamilton-Temple Blackwood, 1st Marquis of
17.E4	Elgin, James Bruce, 8th Earl of
17.M2	Maitland, Sir Thomas
17.W4	Weld, Sir Frederick Aloysius
	Political history. Imperial federation
	Cf. JN248 Political institutions and public administration
18	General works
18.2.A-Z	Relations with Commonwealth countries. By region or country, A-Z
	England
20	Periodicals. Societies
	Museums, exhibitions, etc.
22.A1	General works
22.A2-Z	By city and museum, A-Z
	Collections
25	Official records. Sources and documents
25.A2	Deputy Keeper. By date
25.B1	Record Commission. By date
25.B5	Chronicles. By number

	England
	Collections
	Official records. Sources and documents -- Continued
25.C1	Calendars. By date
	Class here calendars and inventories of the pre-ca. 1800 official records enumerated below. Order of entry is generally based on Scargill-Birds' Guide to the documents in the Public Record Office (1908)
	For calendars and inventories of post-ca. 1800 official records see CD1040+
25.C3	Calendarium genealogicum. Genealogical abstracts of the Inquisitions post mortem, etc., Henry III and Edward I
	Edited by Charles Roberts.
25.C58	Calendar of documents relating to Scotland preserved in Her Majesty's Public Record Office. 1108-1509
25.C6	Calendar of entries in the Papal Registers relating to Great Britain and Ireland 1198-1471
	Edited by W.H. Bliss and J.A. Twemlow
25.C7	Registers of the Privy Council. 1542-1627
	Edited by J.R. Dasent
25.C8	Charter Rolls. 11 Henry III to 28 Edward I. 1257-1516
	Patent Rolls
25.C91	Henry III. 1216-1272
25.C915	Edward I. 1272-1307
25.C917	Edward II. 1307-1327
25.C919	Edward III. 1327-1377
25.C92	Richard II. 1377-1399
25.C922	Henry IV. 1399-1413
25.C924	Henry V. 1413-1422
25.C928	Henry VI. 1422-1461
25.C93	Edward IV. 1461-1477
25.C94	Edward IV, Edward V, Richard III. 1476-1485
25.C945	Henry VII. 1485-1509
25.C95	Edward VI. 1547-1553
25.C952	Philip and Mary. 1553-1558
25.C953	Elizabeth. 1558-1603
	Close Rolls
25.D314	Henry III. 1227-1272
25.D315	Edward I. 1272-1307
25.D317	Edward II. 1307-1327
25.D319	Edward III. 1327-1377
25.D32	Richard II. 1377-1399
25.D322	Henry IV. 1399-1413
25.D324	Henry V. 1413-1422
25.D325	Henry VI. 1422-1477
25.D328	Edward IV. 1461-1476

England
  Collections
    Official records. Sources and documents
      Calendars
        Close Rolls -- Continued

25.D3285	Edward IV, Edward V, Richard III. 1476-1485
25.D3286	Henry VII. 1485-1500
25.D33	Calendar of the Fine rolls preserved in the Public Record Office. 1272-1509
25.D36	Calender of the liberate rolls preserved in the Public Record Office. 1226-1272
25.D37	Calender of Chancery warrants preserved in the Public Record Office. 1244-1326
25.D38	Calendar of various Chancery rolls. 1277-1326

        Inquisitions Post Mortem

25.D5	Henry III, Edward I, Edward II, Edward III
25.D52	Henry III
25.D6	Calendar of inquisitions miscellaneous (Chancery) preserved in the Public Record Office. 1219-1337
25.D7	Inquisitions and assessments relating to feudal aids. 1284-1431

        Calendars of State Papers, etc.

25.E1	Letters and Papers (Foreign and Domestic). Henry VIII. 1509-1546

        State Papers (Domestic)

25.E3	Edward VI to James I and addenda. 1547-1625
25.E5	Charles I. 1625-1649
25.E7	Commonwealth. 1649-1660
25.E9	Committee for the advance of money. 1642-1656
25.F1	Committee for Compounding. 1643-1660
25.F3	Charles II. 1660-1685
25.F4	James II. 1685-1689
25.F5	William and Mary. 1689-1695
25.F52	William III. 1695-1702
25.F6	Anne. 1702-1714
25.F68	George I. 1714-1727
25.F7	George III. 1760-1775
25.G3	State Papers Scotland (and relating to Mary, Queen of Scots). 1509-1603
25.G4	State Papers Scotland. 1688-1782
25.G7	State Papers Ireland (and of the reigns of Henry VIII, Edward VI, Mary, Elizabeth). 1509-1603
25.G9	State Papers Ireland (and of James I). 1603-1625
25.G92	State Papers Ireland. 1625-1670
25.H3	Calendar of state papers, foreign series, of the reign of Edward VI. 1547-1553

England
 Collections
  Official records. Sources and documents
   Calendars
    Calendars of State Papers, etc. -- Continued

25.H33	Calendar of state papers, foreign series, of the reign of Mary. 1553-1558
25.H36	Calendar of state papers, foreign series, of the reign of Elizabeth. 1558-1580
25.H4	Prospectus. Calendar of state papers, Colonial series
25.H5	Calendar of state papers, Colonial series, 1574-1738
25.H55	Journal of the commissioners for trade and plantations. 1704-1782
25.H6	Acts of the Privy council of England. Colonial series. 1613-1783
25.J1	Calendar of letters, despatches, and state papers relating to the negotiations between England and Spain preserved in the archives at Simancas and elsewhere. 1485-1558
25.J3	Calendar of letters and state papers relating to English affairs ... Simancas. 1558-1603
25.J4	Calendar of state papers and manuscripts existing in the archives and collections of Milan. 1385-1618
25.J5	Calendar of state papers and manuscripts relating to English affairs preserved ... Venice. 1202-1672
25.J6	Calendar of Carew manuscripts, preserved in the archiepiscopal library at Lambeth. 1515-1624
25.J7	Calendars of Treasury books and papers. 1556-1728
25.J72	Calendars of Treasury books and papers. 1729-1745
25.J76	Treasury Board papers. 1745-1800
25.Z5	Other. By date
26	Other collections
27	Collected works of individual authors
	Including addresses, essays, lectures
27.5	General works

Description and travel see DA605+
History
 Biography (Collective)
  For individual biography, see the special period, reign or place

28	General works
	Dictionary of National Biography
28.D4	Original. By date
	Including reprints of the original edition combined with supplementary volumes as a single set
28.D52	Abridgment or condensed version. By date

England
  History
    Biography (Collective)
      General works
        Dictionary of National Biography -- Continued

28.D525	Supplementary works. By date
28.D53	Criticism, indexes
28.1	Rulers, kings, etc.
28.2	Queens
28.3	Princes and princesses
	Houses, noble families, etc.
28.35.A1	Collective
28.35.A2-Z	Individual, A-Z
	e.g.
28.35.C45	Churchill family
28.4	Public men
28.7	Women
28.8	Other classes
28.9	Other
30	General works
	Compends
32.A1	Compilations, anthologies, etc.
32.A2-Z	General
32.3	Pictorial works
32.5	Source books
32.7	Syllabi
32.8	Stories
32.9	Rhymes
33	Comic and satiric works
34	Dictionaries. Chronological tables, outlines, etc.
35	Pamphlets, etc.
	General special
	Political and institutional history
	For specific periods, reigns, etc., see the period or reign
	For political parties see JN1111+
40	General works
41	Medieval
42	Modern
44	Special topics (not A-Z)
	Diplomatic history. Foreign and general relations
	For general works on the diplomatic history of a period, see the period
	For works on relations with a specific country regardless of period see DA47+
45	General works

	England
	History
	General special
	Diplomatic history. Foreign and general relations -- Continued
(46)	Biography and memoirs
	see DA28+, and biography numbers under special periods, reigns, etc.
	Relations with individual regions or countries
(47)	Europe
	see D34, D1065
47.1	France
47.2	Germany
47.3	Netherlands
47.6	Rome
47.65	Russia
47.7	Scandinavia
47.8	Spain
	United States see E183.8.A+
47.9.A-Z	Other regions, A-Z
	Military history
49	Periodicals. Societies. Serials
50	General works
52	Dictionaries
54	Biography (Collective)
58	Roman
59	Anglo-Saxon
60	Medieval
	Modern
65	General works
	16th and 17th centuries
66	General works
	Biography and memoirs
66.1.A1	Collective
66.1.A2-Z	Individual, A-Z
	e.g.
66.1.G2	Gage, Sir Henry
	18th century
67	General works
	Biography and memoirs
67.1.A1	Collective
67.1.A2-Z	Individual, A-Z
	e.g.
67.1.W8	Wolfe, James
	19th century
68	General works
	Biography and memoirs

	England
	History
	General special
	Military history
	Modern
	19th century
	Biography and memoirs -- Continued
	1801-1825. Napoleonic period
68.12.A1	Collective
68.12.A2-Z	Individual, A-Z
	e.g.
68.12.M8	Moore, Sir John
68.12.N2	Napier, Sir Charles James
68.12.W4	Wellington, Arthur Wellesley, 1st Duke of
	1825-1850. Mid-century
68.22.A1	Collective
68.22.A2-Z	Individual, A-Z
	e.g.
68.22.C5	Clyde, Colin Campbell, Baron
	Havelock, Sir Henry see DS475.2.H2
68.22.V5	Vicars, Hedley Shafto J.
	1850-1900
68.32.A1	Collective
68.32.A2-Z	Individual, A-Z
	e.g.
68.32.B2	Baden-Powell, Robert Stephenson S.B., Baron
	French, John Denton Pinkstone see DA68.32.Y8
68.32.G5	Gordon, Sir Charles Alexander
68.32.G6	Gordon, Charles George
68.32.K6	Kitchener, Horatio Herbert K., 1st Earl
68.32.R6	Roberts, Frederick Sleigh Roberts, 1st Earl
68.32.W7	Wolseley, Garnet Joseph W., Viscount
68.32.Y8	Ypres, John Denton P.F., 1st Earl of
	20th century
	Cf. DA566.5 Military and naval history (20th century)
69	General works
	Biography and memoirs
69.3.A1	Collective
69.3.A2-Z	Individual, A-Z
	e.g.
69.3.A57	Alexander, Harold Rupert L.G. Alexander, 1st Earl
69.3.A6	Allenby, Edmund Henry H. Allenby, 1st Viscount

	England
	History
	General special
	Military history
	Modern
	20th century
	Biography and memoirs
	Individual, A-Z -- Continued
69.3.H3	Haig, Douglas Haig, 1st Earl
69.3.M56	Montgomery, Bernard Law Montgomery, 1st Viscount
69.3.W37	Wavell, Archibald Percival Wavell, 1st Earl of
	Naval history
70	General works
72	Dictionaries
74	Biography (Collective)
77	General special
80	Medieval
	Modern
85	General works
	16th-17th centuries
86	General works
	Biography and memoirs
86.1.A1	Collective
86.1.B6	Blake, Robert
	Elizabeth, 1558-1603
86.21	Collective
86.22.A-Z	Individual, A-Z
	e.g.
86.22.C8	Cumberland, George Clifford, 3d Earl of
86.22.D7	Drake, Sir Francis
86.22.H3	Hawkins, Sir John
86.22.R2	Raleigh, Sir Walter
86.62	Later Stuart, 1660-1714
86.8.A-Z	Individual battles, A-Z
	Subarrange by author, A-Z
	18th century
87	General works
	Biography and memoirs
87.1.A1	Collective
87.1.A2-Z	Individual, A-Z
	e.g.
87.1.A6	Anson, George Anson, Baron
87.1.B6	Bligh, William
87.1.B8	Byng, John
87.1.C7	Collingwood, Cuthbert Collingwood, Baron
87.1.N4	Nelson, Horatio Nelson, Viscount

England
  History
    General special
      Naval history
        Modern
          18th century
            Biography and memoirs
              Individual, A-Z -- Continued

87.1.S2	St. Vincent, John Jervis, Earl
87.1.V5	Vernon, Edward
87.5.A-Z	Individual battles, A-Z
	Subarrange by author, A-Z
87.7	Other special
	Including mutinies of 1797

          19th century

88	General works
	Biography and memoirs
88.1.A1	Collective
88.1.A2-Z	Individual, A-Z
	e.g.
88.1.B4	Beresford, Charles William D. Beresford, Baron
88.1.D9	Dundonald, Thomas Cochrane, 10th Earl of
88.1.G2	Gambier, James Gambier, Baron
88.1.K3	Keppel, Sir Henry
88.1.N2	Napier, Sir Charles
88.1.P14	Paget, Lord Clarence Edward
88.1.P6	Popham, Sir Home Riggs
88.5	Individual battles. By date
	Subarrange by author, A-Z
	e.g.
88.5 1805	Trafalgar

          20th century
            Cf. DA566.5 Military and naval history (20th century)

89	General works
	Biography and memoirs
89.1.A1	Collective
89.1.A2-Z	Individual, A-Z
	e.g.
89.1.B4	Beatty, David Beatty, 1st Earl
89.1.F5	Fisher, John Arbuthnot Fisher, Baron
89.1.J4	Jellicoe, John Rushworth Jellicoe, 1st Earl

      Air Force history
        Cf. UG635.A+ Military aeronautics

89.5	General works
	Biography and memoirs
89.6.A1	Collective

England
  History
    General special
      Ethnography
        Elements in the population
          By element, A-Z -- Continued
            East Indians see DA125.S57

125.F7	French
125.G4	Germans
125.G7	Greeks
	Hindus see DA125.S57
125.H84	Huguenots
125.I68	Iranians
125.I7	Irish
125.I85	Italians
125.J36	Japanese
	Jews see DS135.E5+
125.J8	Jutes
125.L36	Latvians
125.L58	Lithuanians
125.M38	Mauritians
125.M87	Muslims
125.N4	Negroes. Blacks
	Pakistanis see DA125.S57
125.P6	Poles
125.Q34	Quakers
125.R65	Romanians
125.R8	Russians
125.S3	Scots
	Sikhs see DA125.S57
125.S57	South Asians
	Including Bengali, East Indians, and Pakistanis
125.S62	Spaniards
125.S88	Swedes
125.S9	Swiss
125.U38	Ukrainians
125.V53	Vietnamese
125.W4	West Indians
125.Y45	Yemenis

          By period
            Early and medieval to 1485

129	Dictionaries
129.5	Historiography
130	General works
	Earliest to 1066
134	Sources and documents
135	General works

England
  History
    By period
      Early and medieval to 1485
        Earliest to 1066 -- Continued
          Celts. Pre-Romans (and Romans)

140	General works
141	General special
	e.g. Bladud
142	Stonehenge
	Cf. GN805+ Prehistoric remains
143.A-Z	Other local, A-Z
	Romans
145	General works
	Biography and memoirs
145.2	Collective
145.3.A-Z	Individual, A-Z
	e.g.
145.3.B6	Boadicea, Queen, d. 62
146	Hadrian's Wall
147.A-Z	Local, A-Z
	e.g.
147.L4	Leigh, North
	London see DA677.1
	Saxons, 445-1066
150	Sources and documents. Chronicles
152	General works
152.2	Social life and customs. Civilization
	445-871
	General works see DA152
152.3	Hengist and Horsa
152.5.A-Z	Biography, A-Z
	e.g.
152.5.E2	Edmund, Saint, King of East Anglia
	871-1066
	General works see DA152
153	Alfred, 871-901
154	Edward the Elder, 901-925
154.1	Athelstan, 925-940
154.2	Edmund I, 940-946
154.3	Edred, 946-955
154.4	Edwy, 955-959
154.5	Edgar, 959-975
154.6	Edward the Martyr, 975-978
154.7	Ethelred II the Unready, 978-1016
	Sweyn, 1013-1014 see DA159
154.75	Edmund II Ironside, 1016

England
 History
  By period
   Early and medieval to 1485
    Earliest to 1066
     Saxons, 445-1066
      871-1066 -- Continued
       Danish rule, 1017-1042 (General works and
        individual rulers) see DA158+

154.8	Edward the Confessor, 1042-1066
154.85	Harold II, 1066
	Biography of contemporaries
154.88	Collective
154.9.A-Z	Individual, A-Z
	e.g.
154.9.H4	Hereward
155	Antiquities
	Danish invasions, rule, etc.
158	General works
159	Sweyn, 1013-1014
160	Canute, 1017-1035
161	Harold I, 1037-1040
162	Hardicanute, 1040-1042

    Medieval, 1066-1485

170	Sources and documents. Contemporary works
175	General works
176	General special
177	Biography (Collective)
185	Social life and customs. Civilization
188	Royal forests
	Normans, 1066-1154
190	Sources and documents (Domesday book, etc.)
195	General works
195.8	Battle of Stamford Bridge, 1066
196	Battle of Hastings, 1066
197	William I, 1066-1087
197.5	William II, 1087-1100
198	Henry I, 1100-1135
	Stephen, 1135-1154
198.5	General works
198.6	Matilda, Princess of England, Consort of
	Geoffrey, Count of Anjou
	Biography of contemporaries
198.9	Collective
199.A-Z	Individual, A-Z

    Angevins, 1154-1216

England
History
By period
Early and medieval to 1485
Medieval, 1066-1485
Angevins, 1154-1216 -- Continued

200	Sources and documents. Contemporary works
	For Magna Carta, see JN147, Political science; KD3944+, Law
205	General works
206	Henry II, 1154-1189
207	Richard I, 1189-1199
208	John, 1199-1216
209.A-Z	Biography of contemporaries, A-Z
	e.g.
209.E6	Eleanor of Aquitaine, Consort of Henry II
209.G5	Giraldus Cambrensis
209.T4	Thomas à Becket, Saint, Abp. of Canterbury

Plantagenets, 1216-1399

220	Sources and documents. Contemporary works
225	General works
	Henry III, 1216-1272
227	General works on life and reign
227.5	Barons' War, 1263-1267
228.A-Z	Biography and memoirs of contemporaries, A-Z
	e.g.
228.G8	Grosseteste, Robert, Bp. of London
228.L3	Langton, Stephen, Cardinal, Abp. of Canterbury
228.M7	Montfort, Simon of, Earl of Leicester
229	Edward I, 1272-1307
230	Edward II, 1307-1327
231.A-Z	Biography and memoirs of contemporaries, 1272-1327, A-Z
	e.g.
231.G2	Gaveston, Piers, Earl of Cornwall
233	Edward III, 1327-1377
234	Edward, Prince of Wales, called the Black Prince
235	Richard II, 1377-1399
	Including Tyler's insurrection, 1381, etc.
237.A-Z	Biography and memoirs of contemporaries, A-Z
	e.g.
237.J64	John, of Gaunt, Duke of Lancaster
237.T9	Tyler, Wat
237.W8	Wykeham, William of, Bp. of Winchester

Lancaster-York, 1399-1485

240	Sources and documents. Contemporary works
245	General works

England
History
By period
Early and medieval to 1485
Medieval, 1066-1485
Lancaster-York, 1399-1485 -- Continued

247.A-Z	Biography and memoirs of contemporaries, A-Z
	e.g.
	Bedford, John Plantagenet, Duke of see DA247.J6
247.G2	Gascoigne, Sir William
247.H8	Humphrey, Duke of Gloucester
247.J6	John Plantagenet, Duke of Bedford
247.M3	Margaret of Anjou, Consort of Henry VI
247.R7	Rotherham, Thomas, Abp. of York
247.S4	Shore, Jane
250	Wars of the Roses, 1455-1485
255	Henry IV, 1399-1413
256	Henry V, 1413-1422
257	Henry VI, 1422-1461
258	Edward IV, 1461-1483
259	Edward V, 1483
260	Richard III, 1483-1485. Battle of Bosworth Field, 1485

Modern, 1485-

300	General works. Collections
302	Compends
	Biography and memoirs (Collective)
304	General works
	Houses, noble families, etc.
305	Collective
306.A-Z	Special, A-Z
307	Public men
308	Women

Tudors, 1485-1603

310	Sources and documents. Contemporary works
314	Historiography
315	General works
316	Pamphlets, etc.
	Biography and memoirs
	Collective
317	General works
317.1	Kings, queens, etc.
317.15.A-Z	Houses, noble families, etc., A-Z
317.2	Public men
317.3	Women

	England
	History
	By period
	Modern, 1485-
	Tudors, 1485-1603
	Biography and memoirs -- Continued
317.8.A-Z	Individual, A-Z
	e.g.
317.8.C8	Cranmer, Thomas, Abp. of Canterbury
317.8.P6	Pole, Reginald, Cardinal
320	Social life and customs. Civilization. Intellectual life
325	Early Tudors
	Henry VII, 1485-1509
330	General works
330.8.A-Z	Biography and memoirs of contemporaries, A-Z
	e.g.
330.8.R5	Richmond, Margaret (Beaufort) Tudor, Countess of
	Henry VIII, 1509-1547
331	Sources and documents. Contemporary works
332	General works on life and reign
	Biography
	Queens
333.A2	Collective
333.A6	Catharine, of Aragon
333.B6	Anne Boleyn
333.C44	Anne of Cleves
333.H7	Howard, Catharine
333.P3	Catharine Parr
	Public men
334.A1	Collective
334.A2-Z	Individual, A-Z
334.C9	Cromwell, Thomas, Earl of Essex
334.M8	More, Sir Thomas, Saint
	Cf. B785.M8+ Philosophy
	Cf. HX810.5 Utopias
	Cf. PA8553 Latin literature
	Cf. PR2321+ English literature
334.W8	Wolsey, Thomas, cardinal
335.A-Z	Other, A-Z
337	1509-1527
338	1527-1533. Divorce, etc.
339	1533-1547
	1547-1558
340	General works
	Edward VI, 1547-1558
345	General works on life and reign

England
History
By period
Modern, 1485-
Tudors, 1485-1603
1547-1558
Edward VI, 1547-1558 -- Continued
Biography and memoirs of contemporaries

345.1.A1	Collective
345.1.A2-Z	Individual, A-Z
	e.g.
345.1.D9	Dudley, Lady Jane (Lady Jane Grey)

Mary I, 1553-1558

347	General works works on life and reign
347.1.A-Z	Biography and memoirs of contemporaries, A-Z

Elizabeth I, 1558-1603. Elizabethan age

350	Sources and documents. Contemporary works
352	Pamphlets. By date
355	General works works on life and reign
356	General special
357	Compends

Biography and memoirs of contemporaries
Cf. DA86.21+ Elizabethan admirals

358.A1	Collective
358.A2-Z	Individual, A-Z
	e.g.
358.B3	Bacon, Francis, Viscount St. Albans
	Cf. B1197 Philosophy
358.B9	Burghley, William Cecil, Baron
358.D8	Dudley, Amy (Robsart), Lady
358.E8	Essex, Robert Devereux, Earl of
358.G5	Gilbert, Sir Humphrey
358.L5	Leicester, Robert Dudley, Earl of
358.O8	Oxford, Edward De Vere, Earl of
358.S2	Salisbury, Robert Cecil, 1st Earl of
358.S5	Sidney, Sir Philip
358.W2	Walsingham, Sir Francis
360	Armada

17th century, 1603-1702

370	Sources and documents. Contemporary works
375	General works

Biography and memoirs
Collective

377	General works
377.1	Rulers, kings, etc.
377.2.A-Z	Houses, noble families, etc., A-Z
377.3	Public men

	England
	History
	By period
	Modern, 1485-
	17th century, 1603-1702
	Biography and memoirs
	Collective -- Continued
377.5	Women
378.A-Z	Individual, A-Z
	e.g.
378.P4	Pembroke, Anne (Clifford) Herbert, Countess of
378.P7	Prynne, William
380	Social life and customs. Civilization
	Early Stuarts, 1603-1642
385	Sources and documents. Contemporary works
390	General works
390.1.A-Z	Biography and memoirs, A-Z
	e.g.
390.1.C7	Coke, Sir Edward
390.1.D9	Dudley, Sir Robert, styled Duke of
	Northumberland and Earl of Warwick
	James I, 1603-1625
391	General works on life and reign
	Biography and memoirs of contemporaries
391.1.A1	Collective
391.1.A2-Z	Individual, A-Z
	e.g.
391.1.A6	Anne of Denmark, Consort of James I
391.1.B9	Buckingham, George Villiers, 1st Duke of
391.1.H5	Henry Frederick, Prince of Wales
391.1.S8	Southampton, Henry Wriothesley, 3d Earl of
391.1.S9	Stuart, Lady Arabella
	Gunpowder plot, 1605
392	General works
392.1.A-Z	Biography of participants, A-Z
	e.g.
392.1.D5	Digby, Sir Everard
392.1.G3	Gerard, John
394	Pamphlets, 1603-1624. By date
	Charles I, 1625-1649
395	General works on reign
	Biography and memoirs
396.A1	General collective
396.A2	Charles I
396.A22	Special
396.A3	Sermons, pamphlets, etc.
396.A5	Henrietta Maria, Consort of Charles I

England

History

By period

Modern, 1485-

17th century, 1603-1702

Early Stuarts, 1603-1642

Charles I, 1625-1649

Biography and memoirs -- Continued

396.A6	Children of Charles I
396.A8-Z	Contemporaries, A-Z
	e.g.
396.H18	Hampden, John
396.L3	Laud, William, Abp. of Canterbury
396.P9	Pym, John
396.S8	Strafford, Thomas Wentworth, 1st Earl of
396.W6	William, John, Abp. of York
397	General special
398	Pamphlets, 1625-1641. By date

Civil War and Commonwealth, 1642-1660

400	Sources and documents. Contemporary works
403	Historiography
405	General works
406	General special

Biography and memoirs of contemporaries

407.A1	Collective
407.A2-Z	Individual, A-Z
	e.g.
407.A74	Albemarle, George Monk, 1st Duke of
407.F2	Fairfax, Thomas Fairfax, Baron
407.P4	Peters, Hugh
407.R9	Rupert, Prince, Count Palatine
407.S5	Shaftesbury, Anthony Ashley Cooper, 1st Earl of
407.S6	Sidney, Algernon
407.V2	Vane, Sir Henry

Civil War, 1642-1649

Including local history

410	Sources and documents
411	Contemporary newspapers
412	Pamphlets, 1642-February 1649. By date
413	Historiography
415	General works
417	Battle of Marston Moor, 1644

Biography and memoirs

419.A1	Collective
419.A2-Z	Individual, A-Z
	e.g.

England
History
By period
Modern, 1485-
17th century, 1603-1702
Civil War and Commonwealth, 1642-1660
Civil War, 1642-1649
Biography and memoirs
Individual, A-Z -- Continued

419.S6	Slingsby, Sir Henry, Bart.
419.W2	Waller, Sir William
	Regicides
419.5.A1	Collective
419.5.A2-Z	Individual, A-Z
	e.g.
419.5.G6	Goffe, William
419.5.H3	Harrison, Thomas
	Commonwealth, 1649-1660
420	Sources and documents. Contemporary works
421	Contemporary newspapers
422	Pamphlets, March 1649-1660. By original date of publication
	Subarrange by author
425	General works
	Cromwell, Oliver
426	General works
427	Special
427.1	Pamphlets. By date
(427.2)	Fiction
	see PA-PZ
428	Compends
428.1	Essays, lectures, etc.
428.5	Cromwell, Richard
429.A-Z	Biography and memoirs of contemporaries, A-Z
	e.g.
429.R7	Rogers, John
429.W5	Winstanley, Gerrard
	Later Stuarts, 1660-1685
430	Sources and documents. Contemporary works
431	Contemporary newspapers
432	Pamphlets. By date
435	General works
	Biography and memoirs of contemporaries
437.A1	Collective
437.A2-Z	Individual, A-Z
	e.g.
437.D4	Devonshire, William Cavendish, 1st Duke

England
  History
    By period
      Modern, 1485-
        17th century, 1603-1702
          Later Stuarts, 1660-1685
            Biography and memoirs of contemporaries
              Individual, A-Z -- Continued

437.P5	Peterborough, Charles Mordaunt, 3d Earl
440	Social life and customs. Civilization

          Charles II, 1660-1685

445	General works on life and reign
446	Personal special

            Biography and memoirs of contemporaries

447.A3	Collective
447.A4-Z	Individual, A-Z
447.A72	Arlington, Henry Bennet
447.B9	Buckingham, George Villiers, 2d Duke
447.C3	Catharine of Braganza, Consort of Charles II
447.C6	Clarendon, Edward Hyde, 1st Earl of
447.D7	Downing, Sir George, Bart.
447.E9	Evelyn, John
447.G7	Gramont, Philibert, comte de
447.G9	Gwyn, Nell
447.J4	Jeffreys, George Jeffreys, Baron
447.L4	Leeds, Thomas Osborne, 1st Duke of
447.P4	Pepys, Samuel
447.R4	Reresby, Sir John, 2d Bart.
447.R6	Rochester, John Wilmot, 2d Earl of
447.T2	Temple, Sir William, Bart.
448	General special
	Anglo-Dutch War, 1672-1674 see DJ193
448.9	Monmouth and Monmouth's rebellion, 1685

         James II, 1685-1688

450	General works on life and reign
452	Other

         William and Mary, 1689-1702
           For biography see DA462.A2
           Cf. DJ186+ Reign of William III in Holland

460	General works on reign
461	Lancaster plot, 1689-1694
461.3	Versailles conspiracy, 1695
461.5	Conspiracy of 1696
	Biography and memoirs of contemporaries
462.A2	William III
462.A3	Mary II

	England
	History
	By period
	Modern, 1485-
	17th century, 1603-1702
	Later Stuarts, 1660-1685
	William and Mary, 1689-1702
	Biography and memoirs of contemporaries -- Continued
462.A4-Z	Other individual, A-Z
	e.g.
462.M3	Marlborough, John Churchill, 1st Duke
462.M4	Marlborough, Sarah (Jennings) Churchill, Duchess of
462.P7	Portland, William Bentinck, 1st Earl
463	Pamphlets. By date
	Subarrange by author
	Late modern, 1702-
470	General works
472	Compends
	18th century
	Including House of Hanover (Windsor)
480	General works
	Biography and memoirs
483.A1	Collective
483.A2-Z	Individual, A-Z
	e.g.
483.A7	Argyll, John Campbell, 2d Duke of
483.C5	Chandos, James Brydges, 1st Duke of
483.C6	Chudleigh, Elizabeth, Countess of Bristol ("Duchess of Kingston")
483.D3	Delany, Mary (Granville) Pendarves
483.H3	Hamilton, Emma, Lady
483.H8	Huntingdon, Selina (Shirley) Hastings, Countess of
483.N2	Nash, Richard
483.P6	Pitt, William, 1st Earl of Chatham
483.P6A2	Correspondence
483.P62	Pamphlets
483.W2	Walpole, Horace, 4th Earl of Orford
	For his memoirs of the reign of George III see DA506.W2
485	Social life and customs. Civilization
486	Other
	Anne, 1702-1714
490	Sources and documents
495	General works on life and reign

England
History
By period
Modern, 1485-
Late modern, 1702-
18th century
Anne, 1702-1714 -- Continued

496	Pamphlets. By original date of publication
	Subarrange by author
	Biography and memoirs of contemporaries
497.A1	Collective
497.A3	Children of Anne. William, Duke of Gloucester
497.A4-Z	Individual, A-Z
497.O8	Oxford, Robert Harley, 1st Earl of
497.S3	Sacheverall, Henry
497.S8	Stanhope, James Stanhope, 1st Earl of

1714-1760

498	General works
499	George I, 1714-1727
500	George II, 1727-1760
	Biography and memoirs
501.A1	Collective
501.A2	George I
501.A3	George II
501.A33	Carolina, Consort of George II
501.A35	Frederick Louis, Prince of Wales
	William Augustus, Duke of Cumberland see DA501.C9
501.A4-Z	Other, A-Z
501.A8	Atterbury, Francis, Bp. of Rochester
501.B6	Bolingbroke, Henry St. John, Viscount
501.C5	Chesterfield, Philip Dormer Stanhope, 4th Earl of
501.C9	Cumberland, William Augustus, Duke of
501.M7	Montagu, Lady Mary (Pierrepont) Wortley
501.T3	Temple, Richard Temple Grenville-Temple, Earl
501.W2	Walpole, Robert, 1st Earl of Orford
503	Pamphlets. By original date of publication
	Subarrange by author
	Cf. DD412 Seven Years' War, 1756-1763

George III, 1760-1820

505	General works
	Biography and memoirs of contemporaries
506.A1	Collective
506.A2	George III
506.A3	Charlotte, Consort of George III

England
  History
    By period
      Modern, 1485-
        Late modern, 1702-
          18th century
            George III, 1760-1820
              Biography and memoirs of contemporaries --
                Continued

506.A6	Edward Augustus, Duke of Kent
506.A7	Frederick Augustus, Duke of York and Albany
506.A71	Henry Frederick, Duke of Cumberland
506.A72	Mary Anne (Thompson) Clarke
506.A74	Maria, Duchess of Gloucester
506.A8	Amelia, Princess of England
506.A82-Z	Other, A-Z
	e.g.
506.B9	Burke, Edmund
506.C8	Cornwallis, Charles Cornwallis, 1st Marquis
506.F7	Fox, Charles James
506.F8	Francis, Sir Philip
506.M5	Melville, Henry Dundas, 1st Viscount
506.N2	Napier, Lady Sarah (Lennox) Bunbury
506.N7	North, Frederick North, Baron
	Pindar, Peter see DA506.W8
506.T6	Tooke, John Horne
506.W2	Walpole, Horace, 4th Earl of Orford
	Including memoirs of the reign of George III
	For Walpole's biography see DA483.W2
506.W8	Wolcot, John (pseud. Peter Pindar)

             Contemporary works

506.5	Collections
507	Pamphlets. By date
	Subarrange by author
	Letters of Junius
508.A2	Editions. By date
508.A3	Selections, extracts, etc. By date
508.A4A-.A4Z	Translations. By language, A-Z
508.A5	Criticism, pamphlets, etc.
508.A6	Authorship in general. By author of work
508.A7-Z	Authorship, particular theories
508.F8	Francis, Sir Philip
508.P3	Paine, Thomas
509	Collected works of statesmen, etc.
	For memoirs, journals, letters, etc. see
	DA506.A1+
	For Edmund Burke's work see DA506.B9

England
History
By period
Modern, 1485-
Late modern, 1702-
18th century
George III, 1760-1820 -- Continued
1760-1789

510	General works
512.A-Z	Biography and memoirs, A-Z
	e.g.
512.G6	Gordon, Lord George
512.L3	Lansdowne, William Petty, 1st Marquis of
512.W6	Wilkes, John

1789-1820

520	General works
521	1811-1820. Regency

For the proposed French invasion see
DC220.3

Biography and memoirs

522.A1	Collective
522.A2-Z	Individual, A-Z
	e.g.
522.C2	Canning, George
522.C5	Cobbett, William
522.E7	Erskine, Thomas Erskine, Baron
522.H85	Huskisson, William
522.L7	Liverpool, Robert Banks Jenkinson, 2d Earl of
	Pitt, William 1759-1806
522.P4	Letters. By date
522.P45	Speeches. By date
522.P5	Pamphlets. By date
522.P6	Biography
522.S4	Sheridan, Richard Brinsley Butler
522.W6	Wilberforce, William

Cf. HT1029.A4+ Anti-slavery

19th century

529	Dictionaries
530	General works
531	Pamphlets. By date

Biography and memoirs
Collective

531.1	General works
531.2	Public men

Individual biography
see DA536+

	England
	History
	By period
	Modern, 1485-
	Late modern, 1702-
	19th century -- Continued
533	Social life and customs. Civilization. Intellectual life
	1801-1837
535	General works
	Biography and memoirs, 1801-1837/1850
536.A1	Collective
536.A2-Z	Individual, A-Z
	e.g.
536.B66	Blessington, Marguerite, Countess of
536.B7	Brougham and Vaux, Henry Peter Brougham, Baron
536.C6	Cobden, Richard
536.G8	Greville, Charles Cavendish Fulke
536.G84	Grey, Charles Grey, 2d Earl
(536.M15)	Macaulay, Thomas Babington Macaulay
	see DA3.M3
536.P2	Palmerston, Henry John Temple, 3d Viscount
536.P3	Peel, Sir Robert, Bart.
536.R9	Russell, John Russell, 1st Earl
536.S8	Stanhope, Lady Hester Lucy
	1789-1820 see DA520+
	George IV, 1820-1830
537	General works works on reign
	Cf. DA521 Regency
	Biography and memoirs of contemporaries
538.A1	George IV
538.A2	Caroline Amelia Elizabeth, Consort of George IV
538.A22	Divorce
(538.A25)	Fiction
	see class P-PZ
538.A3	Lady Anne Hamilton
538.A31	Miss C.E. Cary
538.A35	Mary (Darby) Robinson
538.A4	Charlotte Augusta, of Wales, Consort of Prince Leopold of Saxe-Coburg-Saalfeld
538.A5-Z	Other, A-Z
	e.g.
538.B6	Brummell, George Bryan
538.F5	Fitzherbert, Maria Anne (Smythe)
	William IV, 1830-1837

	England
	History
	By period
	Modern, 1485-
	Late modern, 1702-
	19th century
	1801-1837
	William IV, 1830-1837 -- Continued
539	General works on life and reign
540	Era of reform, 1832-1837
	Biography and memoirs of contemporaries
541.A1	Collective
541.A2-Z	Individual, A-Z
	e.g.
541.A4	Adelaide, Consort of William IV
542	Pamphlets, etc.
	Victorian era, 1837-1901
550	General works
551	Pamphlets, etc.
	Victoria
552	Journal, letters, etc.
553	Memoirs by contemporaries
554	Biography
555	Personal special
556	Compends
557	Juvenile works
558	Pamphlets, etc.
558.5	Jubilee pamphlets
559.A-Z	Other royal biography, A-Z
	e.g.
559.A1	Albert, Consort of Victoria
559.A3	Alice, Consort of Louis IV, Grand Duke of
	Hesse-Darmstadt
559.A7	Arthur, Duke of Connaught
559.G4	George, 2d Duke of Cambridge
559.L6	Louise, Duchess of Argyll
559.V5	Victoria Maria Louisa, Duchess of Kent
559.5	The court
559.7	1837-1850
	For Chartism, see HD8396
	1850-1901
560	General works
561	Pamphlets, etc.
	South African War see DT1890+
	Biography and memoirs
562	Collective
	Gladstone

England
History
By period
Modern, 1485-
Late modern, 1702-
19th century
Victorian era, 1837-1901
Biography and memoirs
Gladstone -- Continued

563	Speeches, letters, etc.
563.3	Memoirs by contemporaries
563.35	Cartoons, etc.
563.4	Biography
563.5	Special works
563.6	Compends
563.8	Pamphlets, etc.
563.9	Catherine (Glynn) Gladstone
564.A-Z	Other prime ministers, A-Z
	e.g.
564.B3	Beaconsfield, Benjamin Disraeli, 1st Earl of
	Disraeli, Benjamin see DA564.B3
564.R7	Rosebery, Archibald Philip Primrose, 5th Earl of
564.S2	Salisbury, Robert Arthur Talbot Gascoyne-Cecil, 3d Marquis of
565.A-Z	Contemporaries, A-Z
	e.g.
565.B8	Bright, John
565.B85	Bryce, James Bryce, Viscount
565.C4	Chamberlain, Joseph
565.C6	Churchill, Lord Randolph Henry Spencer
565.C95	Curzon, George Nathaniel Curzon, 1st Marquis
565.L9	Lytton, Edward George E. Lytton Bulwer-Lytton, Baron
565.M16	McCarthy, Justin
565.M78	Morley, John Morley, Viscount
565.R8	Russell, George William Erskine
565.T2	Temple, Sir Richard, Bart.
	20th century
566	General works
566.2	General special
566.3	Pamphlets, etc.
566.4	Social life and customs. Civilization. Intellectual life

	England
	History
	By period
	Modern, 1485-
	Late modern, 1702-
	20th century -- Continued
566.5	Military and naval history
	Cf. DA69+ Military history (20th century)
	Cf. DA89+ Naval history (20th century)
566.7	Political and diplomatic history
566.8	Caricature, satire, etc.
	Biography and memoirs
566.9.A1	Collective
566.9.A2-Z	Individual, A-Z
	e.g.
	Asquith, H.H. (Herbert Henry) see DA566.9.O7
566.9.B15	Baldwin, Stanley Baldwin, 1st Earl
566.9.B2	Balfour, Arthur James Balfour, 1st Earl
566.9.B37	Beaverbrook, William Maxwell Aitken, Baron
566.9.B5	Birkenhead, Frederick Edwin Smith, 1st Earl of
566.9.C43	Chamberlain, Sir Austen
566.9.C5	Churchill, Winston, Sir, 1874-1965
566.9.E28	Eden, Anthony
566.9.G8	Grey, Edward Grey, 1st Viscount
	Isaacs, Rufus, Marquess of Reading see
	DA566.9.R3
566.9.L5	Lloyd George, David
566.9.M25	MacDonald, James Ramsey
566.9.N7	Northcliffe, Alfred Harmsworth, Viscount
566.9.O7	Oxford and Asquith, Herbert Henry Asquith, 1st
	Earl of
566.9.R3	Reading, Rufus Daniel Isaacs, 1st Marquis of
	Edward VII, 1901-1910
567	Biography
	Biography and memoirs of contemporaries
568.A1	Collective
568.A2	Alexandra, Consort of Edward VII
568.A3-.A5	Other royal
568.A6-Z	Other, A-Z
570	Reign
	George V, 1910-1936
573	Biography
	Biography and memoirs of contemporaries
574.A1	Collective
574.A2	Mary, Consort of George V
	Other royal
574.A33	Henry, Duke of Gloucester

England
History
By period
Modern, 1485-
Late modern, 1702-
20th century
George V, 1910-1936
Biography and memoirs of contemporaries
Other royal -- Continued

574.A34	Alice, Duchess of Gloucester
574.A36	George, Duke of Kent
574.A37	Marina, Duchess of Kent
574.A4	Mary, Princess of Great Britain
574.A45A-.A45Z	Other royal, A-Z
574.A5-Z	Other
574.A8	Astor, Nancy Witcher (Langhorne), Viscountess
574.M6	Mosley, Sir Oswald, Bart.
576	Reign
577	Period of World War I, 1914-1919
	For the war itself see D501+
578	1920-1939
	Edward VIII, 1936
580	Biography
581.A-Z	Biography and memoirs of contemporaries, A-Z
	e.g.
581.W5	Windsor, Wallis Warfield, Duchess of
583	Reign
	George VI, 1937-1952
584	Biography
	Biography and memoirs of contemporaries
585.A1	Collective
585.A2	Elizabeth, Consort of George VI
585.A5A-.A5Z	Other royal, A-Z
585.A5M3	Margaret, Princess of Great Britain
585.A6-Z	Other, A-Z
	e.g.
585.A8	Attlee, Clement Richard
585.B4	Bevin, Ernest
585.C5	Chamberlain, Neville
585.C7	Cripps, Sir Richard Stafford
586	Reign
587	Period of World War II, 1939-1945
	1945-1952. Postwar period
588	General works
588.3	Pamphlets, etc.
	1952-

England
History
By period
Modern, 1485-
Late modern, 1702-
20th century
1952- -- Continued
589.3	Addresses, essays, lectures
589.4	Social life and customs. Civilization. Intellectual life
589.7	Political history
589.8	Foreign and general relations
	Elizabeth II, 1952-
590	Biography
	Biography and memoirs of contemporaries
591.A1	Collective
591.A2	Philip, Prince
591.A3-.A45	Other royal
591.A33	Charles, Prince of Wales
591.A34	Anne, Princess of Great Britain
591.A45A-.A45Z	Other, A-Z
591.A5-Z	Other contemporaries, A-Z
	e.g.
591.H4	Heath, Edward
591.T47	Thatcher, Margaret
591.W5	Wilson, Harold
592	Reign
600	Historical geography
	Description and travel
605	History of travel
	By period
610	Through 1600
615	1601-1700
620	1701-1800
625	1801-1900
630	1901-1945
631	1946-1970
632	1971-
640	Gazetteers. Dictionaries, etc.
645	Place names
	Special see DA670+
650	Guidebooks
655	Preservation of historic monuments, etc.
	Castles, halls, cathedrals, etc.
660	General works
662.A-Z	By county, A-Z

	England
	Castles, halls, cathedrals, etc. -- Continued
664.A-Z	By manor hall, etc., A-Z
	e.g.
	For manors, halls, etc. in cities or towns see DA690.A+
664.C36	Chatsworth
665	Watering places
667	Picturesque places, rural scenery, etc.
668	British Islands (Collectively)
	Including Hebrides, Orkneys, Shetlands, Channel Islands, Isle of Man, etc.
669	Historical accounts of disasters (Collectively)
	Including earthquakes, fires, floods, storms, etc.
	For individual disasters see DA670+
	Local history and description
	Counties, regions, etc., A-Z
	e.g.
670.A1	Collective
670.A29	Airedale
670.A96	Axholme, Isle of
670.B25	Bedford Level
	Bedfordshire
670.B29	Serials
670.B3	Nonserials
670.B4	Berkshire
670.B55	Black Country (District)
670.B9	Buckinghamshire
670.C2	Cambridgeshire
670.C4	Channel Islands
670.C44	Charnwood Forest
	Cheshire
670.C5	Serials
670.C6	Nonserials
670.C62	Chiltern Hills (Chilterns)
670.C63	Cleveland (District)
670.C7	Coniston
	Cornwall
670.C78	Serials
670.C8	Nonserials
670.C83	Cotswold Hills
670.C86	Cranborne Chase
670.C88	Craven (District)
	Cumberland
670.C89	Serials
670.C9	Nonserials
670.C93	Cumbria
670.D2	Dartmoor

England
    Local history and description
        Counties, regions, etc., A-Z -- Continued

670.D25	Dean, Forest of
670.D31	Dee River
	Derbyshire
	Including Peak District
670.D42	Serials
670.D43	Nonserials
	Devonshire
670.D49	Serials
670.D5	Nonserials
	Dorsetshire
670.D69	Serials
670.D7	Nonserials
670.D9	Durham
	East Anglia
670.E13	Serials
670.E14	Nonserials
670.E7	Essex
670.E87	Exe River
670.E9	Exmoor
670.F33	Fens (Fenland)
670.F98	Furness
	Gloucestershire
670.G4	Serials
670.G5	Nonserials
	Guernsey
670.G8	Serials
670.G9	Nonserials
670.H18	Hallamshire
670.H2	Hampshire
670.H3	Hayling Island
670.H4	Herefordshire
	Hertfordshire
670.H49	Serials
670.H5	Nonserials
670.H7	Holderness
670.H8	Huntingdonshire
	Isle of Wight see DA670.W6
670.J5	Jersey
	Kent
670.K2	Serials
670.K3	Nonserials
670.L1	Lake District
	Lancashire
670.L19	Serials

DA

	England
	Local history and description
	Counties, regions, etc., A-Z
	Lancashire -- Continued
670.L2	Nonserials
670.L26	Land's End (District)
	Leicestershire
670.L49	Serials
670.L5	Nonserials
	Lincolnshire
670.L69	Serials
670.L7	Nonserials
670.L77	Lizard Head
670.L96	Lundy Island
670.M07	Malvern Hills
	Man, Isle of
670.M1	Serials
670.M2	Nonserials
670.M5	Mendip Hills
670.M6	Middlesex
670.M7	Monmouthshire
670.M9	Mowbray, Vale of
670.N5	New Forest
670.N53	Nidderdale
	Norfolk
670.N59	Serials
670.N6	Nonserials
	Northamptonshire
670.N69	Serials
670.N7	Nonserials
670.N73	Northern England
	Including Northeast and Northwest England
	Northumberland
670.N79	Serials
670.N8	Nonserials
	Nottinghamshire
670.N89	Serials
670.N9	Nonserials
670.O9	Oxfordshire
	Peak District see DA670.D42+
670.P4	Pennine Chain
670.P98	Purbeck, Isle of
670.Q2	Quantock Hills
670.R5	Richmondshire
670.R6	Rochford Hundred
670.R82	Rossendale Forest
	Rutlandshire

England
  Local history and description
    Counties, regions, etc., A-Z
      Rutlandshire -- Continued

670.R89	Serials
670.R9	Nonserials
	Salop see DA670.S39+
670.S2	Scilly Islands
670.S29	Severn River
670.S35	Sherwood Forest
	Shropshire. Salop
670.S39	Serials
670.S4	Nonserials
	Somersetshire
670.S49	Serials
670.S5	Nonserials
	Staffordshire
670.S69	Serials
670.S7	Nonserials
	Suffolk
670.S89	Serials
670.S9	Nonserials
	Surrey
670.S95	Serials
670.S96	Nonserials
	Sussex
670.S97	Serials
670.S98	Nonserials
670.T15	Teesdale
670.T2	Thames River
670.T3	Thanet, Isle of
670.T9	Tyne River
670.W3	Warwickshire
670.W47	Wensleydale
670.W48	Wessex
	For description and travel see DA670.D69+
670.W496	Westmoreland
670.W56	Wharfedale
670.W6	Wight, Isle of
	Wiltshire
670.W69	Serials
670.W7	Nonserials
	Worcestershire
670.W89	Serials
670.W9	Nonserials
670.W97	Wye River
670.W98	Wythburn

England
  Local history and description
    Counties, regions, etc., A-Z -- Continued
      Yorkshire

670.Y59	Serials
670.Y6	Nonserials

London

675	Periodicals. Societies. Serials
	Museums, exhibitions, etc.
675.5.A1	General works
675.5.A2-Z	By museum, A-Z
676	Sources and documents
	Biography and memoirs
676.8.A1	Collective
676.8.A2-Z	Individual, A-Z
676.85	Historiography
	Ethnography
676.9.A1	General works
676.9.A5-Z	Individual elements in the population, A-Z
676.9.A72	Arabs
676.9.A75	Armenians
676.9.A77	Assyrians
676.9.B35	Bangladeshis
676.9.B44	Bengali (South Asian people)
676.9.B55	Blacks
676.9.C88	Cypriotes
676.9.C93	Czechs
676.9.D8	Dutch
676.9.E95	Europeans
676.9.F74	French
676.9.G47	Germans
676.9.I73	Iraqis
676.9.I75	Irish
676.9.L38	Latin Americans
676.9.M3	Maltese
676.9.M38	Mauritians
	Negroes see DA676.9.B55
676.9.O23	Oceanians
676.9.P34	Pakistanis
676.9.P6	Poles
676.9.S6	South Asians
676.9.S63	Spaniards
676.9.S75	Sri Lankans
676.9.T87	Turks
676.9.W36	Welsh
676.9.W4	West Indians
	History, antiquities, description

	England
	London
	History, antiquities, description -- Continued
677	General works
677.1	Antiquities
678	Compends. Juvenile works
679	Guidebooks
679.A11-.A19	Directories
	Pictorial works see DA680+
	By period
680	Medieval through 1600
681	1601-1700
682	1701-1800
683	1801-1900
684	1901-1950
684.2	1951-1980
684.25	1981-
685.A-Z	Parishes, boroughs, streets, etc., A-Z
	e.g.
685.A1	General
685.A3	Aldersgate
685.B65	Bloomsbury
685.C5	Chelsea
685.C55	Chingford
685.E1	East London. East End of London
685.F5	Fleet Street
685.G68	Greenwich
	Hampstead
685.H22	Serials
685.H23	Monographs
685.H9	Hyde Park
685.K5	Kensington
685.L7	Lincoln's Inn Fields
685.M2	Marylebone
685.P5	Piccadilly
685.S6	Soho Square
685.S65	South London
685.S7	Southwark
685.T7	Tottenham
685.W5	Westminster
	Institutions
686	General works
687.A-Z	Individual, A-Z
	e.g.
687.A45	Albany (Chambers)
687.B9	Buckingham Palace
687.C4	Charterhouse

	England
	London
	Institutions
	Individual, A-Z -- Continued
687.C9	Crystal Palace, Sydenham
687.D7	No. 10 Downing Street
	Gray's Inn see KD504.G7
687.H7	Holland House
	Inner Temple see KD504.I5
	Inns of Chancery see KD502
	Inns of Court see KD502
	Lincoln's Inn see KD504.I5
	Middle Temple see KD504.M5
687.S14	Saint Paul's Cathedral
	Staple Inn see KD505.S7
687.S83	Stationers' Hall
687.T2	Temple Church
687.T7	Tower of London
687.W5	Westminster Abbey
687.W6	Westminster Palace. Houses of Parliament
687.W65	Whitehall Palace
688	Social life and customs. Culture. Intellectual life
689.A-Z	Other, A-Z
689.B8	Bridges
	Including London Bridge, etc.
689.C3	Cemeteries
689.C4	Cheapside Cross
	Church records and registers see CS436.L7A1+
689.G3	Gardens
	Including Vauxhall, etc.
689.H48	Historic houses
689.H5	Historic markers
689.H8	Hotels, taverns, etc.
689.L5	Literary landmarks
689.M37	Markets
689.M7	Monuments, statutes, etc.
689.O63	Open spaces
689.P17	Palaces (General)
689.P2	Parks (General)
689.P6	Port of London
689.S7	Squares
689.U5	Underground areas
689.W2	Water
690.A-Z	Other cities, towns, etc., A-Z
	e.g.
690.A1	Collective
690.A14	Abingdon

England

Other cities, towns, etc., A-Z -- Continued

690.A79	Arundel
690.B22	Banbury
690.B26	Barnstaple
690.B29	Basingstoke
690.B3	Bath
690.B6	Birmingham
690.B65	Bolton
690.B68	Boston
690.B685	Bournemouth
690.B7	Bradford (Yorkshire)
690.B78	Brighton
690.B8	Bristol
690.B84	Bristow
690.B92	Burford
690.B97	Bury Saint Edmunds
690.B98	Buxton
	Cambridge
690.C19	Serials
690.C2	Nonserials
690.C3	Canterbury
690.C335	Carlisle
(690.C46)	Chatsworth
	see DA664.C36
690.C48	Cheltenham
690.C49	Chepstow
690.C5	Chester
690.C59	Church Stretton
690.C6	Cinque Ports
690.C7	Colchester
690.C75	Coventry
690.C79	Crowland Abbey
690.C8	Croydon
690.D4	Derby
690.D63	Dorchester
690.D7	Dover
690.D96	Durham
690.E4	Ely
690.E9	Exeter
690.G45	Glastonbury
690.G5	Gloucester
690.G8	Gravesend
	Greenwich see DA685.G68
690.H17	Halifax
690.H2	Hampton Court
690.H35	Hastings

England

Other cities, towns, etc., A-Z -- Continued

690.H54	Hereford
690.H9	Hull
690.I6	Ipswich
690.K4	Kenilworth
690.L15	Lacock
	Including the village and abbey
690.L2	Lancaster
690.L35	Leamington
	Leeds
690.L39	Serials
690.L4	Nonserials
690.L5	Leicester
690.L67	Lincoln
690.L8	Liverpool
690.L85	Ludlow
690.M2	Maidstone
690.M3	Malvern
690.M4	Manchester
690.M42	Margate
690.M46	Marlborough
690.M48	Matlock
690.N53	Newark
690.N55	Newbury
690.N58	Newcastle-under-Lyme
690.N6	Newcastle-upon-Tyne
690.N8	Northampton
690.N87	Northowram
690.N92	Nottingham
	Oxford
690.O97	Serials
690.O98	Nonserials
690.P48	Petworth
690.P7	Plymouth
690.P95	Prestwich
690.R28	Reading
690.R5	Richmond
690.R6	Rochester
690.R9	Rye
690.S13	Saint Albans
690.S16	Salisbury
	Including old and new Sarum
690.S28	Scarborough
690.S54	Sheffield
690.S58	Shrewsbury
	Southampton

England
　　Other cities, towns, etc., A-Z
　　　　Southampton -- Continued
690.S69　　　　　Serials
690.S7　　　　　　Nonserials
690.S75　　　　Southport
690.S8　　　　　Stamford
690.S92　　　　Stratford-upon-Avon
690.T36　　　　Tewkesbury
690.T69　　　　Torquay
690.T92　　　　Tunbridge Wells
690.W14　　　　Wakefield
690.W28　　　　Warrington
690.W3　　　　　Warwick
690.W67　　　　Winchester
690.W76　　　　Windsor
690.W927　　　Worthing
690.Y2　　　　　Yarmouth
690.Y6　　　　　York
　　Wales
700　　　　　Periodicals. Societies. Collections
708　　　　　General works
709　　　　　Compends
710　　　　　Biography (Collective)
711　　　　　Antiquities
　　　　　　　Cf. DA740+ Local history and description
711.5　　　　Social life and customs. Civilization
712　　　　　Ethnography. Races
713　　　　　Pamphlets, etc.
　　　　History
713.5　　　　　Study and teaching
714　　　　　　General works
　　　　　　By period
715　　　　　　　Early and medieval
　　　　　　　　Biography
716.A1　　　　　　Collective
716.A2-Z　　　　　Individual, A-Z
　　　　　　　　　　e.g.
716.G5　　　　　　　Glendower, Owen
　　　　　　　Modern
720　　　　　　　General works
　　　　　　　　19th-20th centuries
　　　　　　　　　Including Rebecca Riots, 1839-1844, etc.
722　　　　　　　　General works
　　　　　　　　Biography and memoirs
722.1.A1　　　　　　Collective

Wales
   History
      By period
         Modern
            19th-20th centuries
               Biography and memoirs -- Continued

722.1.A2-Z	Individual, A-Z
	e.g.
722.1.T9	Turner, Sir Llewelyn
	Description and travel
725	Through 1700
727	1701-1800
730	1801-1950
731	1951-1980
731.2	1981-
734	Gazetteers. Dictionaries, etc. Place names
735	Guidebooks
	Castles, halls, etc.
737	General works
738.A-Z	Special, A-Z
	Local history and description
740.A-Z	Counties, regions, etc., A-Z
	e.g.
740.A5	Anglesey
740.B7	The Border
740.B8	Brecknockshire
740.C3	Cardiganshire
740.C34	Carmarthenshire
740.C35	Carnarvonshire (Caenarvonshire)
740.C6	Clwyd Valley
740.D3	Denbighshire
740.F6	Flintshire
740.G5	Glamorganshire
740.L7	Llandaff (Diocese)
740.M4	Merionethshire
740.M7	Montgomeryshire
740.P3	Pembrokeshire
740.P8	Powys
740.R3	Radnorshire
740.S6	Snowdonia
745.A-Z	Cities, towns, etc., A-Z
	e.g.
745.C2	Cardiff
745.C3	Carnarvon (Caernarfon)
745.H2	Harlech
745.L7	Llandudno
745.W9	Wrexham

	Scotland
750	Periodicals. Societies. Serials
	Museums, exhibitions, etc.
751	General works
751.5.A-Z	Individual. By place, A-Z
(753)	Yearbooks
	see DA750
	Sources and documents
755	Nonofficial
757	Official
757.5	General works
757.7	Historical geography
	Description and travel see DA850+
	History
757.9	Dictionaries. Chronological tables, outlines, etc.
	Biography (Collective)
	For individual biography, see the special period, reign, or place
758	General works
758.1	Public men
758.2	Rulers, kings, etc.
	For the House of Stuart, see DA758.3.S8; for early Stuarts, see DA783.5+; for later Stuarts, see DA784+
	For English sovereigns see DA385+
	Houses, noble families, etc.
	Including biographical memoirs
758.3.A1	Collective
758.3.A2-Z	Individual houses, etc., A-Z
	e.g.
758.3.M3	Mar, Earls of
758.3.S8	Stuart, House of
758.4	Women
	Historiography
759	General works
	Biography of historians
759.5	Collective
759.7.A-Z	Individual, A-Z
760	General works
761	Popular works
762	Compends. Juvenile works
763	Pamphlets, etc.
	General special
765	Political and diplomatic history. Home rule
	Cf. DA775 Special periods, reigns, etc.
767	Military history

	Scotland
	History
	General special -- Continued
	Antiquities
	Cf. DA777.5+ Roman antiquities
	Cf. DA880.A+ Local history and description
770	General works
	Biography of archaeologists
771.A2	Collective
771.A3-Z	Individual, A-Z
	e.g.
771.L3	Laing, David
	Social life and customs. Civilization. Intellectual life.
	National characteristics
772	General works
773	Court life and coronations
	Ethnography
774	General works
774.4.A-Z	Individual elements in the population, A-Z
774.4.A74	Asians
774.4.C55	Chileans
774.4.I72	Irish
774.4.I732	Italians
774.4.T72	Travellers (Nomadic people)
774.5	Scots outside of Scotland (General)
	For Scots in a particular country, see the country
	By period
	Early and medieval to 1603
774.8	Historiography
775	General works
	Early to 1057
	Including antiquities
777	General works
777.3	Earliest to 844
	Roman period
	Including antiquities
777.5	General works
777.7.A-Z	Local, A-Z
	e.g.
777.7.M66	Mons Graupius
	844-1057
	General works see DA777+
778	Kenneth I MacAlpin, 844-860
778.1	Constantine II, 863-877
778.2	Constantine III, 900-942
778.3	Malcolm I, 942-954
778.33	Indulph, 954-962

	Scotland
	History
	By period
	Early and medieval to 1603
	Early to 1057
	844-1057 -- Continued
778.35	Duff, 962-967
778.37	Culen, 967-971
778.4	Kenneth II, 971-995
778.45	Constantine IV, 995-997
778.5	Kenneth III, 997-1005
778.6	Malcolm II, 1005-1034
778.7	Duncan I, 1034-1040
778.8	Macbeth, 1040-1057
778.9.A-Z	Biography of contemporaries, A-Z
	1057-1603
779	General works
	1057-1278
780	General works
781	Malcolm III Canmore, 1057-1093
781.5	Edgar, 1097-1107
781.7	Alexander I, 1107-1124
782	David I, 1124-1153
782.2	Malcolm IV, 1153-1165
782.4	William IV, the Lion, 1165-1214
782.6	Alexander II, 1214-1249
782.8	Alexander III, 1249-1286
782.9.A-Z	Biography of contemporaries, A-Z
	e.g.
782.9.M3	Margaret, Consort of Malcolm III
	1278-1488
783	General works
	War of Independence, 1285-1371
783.2	General works
783.25	John Baliol, 1292-1296
	Sir William Wallace, 1296-1305
	Including Rising, 1297-1304
783.3	General works
783.35	Special events
	1306-1371. 14th century
783.38	General works
	Robert I (Robert Bruce), 1306-1329
783.4	General works
783.41	Special events
	e.g. Battle of Bannockburn, 1314
783.43	David II, 1329-1371
783.45.A-Z	Biography of contemporaries, A-Z

Scotland
History
By period
Early and medieval to 1603
1057-1603
1278-1488 -- Continued
1371-1488. Early Stuarts
Cf. DA758.3.S8 House of Stuart
783.5	General works
783.52	Social life and customs. Civilization. Intellectual life
783.53	Robert II, 1371-1390
	Including Battle of Otterburn, 1388, etc.
783.57	Robert III, 1390-1406
	Including Battle of Perth, 1396, etc.
783.6	James I, 1406-1437
783.7	James II, 1437-1460
783.8	James III, 1460-1488
783.9.A-Z	Biography of contemporaries, A-Z
	e.g.
783.9.C7	Crawford, Alexander Lindsay, 4th Earl of
	1488-1603
784	General works
784.3.A-Z	Biography and memoirs of contemporaries, A-Z
	e.g.
784.3.A4	Albany, John Stewart, Duke of
	James IV, 1488-1513
784.5	General works
784.6	Battle of Flodden, 1513
784.7	James V, 1513-1542
	1542-1603
785	General works
	Mary Stuart, 1542-1567
786	General works on reign
787.A1	History and biography
787.A2	Pamphlets, etc.
787.A3	Special works
	Including iconography
787.A36	Casket letters
787.A5	Compends. Juvenile works
787.A6-Z	Biography of contemporaries, A-Z
	e.g.
787.B7	Bothwell, James Hepburn, 4th Earl of
787.B9	Buchanan, George
787.R6	Rizzio, David
	1567-1603. James VI
788	General works

	Scotland
	History
	By period
	Early and medieval to 1603
	1057-1603
	1488-1603
	1542-1603
	1567-1603. James VI -- Continued
789	Gowrie Conspiracy, 1600
790.A-Z	Biography and memoirs of contemporaries, A-Z
	e.g.
790.M3	MacGregor, Alasdair Roy
	1603-1707/1745
800	General works
	Biography and memoirs
802.A1	Collective
802.A2-Z	Individual, A-Z
	1603-1692
803	General works
803.1	Pamphlets. By date
	1603-1625
803.15	General works
803.2.A-Z	Biography and memoirs, A-Z
	1625-1660
	Including 1625-1688
803.3	General works
	1637-1649
803.6	General works
803.7.A-Z	Biography and memoirs, A-Z
	e.g.
803.7.A3	Montrose, James Graham, 1st Marquis of
803.7.A4	Argyll, Archibald Campbell, Marquis of
803.73	1637-1643
803.8	1649-1660
	1660-1692/1715
804	General works
	Biography and memoirs
804.1.A1	Collective
804.1.A2-Z	Individual, A-Z
	e.g.
804.1.D9	Dundee, John Graham of Claverhouse,
	Viscount
804.1.F6	Fletcher, Andrew
804.6	Revolution, 1688
804.7	Glencoe massacre
	1692-1707
805	General works

	Scotland
	History
	By period
	1603-1707/1745
	1692-1707 -- Continued
807	Union, 1707
	18th century
809	General works
	Biography and memoirs
810.A1	Collective
810.A2-Z	Individual, A-Z
	e.g.
810.E7	Erskine, Henry
810.K3	Kames, Henry Home, Lord
810.M3	Macgregor, Robert (Rob Roy)
	Rob Roy see DA810.M3
811	Pamphlets, etc.
812	Social life and customs. Civilization. Intellectual life
	1707-1745. Jacobite movements
813	General works
	Biography and memoirs
814.A1	Collective
814.A3	James, Prince of Wales, the Old Pretender
814.A4	Clementina, Consort of James
814.A5	Charles Edward, the Young Pretender
814.A52	Albany, Charlotte Stuart, called Duchess of
814.A55	Albany, Louise Maximiliane C.E., Princess of
	Stolberg, known as Countess of
814.A6	Henry Benedict M.C. Stuart, Cardinal York
814.A8-Z	Other, A-Z
	e.g.
814.L8	Lovat, Simon Fraser, Baron
814.M14	Macdonald, Flora
814.2	1707
814.3	1714. Battle of Sheriffmuir
814.4	1719
814.5	1745-1746. Battle of Cullodon, 1746
	19th century
815	General works
	Biography and memoirs
816.A1	Collective
816.A2-Z	Individual, A-Z
	e.g.
816.C6	Cockburn, Henry Cockburn, Lord
816.M3	Marwick, Sir James David
817	Pamphlets, etc.
818	Social life and customs. Civilization

	Scotland
	History
	By period -- Continued
	20th century
821	General works
822.A-Z	Biography and memoirs, A-Z
824	Pamphlets, etc.
826	Social life and customs. Civilization. Intellectual life
	Description and travel
850	History of travel
	By period
855	Through 1800
865	1801-1900
866	1901-1950
867	1951-1980
867.5	1981-
869	Gazetteers. Dictionaries, etc. Place names
870	Guidebooks
873	Preservation of historic monuments, historic houses, etc.
	Castles, halls, etc.
875	General works
877.A-Z	Special, A-Z
	e.g.
	Cf. DA890.A+ Cities and towns of Scotland
877.G6	Glamis Castle
878	Islands of Scotland (Collective)
	For individual islands or groups of islands see
	DA880.A+
880.A-Z	Counties, regions, etc., A-Z
	e.g.
880.A1	Aberdeenshire
880.A5	Angus. Forfar
880.A6	Argyleshire
880.A7	Arran
880.A9	Ayrshire
880.B2	Banffshire
880.B5	Berwickshire
880.B72	Borders Region. Scottish Borders
880.B76	Breadalbane
880.B8	Buchan
880.B9	Buteshire
880.C1	Caithness
880.C5	Clackmannanshire
880.C6	Clyde River. Firth of Clyde
880.D8	Dumbartonshire
880.D88	Dumfriesshire
880.E2	East Lothian. Haddington

	Scotland
	Counties, regions, etc., A-Z -- Continued
	Edinburghshire see DA880.M6
	Elginshire see DA880.M8
880.F4	Fife
	Forfarshire see DA880.A5
880.G1	Galloway
880.G7	Grampians
	Haddingtonshire see DA880.E2
880.H4	Hebrides
	Highlands. Clans
880.H6	History
880.H7	Description
880.H76	Tartans of clans
880.I6	Inverness-shire
880.I7	Iona
880.K5	Kincardineshire
880.K53	Kinross-shire
880.K56	Kintyre
880.K6	Kirkcudbrightshire
880.K75	Knoydart
880.L2	Lanarkshire
	Linlithgowshire see DA880.W4
880.L8	Lochaber
880.L9	Lorne (District)
880.M6	Midlothian. Edinburghshire
880.M8	Moray. Elginshire
880.N3	Nairnshire
	Orkney Islands
880.O5	Serials
880.O6	Nonserials
880.P3	Peeblesshire
880.P4	Perthshire
880.R4	Renfrewshire
880.R7	Ross and Cromarty
880.R8	Roxburghshire
880.S2	Saint Kilda, Hebrides
	Scottish Borders see DA880.B72
880.S4	Selkirkshire
880.S5	Shetland Islands
880.S6	Skye
880.S8	Stirlingshire
880.S96	Sutherland
880.T8	Trossachs
880.T9	Tweed River and Valley
880.U48	Ulva
880.W4	West Lothian. Linlithgowshire

	Scotland
	Counties, regions, etc., A-Z -- Continued
880.W5	Wigtownshire
880.Y2	Yarrow
890.A-Z	Cities, towns, etc., A-Z
	e.g.
890.A2	Aberdeen
890.A5	Arbroath
890.D75	Dryburgh Abbey
890.D79	Dumfries
890.D797	Dunblane
890.D9	Dunfermline
890.D92	Dunkeld
	Edinburgh
890.E2	History
890.E3A1-.E3A19	Directories
890.E3A2-.E3Z	Description. Guidebooks
890.E4A-.E4Z	Special, A-Z
890.E4C3	Castle
890.E4H7	Holyrood Palace and Abbey
890.E4M27	Marchmont
890.E4S1	Saint Giles
	Glasgow
890.G49	Serials
890.G5	Nonserials
890.G8	Gretna Green
890.H2	Haddington
890.H3	Hawick
890.I6	Inverness
890.K48	Kilmarnock
890.K53	Kirkwall
890.L3	Langholm
890.L5	Leith
890.L75	Linlithgow
890.M5	Melrose
890.N75	North Queensferry
890.P1	Paisley
890.P3	Peebles
890.P4	Perth
890.S2	Saint Andrews
890.S8	Stirling
890.S85	Strathblane
890.W5	Whithorn priory
	Ireland
900	Periodicals. Societies. Serials
903	Minor periodicals
905	Sources and documents

	Ireland -- Continued
906	General works
	Biography (Collective) see DA916
	Historiography
908	General works
	Biography of historians
908.5	Collective
908.7.A-Z	Individual, A-Z
	History
	Study and teaching
909	General works
909.2.A-Z	By region or country, A-Z
909.5.A-Z	Individual schools, A-Z
910	General works
	Popular works
911	General
911.2	Stories from Irish history
911.5	Comic and satiric works
912	Compends
913	Addresses, essays, lectures
	General special
	Military history
914	General works
915.A-Z	Biography and memoirs, A-Z
916	Biography (Collective)
	For individual biography, see the special period, reign, or place
916.1	Rulers, kings, viceroys, etc.
916.3	Houses, noble families, etc.
916.4	Public men
916.7	Women
916.8	Other
	Including Irish in other countries
920	Antiquities
	Including pre-Celtic
	Cf. DA990.A+ Local history and description
	Social life and customs. Civilization. National characteristics
925	General works
926.A-Z	Special topics, A-Z
	Ethnography
927	General works
927.4.A-Z	Individual elements in the population, A-Z
927.4.T72	Travellers (Nomadic people)
	By period
	To 1172
930	General works

	Ireland
	History
	By period
	To 1172 -- Continued
930.5	Social life and customs. Civilization. Intellectual life
931	Pagan Ireland, to 433
	Christian Ireland, 433-1172
932	General works
932.2.A-Z	Biography and memoirs, A-Z
932.4	433-795
932.6	Danish wars, 795-1014
	1172-1603
933	General works
933.2	Social life and customs. Civilization. Intellectual life
	Biography and memoirs
933.25	Collective
933.26.A-Z	Individual, A-Z
933.3	English conquest, 1154-1189
	1189-1485
934	General works
934.5	Invasion by Edward Bruce, 1315
	Including biography of Bruce
	1485-1603. Tudors
935	General works
936.A-Z	Biography and memoirs of contemporaries, A-Z
	e.g.
936.K5	Kildare, Gerald Fitzgerald, 8th Earl of
	1558-1603. Elizabeth
937	General works
937.3	Tyrone's Rebellion, 1597-1603
937.5.A-Z	Biography and memoirs of contemporaries, A-Z
	e.g.
937.5.D4	Desmond, Katherine (Fitzgerald) Fitzgerald, Countess of
937.5.O3	O'Donnell, Hugh Roe
	Modern, 1603-
938	General works
	17th century
940	General works
940.3	Social life and customs. Civilization. Intellectual life
940.5.A-Z	Biography and memoirs, A-Z
	e.g.
940.5.C7	Cork, Richard Boyle, 1st Earl of
940.5.O5	O'Neill, Owen Roe
940.5.O7	Ormonde, James Butler, 1st Duke of
941.3	1603-1625. James I
	1625-1649. Charles I

Ireland
  History
    By period
      Modern, 1603-
        17th century
          1625-1649. Charles I -- Continued

941.5	General works
943	1641-1649. Irish Confederation, 1642-1648
	Including the Rebellion of 1641, etc.
944.4	1649-1660. Cromwell
944.5	1660-1685. Charles II
944.7	1685-1688. James II
945	1688-1691
	Including the Siege of Londonderry, 1688-1689; Battle of the Boyne, 1690; Siege of Limerick, 1690; etc.
946	1691-1700
	18th century
947	General works
947.Z9	Pamphlets, etc.
947.3	Social life and customs. Civilization. Intellectual life
948.A2	General special
	Biography and memoirs
948.A5	Collective
948.3.A-Z	Individual, A-Z
	e.g.
948.3.C9	Curran, John Philpot
948.3.F6	Flood, Henry
948.3.G7	Grattan, Henry
	1782-1800
948.4	General works
	1791-1800
948.5	General works
948.6.A-Z	Biography and memoirs, A-Z
	e.g.
948.6.E5	Emmet, Robert
948.6.F5	Fitzgerald, Lord Edward
948.6.T6	Tone, Theobald Wolfe
	1798-1800
	Including Rebellion of 1798
949	General works
949.5	Union, 1801
	19th century. Irish question
	Cf. JN1411 Political institutions and public administration
	Cf. KDK1200+ Constitutional history
949.7	Dictionaries
950	General works

Ireland
  History
    By period
      Modern, 1603-
        19th century. Irish question -- Continued

950.1	Social life and customs. Civilization. Intellectual life 1800-1848
950.2	General works
	Biography and memoirs
950.21	Collective
	Individual
950.22	O'Connell, Daniel
950.23.A-Z	Other, A-Z
	e.g.
950.23.D2	Davis, Thomas Osborne
950.23.D7	Drummond, Thomas
950.23.M6	Mitchel, John
950.23.S5	Sheil, Richard Lalor
950.29	Pamphlets. By date
950.3	1800-1829. Catholic emancipation
	Union, 1801 see DA949.5
950.4	Tithe War, 1829-1838
950.5	1838-1848
950.7	Famine, 1845-1847
	1848-1900
951	General works
	Biography and memoirs
952.A1	Collective
952.A2-Z	Individual, A-Z
	e.g.
952.O3	O'Donovan Rossa, Jeremiah
952.R3	Redmond, John Edward
953	Pamphlets. By date
954	Fenians
955	1848-1868
	1868-1900
957	General works
957.5	Parnell Commission
957.9	Other
	Biography and memoirs
958.A1	Collective
958.A2-Z	Individual, A-Z
	e.g.
958.D2	Davitt, Michael
958.H4	Healy, Timothy Michael
958.O3	O'Brien, William
958.O5	O'Connor, Thomas Power

	Ireland
	History
	By period
	Modern, 1603- -- Continued
	20th century
959	General works
959.1	Social life and customs. Civilization
	1901-1922
960	General works
962	1914-1921. Period of World War I, 1914-1918
	Including Easter Rising, 1916; War of Independence, 1919-1921
963	1922-
	Including Irish Free State, 1922-1937; Eire, 1937-1949; Republic of Ireland, 1949-
	Diplomatic history. Foreign and special relations
964.A2	General works
964.A3-Z	Relations with individual regions or countries, A-Z
	Biography and memoirs
965.A1	Collective
965.A3-Z	Individual, A-Z
	e.g.
965.C25	Carson, Sir Edward Henry
965.C3	Casement, Sir Roger
965.C6	Collins, Michael
965.C7	Connolly, James
965.D4	DeValera, Eamonn
965.G8	Griffith, Arthur
965.H9	Hyde, Douglas
965.P4	Pearse, Padraic
965.P6	Plunkett, Sir Horace Curzon
	21st century
966	General works
966.2	Social life and customs. Civilization. Intellectual life
969	Description and travel
	By period
970	Through 1700
972	1701-1800
975	1801-1900
977	1901-1950
978	1951-1980
978.2	1981-
979	Gazetteers. Dictionaries, etc. Place names
979.5	Directories
980	Guidebooks
982	Pictorial works
	Castles, halls, etc.

Ireland
    Description and travel
        Castles, halls, etc. -- Continued

985	General works
987.A-Z	Individual, A-Z
	e.g.
987.D8	Dungory Castle
988	Islands of Ireland (Collective)
990.A-Z	Counties, regions, etc., A-Z
	e.g.
990.A6	Antrim
990.A8	Aran Islands
990.A85	Armagh
990.B65	Blasket Islands
990.C28	Carlow
990.C59	Clare
990.C6	Connacht (Connaught) Province
990.C7	Connemara (District)
	Cork
990.C78	Periodicals. Societies. Serials
990.C79	History and description
990.D6	Donegal
990.D7	Down
990.D8	Dublin
	Cf. DA995.D75+ Dublin (City)
990.G18	Galway
990.K4	Kerry
990.K45	Killarney, Lakes of
	King's see DA990.O3
990.L5	Leinster
	Including life of Art McMurrough, King
990.L55	Leitrim
990.L6	Leix (Laoighis), Queen's
990.L7	Limerick
990.L8	Londonderry
990.M3	Mayo
990.M7	Monaghan
990.M8	Munster
	Northern Ireland see DA990.U45+
990.O3	Offaly. King's
	Queen's see DA990.L6
990.R7	Roscommon
990.S6	Sligo
990.T3	Tara
990.T5	Tipperary
990.T9	Tyrone
	Northern Ireland (Ulster)

	Ireland
	Counties, regions, etc., A-Z
	Northern Ireland (Ulster) -- Continued
990.U45	Periodicals. Societies. Serials
	Biography
990.U452A1- .U452A19	Collective
990.U452A2-.U452Z	Individual, A-Z
990.U46	History and description
990.W3	Waterford
990.W5	Wexford
990.W6	Wicklow
995.A-Z	Cities, towns, etc., A-Z
	e.g.
995.A72	Armagh
995.B21	Bandon
995.B5	Belfast
995.C3	Carrickfergus
995.C4	Cashel
995.C7	Cork
	Derry see DA995.L75
	Dublin
995.D75	History
995.D8	Description
995.D9A-.D9Z	Special, A-Z
	e. g.
995.D9C32	Cabra
995.D9D8	Dublin Castle
995.D9I53	Inchicore
995.D9K5	King's Inns
995.D9M68	Mountjoy Square
995.D9N44	Nelson Pillar
995.E6	Enniskillen
995.G18	Galway
995.L7	Limerick
995.L75	Londonderry. Derry
995.W32	Waterford

History of Central Europe
  Cf. DJK1+ Eastern Europe

1001	Periodicals. Societies. Serials
1004	Congresses
1005	Sources and documents
1006	Gazetteers. Dictionaries, etc.
1007	Place names (General)
1008	Guidebooks
1009	General works
1010	Pictorial works
1012	Historic monuments, landmarks, scenery, etc.
	For local, see individual countries, regions, etc.
1013	Historical geography
	Description and travel
1014	Early through 1980
1015	1981-
1023	Antiquities
	For local antiquities, see individual countries, regions, etc.
1024	Social life and customs. Civilization. Intellectual life
	For specific periods, see the period
	Ethnography
1026	General works
1028.A-Z	Individual elements in the population, A-Z
1028.C75	Croats
1028.P64	Poles
1028.S84	Swedes
1028.T38	Tatars
	History
	Periodicals, societies, serials see DAW1001
1031	Biography (Collective)
	For individual biography, see the specific period, reign or place
	Historiography
1032	General works
	Biography of historians, area studies specialists, archaeologists, etc.
1033	Collective
1034.A-Z	Individual, A-Z
	Study and teaching. Area studies
1035	General works
1036.A-Z	By region or country, A-Z
1038	General works
1042	Political history
	By period, see the specific period
1044	Foreign and general relations
	By period, see the specific period
1045.A-Z	Relations with specific countries, A-Z
	By period

History
By period -- Continued
1046   Early and medieval to 1500
For the Holy Roman Empire see DD125+
1047   1500-1815
For the Austro-Hungarian Empire see DB1+
1048   1815-1918
1049   1918-1945
1050   1945-1989
1051   1989-

DAW, DB

DAW, DB

	History
	By period
	1521-
	1521-1648
	Rudolf II, 1576-1622 -- Continued
	Biography and memoirs of contemporaries
65.53	Collective
65.54.A-Z	Individual, A-Z
65.6	Mathias, 1612-1619
65.7	1618-1648
	For works on the Thirty Years' War see D251+
65.75	Ferdinand II, 1619-1637
65.8	Ferdinand III, 1637-1657
65.9.A-Z	Biography and memoirs of contemporaries not identified with special reigns, A-Z
	1648-1740
66	General works
66.5	General special
66.8.A-Z	Biography and memoirs, A-Z
	e.g.
	Cf. DB67.8, DB69.5
66.8.S8	Starhemberg, Guido, graf
	Leopold I, 1657-1705
67	General works on life and reign
67.3	General special
67.8.A-Z	Biography and memoirs of contemporaries, A-Z
	e.g.
67.8.C4	Charles V, Duke of Lorraine
67.8.L74	Lobkowitz, Wenzel Franz E., fürst von
	Joseph I, 1705-1711
68	General works on life and reign
	Karl VI, 1711-1740
69	General works on life and reign
69.3	General special
	e.g. Pragmatic sanction
	Cf. JN1625 Political history
69.5.A-Z	Biography and memoirs of contemporaries, A-Z
	1740-1792
69.7	General works
69.8	General special
69.9.A-Z	Biography and memoirs, A-Z
	Cf. DB73, DB74.7
	Maria Theresia, 1740-1780
70	General works on reign
71	Biography of Maria Theresia

History
By period
1521-
19th century
Ferdinand I, 1835-1848 -- Continued
82.5   Pamphlets, etc.
83   Revolution, 1848
Franz Joseph I, 1848-1916
85   General works on life and reign
86   General special
Austro-Sardinian War, 1848-1849 see DG553+
Schleswig-Holstein War, 1864 see DL236+
War with Italy, 1866 see DG558
War with Prussia, 1866 see DD436+
86.7   Period of World War I, 1914-1918
For the war itself see D501+
Biography
87   Franz Joseph I
88   Elisabeth, Consort of Francis Joseph I
89.A-Z   Other members of the royal family, A-Z
e.g.
89.F7   Franz Ferdinand, Archduke
89.R8   Rudolf, Crown Prince
90.A-Z   Biography and memoirs of contemporaries, A-Z
e.g.
90.B6   Beust, Friedrich Ferdinand, graf von
90.C7   Conrad von Hötzendorf, Franz, graf
90.F5   Fischhof, Adolf
90.R2   Radetzky von Radetz, Johann Joseph W.A. F.K,
graf
90.S3   Schönerer, Georg, ritter von
90.T4   Tegetthof, Wilhelm von
20th century
91   General works
91.2   Social life and customs. Civilization. Intellectual life
Karl I, 1916-1918
92   General works on life and reign
93   General special
93.5   Zita, Consort of Karl I
Republic, 1918-
96   General works
97   Other
Biography and memoirs
98.A1   Collective
98.A2-Z   Individual, A-Z
e.g.
98.D6   Dollfuss, Engelbert

Local history and description
Provinces, regions, etc.
Carniola, Littoral, Julian March -- Continued
Görz and Gradiska (General and Slovenia) see
DR1475.G67
Croatia and Slavonia see DR1502+
Dalmatia see DR1620+

441-450.7	Danube River
	For the Danube Valley (General) see DJK76.2+
	Cf. DR49+ Lower Danube Valley
441	Periodicals. Societies. Serials
443	Sources and documents. Collections
445	Guidebooks
446	Description and history (General)
	Description and travel
447	Early and medieval
448	1601-1800
449	1801-1945
449.2	1946-
450	Antiquities
450.5	Social life and customs. Civilization. Intellectual life
450.7	Ethnography

Dinaric Alps see DR1350.D55
Galicia see DK4600.G34+
Hercegovina see DR1775.H47
Hungary see DB901+
Illyrian Provinces, 1809-1814 and Illyria (Kingdom) see
DR1350.I45

(540.5)	Liechtenstein
	see DB881+
(541-560)	Moravia
	see DB2300+
601-620	Salzburg (Table D-DR6)
621-640	Salzkammergut (Table D-DR6)
	Silesia
	see DB2500.S54 (Czechoslovakia); DK4600.S42+ (General, and Poland); DK4600.C54 (Cieszyn Silesia)
(661-680)	Slovakia
	see DB2700+
681-700	Styria (Table D-DR6)
	For Lower Styria (Slovenia) see DR1475.S89
	Sudetenland. Sudetes (Sudetic Mountains)
	see DB2500.S94 (General, and Czechoslovakia); DK4600.S7 (Poland)
(721-740)	Transylvania
	see DR279+

	Local history and description
	Vienna
	Sections, districts, etc., A-Z -- Continued
857.A3-Z	Individual, A-Z
857.B45	1. Bezirk
857.B452	2. Bezirk
857.B453	3. Bezirk
857.B454	4. Bezirk
857.B455	5. Bezirk
857.B456	6. Bezirk
857.B457	7. Bezirk
857.B458	8. Bezirk
857.B459	9. Bezirk
857.B46	10. Bezirk
857.B461	11. Bezirk
857.B462	12. Bezirk
857.B463	13. Bezirk
857.B464	14. Bezirk
857.B465	15. Bezirk
857.B466	16. Bezirk
857.B467	17. Bezirk
857.B468	18. Bezirk
857.B469	19. Bezirk
857.B47	20. Bezirk
857.B471	21. Bezirk
857.B472	22. Bezirk
857.B473	23. Bezirk
857.B474	24. Bezirk
857.B475	25. Bezirk
857.B476	26. Bezirk
857.B477	27. Bezirk
857.B478	28. Bezirk
	Streets, suburbs, etc.
858.A2	Collective
858.A3-Z	Individual, A-Z
	Buildings. Churches, theaters, etc.
859.A2	General works
859.A3-Z	Individual, A-Z
860	Other special (not A-Z)
	Budapest see DB981+
879.A-Z	Other cities, towns, etc., A-Z
	e.g.
879.A8	Aussee. Bad Aussee
	Bad Aussee see DB879.A8
	Bad Gastein see DB879.G2
	Bolzano. Bozen see DG975.B68
	Brasov see DR296.B74

	Local history and description
	Other cities, towns, etc., A-Z -- Continued
879.B49	Braunau
879.B5	Bregenz
	Brixen, Bressanone see DG975.B855
	Brno see DB2650.B75
	Brünn. Brno see DB2650.B75
	Dubrovnik see DR1645.D8
879.G2	Gastein. Bad Gastein
	Gorizia. Görz see DG975.G67
	Görz see DG975.G67
879.G8	Graz. Gratz
879.I6	Innsbruck
	Kraków see DK4700+
879.K9	Kremsmünster
(879.K93)	Kronstadt. Brasov. Stalin
	see DR296.B74
879.L6	Linz
	Meran see DG975.M52
	Pergine see DG975.P37
	Ragusa. Dubrovnik see DR1645.D8
879.S18	Salzburg
	Trent see DG975.T788
	Trieste see DG975.T825
	Zagreb see DR1638

	History of Liechtenstein
881	Periodicals. Societies. Serials
885	Guidebooks
886	General works
887	Pictorial works
888	Description and travel
889	Antiquities
	History
891	General works
	Foreign and general relations
893	General works
894.A-Z	Relations with individual regions or countries, A-Z
898.A-Z	Local, A-Z

DAW, DB

	History of Hungary
901	Periodicals. Societies. Serials
	Museums, exhibitions, etc.
902	General works
902.2.A-Z	Individual. By place, A-Z
903	Sources and documents
	Collected works
903.5	Several authors
903.7	Individual authors
904	Gazetteers. Dictionaries, etc.
905	Guidebooks
906	General works
906.5	Pictorial works
	Historic monuments, landmarks, scenery, etc. (General)
	For local see DB975.A+
906.6	General works
906.7	Preservation
906.75	Historical geography
	Description and travel
906.9	History of travel
907	Early through 1526
910	1527-1800
914	1801-1900
916	1901-1918
917	1919-1980
917.3	1981-
	Ethnography. Races. Magyars
919	General works
919.15	National characteristics
919.2.A-Z	Individual elements in the population, A-Z
919.2.A64	Armenians
919.2.C76	Croats
919.2.G3	Germans
919.2.G74	Greeks
919.2.J39	Jazyge
919.2.K57	Kipchak
919.2.M34	Macedonians
919.2.P34	Palocs
919.2.P66	Poles
919.2.R8	Romanians
919.2.S27	Sarmatians
919.2.S4	Serbs
919.2.S52	Slavs
919.2.S53	Slavs, Southern
919.2.S55	Slovaks
919.2.S57	Slovenes
	Southern Slavs see DB919.2.S53

Ethnography. Races. Magyars
Individual elements in the population, A-Z -- Continued

919.2.S94	Szeklers
919.2.Y8	Yugoslavs
919.5	Hungarians in foreign countries (General)
	For Hungarians in a particular country, see the country
920	Antiquities
	Counties, regions, etc. see DB975.A+
	Cities, towns, etc. see DB999.A+
920.5	Social life and customs. Civilization. Intellectual life

History

921	Dictionaries. Chronological tables, outlines, etc.

Biography (Collective)
For individual biography, see the period, reign, or place

922	General works
922.1	Rulers, kings, etc.
922.3	Houses, noble families, etc.
922.4	Public men
922.7	Women

Historiography

923	General works

Biography of historians

923.5	Collective
923.7.A-Z	Individual, A-Z
923.8	Study and teaching

General works

924	Through 1800. Chronicles
925	1801-
925.1	Compends
925.3	Addresses, essays, lectures
925.5	Military history

Political and diplomatic history. Foreign and general
relations
For general works on the diplomatic history of a period, see the
period
For works on relations with a specific country regardless
of period see DB926.3.A+

926	General works
926.3.A-Z	Relations with individual regions or countries, A-Z

By period
Early to 896

927	General works
927.3	Origins
927.5	Roman period
928	Migrations

Árpád dynasty, 896-1301

929.A3	Sources and documents

History
By period
Arpád dynasty, 896-1301 -- Continued

929.A4-Z	General works
	Biography and memoirs
929.18	Collective
929.2.A-Z	Individual, A-Z
929.25	Arpád, 896-907
929.28	Taksony, 952-972
	Including the Battle of Lechfeld, 955
929.3	Géza, 972-977
	István, Saint, 997-1038
929.35	General works
929.36	Introduction of Christianity, ca. 1000
929.4	Lázló I, 1077-1095
929.45	Kálman, 1095-1116
929.47	István II, 1116-1131
929.5	Béla III, 1173-1196
	András (Endre) II, 1205-1235
929.6	General works
929.65	Aranybulla (Golden Bull), 1222
	Béla IV, 1235-1270
929.7	General works
929.75	Mongol invasion, 1241-1242
929.8	András III, 1290-1301
	Elective kings, 1301-1526
929.95	Sources and documents
930	General works
930.15	Social life and customs. Civilization. Intellectual life
930.2	Károly Róbert I, 1308-1342
930.3	Lajos I, Nagy, 1342-1382
	For his reign in Poland see DK4249
930.4	Sigismund, 1387-1437
	For general works on life and reign in Germany see DD170+
	The Hunyadi
930.5	General works
930.7	Hunyadi, János, 1444-1456
931	Mátyás I, Corvinus, 1458-1490
	Ulászló (Vladislav) II, 1490-1516
931.4	General works
931.5	Dózsa Uprising, 1514
	For his biography see DB931.9.D69
931.7	Lajos (Ludvik) II, 1516-1526
	Biography and memoirs
931.8	Collective

History
By period
Elective kings, 1301-1526
Biography and memoirs -- Continued
931.9.A-Z   Individual, A-Z
    e.g.
931.9.B5   Beatrix, Queen, Consort of Mátyás I
931.9.D69   Dózsa, György
Turkish occupation, 1526-1699
931.94   Sources and documents
931.95   General works
931.96   Social life and customs. Civilization. Intellectual life
1526-1606
932   General works
932.12   Social life and customs. Civilization. Intellectual life
Biography and memoirs
932.15   Collective
932.2.A-Z   Individual, A-Z
    e.g.
932.2.B63   Bocskai, István, Prince of Transylvania
932.2.Z75   Zřinyi, Miklos, grof, 1508-1566
932.25   János I Zápolya, 1526-1540
932.28   Fifteen Years' War, 1591-1606
1606-1699/1711
932.3   General works
932.35   Social life and customs. Civilization. Intellectual life
932.4   Ferenc II Rákóczi
Including the Rákóczi Uprising, 1703-1711
Biography and memoirs
932.47   Collective
932.48.A-Z   Individual, A-Z
    e.g.
932.48.E8   Esterházy, Miklós
932.48.T45   Thököly, Imre, késmárki gróf
932.48.Z75   Zřinyi, Miklös, gróf, 1620-1664
1711-1792. Age of absolutism
932.49   Sources and documents
932.5   General works
932.7   Social life and customs. Civilization. Intellectual life
Biography and memoirs
932.8   Collective
932.9.A-Z   Individual, A-Z
    e.g.
932.9.M3   Martinovics, Ignác József
1792-1918. 19th century
932.95   Sources and documents
933   General works

	History
	By period
	1792-1918. 19th century -- Continued
933.15	Social life and customs. Civilization. Intellectual life
	Biography and memoirs
933.2	Collective
933.3.A-Z	Individual, A-Z
	e.g.
933.3.D2	Deák, Ferencz
933.3.E6	Eötvös, József, báró
933.3.S8	Széchenyi, István, gróf
933.3.T3	Táncsics, Mihály
933.3.W5	Wesselényi, Miklós, báró
933.5	1792-1825
934	1825-1848. Age of reform
	Revolution of 1848-1849
934.5	Sources and documents
935	General works
	Kossuth, Lajos
937	General biography and criticism
937.3	Visit to the United States
937.6	Addresses, essays, lectures
937.8	Other
937.82	Personal narratives
937.83.A-Z	Local revolutionary history. By place, A-Z
	Foreign participation and public opinion
938	General works
939.A-Z	By region or country, A-Z
939.5.A-Z	Other special topics, A-Z
939.5.I53	Influence
939.5.M55	Minorities
939.5.R44	Religious aspects
	1849-1918
940	General works
940.5	Social life and customs. Civilization. Intellectual life
	Biography and memoirs
941.A1	Collective
941.A2-Z	Individual, A-Z
	e.g.
941.A6	Andrássy, Gyula, gróf
941.A8	Apponyi, Albert, gróf
941.T58	Tisza, István, gróf
943	1849-1867
945	1867-1918. Dual monarchy
	20th century
946	Sources and documents
947	General works

History
  By period
    20th century -- Continued

949.2	Social life and customs. Civilization. Intellectual life
950.A1	Biography (Collective)
	For individual biography, see the individual period
953	1914-1918. Period of World War I
	For the war itself see D501+
	1918-1945. Revolution. Counterrevolution, and the Regency
954	Sources and documents
955	General works
955.3	Social life and customs. Civilization. Intellectual life
955.4	Foreign and general relations
	Biography and memoirs
955.5	Collective
955.6.A-Z	Individual, A-Z
	e.g.
955.6.B47	Bethlen, István, gróf
955.6.H67	Horthy, Miklós, nagybányai
955.6.K37	Károlyi, Mihály, gróf
955.6.K83	Kun, Béla
955.7	1919-1920. Revolution and counterrevolution
955.8	1939-1945. Period of World War II
	For the war itself see D731+
	1945-1989. People's Republic
955.9	Sources and documents
956	General works
956.3	Social life and customs. Civilization. Intellectual life
956.4	Foreign and general relations
	Biography and memoirs
956.5	Collective
956.6.A-Z	Individual, A-Z
	e.g.
956.6.K33	Kádár, János
956.6.N33	Nagy, Imre
956.6.R34	Rákosi, Mátyás
	Revolution of 1956
956.7	Sources and documents
957	General works
957.3	Personal narratives
957.4.A-Z	Local revolutionary history. By place, A-Z
957.5.A-Z	Special topics, A-Z
957.5.E95	Executions
957.5.F67	Foreign public opinion
957.5.F74	Press
957.5.R43	Refugees

History
  By period
    20th century -- Continued
      1989-

957.9	Sources and documents
958	General works
958.2	Social life and customs. Civilization. Intellectual life
958.3	Political history
958.4	Foreign and general relations
	Biography and memoirs
958.5	Collective
958.6.A-Z	Individual, A-Z

Local history and description
  Counties, regions, etc.

974.9	Collective
975.A-Z	Individual, A-Z
975.B15	Bácska
	For Bačka (General, and Serbia) see DR2105.B32
975.B2	Banat
	For Banat (General, and Romania) see DR281.B25
	For Serbian Banat see DR2105.B35
975.B3	Baranya
	For Baranja (Croatia) see DR1637.B37
975.B32	Baranyai Szerb-Magyar Köztársaság
975.H4	Hegyalja
975.M4	Mecsek Mountains
	Military Frontier (Territory) see DR1350.M54
975.S9	Szabolcs-Szatmár
975.V4	Vertes Mountains

    Budapest

981	Periodicals. Societies. Serials
981.2	Museums, exhibitions, etc.
	Subarrange by author
981.3	Sources and documents
	Collected works (nonserial)
981.5	Several authors
981.6	Individual authors
983	Directories. Dictionaries. Gazetteers
983.5	Guidebooks
983.7	General works
	Description
984	Early and medieval
984.2	17th-18th centuries
984.3	19th century
984.4	20th century
985	Monumental and picturesque. Pictorial works
987	Antiquities

	Local history and description
	Budapest -- Continued
988	Social life and customs. Civilization. Intellectual life
	Ethnography
988.3	General works
988.5.A-Z	Individual elements in the population, A-Z
	History
988.7	Biography (Collective)
989	General works
	By period
989.5	Early and medieval
990	17th-18th centuries
991	19th century
992	20th century
	Sections, districts, suburbs, etc. Kerultetek (i.e. numbered city sections) and named city sections
993	Collective
993.2.A-Z	Individual, A-Z
993.2.A01-.A22	Kerulet
993.2.K57	Kispest
993.2.V37	Városliget
	Statues, etc.
993.5	Collective
993.7.A-Z	Individual, A-Z
	Parks, squares, cemeteries, etc.
994	Collective
994.2.A-Z	Individual, A-Z
	Streets, bridges, etc.
995	Collective
995.2.A-Z	Individual, A-Z
	Buildings. Palaces, etc.
996	Collective
997.A-Z	Individual, A-Z
	Other cities, towns, etc.
998.9	Collective
999.A-Z	Individual, A-Z

History of Czechoslovakia
    Class here general works on Czechoslovakia, on Bohemia, and on
      the Czech Republic
    For Moravia see DB2300+
    For Slovakia see DB2700+

2000	Periodicals. Societies. Serials
	Museums, exhibitions, etc.
2001	General works
2002.A-Z	Individual. By place, A-Z
2003	Congresses
2004	Sources and documents
	Collected works (nonserial)
2005	Several authors
2006	Individual authors
2007	Gazetteers. Dictionaries, etc.
2008	Place names (General)
2009	Directories
2010	Guidebooks
2011	General works
2012	General special
2013	Pictorial works
	Historic monuments, landmarks, scenery, etc. (General)
	For local see DB2500.A+
2015	General works
2016	Preservation
2017	Historical geography
	Description and travel
2018	History of travel
2019	Early through 1900
2020	1901-1945
2021	1946-1976
2022	1977-
2030	Antiquities
	For local antiquities see DB2500.A+
2035	Social life and customs. Civilization. Intellectual life
	For specific periods, see the period or reign
	Ethnography
2040	General works
2041	National characteristics
2042.A-Z	Individual elements in the population, A-Z
2042.A8	Austrians
2042.B44	Belarusians
2042.B85	Bulgarians
2042.C44	Celts
2042.G4	Germans
	Gypsies in the Czech Republic see DX222
	Gypsies in Slovakia see DX222.5

Ethnography
  Individual elements in the population, A-Z -- Continued
2042.H8	Hungarians
	Jews see DS135.C95+
2042.M33	Macedonians
2042.P6	Poles
	Romanies in the Czech Republic see DX222
	Romanies in Slovakia see DX222.5
2042.R77	Russians
2042.R8	Ruthenians
2042.S5	Slovaks
2042.S6	Sorbs
2042.U5	Ukrainians
2043	Czechoslovaks in foreign countries (General)

      For Czechoslovaks in a particular country, see the country
      For Slovaks in foreign countries (General) see DB2743

History
  Periodicals. Societies. Serials see DB2000

2044	Dictionaries. Chronological tables, outlines, etc.
	Biography (Collective)

      For individual biography, see the specific period, reign, or place

2045	General works
2046	Rulers, kings, etc.
2047	Queens. Princes and princesses
	Houses, noble families, etc.
2048	Collective
2049.A-Z	Individual houses, families, etc., A-Z
2050	Statesmen
2051	Women
	Historiography
2055	General works
	Biography of historians and area studies specialists
2056	Collective
2057.A-Z	Individual, A-Z
	Study and teaching
2059	General works
2060.A-Z	By region or country, A-Z
	Subarrange by author
	General works
2061	Through 1800
2062	1801-1976
2063	1977-
2064	Pictorial works
2065	Juvenile works
2066	Addresses, essays, lectures. Anecdotes, etc.
2068	Philosophy of Czechoslovak history

History -- Continued
 Military history
  For specific periods, including individual campaigns and
   engagements, see the period or reign
2069   Sources and documents
2070   General works
    By period
2071   Early through 1620
2072   1620-1918
2073   1918-
 Political history
  For specific periods, see the period or reign
2074   Sources and documents
2075   General works
 Foreign and general relations
  For general works on the diplomatic history of a period, see the
   period
  For works on relations with a specific country regardless
   of period see DB2078.A+
2076   Sources and documents
2077   General works
2078.A-Z   Relations with individual regions or countries, A-Z
 By period
  Early and medieval to 1526
2080   Sources and documents
2081   General works
2082   General special
2082.4   Addresses, essays, lectures
2082.45   Social life and customs. Civilization. Intellectual life
2082.5   Political history
2083   Biography (Collective)
    Great Moravian Empire, 9th century see DB2385+
    Přemyslid Dynasty, 9th/10th century-ca. 1310
2085   Sources and documents
2086   General works
2087   General special
2087.5   Addresses, essays, lectures
2088   Social life and customs. Civilization. Intellectual life
2088.5   Military history
2088.7   Political history
2089   Foreign and general relations
     Biography and general memoirs
2090   Collective
2091.A-Z   Individual, A-Z
      e.g.
2091.P74   Přemysl II (Otakar)
    Luxemburg Dynasty, 1311-1437

History
  By period
    Early and medieval to 1526
      Luxemburg Dynasty, 1311-1437 -- Continued

2095	Sources and documents
2096	General works
2097	General special
2097.5	Addresses, essays, lectures
2098	Social life and customs. Civilization. Intellectual life
2098.5	Military history
2098.7	Political history
2099	Foreign and general relations
	Biography and memoirs
2100	Collective
2101.A-Z	Individual, A-Z
2102	Jan Lucemburský, 1310-1346
2103	Karel IV, 1346-1378
2104	Vaclav IV, 1378-1419
	Hussite Wars, 1419-1436
2105	Sources and documents
2106	General works
2107	General special
2107.5	Addresses, essays, lectures
2108	Social life and customs. Civilization. Intellectual life
2108.5	Military history
2108.7	Political history
2109	Foreign and general relations
	Biography and memoirs
2110	Collective
2111.A-Z	Individual, A-Z
	e.g.
2111.Z45	Zelivský, Jan
2111.Z59	Zižka z Trocnova, Jan
	1437-1526
2115	Sources and documents
2116	General works
2117	General special
2117.5	Addresses, essays, lectures
2118	Social life and customs. Civilization. Intellectual life
2118.7	Political history
2119	Foreign and general relations
	Biography and memoirs
2120	Collective
2121.A-Z	Individual, A-Z
	Jiří z Poděbrad (The Hussite King), 1458-1471
2125	Sources and documents
2126	General works on life and reign

History
 By period
  Early and medieval to 1526
   1437-1526
    Jiří z Poděbrad (The Hussite King), 1458-1471 --
     Continued

2127	General special
2127.5	Addresses, essays, lectures
2128	Social life and customs. Civilization. Intellectual life
2128.7	Political history
2129	Foreign and general relations
	Biography and memoirs
2130	Collective
2131.A-Z	Individual, A-Z
2133	1471-1526

Hapsburg rule, 1526-1918

2135	Sources and documents
2136	General works
2137	General special
2137.5	Addresses, essays, lectures
2138	Social life and customs. Civilization. Intellectual life
2138.7	Political history
2139	Foreign and general relations
	Biography and memoirs
2140	Collective
2141.A-Z	Individual, A-Z
	1526-1618
2145	Sources and documents
2146	General works
2147	General special
2147.5	Addresses, essays, lectures
2148	Social life and customs. Civilization. Intellectual life
2148.7	Political history
2149	Foreign and general relations
	Biography and memoirs
2150	Collective
2151.A-Z	Individual, A-Z
	e.g.
2151.R83	Rudolf II

Period of Thirty Years' War. Uprising of the Czech
 Estates. 1618-1648
  For the Thirty Years' War (General) see D251+

2155	Sources and documents
2156	General works
2157	General special
2157.5	Addresses, essays, lectures
2158	Social life and customs. Civilization. Intellectual life

History
  By period
    Hapsburg rule, 1526-1918
      Period of Thirty Years' War. Uprising of the Czech
        Estates. 1618-1648 -- Continued

2158.7	Political history
2159	Foreign and general relations
	Biography and memoirs
2160	Collective
2161.A-Z	Individual, A-Z
2162	Battle of Bílá Hora (Battle of White Mountain or Weisser Berg)
	1648-1815
2165	Sources and documents
2166	General works
2167	General special
2167.5	Addresses, essays, lectures
2168	Social life and customs. Civilization. Intellectual life
2168.7	Political history
2169	Foreign and general relations
	Biography and memoirs
2170	Collective
2171.A-Z	Individual, A-Z
	Period of national awakening, 1815-1918
2175	Sources and documents
2176	General works
2177	General special
2177.5	Addresses, essays, lectures
2178	Social life and customs. Civilization. Intellectual life
2178.7	Political history
2179	Foreign and general relations
	Biography and memoirs
2180	Collective
2181.A-Z	Individual, A-Z
	e.g.
2181.H39	Havlíček-Borovský, Karel
2181.J85	Jungman, Josef
2181.P35	Palacký, František
	For Palacký as a historian see DB2057.A+
2182	Revolution of 1848
	Czechoslovak Republic, 1918-1992
	Including the Czechoslovak Socialist Republic
2185	Sources and documents
2186	General works
2187	General special
2187.5	Addresses, essays, lectures
2188	Social life and customs. Civilization. Intellectual life

	History
	By period
	Czechoslovak Republic, 1918-1992
	1945-1968 -- Continued
2217.5	Addresses, essays, lectures
2218	Social life and customs. Civilization. Intellectual life
2218.7	Political history
2219	Foreign and general relations
	Biography and memoirs
2220	Collective
2221.A-Z	Individual, A-Z
	e.g.
2221.D93	Dubček, Alexander
2221.H96	Husák, Gustav
2222	Coup d'etat, 1948
	1968-1989
2225	Sources and documents
2226	General works
2227	General special
2227.5	Addresses, essays, lectures
2228	Social life and customs. Civilization. Intellectual life
2228.7	Political history
2229	Foreign and general relations
	Biography and memoirs
2230	Collective
2231.A-Z	Individual, A-Z
2232	Soviet intervention, 1968. Prague spring
2233	Velvet Revolution, 1989
	1989-1993
2235	Sources and documents
2236	General works
2238	Social life and customs. Civilization. Intellectual life
2238.7	Political history
2239	Foreign and general relations
	Biography and memoirs
2240	Collective
2241.A-Z	Individual, A-Z
	e.g.
2241.H38	Havel, Václav
	1993- . Independent Czech Republic
2242	Sources and documents
2243	General works
2244	Social life and customs. Civilization. Intellectual life
2244.7	Political history
2245	Foreign and general relations
	Biography and memoirs
2246	Collective

History
  By period
    1993-   . Independent Czech Republic
      Biography and memoirs -- Continued

2247.A-Z	Individual, A-Z

Local history and description of the Czech lands
  For local history and description of Slovakia see DB3000+
Moravia

2300	Periodicals. Societies. Serials
	Museums, exhibitions, etc.
2301	General works
2302.A-Z	Individual. By place, A-Z
2303	Congresses
2304	Sources and documents
	Collected works (nonserial)
2305	Several authors
2306	Individual authors
2307	Gazetteers. Dictionaries, etc.
2308	Place names (General)
2309	Directories
2310	Guidebooks
2311	General works
2312	General special
2313	Pictorial works
2315	Historic monuments, landmarks, scenery, etc. (General)
	For local see DB2500.A+
2316	Preservation
2317	Historical geography
	Description and travel
2318	History of travel
2319	Early through 1900
2320	1901-1945
2321	1946-1976
2322	1977-
2330	Antiquities
	For local antiquities see DB2500.A+
2335	Social life and customs. Civilization. Intellectual life
	For specific periods, see the period or reign
	Ethnography
2340	General works
2341	National characteristics
2342.A-Z	Individual elements in the population, A-Z
2342.C76	Croats
2342.G47	Germans
	History
	Periodicals. Societies. Serials see DB2300

DAW, DB

Local history and description of the Czech lands
  Moravia
    History -- Continued
2345   Biography (Collective)
                    For individual biography, see the specific period, reign, or
                    place
                Historiography
2355   General works
                Biography of historians and area studies specialists
2356   Collective
2357.A-Z   Individual, A-Z
                Study and teaching
2359   General works
2360.A-Z   By region or country, A-Z
                    Subarrange by author
                General works
2361   Through 1800
2362   1801-1976
2363   1977-
2364   Pictorial works
2365   Juvenile works
2366   Addresses, essays, lectures. Anecdotes, etc.
2370   Military history
                For specific periods, including individual campaigns and
                    engagements, see the period or reign
2374   Political history
                For specific periods, see the period or reign
2375   Foreign and general relations
                For general works on the diplomatic history of a period, see
                    the period
                For works on relations with a specific country
                    regardless of period see DB2376.A+
2376.A-Z   Relations with individual regions or countries, A-Z
            By period
                Early to 1000. Great Moravian Empire
2385   Sources and documents
2386   General works
2387   General special
2387.5   Addresses, essays, lectures
2388   Social life and customs. Civilization. Intellectual life
2388.7   Political history
2389   Foreign and general relations
                Biography and memoirs
2390   Collective
2391.A-Z   Individual, A-Z
                    e.g.
2391.S93   Svatopluk

Local history and description of the Czech lands
   Moravia
     History
      By period -- Continued
        1000-1800

2395	Sources and documents
2396	General works
2397	General special
2397.5	Addresses, essays, lectures
2397.7	Social life and customs. Civilization. Intellectual life
2398	Political history
	Biography and memoirs
2400	Collective
2401.A-Z	Individual, A-Z

        19th century

2405	Sources and documents
2406	General works
2407	General special
2407.5	Addresses, essays, lectures
2408	Political history
	Biography and memoirs
2410	Collective
2411.A-Z	Individual, A-Z

        20th century

2415	Sources and documents
2416	General works
2417	General special
2417.5	Addresses, essays, lectures
2418	Political history
	Biography and memoirs
2420	Collective
2421.A-Z	Individual, A-Z
2500.A-Z	Counties, regions, mountains, rivers, etc., A-Z

         Class here geographical features of the Czech lands and those
           shared by the Czech lands and Slovakia, but lying
           principally in the Czech lands
         e.g.
         For areas entirely or largely in Slovakia see DB3000+
         Beskids see DB3000.B4
          For Beskids (General, and Poland) see DK4600.B4
         Bohemian Forest see DB2500.C463

2500.B75	Brno region (Brünn region)
	Carpathian Mountains see DJK71+
2500.C462	Ceskomoravská vysočina
2500.C463	Cesky les (Bohemian Forest. Böhmerwald)
2500.C464	Cesky ráj

Local history and description of the Czech lands
Counties, regions, mountains, rivers, etc., A-Z -- Continued

2500.C465	Ceský Těšín region
	For Cieszyn region (General, and Poland) see DK4600.C54+
2500.C54	Cheb region (Egerland)
	For Egerland in Germany see DD801.A+
	Eger River and Valley see DB2500.O57
	Egerland see DB2500.C54
	Elbe River and Valley see DB2500.L33
2500.E53	Elbe Sandstone Rocks
	Cf. DD801.S281 Saxon Switzerland
	Isera Mountains see DB2500.J58
2500.J47	Jeseníky Mountains (Altvatergebirge)
2500.J553	Jihočeský kraj
2500.J555	Jihomoravský kraj
2500.J58	Jizera Mountains (Isergebirge)
	For Isera Mountains (General, and Poland) see DK4600.I9
2500.J582	Jizera River and Valley (Iser)
2500.K37	Karlovy Vary region (Karlsbad region)
	Karpaty see DJK71+
2500.K75	Krkonoše (Riesengebirge). Krkonoše region. Podkrkonošský kraj
	For Krkonose in Poland see DK4600.K77
2500.K758	Krušné hory (Ore Mountains. Erzgebirge)
2500.L33	Labe River and Valley
	For Elbe River (General, and Germany) see DD801.E3
	Lusatian Mountains see DB2500.L98
2500.L98	Luzické hory
	Northern Bohemia see DB2500.S48
2500.O57	Ohře River and Valley (Eger)
	Ore Mountains see DB2500.K758
2500.O75	Orlické hory (Adlergebirge)
	Podkarpatská Rus see DK508.9.Z35
	Podrkonošský kraj see DB2500.K75
	Ruthenia see DK508.9.Z35
2500.R83	Rychlesbské hory
2500.S48	Severočeský kraj. Northern Bohemia
2500.S49	Severomoravský kraj
	Silesia see DB2500.S54
2500.S54	Slezsko
	For Silesia (General, and Poland) see DK4600.S42+
2500.S65	Snězka (Sniezka. Schneekoppe)
2500.S76	Stredocesky kraj
2500.S94	Sudety (Sudetenland)
	For Sudetes in Poland see DK4600.S656; DK4600.S7

DAW, DB

Local history and description of the Czech lands
Counties, regions, mountains, rivers, etc., A-Z -- Continued

2500.S96	Sumava
2500.V57	Vltava River and Valley (Moldau)
2500.V93	Východočeský kraj
2500.Z36	Západočeský kraj
	Prague (Praha)
2600	Periodicals. Societies. Serials
2601	Museums, exhibitions, etc.
	Subarrange by author
2603	Sources and documents
	Collected works (nonserial)
2604	Several authors
2605	Individual authors
2606	Directories. Dictionaries. Gazetteers
2607	Guidebooks
2610	General works
	Description
2611	Early and medieval
2612	16th-19th century
2613	1901-1976
2614	1977-
2620	Pictorial works
2621	Antiquities
2622	Social life and customs. Civilization. Intellectual life
	Ethnography
2623	General works
2624.A-Z	Individual elements in the population, A-Z
2624.A9	Austrians
2624.G4	Germans
	Jews see DS135.C95+
2624.R87	Russians
2624.R9	Ruthenians
2624.S5	Slovaks
2624.U5	Ukrainians
	History
2625	Biography (Collective)
	For individual biography, see the specific period
2626	General works
	By period
2627	Early and medieval
2628	16th-19th century
2629	20th century
	Sections, districts, suburbs, etc.
2630	Collective
2631.A-Z	Individual, A-Z
	e.g.

	Local history and description of the Czech lands
	Prague (Praha)
	Sections, districts, suburbs, etc.
	Individual, A-Z -- Continued
2631.M35	Malá Strana
	Monuments, statues, etc.
2632	Collective
2633.A-Z	Individual, A-Z
	Parks, squares, cemeteries, etc.
2634	Collective
2635.A-Z	Individual, A-Z
	Streets. Bridges
2636	Collective
2637.A-Z	Individual, A-Z
	Buildings
2648	Collective
2649.A-Z	Individual, A-Z
2650.A-Z	Other cities and towns, A-Z
	e.g.
	For castles, manors, etc. outside cities see DB2500.A+
	For cities and towns in Slovakia see DB3150.A+
2650.B75	Brno (Brünn)
2650.C463	Ceské Budejovice (Budweiss)
2650.C467	Ceský Těšín
	For Cieszyn, Poland see DK4800.C5
2650.L53	Liberec (Reichenberg)
2650.O46	Olomouc (Olmutz)
	Pilsen see DB2650.P49
2650.P49	Plzeň
	Prague see DB2600+
	Praha see DB2600+
	Slovakia
2700	Periodicals. Societies. Serials
	Museums, exhibitions, etc.
2701	General works
2702.A-Z	Individual. By place, A-Z
2703	Congresses
2704	Sources and documents
	Collected works (nonserial)
2705	Several authors
2706	Individual authors
2707	Gazetteers. Dictionaries, etc.
2708	Place names (General)
2709	Directories
2710	Guidebooks
2711	General works
2712	General special

Slovakia -- Continued

2713	Pictorial works
	Historic monuments, landmarks, scenery, etc. (General)
	For local see DB3000+
2715	General works
2716	Preservation
2717	Historical geography
	Description and travel
2718	History of travel
2719	Early through 1900
2720	1901-1945
2721	1946-1976
2722	1977-
2730	Antiquities
	For local antiquities see DB3000+
2735	Social life and customs. Civilization. Intellectual life
	For specific periods, see the period or reign
	Ethnography
2740	General works
2741	National characteristics
2742.A-Z	Individual elements in the population, A-Z
2742.A8	Austrians
2742.C74	Croats
2742.C9	Czechs
2742.G4	Germans
	Gypsies in the Czech Republic see DX222
	Gypsies in Slovakia see DX222.5
2742.H8	Hungarians
	Jews see DS135.C95+
2742.P6	Poles
	Romanies in the Czech Republic see DX222
	Romanies in Slovakia see DX222.5
2742.R8	Ruthenians
2742.T47	Thracians
2742.U6	Ukrainians
2743	Slovaks in foreign countries (General)
	For Slovaks in a particular country, see the country
	History
	Periodicals. Societies. Serials see DB2700
2744	Dictionaries. Chronological tables, outlines, etc.
	Biography (Collective)
	For individual biography, see the specific period, reign, or place
2745	General works
2746	Rulers, kings, etc.
2747	Queens. Princes and princesses
	Houses, noble families, etc.

	Slovakia
	History
	Biography (Collective)
	Houses, noble families, etc. -- Continued
2748	Collective
2749.A-Z	Individual houses, families, etc., A-Z
2750	Statesmen
2751	Women
	Historiography
2755	General works
	Biography of historians and area studies specialists
2756	Collective
2757.A-Z	Individual, A-Z
	Study and teaching
2759	General works
2760.A-Z	By region or country, A-Z
	Subarrange by author
	General works
2761	Through 1800
2762	1801-1976
2763	1977-
2764	Pictorial works
2765	Juvenile works
2766	Addresses, essays, lectures. Anecdotes, etc.
2768	Philosophy of Slovak history
	Military history
	For specific periods including individual campaigns and
	engagements, see the period or reign
2769	Sources and documents
2770	General works
	By period
2771	Early through 1620
2772	1621-1918
2773	1918-
	Political history
	For specific periods, see the period or reign
2774	Sources and documents
2775	General works
	Foreign and general relations
	For general works on the diplomatic history of a period, see
	the period
	For works on relations with a specific country
	regardless of period see DB2778.A+
2776	Sources and documents
2777	General works
2778.A-Z	Relations with individual regions or countries, A-Z
	By period

Slovakia
　History
　　By period -- Continued
　　　Early and medieval to 1800
2785　　　　　　　Sources and documents
2786　　　　　　　General works
2787　　　　　　　General special
2787.5　　　　　　Addresses, essays, lectures
2788　　　　　　　Social life and customs. Civilization. Intellectual life
2788.5　　　　　　Military history
2788.7　　　　　　Political history
2789　　　　　　　Foreign and general relations
　　　　　　　　Biography and memoirs
2790　　　　　　　　Collective
2791.A-Z　　　　　　Individual, A-Z
　　　　　　　1800-1918
2795　　　　　　　Sources and documents
2796　　　　　　　General works
2797　　　　　　　General special
2797.5　　　　　　Addresses, essays, lectures
2798　　　　　　　Social life and customs. Civilization. Intellectual life
2798.5　　　　　　Military history
2798.7　　　　　　Political history
2799　　　　　　　Foreign and general relations
　　　　　　　　Biography and memoirs
2800　　　　　　　　Collective
2801.A-Z　　　　　　Individual, A-Z
　　　　　　　Czechoslovak Republic, 1918-1992
2805　　　　　　　Sources and documents
2806　　　　　　　General works
2807　　　　　　　General special
2807.5　　　　　　Addresses, essays, lectures
2808　　　　　　　Social life and customs. Civilization. Intellectual life
2808.7　　　　　　Political history
2809　　　　　　　Foreign and general relations
　　　　　　　　Biography and memoirs
2810　　　　　　　　Collective
2811.A-Z　　　　　　Individual, A-Z
　　　　　　　　　e.g.
2811.H65　　　　　　　Hlinka, Andrej
2813　　　　　　　　1918-1939
　　　　　　　Period of World War II. Slovak Independence, 1939-
　　　　　　　　1945
2815　　　　　　　Sources and documents
2816　　　　　　　General works
2817　　　　　　　General special
2817.5　　　　　　Addresses, essays, lectures

Slovakia
  History
    By period
      Czechoslovak Republic, 1918-1992
        Period of World War II. Slovak Independence, 1939-
          1945 -- Continued

2818	Social life and customs. Civilization. Intellectual life
2818.7	Political history
2819	Foreign and general relations
	Biography and memoirs
2820	Collective
2821.A-Z	Individual, A-Z
	e.g.
2821.T57	Tiso, Josef
2822	Uprising, 1944
	1945-1968
2825	Sources and documents
2826	General works
2827	General special
2827.5	Addresses, essays, lectures
2828	Social life and customs. Civilization. Intellectual life
2828.7	Political history
2829	Foreign and general relations
	Biography and memoirs
2830	Collective
2831.A-Z	Individual, A-Z
	1968-1992
2835	Sources and documents
2836	General works
2837	General special
2837.5	Addresses, essays, lectures
2838	Social life and customs. Civilization. Intellectual life
2838.7	Political history
2839	Foreign and general relations
	Biography and memoirs
2840	Collective
2841.A-Z	Individual, A-Z
2842	Soviet intervention, 1968
2844	1989-1992
	1993- . Independent republic
2845	Sources and documents
2846	General works
2847	Social life and customs. Civilization. Intellectual life
2848	Political history
2849	Foreign and general relations
	Biography and memoirs
2849.5	Collective

DAW, DB

	Slovakia
	History
	By period
	1993- . Independent republic
	Biography and memoirs -- Continued
2850.A-Z	Individual, A-Z
	Local history and description
3000.A-Z	Counties, regions, mountains, rivers, etc., A-Z

Class here the geographical features of Slovakia, as well as those shared by Slovakia and the Czech lands, but lying principally in Slovakia

e.g.

For areas entirely or largely in the Czech lands see DB2500.A+

3000.B4	Beskids

For Beskids (General, and poland) see DK4600.B4

3000.B55	Bílé Karpaty
	Carpathian Mountains see DJK71+
	Danube see DB3000.D85
3000.D85	Danaj River and Valley

For the Danube River (General) see DJK76.2+

Little Carpathian Mountains see DB3000.M35

3000.M35	Malé Karpaty
3000.O73	Orava River, Valley and Reservoir
	Slovak Ore Mountains see DB3000.S56
3000.S56	Slovenské Rudohorie
3000.S65	Spiš
3000.S76	Středoslovenský kraj
3000.T37	Tatra Mountains

For Tatra Mountains in Poland see DK4600.T3

3000.V35	Váh River and Valley
3000.V93	Východoslovenský kraj
	White Carpathian Mountains see DB3000.B55
3000.Z36	Západoslovenský kraj
	Bratislava (Pressburg)
3100	Periodicals. Societies. Serials
3101	Museums, exhibitions, etc.
	Subarrange by author
3103	Sources and documents
	Collected works (nonserial)
3104	Several authors
3105	Individual authors
3106	Directories. Dictionaries. Gazetteers
3107	Guidebooks
3110	General works
	Description
3111	Early and medieval

	Slovakia
	Local history and description
	Bratislava (Pressburg)
	Description -- Continued
3112	16th-19th centuries
3113	1901-1976
3114	1977-
3120	Pictorial works
3121	Antiquities
3122	Social life and customs. Intellectual life
	Ethnography
3123	General works
3124.A-Z	Individual elements in the population, A-Z
3124.A8	Austrians
3124.C9	Czechs
3124.G4	Germans
	Gypsies in the Czech Republic see DX222
	Gypsies in Slovakia see DX222.5
3124.H8	Hungarians
	Jews see DS135.C95+
	Romanies in the Czech Republic see DX222
	Romanies in Slovakia see DX222.5
3124.R97	Ruthenians
3124.U67	Ukrainians
	History
3125	Biography (Collective)
	For individual biography, see the specific period
3126	General works
	By period
3127	Early and medieval
3128	16th-19th centuries
3129	20th century
	Sections, districts, suburbs, etc.
3130	Collective
3131.A-Z	Individual, A-Z
	Monuments, statues, etc.
3132	Collective
3133.A-Z	Individual, A-Z
	Parks, squares, cemeteries, etc.
3134	Collective
3135.A-Z	Individual, A-Z
	Streets. Bridges
3136	Collective
3137.A-Z	Individual, A-Z
	Buildings
3138	Collective
3139.A-Z	Individual, A-Z

Slovakia
Local history and description -- Continued
3150.A-Z   Other cities and towns, A-Z
                                    e.g.
3150.B35   Banská Bystrica
                                 Bratislava see DB3100+
3150.K65   Komárno
3150.K67   Košice
                                 Martin see DB3150.T97
3150.N57   Nitra
3150.T74   Trenčín
3150.T97   Turčiansky Sväty Martin. Martin

	History of France
1	Periodicals. Serials
2	Societies
3	Sources and documents
	Collected works
4	Several authors
5	Individual authors
14	Gazetteers. Dictionaries, etc. Place names
15	Directories
16	Guidebooks
17	General works
18	Compends
19	Historical accounts of disasters caused by the elements
	Including earthquakes, fires, floods, storms, etc. (General)
	For individual disasters see DC600+
20	Pictorial works
	Historic monuments, landmarks, scenery, etc. (General)
	For local see DC600+
20.2	General works
20.3	Preservation
20.5	Historical geography
20.7	Geography
	Description and travel
21	Earliest through 686
22	687-1514
23	1515-1588
24	1589-1714
25	1715-1788
26	1789-1815
27	1816-1870
28	1871-1945
29	1946-1974
29.3	1975-
	Antiquities
	For local see DC600+
	Cf. DC63 Roman, Celtic, etc., antiquities
30	Periodicals. Collections, etc.
31	General works
	Social life and customs. Civilization. Intellectual life
33	General works
33.15	Regal antiquities. Ceremonials, pageants, etc. Court life
	By period
33.2	Early and medieval
33.3	Renaissance period. 16th century

	Social life and customs. Civilization. Intellectual life
	By period -- Continued
33.4	17th-18th centuries
	For Louis XIV see DC128
	For Louis XV see DC133.8
	For Louis XVI see DC136+
33.5	1789-1830
	Cf. DC159 Social life and customs, 1789-1815
	Cf. DC256.5 Social life and customs, 1815-1830
33.6	1831-1900
33.7	1901-2000
33.8	2001-
33.9	French culture in foreign countries (General)
	Including general works on the French in foreign countries
	For the French in a particular country, see the country
	Ethnography
	Including national characteristics
34	General works
34.5.A-Z	Individual elements in the population, A-Z
	For individual elements in the population of a particular place, see the place
34.5.A37	Africans
34.5.A4	Algerians, Arab
34.5.A42	French Algerians
34.5.A44	Americans
34.5.A46	Antilleans
34.5.A67	Arabs
34.5.A7	Armenians
34.5.A8	Asians
34.5.B37	Basques
34.5.B55	Blacks
34.5.B75	British
34.5.B8	Bulgarians
34.5.C3	Cagots
34.5.C34	Cameroonians
34.5.C65	Congolese (Brazzaville)
34.5.C66	Congolese (Democratic Republic)
34.5.E35	Egyptians
34.5.F6	Foreign population (General)
34.5.G3	Germans
34.5.H3	Haitians
34.5.H54	Hmong (Asian people)
34.5.H86	Hungarians
34.5.I54	Indochinese
34.5.I7	Irish
34.5.I8	Italians
34.5.K3	Kabyles

Ethnography
    Individual elements in the population, A-Z -- Continued
34.5.K34	Kalmyks
34.5.K67	Koreans
34.5.L36	Laotians
34.5.L38	Latvians
34.5.L4	Lebanese
34.5.M34	Malians
34.5.M38	Mauritians
34.5.M7	Moroccans
34.5.M87	Muslims
	Negroes see DC34.5.B55
34.5.N67	North Africans
34.5.P54	Pieds-Noirs
34.5.P6	Poles
34.5.P67	Portuguese
34.5.R45	Reunionese
34.5.R6	Romanians
34.5.R8	Russians
34.5.S45	Senegalese
34.5.S57	Slovenes
34.5.S65	Spaniards
34.5.T84	Tunisians
34.5.T87	Turks
34.5.U37	Ukrainians
34.5.V53	Vietnamese
34.5.Y84	Yugoslavs

    French people in foreign countries (General) see DC33.9
    History

35	Dictionaries. Chronological tables, outlines, etc.
35.5	Albums. Pictorial atlases. Collections of historical prints and portraits, etc.
36	Biography (Collective)
	For individual biography, see the period, reign, or place
36.1	General special
	e.g. Les batards de la Maison de France
36.2	Women
36.3	Favorites
36.4	Public men
36.6	Rulers, kings, etc.
36.7	Queens, princesses, etc.
36.8.A-Z	Houses, noble families, etc., A-Z
	e.g.
36.8.A6	Anjou, House of
36.8.B7	Bourbon, House of
36.8.C6	Conde family
36.8.O7	Orléans, House of

	History
	Biography (Collective)
	Houses, noble families, etc., A-Z -- Continued
36.8.V3	Valois, House of
	Historiography
36.9	General works
	Biography of historians
36.95	Collective
36.98.A-Z	Individual, A-Z
	e.g.
36.98.F7	Froissart, Jean
36.98.H8	Houssaye, Henry
36.98.L3	Lavisse, Ernest
36.98.M5	Michelet, Jules
	Peiresc, Nicolas Claude F. de see DC121.8.P4
36.98.T4	Thierry, Augustin
	Study and teaching
36.983	General works
36.985.A-Z	Local, A-Z
	Subarrange by author
	General works
37	To 1815. Chronicles
38	1815-
39	Compends
40	Pamphlets, etc.
40.5	Anecdotes, etc.
41.A-Z	Special, A-Z
	For elements in the population see DC34.5.A+
41.R4	Regionalism
	General special
	Military history
	For individual campaigns and engagements, see the special period
44	Sources and documents
	Biography (Collective)
44.5	General works
44.8	Officers
45	General works
45.5	Compends
45.7	General special
45.9	Pamphlets, etc.
	By period
	For the military history of special periods, reigns, etc., see the period or reign
46	Early to Reformation
46.5	16th century
46.7	17th-18th centuries

History
  General special
    Military history
      By period -- Continued

47	19th-20th centuries
	Naval history
	For individual campaigns and engagements, see the special period
49	Sources and documents
49.5	Biography (Collective)
	General works
50.A2	Early works to 1800
50.A3-Z	1801-
51	Early and medieval
51.5	15th-16th centuries
52	17th-18th centuries
	Cf. DC139+ French Revolution
53	19th-20th centuries
	For general modern see DC50.A2+
	For 20th century see DC368
55	Political and diplomatic history. Foreign and general relations
	For general works on the political and diplomatic history of a period, see the period
	For works on relations with a specific country regardless of period see DC59.8.A+
56	Early and medieval
57	1515-1789. Early modern
	For general modern see DC55
58	19th-20th centuries
59	Special topics
	Church and state see BR840+
59.8.A-Z	Relations with individual regions or countries, A-Z
	By period
	Early and medieval to 1515
60	Sources and documents
	Cf. DC3 Sources and documents
60.5	Selections, extracts, etc.
60.6	Dictionaries
	General works
60.8	Through 1800. Chronicles
61	1801-
	Social life and customs. Civilization. Intellectual life see DC33.2
	Gauls. Celts
62.A2	Collections
62.A3-Z	General works

History
By period
Early and medieval to 1515
Carolingians, 687-987
Sources and documents -- Continued
Chronicles

70.A2	9th century
70.A3	10th century
70.A4-Z	General works
70.6	Pepin of Heristal, 687-714
70.8	Childebrand
	Charles Martel, 715-741
71	General works on life and reign
71.5	Battle of Poitiers (Tours), 732
	Pepin le Bref, 752-768
72	General works on life and reign
	Cf. DD132 Reign in Germany
	Charlemagne, 768-814
	Cf. DD133 Reign in Germany
73.A2	Sources and documents
	General works on life and reign
73.A3-Z	Modern
	Contemporary and medieval
	Einhard
73.2	Complete works
73.3	Vita Caroli Magni
	Translations
73.32	English
73.33	French
73.34	German
73.35.A-Z	Other languages, A-Z
	e.g.
73.35.D3	Danish
73.4	Biography and criticism
73.5	Vita Caroli Magni sec. XII
73.55	Criticisms, etc.
73.6	Other vitae
73.7	Personal special
73.8	Pamphlets, etc.
73.9	Carloman, 768-771
73.95.A-Z	Biography and memoirs of contemporaries, A-Z
	e.g.
73.95.R6	Roland
	Louis I le Pieux, 814-840
74	General works
	General works on life and reign in Germany see DD134+

History
  By period
    Early and medieval to 1515
      Carolingians, 687-987
        Louis I le Pieux, 814-840

74.5.A-Z	Biography and memoirs of contemporaries, A-Z
	e.g.
74.5.J8	Judith, Empress, Consort of Louis le Pieux
75	Treaty of Verdun, 843

          For legal works, including texts of the treaty and
            related documents see KZ1328.2
        Charles I (II) le Chauve, 840-877

76	General works on life and reign
76.3	General special
	Biography and memoirs
76.4	Collective
76.42.A-Z	Individual, A-Z
77	Louis II le Bègue, 877-879
77.3	Louis III, 879-882
77.5	Carloman, 882-884
	Karl II (III) der Dicke, 884-887
77.8	General works on life and reign
	General works on life and reign in Germany see
	DD134.6
77.9	Siege of Paris, 885-886
78	Eudes, 888-898
79	Charles III le Simple, 898-922
79.5	Robert I, 922-923
79.7	Raoul (Rodolphe), 923-936
80	Louis IV (Louis d'Outremer), 936-954
81	Lothaire, 954-986
81.5	Louis V, 986-987
	Capetians, 987-1328
82.A2	Sources and documents
82.A3-Z	General works
83	General special
	Wars with Albigenses
83.2	Sources and documents
83.3	General works
84	Hugues Capet, 987-996
85	Robert II, 996-1031
	Henri I, 1031-1060
85.6	General works on life and reign
85.8.A-Z	Biography and memoirs of contemporaries, A-Z
	e.g.
85.8.A54	Anne, Consort of Henry I
86	Dukes of Normandy

History
By period
Early and medieval to 1515
Capetians, 987-1328 -- Continued
Philippe I, 1060-1108

87	General works on life and reign
87.7.A-Z	Biography and memoirs of contemporaries, A-Z
	e.g.
87.7.H8	Hugo, Abp. of Lyons
	Louis VI, 1108-1137
88	General works on life and reign
88.5	Political and diplomatic history
88.7.A-Z	Biography and memoirs of contemporaries, A-Z
	Louis VII, 1137-1180
89	General works on life and reign
89.7.A-Z	Biography and memoirs of contemporaries, A-Z
	e.g.
89.7.S8	Suger, Abbot of Saint Denis
	Philippe II Auguste, 1180-1223
90.A2	Sources and documents
90.A3-Z	General works on life and reign
90.7.A-Z	Biography and memoirs of contemporaries, A-Z
	e.g.
90.7.I6	Ingeborg, Consort of Philip II
90.8	Louis VIII, 1223-1226
	Louis IX, Saint, 1226-1270
91.A2	Sources and documents
91.A3-Z	General works on life and reign
91.3	Peace of Paris, 1258
	For legal works on the Treaty of Paris, 1258 see KZ1329.3
91.5	Personal special
	e.g. Heart of St. Louis
91.6.A-Z	Biography and memoirs of contemporaries, A-Z
	e.g.
91.6.B5	Blanche of Castille, Consort of Louis VIII
91.6.J6	Joinville, Jean, sire de
91.7	Philippe III, 1270-1285
92	Philippe IV, 1285-1314
	Louis X, 1314-1316
93	General works on life and reign
93.3	Jean I, b. 1316
93.4	Philippe V, 1316-1322
93.7	Charles IV, 1322-1328
94.A-Z	Biography and memoirs, 1270-1328, A-Z
	e.g.
94.A4	Accorre, Renier

History
  By period
    Early and medieval to 1515
      Capetians, 987-1328
        Biography and memoirs, 1270-1328, A-Z -- Continued

94.C4	Charles, Count of Valois
	1328-1515
95.A2	Sources and documents
95.A3-Z	General works
95.45	Military history
95.5	Political and diplomatic history
95.6	Special topics
95.7.A-Z	Biography and memoirs, A-Z
	Hundred Years' War, 1339-1453
96.A2	Contemporary and early works
96.A3-Z	General works
96.5	General special
97.A-Z	Biography and memoirs, A-Z
	Particularly of first half of the war
	e.g.
97.D8	Du Guesclin, Bertrand, comte de Longueville
	14th century
97.5	General works
	Philippe VI, 1328-1350
98	General works on life and reign
98.3	General special
98.5.A-Z	Special events, battles, etc., A-Z
	e.g.
98.5.C2	Calais, Siege of, 1346
98.5.C8	Crecy, Battle of, 1346
98.7.A-Z	Biography and memoirs of contemporaries, A-Z
	e.g.
98.7.C4	Cayon, Jean
	Jean II, 1350-1364
99	General works on life and reign
99.2	General special
99.3	La Jacquerie, 1358
99.5.A-Z	Other events, battles, etc., A-Z
	e.g.
99.5.B7	Bretigny, Peace of, 1360
	For legal works on the Treaty of Bretigny, 1360 see KZ1329.8.B74
99.5.P6	Poitiers, Battle of, 1356
99.5.S3	Saintes, Battle of, 1351
99.7.A-Z	Biography and memoirs of contemporaries, A-Z
	e.g.
99.7.L4	Le Coq, Robert, Bp.

DC

History
  By period
    Early and medieval to 1515
      1328-1515
        14th century -- Continued
          Charles V, 1364-1380

100	General works on life and reign
100.3	General special
100.5.A-Z	Special events, battles, etc., A-Z
100.7.A-Z	Biography and memoirs of contemporaries, A-Z

Charles VI, 1380-1422

101	General works on life and reign
101.A2	Contemporary and early
101.3	General special
101.5.A-Z	Special events, battles, etc., A-Z
101.5.A2	Agincourt, Battle of, 1415
101.5.C33	Cabochien Uprising, 1413
101.5.R8	Roosebeke, Battle of, 1382
101.5.T7	Troyes, Peace of, 1420

For legal works on the Treaty of Troyes, 1420
see KZ1329.8.T76

Biography and memoirs of contemporaries

101.6	Collective
101.7.A-Z	Individual, A-Z

e.g.

101.7.I7	Isabeau, of Bavaria, Consort of Charles VI
101.7.M6	Montreuil, Jean de
101.7.O6	Orgemont, Nicolas d'
101.7.O7	Orléans, Louis de France, duc d'

15th century

101.9	General works

Charles VII, 1422-1461

102	General works on life and reign
102.A2	Contemporary and early
102.A3	General special
102.5	Special events, battles, etc.

Arrange chronologically by affixing to .5 the last two
digits of the date
e.g.

102.527	Siege of Montargis, 1427
102.528	Siege of Orléans, 1428-1429
102.535	Congress and Peace of Arras, 1435

For legal works on the Treaty of Arras, 1435
see KZ1329.8.A77

102.544	Siege of Metz, 1444

Biography and memoirs of contemporaries

102.8.A1	Collective

History
  By period
    Early and medieval to 1515
      1328-1515
        15th century -- Continued
          Louis XII, 1498-1515

108	General works on life and reign
108.A2	Contemporary and early
108.2	Jeanne, Consort of Louis XII
108.3	Anne de Bretagne
108.8	Letters of Louis XII
109	Other special
	e.g. The Armagnacs
	Cf. DC611.A7265+ Armagnac, former province

    Modern, 1515-
      Including works on the modern period in general

110	General works
	1515-1589. 16th century
	Including wars in Italy, conflict with Austria, Renaissance and Reformation, religious wars, etc.
111.A2	Sources and documents
111.A3-Z	General works
111.3	General special
111.5	Political and diplomatic history. Foreign and general relations
	Social life and customs. Civilization. Intellectual life see DC33.3
	Biography and memoirs of contemporaries
112.A1	Collective
112.A2-Z	Individual, A-Z
112.A6	Antoine de Bourbon, King of Navarre
112.A8	Aubigné, Théodore Agrippa d'
112.B6	Bourbon, Charles, duc de
112.C6	Coligny, Gaspard de, seigneur de Châtillon
	Guise, Dukes and Duchesses of
112.G8	General works
112.G81	Guise, Antoinette (de Bourbon), duchesse de
112.G83	Guise, Charles de, cardinal de Lorraine
112.G85	Guise, François de Lorraine
112.G9	Guise, Henri, duc de
112.J4	Jeanne d'Albret, Queen of Navarre
112.L45	La Noue, François de
112.L6	L'Hospital, Michel de
112.L8	Louise de Savoie, Duchess of Angoulême
112.M2	Marguerite d'Angoulême, Queen of Navarre
112.M9	Mornay, Philippe de, seigneur de Plessis-Marly, called du Plessis-Mornay

History
By period
Modern, 1515-
1515-1589. 16th century
Biography and memoirs of contemporaries
Individual, A-Z -- Continued
112.R4   Renée, of France, Consort of Hercules II, Duke of
Ferrara
112.V75   Villeroy, Nicolas de Neuf-ville, seigneur de
François I, 1515-1547
113.A2   Sources and documents
113.A3   Contemporary and early works
113.A4-Z   General works on life and reign
113.3   General special
113.5   Diplomatic history. Foreign and general relations
Including Peace of Cambrai, 1529 (Ladies' Peace);
Peace of Madrid, 1526
For legal works on the Treaty of Cambrai, 1529
see KZ1329.8.C36
For legal works on the Treaty of Madrid, 1526 see
KZ1329.8.M33
Henri II, 1547-1559
114   General works on life and reign
Including Peace of Cateau-Cambrésia, 1559
For legal works on the Treaty of Cateau-
Cambrésis, 1559 see KZ1329.8.C38
114.3   General special
114.5   Diane de Poitiers, Duchess of Valentinois
115   François II, 1559-1560
Charles IX, 1560-1574
116   General works on life and reign
116.5   General special
116.7   Diplomatic history. Foreign and general relations
117.A-Z   Special events, A-Z
e.g.
117.L3   Siege of La Rochelle, 1573
118   Massacre of St. Bartholomew, 1572
Henri III, 1574-1589
119   General works on life and reign
119.7   Louise of Lorraine, Consort of Henry III
119.8   Catherine de Médicis, Consort of Henry II
120   Holy League, 1576-1593
1589-1715
120.8   Historiography
121   General works
121.3   General special
121.5   Diplomatic history. Foreign and general relations

History
  By period
    Modern, 1515-
      1589-1715 -- Continued

121.7	Social life and customs. Civilization. Intellectual life
	Biography and memoirs
121.8.A2	Collective
121.8.A3-Z	Individual, A-Z
	e.g.
121.8.E7	Epernon, Jean Louis de Nogaret, duc d'
121.8.F2	Fabert, Abraham de
121.8.L3	La Rochefoucauld, François de, Cardinal
121.8.L6	Louise de Coligny, Consort of William I, Prince of Orange
121.8.P3	Pasquier, Nicolas
121.8.P4	Peiresc, Nicolas Claude Fabri de
121.9.A-Z	Local, A-Z
	e.g.
121.9.N2	Narbonne
	Henri IV, 1589-1610
122	General works on reign
122.3	General special
	Edict of Nantes see BR845
122.5	Diplomatic history. Foreign and general relations
122.8	Biography of Henri IV
	Biography and memoirs of contemporaries
122.9.A2	Collective
122.9.A3-Z	Individual, A-Z
	e.g.
122.9.B3	Bassompierre, François de
122.9.C7	Condé, Charlotte Catherine (de la Trémoille), princesse de
122.9.E7	Estrées, Gabrielle d'
122.9.M2	Marguerite de Valois, Consort of Henry IV
122.9.M3	Marie de Médicis, Consort of Henry IV
122.9.O7	Ossat, Arnaud d', Cardinal
122.9.S9	Sully, Maximilien de Béthune, duc de
	Louis XIII, 1610-1643
123	General works on reign
123.A2	Collections
123.2	Regency of Marie de Médicis
	For biography see DC122.9.M3
123.3	Special topics
123.5	Diplomatic history. Foreign and general relations
123.8	Biography of Louis XIII
	Biography and memoirs of contemporaries, A-Z
	e.g.

History
By period
Modern, 1515-
1589-1715
Louis XIII
Biography and memoirs of contemporaries
Anne, Consort of Louis XIII see DC124+

123.9.C4	Chevrèuse, Marie de Rohan, duchesse de
123.9.C6	Concini, Concino maréchal d'Ancre
123.9.L5	Le Clerc du Tremblay, François
123.9.R5	Richelieu, Armand Jean du Plessis, Cardinal, duc de
123.9.R7	Rohan, Henri, duc de

Anne d'Autriche, 1643-1661

124	General works on life and regency
124.3	Biography
124.4	Fronde, 1649-1653
124.45	War with Spain. Peace of the Pyrenees, 1659

Louis XIV, 1643-1715

124.5	Sources and documents
125	General works on reign
126	General special
	Including court life
	For general works on the French court and society, Louis XIV-Louis XVI see DC33.4
127.A-Z	Special topics, A-Z
127.C3	Camisards, Revolt of
	Revocation of Edict of Nantes see BR845
127.3	Diplomatic history. Foreign and general relations
127.6	Military history
127.8	Naval history
128	Social life and customs. Civilization. Intellectual life
	For court life see DC126
128.5	Public opinion formation. Internal propaganda
129	Biography and writings of Louis XIV
	Biography and memoirs of contemporaries
130.A2	Collective
130.A3-Z	Individual, A-Z
	e.g.
130.B4	Berwick, James Fitz-James, 1st Duke of
130.B9	Bussy, Roger de Rabutin
130.C2	Caylus, Marie Marguerite
130.C6	Colbert, Jean Baptiste
130.C7	Condé, Louis II de Bourbon, prince de
130.C77	Coulanges, Philippe Emmanuel
130.F6	Forbin, Claude, comte de

History
  By period
    Modern, 1515-
      1589-1715
        Louis XIV, 1643-1715
          Biography and memoirs of contemporaries
            Individual, A-Z -- Continued

130.L2	La Fayette, Marie Madeleine (Pioche de La Vergne), comtesse de
130.L4	La Vallière, Louise Françoise de La Baume Le Blanc, duchesse de
130.L5	Lenclos, Anne, called Ninon de
130.L7	Louis, Duke of Burgundy, dauphin
130.M2	Maintenon, Françoise d'Aubigné, marquise de
130.M25	Man in the iron mask
130.M37	Marie-Thérèse, Consort of Louis XIV
130.M38	Mattioli, Ercole Antonio
	Mazarin, Jules, cardinal
130.M4	General works
130.M43	Mazarinades
130.M78	Montespan, Françoise-Athénaïs de Rochechouart de Mortemart, marquise de
130.M8	Montpensier, Anne Marie L. d'Orléans, duchesse de
130.O7	Orléans, Élisabeth Charlotte, duchesse d'
130.R45	Retz, Jean François P. de Gondi, cardinal de
130.S2	Saint-Simon, Louis de Rouvoy, duc de
130.S5	Sévigné, Marie de Rabutin-Chantal, marquise de
130.T2	Tallemant des Réaux, Gédéon
130.T9	Turenne, Henri de La Tour d'Auvergne, vicomte de
130.V3	Vauban, Sébastien Le Prestre de
	1715-1789. 18th century
131	General works
131.5	Diplomatic history. Foreign and general relations
	Cf. DC57 Early modern, 1515-1789
	Biography
131.8	Collective
131.9.A-Z	Individual, A-Z
132	Regency of Philippe, duc d'Orléans, 1715-1723
	Louis XV, 1715-1774
133	General works on reign
133.3	General special
	Including court life
	For general works on the French court and society, Louis XIV-Louis XVI see DC33.4
133.4	Political history

History
By period
Modern, 1515-
1715-1789. 18th century
Louis XV, 1715-1774 -- Continued

133.5	Diplomatic history. Foreign and general relations
133.6	Military history
(133.7)	Naval history
	see DC52
133.8	Social life and customs. Civilization. Intellectual life
	For court life see DC133.3
	Biography
134	Louis XV
134.5	Marie Leszczynska
134.7	Louis, dauphin
	Contemporaries
135.A1	Collective
135.A2-Z	Individual, A-Z
	e.g.
135.A3	Aguesseau, Henri François d'
135.C5	Choiseul Stainville, Etienne François, duc de
135.D8	Du Barry, Jeanne Bécu, comtesse
135.D85	Dubois, Guillaume, Cardinal
135.E6	Eon de Beaumont, Charles Geneviève L.A.A.T. d'
135.E7	Epinay, Louise Florence P.T. d'Esclavelles, marquise d'
135.L5	Lespinasse, Julie Jeanne E. de
135.P8	Pompadour, Jeanne Antoinette (Poisson), marquise de
135.R5	Richelieu, Louis François A. du Plessis, duc de
135.S3	Saxe, Maurice, comte de
	Louis XVI, 1774-1789/1793
136.A2	Sources and documents
136.A3-Z	General works on reign
	For general works on the French court and society, Louis XIV-Louis XVI see DC33.4
	For works on the last years of the reign and life of Louis XVI see DC137+
136.5	Political history
136.6	Diplomatic history. Foreign and general relations
	The Court; social life and customs see DC136+
136.9	Other
	Biography and memoirs
	Louis XVI
137	General biography
137.05	Flight

History
By period
Modern, 1515-
1715-1789. 18th century
Louis XVI, 1774-1789/1793
Biography and memoirs
Louis XVI -- Continued

137.07	Imprisonment
137.08	Trial and death
137.09	Other
	Marie Antoinette
137.1	General biography
137.15	Affair of the diamond necklace
137.17	Imprisonment, trial, death
	For works dealing with the last year of the royal family see DC137.07
137.18	Death
137.19	Other
137.2	Angoulême, Marie Thérèse C., duchesse d'
137.25	Louis-Joseph-Xavier, Dauphine of France
137.3	Louis XVII
	Lost Dauphin controversy and claimants
137.36	General works
137.37	Naundorf, Karl Wilhelm
137.38.A-Z	Other claimants, A-Z
137.4	Elisabeth, Princess of France
	Contemporaries
137.5.A1	Collective
137.5.A2-Z	Individual, A-Z
	e.g.
137.5.B6	Biron, Armand-Louis de Gontaut, duc de
137.5.F4	Fersen, Hans Axel von, grefve
137.5.L2	Lamballe, Marie Thérèse L. de Savoie-Carignan, princesse de
137.5.L3	La Motte, Jeanne de Saint-Rémy de Valois, comtesse de
137.5.M3	Malesherbes, Chrétien Guillaume de Lamoignon de
137.5.S8	Suffren de Saint-Tropez, Pierre André de
137.5.T9	Turgot, Anne Robert J., baron de l'Aulne
138	Antecedent history and causes of the Revolution
	Revolutionary and Napoleonic period, 1789-1815
139	Periodicals. Societies. Serials
	Museums, exhibitions, etc.
139.5	General works
139.7.A-Z	Individual. By place, A-Z
140	Contemporary newspaper literature, journals, etc.

	History
	By period
	Revolutionary and Napoleonic period, 1789-1815 --
	Continued
	Almanacs
140.4	Collective
140.5.A-Z	Individual, A-Z
140.8	Anecdotes
(140.9)	Poems, songs, and other illustrative literature
	see class P
141	Sources and documents. Collections
	Including special periods
	Cahiers
141.3.A1-.A3	General collections
141.3.A4	Digests, résumés, extracts
141.3.A5	Introductions. Guides
141.3.A6-Z	Special local
	Laws, decrees, etc.
141.5	Official (Promulgated by the assemblies)
141.7	Selections, etc., by individuals
141.8	Condemnations, confiscations, etc. (Persons and property)
	Collected works
142	Several authors
143	Individual authors
	For works of authors contemporary to the Revolution and Empire, such as Mirabeau, Robespierre, etc. see DC146.A+
	Biography, memoirs, etc., of contemporaries
145	Collective
146.A-Z	Individual, A-Z
	e.g.
146.C45	Chimay, Jeanne Marie I.T. (de Cabarrus), princesse de
146.C69	Condorcet, Marie Jean A.N.C., marquis de
146.C8	Corday d'Armont, M.A. Charlotte de
146.D2	Danton, Georges Jacques
146.D5	Desmoulins, Camille
146.D9	Dumouriez, Charles François D
146.G3	Genlis, Stéphanie Félicité D. de Saint-Aubin, comtesse de
146.H7	Hoche, Lazare
146.L2	Lafayette, Marie Joseph P.Y.R.G. du Motier, marquis de
	Cf. E207.L2 His career in America
146.M3	Marat, Jean Paul
146.M7	Mirabeau, Honoré Gabriel R., comte de

History
  By period
   Revolutionary and Napoleonic period, 1789-1815
    General special
     Diplomatic history. Foreign relations
      Emigrés
       Indemnity -- Continued

158.15	Separate documents
158.17	General works
158.2	Religious history during the Revolution
158.5	Parties. Clubs. Societies (General)
	e.g. Royalist conspiracies
158.6.A-Z	Individual clubs or societies. By name, A-Z
	e.g.
158.6.P4	Philadelphes
158.6.S6	Société populaire de la section Le Pelletier
158.8	Other
	Including aliens, foreign public opinion, the middle class, women, Blacks, prisons, sansculottes, etc., during the Revolution
159	Social life and customs
	Cf. DC202.9 Social life and customs during the Empire
	Celebrations. Anniversaries
160	General works
160.2	1889
160.3	1989
	By period
	Assemblies to Directory, 1787/1789-1795
161	General works
162	General special
163	1787-June 17, 1789
	Including the year 1789
163.4	Assembly of Notables, 1787
163.7	States-General, May 1789
	Constituent Assembly, June 17, 1789-September 30, 1791
165	General works
165.5	Pamphlets, etc.
166	Special. June 17-July 14, 1789
166.062	Tennis-court oath, June 20
166.0623	Séance royale, June 23
166.0627	Fusion of orders, June 27
	Fall of the Bastille, July 14, 1789
167	General works
167.5	History of the Bastille
168	Special. July 17-December 31, 1789

History
By period
Revolutionary and Napoleonic period, 1789-1815
By period
Assemblies to Directory, 1787/1789-1795
Convention, September 22, 1792-October 1795
Reign of Terror, June 2, 1793-July 28, 1794
Special events -- Continued

184	1793
185	January-July 29, 1794
185.0727	9th thermidor
185.5	July 28,1794-October 1795
	Special events
185.7	1794
185.9	January-October, 1795
	Directory, October 1795-November 9, 1799
186	General works
186.5	General special
187	Year IV (1796)
	Special
187.7	13th vendémiaire
187.8	Babeuf's conspiracy
	Including Francois Noël Babeuf, also known as Gracchus or Caius Gracchus Babeuf
188	Year V (1797)
188.7	18th fructidor
189	Year VI (1798)
189.7	Special
190	Year VII and VIII (1799)
190.6	30th prairial
190.8	18th brumaire
	Consulate, 1799-1804
	For works treating the Consulate and Revolution together, or the Consulate, Revolution, and Empire together see DC139+
	For works treating the Consulate and Empire together see DC197+
191	General works
192	General special
192.4	Constitution of the year VIII
192.5	Royalist insurrection, 1800
192.6	Concordat, July 1801
192.8	The conspiracies of 1802
	Including attempted assassination of Napoleon
193	Life consulate, August 2, 1802
193.2	Expedition to Santo Domingo, 1803

History
By period
Revolutionary and Napoleonic period, 1789-1815
By period
Consulate, 1799-1804 -- Continued
193.4 Conspiracies (Cadoudal-Pichegru, 1803-1804)
Cf. DC192.8 Conspiracies of 1802
193.5 Duc d'Enghien (Louis Antoine Henri de Bourbon-Condé)
193.8 Other
Local history, 1789-1804
Paris
Cf. DC26 Description and travel in France, 1789-1815
Cf. DC33.5 Social life and customs in France, 1789-1830
Cf. DC731 Paris, 1789-1815
194.A2 Sources and documents
194.A3-Z General works
195.A-Z Other (Departments, cities, etc.), A-Z
Empire (First). Napoleon I, 1804-1815
Including works treating the Consulate and Empire together
197 Periodicals. Sources and documents. Collections
197.5 Minor collections
Memoirs and biography of contemporaries
Cf. DC145+ Biography, 1789-1815
198.A1 Collective
198.A2-Z Individual, A-Z
e.g.
Bernadotte, Jean Baptiste (Karl XIV Johan, King of Sweden and Norway) see DL820
198.C25 Cambronne, Pierre Jacques E., baron de
Coigny, Aimée de, 1769-1820 see DC198.F61
198.D2 Davout, Louis Nicolas, duc d'Auerstaedt et prince d'Eckmühl
198.F61 Fleury, Anne Françoise Aimée de Franquetot de Coigny, duchesse de, 1769-1820
198.F7 Fouché, Joseph, duc d'Otrante
198.M8 Murat, Joachim (Joachim Murat, King of Naples)
Cf. DG848.45 Murat as King of Naples
198.N6 Ney, Michel, duc d'Elchingen, Prince de la Moskowa
199 Collections of letters, etc.
201 General works
202 General special
Including prisoners of war

	History
	By period
	Revolutionary and Napoleonic period, 1789-1815
	By period
	Empire (First). Napoleon I, 1804-1815
	General special -- Continued
202.1	Military history
	For general history and description see DC201
	Cf. DC151+ Military history, 1789-1815
	Cf. DC227+ Napoleonic wars
202.3	Naval history
	Cf. DC153 Naval history, 1789-1815
202.5	Political history
	Cf. DC155 Political and administrative history,
	1789-1815
202.7	Diplomatic history
	Class here general works only
	For special treaties and events see DC220+
	Cf. DC157+ Diplomatic history, 1789-1815
202.8	Colonial policy
	Cf. JV1800+ History of French colonization
202.9	Social life and customs. Culture
	Biography of Napoleon
203	General works
203.2	Anecdotes
203.4	Caricature and satire
203.8	Napoleon in literature and art
203.9	Other special topics
204	Napoleon's relations with women
	Personal special
205	Life before 1804
206	Coronation, 1804
209	1814-1821
211	Captivity, 1815-1821. St. Helena. Elba
	For the return from Elba see DC238
212	Illness and death
212.5	Burial in France, 1840
	Cf. DC782.I5 Hôtel des invalides
	Writings of Napoleon
213.A1	Complete works
213.A2-Z	Correspondence and decrees
213.2	Memoirs
214.A-Z	Selections, sayings, opinions, etc. By editor, A-Z
	For military maxims see U19
214.3	Will
214.5	Spurious and doubtful
215	Letters to Napoleon

History
By period
Revolutionary and Napoleonic period, 1789-1815
By period
Empire (First). Napoleon I, 1804-1815
Writings of Napoleon -- Continued
215.5 Criticism of writings
Bonaparte family
216 General works
216.1 Joséphine
216.2 Marie Louise
216.3 Napoleon II (François Charles J. Bonaparte, herzog von Reichstadt)
216.35 Eugène de Beauharnais
216.4 Hortense
216.5 Joseph
Cf. DG848.44 Kingdom of Naples under his administration
Cf. DP207+ As king of Spain, 1806-1808
216.6 Lucien
216.7 Louis
216.8 Jérôme
Sisters
General works see DC216+
216.83 Elisa
216.85 Caroline
216.87 Pauline
Father and mother of Napoleon
216.88 General works
216.89 Carlo Maria Bonaparte
216.9 Maria Letizia (Ramolino) Bonaparte
216.95.A-Z Other, A-Z
e.g.
216.95.L4 Léon, Charles, called Comte Léon
217 Other material
Wars in the provinces
218 Vendean wars
Including later wars
218.1 Collective biography of participants
218.2.A-Z Contemporary records, narratives, memoirs, etc., A-Z
e.g.
218.2.C4 Charette de la Contrie, François Athanase
218.2.L3 La Rochejaquelein, Henri du Vergier, comte de
218.3.A-Z Individual events, battles, etc., A-Z
218.3.M66 Montreuil-Bellay, Battle of, 1793
218.3.Q5 Quiberon Expedition, 1795

History
By period
Revolutionary and Napoleonic period, 1789-1815
By period
Empire (First). Napoleon I, 1804-1815
Wars in the provinces
Vendean wars -- Continued
218.5	Chouans
219	Avignon and Comtat-Venaissin

Revolutionary wars, 1792-1802
220	First and Second Coalitions, 1792-1802
220.1	General special
220.15	Pamphlets, etc.
220.2	Campaign of 1792
220.3	Proposed invasion of England
220.5	Campaign of 1793
220.6	Campaign of 1794-1795
220.8	Campaign of 1796 (other than Italian)
221	Second coalition, 1799-1802
221.5	General special
222.A-Z	Individual events, battles, etc., A-Z
	e.g.
222.B3	Basel, Treaty of, 1795
222.C3	Campo-Formio, Peace of, 1797
222.F6	Fleurus, Battle of, 1794
222.J4	Jemappes, Battle of, 1792
222.L8	Lunéville, Treaty of, 1801
222.R3	Rastatt, Congress of, 1797-1799
222.S8	Switzerland, Invasion of, 1799-1801
222.T7	Toulon, Siege of, 1793
222.V15	Valenciennes, Siege of, 1793
222.V2	Valmy, Battle of, 1792
222.W37	Wattignies (France), Battle of, 1793
222.Z8	Zurich, Battle of, September 25-26, 1799
222.5	Treaty of Amiens, 1802

Wars in Italy
223	General works
223.4	First campaign, 1796-1797
223.5	Pamphlets, etc.
223.7	Second campaign, 1800. Battle of Marengo, June 14
224.A-Z	Individual events, battles, etc., A-Z
224.C58	Civita Castellana, Battle of, 1798
224.G4	Genoa, Siege of, 1800
224.M36	Mantua, Siege of, 1799
	Marengo, Battle of see DC223.7
224.P27	Pasque veronesi, Verona, 1797
224.P3	Peschiera, Siege of, 1801

History
By period
Revolutionary and Napoleonic period, 1789-1815
Revolutionary wars, 1792-1802
Wars in Italy
Individual events, battles, etc., A-Z -- Continued

224.R54	Rigutino, Battle of, 1799
224.T73	Trebbia River, Battle of, 1799
224.8	Pamphlets, etc.

Expedition to Egypt and Syria, 1798-1801
Including occupation of Egypt, 1798-1799
Cf. DT103 Egypt, 1798-1805

225	General works
226.A-Z	Individual events, battles, etc., A-Z
	e.g.
226.A3	Alexandria, Battle of, 1801
226.E4	El-Arish, Convention of, 1800
226.M3	Malta, 1798
226.N5	Nile, Battle of the, 1798

Napoleonic wars, 1800-1815
Cf. DC151+ Military history, 1789-1815

226.2	Sources and documents
226.3	General works
226.4	General special
226.5	Personal narratives
226.6.A-Z	Special topics, A-Z
	Participation, Foreign
226.6.P36	General works
226.6.P362A-.P362Z	By region or country, A-Z
226.6.P74	Prisoners and prisons

Third Coalition, 1805. German-Austrian campaign

227.A1-.A2	Sources and documents
227.A5-Z	General works
227.5.A-Z	Individual events, battles, etc., A-Z
	e.g.
227.5.A8	Austerlitz, Battle of, December 12
227.5.D8	Dürnstein, Battle of, November 11
227.5.E6	Elchingen, Battle of, October 14
227.5.P8	Pressburg, Treaty of, December 26
227.5.U6	Ulm, Capitulation of, October 17

Campaigns in Italy, 1805-1815

228	General works
228.5.A-Z	Individual events, battles, etc. A-Z
228.5.M35	Maida, Battle of, 1806

Campaigns against Prussia, Poland and Russia, 1806-1807

229	General works

	History
	By period
	Revolutionary and Napoleonic period, 1789-1815
	Napoleonic wars, 1800-1815
	Campaigns against Prussia, Poland and Russia, 1806-1807 -- Continued
230.A-Z	Individual events, battles, etc., A-Z
	e.g.
230.A8	Auerstedt, Battle of, 1806
230.E8	Eylau (Preussisch), Battle of, 1807
230.F7	Friedland, Battle of, 1807
230.J4	Jena, Battle of, 1807
230.K6	Königsberg, Treaty of, 1807
230.L8	Lübeck, Battle of, 1806
230.P6	Pultusk, Battle of, 1807
230.T5	Tilsit, Treaty of, 1807
	Campaigns against Portugal and Spain. Peninsular War, 1807-1814
	Including narratives and letters by officers, etc., other than English
231	General works
232	Special English material
	Including Wellingtoniana and narratives and letters by English officers, etc.
	Cf. DA68.12.W4 Biography of Wellington, Arthur Wellesley, Duke of, 1769-1852
232.5	Pamphlets, etc.
233.A-Z	Individual events, battles, etc., A-Z
233.A5	Albuera, Battle of, 1811
233.B26	Badajoz, Battle of, 1812
233.B3	Bailén (Spain), Battle of, 1808
233.B8	Bussaco, Battle of, 1810
233.C5	Cintra, Convention of, 1808
233.C55	Ciudad-Rodrigo, Siege of, 1810
233.C7	Corunna, Battle of, 1809
233.F84	Fuentes de Oñoro, Battle of, 1811
233.J34	Jaén, Occupation of, 1808-1813
233.M3	Madrid, Occupation of, 1808-1813
233.O7	Orthez, Battle of, 1814
233.P67	Porto, Occupation of, 1808-1809
233.S2	Salamanca, Battle of, 1812
233.S3	Saragossa, Siege of, 1808-1809
233.S57	Sitges, Occupation of, 1808-1814
233.T7	Tortosa, Siege of, 1810-1811
233.V27	Vimeiro, Battle of, 1808
233.V3	Vitoria, Battle of, 1813
233.5.A-Z	Special topics, A-Z

History
By period
Revolutionary and Napoleonic period, 1789-1815
Napoleonic wars, 1800-1815
Campaigns against Portugal and Spain. Peninsular
War, 1807-1814
Special topics, A-Z -- Continued

233.5.G8	Guerrillas
233.5.U53	Underground movements

German and Austrian campaign, 1809

234	General works

Individual events, battles, etc.

234.3	Abensberg, Battle of, April 20. Eggmühl (Eckmühl), Battle of, April 22
234.6	Aspern, Battle of, May 21-22
234.63	Sankt Michael in Obersteiermark, Battle of, May 25
234.65	Graz, Battle of, June 15-26
234.8	Wagram, Battle of, July 5-6
234.85	Znojmo, Battle of, July 10-11
234.87	Walcheren Expedition, July-Sept.
234.9	Treaty of Vienna, (Treaty of Schönbrunn), December 14

Russian campaign, 1812

235	General works
235.1	General special
	e.g. Guerrillas
235.3	Preparations. "Fürstentag" in Dresden, 1812
235.5.A-Z	Individual events, battles, etc., A-Z
	e.g.
235.5.B7	Borodino, Battle of, September 7
235.5.M8	Burning of Moscow
235.8	Pamphlets, etc.

1813-1814. War of Liberation

236	General works
236.1	General special

Campaign in Saxony, Germany, 1813

236.3	General works

Battle of Leipzig, October 16-19

236.5	Sources and documents
236.55	Contemporary accounts. Personal narratives
236.6	General works
236.65	Pamphlets
236.68	Special topics (not A-Z)
236.7.A-Z	Other battles, events, etc., A-Z
	e.g.
236.7.B3	Bautzen, May 20
236.7.D8	Dresden, August 27

History
  By period
    Revolutionary and Napoleonic period, 1789-1815
      Napoleonic wars, 1800-1815
        1813-1814. War of Liberation
          Campaign in Saxony, Germany, 1813
            Other battles, events, etc., A-Z -- Continued

236.7.L8	Lützen, May 2
	Campaign in Poland, 1813
236.72	General works
236.73.A-Z	Individual events, battles, etc., A-Z
236.73.T67	Toruń
236.73.Z35	Zamość
	1814
236.75	General works
236.8.A-Z	Individual events, battles, etc., A-Z
	e.g.
236.8.B2	Bayonne, Siege of
236.8.B38	Belfort, Siege of, 1813-1814
236.8.B4	Belgium, Campaign in
236.8.C5	Châtillon-sur-Seine Congress, February 3-March 31
	For legal works on the Congress of Châtillon-sur-Seine, 1814 see KZ1346.3
236.8.H2	Hamburg, Siege of, 1814
236.8.P4	Pfalzburg, Siege of
236.8.S4	Sens-sur-Yonne, Sieges of
237	Paris in 1814
238	Abdication (April 6, 1814) and Elba
238.5	Treaty of Paris, 1814
	For legal works, including texts of the treaty and related documents see KZ1348
	1815. First restoration and Hundred days
	Including Paris in 1815
239	General works
240	Individual events. By date
	e.g.
240 Nov. 20	Treaty of Paris, 1815
	For legal works, including texts of the treaty and related documents see KZ1355.5
240 June 22	Second abdication of Napoleon
	Battle of Waterloo, June 18, 1815
241	Sources and documents
241.5	Contemporary accounts. Personal narratives
242	General works
243	Pamphlets, etc.
244	Special topics

History

By period

Revolutionary and Napoleonic period, 1789-1815

Napoleonic wars, 1800-1815

1815. First restoration and Hundred days

Battle of Waterloo, June 18, 1815 -- Continued

244.5	The battlefield
	Including museums
244.7	Other
	Including Gordon Highlanders at battles of Quatre Bras and Waterloo
245	Austria and Italy in their relation to Napoleonic history
249	Congress of Vienna, 1814-1815

For legal works on the Congress of Vienna, 1814-1815 see KZ1355

For legal works on the Holy Alliance Treaty, 1815, including texts of the treaty and related works see KZ1358+

For legal works on the Ionian Islands Treaty, 1815, including texts of the treaty and related works see KZ1370.I56+

19th century

251	General works
252	General special
252.5	Pamphlets, etc.
252.7	Military history

Biography and memoirs

19th century as a whole

254.A2	Collective
254.A3-Z	Individual, A-Z
	e.g.
254.C7	Crémieux, Adolphe Isaac M.

Early 19th century

255.A2	Collective
255.A3-Z	Individual, A-Z
	e.g.
255.C4	Chateaubriand, François Auguste R., vicomte de

For literary criticism of his Mémoires d'outre-tombe see PQ2205

255.C7	Constant de Rebecque, Henri Benjamin
255.G8	Guizot, François Pierre G.
255.L4	Lamennais, Hugues Félicité R. de
255.M3	Mathilde Bonaparte, princess
255.M7	Montalembert, Charles Forbes R. de Tryon, comte de
255.R3	Récamier, Jeanne Françoise J.A. (Bernard)

History
  By period
    19th century
      Biography and memoirs
        Early 19th century
          Individual, A-Z -- Continued

255.T3	Talleyrand-Périgord, Charles Maurice de, prince de Bénévent

        Later 19th century
          see DC280.5, DC342.8
      Restoration, 1815-1830
        Including reign of Louis XVIII

256	General works
256.5	Social life and customs. Civilization
256.8	General special
257	Biography of Louis XVIII, 1815-1824

        Charles X, 1824-1830

258	General works on reign
259	Biography
259.5	Personal special
260.A-Z	Biography and memoirs of contemporaries, A-Z
	e.g.
260.B5	Berry, Marie Caroline F.L. de Naples, duchesse de
260.F5	Feuchères, Sophie (Dawes), baronne de
260.J6	Joséphine, Consort of Louis XVIII
260.P4	Périer, Casimir Pierre
261	July Revolution, 1830
262	Pamphlets, etc.

      July monarchy, 1830-1848

265	Sources and documents
266	Reign of Louis Philippe
266.5	Political and diplomatic history
267	General special
267.8	Abdication, etc.
	Cf. KJV4126.A23 Constitutional law

        Biography

268	Louis Philippe
269.A-Z	Contemporaries, A-Z
	e.g.
269.B9	Bugeaud de la Piconnerie, Thomas Robert, duc d'Isly
269.C3	Carrel, Armand
269.M3	Marie Amélie, Consort of Louis Philippe
269.O68	Orléans, Ferdinand Philippe L.C.H., duc d'
269.T3	Talleyrand-Périgord, Dorothée (von Biron), duchesse de

      February Revolution and Second Republic

History
  By period
    19th century
      February Revolution and Second Republic -- Continued
      Revolution, 1848

270	General works. Paris
271.A-Z	Other local, A-Z
	Second Republic, 1848-1851
271.5	Sources and documents
272.A2	Periodicals
272.A3-Z	General works
272.5	General special
272.7	Provisional government
	Cf. KJV4129.P76 Constitutional law
273	Outbreaks of May and June 1848
273.6	Foreign affairs
274	Coup d'état, December 2, 1851
274.5	General special
	Second Empire, 1852-1870
275	Sources and documents
275.2	Minor collections
	Including works of Napoleon III
276	General works
276.5	General special
277	Political and diplomatic history
277.5	Military history
277.8	Naval history
278	Social life and customs. Civilization
279	Other
	Biography and memoirs
280	Napoleon III
	For his works see DC275.2
280.2	Eugénie, Consort of Napoleon III
280.3	Louis Napoleon, prince imperial
280.4	Family (Napoleon III and his court)
	Contemporaries, 1830-1870
280.45	Collective
280.5.A-Z	Individual, A-Z
	e.g.
280.5.A8	Aumale, Henri Eugène P.L. d'Orléans, duc d'
280.5.B3	Bazaine, Achille François
280.5.C38	Chambord, Henri Charles F.M.D. d'Artois, duc de Bordeaux, comte de ("Henri of France," "Henry V")
280.5.F3	Favre, Jules
280.5.M7	Morny, Charles Auguste L.J., duc de
280.5.T5	Thiers, Adolphe

History
By period
19th century -- Continued
Franco-German or Franco-Prussian War, 1870-1871

281	Periodicals. Societies. Serials
282	Sources and documents
285	Memoirs. Personal narratives
289	General works
290	Compends
291	Pamphlets, etc.
292	Causes

e.g. Spanish succession
Cf. DC300 Diplomatic history of the war
Military history

293	General works
293.05	Pamphlets, etc.

French army

293.1	General works. Causes of defeat, etc.
294	Regular army
294.A 1st	1. corps d'armée
294.B 1st	1. division
294.C 1st	1. brigade
294.D 1st	1. régiment d'infanterie
294.F 1st	1. division de cavalerie
294.H 1st	1. bataillon de chasseurs à pied
294.K 1st	1. régiment de chasseurs
294.L 1st	1. régiment de cuirassiers
294.M 1st	1. régiment de dragons
294.N 1st	1. régiment de hussards
294.R 1st	1. régiment d'artillerie

Volunteer troops, irregulars, etc.

295.A2A-.A2Z	Garde nationale mobile, A-Z
295.B2A-.B2Z	Garde nationale mobilisée, A-Z
295.C2A-.C2Z	Garde nationale, A-Z
295.F2A-.F2Z	Francs-tireurs
295.H2A-.H2Z	Corps francs, A-Z
295.5	Other

German army

296	General works
297	Prussian army
297.1	Baden army
297.2	Bavarian army
297.4	Hessian army
297.6	Saxon army
297.8	Württemberg army
297.9	Other
298	Naval history

History
  By period
    19th century
      Franco-German or Franco-Prussian War, 1870-1871 --
        Continued

299	Political history
	Cf. DC310 Gouvernement de la défense nationale
300	Diplomatic history
	Including general relations of Second Empire with Germany
	Campaigns and battles
	Army of the Rhine
301	General works
301.5	Pamphlets, etc.
302	Saarbrücken, August 2, 1870
302.3	Weissenburg, August 4, 1870
302.5	Wörth, August 6, 1870
302.6	Pamphlets, etc.
302.7	Spicheren, August 12, 1870
302.9	Pont-à-Mousson, August 12, 1870
303	Colombey-Nouilly, August 14, 1870
303.2	Vionville (Rezonville), Mars-la-Tour, August 16, 1870
303.4	Gravelotte, August 18, 1870
303.6	Beaumont, August 30, 1870
303.8	Noisseville, August 31-September 1, 1870
304	Metz, 1870
304.5	Bazaine affair
	Operations in the provinces
305	General works
305.1	Nord
305.3	Ouest
	Loire (Armées de la Loire)
305.5	General works
305.6	Battle of Orléans, 1870
305.7	Vosges. Siege of Dijon, 1870-1871
305.8	German communications
	Est
305.9	General works
305.92	Belfort (Siege and battle), 1870-1871
	Sedan (Armée de Châlons), September 1, 1870
306	General works
306.5	Pamphlets, etc.
307	Celebrations. By date and place
	e.g.
307 1895.C4	Chicago
308	Siege of Strassburg (Strasbourg), 1870

History
  By period
    19th century
      Franco-German or Franco-Prussian War, 1870-1871
        Campaigns and battles -- Continued

309.A-Z	Other battles, sieges, etc., A-Z
	e.g.
309.A5	Amiens (Villers-Bretonneux), Battle of, November 27, 1870
309.B4	Beaune-la-Rolande, Battle of, November 28, 1870
309.B5	Bitche (Bitsch), Siege of, 1870-1871
309.C4	Châteaudun, Siege of, 1870
309.C7	Coulmiers, Battle of, November 9, 1870
309.C8	Cussey, Battle of, October 22, 1870
309.D3	Dammartin-en-Goële, Occupation of, 1870-1871
309.E8	Epinal, Battle of, October 12, 1870
309.L2	Landrecies, Siege of, 1871
309.L7	Loigny-Poupry, Battle of, December 12, 1870
309.L8	Longwy, Siege of, 1871
309.M4	Mézières, Siege of, 1870-1871
309.M8	Montmédy, Siege of, 1870
309.N3	Neubreisach (Neuf-Brisach), Siege of, 1870
309.P2	Pas-de-Calais, Invasion of, 1870-1871
309.P4	Peronne, Siege of, 1870
309.R2	Rambervillers, Battle of, October 9, 1870
309.R8	Rouen, Occupation of, 1870-1871
309.S3	Sélestat (Schlettstadt), Siege of, 1870
309.V4	Verdun, Siege of, 1870
310	Gouvernement de la défense nationale
	Siege of Paris (and Commune), 1870-1871
311.A2	Sources and documents
311.A3-Z	General works
312	General special
313	Other special
	e.g. Marine
314	Personal narratives
315	Pamphlets, etc.
315.5	Pictorial works
	Commune, 1871
316	General works
317	General special
318	Pamphlets, etc.
319	Minor operations in connection with Siege of Paris
320	Medical and sanitary services. Hospital services
321	Alsace-Lorraine annexation question
323	German occupation and evacuation

History
  By period
    19th century
      Franco-German or Franco-Prussian War, 1870-1871 --
        Continued

(324)	War indemnity
	see HJ8645
325	Results of the war, etc.
326	Reparation of damages
326.5.A-Z	Special topics, A-Z
326.5.P74	Press coverage
326.5.P82	Public opinion
	Later 19th century
330	General works
331	General special
	Third Republic, 1871-1940
334	Periodicals. Sources and documents. Collections
335	General works
337	General special
338	Social life and customs. Civilization
339	Military history
339.5	Naval history
	Political and diplomatic history
340	General works
341	Diplomatic history
	Biography and memoirs
	Collective
342	General works
342.1	Public men
342.3	Women
342.8.A-Z	Individual, A-Z
	e.g.
	Cf. DC280.5.A+ Biography, 1830-1870
342.8.B7	Boulanger, Georges Ernest J.M.
	Brazza, Pierre Savorgnan de see DT546.267.B72
342.8.C6	Clemenceau, Georges Eugène B.
342.8.F4	Ferry, Jules François C.
342.8.F6	Foch, Ferdinand
342.8.F62	Pamphlets, etc.
342.8.G2	Gallieni, Joseph Simon
342.8.G3	Gambetta, Léon Michel
342.8.J4	Jaurès, Jean Léon
342.8.J6	Joffre, Joseph Jacques C.
342.8.L6	Louis, Georges
342.8.L8	Lyautey, Louis Hubert G.
342.8.P3	Paris, Louis Philippe A. d'Orléans, comte de
342.8.P4	Pétain, Henri Philippe B.O.

DC

History
　By period
　　20th century
　　　Biography and memoirs
　　　　Individual, A-Z -- Continued
　　　　　Gaulle, Charles de see DC420+
373.H4　　　　Herriot, Edouard
373.L33　　　　Lattre de Tassigny, Jean Joseph M.G. de
373.L35　　　　Laval, Pierre
373.L4　　　　Leclerc de Hautecloque, Philippe
373.M3　　　　Maurras, Charles Marie P.
373.R45　　　　Reynaud, Paul
373.T5　　　　Thomas, Albert
375　　　Loubet, Emile, 1899-1906
380　　　Fallières, Clément Armand, 1906-1913
　　　Poincaré, Raymond, 1913-1920
385　　　　General works
387　　　　Period of World War I, 1914-1918
　　　　　For the war itself see D501+
　　　Reconstruction, 1919-1940
389　　　　General works
391　　　　Deschanel, Paul Eugène L., 1920
393　　　　Millerand, Alexandre, 1920-1924
394　　　　Doumergue, Gaston, 1924-1931
395　　　　Doumer, Paul, 1931-1932
396　　　　Lebrun, Albert François, 1932-1940
397　　　1940-1946
　　　　Including the period of World War II, 1939-1945, totalitarian
　　　　　state, Pétain, interim regime
　　　Fourth Republic, 1947-1958. Post-war period
398　　　　Periodicals. Sources and documents. Collections
400　　　　General works
401　　　　General special
402　　　　Social life and customs. Civilization
403　　　　Military and naval history
404　　　　Political and diplomatic history
　　　　Biography and memoirs
406　　　　　Collective
407.A-Z　　　　Individual, A-Z
　　　　　　e.g.
407.M4　　　　　Mendès-France, Pierre
407.P5　　　　　Pinay, Antoine
407.S3　　　　　Schuman, Robert
408　　　　Auriol, Vincent, 1947-1953
409　　　　Coty, René, 1954-1958
　　　Fifth Republic, 1958-
411　　　　Periodicals. Sources and documents. Collections

Local history and description
  Larger geographical divisions
    North. Northeast -- Continued

601.4	Antiquities
601.45	Social life and customs. Civilization
	History
601.5	General
	By period
601.7	Medieval and early modern
601.8	Modern
601.9	Special topics (not A-Z)
	East
603.1	Periodicals. Societies. Serials
603.3	General works. Description and travel. Guidebooks
	History
603.8	Modern
603.9	Special topics (not A-Z)
	Central
605.1	Periodicals. Societies. Serials
605.3	General works. Description and travel. Guidebooks
605.4	Antiquities
605.5	History
605.9	Special topics (not A-Z)
	South. Gulf of Lyons
607.1	Periodicals. Societies. Serials
607.2	Sources and documents
607.23	Gazetteers. Directories. Dictionaries
607.25	Biogaphy (Collective)
607.3	General works. Description and travel. Guidebooks
607.4	Antiquities
607.45	Social life and customs. Civilization
	History
607.5	General works
	By period
607.7	Medieval and early modern
	Modern
607.8	General works
	Biography and memoirs
607.82	Collective
607.83.A-Z	Individual, A-Z
607.9	Special topics (not A-Z)
	Riviera
	Cf. DG975.R6 Italian Riviera
608.3	General works. Description and travel. Guidebooks
608.45	Social life and customs. Civilization
	History
608.5	General works

	Local history and description
	Larger geographical divisions
	South. Gulf of Lyons
	Riviera
	History -- Continued
	By period
608.8	Modern
608.9	Special topics (not A-Z)
	West. Southwest
609.1	Periodicals. Societies. Serials
609.15	Congresses
609.2	Sources and documents
609.3	General works. Description and travel. Guidebooks
609.4	Antiquities
609.45	Social life and customs. Civilization
	History
609.5	General works
	By period
609.7	Medieval and early modern
	Modern
609.8	General works
	Biography and memoirs
609.82	Collective
609.83.A-Z	Individual, A-Z
	Regions, provinces, departments, etc., A-Z
	For works limited to local history between 1589 and 1715 see DC121.9.A+
	For works limited to local history during the Revolution and Consulate see DC195.A+
	For works limited to local history during the February Revolution of 1848 see DC271.A+
611.A16	Agenais
611.A26-.A27	Ain
611.A26	Periodicals. Societies. Serials
611.A261	Sources and documents
611.A2615	Congresses
611.A262	Gazetteers. Directories. Dictionaries, etc.
611.A263	Biography (Collective)
611.A264	General works. Description and travel. Guidebooks
611.A265	Antiquities
611.A266	Social life and customs. Civilization
611.A27	History. Biography. Special topics
611.A298-.A299	Aisne
	Including old district, Thiérache
611.A298	Periodicals. Sources. Antiquities
611.A299	General works. Description and travel. History
611.A3	Alais

Local history and description
  Regions, provinces, departments, etc., A-Z -- Continued

611.A33-.A35	Albigeois
611.A33	Periodicals. Sources. Gazetteers
611.A34	General works. Description and travel
	Including biography, guidebooks, antiquities, social life and customs, civilization
611.A35	History. Special topics
611.A435-.A437	Allier
611.A435	Periodicals. Sources. Gazetteers. Directories
611.A436	General works. Description and travel
	Including biography, guidebooks, antiquities, social life and customs, civilization
611.A437	History. Special topics
611.A553-.A557	Alpes (Basses-, Hautes-, Maritimes)
	Cf. DQ820+ Swiss Alps
611.A553	Periodicals. Societies. Serials
611.A554	Sources and documents
611.A555	Gazetteers. Dictionaries, etc.
611.A556	Description and travel. History
611.A557	Other
	Alsace see DC647+
611.A60-.A609	Anjou (Table D-DR11)
611.A645-.A655	Aquitaine
611.A645	Periodicals. Societies. Serials
611.A646	Sources and documents
611.A647	Collected works
611.A648	Biography
611.A649	Gazetteers. Directories, etc.
611.A65	General works. Description and travel. Guidebooks
611.A652	Antiquities
611.A653	Social life and customs. Civilization
611.A654	Ethnography
611.A655	History
611.A66	Arcachon Basin
611.A67	Ardèche
611.A673-.A678	Ardennes
611.A673	Periodicals. Societies. Serials
611.A676	General works. Description and travel. Guidebooks
611.A677	Antiquities. Civilization. Social life and customs
611.A678	History
611.A7	Ariège (Department)
	For description and travel before 1790 see DC611.F67
611.A7263	Arles
611.A7265-.A7295	Armagnac (Comté and family)
	Cf. DC109 Armagnacs in the 15th century
611.A7265	Periodicals. Sources. Biography. General works

	Local history and description
	Regions, provinces, departments, etc., A-Z
	Armagnac (Comté and family) -- Continued
611.A727	Social life and customs
611.A7295	History
611.A8	Artois (Province)
	Cf. DC611.P281+ Pas-de-Calais
611.A887-.A896	Aube
611.A887	Periodicals. Societies. Serials
611.A888	Sources and documents
611.A889	Gazetteers
611.A89	Biography (Collective)
611.A891	General works. Description and travel. Guidebooks
611.A892	Antiquities
611.A8925	Social life and customs. Civilization
611.A893	History (General)
	By period
611.A894	Early
611.A895	Medieval
611.A896	Modern
611.A92-.A925	Aude
611.A92	Periodicals. Societies. Sources
611.A922	Dictionaries. Gazetteers
611.A923	General works. Description and travel. Guidebooks
611.A924	History
611.A925	Other
611.A94-.A946	Auvergne
611.A94	Periodicals. Societies. Serials
611.A941	Sources and documents
611.A942	General works. Description and travel. Guidebooks
611.A943	Biography (Collective)
611.A945	History
611.A9455	Social life and customs
611.A946	Special topics (not A-Z)
611.A954	Avesnes
611.A961-.A963	Aveyron (Table D-DR12)
611.B25	Barrois. Bar (County or Duchy)
611.B31-.B319	Basque District
	For works treating both French and Spanish Districts see DP302.B41+
611.B31	Periodicals. Societies. Serials
611.B312	Sources and documents
611.B3123	Gazetteers, directories, dictionaries, etc.
611.B3125	Biography (Collective)
611.B313	General works. Description and travel. Guidebooks
611.B314	Antiquities
	History

Local history and description
  Regions, provinces, departments, etc., A-Z
    Basque District
      History -- Continued

611.B315	General works
611.B316-.B318	By period
	Including history and description and travel
611.B316	Early
611.B317	Medieval and early modern
611.B318	Modern
611.B319	Special topics (not A-Z)
	Basses-Alpes see DC611.A553+
	Bayonne (Diocese)
611.B34	Periodicals. Societies. Serials
611.B35	Sources and documents
611.B356	Gazetteers. Dictionaries, etc.
611.B36	General works. Description and travel. History
611.B37-.B375	Béarn
611.B37	Periodicals. Societies. Sources
611.B372	General works. Description and travel. Guidebooks
611.B373	General history
611.B375	Other
611.B377	Beauce
611.B38	Beaujolais
611.B395	Beauvais
611.B425-.B427	Belfort (Table D-DR12)
611.B522	Bernaville
611.B531-.B533	Berry
611.B531	Periodicals. Societies. Sources
611.B532	General works. Description and travel. Guidebooks
611.B533	History
611.B574	Béziers
611.B577	Bidasoa River and Valley
	Cf. DP302.B64 General and Spain
611.B6	Boisbelle (Cher)
611.B751-.B752	Bouches-du-Rhône
611.B751	Periodicals. Societies. Sources
611.B752	General works. Description and travel. History
	Bouillon see DH801.B6
	Boulogne see DC801.B75+
611.B764-.B767	Bourbonnais
611.B764	Periodicals. Societies. Sources
611.B765	General works. Description and travel. Guidebooks
611.B766	Antiquities
611.B7665	Social life and customs
611.B767	History
611.B771-.B787	Burgundy (Bourgogne)

Local history and description
Regions, provinces, departments, etc., A-Z
Burgundy (Bourgogne) -- Continued

611.B771	Periodicals. Societies. Serials
611.B772	Sources and documents
611.B7723	Gazetteers. Directories. Place names, etc.
611.B7725	Biography (Collective)
611.B773	General works. Description and travel
611.B774	Antiquities
611.B7742	Social life and customs
	History
611.B7743	Historiography
	Biography of historians, area studies specialists,
	archaeologists, etc.
611.B7745	Collective
611.B7747A-.B7747Z	Individual, A-Z
611.B775	General works
	By period
611.B776	Early and medieval to 1477
611.B777	Early to 843
611.B778	843-1032
	For House of Savoy see DG611.5
611.B779	1032-1361, Dukes of the Capetian dynasty
611.B78	1361-1477, Dukes of Burgundy
611.B781	1467-1477, Charles le Téméraire
	For Wars of Burgundy see DQ101+
611.B782	1477-1789
611.B785	1789-
611.B787	Other special
611.B841-.B9173	Brittany (Bretagne)
611.B841	Periodicals. Societies. Serials
611.B842	Sources and documents
611.B843	Collected works
611.B844	Pamphlets, etc.
611.B845	Biography (Collective)
611.B846	Gazetteers. Directories, etc.
611.B847	General works
611.B848	Description and travel
	Including the picturesque
611.B85	Antiquities
611.B851	Social life and customs. Civilization
611.B852	Ethnography
611.B854	History
611.B855	General special
	By period
611.B856	Early to 877. Armorica
611.B863-.B909	877-1492

Local history and description
  Regions, provinces, departments, etc., A-Z
    Brittany (Bretagne)
      History
        By period
          877-1492 -- Continued
            General works see DC611.B854

611.B864	General special
611.B865	Alain III, 877-907
611.B866	Alain IV, 937-952
611.B867	Conan I, 952-992
611.B868	Geoffroy I, 992-1008
611.B869	Alain V, 1008-1040
611.B87	Conan II, 1040-1066
611.B871	Hoël V, 1066-1084
611.B873	Alain VI, 1084-1112
611.B874	Conan III, 1112-1148
611.B876	Conan IV, 1156-1169
611.B877	Geoffroy II, 1169-1186
611.B878	Arthur I, 1196-1203
611.B879	Constance
611.B881	Alix
611.B882	Pierre I de Dreux, 1213-1237
611.B884	Jean I, 1237-1286
611.B885	Jean II, 1286-1305
611.B887	Arthur II, 1305-1312
611.B888	Jean III, 1312-1341
611.B89	Jean de Montfort
611.B891	Charles de Blois
611.B895	Period of Hundred Years' War
611.B897	Interregnum, 1345-1364
611.B898	Jean IV, 1364-1399
611.B899	Jean V, 1399-1442
611.B9	François I, 1442-1450
611.B902	Pierre II, 1450-1457
611.B904	Françoise d'Amboise
611.B905	Arthur III de Richemont, 1457-1458
611.B906	François II, 1458-1488
611.B908	Anne, Consort of Louis XII, 1488-1492
611.B909	Period during which union with France was effected, 1458-1492
611.B91	Union with France, 1492-1789
611.B915	1789-1815
611.B916	1815-1945
611.B917	1945-
	Biography and memoirs
611.B9172	Collective

Local history and description
  Regions, provinces, departments, etc., A-Z
    Brittany (Bretagne)
      History
        By period
          1945-
            Biography and memoirs -- Continued

611.B9173A-.B9173Z	Individual, A-Z
611.B92	Brie
	Cf. DC611.S45+ Seine-et-Marne
611.B923	Brivadois
611.B931-.B933	Bugey (Table D-DR12)
	Burgundy see DC611.B771+
611.C166-.C168	Calvados
611.C166	Periodicals. Sources. Gazetteers
611.C167	General works. Description and travel
	Including biography, guidebooks, antiquities, social life and customs, civilization
611.C168	History. Special topics
611.C2	Camargue
611.C228-.C23	Cantal
611.C228	Sources
611.C229	History
611.C23	Description and travel
	Carcassonne see DC801.C22+
611.C29	Carlat (Comté)
611.C32	Causses
611.C33	Cauterets Valley
611.C34	Caux
	Cf. DC611.S44+ Seine-Inférieure
611.C395	Cerdagne
	For works treating both the French and Spanish regions see DP302.C715
611.C423-.C425	Cévennes Mountains (Table D-DR12)
611.C44-.C4986	Champagne. Champagne-Ardenne
611.C44	Periodicals. Serials
611.C445	Societies
611.C446	Sources and documents
611.C447	Collected works
611.C448	Biography
611.C449	Gazetteers, etc.
611.C45	General works
611.C451	Description and travel
611.C453	Antiquities
611.C455	Ethnography
	History
611.C456	General works

Local history and description
  Regions, provinces, departments, etc., A-Z
    Champagne. Champagne-Ardenne
      HIstory -- Continued
        By period
          Early and medieval to 1314

611.C457	General works
611.C46	Earliest to 814
611.C462	Counts of Troyes, 814-923
611.C464	Counts of Vermandois, 923-1019
611.C465	Herbert I, 923-943
611.C466	Robert II, 943-968
611.C467	Herbert II, 968-993
611.C468	Etienne I, 993-1019
611.C47	Counts of Blois, 1019-1314
611.C471	Eudes I, 1019-1037
611.C472	Etienne II, 1037-1048
611.C473	Eudes II, 1048-1063
611.C474	Thibaud I, 1063-1089
611.C475	Eudes III, 1090-1093
611.C476	Hugues, 1093-1125
611.C477	Thibaud II, 1125-1152
611.C478	Henri I, 1152-1181
611.C479	Henri II, 1181-1197
611.C48	Thibaud III, 1197-1201
611.C482	Thibaud IV, 1201-1253
611.C484	Blanche de Navarre, 1201-1222
611.C485	Thibaud V, 1253-1270
611.C486	Marguérite de Bourbon, 1253-1256
611.C487	Henri III, 1270-1274
611.C488	Jeanne, 1274-1305
611.C489	Louis, 1305-1314
611.C49	Union with France to Revolution, 1314-1789
611.C492	Period of Hundred Years' War, 1328-1453
611.C494	1461-1610, Louis XI to Henri IV
611.C496	1610-1789, Louis XIII to Louis XVI
611.C498	1789-1815

19th-20th centuries

611.C4983	General works
	Biography and memoirs
611.C4985	Collective
611.C4986A-.C4986Z	Individual, A-Z
611.C51-.C52	Charente (and Charente-Inférieure)

For Poitou-Charentes see DC611.P731+

611.C51	Periodicals. Societies. Serials

	Local history and description
	Regions, provinces, departments, etc., A-Z
	Charente (and Charente-Inférieure) -- Continued
611.C52	Description and travel. History
	Including biography, guidebooks, antiquities, social life and customs, civilization
611.C56-.C563	Cher
611.C56	Periodicals. Societies. Serials
611.C562	General works. Description and travel. Guidebooks
611.C563	History
611.C65	Clermontois
611.C753	Cornouaille
611.C77-.C779	Corrèze (Table D-DR11)
611.C8-.C8355	Corsica
611.C8	Periodicals. Societies. Serials
611.C801	Sources and documents
611.C802	Collected works
611.C804	Pamphlets, etc.
611.C806	Biography and memoirs (Collective)
611.C808	Gazetteers. Directories, etc.
611.C81	General works
	Description and travel
611.C811	Through 1815
611.C812	1816-
611.C815	Antiquities
611.C816	Social life and customs. Civilization
611.C818	Ethnography
611.C82	History
611.C822	General special
	By period
611.C826	Early and medieval
611.C828	16th-17th centuries
611.C83	Modern
611.C831	18th century
	Biography and memoirs
611.C8314	Collective
611.C8315A-.C8315Z	Individual, A-Z
611.C832	Theodor I (baron Neuhof), 1736-1738
611.C833	Annexation to France, 1768
611.C834	Period of the French Revolution
611.C835	19th-20th centuries
	Biography and memoirs
611.C8354	Collective
611.C8355A-.C8355Z	Individual, A-Z
611.C842-.C85	Côte d'Or
611.C842	Periodicals. Societies. Serials
611.C843	Sources. Gazetteers. Directories. Biography

Local history and description
Regions, provinces, departments, etc., A-Z
Côte d'Or -- Continued

611.C844	General works. Description and travel. Guidebooks
611.C845	Antiquities
611.C846	History (General)
611.C847	History (Early)
611.C848	History (Medieval and early modern)
611.C849	History (Modern)
611.C86	Cotentin
611.C87	Côtes-du-Nord. Cotes-d'Amor
611.C9-.C909	Creuse
611.C9	Periodicals. Societies. Serials
611.C9023	Gazetteers, directories, dictionaries, etc.
611.C903	General works. Description and travel. Guidebooks
611.C904	Antiquities
611.C9045	Social life and customs. Civilization
611.C905	History (General)
	By period
611.C906	Early
611.C907	Medieval and early modern
611.C908	Modern
611.C909	Biography
611.D241-.D305	Dauphiné
611.D241	Periodicals. Societies. Serials
611.D242	Sources and documents
611.D243	Collected works
611.D244	Pamphlets, etc.
611.D245	Biography and memoirs
611.D246	Gazetteers. Directories, etc.
611.D247	General works
611.D248	Description and travel
611.D25	Antiquities
611.D251	Social life and customs. Civilization
611.D252	Ethnography
611.D254	History
	By period
611.D26	Early and medieval to 1032
611.D27	Under Germany, 1032-1350
611.D271	First dynasty of Dauphins, 1063-1162
611.D272	Guigue II, 1063-1080
611.D273	Guigue III, 1080-1125
611.D274	Guigue IV, 1125-1143
611.D275	Guigue V, 1143-1162
611.D276	Second dynasty of Dauphins, 1192-1281
611.D277	André, 1192-1237
611.D278	Guigue VI, 1237-1269

Local history and description
Regions, provinces, departments, etc., A-Z
Dauphiné
History
By period
Under Germany, 1032-1350
Second dynasty of Dauphins, 1192-1281 --
Continued

611.D279	Jean I, 1269-1281
611.D28	Third dynasty of Dauphins, 1281-1350
611.D281	Humbert I, 1281-1307
611.D282	Jean II, 1307-1319
611.D283	Guigue VII, 1319-1333
611.D284	Humbert II, 1333-1350
611.D29	Union with France, 1350-1789
611.D3	15th-16th centuries
611.D302	17th-18th centuries
611.D305	1789-
	Deux-Sèvres see DC611.S51+
611.D5	Dinan (District)
611.D663	Dole
611.D69	Dombes
611.D695	Donges (Vicomté)
611.D7	Dordogne (Department, River, and Valley)
611.D75	Doubs
611.D781-.D786	Drôme
611.D781	Periodicals. Societies. Serials
611.D782	Gazetteers. Directories. Dictionaries
611.D783	General works. Description and travel. Guidebooks
611.D784	Antiquities. Social life and customs
611.D785	History
611.D786	Special topics (not A-Z)
611.D921-.D923	Dunois (Table D-DR12)
	Escaut see DH801.S35
611.E75	Essonne
611.E86-.E89	Eure
611.E86	Periodicals. Societies. Collections. Sources. Gazetteers
611.E87	General works. Description and travel. Guidebooks
611.E88	Antiquities
611.E885	Social life and customs
611.E889	History
611.E91-.E94	Eure-et-Loir
611.E91	Periodicals. Societies. Serials
611.E93	General works. Description and travel. Guidebooks
611.E94	History
611.F497-.F499	Finistère (Table D-DR12)

	Local history and description
	Regions, provinces, departments, etc., A-Z -- Continued
	Flandre-Wallone see DC611.N821+
611.F67	Foix (Comté)
611.F71-.F719	Forez (Table D-DR11)
611.F811-.F819	Franche-Comté
611.F811	Periodicals. Societies. Serials
611.F812	Sources and documents
611.F8123	Gazetteers. Directories. Dictionaries
611.F813	General works. Description and travel. Guidebooks
611.F814	Antiquities
611.F815	History (General)
	By period
611.F816	Early
611.F817	Medieval and early modern
611.F818	Modern
	Biography and memoirs
611.F8182	Collective
611.F8183A-.F8183Z	Individual, A-Z
611.F819	Special topics (not A-Z)
611.G215-.G217	Gard
611.G215	Periodicals. Societies. Serials
611.G216	History
611.G217	Description and travel
611.G23	Garrone, Haute-
611.G24-.G26	Gascony and Guyenne
611.G24	Periodicals. Societies. Collections
611.G25	History
611.G26	Description and travel
611.G3	Gatinais
611.G35	Gers
611.G4	Gévaudan
611.G5	Gironde
611.G7	Groix, Isle of
	Guyenne see DC611.G24+
	Haut-Rhin see DC611.R44
	Haute-Garonne see DC611.G23
	Haute-Loire see DC611.L817+
	Haute-Marne see DC611.M365+
	Haute-Saône see DC611.S336+
	Haute-Savoie see DC611.S36+
	Haute-Vienne see DC611.V6
	Hautes-Alpes see DC611.A553+
611.H38	Hauts-de-Seine
611.H51-.H53	Hérault (Table D-DR12)
611.I26-.I27	Ile-de-France
611.I26	Periodicals. Sources and documents

Local history and description
    Regions, provinces, departments, etc., A-Z
      Ile-de-France -- Continued

611.I27	General works. Description and travel. History
	Including biography, guidebooks, antiquities, social life and customs, civilization
611.I29-.I3	Ille-et-Vilaine
611.I29	Periodicals. Serials. Sources and documents. Congresses
611.I3	General works. Description and travel. History
	Including biography, guidebooks, antiquities, social life and customs, civilization
611.I36-.I38	Indre (Départment)
611.I36	Periodicals. Societies. Serials
611.I363	Collective biography
611.I37	General works. Description and travel. Guidebooks
611.I38	History
611.I41-.I43	Indre-et-Loire (Table D-DR12)
611.I7-.I75	Isère (Department)
611.I7	Periodicals. Societies. Serials
611.I723	Gazetteers, directories, dictionaries, etc.
611.I73	General works. Description and travel. Guidebooks
611.I74	Antiquities
611.I745	Social life and customs. Civilization
611.I75	History
611.J8-.J88	Jura (Department). Jura Mountains
611.J8	Periodicals. Societies. Serials
611.J83	Description
611.J84	Antiquities
611.J845	Social life and customs. Civilization
611.J85	History (General)
611.J88	History (Modern)
611.L255-.L257	Landes (Table D-DR12)
611.L27-.L271	Langres
611.L27	Periodicals. Societies. Serials
611.L271	General works. Description and travel. History
611.L285-.L323	Languedoc
611.L285	Periodicals. Societies. Serials
611.L286	Sources and documents
611.L287	Collected works
611.L288	Pamphlets, etc.
611.L289	Biography (Collective)
611.L29	Gazetteers. Directories, etc.
611.L291	General works
611.L292	Description and travel
611.L294	Antiquities
611.L295	Social life and customs. Civilization

Local history and description
  Regions, provinces, departments, etc., A-Z
    Languedoc -- Continued

611.L296	Ethnography
611.L298	History
611.L299	General special
	By period
611.L3	Early and medieval to 1229
	1229-1789 see DC611.L298
611.L313	Period of Hundred Years' War, 1328-1453
611.L317	1453-1610
611.L319	1610-1789
611.L32	1789-
	Biography and memoirs
611.L322	Collective
611.L323A-.L323Z	Individual, A-Z
611.L4	Laonnais
611.L731-.L735	Limousin
611.L731	Periodicals. Societies. Collections
611.L732	General works. Description and travel. Guidebooks
611.L733	Antiquities
611.L7335	Social life and customs. Civilization
611.L734	History (General)
611.L735	Special topics (not A-Z)
611.L80-.L809	Loire (Department) (Table D-DR11)
611.L81	Loire River. Loire River Valley
611.L817-.L824	Loire, Haute-
611.L817	Periodicals. Sources and documents
611.L819	Dictionaries. Gazetteers
611.L82	General works. Description and travel. Guidebooks
611.L821	Antiquities
611.L8215	Social life and customs
611.L824	History
611.L826-.L829	Loire-Inférieure. Loire-Atlantique
611.L826	Periodicals. Societies. Serials
611.L827	General works. Description and travel. Guidebooks
611.L828	Antiquities
611.L829	History
611.L83-.L831	Loiret
611.L83	Periodicals. Serials. Sources and documents. Congresses
611.L831	General works. Description and travel. History
	Including biography, guidebooks, antiquities, social life and customs, civilization
611.L832-.L835	Loire-et-Cher
611.L832	Periodicals. Societies. Serials
611.L833	History

Local history and description
Regions, provinces, departments, etc., A-Z
Loire-et-Cher -- Continued

611.L835	Description and travel
(611.L84)	Lorraine
	see DC652+
611.L881-.L883	Lot (Table D-DR12)
611.L884-.L886	Lot-et-Garonne (Table D-DR12)
611.L924-.L926	Lozère
611.L924	Periodicals. Societies. Serials
611.L925	History
611.L926	General works. Description and travel. Guidebooks
611.L95-.L97	Lyonnais
611.L95	Periodicals. Societies. Serials
611.L96	General works. Description and travel. Guidebooks
611.L97	History
611.M221-.M229	Maine
611.M221	Periodicals. Societies. Serials
611.M222	Sources and documents
611.M223	General works. Description and travel. Guidebooks
611.M224	Antiquities
611.M225	History (General)
611.M226	History (Early)
611.M227	History (Medieval and early modern)
611.M228	History (Modern)
611.M229	Biography
611.M24-.M249	Maine-et-Loire (Table D-DR11)
611.M267-.M275	Manche
611.M267	Periodicals. Societies. Serials
611.M268	Sources and documents
611.M269	General works. Description and travel. Guidebooks
611.M271	History (General)
611.M272	History (Early)
611.M273	History (Medieval and early modern)
611.M274	History (Modern)
611.M275	Other
611.M31-.M319	Marche (Table D-DR11)
	Maritime Alps see DC611.A553+
611.M352-.M36	Marne
611.M352	Periodicals. Societies. Serials
611.M354	General works. Description and travel. Guidebooks
611.M355	Antiquities. Social life and customs. Civilization
611.M356	History (General)
611.M358	History (Medieval and early modern)
611.M359	History (Modern)
611.M36	Other
611.M365-.M374	Marne, Haute-

Local history and description
Regions, provinces, departments, etc., A-Z
Marne, Haute- -- Continued

611.M365	Periodicals. Societies. Serials
611.M367	Sources and documents
611.M3673	Gazetteers. Directories. Dictionaries
611.M369	History (General)
611.M3705	Social life and customs. Civilization
611.M373	History (Medieval and early modern)
611.M374	History (Modern)
611.M4	Marne River. Marne River Valley
611.M43-.M45	Maurienne
611.M43	Periodicals. Societies. Serials
611.M44	Sources and documents
611.M45	Description and travel
611.M466-.M4693	Mayenne
611.M466	Periodicals. Societies. Sources and documents. Collections
611.M467	Gazetteers. Directories. Dictionaries
611.M468	General works. Description and travel. Guidebooks
611.M469	History, etc.
611.M4692	Collective biography
611.M4693A- .M4693Z	Individual biography, A-Z
611.M573	Meurthe
611.M591-.M593	Meurthe-et-Moselle (Table D-DR12)
611.M597-.M6	Meuse
611.M597	Periodicals. Societies. Serials
611.M598	General works. Description and travel. Guidebooks
611.M599	Antiquities
611.M6	History
611.M68	Mont Blanc. Mont Blanc Region
611.M695	Montagnes Noires (Brittany)
611.M831-.M833	Morbihan (Table D-DR12)
611.M859	Morinie
611.M891-.M893	Morvan (Table D-DR12)
611.M897-.M91	Moselle (Department, River, and Valley)
611.M897	Periodicals. Societies. Serials
611.M898	General works. History and description
611.M9	Biography (Collective)
611.M91	Other
	Cf. DC611.M591+ Meurthe-et-Moselle
	Cf. DD801.M7 Moselle River (Germany)
611.M925	Mouthier-en-Bresse
611.N217-.N219	Narbonne (Table D-DR12)
611.N324	Navarre, French
611.N542-.N544	Nièvre (Dept.)

Local history and description
Regions, provinces, departments, etc., A-Z
Nièvre (Dept.) -- Continued

611.N542	Periodicals. Sources and documents
611.N543	General works. Description and travel. Guidebooks
611.N544	History
611.N73-.N737	Nivernais
611.N73	Periodicals. Societies. Serials
611.N731	Sources and documents
611.N732	Biography (Collective)
611.N733	General works. Description and travel. Guidebooks
611.N734	History (General)
611.N7345	Civilization
611.N736	Gazetteers. Directories. Guidebooks
611.N737	Special topics (not A-Z)
611.N821-.N823	Nord (Dept.) Nord-Pas-de-Calais
611.N821	Periodicals. Societies. Serials
611.N8213	Museums. Exhibitions
611.N8215	Congresses
611.N822	General works. Description and travel. Guidebooks
611.N823	History. Antiquities. Civilization
611.N841-.N899	Normandy
611.N841	Periodicals. Societies. Serials
611.N842	Sources and documents
611.N843	Collected works
611.N844	Pamphlets, etc.
611.N845	Biography (Collective)
611.N846	Gazetteers. Directories, etc.
611.N847	General works
611.N848	Description and travel
611.N85	Antiquities
611.N851	Social life and customs. Civilization
611.N852	Ethnography
611.N854	History
611.N855	General special
	By period
611.N856	Early and medieval to 1204
611.N86	Earliest to 911
611.N862	Norman princes, 911-1106
611.N863	Rollon, 911-931
611.N864	Guillaume I, 927-942
611.N865	Richard I, 942-996
611.N866	Richard II, 996-1026
611.N867	Richard III, 1026-1027
611.N868	Robert I, 1027-1035
611.N869	Guillaume II (William I of England), 1035-1087
611.N87	Robert II, 1087-1106

Local history and description
    Regions, provinces, departments, etc., A-Z
      Normandy
        History
          By period -- Continued

611.N872	Anglo-Norman kings, 1106-1204
611.N874	Henry I, 1106-1135
611.N8743	Stephen, 1135-1144
611.N8746	Geoffroy, 1144-1151
611.N875	Henry II, 1151-1189
611.N876	Richard IV (I of England), 1189-1199
611.N877	John, 1199-1204
611.N878	Conquest of Normandy by Philippe Auguste, 1200-1204
	Capetians, 1204-1329
611.N8795	Sources and documents
611.N88	General works
611.N89	1329-1461
	Biography and memoirs
611.N8925	Collective
611.N8926A-.N8926Z	Individual, A-Z
	1461-1790
611.N893	Sources and documents
611.N894	General works
	Biography and memoirs
611.N895	Collective
611.N896A-.N896Z	Individual, A-Z
611.N897	Napoleonic period
611.N898	19th century
611.N899	20th century
611.O36-.O38	Oise (Table D-DR12)
611.O61-.O65	Orléanais
611.O61	Periodicals. Societies. Serials
611.O62	Gazetteers. Directories. Dictionaries
611.O63	General works. Description and travel. Guidebooks
611.O64	History
611.O65	Special topics (not A-Z)
611.O74-.O76	Orne (Table D-DR12)
611.O795	Ossau Valley
611.P281-.P286	Pas-de-Calais
611.P281	Periodicals. Societies. Serials
611.P283	Gazetteers. Directories, etc.
611.P284	Biography
611.P285	General works. Description and travel. Guidebooks
611.P286	History
	Pays Basque see DC611.B31+
611.P42-.P425	Perche

	Local history and description
	Regions, provinces, departments, etc., A-Z
	Perche -- Continued
611.P42	Periodicals. Sources. Documents. Gazetteers.
	Biography
611.P422	General works. Description and travel. Guidebooks
611.P423	Antiquities
611.P424	History
611.P425	Special topics (not A-Z)
611.P44-.P449	Périgord (Table D-DR11)
611.P58-.P589	Picardy (Table D-DR11)
611.P731-.P78	Poitou
	Including Poitou-Charentes
611.P731	Periodicals. Societies. Serials
611.P732	Sources and documents
611.P733	Collected works
611.P734	Pamphlets, etc.
	Biography
611.P736	Collective
611.P737A-.P737Z	Individual, A-Z
611.P738	Gazetteers. Directories, etc.
611.P739	General works
611.P74	Description and travel
611.P742	Antiquities
611.P743	Social life and customs. Civilization
611.P744	Ethnography
611.P745	History
611.P746	General special
	By period
611.P747	Early and medieval
611.P748	Celtic and Gallo-Roman period
611.P749	Merovingian period
611.P75	Counts of Poitou, 778-1204
611.P765	Poitou Angevin and English, 1152-1204
611.P772	1203-1339 (Alfonse, 1228-1271)
611.P775	Hundred Years' War to Reformation
611.P777	Annexation to crown of France, 1416-
611.P778	Reformation and religious wars
611.P78	17th-18th centuries
611.P8045-.P805	Ponthieu (Comté)
611.P8045	Civilization
611.P805	History
(611.P817-.P819)	Ponts
611.P9	Privas
611.P951-.P979	Provence
611.P951	Periodicals. Societies. Serials
611.P952	Sources and documents

Local history and description
  Regions, provinces, departments, etc., A-Z
    Provence -- Continued

611.P953	Collected works
611.P954	Pamphlets, etc.
611.P955	Biography (Collective)
611.P956	Gazetteers. Directories, etc.
611.P957	General works
611.P958	Description and travel
611.P96	Antiquities
611.P961	Social life and customs. Civilization
611.P962	Ethnography
	History
	Study and teaching
611.P9635	General works
611.P9636A-.P9636Z	By region or country, A-Z
611.P964	General works
611.P965	General special
	By period
611.P966	Early and medieval to 1486
611.P967	Early to 933
611.P969	Feudal period: Boson dynasty, 934-1113
611.P97	Bérenger dynasty; Counts of Barcelona, 1113-1246
611.P972	Anjou dynasty, 1246-1481
611.P974	Union with France, 1486-1789
611.P976	1486-1610
611.P977	1610-1789
611.P978	1789-1815
611.P979	1815-
	Mainly with modern departments and southern France, e.g. DC611.A553+ DC611.B751+ DC611.V281+
611.P9798	Puy-de-Dôme
611.P98-.P989	Pyrenees (General, and French). Pyrénées-Atlantiques. Hautes Pyrénées (Table D-DR11)
	For Spanish Pyrenees see DP302.P8
611.Q4	Quercy
611.R237	Rance River (Côtes-du-Nord)
611.R281-.R282	Ré Island
611.R281	Periodicals. Serials. Sources and documents. Congresses
611.R282	General works. Description and travel. History
	Including biography, guidebooks, antiquities, social life and customs, civilization
611.R43	Rethelois
611.R435	Retz
611.R44	Rhin, Haut-
611.R46-.R465	Rhône (Department)

	Local history and description
	Regions, provinces, departments, etc., A-Z
	Rhône (Department) -- Continued
611.R46	Periodicals. Societies. Serials
611.R463	General works. Description and travel. Guidebooks
611.R465	History
611.R478	Rhône River. Rhône River Valley
611.R85-.R87	Roussillon
611.R85	Sources and documents
611.R855	Biography (Collective)
611.R86	History
611.R87	Miscellanea
611.S101-.S104	Saint A
	Subarrange by first letter following A
611.S115-.S128	Saint B
	Subarrange by first letter following B, e.g.
611.S126	Saint-Brieuc
611.S129-.S143	Saint C
	Subarrange by first letter following C
611.S144-.S148	Saint D
	Subarrange by first letter following D
611.S149-.S153	Saint E
	Subarrange by first letter following E, e.g.
611.S152	Saint-Etienne (Loire)
611.S154-.S16	Saint F
	Subarrange by first letter following F
611.S161-.S169	Saint G
	Subarrange by first letter following G
611.S17-.S174	Saint H
	Subarrange by first letter following H
611.S175-.S178	Saint I
	Subarrange by first letter following I
611.S179-.S183	Saint J
	Subarrange by first letter following J
611.S184-.S192	Saint K
	Subarrange by first letter following K
611.S193-.S208	Saint L
	Subarrange by first letter following L
611.S209-.S224	Saint M
	Subarrange by first letter following M
611.S225-.S236	Saint N
	Subarrange by first letter following N
611.S237-.S24	Saint O
	Subarrange by first letter following O
611.S241-.S25	Saint P
	Subarrange by first letter following P

Local history and description
   Regions, provinces, departments, etc., A-Z -- Continued

611.S251-.S255	Saint Q
	Subarrange by first letter following Q
611.S256-.S265	Saint R
	Subarrange by first letter following R
611.S266-.S278	Saint S
	Subarrange by first letter following S
611.S279-.S29	Saint T
	Subarrange by first letter following T
611.S291-.S292	Saint U
	Subarrange by first letter following U
611.S293-.S299	Saint V
	Subarrange by first letter following V
611.S3	Saint W
	Subarrange by author
611.S302	Saint X
	Subarrange by author
611.S304	Saint Y
	Subarrange by author
611.S306	Saint Z
	Subarrange by author
611.S31-.S318	Sainte A-Sainte Z
	e.g.
611.S317	Sainte-Ramée
611.S321-.S33	Single words beginning Saint...
	e.g.
611.S325-.S327	Saintonge
611.S325	Periodicals. Societies. Serials
611.S326	Biography
611.S327	General works. Description and travel. History
	Including biography, guidebooks, antiquities, social life and customs, civilization
611.S336-.S338	Saône, Haute- (Table D-DR12)
611.S339	Saône River
611.S34-.S345	Saône-et-Loire
611.S34	Periodicals. Societies. Serials
611.S3423	Gazetteers, directories, dictionaries, etc.
611.S343	General works. Description and travel. Guidebooks
611.S344	Antiquities
611.S345	History
611.S351-.S353	Sarthe (Table D-DR12)
611.S36-.S369	Savoie. Haute-Savoie (Table D-DR11)
	Cf. DC611.T169+ Tarentaise
611.S38	Sedan
611.S4	Seine (Department)
611.S44-.S444	Seine-Inférieure. Seine-Maritime

Local history and description
   Regions, provinces, departments, etc., A-Z
      Seine-Inférieure. Seine-Maritime -- Continued

611.S44	Periodicals. Societies. Serials
611.S441	Gazetteers, directories, dictionaries, etc.
611.S442	General works. Description and travel. Guidebooks
611.S443	Antiquities
611.S444	History
611.S45-.S455	Seine-et-Marne
611.S45	Periodicals. Societies. Serials
611.S451	Antiquities
611.S452	General works. Description and travel. Guidebooks
611.S454	History
611.S455	Other
611.S458-.S46	Seine-et-Oise
611.S458	Periodicals. Societies. Serials
611.S459	Biography
611.S46	General works. Description and travel. History
	Including guidebooks, antiquities, social life and customs, civilization
611.S461	Seine River
611.S476-.S478	Senlis (Table D-DR12)
611.S49	Sennecey-le-Grand
611.S51-.S513	Sèvres, Deux-
611.S51	Periodicals. Societies. Serials
611.S512	General works. Description and travel. Guidebooks
611.S513	History
611.S682-.S684	Soissons (Table D-DR12)
611.S8	Somme
611.T169-.T171	Tarentaise (Table D-DR12)
611.T183-.T184	Tarn
611.T183	Periodicals. Serials. Sources and documents. Congresses
611.T184	General works. Description and travel. History
	Including biography, guidebooks, antiquities, social life and customs, civilization
611.T187-.T189	Tarn-et-Garonne (Table D-DR12)
	Thiérache see DC611.A298+
611.T717-.T719	Toulouse (Table D-DR12)
611.T721-.T781	Touraine
611.T721	Periodicals. Societies. Serials
611.T722	Sources and documents
611.T723	Collected works
611.T724	Pamphlets, etc.
611.T725	Biography (Collective)
611.T726	Gazetteers. Directories, etc.
611.T727	General works

Local history and description
    Regions, provinces, departments, etc., A-Z
      Touraine -- Continued

611.T728	Description and travel
611.T73	Antiquities
611.T731	Social life and customs. Civilization
611.T732	Ethnography
611.T734	History
611.T735	General special
	By period
611.T736	Early and medieval
611.T738	Under Gaul
611.T739	Gallo-Roman
611.T74	Merovingian and Carolingian
611.T743	Comté de Tours
611.T745	Thibaud I, 940-978
611.T746	Eudes I, 978-995
611.T747	Thibaud II, 995-1004
611.T748	Eudes II, 1004-1037
611.T749	Thibaud III, 1037-1044
611.T75	Geoffroy I Martel, 1044-1060
611.T751	Geoffroy II le Barbu (d. 1103?)
611.T752	Foulque IV le Réchin, d. 1109
611.T753	Geoffroy III, Martel, d. 1106
611.T754	Foulque V le Jeune, 1109-1129
611.T755	Geoffroy IV le Bel, Plantagenet, 1129-1151
611.T756	Geoffroy V Plantagenet, 1151-1158
611.T758	1158-1204. English period
611.T76	1204-1360
611.T77	Duchy, 1360-1584
611.T78	Union with France, 1584-1789
611.T781	1789-
611.T92	Trièves
611.V12	Val-de-Marne
611.V13	Val-d'Oise
611.V14	Valence
611.V151	Valenciennes
611.V21	Valois
611.V281-.V283	Var (Table D-DR12)
611.V356-.V357	Vaucluse
611.V356	Periodicals. Serials. Sources and documents. Congresses
611.V357	General works. Description and travel. History Including biography, guidebooks, antiquities, social life and customs, civilization
611.V358-.V359	Vaudois valleys

Local history and description
Regions, provinces, departments, etc., A-Z
Vaudois valleys -- Continued

611.V358	Periodicals. Serials. Sources and documents. Congresses
611.V359	General works. Description and travel. History
	Including biography, guidebooks, antiquities, social life and customs, civilization
611.V433-.V435	Velay (Table D-DR12)
611.V44	Venaissin
611.V45-.V459	Vendée
611.V45	Periodicals. Societies. Serials
611.V452	Sources and documents
611.V4523	Gazetteers, directories, dictionaries, etc.
611.V4525	Biography (Collective)
611.V453	General works. Description and travel. Guidebooks
611.V454	Antiquities
611.V4545	Social life and customs. Civilization
611.V455	History (General)
611.V456	History (Early)
611.V457	History (Medieval and early modern)
611.V458	History (Modern)
611.V4583A-.V4583Z	Individual biography, A-Z
611.V459	Special topics (not A-Z)
611.V464-.V466	Vendôme (Table D-DR12)
611.V5	Vermandois
611.V58	Vienne
611.V6	Vienne, Haute-
611.V8	Vivarais
611.V961-.V963	Vosges (Dept.) (Table D-DR12)
	Vosges Mountains see DC645+
611.Y54-.Y56	Yonne
611.Y54	Periodicals. Societies. Sources
611.Y55	Gazetteers. Collective biography
611.Y56	General works. Description and travel. History. Antiquities
611.Y9	Yvelines
	Alsace-Lorraine
	For individual departments composing this region, see DC611.M897+, DC611.R44, etc.
630	Periodicals. Societies. Serials
631	Sources and documents
632	Gazetteers. Directories
633	General works
634	Description and travel
635	Antiquities
636	Social life and customs. Civilization

	Local history and description
	Alsace-Lorraine -- Continued
	History
637	Biography (Collective)
	By period
639	Early and medieval
640	1500-1789
641	1789-1871
642	1871-1945
643	1945-
	Special regions, etc.
645	Vosges Mountains
	Other regions see DC611.A+
	Cites, towns, etc. see DC801.A+
	Alsace
647	Periodicals. Societies. Serials
647.3	Sources and documents
647.6	Gazetteers. Directories, etc.
648	General works
648.3	Description and travel
648.6	Antiquities
649	Social life and customs. Civilization
	History
649.5	Biography (Collective)
650	General works
	By period
650.2	Early and medieval
650.3	1500-1789
	Biography and memoirs
650.34	Collective
650.36.A-Z	Individual, A-Z
650.4	1789-1871
650.5	1871-1945
	Biography and memoirs
650.53	Collective
650.54.A-Z	Individual, A-Z
650.6	1945-
	Lorraine
652	Periodicals. Societies. Serials
652.2	Congresses
652.3	Sources and documents
652.6	Gazetteers. Directories, etc.
653	General works
653.3	Description and travel
653.6	Antiquities
654	Social life and customs. Civilization
	History

Local history and description
  Alsace-Lorraine
    Lorraine
      History -- Continued
654.5	Biography (Collective)
655	General works
	By period
655.2	Early and medieval
655.3	1500-1789
655.4	1789-1871
655.5	1871-1945
	Biography and memoirs
655.53	Collective
655.54.A-Z	Individual, A-Z
655.6	1945-
	Paris
701	Periodicals. Societies. Serials
702	Sources and documents
703	Collected works
704	Directories. Dictionaries
	Biography and memoirs
705.A1	Collective
705.A2-Z	Individual, A-Z
707	General works. Description and travel. Pictorial works
708	Guidebooks
709	Pamphlets, etc.
711	Antiquities. Museums
715	Social life and customs. Culture. Civilization
	Ethnography
717	General works
718.A-Z	Individual elements in the population, A-Z
718.A34	Africans
718.A36	Afro-Americans. African Americans
718.A4	Algerians
718.A44	Americans (U.S.)
718.A5	Antilleans
718.A72	Arabs
718.A73	Argentines
718.A74	Asians
718.B56	Blacks
718.B72	Bretons
718.B74	British
718.C45	Chileans
718.C47	Chinese
718.C64	Columbians
718.C67	Corsicans
718.C83	Cubans

Local history and description
  Paris
    Ethnography
      Individual elements in the population, A-Z -- Continued

718.G47	Germans
718.G7	Greeks
718.H84	Hungarians
718.I24	Icelanders
718.I73	Italians
718.J37	Japanese
718.K67	Koreans
718.L37	Latin Americans
718.L43	Lebanese
718.L55	Limousins
718.M87	Muslims
718.N64	North Africans
718.N67	Norwegians
718.P64	Poles
718.P67	Portuguese
718.R75	Romanians
718.R8	Russians
718.S35	Senegalese
718.S65	Spaniards
718.S95	Swiss
718.T64	Togolese
718.T85	Tunisians
718.T87	Turks
718.V53	Vietnamese
719	Political history

History
  General works see DC707

723	General special

  By period
    Including description and social life and customs

725	Earliest to 1515
727	16th century
729	17th-18th centuries
731	1789-1815
733	1815-1870
735	1871-1914

      Description see DC707
      Social life and customs see DC715
      Siege of Paris see DC311+
      Commune see DC316+

736	1914-1921
737	1922-

Sections, districts, etc.

Local history and description
Paris
Sections, districts, etc. -- Continued
Arrondissements, faubourgs, etc.

752.A-Z	Individual, A-Z
752.A01	1er Arrondissement. Louvre
752.A02	2e Arrondissement. Bourse
752.A03	3e Arrondissement. Temple
752.A04	4e Arrondissement. Hôtel-de-Ville
752.A05	5e Arrondissement. Panthéon
752.A06	6e Arrondissement. Luxembourg. Saint-Sulpice
752.A07	7e Arrondissement. Palais Bourbon
752.A08	8e Arrondissement. Elysée
752.A09	9e Arrondissement. Opéra
752.A10	10e Arrondissement. Enclos-Saint-Laurent
752.A11	11e Arrondissement. Popincourt
752.A12	12e Arrondissement. Reuilly-Bois de Vincennes
752.A13	13e Arrondissement. Gobelins
752.A14	14e Arrondissement. Observatoire
752.A15	15e Arrondissement. Vaugirard
752.A16	16e Arrondissement. Passy
752.A17	17e Arrondissement. Batignolles-Monceau
752.A18	18e Arrondissement. Butte-Montmartre
752.A19	19e Arrondissement. Buttes-Chaumont
752.A20	20e Arrondissement. Ménilmontant
	Batignolle-Monceau see DC752.A17
752.B45	Belleville
	Bourse see DC752.A02
	Butte-Montmartre see DC752.A18
	Buttes-Chaumont see DC752.A19
752.C45	Chaillot
752.D43	Défense
	Elysée see DC752.A08
	Enclos-Saint-Laurent see DC752.A10
752.F68	Faubourg-Saint-Antoine
752.F7	Faubourg-Saint-Germain
	Gobelins see DC752.A13
752.G67	Goutte d'or
752.H34	Les Halles
	Hôtel-de-Ville see DC752.A04
752.I4	Ile de la Cité
752.I45	Ile Saint-Louis
	La Défense see DC752.D43
	La Villette see DC752.V54
752.L38	Latin Quarter. Quartier latin
	Left Bank see DC752.R52
	Louvre see DC752.A01

Local history and description
  Paris
    Sections, districts, etc.
      Arrondissements, faubourgs, etc.
        Individual, A-Z -- Continued

	Luxembourg see DC752.A06
752.M37	Marais
	Ménilmontant see DC752.A20
(752.M7)	Montmartre
	see DC752.A18
752.M8	Montparnasse
	Observatoire see DC752.A14
	Opéra see DC752.A09
	Palais Bourbon see DC752.A07
	Panthéon see DC752.A05
	Passy see DC752.A16
	Popincourt see DC752.A11
752.Q2	Quartier Barbette
	Quartier de Chaillot see DC752.C45
	Quartier du Marais see DC752.M37
	Quartier du Val-de-Grâce see DC752.V3
	Quartier La Villette see DC752.V54
	Quartier latin see DC752.L38
752.Q67	Quartier Saint-Georges
	Quartier Saint-Germain-des-Prés see DC752.S25
752.Q8	Quartier Saint Victor
	Reuilly-Bois de Vincennes see DC752.A12
752.R52	Rive gauche. Left Bank
752.S25	Saint-Germain des-Prés
752.S48	Saint-Merri
	Saint-Sulpice see DC752.A06
	Temple see DC752.A03
752.V3	Val-de-Grâce
	Vaugirard see DC752.A15
752.V54	La Villette
753	Catacombs. The underground city
755	Cemeteries
757	Fountains
	Parks (General)
759	General works
760.A-Z	Individual, A-Z
	e.g.
760.M6	Montsouris
	Streets, bridges, waterfront, etc.
761	General works
762.A-Z	Individual, A-Z
	e.g.

	Local history and description
	Paris
	Sections, districts, etc.
	Streets, bridges, waterfront, etc.
	Individual, A-Z -- Continued
762.P6	Place Vendôme
762.P7	Pont neuf
762.R75	Rue du Bac
	Suburbs. Communes suburbaines
768	General works
769.A-Z	Individual, A-Z
	e.g.
769.A8	Auteuil
769.P3	Passy
	Buildings
	Cf. NA1050, NA4298.P2, NA5550, Architecture
771	General works
	Churches, monasteries, etc.
	General works
774.A-Z	Individual, A-Z
	e.g.
774.M2	Madeleine, La
774.N7	Notre-Dame (Cathedral)
774.N8	Notre-Dame des champs
774.S3	Sainte-Chapelle
777	Halls and markets
	Public buildings, palaces, etc.
781	General works
782.A-Z	Individual, A-Z
	e.g.
782.E4	Palais de l'Elysée
782.I5	Hôtel des invalides
	Cf. DC212.5 Burial of Napoleon
782.T9	Tuileries
782.V5	Hôtel de ville
	Theaters
785	General works
786.A-Z	Individual, A-Z
789.A-Z	Other buildings, A-Z
	e.g.
789.B2	Château de Bagatelle
790.A-Z	Other, A-Z
	e.g.
790.A6	Arc de triomphe de l'Etoile
790.C6	Colonne Vendôme
	Other cities, towns, etc., A-Z
	e.g.

Local history and description
 Other cities, towns, etc., A-Z -- Continued

801.A325	Aix-en-Provence
801.A51	Amiens
801.A55	Angers
801.A6	Annecy
	Arles
801.A7	Periodicals. Societies. Sources and documents
801.A71	Description and travel. Guidebooks

    Including biography, antiquities, social life and customs,
     civilization

801.A72	History
801.A79	Arras
801.A96	Avignon
801.B45	Beauvais
801.B66	Blois
801.B71-.B73	Bordeaux (Table D-DR12)
801.B75-.B77	Boulogne-sur-Mer (Table D-DR12)
801.B83-.B85	Brest (Table D-DR12)
801.C11	Caen
801.C19	Cannes
801.C22-.C24	Carcassonne
801.C22	Periodicals. Societies. Serials
801.C23	Museums. Antiquities
801.C24	General works. Description and travel. History

    Including biography, guidebooks, social life and customs,
     civilization, special topics

801.C28	Carnac
801.C32-.C34	Châlons-sur-Marne (Table D-DR12)
801.C42	Chantilly
801.C47-.C48	Chartres (City)
801.C47	Serials
801.C48	Monographs
	Chartres (Diocese) see DC611.E91+
	Château de Fontainebleau see DC801.F67
	Château de Saint Germain-en-Laye see DC801.S19
	Château de Versailles see DC801.V55+
801.C56-.C58	Clermont-Ferrand (Table D-DR12)
801.C657	Colmar
801.C7	Compiègne
801.D4	Deauville
801.D56	Dieppe
801.D59-.D61	Dijon
801.D59	Periodicals. Societies. Serials. Sources
801.D6	General works. Description and travel. Guidebooks
801.D61	History
801.D72	Douai

	Local history and description
	Other cities, towns, etc., A-Z -- Continued
801.E71	Ermenonville
801.F67	Fontainebleau
801.G399-.G4	Gien
801.G399	Serials
801.G4	Monographs
801.G81-.G83	Grenoble (Table D-DR12)
801.H38	Havre
801.L15-.L4339	La A - La Z
	e.g.
801.L43	La Rochelle
801.L434-.L4624	Laa - Laz
	e.g.
801.L4375	Laon
801.L4626-.L6469	Le A - Le Z
	e.g.
	Le Havre see DC801.H38
801.L48-.L49	Le Mans
801.L48	Periodicals. Serials. Sources and documents. Congresses
801.L49	General works. Description and travel. History
	Including biography, guidebooks, antiquities, social life and customs, civilization
801.L6462	Le Vésinet
801.L647-.L652	Lea - Lerz
801.L653-.L655	Les A - Les Z
	e.g.
801.L6534	Les Baux-de-Provence
801.L656-.L6639	Lesa - Lez
	e.g.
801.L658	Levroux
801.L68-.L689	Lille (Table D-DR11)
801.L71-.L73	Limoges (Table D-DR12)
801.L78	Lisieux
801.L79	L'Isle-Adam
	Lyon
801.L96	Periodicals. Societies. Serials
801.L961	Sources and documents
801.L9615	Biography (Collective)
801.L9623	Gazetteers, directories, dictionaries, etc.
801.L963	General works. Description and travel. Guidebooks
801.L964	Antiquities
801.L9645	Social life and customs
801.L9646	Ethnography
801.L965	History (General)
	By period

Local history and description
  Other cities, towns, etc., A-Z
    Lyon
      History (General)
        By period -- Continued

801.L966	Early
801.L967	Medieval and early modern
801.L968	Modern
	Biography and memoirs
801.L9682	Collective
801.L9683.A-Z	Individual, A-Z
	Mans, Le see DC801.L48+
801.M34-.M38	Marseille
801.M34	Periodicals. Societies. Serials
801.M345	Sources and documents
801.M35	Directories, etc.
801.M355	Antiquities
801.M36	History and description
801.M37	By period
801.M38	Special topics (not A-Z)
801.M54	Mentone (Menton)
801.M65	Metz
801.M7515	Mont-Saint-Michel
801.M93	Mulhouse
801.N16	Nancy
801.N2	Nantes
801.N68	Nice
801.N71-.N72	Nîmes
801.N71	Periodicals. Sources and documents
801.N72	General works. History. Description and travel
	Including biography, civilization, social life and customs, etc.
801.O6-.O64	Orléans
801.O6	Periodicals. Sources and documents
801.O63	General works. Description and travel. Guidebooks
801.O64	History
801.P32	Pau
801.P77	Poitiers
801.R16	Rambouillet
801.R35-.R36	Reims
801.R35	Periodicals. Serials. Sources and documents. Congresses
801.R36	General works. Description and travel. History
	Including biography, guidebooks, antiquities, social life and customs, civilization
	Rochelle, La see DC801.L43
801.R84-.R86	Rouen (Table D-DR12)

Local history and description
Other cities, towns, etc., A-Z -- Continued

801.S1003	Sablé-sur-Sarthe
801.S11-.S12	Saint A
	e.g.
801.S113	Saint-Antoine-de-Viennois (Isère)
801.S121-.S14	Saint B
801.S141-.S158	Saint C
	e.g.
801.S141	Saint-Calais
801.S15	Saint-Cloud
801.S159-.S17	Saint D
	e.g.
801.S16	Saint-Denis
801.S168	Saint-Dizier
801.S171-.S175	Saint E
	e.g.
801.S173	Saint-Etienne (Loire)
801.S176-.S185	Saint F
	e.g.
801.S18	Saint-Florent-lès-Saumur
801.S186-.S195	Saint G
	e.g.
801.S19	Saint-Germain-en-Laye
801.S192	Saint-Gilles
801.S196-.S2	Saint H
801.S201-.S205	Saint I
801.S206-.S21	Saint J
	e.g.
801.S207	Saint-Jean d'Angély
801.S211-.S212	Saint K
801.S213-.S23	Saint L
801.S231-.S25	Saint M
	e.g.
801.S234-.S235	Saint-Malo
801.S251-.S27	Saint N
801.S271-.S275	Saint O
	e.g.
801.S273	Saint-Omer
801.S276-.S285	Saint P
801.S286-.S29	Saint Q
	e.g.
801.S288	Saint-Quentin (Aisne)
801.S291-.S3	Saint R
801.S301-.S32	Saint S
	e.g.
801.S304	Saint-Sauveur-en-Rue

	Local history and description
	Other cities, towns, etc., A-Z -- Continued
801.S321-.S335	Saint T
801.S336	Saint U
801.S337-.S35	Saint V
801.S351	Saint W
801.S353	Saint X
801.S355	Saint Y
801.S357	Saint Z
801.S365	Sainte-Menehould
801.S3655	Saintes
801.S3664	Saïx
801.S443	Sélestat
801.S5	Sens-sur-Yonne
801.S65	Soissons
801.S77	Strasbourg
801.T72	Toulon
801.T724-.T726	Toulouse (Table D-DR12)
801.T74	Tours
801.T86-.T87	Troyes
801.T86	Periodicals. Serials. Sources and documents. Congresses
801.T87	General works. Description and travel. History
	Including biography, guidebooks, antiquities, social life and customs, civilization
801.V45	Verdun
801.V55-.V57	Versailles. Trianons (Table D-DR12)
	Vésinet, Le see DC801.L6462
(900)	French colonies
	Collective see JV1800+
	Individual colonies
	see subclasses D-F
	Andorra
921	Periodicals. Societies. Serials
922	Sources and documents
923	Directories. Dictionaries
924	General works. Description and travel
	For 20th century description and travel see DC928
925	History (General)
	By period
926	Early
927	Medieval and early modern
928	Modern
930	Special topics (not A-Z)
932.A-Z	Local history and description, A-Z
	e. g.
932.C35	Canillo Parish

	Andorra
	Local history and description, A-Z -- Continued
932.S35	Sant Julia de Loria
	Monaco
941	Periodicals. Societies. Serials
942	Sources and documents
	Biography
943.A1	Collective
943.A2-Z	Individual, A-Z
	e.g.
943.G7	Grace, Princess of Monaco, 1929-1982
943.G74	Grimaldi family
943.M6	Monaco, Catherine Charlotte de Gramont, princesse de
943.R3	Rainier III, Prince of Monaco, 1923-
945	General works. History and description
946	Monte Carlo
947	Other special
	Nice see DC801.N68

DD

Ethnography

    Individual elements in the population, A-Z -- Continued

78.I73	Iraqis
78.I77	Italians
78.K67	Koreans
78.K87	Kurds
78.L37	Latvians
78.M3	Marcomanni
	Cf. DD801.B348 Races of Bavaria
78.M64	Moldavians
78.M67	Moroccans
78.M87	Muslims
78.O24	Obodrites
78.P64	Poles
78.P67	Portuguese
78.R65	Romanians
78.R86	Russian Germans
78.R87	Russians
78.S27	Savoyards
78.S3	Saxons
78.S46	Senegalese
78.S5	Slavs
78.S6	Sorbs. Wends
78.S7	South Asians
78.S8	Suevi
78.S93	Swedes
78.T45	Thais
78.T87	Turks
78.U3	Ubii
78.U47	Ukrainians
78.V54	Vietnamese
	Wends see DD78.S6
78.W5	Westphalians

Germans in foreign countries (General) see DD68

History

84	Dictionaries. Chronological tables, outlines, etc.
	Biography (Collective)
	For individual biography, see special period, reign, or place
85	General works
85.2	Women
85.4	Public men
85.6	Rulers, emperors, etc.
85.7	Queens, princesses, etc.
85.8.A-Z	Houses, noble families, etc., A-Z
	e.g.
85.8.L4	Leiningen, House of
	Historiography

DD

History
By period
Early and medieval to 1519
Medieval Empire, 481-1273
Hohenstaufen period, 1125-1273
Friedrich II, 1215-1250 -- Continued

152.5	Heinrich Raspe IV, von Thüringen, 1246-1247
153	Wilhelm von Holland
154	Konrad IV, 1250-1254
155	Interregnum, 1254-1273. League of the Rhine cities, 1254

Houses of Habsburg and Luxemburg, 1273-1519

156.A2	Sources and documents
156.A3-Z	General works
157	General special
158.A-Z	Biography, A-Z
	e.g.
158.B3	Berthold VII, Count of Henneberg
159	Rudolf I, 1273-1291
160	Adolf, 1292-1298
161	Albrecht I, 1298-1308
162	Heinrich VII, 1308-1313
	Ludwig IV (der Baier), 1314-1347
163	General works on life and reign
163.5	General special
164	Friedrich III der Schöne, 1314-1330
165	Karl IV, 1347-1378
166	Günther, 1349
167	Wenzel, 1378-1400
168	Ruprecht, 1400-1410
169	Jobst, 1410-1411
	Sigismund, 1411-1437
170	General works on life and reign
170.3	General special
	1438-1519. 15th century
171.A2	Sources and documents
171.A3-Z	General works
171.5.A-Z	Biography, A-Z
	e.g.
171.5.R2	Rechberg, Hans von
172	Albrecht II, 1438-1439
	Friedrich III (IV), 1440-1493
173	General works on life and reign
173.5	General special
	Maximilian I, 1493-1519
174	General works on life and reign
174.3	General special

History
  By period
    Modern, 1519-
      1519-1648. Reformation and Counter-reformation
        Maximilian II, 1564-1576 -- Continued

186.5	General special
187	Rudolf II, 1576-1612
187.8	Matthias, 1612-1637
188	Ferdinand II, 1619-1637
	For his reign see DD189
188.5	Ferdinand III, 1637-1657
	Class here biography only
	For his reign see DD189
188.7	Ferdinand IV, 1653-1654
	Including election, biography, etc.
189	Period of the Thirty Years' War, 1618-1648
	For the war itself see D251+
	1648-1740
190.A2	Sources and documents
190.A3-Z	General works
	Biography and memoirs
190.3.A1	Collective
190.3.A2-Z	Individual, A-Z
	e.g.
190.3.J6	Josef Clemens, Abp. and Elector of Cologne
190.3.K4	Karl Ludwig, Elector Palatine
190.3.M3	Manteuffel, Ernst Christoph, graf von
190.35	1648-1658
190.4	1658-1705
	For biography of Leopold I see DB67+
190.6	1705-1711
	For biography of Joseph I see DB68+
190.8	1711-1740
	For biography of Karl VI see DB69+
	1740-1789. 18th century
191	Sources and documents
	Biography and memoirs
192.A1	Collective
192.A2-Z	Individual, A-Z
	e.g.
192.L4	Laukhard, Friedrich Christian
192.M6	Möser, Justus
192.S29	Schönborn, Friedrich Karl, graf von, bp.
193	General works
193.5	Social life and customs. Civilization. Intellectual life
194	Karl VII, 1742-1745
195	Franz I, 1745-1765

	History
	By period
	Modern, 1519-
	1740-1789. 18th century -- Continued
196	1765-1790
	For biography of Joseph II see DB74+
	1789-1815. French Revolutionary and Napoleonic period
197	General works
	Cf. DC139+ France, 1789-1815
197.5	Political and diplomatic history
	1789-1806
198	General works
198.4	1790-1792
	For biography of Leopold II see DB74.8
198.7	1792-1806
	For biography of Franz II see DB81
199	1806-1815
	Including Confederation of the Rhine, 1806-1813, etc.
	19th century
201	Sources and documents
203	General works
204	General special
	Biography and memoirs
205.A2	Collective
205.A3-Z	Individual, A-Z
	e.g.
205.B6	Blum, Robert
	Dahlberg, Karl Theodor von see DD205.K3
205.G6	Görres, Johann Joseph von
205.H7	Hohenlohe-Schillingsfürst, Chlodwig Karl V., fürst
	zu
205.J3	Jahn, Friedrich Ludwig
205.K3	Karl Theodor, Abp. and Elector of Mainz
205.K7	Krupp, Alfred
205.W4	Windthorst, Ludwig Josef F.G.
206	1815-1848
	1848-1849
207	General works
207.5	Special aspects
208	Prussia and Berlin
208.5	Other
209.A-Z	Local, A-Z
	1850-1871
210	General works
211.A-Z	Biography and memoirs, A-Z
	e.g.
211.J2	Jacoby, Johann

DD

History
By period
Modern, 1519-
New Empire, 1871-1918 -- Continued
222	General special
	Wilhelm I, 1871-1888
223	General works on life and reign
	Cf. DD225 Political history of reign
223.7	Augusta, Consort of William I
223.8	Other members of royal family
223.9	Special topics
	Including Drei-kaiser-jahr (1888); Elise Radziwill, Polish princess; war scare of 1875; etc.

DD

	Friedrich III, 1888
224	General works on life and reign
224.3	Writings, speeches, diaries, etc.
224.6	Illness
224.8	Pamphlets, etc.
224.9	Victoria, Consort of Frederick III
224.92	Henry, Prince of Prussia
224.95	Victoria, Princess of Prussia
225	Political history, Wilhelm I and Friedrich III
226	Special topics
	Including courts and courtiers
	Kulturkampf see DD118
	Wilhelm II, 1888-1918
228	General works on reign
228.2	General special
228.3	Social life and customs. Civilization. The court
228.5	Political history
228.6	Diplomatic history
	Individual countries see DD120.A+
228.8	Period of World War I, 1914-1918
	For the war itself see D501+
228.9	Abdication and flight of Wilhelm II
	Biography
	Wilhelm II
229	General works
229.1	Letters (Collections). By imprint date
229.2	Portraits, caricatures, etc.
229.3	Speeches (Collective and individual), etc.
	Alphabetically by title
229.5	Pamphlets, etc.
	Imperial family
229.6	General works
229.7	Auguste Viktoria, Consort of Wilhelm II
229.8.A-Z	Other members of family, A-Z

History
By period
Modern, 1519-
20th century
Revolution and Republic, 1918-
By period
Hitler, 1933-1945. National socialism
The Nazi Party (Nationalsozialistische Deutsche
Arbeiter-Partei) -- Continued

253.2	Serials. Party documents. By title
	Including serials entered under the party name
	without subheading
253.25	General works
	Including party organization
	Party meetings (Reichsparteitage)
253.27	General works
253.28	Individual meetings. By date
	Meetings were held in 1923, 1926, 1927, 1929,
	1933-1938
	Administrative offices of the party
253.29	General works
253.3.A-Z	Individual offices, A-Z
	By subhead descriptive of the Reich, if
	possible
	Offices are variously styled Ämter,
	Beauftragte, Dienststellungen,
	Hauptämter, Institute, Kanzleien,
	Kommissionen, Reichsführungen,
	Reichsleitungen, etc.
	For works where subject matter is not
	dominated by party interests, see the
	subject
	Territorial divisions of the party, its
	Hoheitsgebiete
253.39	General works
253.4.A-Z	By Gau, A-Z
	Under each Gau:
	.A1 Serials. Collections
	.A5-.Z General works
	e.g.
253.4.B3	Gau Baden
253.4.B3A1	Serials. Collections
253.4.B3A2-.B3Z	General works
	Auslandsorganisation
	Rated as a Gau
253.412	Arbeitsbereich. General government
253.413	Landesgruppen

History
  By period
    Modern, 1519-
      20th century
        Revolution and Republic, 1918-
          By period
            Hitler, 1933-1945. National socialism
              The Nazi Party (Nationalsozialistische Deutsche
                Arbeiter-Partei)
                Territorial divisions of the party, its
                  Hoheitsgebiete -- Continued

253.42.A-Z	By Kreis, A-Z
	Under each Kreis:
	.A1 Serials. Collections
253.43.A-Z	By Ortsgruppe, A-Z
	Under each Ortsgruppe:
	.A1 Serials. Collections
253.44.A-Z	By Zelle, A-Z
	Under each Zelle:
	.A1 Serials. Collections
253.45.A-Z	By Block, A-Z
	Under each Block:
	.A1 Serials. Collections
253.46	Branches of the party, its Gliederungen
	Individual formations
	Bund der Jungmädel
253.47.A1	Serials. Collections
253.47.A2-Z	General works
	Bund Deutscher Mädel
253.48.A1	Serials. Collections
253.48.A2-Z	General works
	Deutsches Jungvolk
253.49.A1	Serials. Collections
253.49.A2-Z	General works
	Dozentenbuch see L33
	Frauenschaft see DD253.58.A1+
	Hitler-Jugend
	Cf. HQ799.A+ Youth of Germany
253.5.A1	Serials. Collections
253.5.A2-Z	General works
253.53.A-Z	Local, A-Z
	Kraftfahrerkorps
253.56.A1	Serials. Collections
253.56.A2-Z	General works
	Marinesturmabteilung see DD253.73
	Nationalsozialistische Frauenschaft
253.58.A1	Serials. Collections

History
  By period
    Modern, 1519-
      20th century
        Revolution and Republic, 1918-
          By period
            Hitler, 1933-1945. National socialism
              The Nazi Party (Nationalsozialistische Deutsche
                Arbeiter-Partei)
                Branches of the party, its Gliederungen
                  Individual formations
                    Nationalsozialistische Frauenschaft --
                      Continued

253.58.A2-Z	General works
	Dozentenbuch see L33
	Schutzstaffel
253.6.A1	Serials. Collections
253.6.A2-Z	General works
	Local
253.62.A-Z	By key word, A-Z
	e.g.
253.62.R5	Rhine
253.63	By number, A-Z
	e.g.
253.63 39th	39th
	Waffenschutzstaffel
	Cf. D757.85 World War II
253.65.A1	Serials. Collections
253.65.A2-Z	General works
	Studentenbund see LA729.A1+
253.7	Sturmabteilung
253.73	Marinesturmabteilung
253.76	Affiliated organizations not elsewhere provided for
253.8.A-Z	Individual organizations. By key word, A-Z
	e.g.
253.8.K7	Kriegerbund
253.8.S8	Stahlhelm
	Propaganda in other countries
254	General works
255.A-Z	Individual regions or countries, A-Z
(256)	Period of World War II, 1939-1945
	see D731+ for the war itself; DD253 for contemporary works on the Hitler period; DD256.45+ for postwar works on the Hitler period

History
  By period
    Modern, 1519-
      20th century
        Revolution and Republic, 1918-
          By period
            Hitler, 1933-1945. National socialism -- Continued
              Resistance movements against National Socialist
                regime

256.3	General works
256.35	Assassination attempts against Hitler
256.4.A-Z	Local, A-Z
	Postwar works on the Hitler period
	For contemporary works on the Hitler period see DD253.A1+
256.45	Periodicals. Societies. Serials
256.46	Congresses
	Sources and documents see DD253.A1+
256.47	Dictionaries
256.48	Historiography
256.49	Study and teaching
256.5	General works
256.6	Social life and customs. Civilization. Intellectual life
256.7	Political history
256.8	Foreign and general relations
	Biography and memoirs see DD243+
	Propaganda see DD254
	Resistance movements see DD256.3+
	Period of Allied occupation, 1945-1990
257.A1	Periodicals. Societies
257.A2-Z	General works
257.2	General special
257.25	Reunification question
257.4	Political and diplomatic history
	Biography and memoirs see DD243+
	West Germany
258	Periodicals. Societies. Serials
258.2	Congresses
258.23	Gazetteers. Dictionaries, etc.
258.24	Directories
258.25	Guidebooks
258.3	General works
258.35	Pictorial works
	Description and travel
258.39	History of travel
258.4	Through 1980

	West Germany
	Description and travel -- Continued
258.42	1981-
258.45	Antiquities
	For local antiquities see DD801.A+
	Ethnography
258.5	General works
258.55.A-Z	Individual elements in the population, A-Z
258.55.E35	Egyptians
258.55.G74	Greeks
258.55.P64	Poles
258.55.P67	Portuguese
258.55.R87	Russian Germans
258.55.T87	Turks
258.55.V53	Vietnamese
258.55.Y83	Yugoslavs
	History
	Periodicals. Societies. Serials see DD258
258.6	Biography (Collective)
258.7	General works
258.75	Political history
	Foreign and general relations
	For general works on the diplomatic history of a period, see the period
	For works on relations with a specific country regardless of the period see DD258.85.A+
258.8	General works
258.85.A-Z	Relations with individual regions or countries, A-Z
	By period
258.9	Through 1949
	Konrad Adenauer, 1949-1963
	For biography of Adenauer see DD259.7.A+
259	General works on life and administration
259.2	General special
259.25	Social life and customs. Civilization. Intellectual life
259.4	Political history
259.5	Foreign and general relations
	Biography and memoirs
259.63	Collective
259.7.A-Z	Individual, A-Z
	1963-
260	General works
260.2	General special
260.3	Social life and customs. Civilization. Intellectual life
260.4	Political history
260.5	Foreign and general relations
	Biography and memoirs

Prussia
  History
    By period
      Modern, 1640-
        18th century
          Friedrich II der Grosse, 1740-1786 -- Continued

403	General works on reign
403.8	General special
	Biography
404	Friedrich II
404.5	Elisabeth Christine
404.7	Friedrich II in literature and art
	Works
	Complete and posthumous works
405	In French. By editor or date
405.1	In German
	By editor or date
405.12	In English
	By editor or date
	Political correspondence
405.2	In French
	By editor or date
405.22	In German
	By editor or date
405.23	In English
	By editor or date
	Selections (not confined to any one subject elsewhere classified)
405.3	In French
	By editor or date
405.32	In German
	By editor or date
405.33	In English
	By editor or date
405.34	In other languages (not A-Z)
	By editor or date
	Memoirs
405.5	In French
	By editor or date
405.52	In German
	By editor or date
405.53	In English
	By editor or date
	Correspondence (other than political)
405.6	In French
	By editor or date

Prussia
  History
    By period
      Modern, 1640-
        18th century
          Friedrich II der Grosse, 1740-1786
            Works
              Correspondence (other than political) --
                Continued
405.62   In German
                By editor or date
405.63   In English
                By editor or date
405.8   Doubtful and spurious
                By title and date
            Silesian wars, 1740-1745
406   General works
406.5   Diplomatic history
407.A-Z   Special events, battles, etc., A-Z
407.F8   Füssen, Treaty of, 1745
407.H7   Hohenfriedeberg, Battle of, 1745
407.K4   Kesselsdorf, Battle of, 1745
407.S65   Soor, Battle of, 1745
407.5   Peace of Dresden, 1745
                Cf. DD801.S398 Saxony
            Austrian succession, 1740-1748
              see DB72
408   1745-1756
            Seven Years' War, 1756-1763
                Cf. DA500 England during Seven Years' War
                Cf. DC133+ France under Louis XV, 1715-1774
409   Sources and documents
410.A-Z   Memoirs of contemporaries, A-Z
                Cf. DD402.A1+ Biography of contemporaries,
                  1740-1786
411   General works
411.5   General special
412   Pamphlets, etc.
                Cf. DA67+ English military history (18th
                  century)
                Cf. DA503 English pamphlets, 1714-1760
412.6.A-Z   Special events, battles, etc., A-Z
412.6.H7   Hochkirch, Battle of, 1758
412.6.K8   Kunersdorf, Battle of, 1759
412.6.L6   Leuthen, Battle of, 1757
412.6.M55   Minden, Battle of, 1759
412.6.P7   Prague, Battle of, 1757

Prussia
History
By period
Modern, 1640-
18th century
Friedrich II der Grosse, 1740-1786
Seven Years' War, 1756-1763
Special events, battles, etc., A-Z -- Continued

412.6.R7	Rossbach, Battle of, 1757
412.6.T6	Torgau, Battle of, 1760
412.8	Peace of Hubertsburg, 1763
	For Treaty of Paris see D297+
413	1763-1778
413.2	1778-1786
	Friedrich Wilhelm II, 1786-1797
414	General works on life and reign
414.9.A-Z	Biography and memoirs of contemporaries, A-Z
	e.g.
414.9.L5	Lichtenau, Wilhelmine (Enke), gräfin von
414.9.L6	Louis Ferdinand, Prince of Prussia
	19th century
415	Sources and documents
416.A-Z	Biography and memoirs, A-Z
	e.g.
	Cf. DD205.A2+ German 19th century biography
416.B3	Bernhardi, Theodor von
416.B4	Bernstorff, Albrecht, graf von
416.B8	Bunsen, Christian Karl J., freiherr von
416.R2	Radziwill, Luise, ksiezna
416.S8	Stein, Heinrich Friedrich K., freiherr vom und zum
417	General works
	1789-1815. Period of the French Revolution
	Cf. DC139+ French Revolutionary and
	Napoleonic period
418	Sources and documents
	Biography and memoirs
418.6.A2	Collective
418.6.A3-Z	Individual, A-Z
	e.g.
418.6.B6	Blücher, Gebhard Leberecht von
418.6.B7	Boyen, Hermann von
418.6.G6	Gneisenau, August Wilhelm A., graf Neithardt von
418.6.S3	Scharnhorst, Gerhard Johann D. Von
418.6.S33	Schill, Ferdinand Baptista von
418.6.Y7	Yorck von Wartenburg, Hans David L., graf
419	General works

Prussia

History

By period

Modern, 1640-

19th century

1789-1815. Period of the French Revolution --
Continued

Military history see DC236+

Friedrich Wilhelm III, 1797-1840

420	General works on life and reign
	Biography and memoirs
421	Friedrich Wilhelm III
421.3	Luise, Consort of Frederick William III
421.4	Auguste, Princess of Liegnitz, Consort of Frederick William III
422.A-Z	Contemporaries, A-Z
	e.g.
	Cf. DD205.A2+ German 19th century biography
422.C5	Clausewitz, Karl von
422.H2	Hardenberg, Karl August, Fürst von
422.H8	Humboldt, Wilhelm, Freiherr von
422.M35	Marwitz, Friedrich August L. von der
423	Confederation, 1816-1866
	Friedrich Wilhelm IV, 1840-1861
424	General works on reign
424.3	Pamphlets, etc.
	Biography and memoirs
424.8	Friedrich Wilhelm IV
424.9.A-Z	Contemporaries, A-Z
	e.g.
	Cf. DD205.A2+ German 19th century biography
424.9.F7	Friedrich Karl, Prince of Prussia
424.9.H2	Hansemann, David Justus L.
424.9.M2	Manteuffel, Edwin Karl R., freiherr von
	Wilhelm I, 1861-1888
425	General works on reign as king of Prussia
	Biography see DD223+
	Biography and memoirs of contemporaries see DD219.A+
429	General special
431	Prussia during the war with Denmark, 1864
	For general works on the war see DL236+
	Austro-Prussian War, 1866
436	Sources and documents
437.A-Z	Memoirs and reminiscences, A-Z
438	General works

Local history and description
Larger geographic divisions
Northeast -- Continued

711	Periodicals. Societies. Serials
714	General works. Description and travel. Guidebooks
714.5	Antiquities
714.7	Social life and customs. Civilization. Intellectual life
	History
715	General works
	By period
716	Early and medieval
717	16th-18th centuries
718	19th-20th centuries
719	Special topics (not A-Z)
721-729	Northwest
	Including North Sea Region
721	Periodicals. Societies. Serials
724	General works. Description and travel. Guidebooks
724.5	Antiquities
724.7	Social life and customs. Civilization. Intellectual life
	History
725	General works
	By period
726	Early and medieval
727	16th-18th centuries
728	19th-20th centuries
729	Special topics (not A-Z)
	Eastern see DD280+
	West see DD258+
781-789	Southern
781	Periodicals. Societies. Serials
784	General works. Description and travel. Guidebooks
784.5	Antiquities
784.7	Social life and customs. Civilization. Intellectual life
784.8	Ethnography
	History
785	General works
	By period
786	Early and medieval
787	16th-18th centuries
788	19th-20th centuries
801.A-Z	States, provinces, regions, etc., A-Z
801.A28	Allgäu Alps
801.A44	Alps, Bavarian
801.A47	Ammersee
801.A48	Amrum
801.A53	Angeln

Local history and description
States, provinces, regions, etc., A-Z -- Continued

801.A7-.A79	Anhalt (Table D-DR13)
801.A85	Ansbach
801.B1-.B19	Baden (Table D-DR13)
801.B23-.B239	Baden-Württemberg (Table D-DR13 modified)

        Established in 1952 by the reunion of Württemberg and
            Baden which in 1945 had been divided into three parts
            named Württemberg-Baden, Württemberg-Hohenzollern,
            and Baden

801.B23	Periodicals. Societies. Serials
801.B231	This number not used
801.B24	Bamburg
801.B25	Bardengau
801.B31-.43	Bavaria (Bayern)
801.B31	Periodicals. Societies. Serials
801.B32	Sources and documents
801.B322	Collections
801.B33	Gazetteers. Dictionaries, etc.
801.B335	Biography (Collective)
	Including House of Wittelsbach
801.B34	General works. Description and travel
801.B345	Antiquities
801.B347	Social life and customs. Civilization
801.B348	Ethnography
801.B35	History
	By period
801.B36	Earliest to 1180
801.B361	Individual rulers. By date of accession
801.B362	Wittelsbach period, 1180-1508
801.B365	Individual rulers. By date of accession
801.B37	1508-1806
801.B371	Wilhelm IV, 1508-1550
801.B372	Albrecht V, 1550-1579
801.B3725	Wilhelm V, 1579-1597
801.B373	Maximilian I, 1597-1651
801.B3733	Ferdinand Maria, 1651-1679
801.B3735	Maximilian II, 1679-1726
801.B3738	Karl Albrecht, 1726-1745
801.B374	Maximilian III, 1745-1777
801.B375	Karl Theodor, 1777-1799
801.B376	Bavarian succession, 1778-1779
801.B377A-.B377Z	Biography and memoirs of contemporaries, 1508-1799, A-Z
	1792-1815 see DD801.B381
801.B378	19th century
	Maximilian I, 1799/1806-1825

Local history and description
  States, provinces, regions, etc., A-Z
    Bavaria (Bayern)
      History
        By period
          19th century
            Maximilian I, 1799/1806-1825 -- Continued

801.B38	General works on life and reign
801.B381	1792/1799-1815
801.B382	Ludwig I, 1825-1848
801.B383A-.B383Z	Biography and memoirs of contemporaries, 1806-1848, A-Z
801.B385	Maximilian II, 1848-1864
801.B387	Ludwig II, 1864-1886
801.B39	Luitpold, 1886-1912
801.B395	Biography and memoirs of contemporaries, 1848-1912, A-Z
801.B397	20th century
801.B4	Ludwig III, 1912-1918
801.B41	Period of World War I, 1914-1918
801.B42	1919-1945
801.B422	Period of World War II, 1939-1945
801.B423	Period of Allied occupation, 1945-
801.B43A-.B43Z	Biography and memoirs, A-Z
	e.g.
801.B43R8	Rupprecht, Crown Prince of Bavaria
801.B44-.B449	Bavaria, Lower (Table D-DR13)
801.B45-.B459	Bavaria, Upper (Table D-DR13)
	Bavarian Alps see DD801.A44
	Bayern see DD801.B31+
801.B47	Berg (Duchy)
801.B48	Bergisches Land
801.B63-.B64	Black Forest (Schwarzwald)
801.B63	Periodicals. Serials. Sources and documents. Congresses
801.B64	General works. Description and travel. History
	Including antiquities, social life and customs, civilization, biography
	Bodensee see DD801.C7+
801.B68-.B689	Brandenburg (Table D-DR13)
801.B7-.B79	Breisgau (Table D-DR13)
801.B793	Bremen
801.B8-.B89	Brunswick (Table D-DR13)
801.C48	Chiemgau
801.C7-.C79	Constance, Lake, and adjacent territory (Table D-DR13)
	Including Bishopric
801.C83	Cottbus (Bezirk)

Local history and description

States, provinces, regions, etc., A-Z -- Continued

801.D56-.D562	Dithmarschen
801.D56	Periodicals. Serials. Sources and documents. Congresses
801.D562	General works. Description and travel. History Including antiquities, social life and customs, civilization, biography
801.D74	Dresden (Bezirk)
801.D85	Düren
801.D86	Düsseldorf (Regierungsbezirk)
801.E23	East Friesland (Ostfriesland) Including East Frisian Islands
801.E25	Eider River and Valley
801.E26	Eiderstedt (Germany)
801.E272	Eifel
801.E3	Elbe River (General, and Germany) For Elbe River in Czechoslovakia see DB2500.L33
801.E462	Ems River and Valley
801.E72	Erfurt (Bezirk)
801.E772	Erzgebirge (Ore Mountains)
801.F45	Fichtelgebirge
801.F5	Finkenwärder
801.F53	Fläming
801.F55	Fohr Island
801.F56-.F569	Franconia (Franken) (Table D-DR13)
801.F57	Franconia, Lower
801.F573	Franconia, Middle
801.F575	Franconia, Upper
	Franken see DD801.F56+
801.F63	Frankenwald
801.F64	Frankfurt an der Oder (Bezirk)
801.F661-.F662	Fränkische Schweiz
801.F661	Periodicals. Societies. Museums
801.F662	General works. Description and travel. History Including antiquities, social life and customs, civilization, biography
	Friesland, East see DD801.E23
	Friesland, North see DD801.N56
801.G4	Gera (Bezirk)
	Glatz (Grafschaft). Klodzko see DK4600.K53+
801.G64	Göppingen (Bezirk)
801.H14	Halle (Bezirk)
801.H15	Hallig Island
	Hamburg see DD901.H2+
801.H16	Hanau-Lichtenberg
801.H164-.H1649	Hanover (Table D-DR13)

Local history and description
States, provinces, regions, etc., A-Z -- Continued

801.H17-.H25	Hansa towns. Hanseatic League
801.H17	Periodicals. Societies. Serials
801.H175	Congresses
801.H18	Sources and documents
801.H19	Gazetteers, directories, dictionaries, etc.
801.H2	General works. Description and travel. Guidebooks
	History
801.H21	General works
	By period
801.H22	Early and medieval
801.H23	16th-18th centuries
801.H24	19th-20th centuries
801.H25	Special topics (not A-Z)
801.H3-.H39	Harz Mountains (Table D-DR13)
801.H3982	Helgoland
801.H5-.H59	Hesse (Table D-DR13)
	Including Hesse (Grand Duchy), Hesse-Darmstadt, Hesse-Kassel, Hesse-Nassau, Nassau (Duchy), and Hesse-Homburg
801.H632	Hiddensee
801.H641	Hildesheim
801.H7	Hohenlohe
801.H742	Hohenzollern
	Hohes Venn see DH801.H35
801.H8	Hunsrück
801.J862	Julich
801.K34	Karl-Marx-Stadt (Bezirk)
801.K36	Karwendelgebrige
801.K38	Kassel (Bezirk)
801.K58	Klötze
801.K6	Könnigssee
801.K9	Kyffhäuser Mountains
801.L29	Landsberg am Lech
801.L36	Lauenberg
	Lausitz see DD801.L85+
801.L43	Lech River and Valley
801.L45	Leipzig (Bezirk)
801.L7-.L79	Lippe (Table D-DR13)
	Lower Bavaria see DD801.B44+
	Lower Franconia see DD801.F57
	Lower Saxony see DD801.N4
801.L82	Ludwigsburg
801.L83-.L839	Lüneburg (Regierungsbezirk). Lüneburg Heath (Lüneburger Heide) (Table D-DR13)
801.L85-.L859	Lusatia (Lausitz) (Table D-DR13)

Local history and description
States, provinces, regions, etc., A-Z -- Continued

801.L862	Lusatia, Lower
801.L872	Lusatia, Upper
801.M16	Magdeburg (Bezirk)
801.M2	Main River and Valley
801.M3-.M39	Mecklenburg-Vorpommern. Mecklenburg (Table D-DR13)
	Including Mecklenburg-Schwerin
801.M5	Mecklenburg-Strelitz
	Middle Franconia see DD801.F573
801.M66	Moers
801.M7	Moselle River and Valley
	Cf. DC611.M897+ France
801.M952	Münsterland
801.N3	Nahe River and Valley
	Nassau (Duchy) see DD801.H5+
801.N35	Neckar River and Valley
801.N37	Neubrandenburg (Bezirk)
801.N4	Niedersachsen (Lower Saxony)
801.N56	North Friesland (Nordfriesland)
	Including North Frisian Islands
801.N6	North Rhine-Westphalia
801.O24	Oberbergischer Kreis
	Oberpfalz see DD801.P5
801.O3	Odenwald
	Oder-Neisse area see DK4600.O33+
801.O42-.O43	Oldenburg
801.O42	Periodicals. Serials. Sources and documents. Congresses
801.O43	General works. Description and travel. History
	Including antiquities, social life and customs, civilization, biography
	Ore Mountains see DD801.E772
801.O84	Osnabrück (District)
801.P4-.P49	Palatinate (Pfalz). Rhineland Palatinate (Table D-DR13)
801.P5	Palatinate, Upper
	Pfalz see DD801.P4+
801.P66	Potsdam (Bezirk)
801.R12	Rappoltstein
801.R15	Ratzeburg
801.R2	Regnitz River and Valley
801.R3	Reuss (Elder line)
801.R4	Reuss (Younger line)
801.R682	Rhine Province. Rhineland
	Rhine River and Valley
801.R7	Periodicals. Societies. Serials

Local history and description
    States, provinces, regions, etc., A-Z
        Rhine River and Valley -- Continued

801.R713	Museums, exhibitions, etc.
	Subarrange by author
801.R718	Biography (Collective)
801.R725	Social life and customs. Civilization. Intellectual life
801.R74	General works. Description and travel. Guidebooks.
	Geography
	History
801.R744	General works
	By period
801.R745	Early and medieval
801.R748	16th-18th centuries
801.R75	19th-20th centuries
801.R76	Special topics (not A-Z)
	Rhineland Palatinate see DD801.P4+
801.R78	Rhön
801.R796	Rosenheim
801.R797	Rostock (Bezirk)
801.R7982	Rügen (Island)
801.R8	Ruhr River and Valley
801.S13-.S139	Saar River and Valley (Table D-DR13 modified)
801.S13	Periodicals. Societies. Serials
801.S131	This number not used
801.S14-.S149	Saarland (Table D-DR13)
	Sächsische Schweiz see DD801.S281
801.S1672	Sauerland
801.S17	Saxe-Altenburg
801.S2-.S21	Saxe-Coburg-Gotha
801.S2	Periodicals. Sources and documents. Collections
801.S21	History
801.S23	Saxe-Meiningen
801.S26	Saxe-Weimar (-Eisenach)
801.S281	Saxon Switzerland (Sächsische Schweiz)
	Cf. DB2500.E53 Elbe Sandstone Rocks
801.S31-.S46	Saxony
	Including Saxony-Anhalt
801.S31	Periodicals. Societies. Serials
801.S32	Sources and documents
801.S322	Collections
801.S33	Gazetteers, dictionaries, etc.
801.S34	General works. Description and travel
801.S345	Antiquities
801.S347	Social life and customs. Civilization
801.S348	Ethnography
801.S35	History

Local history and description
States, provinces, regions, etc., A-Z
Saxony
History
801.S352	General special
801.S354	Military history
801.S357	Reigning houses, etc.
	By period
801.S36	Early and medieval
801.S361	Earliest to 806
801.S362	806-1089
801.S364	1089-1288
801.S367	Individual reigns. By date
801.S37	1288-1485
801.S375	Individual reigns. By date
801.S38	1485-1694
801.S382	Friedrich III, 1486-1525
801.S383	Johann, 1525-1532
801.S384	Johann Friedrich, 1532-1547
801.S386	Moritz, 1547-1553
801.S387	August, 1553-1586
801.S388	Christian I, 1586-1591
801.S389	Christian II, 1591-1611
801.S39	Johann Georg I, 1611-1656
801.S392	Johann Georg II, III, IV, 1656-1694
801.S393	Modern
801.S394	1694-1763
	Friedrich August I, 1694-1733
801.S395	General works on life and reign
	Cf. DK4315 Reign in Poland
801.S396	General special
	Friedrich August II, 1733-1763
801.S397	General works on life and reign
	Cf. DK4325 Reign in Poland
801.S398	General special
801.S399	Friedrich Christian, 1763
801.S4A-.S4Z	Biography and memoirs of contemporaries, A-Z
	e.g.
801.S4B7	Brühl, Heinrich Reichsgraf von
801.S4M3	Maria Antonia Walpurgis, Consort of Friedrich Christian
	Friedrich August I, 1763-1827
801.S401	General works on life and reign
801.S403	1763-1806
801.S405	1789-1806
801.S406	1806-1815/1827

Local history and description
  States, provinces, regions, etc., A-Z
    Saxony
      History
        By period
          Modern
            Friedrich August I, 1763-1827 -- Continued

801.S409A-.S409Z	Biography and memoirs of contemporaries, A-Z
	e.g.
801.S409F8	Funck, Karl Wilhelm F. von
801.S409O6	Oppel, Julius Wilhelm von
801.S41	1827-1902. 19th century
801.S412	Anton, 1827-1836
801.S414	Friedrich August II, 1836-1854
801.S416	Johann, 1854-1873
801.S42	Albrecht, 1873-1902
801.S425	1902-1990. 20th century
801.S43	Georg, 1902-1904
801.S44	Frederick Augustus III, 1904-1918
	Including period of World War I
801.S45	Affair of Louisa of Tuscany, formerly Louise Antoinette Marie, Archduchess of Austria
801.S453	1919-1933. Free state in Weimar Republic
801.S455	1933-1945
801.S457	1945-1952
801.S458	1952-1990. Region in East Germany
801.S46	1990-
(801.S58)	Saxon Switzerland
	see DD801.S281
	Saxony, Lower see DD801.N4
801.S62-.S63	Schaumburg-Lippe
801.S63	General works. Description and travel. History
	Including antiquities, social life and customs, civilization, biography
801.S633-.S6339	Schleswig-Holstein (Table D-DR13)
	Schwaben see DD801.S942
801.S65	Schwarzburg-Rudolstadt
801.S68	Schwarzburg-Sondershausen
	Schwarzwald see DD801.B63+
801.S69	Schwerin (Bezirk)
801.S7	Siebengebirge
801.S8	Spessart Mountains
801.S82	Spree Forest
801.S83	Stade
801.S833	Staffelstein
801.S835	Starnberger See
801.S838	Steigerwald

Local history and description
    States, provinces, regions, etc., A-Z -- Continued

801.S86	Suhl (Bezirk)
801.S942	Swabia (Schwaben)
801.S96	Sylt
801.T27	Taunus Mountains
801.T3	Teck
801.T314	Tegernsee
	Teutoburger Wald see DD801.W5
801.T36	Tharandter Wald
801.T4-.T49	Thuringia (Thuringian States) (Table D-DR13)
801.T5	Thuringian Forest
801.T8	Tübingen (Grafschaft)
801.U5	Unstrut River and Valley
	Upper Bavaria see DD801.B45+
	Upper Franconia see DD801.F575
	Upper Lusatia see DD801.L872
	Upper Palatinate see DD801.P5
801.V7	Vogtland
	Vosges Mountains see DC645
801.W2-.W29	Waldeck (Table D-DR13)
	Warthegau see DK4600.W55+
801.W5	Weser Mountains. Weser River and Valley. Teutoburg Forest
	For the Battle of Teutoburger Wald see DD123
801.W53	Westerwald
801.W54-.W549	Westphalia (Table D-DR13)
801.W59	Wursten
801.W6-.W82	Württemberg
801.W6	Periodicals. Societies. Serials
801.W61	Sources and documents
	Collected works
801.W612	Several authors
801.W614	Individual authors
801.W62	Biography (Collective)
801.W625	Gazetteers. Dictionaries, etc.
801.W627	Guidebooks
801.W63	General works
	Description and travel
801.W634	Through 1800
801.W635	1801-1900
801.W636	1901-
801.W64	Monumental and picturesque
	Including castles, ruins, etc.
801.W645	Antiquities
801.W647	Social life and customs. Civilization
801.W648	Ethnography

	Local history and description
	States, provinces, regions, etc., A-Z
	Württemberg -- Continued
801.W65	History
801.W652	General special
801.W653	Pamphlets, etc.
801.W654	Military history
801.W656	Political history
801.W657	Reigning houses
	By period
	Early and medieval
801.W66	General works
801.W662	Earliest to 1241
801.W663A-.W663Z	Individual counts, A-Z
801.W664-.W688	1241-1495
	General works see DD801.W66+
801.W665	Ulrich I, 1241-1265
801.W666	Ulrich II, 1265-1279
801.W669	Eberhard I, 1265/1279-1325
801.W671	Ulrich III, 1325-1344
801.W673	Eberhard II, 1344-1392
801.W675	Ulrich IV, 1344-1366
801.W677	Eberhard III, 1392-1417
801.W678	Eberhard IV, 1417-1419
801.W68	1419-1482, Division and reunion
801.W683	Henriette, Consort of Eberhard IV
801.W684	Ludwig I, 1442-1450
801.W685	Ulrich V, 1442-1480
801.W686	Ludwig II der Jüngere, 1450-1457
801.W687	Eberhard II der Jüngere, 1480-1482
801.W688	Eberhard V (I as Duke), 1457-1496
	Modern
801.W69	1495-1806
801.W693	Eberhard II, 1496-1498
801.W694	Ulrich, 1498-1550
801.W696	Christoph, 1550-1568
801.W698	Ludwig, 1568-1593
801.W7	Friedrich I, 1593-1608
801.W702	Period of Thirty Years' War, 1618-1648
801.W704	Johann Friedrich, 1608-1628
801.W71	Eberhard III, 1628-1674
801.W713	Ludwig Friedrich, 1628-1633
801.W714	Julius Friedrich, 1628-1633
801.W717	Wilhelm Ludwig, 1674-1677
801.W72	Eberhard Ludwig, 1677-1733
801.W723	Friedrich Karl, 1677-1693
801.W725	Karl Alexander, 1733-1737

Local history and description
States, provinces, regions, etc., A-Z
Württemberg
History
By period
Modern
1495-1806 -- Continued

801.W73	Karl Eugen, 1737-1793
801.W734	Karl Rudolf, 1737-1738
801.W735	Friedrich Karl, 1738-1744
801.W737	Ludwig Eugen, 1793-1795
801.W738	Friedrich Eugen, 1795-1797
801.W739A-.W739Z	Biography and memoirs, A-Z
	e.g.
801.W739S7	Süss-Oppenheimer, Joseph
801.W74	19th-20th centuries
801.W745	Biography (Collective)
801.W75	Friedrich I, 1797-1816
	Wilhelm I, 1816-1864
801.W76	General works on life and reign
801.W762	Catharine, Consort of William I
	Cf. DK190.6.C2 Sister of Alexander I of Russia
801.W763	Pauline, Consort of William I
801.W764A-.W764Z	Biography and memoirs, A-Z
801.W765	1871-1917
801.W77	Karl I, 1864-1891
	Wilhelm II, 1891-1918
801.W78	General works on life and reign
801.W79	Period of World War I, 1914-1918
801.W8	1918-
	Class here works on the period of German Revolution, Republic, etc.
801.W82A-.W82Z	Biography and memoirs, A-Z
	e.g.
801.W82B55	Bolz, Eugene Anton
801.W82M3	Maier, Reinhold
	Berlin
851	Periodicals. Societies. Serials
852	Sources and documents
853	Collected works
854	Directories. Dictionaries
	Biography
857.A2	Collective
857.A3-Z	Individual, A-Z
859	Guidebooks
860	General works. Description

Local history and description

Bonn -- Continued

Sources and documents

900.25	Several authors
900.26	Individual authors
900.27	Directories. Dictionaries. Gazetteers
900.28	Guidebooks
900.29	General works
900.3	Description
900.33	Pictorial works
900.34	Antiquities
900.35	Social life and customs. Intellectual life. Civilization

History

900.38	Biography (Collective)
	For individual biography, see the specific period
900.4	General works

By period

900.42	Early and medieval
900.43	1519-1949
900.45	1949-

Sections, districts, suburbs, etc.

900.6	Collective
900.62.A-Z	Individual, A-Z

Streets. Bridges

900.7	Collective
900.72.A-Z	Individual, A-Z

Buildings

900.75	Collective
900.76.A-Z	Individual, A-Z

Other cities, towns, etc., A-Z

e.g.

901.A1	General
901.A25-.A26	Aachen (Aix-la-Chapelle) (Table D-DR14)
901.A283	Aalen
901.A28739	Aldenhoven
901.A35	Altenburg
901.A91-.A92	Augsburg (Table D-DR14)
901.B109	Bad Bentheim
901.B11255	Bad Endorf
	Bad Kissingen see DD901.K6
	Bad Nauheim see DD901.N25
901.B119	Bad Windsheim
901.B12-.B13	Baden (Table D-DR14)
901.B2	Bamberg
901.B4	Bayreuth
901.B443	Berchtesgaden
901.B4487	Betzenstein

Local history and description
Other cities, towns, etc., A-Z -- Continued

901.B56	Bochum
	Bonn see DD900.2+
901.B63	Bramstedt
901.B65	Brandenburg
	Braunschweig see DD901.B95
901.B7-.B79	Bremen (Table D-DR13)
901.B82	Bremerhaven
	Breslau see DK4780
901.B8914	Brückenau
901.B95	Brunswick (Braunschweig)
901.B9675	Buhlenberg
901.B9677	Buldern
901.B9678	Bühlstadt
901.B976	Burghausen
901.B9774	Burhave (Butjadingen)
901.C65	Coburg
	Colmar see DC801.C657
901.C7-.C79	Cologne (Köln) (Table D-DR13 modified)
	History
	By period
901.C765	Period of the Reformation
901.C777	1789-1815
	Sections, districts, suburbs, etc.
901.C785	Collective
901.C7852A-.C7852Z	Individual, A-Z
901.C85	Constance (Konstanz)
	Danzig see DK4650+
901.D3	Darmstadt
901.D43	Detmold
901.D6	Dortmund
901.D7-.D79	Dresden (Table D-DR13)
901.D95	Duesseldorf (Düsseldorf)
901.D96	Duingen
901.D97	Duisburg
901.E2	Eberbach
901.E23436	Egelsbach
901.E25	Eichstätt
	Elbing (Elblag) see DK4800.E4
901.E5	Emden
901.E6	Erfurt
901.E75	Essen
901.F5	Flensburg
901.F7-.F79	Frankfurt am Main (Table D-DR13)
901.F85	Freiberg
901.F87	Freiburg im Breisgau

Local history and description
    Other cities, towns, etc., A-Z -- Continued

901.F892	Friedberg (Hesse)
901.F894125	Frielendorf
901.F8942	Fuerstenau (Fürstenau)
901.F8943	Fuerth (Fürth)
901.F9	Fulda
901.G346	Geldern
901.G44	Giessen
901.G55	Goettingen (Göttingen)
901.G68	Goslar
	Gottorf Castle see DD901.S2
901.G8	Greifswald
901.G88	Guben
901.H17	Halberstadt
901.H19	Halle
901.H2-.H29	Hamburg (Table D-DR13)
901.H32	Hameln
901.H325	Hamm
901.H35	Hanau
901.H4-.H49	Hanover (Table D-DR13)
901.H522	Hedehusum
901.H523	Heek
901.H55-.H56	Heidelberg (Table D-DR14)
901.H612	Heiden über Detmold
901.H62	Heilbronn (Württemberg)
901.H64	Heilsbronn (Bavaria)
901.H657	Hersfeld
901.H66	Hildesheim
901.H68	Hirsau
901.H69	Hirschau
901.H73	Hoechst am Main (Höchst am Main)
901.H755	Hof
901.H784	Hollingstedt
901.H855	Höxter
901.H857	Hüfingen
901.H96	Husum
901.I594	Immendingen
901.I63	Ingelheim am Rhein
901.I8	Iserlohn
901.I823	Isinger
901.J4	Jena
901.J85	Jünkerath
901.J86	Junkersdorf
901.K3	Karlsruhe
901.K33	Kassel
901.K48-.K49	Kiel (Table D-DR14)

	Local history and description
	Other cities, towns, etc., A-Z -- Continued
901.K6	Kissingen, Bad
901.K75-.K76	Koblenz (Table D-DR14)
	Köln see DD901.C7+
(901.K8)	Königsberg
	see DK651.K1213
	Konstanz see DD901.C85
901.K9	Krefeld
	Landeshut see DK4800.K34
901.L2649	Langenhain (Ober-Mörlen)
901.L37	Lauterbach
901.L496	Leipheim
901.L5-.L59	Leipzig (Table D-DR13)
	Leszno (Lissa) see DK4800.L48
	Liegnitz see DK4800.L44
901.L817	Ludwigsburg
901.L82	Ludwigshafen am Rhein
901.L83-.L84	Luebeck (Lübeck) (Table D-DR14)
901.L93	Lueneburg (Lüneburg)
901.L934	Luenen (Lünen)
901.L936	Luetau (Lütau)
901.L95	Luhe
901.L968	Lühen
901.L97	Lustadt
901.M15	Magdeburg
	Mainz
901.M2	Periodicals. Societies. Serials
901.M21	General works. Description and travel. History
	Including antiquities, social life and customs, civilization, biography
901.M2618	Malente-Gremsuhlen
901.M27	Mannheim
901.M275	Marburg
	Marienburg, Malbork see DK4800.M35+
901.M2837	Markgröningen
	Mechtal (Silesia) see DK4800.M35+
901.M5	Meissen
(901.M54-.M56)	Metz
	see DC801.M65
901.M585	Mönchengladbach
	Formerly München-Gladbach
901.M62513	Moordorf
(901.M63-.M66)	Muehlhausen (Mülhausen)
	see DC801.M93
901.M693	Muehlheim an der Ruhr (Mülheim an der Ruhr)
901.M696	Muenster (Münster)

Local history and description
    Other cities, towns, etc., A-Z -- Continued
       Munich

901.M71	Periodicals. Societies. Serials
901.M72	Sources and documents
901.M73	Collected works
901.M74	Dictionaries. Directories
901.M76	Guidebooks
901.M77	General works. Description
901.M79	Pictorial works
901.M8	Antiquities
901.M83	Social life, customs, etc. Culture
	History and description
	General works see DD901.M77
	By period
901.M86	Early
901.M87	16th-18th centuries
901.M88	1789-1815
901.M89	1815-1871
901.M9	1871-1950
901.M912	1951-
	Sections, districts, etc.
901.M92A1	General works
901.M92A2-.M92Z	Individual, A-Z
	Buildings
901.M93	General works
901.M94A-.M94Z	Individual, A-Z
901.M95	Other
901.M98	Mussbach
901.N25	Nauheim. Bad
901.N3	Naumburg
	Neisse see DK4800.N9
901.N91-.N92	Nuremberg (Table D-DR14)
901.O2	Oberammergau
901.O4	Oldenburg
901.O75	Osnabrück
901.P1	Paderborn
901.P5	Pforzheim
	Posen see DK4750
901.P8	Potsdam
901.R4	Ratisbon. Regensburg
901.R42	Ravensberg
901.R425	Recklinghausen
	Regensburg see DD901.R4
901.R8	Rostock
901.R85	Rothenburg ob der Tauber
901.S129	Saarbrücken

Local history and description

Other cities, towns, etc., A-Z -- Continued

901.S15	Saverne (Alsace)
901.S2	Schleswig
	Sélestat see DC801.S443
901.S6	Soest
901.S7	Spires (Speyer)
	Steglitz see DD883.A+
	Stettin see DK4800.S93+
901.S8	Stralsund
	Strassburg see DC801.S77
901.S96-.S97	Stuttgart (Table D-DR14)
901.T789	Treuchtlingen

Trier (Treves)

901.T8	Periodicals. Societies. Serials
901.T81	General works. Description and travel. History

Including antiquities, social life and customs, civilization, biography

901.T88	Trifels
901.T9	Tuchel
901.T91-.T92	Tuebingen (Tübingen) (Table D-DR14)
901.T975	Tuttlingen
901.U26	Uebach
901.U3	Ueberlingen
901.U4	Ulm
901.U47	Unna
901.W4	Weimar
901.W47	Wernigerode
901.W55	Wetzlar
901.W57	Wiedenbruck
901.W58	Wiesbaden
901.W62	Wismar

Worms

901.W71	Periodicals
901.W72	General works. Description and travel. Guidebooks. Geography

History

901.W74	General works

By period

901.W75	Early through 17th century
901.W76	18th-21st centuries
901.W77	Worpswede

Wuerzburg (Würzburg)

901.W91	Museums, exhibitions, etc.

Subarrange by author

901.W92	General works. Description and travel. Guidebooks. Geography

Local history and description
Other cities, towns, etc., A-Z
Wuerzburg (Würzburg) -- Continued
History

901.W93	General works
901.W935	Biography (Collective)
901.W95	Social life and customs. Civilization. Intellectual life
901.X3	Xanten
	Zabern see DD901.S15
901.Z9	Zwickau
(905)	German colonies

         For collective, see JV2000+
         For individual colonies, see Classes D-F

History of the Greco-Roman world
    Including the Mediterranean Region
    Class here general classical antiquities and history
    For Greek antiquities and history see DF10+
    For Roman antiquities and history see DG11+
    Cf. CC1+ Classical archaeology
    Cf. JC51+ Ancient state
    Cf. PA1+ Classical philology

1	Periodicals. Serials
2	Societies
	Museums, exhibitions, etc. see DE46
2.5	Congresses
	Collected works
3	Several authors
3.5	Pamphlets, etc.
4	Individual authors
5	Dictionaries. Encyclopedias
6	Tables, outlines, etc.
7	Biography (Collective)

        Cf. D107 Rulers, kings, etc., in works covering ancient and
          modern history

7.P5	Plutarch's lives (English translation)

        For texts and other translations see PA4369.A2+

Historiography

8	General works
	Biography of historians and archaeologists
9.A1	Collective
9.A2-Z	Individual, A-Z
	Study and teaching
15	General works
15.5.A-Z	By region or country, A-Z

        Subarrange by author

Geography
    Cf. D973 Modern geography
    Cf. G83+ Ancient geography
    Periodicals and societies see DE1

23	Sources and documents. Collections. Classical authors
24	Collected works (Modern)
25	Dictionaries
	Comprehensive works. Orbis antiquus
27	Classical authors
	Modern authors
28	Through 1800
29	1801-
31	General special

Description and travel
    see D911, D971+, DS45+

Antiquities. Civilization. Culture
  For classical antiquity in modern literature, see PN883; PR127
  Cf. CC1+ Archaeology
  Cf. N5320+ Ancient art
  Periodicals and societies see DE1

46	Museums. Exhibitions, etc.
46.5.A-Z	Individual. By place, A-Z

  Collected works see DE3+
  Dictionaries and encyclopedias see DE5

57	Works through 1800
58	General special
	Works, 1801-
59	General works
59.5	Preservation
59.7	Expertising
60	General special
61.A-Z	Special topics, A-Z
61.A4	Agora. Market place
61.A55	Amphoras
61.A77	Art
61.B87	Burial
61.C4	Children
61.D5	Diptychs
61.E25	Ecology
61.E5	Elephants
61.F2	Family
61.F66	Food
61.F67	Forgeries
61.H35	Harbors
61.H38	Heracles
61.H42	Heroes
61.H7	Hotels, taverns, etc.
61.H86	Hunting
61.I48	Implements, utensils, etc.
61.I58	Intellectuals
61.L32	Labor. Working class
61.L34	Lamps
61.M36	Marble
61.M5	Military antiquities, etc.
61.M65	Monuments
61.N3	Naval antiquities, etc.
61.P42	Peace
61.P5	Pirates
61.P63	Population
61.P66	Pottery
61.P75	Propaganda
61.P8	Public and political antiquities

Antiquities. Civilization. Culture
    Works, 1801-
        Special topics, A-Z -- Continued

61.R44	Religious life and customs
61.S43	Seafaring life
61.S48	Sepulchral monuments
	Slavery see HT863
61.S7	Spectacles, circuses, etc.
61.T33	Tablets (Paleography)
61.T4	Temples
61.T43	Terra-cotta sculpture
61.U53	Underwater antiquities
	Utensils see DE61.I48
61.W35	War
61.W54	Wine and wine making
61.Y68	Youth
71	Social life and customs. Civilization. Culture

        Cf. CB311+ History of ancient civilization and culture

72	Greco-Roman world in the time of Christ

        Cf. BR170 Relations of Christianity to the Roman Empire
           and Eastern Empire
        Cf. BS2375 Historical criticism of the New Testament
        Cf. BS2410 History of Christianity in New Testament times

Ethnography

73	General works
73.2.A-Z	Individual elements in the population, A-Z
73.2.B55	Blacks
73.2.C37	Carthaginians

        Cf. DT269.C3+ Carthaginian Empire and civilization

73.2.P56	Phoenicians
73.2.S4	Sea peoples
73.2.S9	Swiss

History

80	General works
83	General special
84	Military and naval history
85	Political history

        For specific periods, see the period
        Foreign and general relations
           For general works on the diplomatic history of a period, see
               the period
           For works on relations with a specific country
               regardless of period see DE85.5.A+

85.3	General works
85.5.A-Z	Relations with individual regions or countries, A-Z
	By period

	History
	By period -- Continued
	Ancient to 476. Greco-Roman era
	Cf. DT269.C3+ Carthage
86	General works
87	Pamphlets, etc.
88	Military and naval history
89	Political and diplomatic history
92	Beginning of Christian era
94	476-1517
96	1517-1789
96.5	1789-1815
97	1815-1914
98	1914-1945
100	1945-

Ancient Greece
  Antiquities. Civilization. Culture
    Public and political antiquities -- Continued

83	Administration. Finance. Archons
	Cf. DF277 History and political antiquities of Athens
	Cf. HJ217 Public finance in ancient Greece
85	Federations. Colonies
	Cf. JV93 History of ancient Greek colonization
86	Archives and diplomatics
	For treaties see KL4111+
(87)	Legal antiquities
	see KL4100+
	Military and naval antiquities
	Cf. U33 History of ancient Greek military science
89	General works
89.5	Pamphlets, etc.
90	Naval antiquities alone
	Cf. V37 History of ancient Greek naval science
	Private antiquities
	Including private life
	Cf. DF78 Social life and customs
91	General works
93	Family. Woman. Children
	Cf. HQ510 Social history
	Cf. HQ1134 Women and feminism in ancient Greece
95	Education
	Cf. LA75 History of education
	Cf. LB85.A+ Educators and writers of ancient Greece
(97)	Athletics. Games
	see GV21+
99	Dwellings. Baths, etc.
	Dress and costume see GT550
100	Eating. Drinking. Cooking, etc.
	Funeral customs. Sepulchral customs
	Cf. GT3170 Treatment of the dead in antiquity
101	General works
101.2	Mouthpieces (Grave goods)
101.5	Sepulchral monuments
	Cf. NA6139 Architecture
	Cf. NB143 Bronze sculpture
105	Agriculture
	Cf. HD133+ Land in ancient Greece (Economic history)
	Cf. S429 Production of plants, animals, etc.
	Cf. S490.8+ Production of plants, animals, etc.
107	Commerce. Industries
	Cf. HC37 National production (Economics)
	Cf. HF375+ Commerce in ancient Greece (Economics)

Ancient Greece
  Antiquities. Civilization. Culture -- Continued
109   Other social institutions
         Cf. HN9+ Social problems in ancient Greece
       Religious antiquities
         For Greek mythology see BL780+
121   General works
122   Cultus
123   Festae
124   Mysteries
125   Divination. Oracles
126   Magic
127   Temples. Altars, etc.
129   Other special (not A-Z)
       Art antiquities
130   General works
131   Gargoyles
         Numismatics see CJ301+
         Weights and measures see QC84
         Greek art see N5630+
       Ethnography
135   General works
136.A-Z   Particular tribes and peoples, A-Z
136.A2   Achaeans
136.A3   Aeolians
136.D6   Dorians
136.I6   Ionians
136.M47   Messenians
136.P44   Pelasgi
     History
       Periodicals, societies, collections, dictionaries see DF10+
207   Chronological tables, etc.
       Biography (Collective)
208   General works
208.5   Prosopography
       Source books see DF12
       Historiography
211   General works
         Biography of historians and archaeologists
212.A2   Collective
212.A3-Z   Individual, A-Z
             e.g.
212.B7   Brøndsted, Peter Oluf
212.C8   Curtius, Ernst
212.E82   Evans, Sir Arthur John
212.S4   Schliemann, Heinrich
       Study and teaching

	Ancient Greece
	History
	Study and teaching -- Continued
212.3	General works
212.4.A-Z	By region or country, A-Z
212.5.A-Z	Individual schools, A-Z
	General works
213	Classical authors (Translations)
	For texts of individual authors, see PA
	For texts of several authors see DF12
	Modern authors
213.5	Through 1800
214	1801-
215	Compends. Textbooks. Juvenile works
216	Syllabi, etc.
217	General special
218	Pamphlets, etc.
	By period
	Early to ca. 1100 B.C.
	Bronze Age. Aegean civilization
	Including islands of the Aegean
220	General works
220.3	Minoan civilization. Minoans
	Cf. DF221.C8 Crete
220.5	Mycenaean civilization
	Cf. DF221.M9 Mycenae
221.A-Z	Special local exploration, etc., A-Z
	For antiquities later than Minoan and Mycenean
	ages see DF261.A+
	For medieval and modern period see DF901.A+
	Achaea see DF221.A27
221.A27	Achaia
221.A35	Aegina
221.A42	Agrilitses Mound
221.A45	Aigeira
221.A5	Aïyion
221.A78	Argolis (Province)
221.A8	Argos
221.A84	Asine
221.A87	Attica
221.A95	Ayios Stefanos
221.B63	Boeotia. Voiōtia
221.C56	Chorsiai
221.C6	Corinth
221.C8	Crete
	Including local sites and adjacent islands, e.g. Pseira
	Island

Ancient Greece
History
By period
Early to ca. 1100 B.C.
Special local exploration, etc., A-Z -- Continued
221.C93   Cyclades
Class here works on the Cyclades collectively
For works on an individual island, see the island, e.g.
Naxos Island, DF221.N39
221.D4   Dendra
221.D56   Dimini Site
221.D58   Dimitra Site
221.E65   Enipeus River Valley
221.E7   Eretria
221.G53   Gla Site
221.H25   Hagion Gala
221.H27   Hagiorgitika Site
221.H94   Hymettus Mountain
221.I84   Ithaca Island
221.K33   Kárpathos Island
221.K34   Kastanas Site
221.K36   Kea (Keōs) Island
221.K44   Keros Island
221.K5   Kíthira Island
221.K7   Korakon
221.L37   Lárisa
221.L47   Lerni
221.L477   Leukantion
221.L48   Levkás Island
221.L56   Lithares Site
221.M35   Manika
221.M54   Midea
221.M9   Mycenae
221.N39   Naxos Island
221.N52   Nichoria
221.O4   Olympia
221.P37   Paxos Island
221.P47   Perafi Mountains
221.P49   Pevkakia Magoula Mound
221.P56   Phaestus
221.P58   Phthiōtis
221.P6   Phylakopi
221.P63   Pílos
221.P68   Poliochnē
221.P77   Prósimna
                                    Pseira Island see DF221.C8
221.P94   Pylona

	Ancient Greece
	History
	By period
	Early to ca. 1100 B.C.
	Special local exploration, etc., A-Z -- Continued
221.R56	Rhodes
221.S93	Sybrita
221.S96	Syros Island
221.T33	Thasos
221.T35	Thebes. Thēvai
221.T38	Thera Island
221.T4	Thessaly
	Thēvai see DF221.T35
221.T45	Thorikon
221.T5	Tiryns
221.T8	Troy
	Including Troas
	Voiōtia see DF221.B63
	ca. 1125-500 B.C.
221.2	General works
221.3	Dorian invasions, ca. 1125-1025 B.C.
221.5	Geometric period, ca. 900-700 B.C.
	775-500 B.C. Age of Tyrants. Archaic period
222	General works
222.2	General special
223	Addresses, essays, lectures
224.A-Z	Biography, A-Z
	e.g.
224.P4	Pisistratus
224.S7	Solon
	Persian Wars, 499-479 B.C.
225	General works
225.2	General special
225.25	Pamphlets, etc.
225.3	Ionian revolt, 499-494
225.33	Burning of Sardis, 498
225.35	Capture of Miletus, 494
225.37	Conquest of Thrace, 494-492
225.4	Marathon, 490
225.5	Thermopylae, 480
225.53	Naval battles of Artemisium, 480
225.55	Burning of Athens, 480
225.6	Salamis, 480
225.7	Plataea, 479
225.75	Mycale, 479
225.8	Capture of Sestus, 478
225.9.A-Z	Other special events, A-Z

Ancient Greece

  History

    By period

      Persian wars, 499-479 B.C. -- Continued

226.A-Z	Biography, A-Z
	e.g.
226.M5	Miltiades
226.T45	Themistocles
	Athenian supremacy. Age of Pericles. 479-431 B.C.
227	General works
227.4	Pamphlets, etc.
227.5	General special
	Including the First Delian League, etc.
227.6	Capture of Eion, 476
227.63	Battles of the Eurymedon, 468
227.65	Revolt of Thasos, 465
227.7	Third Messenian War, 464-456
227.75	War with Aegina and Corinth, 459-456
227.77	Athenian expedition to Egypt, 454
227.8	Peace of Cimon/Callias, 449-448 B.C.
227.83	Revolt of Euboa and Megara, 446-445
227.85	Samian War, 440-439
227.9.A-Z	Other special events, A-Z
228.A-Z	Biography, A-Z
	e.g.
228.A7	Aristides, the Just
228.A8	Aspasia
228.P4	Pericles
229	Peloponnesian War, 431-404 B.C.
	For Thucydides use:
	.T5 *English text. By translator, A-Z*
	.T55 *English selections. By translator, A-Z*
	.T56A-.T56Z *Other languages. By language, A-Z, and date*
	.T6 *Biography and criticism*
229.1	Pamphlets, etc.
229.2	General special
229.3	First period, 431-421
229.35	Second period, 421-413
229.37	Third period, 413-404
229.4	Siege and fall of Plataea, 429-427
229.43	Revolt and capitulation of Mytilene, 428-427
229.45	Fortification of Pylus, 425
229.47	Capture of Sphacteria, 425
229.5	Invasion of Boeotia, 424
229.53	Invasion of Thrace, 424

	Ancient Greece
	History
	By period
	Hellenistic period, 323-146 B.C. -- Continued
235.A3-Z	General works
235.3	General special
	323-281. Macedonian hegemony. Struggles of the Diadochi
	Cf. DF261.M2 Macedonia
235.4	General works
235.45	General special
	Biography and memoirs
235.47	Collective
235.48.A-Z	Individual, A-Z
	e.g.
235.48.P9	Pyrrhus, King of Epirus
235.5	Lamian War, 323-322
235.7	Athenian Revolution, 286
	280-220. Aetolian and Achaean leagues
236	General works
236.3	General special
236.4	Galatian Invasion, 279-278
236.5	Chremonidean War, 267-262
236.7	Pamphlets, etc.
237.A-Z	Biography, A-Z
237.A6	Antigonus Gonatas
237.A7	Aratus of Sicyon
	220-146. Macedonian wars and Roman conquest
	Cf. DG250+ Ancient Rome, 753-27 B.C.
238	General works
238.3	General special
238.7	Pamphlets, etc.
238.9.A-Z	Biography, A-Z
238.9.P4	Perseus, King of Macedonia
238.9.P5	Philip V, King of Macedonia
	Roman epoch, 140 B.C.-323/476 A.D.
239	General works
240	General special
241	Pamphlets, etc.
	Local history and description
251	Territories, colonies, regions, etc. (in combinations)
	For particular tribes and people see DF136.A+
261.A-Z	Separate states, territories, islands, etc., A-Z
	Cf. DS156.A+ Ancient states of Asia Minor
261.A17	Achaea. Akhaia

	Ancient Greece
	Local history and description
	Separate states, territories, islands, etc., A-Z -- Continued
261.A177	Aegean Sea Region
	Including islands of the Aegean
	Cf. DF895+ General history and description
	Cf. DS51.A+ Turkish islands of the Aegean
261.A18	Aegina
261.A2	Aetolia
261.A26	Aineia
	Akhaia see DF261.A17
261.A34	Akanthos
261.A36	Akra Soúnion
261.A37	Akrofiri Peninsula
261.A39	Aliki
261.A4	Almyros
261.A47	Amphipolis
261.A5	Andros (Island)
261.A65	Argolis Peninsula
261.A68	Arkadia
261.A7	Asine
	Athens see DF275+
261.A8	Attica. Attikí
261.B5	Boeotia. Voiotia
261.B7	Bosporus (Kingdom)
261.B77	Brauron
261.C28	Caria
261.C36	Cephalonia
261.C38	Chalcidice Peninsula
261.C4	Chalcis
261.C44	Chios Island
261.C5	Claros
261.C6	Clazomenae
261.C64	Corfu Island
261.C64	Corfu Island. Kerkyra
261.C65	Corinth
261.C7	Cos (Island)
261.C8	Crete
261.C93	Cyclades
	Class here works on the Cyclades collectively
	For works on an individual island, see the island, e.g.
	Naxos Island, DF261.N34
261.D3	Delos (Island)
261.D35	Delphi
261.D36	Demetrias
261.D38	Dervéni
261.D53	Dion (Pieria)

Ancient Greece
  Local history and description
    Separate states, territories, islands, etc., A-Z -- Continued

261.D6	Dodona
261.E3	Elatea
261.E4	Eleusis
261.E413	Eleutherna
261.E42	Elis
261.E5	Ephesus
261.E6	Epidaurus
261.E65	Epirus

For Northern Epirus (Albania) see DR996.E64

261.E7	Eretria
261.E9	Euboea
261.F5	Flious
261.G6	Gonnoi
261.G62	Goritsa
261.G64	Gortyna
261.H15	Hagia Triada Site
261.H25	Halieis
261.H32	Hephaisteia
261.I34	Ialysos
261.I58	Iolkos
261.I6	Ionian Islands
261.I85	Isthmia
261.I87	Ithaca Island
261.K377	Kastellorizo (Island). Megisti
261.K38	Kastelos (Chania, Crete)
261.K4	Kavousi
261.K45	Kekhriai
	Kerkyra see DF261.C64
261.K5	Kleitor
261.K55	Knossos
261.K67	Korinthia
261.K87	Kymē (Euboea Island)
261.K9	Kynouria
261.L2	Lakōnia
261.L3	Larissa
261.L34	Lathouresa
261.L49	Lesbos Island
261.L53	Leukantion
261.L63	Locris

	Ancient Greece
	Local history and description
	Separate states, territories, islands, etc., A-Z -- Continued
261.M2	Macedonia
	For modern Greek Macedonia see DF901.M3
	For modern Bulgarian Macedonia see DR95.B55
	For Macedonia (General, and Yugoslavia) see DR2152+
	Cf. DF232.5+ Greek history
261.M3	Mantinea
261.M34	Maronea
261.M39	Megalo Nisi Galanis
261.M4	Megalopolis
	Megisti see DF261.K377
261.M45	Messēnia
261.M46	Metapontum
261.M465	Methana Peninsula
261.M47	Methydrion
261.M49	Midea
261.M5	Miletus
261.M55	Mithimna
	Morea see DF261.P3
261.M9	Myrina
261.N3	Naucratis
261.N34	Naxos Island
261.N45	Nemea
261.N48	New Halos
261.N55	Nikopolis
261.O47	Oiniadai
261.O5	Olympia
261.O53	Olynthus
261.O57	Omólion
261.O75	Oropos
261.O77	Orthagoria
261.P2	Paros
261.P27	Pella
261.P3	Peloponnesus
261.P48	Phaselis
261.P5	Pherae
261.P53	Philippi
261.P55	Phōkis. Phocis
261.P56	Phylla
261.P57	Plataea
261.P6	Potidaea
261.P64	Potidaion
261.P8	Priene
261.P94	Pylos (Eleia, Greece)

Ancient Greece
Local history and description
Separate states, territories, islands, etc., A-Z -- Continued

261.R47	Rhodes
261.S16	Salamis (Island)
261.S2	Samos
261.S3	Samothrace
261.S45	Serrai (Eparchy)
261.S55	Simi
261.S56	Sindos
261.S8	Sparta
261.T15	Tanagra
261.T2	Thasos
261.T3	Thebes
261.T4	Thera
261.T45	Therme
261.T48	Thesprōtia
261.T49	Thessalonikē
261.T5	Thessaly
261.T6	Thrace

For modern Greek Thrace see DF901.T75
For general works on Thrace see DR50+
For Bulgarian Thrace see DR95.T45
For Turkish Thrace see DR701.T5

261.T64	Tinos
261.T75	Torone
261.T8	Troezen
261.V2	Vari
261.V28	Vergina
261.V3	Veroia
261.V56	Vitsa
	Voiotia see DF261.B5
261.V74	Vrokastro Site
	Athens

Cf. DF624 Medieval Athens
Cf. DF915+ Modern Athens

	Antiquities. Culture
275	General works
277	Political antiquities
	History
285	General works
285.5	Historiography
287.A-Z	Localities, buildings, etc., A-Z
287.A2	Acropolis
287.A23	Agora
287.A83	Asklepieion
287.B3	Basilicas

	Ancient Greece
	Local history and description
	Athens
	Localities, buildings, etc., A-Z -- Continued
287.C4	Ceramicus. Kerameikos
287.E6	Erechtheum
287.H4	Hephaisteion
287.M65	Monument of Philopappus
287.O3	Odeum of Pericles
287.O48	Olympieion
287.P3	Parthenon
287.P4	Piraeus
287.P6	Pnyx
287.P75	Propylaea
287.S27	Sanctuary of the Nymph
287.S74	Stoa of Attalos
287.S75	Stoa Poecile
287.T5	Tholos
287.T66	Tourkovouni
287.T68	Tower of the Winds
287.W3	Walls
289	Other special
	Medieval Greece. Byzantine Empire, 323-1453
	Cf. DF750+ General Greek history
501	Periodicals. Societies. Serials
501.5	Congresses. Conferences, etc.
	Sources and documents
503	General works
504	Pamphlets, etc.
504.5	General works
	Historiography
505	General works
	Biography of historians, area studies specialists,
	archaeologists, etc.
505.5	Collective
505.7.A-Z	Individual, A-Z
	e.g.
505.7.J6	Joannes Malalas
505.7.P7	Procopius, of Caesarea
	Study and teaching
505.8	General works
505.82.A-Z	By region or country, A-Z
	Subarrange by author
	Biography (Collective)
	For individual biography, see the specific period, reign, or place
506	General works
506.5	Rulers, kings, etc.

Medieval Greece. Byzantine Empire, 323-1453 -- Continued

518	Historical geography
519	Description and travel
520	Antiquities
	For local antiquities see DF895+
	Social life and customs. Civilization. Intellectual life
	For specific periods, see the period or reign
521	General works
531	General special
(541)	Special topics (not A-Z)
	For specific periods, see the period or reign
	Ethnography
542	General works
542.4.A-Z	Individual elements in the population, A-Z
542.4.B84	Bulgarians
542.4.S62	Slavs
542.4.T87	Turkic peoples
543	Military history
544	Naval history
545	Political history
	Foreign and general relations
	For general works on the diplomatic history of a period, see the period
	For works on relations with a specific country regardless of period see DF547.A+
546	General works
547.A-Z	Relations with individual regions or countries, A-Z
548	Empire and papacy
	Cf. BX1171 Roman Catholic Church and Byzantine Empire
	Cf. D133 Church and state (Medieval Europe)
	History
	General works
	Through 1800. Chronicles
550	Byzantine
551	Other
552	1801-
552.5	Compends
552.8	Pamphlets, etc.
	Eastern Empire, 323/476-1057
553	General works
553.5	Pamphlets, etc.
	323-527
	Class here only history specifically Eastern
	For general history see DG315
555	General works
556	General special

Medieval Greece. Byzantine Empire, 323-1453
   History
   Eastern Empire, 323/476-1057
     527-1057
       720-886. Iconoclasts
        Biography and memoirs -- Continued

581.3	Collective
581.32.A-Z	Individual, A-Z
582	Leo III the Isaurian, 717-741
583	Constantine V Copronymus, 741-775
584	Leo IV Chozar, 775-780
585	Constantine VI, 780-797
586	Irene, 797-802
586.2	Nicephorus I, 802-811
586.4	Stauracius, 811
586.5	Michael I Rhangabe, 811-813
586.7	Leo V the Armenian, 813-820
586.9	Michael II, 820-829
587	Theophilus, 829-842
588	Michael III, 842-867
589	Basil I, 867-886

      886-1057

590	Sources and documents
591	General works
	Biography and memoirs
591.3	Collective
591.32.A-Z	Individual, A-Z
591.35.A-Z	Local, A-Z
592	Leo VI the Philosopher, 886-911
593	Constance VII Porphyrogenitus, 912-959. Alexander, 912-913 (Co-emperor). Romanus I Lecapenus, 920-944 (Co-emperor)
594	Romanus II, 959-963
	Basil II Bulgaroctonus, 963-1025
595	General works
595.5	Nicephorus II Phocas, 963-969
595.7	John I Zimisces, 969-976
596	Constantine VIII, 1026-1028
596.5	Romanus III Argyrus, 1028-1041
597	Michael IV the Paphlagonian, 1034-1041
597.5	Michael V Calaphates, 1041-1042
598	Constantine IX Monomachus, 1042-1054
599	Theodora, 1054-1056
599.5	Michael VI Stratioticus, 1056-1057

     1057-1453

599.8	Sources and documents
	General works

Medieval Greece. Byzantine Empire, 323-1453
    History
       1057-1453
          General works -- Continued
            Through 1800. Chronicles

600	Byzantine
600.5	Other
601	1801-
601.3	Pamphlets, etc.
602	Isaac I Comnenus, 1057-1059
602.5	Constantine X Ducas, 1059-1067
602.7	Romanus IV Diogenes, 1067-1071
603	Michael VII Parapinaces, 1071-1078
604	Nicephorus III Botaniates, 1078-1081
	Alexius I Comnenus, 1081-1118
605	General works
605.3	Anna Comnena, Princess
606	John II Comnenus, 1118-1143
607	Manuel I Comnenus, 1143-1180
608	Alexius II Comnenus, 1180-1183
608.3	Andronicus I Comnenus, 1183-1185
608.5	Isaac II Angelus, 1185-1195, 1203-1204
608.7	Alexius III Angelus, 1195-1203
608.8	Alexius IV Angelus, 1203-1204
608.9	Alexius V Ducas, 1204
609	Empire of Trebizond, 1204-1461
	1204-1261. Latin Empire
610	Sources and documents
	General works
610.8	Through 1800. Chronicles
611	1801-
613	Constitution and organization
614	Baldwin I, 1204-1205
615	Henry, 1205-1216
616	Peter, 1217-1219
617	Robert, 1219-1228
618	Baldwin II, 1228-1261
619	Fall of Empire, 1261
	Individual states and empires
622	Thessalonica (Thessalonike)
623	Achaia-Morea
624	Athens
	Nicaea
625	General works
626	Theodore I Lascaris, 1204-1222
626.3	John III Ducas, 1222-1254
626.5	Theodore II Lascaris, 1254-1258

Medieval Greece. Byzantine Empire, 323-1453
  History
    1057-1453
      1204-1261. Latin Empire
        Individual states and empires
          Nicaea -- Continued

626.7	John IV Lascaris, 1258-1259
626.9	Michael VIII Palaeologus, 1259-1261
628.A-Z	Other mainland states, A-Z
629.A-Z	Island states, A-Z
	e.g.
629.A7	Archipelago
	1261-1453. Palaeologi
630	Sources and documents
	General works
631.A2	Byzantine
631.A3-Z	Other
632	General special
633.A-Z	Local, A-Z
	e.g.
633.A8	Asia Minor
	Biography and memoirs
633.3	Collective
633.32.A-Z	Individual, A-Z
635	Michael VIII Palaeologus, 1261-1282
	Andronicus II Palaeologus, 1282-1328
636	General works
636.5	Catalan Grand Company, 1302-1311
637	Andronicus III Palaeologus, 1328-1341
638	John V Palaeologus, 1341-1391
	John VI Cantacuzenus, 1347-1354 (Coregent)
	Andronicus IV, 1376-1379 (Rival emperor)
639	Manuel II Palaeologus, 1391-1425
	John VII Palaeologus, 1398-1402 (Coregent)
641	John VIII Palaeologus, 1425-1448
642	Constantine XI Dragases, 1448-1453
	1453. Fall of Constantinople
	Cf. DR502 Turkish accounts
	Through 1800
645	Byzantine accounts
647	Other
649	1801-
	Modern Greece
701	Periodicals. Societies. Serials
703	Sources and documents
	Collected works
705	Several authors

DF

Modern Greece
History
By period
1821-
1821-1913. 19th century
War of Independence, 1821-1829
Special topics, A-Z -- Continued
811.C64   Collectibles
Foreign participation
811.F65   General works
811.F652A-.F652Z   By region or country, A-Z
811.I54   Influence
811.P37   Paramilitary forces
811.P48   Philikē Hetaireia
811.P74   Prisoners and prisons
811.R44   Religious aspects
811.S63   Social aspects
811.W64   Women
814   Pamphlets, etc.
Biography
815.A2   Collective
815.A3-Z   Individual, A-Z
e.g.
815.T7   Tompazēs, Iakōbos
Kapodistrias, 1827-1831
816   Sources and documents
817   General works
818   Other
821   1831-1832
Otho I, 1833-1862
823   General works on life and reign
Biography and memoirs
823.2   Collective
823.3.A-Z   Individual, A-Z
823.5   Pamphlets, etc.
823.6   Acarnanian Revolt, 1836
823.65   Revolution, 1848
823.68   Arta Revolt, 1854
823.7   Revolution, 1862
George I, 1863-1913
825   General works on life and reign
825.3   Pamphlets, etc.
826   Annexation of Thessaly and Epirus, 1881
827   War with Turkey, 1897
Cf. DR575 Turkey during war with Greece
1897-1913
831   General works

Modern Greece
  History
    By period
      1821-
        20th century
          George II, 1935-1947
            Civil War, 1944-1949 -- Continued

849.52	General works
849.53.A-Z	Special events, battles, etc., A-Z
	Biography and memoirs
849.57	Collective
849.58.A-Z	Individual, A-Z
	Paul I, 1947-1964
850	General works on life and reign
851	Phreiderikē, Consort of Paul I
	Biography and memoirs of contemporaries
851.3	Collective
851.5.A-Z	Individual, A-Z
	Constantine II, 1964-1967
852	General works on life and reign
	Biography and memoirs of contemporaries
852.3	Collective
852.5.A-Z	Individual, A-Z
	Period of military rule, 1967-1974
853	General works
	Biography and memoirs
853.3	Collective
853.5.A-Z	Individual, A-Z
	Restoration of democracy, 1974-
854	General works
	Biography and memoirs
854.3	Collective
854.32.A-Z	Individual, A-Z
	Local history and description
	Cf. DF251+ Local history and description of ancient Greece
895	Archipelago (Islands of the Aegean)
	Cf. D972 European Orient
	Cf. DF901.C9 Cyclades
901.A-Z	Regions, provinces, islands, etc., A-Z
	e.g.
901.A24	Achaia
901.A25	Achelous River Region
901.A33	Aegina
901.A38	Aigialeia
901.A6	Andros (Island)
	Arcadia see DF901.A73

	Modern Greece
	Local history and description
	Regions, provinces, islands, etc., A-Z -- Continued
901.A73	Arkadia. Arcadia
901.A77	Athos, Mount
	For Athos (Monasteries) see BX385.A8+
901.A8	Attica. Attiki
901.C4	Cephalonia
	Chios see DF901.K55
901.C7	Corfu
901.C76	Cos. Kos
901.C78-.C89	Crete
901.C78	Periodicals. Societies. Serials
901.C786	Place names
901.C79	Biography (Collective)
901.C8	Description and travel
901.C815	Social life and customs. Civilization. Intellectual life
901.C82	History
	Antiquities and ancient history
	Archaeological explorations see DF221.C8
	General ancient history see DF261.C8
901.C825	Early and medieval
901.C826	826-961. Arab rule
901.C827	961-1204. Greek rule
901.C83	1204-1669. Venetian rule
	Cf. DG678.2 Turkish wars, 1453-1571
	Cf. DR534.2+ War of Candia, 1644-1669
901.C835	1669-1898. Turkish rule
	19th century
901.C84	General works
901.C843	1821-1829
	Cf. DF804+ Greek War of Independence, 1821-
	1829
901.C85	1866-1868
901.C851	Pamphlets, etc.
901.C857	1896-1897
	Cf. DF827 War with Turkey, 1897
901.C86	1898-
901.C88A-.C88Z	Counties, regions, etc., A-Z
	For cities see DF951.A+
901.C9	Cyclades
	Cf. D972 European Orient
	Cf. DR701.A2 Aegean Sea
901.D6	Dodecanese
901.D65	Doris
901.E44	Eleia

Modern Greece
Local history and description
Regions, provinces, islands, etc., A-Z -- Continued

901.E6	Epirus
	For Northern Epirus (Albania) see DR996.E64
901.E8	Euboea
901.G6	Gortynia
901.H9	Hydra
901.I4	Ikaria Island
901.I58-.I66	Ionian Islands
901.I58	Periodicals
901.I6	General works. Description and travel
901.I64	History
901.I642	1797-1815
901.I65	1815-1864. British protectorate
901.I66	1864-
901.I695	Ionian Sea
901.I8	Ithaca (Thiaki)
901.K25	Kálimnos Island
901.K27	Kárpathos Island
901.K29	Kastellorizo Island
901.K3	Kastoria (Nomos)
901.K5	Khalkidhikî Peninsula
901.K55	Khîos
901.K57	Kîthira (Island)
	Kos see DF901.C76
901.L28	Lakōnia
901.L35	Lemnos Island
901.L38	Lesbos Island
901.L4	Levkás (Island)
901.M3	Macedonia
	For ancient Greek Macedonia see DF261.M2
	For modern Bulgarian Macedonia see DR95.B55
	For Macedonia (General, and Yugoslavia) see DR2152+
901.M34	Mani
901.M532	Messēnia (Nomos)
901.M9	Mykonos (Island)
901.N3	Naxos (Island)
901.N57	Nisyro
901.O4	Oinousai Islands
901.O6	Olympus, Mount (Thessaly)
901.P24	Parnassus, Mount
901.P26	Paros
901.P27	Patmos
901.P3	Paxos
901.P4	Peloponnesus

Modern Greece
   Local history and description
      Regions, provinces, islands, etc., A-Z -- Continued

901.P6	Poros
	Rhodes
901.R4	Island
901.R42	City
901.R43A-.R43Z	Other cities, A-Z
901.S34	Samos
901.S54	Sīmi Island
901.S6	Skyros
901.S66	Souli
901.S7	Spetsai (Island)
901.S9	Syros
901.T6	Tenos
901.T65	Thasos (Island)
901.T67	Thera Island
901.T68	Thermopylae
901.T7	Thessaly

          For archaeological exploration see DF221.T4
          For general ancient history see DF261.T5

901.T75	Thrace (Western)

          For ancient Greek Thrace see DF261.T6
          For general works on Thrace see DR50+
          For Bulgarian Thrace see DR95.T45
          For Turkish Thrace see DR701.T5

901.T754	Thyreatis
901.Z26	Zagori
901.Z3	Zakinthos Island. Zante
	Zante see DF901.Z3
	Athens
915	Periodicals. Societies. Serials
916	Gazetteers
916.5	Guidebooks
917	General works
	Description
918	Early through 1829
919	1830-
	Antiquities see DF275+
920	Social life and customs. Culture
	History

      Including medieval and modern Athens treated together

921	General works
	Ancient see DF285+
922	Medieval to 1453

         Cf. DF624 Athens (Latin Empire)

923	1453-1829

Modern Greece
 Local history and description
  Athens
   History -- Continued

924	1830-1900
925	1901-
930.A-Z	Localities. Sections, districts, etc., A-Z
	Buildings
935	General works
936.A-Z	Individual, A-Z
951.A-Z	Other cities, towns, etc., A-Z
	e.g.
951.G2	Galaxidi (Galaxeidion)
951.I5	Iōannina (Janina)
951.N4	Néa Erithraía
951.T45	Thessalonike. Salonika

	History of Italy
	For the general history of Italy, including ancient Rome see DG466+
	Ancient Italy. Rome to 476
11	Periodicals. Serials
12	Societies
	Museums, exhibitions, etc.
12.2	General works
12.3.A-Z	Individual. By place, A-Z
12.5	Congresses
13	Sources and documents. Collections. Classical authors
	Collected works
14	Several authors
15	Individual authors
16	Dictionaries
	Geography. Description and travel
	Cf. G83+ History of ancient geography
	Dictionaries see DG16
	General works
27	Classical authors (Translations)
	For texts, see PA
	Itineraria. Roman roads
	Including bridges
	For Roman roads and bridges in specific countries other than Italy, see the country in subclasses DA-DT
28	General works
28.5	General special
29.A-Z	Individual, A-Z
29.A4	Amerina, Via
29.A6	Appian Way (Via Appia)
29.A74	Ardeatina, Via
29.A94	Augusta, Via
29.A96	Aurelia, Via
29.C37	Cassian Way
29.C5	Claudia Augusta, Via
29.C53	Claudia Braccianese, Via. Via Clodia
	Clodia, Via see DG29.C53
29.E34	Egnatia, Via
29.F47	Ferentina, Via
29.F53	Flaminia, Via
29.J85	Julia Augusta, Via (Italy and Austria)
29.L33	Labicana, Via
29.L38	Latina, Via
29.N65	Nomentana, Via
29.P67	Postumia, Via
29.P74	Prenestina, Via
29.R43	Regina, Via

DG

Ancient Italy. Rome to 476
Local history and description
Regions, provinces, etc.
Other
Regions in Italy, A-Z -- Continued

55.C26	Calabria
55.C27	Camonica Valley
55.C28	Campagna di Roma
55.C3	Campania
55.C32	Carpino River Plain
55.C33	Casentino Valley
55.C335	Cassibile Region
55.C34	Castellier degli Elleri Mountain
55.C36	Castelporziano, Tenuta di
55.C45	Chiana River and Valley
55.C63	Como (Province)
55.C64	Conca River Valley
55.C65	Cosenza (Province)
55.C73	Crati River Valley
55.C87	Curone Valley
55.E45	Elba
55.E48	Elsa Valley
55.E54	Emilia-Romagna
55.E87	Etruria. Tuscany
	Cf. DG222.5+ Etruscans
55.E89	Euganean Hills
55.F47	Ferrara Region
55.F53	Fiora River Valley
55.F55	Foglia River Valley
55.F57	Forum Julii (Friuli)
	Cf. DG975.F85 Friuli (City)
55.F73	Friuli (Region)
55.F74	Friuli-Venezia Giulia
55.F83	Fucino Basin
55.G37	Garda, Lake
55.G377	Garza River Valley
55.G73	Grado Lagoon
55.G77	Grosseto (Province)
55.I82	Ischia Island
	Lavoro, Terra di see DG55.S9
55.L5	Liguria
55.L55	Lipari Islands. Aeoliae Insulae
	Including individual islands, e. g. Vulcano Island
55.L57	Liri River Valley
55.L58	Livorno (Province)
55.L6	Lombardy
55.M28	Maggiore, Lake, Region

Ancient Italy. Rome to 476
Local history and description
Regions, provinces, etc.
Other
Regions in Italy, A-Z -- Continued

55.M3	Magna Graecia
55.M35	Mantua (Province)
55.M37	Marches
55.M38	Maremma
55.M43	Messina, Strait of, Region
55.M45	Metauro Valley
55.M63	Modena (Province)
55.M65	Molise
55.N47	Nera River Valley
55.N68	Novara
55.N86	Nuoro Province
55.O74	Orcia River Valley
55.P38	Pavia (Province)
55.P44	Peligna Valley
55.P48	Pesaro e Urbino (Province)
55.P5	Phlegraean Plain
55.P53	Piacenza (Province)
55.P55	Piedmont
55.P57	Pisa (Province)
55.P6	Po Valley
55.P65	Policastro Gulf region
55.P66	Pontine Marshes
55.P68	Pozzuoli Gulf
	Puglia see DG55.A65
55.R5	Reggio Emilia (Province)
55.R54	Rieti (Province)
55.R65	Romagna
55.S13	Sabbia Valley
55.S135	Sabina
55.S16	Salentina Peninsula
55.S2	Sardinia
55.S48	Sibari Plain
55.S5	Sicilia
	Including Sicans, Siculi, etc.
55.S54	Siena (Province)
55.S56	Sinni River Valley
55.S85	Susa Valley
55.S9	Syracuse
55.T47	Terra di Lavoro
55.T52	Tiber River Valley
55.T73	Trentino-Alto Adige
55.T76	Tronto River Valley

Ancient Italy. Rome to 476
Local history and description
Regions, provinces, etc.
Other
Regions in Italy, A-Z -- Continued

55.T87	Turin (Province)
	Tuscany see DG55.E87
55.T95	Tyrrhenian Sea Region
55.U45	Ufita River Valley
55.U63	Umbria
55.V34	Valle d'Aosta
55.V37	Varese (Province)
55.V45	Veneto
55.V47	Venice (Province)
55.V49	Versilia Plain
55.V57	Viterbo (Province)
	Vulcano Island see DG55.L55
55.V59	Vivara Island
59.A-Z	Regions outside of Italy, A-Z

Prefer local history for material relating to the history of
individual countries in the Roman period (except for
such regions as do not correspond to modern
geographical divisions), e.g., DA145+ Roman period
in England
Cf. DG87 Provinces, colonies, municipa (General,
including antiquities)

59.A2	General works
59.A34	Achaia
59.A4	Africa
59.A8	Asia
59.B44	Belgica
59.C9	Cyrene
59.D3	Dacia
	Cf. DR239.2 Dacians
59.D4	Dalmatia
59.D43	Danube River Valley
59.E64	Epirus Vetus
59.G2	Gallia
	Hispania see DP94+
59.I15	Iberia
59.I2	Illyria
	Cf. DR39.5 Illyrians
59.M3	Mauretania
59.M7	Moesia
59.M74	Moselle River and Valley
59.N37	Narbonensis
59.N7	Noricum

	Ancient Italy. Rome to 476
	Local history and description
	Regions, provinces, etc.
	Other
	Regions outside of Italy, A-Z -- Continued
59.P2	Pannonia
59.R5	Rhaetia
	Rhine Valley see DD801.R7+
	Sardinia see DG55.S2
	Sicilia see DG55.S5
59.S9	Syria
	Rome (City) to 476
	Including description, antiquities, views, etc.
	For modern, including medieval see DG803+
	For architectural works with texts see NA310+
61	Periodicals. Societies. Collections
62	Guidebooks. Outlines, etc.
	General works
62.5	Through 1800
63	1801-
63.5	Preservation
64	Minor works. Special (not A-Z)
	Including exhibitions, models, photographs, pictures, etc.
65	Archaeological discoveries
	Sections, districts, etc.
66	Colles, montes, etc.
	Including Capitoline Hill, Palatine Hill, etc.
66.5	Forum Romanum
66.8	Graecostasis
67	Gates (Portae). Walls, aqueducts, bridges, etc.
	Buildings
	Cf. DG133 Temples, altars, etc.
68	General works
68.1	Individual buildings (not A-Z)
	Including Colosseum, Septizonium, Thermae Agrippae, etc.
69	Other special
	Including Arch of Titus, Lapis niger in the Comitiu Flaminia, etc.
70.A-Z	Other cities, towns, etc., A-Z
	For modern history, including ancient and medieval see DG975.A+
70.A1	General works
70.A17	Abbasanta
70.A24	Acquarossa
70.A25	Acquavina (Siena)
70.A26	Adria

DG

Ancient Italy. Rome to 476
Local history and description
Other cities, towns, etc., A-Z -- Continued

70.A27	Aesernia (Isernia)
70.A3	Agrigentum (Agrigento, Girgenti)
70.A47	Akrai (Palazzollo Acreide)
70.A53	Alba Fucens. Alba Funcentia
70.A533	Alba Longa
70.A534	Alba Pompeia (Alba)
70.A535	Albanella
70.A54	Albintimilium
70.A545	Alesa. Halaesa
70.A55	Alife
70.A57	Altinum (Altino)
70.A573	Amelia
70.A576	Amiternum
70.A578	Anagni
70.A58	Ancona
70.A583	Angera
	Ansedonia (Cosa) see DG70.C63
70.A59	Antium. Anzio
	Antemnae see DG66
	Anzio see DG70.A59
70.A6	Aquileia
70.A63	Aquinum (Aquino)
70.A7	Arcevia
70.A72	Ardea
70.A725	Ariccia
70.A73	Arona
70.A74	Arretium (Arezzo)
70.A75	Artena
70.A753	Artimino
70.A76	Ascoli Piceno
70.A77	Ascoli Satriano
70.A774	Asolo
70.A775	Assisi
70.A776	Asti
70.A78	Atella
70.A83	Augustanus Laurentium
70.B16	Bagno di Romagna
70.B17	Bagnolo San Vito
	Including Forcello Site
70.B27	Balone Site
70.B33	Barcola
70.B34	Barletta
70.B36	Basta
70.B4	Belluno

Ancient Italy. Rome to 476
Local history and description
Other cities, towns, etc., A-Z -- Continued

70.B42	Bene Vagienna
70.B43	Beneventum (Benevento)
70.B44	Bergamo
70.B47	Biella
70.B49	Bisignano
70.B5	Bithia
70.B53	Blanda
70.B54	Blera
70.B7	Bologna
70.B72	Bomarzo
70.B75	Boscoreale
70.B78	Bovino
70.B8	Brescia
70.B82	Bressanone
70.B83	Brindisi
	Buccino see DG70.V63
70.B87	Budrio
70.C116	Caelia (Bari Province)
(70.C12)	Caere
	see DG70.C39
70.C125	Cagliari
	Including Tuvixeddu Site, Vico III Lanusei Site
70.C127	Caiazzo
70.C13	Cairano
70.C14	Calatia
70.C15	Cales (Calvi Risorta)
70.C16	Calvatone
70.C17	Camarina
70.C173	Campanella Point
70.C1733	Campassini Site
70.C1735	Canar di San Pietro Polesine Site
70.C1738	Cannae
70.C174	Canosa di Puglia
70.C176	Capannori
70.C18	Capena
70.C19	Capiago Intimiano
70.C195	Capo d'Orlando
70.C197	Capracotta
70.C2	Capri
70.C25	Capua
	Including Santa Maria Capua Vetere
70.C257	Carlino
70.C26	Carrara
70.C263	Carseoli (Carsoli)

DG

Ancient Italy. Rome to 476
Local history and description
Other cities, towns, etc., A-Z

70.C265	Carsulae
70.C27	Cascia
70.C28	Casignana
70.C29	Cassana
70.C3	Castel di Decima
70.C3115	Castel Giorgio
70.C312	Castel Volturno
70.C3125	Castelfranco Emilia
70.C313	Castellaneta
70.C314	Castellaro del Vhó
70.C315	Castiglion Fiorentino
70.C316	Castiglione del Lago
70.C317	Castronuovo di Sicilia
70.C318	Catania
70.C319	Catignano
70.C32	Cattolica
70.C34	Cavallino
	Ceccano see DG70.F33
	Celano see DG70.C54
70.C38	Centuripe
70.C39	Cerveteri (Caere)
70.C393	Cervia
70.C395	Cesena
70.C397	Cesenatico
70.C42	Chianciano Terme
70.C425	Chieri
70.C43	Chieti
70.C44	Chiusi
70.C49	Cittadella
70.C52	Civita di Paterno Site
70.C53	Civitavecchia
70.C54	Cliternum (Celano)
70.C56	Codroipo
70.C568	Colle di Rapino Cave
70.C57	Colle di Val d'Elsa
70.C573	Collemancio (Urbinum Hortense)
70.C574	Comacchio
70.C575	Corchiano
70.C576	Corciano
70.C58	Cornus
70.C59	Corti Site
70.C6	Cortona
70.C62	Corvaro
70.C63	Cosa (Ansedonia)

Ancient Italy. Rome to 476
Local history and description
Other cities, towns, etc., A-Z -- Continued

70.C65	Cottanello
70.C74	Cremona
70.C77	Crotone
70.C78	Crustumerium
70.C9	Cumae
70.C93	Cupra Marittima
70.D47	Desenzano del Garda
	Egnatia see DG70.G57
70.E68	Entella Site
70.E8	Este
70.F33	Fabrateria Vetus (Ceccano)
70.F34	Falerium Vetus (Civita Castellana)
70.F36	Falerone
70.F38	Fanum Fortunae (Fano)
70.F47	Ferentinum Hirpinum
70.F49	Fermo
70.F5	Ferrone Site
70.F53	Ficana
70.F535	Fidenae
70.F54	Fiesole
70.F55	Florence
70.F64	Foligno
70.F66	Fondi
	Forcello Site see DG70.B17
70.F68	Fordongianus
70.F686	Forlì
70.F687	Forlimpopoli
70.F69	Formello
	Forum Corneli see DG70.I47
70.F72	Fossa Necropolis Site
	Frascati see DG70.T8
70.F73	Fregellae
70.G3	Gabii
70.G34	Galeata
70.G37	Gargano Promontory
70.G45	Gela (Sicily)
70.G47	Genoa
70.G5	Ghiaccio Forte
70.G53	Ginosa
70.G55	Gioiosa Ionica
70.G57	Gnathia. Egnatia
70.G65	Golasecca
70.G67	Gonessa
70.G72	Gravina di Puglia

Ancient Italy. Rome to 476
Local history and description
Other cities, towns, etc., A-Z -- Continued

70.G73	Graviscae
70.G75	Greve in Chianti
70.G84	Gubbio
	Halaesa see DG70.A545
70.H48	Heraclea
70.H5	Herculaneum
	Including Villa of the Papyri
	Herdonia see DG70.O7
70.H56	Himera
70.H9	Hyccara
70.I28	Iato Mountain (Sicily)
70.I35	Idoli Lake
(70.I45)	Imera see DG70.H56
70.I47	Imola (Forum Corneli)
70.I57	Interamna Nahars (Terni)
70.I6	Ipponion
	Isernia see DG70.A27
70.I85	Isola Rizza
70.I87	Ittireddu
70.L32	La Giostra Site
70.L33	Lagole
70.L34	Lamezia Terme
70.L35	Lanuvium
70.L36	Laos
70.L365	Larino
70.L37	Laurentum
70.L372	Lavello
70.L373	Lavinium
70.L38	Lecce
70.L383	Lecco
70.L39	Legoli
70.L4	Leontinoi (Lentini)
70.L47	Leuca
70.L52	Licata (Sicily)
70.L53	Licenza
	Lilybaeum see DG70.M356
70.L55	Lipari. Lipari Islands
	Littamum see DG70.S236
70.L6	Locri Epizephyrii
70.L83	Lucca
70.L85	Lucera
70.L87	Lucus Feroniae
70.L92	Luna (Extinct city)
70.M28	Maccaretolo Site

Ancient Italy. Rome to 476
Local history and description
Other cities, towns, etc., A-Z -- Continued

70.M32	Madore Hill Site
	Manicalunga Necropolis Site see DG70.S4
70.M35	Mantua
70.M354	Marianopoli
70.M356	Marsala. Lilybaeum
70.M36	Marzabotto
70.M365	Massa-Carrara
70.M37	Matauros
70.M39	Matelica
70.M43	Medma
70.M44	Megara Hyblaea
70.M46	Merano
70.M5	Messina
70.M52	Metapontum
70.M56	Milan
70.M57	Milazzo (Mylai)
70.M58	Minervino Murge
70.M6	Minturno
70.M62	Mirandola
70.M623	Misenum (Miseno)
70.M63	Modena
70.M635	Mola di Monte Gelato Site
70.M637	Monte Adranone Site
70.M639	Monte Maranfusa Site
70.M64	Monte Romano
70.M643	Montecchio Emilia
70.M644	Montegrotto Terme
70.M645	Montemilone
70.M647	Monterenzio
70.M65	Monteroduni
70.M66	Morgantina (Sicily)
70.M67	Motya (Mozia), San Pantaleo Island (Sicily)
70.M82	Muggia
70.M86	Muro Leccese
70.M87	Musarna (Extinct city)
	Mylai see DG70.M57
70.N35	Naples
70.N37	Narce
70.N39	Nave
70.N4	Naxos
70.N42	Neapolis (Sardinia)
70.N45	Nemi
70.N62	Nocera Superiore
70.N64	Nora (Sardinia)

Ancient Italy. Rome to 476
Local history and description
Other cities, towns, etc., A-Z -- Continued

70.N65	Noto (Sicily)
70.O33	Oderzo
70.O44	Oleggio
	Oplontis see DG70.T67
70.O7	Ordona. Herdonia
70.O73	Oria
70.O75	Ornavasso
70.O76	Orroli
70.O77	Orune
70.O78	Orvieto
70.O785	Osimo
70.O788	Ossaia Site
70.O79	Osteria dell'Osa
70.O8	Ostia
70.O86	Otricoli
70.O93	Ozieri (Sardinia)
70.P25	Padria
70.P27	Padua
70.P3	Paestum
70.P325	Palermo
70.P33	Palestrina (Praeneste)
70.P35	Pantalica
70.P36	Pantelleria Island
70.P38	Parabiago
70.P39	Parre
70.P393	Passignano sul Trasimeno
70.P396	Pegognaga
70.P4	Perugia
70.P43	Pesaro
70.P45	Petruscio Ravine
70.P52	Piazza Armerina
70.P53	Pietrabbondante (Bovianum Vetus)
70.P55	Pietramelara
70.P57	Pisa
70.P58	Pitigliano
70.P59	Plestia
70.P62	Poggio Buco Site
70.P64	Poggio Civitate
70.P65	Poggio Colla Site
70.P66	Poggio Pinci
70.P68	Pomarico Vecchio
70.P685	Pombia
70.P7	Pompeii
70.P74	Ponti di Nona

Ancient Italy. Rome to 476
Local history and description
Other cities, towns, etc., A-Z -- Continued

70.P76	Pontecagnano Faiano
70.P765	Ponza Island
70.P77	Populonia
70.P775	Pordenone
70.P777	Porticello
70.P78	Porto Torres
70.P79	Portus
70.P82	Potentia (Macerata Province)
	Pozzarello Site see DG70.V64
70.P84	Prima Porta
70.P9	Puteoli (Pozzuoli)
70.P95	Pyrgi
70.R34	Ragusa
70.R36	Ravanusa
70.R37	Ravenna
70.R4	Reate (Rieti)
70.R43	Reggio di Calabria
70.R435	Reggio Emilia
70.R46	Remedello Sotto
	Rieti see DG70.R4
70.R54	Rimini
70.R63	Rocca di Papa
70.R65	Roccagloriosa
70.R7	Roselle
70.R72	Rosignano Marittimo
70.R77	Rubiera
70.R8	Rudiae
70.R87	Russi
70.S213	Sabucina
70.S217	Salapia. Salpi
70.S22	Salento
70.S223	Salerno
70.S23	Salò
	Salpi see DG70.S217
70.S236	San Candido. Littamum
70.S238	San Giovanni di Ruoti Site
70.S24	San Giovenale
70.S2415	San Giustino
70.S2417	San Lorenzo di Sebato
70.S242	San Marino
70.S244	San Paolo di Civitate
70.S246	San Piero a Sieve
70.S247	San Severo
70.S248	Sannace Mountain

Ancient Italy. Rome to 476
Local history and description
Other cities, towns, etc., A-Z
Santa Maria Capua Vetere see DG70.C25

70.S249	Santa Marinella
70.S2497	Sant'Angelo in Vado (Tifernum Matarense)
70.S2498	Sant'Angelo Muxaro
70.S25	Sant'Antioco Island
70.S253	Sant'Antonio Abate
70.S255	Sant'Ilario d'Enza
70.S257	Santorso
70.S258	Sanzeno
70.S27	Sarteano
70.S28	Satricum
70.S33	Saturnia
70.S35	Scafati
70.S354	Schiavi d'Abruzzo
70.S36	Scolacium
70.S38	Segesta
70.S385	Segni
70.S39	Segusium (Susa)
70.S4	Selinus

Including Manicalunga Necropolis Site

70.S43	Sepino
70.S437	Sessa Aurunca
70.S44	Sestino
70.S45	Sesto Fiorentino
70.S52	Sibari

Siena see DG70.A25

70.S53	S'Imbalconadu Site
70.S55	Sipontum
70.S56	Sirai Mountain
70.S58	Siris
70.S62	Solunto
70.S64	Sorgenti della Nova Site
70.S645	Sorrento
70.S646	Sorso
70.S647	Sovana
70.S65	Sperlonga
70.S66	Spina
70.S67	Spoleto
70.S77	Stabiae
70.S83	Stróngoli
70.S84	Subiaco
70.S86	Sulcis

Susa see DG70.S39

70.S9	Sybaris

Ancient Italy. Rome to 476
　　Local history and description
　　　Other cities, towns, etc., A-Z -- Continued
　　　　Syracuse see DG55.S9

70.T3	Tarentum (Taranto)
70.T35	Tarquinia
70.T36	Temesa
70.T37	Tergeste (Trieste)
70.T38	Termini Imerese (Sicily)
	Terni see DG70.I57
70.T4	Terracina
70.T45	Tessennano
70.T5	Tharros
70.T55	Thiene
70.T6	Tibur (Tivoli)
	Tifernum Matarense see DG70.S2497
70.T66	Todi
70.T67	Torre Annunziata. Oplontis
70.T675	Torre di Satriano Site
70.T68	Torre Galli Site
70.T69	Torrita di Siena
70.T72	Trapani
70.T74	Trea (Treia)
70.T76	Treviso
70.T77	Tridentum (Trento)
70.T78	Turi
70.T79	Tuscania
70.T8	Tusculum (Frascati)
	Tuvixeddu Site see DG70.C125
70.U34	Ugento
70.U66	Urago d'Oglio
70.U7	Urbs Salvia
70.V2	Vaglio de Basilicata
70.V24	Valéggio sul Mincio
70.V26	Valesio (Extinct city)
70.V3	Veii
70.V33	Velia
70.V332	Velleia (Extinct city)
70.V335	Venosa
70.V34	Verabolo
70.V343	Vercelli
70.V346	Veretum
70.V35	Verona
70.V4	Vetulonia
70.V5	Vicentia (Vicenza)
	Vico III Lanusei Site see DG70.C125
70.V53	Vico Equense

Ancient Italy. Rome to 476
Local history and description
Other cities, towns, etc., A-Z -- Continued

70.V55	Villa di Settefinestre Site
70.V56	Villadose
70.V58	Viterbo
70.V62	Voghenza
70.V63	Volcei (Buccino)
70.V64	Volsinii (Viterbo Province)
	Including Pozzarello Site
70.V65	Volterra
70.V9	Vulci
70.Z8	Zuglio

Antiquities. Civilization. Culture
　　Cf. CC1+ Archaeology
　　Cf. N5740+ Ancient art
　　Periodicals see DG11
　　Societies see DG12
　　Congresses see DG12.5
　　Dictionaries see DG16

75	Outlines, tables, etc.
	General works
76	Through 1800
77	1801-
77.5	Preservation
78	General special
	Including social life and customs
	Cf. DG90+ Private life
	Local see DG51+
79	Pamphlets, etc.
	Public and political antiquities
81	General works
82	General special
	For foreign and general relations see DG214+
	Administration
	For works on political theory see JC81+
83	General works
83.A7	Augustales. Severi augustales
83.A8	Honor bisellii
	Citizenship
	Cf. KJA2930+ Roman law
83.1	General works
83.3	Special classes
	Including Patres, Nobiles, Clientes, Plebs, Equestrian order, etc.
83.5.A-Z	Magistratus. Dignitaries
	Cf. KJA2980+ Roman law

Ancient Italy. Rome to 476
Antiquities. Civilization. Culture
Public and political antiquities
Administration
Magistratus. Dignitaries -- Continued
83.5.A1   General works
83.5.A3   Aediles
83.5.C4   Censores
83.5.C7   Consules
                        Cf. DG202 Fasti consulares
83.5.C85   Curatores rei publicae
83.5.D2   Decemviri
83.5.D23   Decuriones
83.5.D4   Dictatores
83.5.D8   Ducenarii
83.5.I6   Imperatores
83.5.M2   Magistratus municipales
83.5.M23   Magistri officiorum
83.5.N68   Notarii
83.5.P2   Pontifices
83.5.P3   Praefecti Praetores
83.5.P4   Praefectus urbis
83.5.P5   Praesides provinciarum
83.5.P6   Praetores
83.5.P68   Primipili
83.5.P7   Proconsules
83.5.P8   Procurator Caesaris
83.5.Q2   Quaestores
83.5.Q5   Quinquennales
83.5.R3   Reges
83.5.T3   Tetrarchae
83.5.T7   Tribuni
83.5.V5   Vigiles
85   Finance. Economics. Maintenance
87   Provinces. Colonies. Municipia
                    Including antiquities
                    Cf. JV98 Roman colonies and colonization
(88)   Legal antiquities
                    see subclass KJA
89   Military and naval antiquities
                    Including triumphs, trophies, etc.
                        For legal aspects of prisoners of war see KJA3328
                        Cf. U35 Roman military science
                        Cf. V39 Roman naval science
                Private antiquities
                    Including private life
                    Cf. DG78 Social life and customs

Ancient Italy. Rome to 476
Antiquities. Civilization. Culture
Private antiquities -- Continued

90 General works
91 Family. Women. Youth
Cf. HQ511 Family, marriage, home (Ancient Rome)
Cf. HQ1136 Women, feminism (Ancient Rome)
93 Education
Cf. LA81 Education in ancient Rome
Cf. LB91.A+ Theories of education by individual
educators and writers (Ancient Rome)
(95) Athletics. Games. Circuses. Gladiators
see GV31+
Dwellings. Baths, etc.
Including domestic antiquities in general
Cf. NA324 Roman architecture
97 General works
97.2 Amphoras
97.3 Utilitarian ceramics
Including bricks, tiles, etc.
98 Lamps
(99) Dress. Costume
see GT555
101 Eating, cooking (Convivia)
103 Funeral customs. Sepulchral customs
Cf. GT3170 Treatment of the dead in antiquity
105 Agriculture. Land
Cf. HD137+ Land (Economic history of Rome)
Cf. S431 History of Roman agriculture
Cf. S490.8+ Treatises on agriculture by Roman authors
Commerce. Industries
Cf. HC39 Economic history and conditions in ancient
Rome
Cf. HF377+ History of commerce (Ancient Rome)
107 General works
107.8 Storage. Containers
Including barrels, etc.
108 Transportation
Cf. DG28+ Roman roads
Cf. HE175 History of transportation and
communications in Rome
109 Other social institutions
Cf. HN9+ Social history and conditions (Ancient Rome)
Religious antiquities
For Roman mythology see BL798+
121 General works
Cultus

	Ancient Italy. Rome to 476
	Antiquities. Civilization. Culture
	Religious antiquities
	Cultus -- Continued
123	General works
124	Cult of the emperors
125	Festae
127	Mysteries
129	Divination
131	Magic
133	Temples, altars, etc.
135	Other special
135.5	Amphitheaters
135.6	Aqueducts
	Art antiquities
136	General works
137	Art metal-work
	Cf. NK6407.3 Decorative arts
139	Sarcophagi
140	Pottery
141	Mosaic pavements
142	Urns
	Chronology see CE46
	Numismatics see CJ801+
	Tesserae see CJ4865
	Weights and measures see QC84
190	Ethnography
	History
	Periodicals, societies, collections, dictionaries see DG11
201	Chronological tables, etc.
202	Fasti consulares
	Cf. KJA2992 Roman law
	Biography (Collective)
203	General works
203.5	Prosopography, etc.
204.A-Z	Houses, noble families, etc., A-Z
204.A35	Acilii Glabriones family
204.C35	Calpurnii family
204.S35	Scipio family
204.U47	Ulpii family
	Historiography
205	General works
	Biography of historians and archaeologists
206.A2	Collective
206.A3-Z	Individual, A-Z
	e.g.
206.G5	Gibbon, Edward

Ancient Italy. Rome to 476
  History
    Historiography
      Biography of historians and archaeologists
        Individual, A-Z -- Continued

206.M6	Mommsen, Theodor
206.N5	Niebuhr, Barthold Georg
206.P57	Piso Frugi, Lucius Calpurnis, b. ca. 182 B.C.
206.P7	Pozzo, Cassiano del
206.T32	Tacitus, Cornelius
206.5	Study and teaching

      General works

207	Translations of classical authors

        For texts, see PA
       Modern authors

208	Through 1775
209	1776-
210	Compends. Textbooks
210.5	Syllabi, etc.
211	General special
213	Addresses, essays, lectures

      Foreign and general relations
        For general works on the diplomatic history of a period, see
          the period
        For works on relations with countries that became part of the
          Roman Empire, see DG55+
        For works on relations with other countries, regardless
          of the period see DG215.A+

214	Sources and documents
214.5	General works
215.A-Z	Relations with individual regions or countries, A-Z

      By period
        Pre-Roman Italy
          Including Italic peoples (General)

221	General works
221.5	General special
222	Pamphlets, etc.

        Etruria. Etruscans
          For general works on Etruria during the pre-Roman
            through the Roman periods see DG55.E87
          For Etruscan antiquities in ancient Roman cities
            see DG70.A+
          For Villanovan culture see GN780.2.V5

222.5	Periodicals. Societies. Exhibitions
222.7	Sources and documents
223	General works
223.2	General special

Ancient Italy. Rome to 476
History
By period
Pre-Roman Italy
Etruria. Etruscans -- Continued

223.3	Social life and customs. Civilization
223.4	Social conditions
223.5	Political and diplomatic history
223.7.A-Z	Special topics, A-Z
	Art see N5750
223.7.B75	Bronzes
223.7.C47	Chariots
223.7.C65	Commerce
223.7.F5	Fibulae
223.7.F53	Figurines
223.7.G66	Gold jewelry
223.7.H85	Hunting
	Language see P1078
223.7.M47	Merchant marine
223.7.M54	Mineral industries
223.7.M55	Mirrors
223.7.P35	Palaces
223.7.P67	Pottery
	Religion see BL813.E8
223.7.R62	Roads
223.7.S57	Shrines. Temples
223.7.S68	Sports
223.7.S76	Springs
	Temples see DG223.7.S57
223.7.T45	Terra-cotta sculpture
223.7.T6	Tombs
223.7.U7	Urns
223.7.V35	Vases
223.7.V67	Votive offerings
	Cf. BL760.V6 Etruscan religion
225.A-Z	Other peoples, A-Z
225.A45	Aequi
225.A8	Aurunci
225.B79	Bruttii
225.C37	Carthaginians
225.C44	Celts
225.D3	Daunii
225.E43	Egyptians
225.E66	Enotri
225.F3	Falisci
225.F73	Frentani
225.G38	Gauls

DG

	Ancient Italy. Rome to 476
	History
	By period
	Pre-Roman Italy
	Other peoples, A-Z -- Continued
225.G74	Greeks
225.L53	Ligurians
225.L83	Lucani
225.M28	Marrucini
225.M3	Marsi
225.M4	Messapii
225.O8	Oscans
225.P44	Pelasgi
225.P45	Phenicians
225.P47	Picenes
225.S2	Sabines
225.S24	Salassi
225.S26	Samnites
	Sicans see DG55.S5
	Siculi see DG55.S5
225.T38	Tauriani
225.U52	Umbrians (Italic people)
225.V3	Veneti
225.V4	Vestini
225.V55	Vittimuli
225.V64	Volsci
	Kings and Republic, 753-27 B.C.
	Cf. KJA2860 Roman law
	Cf. KJA2870 Roman law
231	General works
231.3	General special
231.7	Pamphlets, etc.
	Foundations and Kings, 753-510 B.C.
233	General works
233.2	General special
233.25	Pamphlets, etc.
233.3	Romulus, 753-716
233.4	Numa Pompilius, 715-673
233.5	Tullus Hostilius, 673-642
233.6	Ancus Marcius, 642-617
233.7	Tarquinius Priscus, 616-579
233.8	Servius Tullius, 578-535
233.9	Tarquinius Superbus, 535-510
	Republic to First Punic War, 509-265 B.C.
235	General works
235.2	General special
235.4	Special events to 343. By date

DG

Ancient Italy. Rome to 476
>History
>>By period
>>>Kings and Republic, 753-27 B.C.
>>>>Conquest of the Mediterranean world, 264-133 B.C.
>>>>200-133 B.C.
>>>>>Biography, A-Z -- Continued

253.S4	Scipio Aemilianus Africanus minor, Publius Cornelius
253.V5	Viriathus

>>>>Fall of the Republic and establishment of the Empire, 133-27 B.C.

253.5	Sources and documents
254	General works
254.2	General special
254.3	Pamphlets, etc.
254.5	The Gracchi, 133-121
255	Jugurthine War, 111-105
255.5	Cimbri and Teutoni, 113-101
	Including Battle of Aquae Sextiae, 102 B.C.

>>>>>Period of Marius and Sulla, 111-78 B.C.

256	General works
256.2	General special
256.5	Marius (Gaius), life and times
256.7	Sulla (Lucius Cornelius), life and times
257	Second Servile War, 103-99
257.3	Social or Marsic War, 90-88
257.5	First Civil War, 88-86
257.6	First Mithridatic War, 88-84
257.8	Second Civil War, 83-78
	Including works covering First and Second Civil Wars
258	Pompey (Gnaeus Pompeius Magnus), life and times
258.3	Third Mithridatic war, 74-61
258.5	Spartacus and the Third Servile War (War of the gladiators), 73-71
259	Conspiracy of Catiline, 65-62
	Biography
260.A1	Collective
260.A2-Z	Individual, A-Z
	e.g.
260.A6	Antonius, Marcus
260.A8	Atticus, Titus Pomponius
260.B3	Balbus, Lucius Cornelius Maior
260.B8	Brutus, Decimus Junius, surnamed Abinus
260.B83	Brutus, Marcus Junius
260.C3	Cato, Marcus Porcius, Uticensis

DG

Ancient Italy. Rome to 476
History
By period
Empire, 27 B.C.-476 A.D.
Constitutional empire, 27 B.C.-284 A.D.
Twelve Caesars (Julius-Domitian), 27 B.C.-96 A.D.
68-96. Flavian emperors -- Continued

290	Titus, 79-81
291	Domitian, 81-96
	Biography, 27 B.C.-96 A.D.
291.6	Collective
291.7.A-Z	Individual, A-Z
	e.g.
291.7.A2	Agricola, Gnaeus (Cn.) Julius
291.7.A3	Agrippa, Marcus Vipsanius
291.7.M3	Maecenas, Gaius (C.) Cilnius
291.7.S4	Sejanus, Lucius Aelius
	96-180
292	General works
	Biography and memoirs
292.5	Collective
292.7.A-Z	Individual, A-Z
293	Narva, 96-98
294	Trajan, 98-117
295	Hadrian, 117-138
296	Antonius Pius, 138-161
297	Marcus Aurelius, 161-180
	180-284
298	General works
	Biography and memoirs
298.5	Collective
298.7.A-Z	Individual, A-Z
299	Commodus, 180-192
300	Septimius Severus, 193-211
301	Caracalla, 211-217
302	Macrinus, 217-218
303	Elagabalus, 218-222
304	Severus Alexander, 222-235
305	235-284
306	Maximinus, 235-238
306.3	Gordianus III, 238-244
306.5	Philippus, 244-249
306.7	Decius, 249-251
307	Gallus, 251-253
307.3	Valerian, 253-260
307.5	Gallienus, 260-268
307.7	Claudius II, 268-270

Ancient Italy. Rome to 476
   History
     By period
       Empire, 27 B.C.-476 A.D.
         Constitutional empire, 27 B.C.-284 A.D.
          180-284
           235-284 -- Continued

308	Aurelian, 270-275
308.3	Tacitus, 275-276
308.5	Florianus, 276
308.7	Probus, 276-282
309	Carus, 282-283
309.3	Carinus and Numerianus, 283-284

          284-476. Decline and fall

310	Sources and documents
311	General works
312	Other
312.5.A-Z	Biography, A-Z
	Prefer individual periods, DG313+
312.5.P7	Praetextatus, Vettius Agorius
312.5.S5	Sidonius, Gaius (C.) Sollius M.A.

         Diocletian, 284-305

313	General works
314	Rival Augusti, 306-324
	Including life of Gaius Galerius Valerius Maximinus
	(Maximinus Daia), d. 313
314.8.A-Z	Biography of contemporaries, A-Z
315	Constantine the Great, 306-337
	Cf. DF557 History specifically Eastern

         337-364

316	General works
316.3	Constantine II, 337-340
316.5	Constans, 337-350
316.7	Constantius II, 353-361
317	Julian, 361-363
317.5	Jovian, 363-364
317.7.A-Z	Other, A-Z

        Valentinian and last emperors. End of the Western
          Empire, 364-476

319	General works
	Biography and memoirs
322	Collective
322.5.A-Z	Individual, A-Z
323	Valentinian I, 364-375
	Valens see DF559

        375-392

325	General works

Ancient Italy. Rome to 476
 History
  By period
   Empire, 27 B.C.-476 A.D.
    284-476. Decline and fall
     Valentinian and last emperors. End of the Western
      Empire, 364-476
      375-392 -- Continued

Medieval and modern Italy, 476-
Description and travel -- Continued

424	1601-1795
425	1796-1815
426	1816-1860
427	1861-1900
428	1901-1918
429	1919-1944
430	1945-1974
430.2	1975-
431	Antiquities

Cf. DG600+ Local history and description

Social life and customs. Civilization

441	General works
442	General special

For brigands see HV6453.A+

443	Early through 1400
445	1401-1600. Renaissance
447	1601-1789
449	1789-1815
450	1816-1945
451	1945-
453	Italian culture in foreign countries

Class here general works, or those in combinations too broad
for any one country

Ethnography

455	General works
457.A-Z	Individual elements in the population, A-Z
457.A35	Africans
457.A7	Albanians
457.A75	Americans
457.A77	Arabs
457.A78	Argentines
457.A79	Armenians
457.C36	Cape Verdeans
457.C47	Chinese
457.C74	Croats
457.E54	English
457.F55	Filipinos
457.F7	Friulians
457.G4	Germans
457.G7	Greeks
457.L3	Ladins
457.M67	Moroccans
457.M87	Muslims
457.N67	North Africans
457.P67	Poles

DG

Medieval and modern Italy, 476-
    Ethnography
        Individual elements in the population, A-Z -- Continued

457.R65	Romanians
457.R78	Russians
457.S45	Senegalese
457.S48	Slavs
457.S5	Slovenes
457.S62	Somalis
457.S67	Spaniards
457.U37	Ukrainians
457.W35	Walsers

    History

461	Dictionaries. Chronological tables, outlines, etc.

      Biography (Collective)
        For individual biography, see the special period, reign, or
          place

463	General works
463.2	Rulers, kings, etc.
463.4	Public men
463.6	Women

        Houses, noble families, etc.

463.7	Collective
463.8.A-Z	Individual, A-Z

          e.g.

463.8.A57	Aosta, Dukes of
463.8.B7	Borgia family
463.8.C24	Cairoli family
463.8.C27	Caprara family
463.8.C7	Colonna family
463.8.E7	Este family
463.8.M35	Malaspina family
463.8.M37	Malatesta family
463.8.M39	Masino, Counts of
463.8.O33	Odescalchi family
463.8.O77	Orsini family
463.8.S4	Sforza family

      Historiography

465	General works

        Biography of historians

465.5	Collective
465.7.A-Z	Individual, A-Z

          e.g.

465.7.B7	Botta, Carlo Giuseppe G.
465.7.G5	Giannone, Pietro, 1676-1748
465.7.G56	Giovio, Paolo, 1483-1552
	Muratori, Lodovico Antonio see DG545.8.M8

Medieval and modern Italy, 476-
  History
    Historiography
      Biography of historians
        Individual, A-Z -- Continued

465.7.R62	Romeo, Rosario
465.7.S72	Spotorno, Giovanni Battista, 1788-1844

      Study and teaching

465.8	General works
465.82.A-Z	By region or country, A-Z

    General works
      Including those beginning with Roman period

466	Through 1800
467	1801-
468	Compends
469	History of two or more provinces, etc.
470	Addresses, essays, lectures (Collectively)
471	Pamphlets, etc.
473	Special aspects

    General special
      Military history
        For individual campaigns and engagements, see the
          special period

480	Sources and documents

        Biography (Collective)

481.A2	General
481.A3-Z	Officers
482	General works

        By period

483	Early and medieval
483.5	1492-1792
484	1792- . 19th-20th centuries
486	Naval history

        For individual campaigns and engagements, see the
          special period
      Political and diplomatic history. Foreign and general
        relations
        Prefer special periods, reigns, etc. in DG500+

491	General works
492	Earliest to 768
493	768-1268
494	1268-1492
495	1492-1789
497	1789-1860
498	1861-1945
(498.2)	1945-

        see DG576.8+

Medieval and modern Italy, 476-
History
General special
Political and diplomatic history. Foreign and general
relations -- Continued

499.A-Z	Relations with individual regions or countries, A-Z
	By period
	Medieval, 476-1492
	General works
500	Through 1800. Chronicles
501	1801-
502	General special
	476-1268
	General works
503.A2	Through 1800. Chronicles
503.A3-Z	1801-
	For Arabs see DG867.1+
	For Normans see DG867.19+
	476-474
504	General works
504.5	Biography (Collective)
505	Odoacer, 476-489
	Gothic Kingdom, 489-553
	Cf. DG657.2 Goths in Milan
506	General works
507	Theodoric, 489-526
508	Amalasuntha, 526-534
	Theodat, 534-536
508.5	General works on life and reign
509	Byzantine War
509.3	Vitiges, 536-539
509.4	Ildibald, 539-541
509.5	Totila, 541-552
509.7	Teja, 552-553
509.9.A-Z	Biography, A-Z
509.9.C3	Cassidorus Senator, Flavius Magnus Aurelius
510	Byzantine Exarchate, 553-568
	Lombard Kingdom, 568-774
	Cf. D145 Lombard migrations
511	General works
511.15	General special
511.2	Pamphlets, etc.
	Biography
511.25	Collective
511.27.A-Z	Individual, A-Z
	Alboin, 568-573
511.4	General works

Medieval and modern Italy, 476-
  History
    By period
      Medieval, 476-1492
        476-1268
          476-474
            Lombard Kingdom, 568-774
              Alboin, 568-573 -- Continued

511.5	Rosamunda, Consort of Alboin
511.6	Cleph, 573-575
511.7	Interregnum, 575-584
511.8	Authari, 584-590
512	Agilulf, 590-615
512.2	Adaloald, 615-625
512.3	Arioald, 625-636
512.4	Rothari, 636-652
512.6	Rodoald, 652-653
512.7	Aribert I, 653-661
512.8	Grimoald, 662-672
513	Berthari, 672-690
513.2	Cunibert, 690-703
513.5	Liutbert, 690-703
513.6	Raginbert, 704
513.7	Aribert II, 704-712
513.8	Ansprand, 712-713
514	Liutprand, 713-744
514.3	Rachis, 744-749
514.4	Aistulf, 749-756
514.5	Desiderius, 756-774
514.7	Lombard principalities, 9th-11th centuries

            Frankish emperors, 774-962

515	General works
517	Bernardo, 810/813-818
517.5	Berengario I, 894-924
517.7	Ugo, 926-947
518	Berengario II, 950-960
519.A-Z	Biography, A-Z

            German emperors, 962-1268

520	General works

            The Commune. Guelfs and Ghibellines
              General works

522	Through 1800. Chronicles
523	1801-
527	11th century
529	12th century

        1268-1492

530	General works

Medieval and modern Italy, 476-
History
By period
Medieval, 476-1492
1268-1492 -- Continued
13th century
General works

531.A2	Through 1800
531.A3-Z	1801-

Biography

531.8.A1	Collective
531.8.A2-Z	Individual, A-Z
	e.g.
531.8.E8	Ezzelino da Romano
531.8.P5	Pier delle Vigne
531.8.U2	Ubaldini, Ottaviano degli, Cardinal

Renaissance. 14th-16th centuries
General works

532	Through 1800
533	1801-

1300-1492. Signorie

534	General works

14th century

535	General works
536.A-Z	Biography, A-Z
	e.g.
536.O66	Orsini, Rinaldo, conte di Tagliacozzo

15th century

537	General works

Biography

537.8.A1	Collective
537.8.A2-Z	Individual, A-Z
	e.g.
537.8.B4	Bēssariōn, originally Jōannēs, cardinal
537.8.B8	Bruni, Leonardo Aretino
537.8.G2	Gattamelata, Stefano Giovanni
537.8.P7	Poggio-Bracciolini
537.8.S3	Sforza, Caterina
537.8.S5	Sigismondo, Pandolfo Malatesta, Lord of Rimini

Modern, 1492-
Including period of Spanish and Austrian supremacy

538	General works

16th century. 1492-1618

539.A2	Sources and documents

General works

539.A3-Z	Through 1800

Medieval and modern Italy, 476-
History
By period
Modern, 1492-
16th century. 1492-1618
General works -- Continued

540	1801-
	Biography and memoirs
540.8.A1	Collective
540.8.A3-Z	Individual, A-Z
	e.g.
540.8.B5	Boccalini, Traiano
540.8.C3	Castiglione, Baldassare, conte
	For literary works see PQ4617.C65
	Cf. BJ601+ Il cortegiano
540.8.C8	Colonna, Vittoria, marchesa di Pescara
540.8.I7	Isabella d'Este, Consort of Giovanni Francesco II
540.8.M7	Morata, Olympia Fulvia
540.8.S7	Strozzi, Filippo
	1492-1527. Invasions
	General works
541.A2	Through 1800
541.A3-Z	1801-
	Biography and memoirs
541.8.A1	Collective
541.8.A2-Z	Individual, A-Z
	e.g.
541.8.B3	Bayard, Pierre du Terrail, seigneur de
541.8.M4	Medici, Giovanni de' (1498-1526)
	17th century
542.5	Historiography
	General works
543	Through 1800
544	1801-
	Biography and memoirs
544.7	Collective
544.8.A-Z	Individual, A-Z
	e.g.
544.8.P27	Paleotti, Cristina (Dudley), marchesa
	18th century
544.9	Sources and documents
545	General works
545.5	Pamphlets, etc.
	Biography and memoirs
545.8.A1	Collective
545.8.A2-Z	Individual, A-Z
	e.g.

Medieval and modern Italy, 476-
  History
    By period
      Modern, 1492-
        18th century
          Biography and memoirs
            Individual, A-Z -- Continued

545.8.G3	Galiani, Ferdinando
545.8.M8	Muratori, Lodovico Antonio

        1792-1815. Napoleonic period

546	Sources and documents
547	General works
547.2	1792-1796
547.25	1796-1797
547.4	1797-1800

        Kingdom of Italy

548	Sources and documents
548.2	Cispadane Republic, 1796
548.4	Transpadane Republic, 1796
548.6	Cisalpine Republic, 1797-1802
548.8	Italian Republic, 1802-1805
549	Kingdom of Italy, 1805-1814

       19th century
        Including 1789-1848

550.5	Historiography
551	General works

        Biography and memoirs

551.7	Collective
551.8.A-Z	Individual, A-Z
	e.g.
551.8.B24	Balbo, Cesare, conte
551.8.G5	Gioberti, Vincenzo
551.8.R5	Ricciardi, Francesco Antonio, conte di
551.8.R65	Rossi, Pellegrino Luigi Edoardo, conte

      1848-1871. Risorgimento. Wars of Independence

552.A15	Periodicals. Societies
552.A155	Congresses
552.A2	Sources and documents
552.A3-Z	General works
552.5	Political and diplomatic history
552.6	Other special

       Biography and memoirs

552.7	Collective
552.8.A-Z	Individual, A-Z
	e.g.
552.8.A985	Azeglio, Massimo Tapparelli, marchese d'
552.8.B5	Bixio, Nino, 1821-1873

Medieval and modern Italy, 476-
> History
>> By period
>>> Modern, 1492-
>>>> 19th century
>>>>> 1848-1871. Risorgimento. Wars of Independence
>>>>>> Biography and memoirs
>>>>>>> Individual, A-Z -- Continued

552.8.C2	Capponi, Gino Alessandro G.G., marchese
552.8.C25	Cattaneo, Carlo, 1801-1869
552.8.C3	Cavour, Camillo Benso, conte di
552.8.G2	Garibaldi, Giuseppe
552.8.M3	Mazzini, Giuseppe
552.8.M4	Minghetti, Marco
552.8.O6	Orsini, Felice
552.9	Caricature and satire

1848-1849. Austro-Sardinian War

553	General works
553.2	1848
553.3	1849
553.5.A-Z	Special events, battles, etc., A-Z
553.5.B74	Brescia, Ten Days, 1849
553.5.C78	Curtatone and Montanara, Battle of, 1848
553.5.C8	Custozza, Battle of, 1848
553.5.M5	Messina, Bombardment, 1848
553.5.N7	Novara, Battle of, 1849
553.5.S5	Sicily, Campaign in, 1849
553.5.V4	Velletri, Battle of, 1849
	French expedition, 1849 see DG798.5

1859-1860

554	General works
554.3	Pamphlets, etc.
554.5.A-Z	Special events, battles, etc., A-Z
554.5.E96	Expedition of the Thousand, 1860
554.5.G2	Gaeta, Siege of, 1860-1861
554.5.M2	Magenta, Battle of, 1859
554.5.M65	Montebello, Battle of, 1859
554.5.S3	San Martino, Battle of, 1859
554.5.S7	Solferino, Battle of, 1859
554.5.V6	Volturno, Battle of, 1860

1871-1947. United Italy (Monarchy)

555	General works
	Biography and memoirs
556.A1	Collective
556.A2-Z	Individual, A-Z
	e.g.
556.C7	Crispi, Francesco

Medieval and modern Italy, 476-
History
By period
Modern, 1492-
1871-1947. United Italy (Monarchy)
Biography and memoirs
Individual, A-Z -- Continued

556.F3	Farini, Domenico
556.M65	Monzani, Cirillo, 1820-1889
556.S6	Spaventa, Silvio

Vittorio Emanuele II, 1861-1878

557	General works on life and reign
557.5	Political and diplomatic history
557.7	Iconography
557.9	Pamphlets, etc.
558	War with Austria, 1866

Includes battles of Custozza, Lissa, etc.

559	Siege and occupation of Rome, 1870

Cf. DG798.7 End of temporal power of Papal
States

Umberto I, 1878-1900

561	General works on life and reign
561.5	Personal special
562	Margherita di Savoia, Consort of Humbert I
564	Political and diplomatic history

Vittorio Emanuele III, 1900-1946

For works on the regency (1944-1946) and reign
(May 9-June 3, 1946) of Umberto II see
DG572
For works on his life see DG575.A4

566	General works on life and reign
568	General special
568.5	Political and diplomatic history

Including general and pre-Fascist

569	Pamphlets, etc.
569.5	Period of World War, 1914-1918

For the war itself see D501+

1919-1945. Fascism

Cf. JN5657.A+ Political parties of Italy

571.A1	Periodicals. Societies. Serials
571.A2	Sources and documents
571.A3-Z	General works
571.16	Historiography
571.5	Caricature and satire
571.7	Resistance movements against Fascist regime
571.75	March on Rome, 1922

Medieval and modern Italy, 476-
 History
  By period
   Modern, 1492-
    1871-1947. United Italy (Monarchy)
     Vittorio Emanuele III, 1900-1946
      1919-1945. Fascism -- Continued

572   Period of World War II, 1939-1945. Interim
        regimes
        Including period of double occupation (Allied and
         German), regency and reign of Umberto II, and
         period of Provisional Government, 1943-1947
        Cf. D731+ World War II
      Biography and memoirs

574   Collective
575.A-Z   Individual, A-Z
        e.g.
575.A1-.A49   Royal family
575.A14   Amedeo, Duke of Aosta
575.A2   Elena, Consort of Victor Emanuel III
        Humbert II see DG575.A4
575.A4   Umberto II
575.A6   Annunzio, Gabriele d'
        Cf. PQ4803+ Annunzio as a writer
575.B2   Badoglio, Pietro
575.B3   Balbo, Italo
575.C52   Ciano, Galeazzo, conte
       D'Annunzio, Gabriele see DG575.A6
       De Gasperi, Alcide see DG575.G3
575.G3   Gasperi, Alcide de
575.G5   Giolitti, Giovanni
575.G8   Guiccioli, Alessandro, marchese, 1843-1929
575.M36   Matteotti, Giacomo
575.M8   Mussolini, Benito
575.N5   Nitti, Francesco Saverio
575.R6   Rosselli, Carlo
575.S29   Salvemini, Gaetano, 1873-1957
575.T6   Togliatti, Palmiro
575.T8   Turati, Filippo
     1948- . Republic
576   Periodicals. Sources and documents. Collections
576.8   General works
576.9   General special
      Social life and customs. Civilization. Intellectual life
       see DG451
577   Political history
577.2   Foreign and general relations

Medieval and modern Italy, 476-
History
By period
Modern, 1492-
1948- . Republic -- Continued
By period
1948-1976

577.5	General works
	Biography and memoirs
578	Collective
579.A-Z	Individual, A-Z
	e.g.
579.E4	Einaudi, Luigi
579.N52	Nicola, Enrico de

1976-1994

581	General works
	Biography and memoirs
582	Collective
583.A-Z	Individual, A-Z
	e.g.
583.S45	Segni, Mario

1994-

583.5	General works
	Biography and memoirs
583.7	Collective
583.8.A-Z	Individual, A-Z
	e.g.
583.8.D55	Dini, Lamberto

Northern Italy

600	General works
600.5	Pictorial works
601	Description and travel
	Guidebooks see DG416
603	Antiquities
605	Social life and customs. Civilization
607	History
609	Other

Piedmont. Savoy

610	Periodicals. Societies. Serials
611	Sources and documents
	Collected works
611.2	Several authors
611.25	Individual authors
	Biography (Collective)
611.3	General works
611.5	House of Savoy
611.6.A-Z	Noble families, A-Z

Northern Italy
Piedmont. Savoy
Biography (Collective) -- Continued
611.7	Public men
611.75	Women
611.8	Gazetteers. Directories. Dictionaries
612	Guidebooks
612.2	General works
612.5	Monumental and picturesque, etc.

Description and travel
613	Through 1860
614	1861-1950
614.2	1951-
615	Antiquities
615.6	Social life and customs. Civilization

History
616	General works on Piedmont-Savoy, or Savoy alone

Early and medieval
617	General works on Piedmont-Savoy, or Savoy alone
617.1	Earliest

Savoy
General works on the counts of Savoy see DG611.5
617.25	Umberto I, 1003-1051
617.27	Adelaide, 1035-1091
617.28	Oddone, d. 1060
617.29	Amedeo I
617.3	Amedeo II, d. 1080
617.32	Umberto II, d. 1103
617.33	Amedeo III, 1103-1148
617.34	Umberto III, 1148-1189
617.37	Tommaso I, 1189-1233
617.38	Amedeo IV, 1233-1253
617.39	Bonifacio, 1253-1263. Tommaso II, regent
617.393	Pietro II, 1263-1268
617.396	Filippo I, 1268-1285
617.4	Amedeo V, 1285-1323
617.43	Edoardo, 1323-1329
617.44	Aimone, 1329-1343
617.45	Amedeo VI, 1343-1383
617.47	Amedeo VII, 1383-1391
617.48	Amedeo VIII, 1391-1439

Piedmont
617.5	General works
617.6	Earliest
617.7	1002-1189
617.8	1189-1311
617.9	1311-1416

Northern Italy
Piedmont. Savoy
History -- Continued
Modern

618	General works
	15th-17th centuries
618.2	General works
618.3	Lodovico I, 1439-1465
618.31	Amedeo IX, 1465-1472
618.32	Filiberto I, 1472-1482
618.33	Carlo I, 1482-1490
618.34	Carlo II, 1490-1496
618.35	Filippo II of Bresse, 1490/1496-1497
618.36	Filiberto II, 1497-1504
618.38	Carlo III, 1504-1553
618.4	Emanuele Filiberto, 1553-1580
618.42	Carlo Emanuele I, 1580-1630
618.44	Vittorio Amedeo I, 1630-1637
618.45	Francesco Giacinto, 1637-1638
618.46	Carlo Emanuele II, 1638-1675
618.48	Christine of France, 1638-1648
	1675-1718 see DG618.53+
	Kingdom of Sardinia, 1718-1860
618.5	General works
	Biography and memoirs
618.52	Collective
618.522.A-Z	Individual, A-Z
	Vittorio Amedeo I, 1675-1730
618.53	General works on life and reign
618.54.A-Z	Biography of contemporaries, A-Z
	e.g.
618.54.A7	Anne Marie d'Orléans, Consort of Victor Amadeus I
618.55	Carlo Emanuele I (III), 1730-1773
618.57	Vittorio Amedeo II, 1773-1796
	Carlo Emanuele II (IV), 1796-1802
618.58	General works
618.59	Marie Clotilda, Consort of Charles Emanuel IV
618.6	Vittorio Emanuel I, 1802-1821
618.62	Carlo Felice, 1821-1831
618.64	Carlo Alberto, 1831-1849
618.66	1848-1849
	Cf. DG553+ Austro-Sardinian War, 1848-1849
618.68	Vittorio Emanuele II, 1849-1860
	Piedmont, 1860-
618.7	General works
618.72	1860-1945

Northern Italy
  Piedmont. Savoy
    History
      Modern
        Piedmont, 1860- -- Continued
          1945-
618.75   General works
              Biography and memoirs
618.77   Collective
618.78.A-Z   Individual, A-Z
  Genoa
      Class here works on the republic, the city, and the province of
        Genoa
631   Periodicals. Societies. Serials
631.2   Sources and documents
      Collected works
631.4   Several authors
631.5   Individual authors
631.6   Directories. Dictionaries
      Biography (Collective)
631.7   General works
        Houses, noble families, etc.
631.8   Collective
631.82.A-Z   Individual, A-Z
            e.g.
631.82.D6   Doria family
631.82.G34   Galliera, Dukes of
631.82.G58   Giustiniani family
632   Guidebooks
632.5   Monumental and picturesque, etc.
632.8   Historical geography
      Description
633   Through 1860
634   1861-1950
634.2   1951-
635   Antiquities
635.6   Social life and customs. Civilization
      Ethnography
635.7   General works
635.8.A-Z   Individual elements in the population, A-Z
635.8.L37   Latin Americans
      History
        General works
636   Modern
636.3   Early to 1800
        Early and medieval
          Including Liguria

	Northern Italy
	Genoa
	History
	Early and medieval -- Continued
637	General works
637.15	Earliest to 774
637.2	774-1064
637.3	1064-1167
	Including First crusade, 1096-1099
637.4	1137-1339. Period of subsequent crusades
637.5	1339-1396. 14th century
	For War of Chioggia, 1378-1389 see DG677.7+
	Biography and memoirs
637.52	Collective
637.53.A-Z	Individual, A-Z
637.55	1392
	15th century
637.57	General works
637.6	1396-1421 (France)
637.7	1421-1458 (Milan)
637.8	1458-1464 (France)
637.9	1464-1499 (Milan)
	Modern
638	General works
	16th century
	General works
638.1	Through 1800
638.12	1801-
638.2	Fieschi Conspiracy, 1547
638.25.A-Z	Biography, A-Z
	e.g.
638.25.D7	Doria, Andrea, principe di Melfi
638.3	17th century
	18th century
638.35	General works
	Biography and memoirs
638.37	Collective
638.38.A-Z	Individual, A-Z
638.4	1789-1814
	1815-1900
638.5	General works
638.6	1815-1848
638.7	1849-1870
639	1901-1945
639.2	1945-
	Sections, districts, suburbs, etc.
643	Collective

	Northern Italy
	Genoa
	Sections, districts, suburbs, etc. -- Continued
643.2.A-Z	Individual, A-Z
	Monuments, statues, etc.
643.4	Collective
643.5.A-Z	Individual, A-Z
	Parks, squares, cemeteries, etc.
643.7	Collective
643.8.A-Z	Individual, A-Z
	Streets. Bridges
644	Collective
644.2.A-Z	Individual, A-Z
	Buildings
644.4	Collective
644.5.A-Z	Individual, A-Z
645	Other
	Milan. Lombardy
651	Periodicals. Societies. Sources and documents
	Collected works
651.4	Several authors
651.5	Individual authors
651.6	Directories. Dictionaries
	Biography (Collective)
651.7	General works
	Houses, noble families, etc.
651.74	Collective
651.75.A-Z	Individual, A-Z
	e. g.
651.75.C33	Cadorna family
652	Guidebooks
652.2	General works
652.5	Monumental and picturesque, etc.
	Description and travel
	Cf. DG659.52+ Milan (City)
653	Through 1860
654	1861-1950
654.2	1951-
655	Antiquities
655.6	Social life and customs. Civilization
	History
	General works
656	Modern
656.3	Early to 1800
	Early and medieval
657	General works
657.1	Early to 452

DG

Northern Italy
Milan. Lombardy
History
Early and medieval -- Continued
657.2   452-774. Huns, Goths, Lombards
657.3   774-1100
                   1101-1237
657.35   General works
657.37   Friedrich I Barbarossa, 1158-1185
657.4   Lombard League, 1167-1183
657.45   Battle of Legnano, 1176
                   1237-1535
657.5   General works
657.65   1237-1311. Terriani period
                   1311-1447
                       Including earlier Visconti period
657.7   General works
                       Biography and memoirs
657.72   Collective
657.73.A-Z   Individual, A-Z
657.75   1447-1450. Ambrosian Republic
                   1447-1535. Sforza (Duchy of Milan)
657.8   General works
657.9.A-Z   Biography, A-Z
                           e.g.
657.9.B4   Beatrice d'Este, Consort of Lodovico Sforza, il
                               Moro, Duke of Milan
657.9.B5   Bianca Maria Visconti, Duchess of Milan
657.9.G3   Galeazzo Maria Sforza, Duke of Milan
657.9.I7   Isabella d'Argona, Consort of Gian Galeazzo
                               Sforza, Duke of Milan
                   Modern
658   General works
                   1535-1714. Spanish period
658.1   General works
                       Biography
658.13   Collective
658.15.A-Z   Individual, A-Z
                   1714-1796. Austrian period
658.2   General works
                       Biography
658.23   Collective
658.25.A-Z   Individual, A-Z
                   1796-1900
658.3   General works
658.4   1796-1815
658.5   1815-1859. Lombardo-Venetian Kingdom

	Northern Italy
	Milan. Lombardy
	History
	Modern
	1796-1900 -- Continued
658.6	1860-1900
658.7.A-Z	Biography, 1796-1900, A-Z
	e.g.
658.7.M3	Maffei, Clara (Carrara-Spinelli), contessa
658.8	1901-
	Milan (City)
659.52	Guidebooks
659.54	Description
659.56	Pictorial works
	Ethnography
659.58	General works
659.6.A-Z	Individual elements in the population, A-Z
659.6.A37	Africans
659.6.C46	Chinese
659.6.F74	French
659.6.S45	Senegalese
	History
659.7	General works
	By period
660	Through 1860
661	1861-1945
	1946-
662	General works
	Biography and memoirs
662.2	Collective
662.25.A-Z	Individual, A-Z
	Sections, districts, suburbs, etc.
663	Collective
663.2.A-Z	Individual, A-Z
	Monuments, statues, etc.
663.3	Collective
663.5.A-Z	Individual, A-Z
	Parks, squares, cemeteries, etc.
663.7	Collective
663.8.A-Z	Individual, A-Z
	Canals
663.9	Collective
663.92.A-Z	Individual, A-Z
	Streets, bridges, gates, etc.
664	Collective
664.2.A-Z	Individual, A-Z
	Buildings

DG

	Northern Italy
	Milan. Lombardy
	Milan (City)
	Buildings -- Continued
664.3	Collective
664.5.A-Z	Individual, A-Z
	Venice
670	Periodicals. Societies. Serials
671	Sources and documents
	Collected works
671.2	Several authors
671.3	Individual authors
	Biography (Collective)
671.4	General works
671.43	Women
671.45	Public men
671.5	Rulers, doges, etc.
671.6.A-Z	Houses, noble families, etc., A-Z
672	Guidebooks
672.2	General works
	Historic monuments, landmarks, etc. (General)
672.4	General works
672.5	Preservation
	Description
673	Through 1860
674	1861-1950
674.2	1951-
674.7	Pictorial works
675	Antiquities
675.6	Social life and customs. Civilization
	Ethnography
675.62	General works
675.63.A-Z	Individual elements in the population, A-Z
675.63.A84	Asians
675.63.C76	Croats
675.63.C94	Cypriotes
675.63.G75	Greeks
	History
	Historiography
675.7	General works
	Biography of historians
675.72	Collective
675.73.A-Z	Individual, A-Z
	General works
676	Modern
676.3	Early to 1800
676.5	Outlines, syllabi, etc.

	Northern Italy
	Venice
	History -- Continued
676.8	Military history
	Political history
	For specific periods, see the period
676.88	Sources and documents
676.9	General works
	Foreign and general relations
	For general works on the diplomatic history of a period, see the period
	For works on relations with a specific country regardless of period see DG676.97.A+
676.93	Sources and documents
676.95	General works
676.97.A-Z	Relations with individual regions or countries, A-Z
	Early and medieval
	General works
677.A2	Through 1800
677.A3-Z	1801-
	Early to 811
677.1.A2	Early works through 1800
677.1.A3-Z	Works, 1801-
	697-810
677.3	General works
677.33	Paolo Lucio Anafesto, 697-717
677.331	Marcello Tegaliano, 717-726
677.332	Orso Ipato, 726-737
677.333	Deodato, 732-755
677.334	Gallo Gaulo, 755-756
677.335	Domenico Monegario, 756-764
677.336	Maurizio Galbajo, 764-787
677.337	Giovanni Galbajo, 787-804
677.338	Obelerio Antenorio, 804-810
	811-991
677.35	General works
677.37	Agnello Partecipazio, 811-827
677.371	Giustiniano Partecipazio, 827-829
677.372	Giovanni Partecipazio I, 828-836
677.373	Pietro Tradonico, 836-864
677.374	Orso Partecipazio I, 864-881
677.375	Giovanni Partecipazio II, 881-883
677.376	Pietro Candiano I, 887
677.377	Pietro Tribuno, 888-912
677.378	Orso Partecipazio II, 912-932
677.379	Pietro Candiano II, 932-939
677.38	Pietro Partecipazio, 939-942

DG

Northern Italy
Venice
History
Early and medieval
811-991 -- Continued
677.381   Pietro Candiano III, 942-959
677.382   Pietro Candiana IV, 959-976
677.383   Pietro Orseolo I, 976-978
677.384   Vitale Candiano, 978-979
677.385   Tribuno Memmo, 979-991
991-1096. Relations with Constantinople
Cf. DF553+ Early history of Eastern Empire
Cf. DR481 Early history of Turkey
677.4   General works
677.43   Pietro Orseolo II, 991-1008
677.44   Ottone Orseolo, 1008-1026
677.45   Pietro Centranico, 1026-1031
677.46   Domenico Flabianico, 1032-1043
677.47   Domenico Contrarini, 1043-1070
677.48   Domenico Selvo, 1071-1084
677.49   Vitale Falier, 1085-1096
1096-1172. Crusades. Normans
677.5   General works
677.53   Vitale Michiel I, 1096-1102
677.531   Ordelafo Falier, 1102-1116
677.532   Domenico Michiel, 1117-1130
677.533   Pietro Polani, 1130-1148
677.534   Domenico Morosini, 1148-1156
677.535   Vitale Michiel II, 1156-1172
1172-1311. 13th century
677.6   General works
677.62   Sebastiano Ziani, 1172-1178
677.63   Orio Malipiero, 1178-1192
677.64   Enrico Dandolo, 1192-1205. Fourth crusade
677.65   Pietro Ziani, 1205-1229
677.66   Jacopo Tiepolo, 1229-1249
677.67   Marino Morosini, 1249-1253
677.671   Renier Zeno, 1253-1268
677.672   Lorenzo Tiepolo, 1268-1275
677.673   Jacopo Contarini, 1275-1280
677.674   Giovanni Dandolo, 1280-1289
677.68   Pietro Gradenigo, 1289-1311. Council of ten
1311-1382. 14th century
Including war with Turks and War of Chioggia, 1378-1380
677.7   General works
677.75   Marino Zorzi, 1311-1312
677.76   Giovanni Soranzo, 1312-1328

Northern Italy
  Venice
    History
      Early and medieval
        1311-1382. 14th century -- Continued

677.79	Francesco Dandolo, 1329-1339
677.793	Bartolomeo Gradenigo, 1339-1342
677.796	Andrea Dandolo, 1343-1354
677.8	Marino Falier, 1354-1355
677.81	Giovanni Gradenigo, 1355-1356
677.82	Giovanni Dolfin, 1356-1361
677.83	Lorenzo Celsi, 1361-1365
677.84	Marco Cornaro. 1365-1368
677.845	Andrea Contarini, 1368-1382

       1381-1501. 15th century

677.85	General works
677.9	Michele Morosini, 1382
677.91	Antonio Venier, 1382-1400
677.92	Michele Steno, 1400-1413
677.93	Tommaso Mocegnigo, 1414-1423
677.94	Francesco Foscari, 1423-1457
677.95	Pasquale Malipiero, 1457-1462
677.96	Cristoforo Moro, 1462-1471
677.97	Nicolò Tron, 1471-1473
677.98	Nicolò Marcello, 1473-1474
677.981	Pietro Mocenigo, 1474-1476
677.982	Andrea Vendramin, 1476-1478
677.983	Giovanni Mocenigo, 1478-1485
677.984	Marco Barbarigo, 1485-1486
677.985	Agostino Barbarigo, 1486-1501
677.99.A-Z	Biography of contemporaries, A-Z
	e.g.
677.99.B3	Barbaro, Francesco
677.99.C6	Celleoni, Bartolomeo
677.99.D37	Dario, Giovanni, 1414?-1494
677.99.G5	Giuliano, Andrea
677.99.Z4	Zeno, Carlo

     Modern

678	General works
678.2	Turkish wars, 1453-1571
	Cf. DR501+ History of Turkey, 1451-1571
678.22	Sources and documents
	General works
678.23	Through 1800
678.235	1801-
	Biography and memoirs
678.24.A1	General works

	Northern Italy
	Venice
	History
	Modern
	16th century
	Biography and memoirs -- Continued
678.24.A2-Z	Individual, A-Z
	e.g.
678.24.B3	Barbaro, Marco Antonio
678.24.S3	Sanuto, Marino
	Leonardo Loredano, 1501-1521
678.25	General works
678.26	League of Cambrai, 1508
678.28	Antonio Grimani, 1521-1523
678.281	Andrea Gritti, 1523-1538
678.282	Pietro Lando, 1539-1545
678.283	Francesco Donato, 1545-1553
678.284	Antonio Marco Trevisan, 1553-1554
678.285	Francesco Venier, 1554-1556
678.286	Lorenzo Priuli, 1556-1559
678.287	Girolamo Priuli, 1559-1567
678.288	Pietro Loredano, 1567-1570
678.289	Alvise Mocenigo I, 1570-1577
678.29	Sebastiano Venier, 1577-1578
678.291	Nicoló da Ponte, 1578-1585
678.292	Pasquale Cicogna, 1585-1595
	1595-1718. 17th century
	General works
678.3	Through 1800
678.31	1801-
	Mariano Grimani, 1595-1605. Papal Conflict
678.315	General works
678.317	Paolo Sarpi
	Class here biographical works
	For his works see DG678.315
678.32	Spanish conspiracy, 1618
	1644-1718. Period of war with Turkey over Candia
	For works on the war itself see DR534.2+
	General works
678.33	Through 1800
678.34	1801-
678.36	Leonardo Donato, 1606-1612
678.361	Marc' Antonio Memmo, 1612-1615
678.362	Giovanni Bembo, 1615-1618
678.363	Nicoló Donato, 1618
678.364	Antonio Priuli, 1618-1623
678.365	Francesco Contarini, 1623-1624

Northern Italy
  Venice
    History
      Modern
        1595-1718. 17th century -- Continued

678.366	Giovanni Cornaro, 1625-1629
678.367	Nicoló Contarini, 1630-1631
678.368	Francesco Erizzo, 1631-1646
678.369	Francesco Molin, 1646-1655
678.37	Carlo Contarini, 1655-1656
678.371	Francesco Cornaro, 1656
678.372	Bertucci Valier, 1656-1658
678.373	Giovanni Pesaro, 1658-1659
678.374	Domenico Contarini, 1659-1675
678.375	Nicolò Sagredo, 1675-1676
678.376	Luigi Contarini, 1684-1688
678.377	Marcantonio Giustiniani, 1684-1688
678.378	Francesco Morosini, 1688-1694
678.379	Silvestro Valier, 1694-1700
678.38	Alvise Mocenigo II, 1700-1709
678.381	Giovanni Cornaro II, 1709-1722
678.39	Peace of Passarowitz, 1718

         1718-1797. Fall of the Republic

678.4	General works
	Biography and memoirs
678.42	Collective
678.43.A-Z	Individual, A-Z
678.45	Alvise Sebastiano Mocenigo III, 1722-1732
678.454	Carlo Ruzzini, 1732-1735
678.457	Alvise Pisani, 1735-1741
678.46	Pietro Grimani, 1741-1752
678.47	Francesco Loredano, 1752-1762
678.474	Marco Foscarini, 1752-1763
678.478	Alvise Mocenigo IV, 1763-1778
678.48	Paolo Renier, 1779-1789
678.49	Ludovico Manin, 1789-1797

         1797-1900

678.5	General works
	1797-1866
678.51	General works
678.53	1797-1814
678.54	1815-1848
	For works dealing with the Lombardo-Venetian Kingdom as a whole see DG658.5
678.55	1848-1866
	Including life of Daniele Manin
678.6	1866-1900

	Northern Italy
	Venice
	History
	Modern
	1797-1900 -- Continued
678.7.A-Z	Biography and memoirs, 1797-1900, A-Z
	e.g.
678.7.M3	Maurogonato, Isacco Pesaro
678.8	1901-
679	Other
	Sections, districts, individual islands, etc.
684.15	Collective
684.16.A-Z	Individual, A-Z
	Monuments, statues, etc.
684.2	Collective
684.22.A-Z	Individual, A-Z
	Parks, squares, cemeteries, etc.
684.3	Collective
684.32.A-Z	Individual, A-Z
	Canals
684.4	Collective
684.42.A-Z	Individual, A-Z
	Streets. Bridges
684.5	Collective
684.52.A-Z	Individual, A-Z
684.6	Lagoons (General)
	Including dikes, levees, etc.
	For threat of destruction see DG672.5
	Buildings
684.7	Collective
684.72.A-Z	Individual, A-Z
	Other cities of the Republic see DG975.A+
	Central Italy
691	General works
691.5	Biography (Collective)
692	Description and travel
	Guidebooks see DG416
694	Antiquities
	Tuscany. Florence
731	Periodicals. Societies. Serials
731.15	Congresses
731.2	Sources and documents
	Collected works
731.4	Several authors
731.5	Individual authors
731.6	Directories

	Central Italy
	Tuscany. Florence -- Continued
	Biography (Collective)
	For individual biography, see the specific period, reign or place
731.7	General works
	Houses, noble families, etc.
731.8	Collective
731.82.A-Z	Individual houses, families, etc., A-Z
732	Guidebooks
732.5	General works
732.7	Preservation of historic monuments, landmarks, scenery, etc.
	Description and travel
733	Through 1860
734	1861-1950
734.2	1951-1980
734.23	1981-
734.4	Pictorial works
735	Antiquities
735.6	Social life and customs. Civilization
	Ethnography
735.7	General works
735.72.A-Z	Individual elements in the population, A-Z
735.72.C48	Chinese
	History
735.8	Historiography
	General works
736	Modern
736.3	Early through 1800
736.5	General special
	Medieval
737.A15	Sources and documents
	General works
737.A2	Through 1800
737.A3-Z	1801-
	Early
	General works
737.2	Through 1800
737.22	1801-
	Biography
737.24.A1	Collective
737.24.A2-Z	Individual, A-Z
	e.g.
737.24.H9	Hugo, of Tuscany
737.24.M4	Matilde, Countess of Tuscany
	14th century

	Central Italy
	Tuscany. Florence
	History
	Medieval
	14th century -- Continued
	General works
737.25	Through 1800
737.26	1801-
	Biography and memoirs
737.27	Collective
737.28.A-Z	Individual, A-Z
	Modern
737.3	General works
	Early modern. Medicean period
737.4	General works
737.42	Biography of Medici family
	15th century
	General works
737.5	Through 1800
737.55	1801-
	Biography and memoirs
737.58.A1	Collective
737.58.A2-Z	Individual, A-Z
	e.g.
737.58.S7	Strozzi, Alessandra (Macinghi)
737.6	Giovanni, d. 1429
737.7	Cosimo il Vecchio, 1429-1464
737.8	Pietro I, 1464-1469
737.9	Lorenzo il Magnifico, 1469-1492
737.95	Pietro II, 1492-1494
737.97	Savonarola, Girolamo, 1452-1498
	16th century
738	General works
738.13	1494-1530
	Biography and memoirs
738.14.A1	Collective
738.14.A2-Z	Individual, A-Z
	e.g.
738.14.B5	Bianca Cappello, Consort of Francesco Maria de' Medici
738.14.G53	Giannotti, Donato, 1492-1573
738.14.G9	Guicciardini, Francesco
738.14.M2	Machiavelli, Niccolò
	For literary works see PQ4627.M2
738.15	Alessandro, 1532-1537
738.17	Cosimo I, 1537-1574
738.19	Francesco Maria, 1574-1587

Central Italy
Tuscany. Florence
History
Modern
Early modern. Medicean period
16th century -- Continued

738.21	Ferdinando I, 1587-1609
	1609-1737
738.22	General works
738.23	Cosimo II, 1609-1621
738.25	Ferdinando II, 1621-1670
738.27	Cosimo III, 1670-1723
738.28	Giovanni Gastone, 1723-1737
	Biography and memoirs
738.29.A1	Collective
738.29.A2-Z	Individual, A-Z
	1737-
738.3	General works
	1737-1801. Lorraine dynasty
738.32	General works
738.33	General special
738.34	Francis II, 1737-1765
738.35	Leopold I, 1765-1790
738.37	Ferdinand III, 1790-1801 (1824)
	Biography and memoirs
738.39.A1	Collective
738.39.A2-Z	Individual, A-Z
	19th century
738.4	General works
	Napoleonic period
738.42	General works
	1801-1807. Kingdom of Etruria
738.43	General works
738.435	Maria Luigia, Consort of Louis I, King of Etruria
738.44	1808-1814. Under France
	1815-1860
738.5	General works
	Biography and memoirs
738.6.A1	Collective
738.6.A2-Z	Individual, A-Z
	e.g.
738.6.R5	Ricasoli, Bettino, barone
	1860-1945
738.7	General works
	Biography and memoirs
738.79.A1	Collective
738.79.A2-Z	Individual, A-Z

DG

	Central Italy
	Tuscany. Florence
	History
	Modern
	1737- -- Continued
	1945-
738.792	General works
	Biography and memoirs
738.793	Collective
738.794.A-Z	Individual, A-Z
739	Other
	Local (Florence)
	Sections, districts, suburbs, etc.
755	Collective
755.3.A-Z	Individual, A-Z
	Monuments, statues, etc.
756	Collective
756.3.A-Z	Individual, A-Z
	Parks, squares, cemeteries, etc.
757.3	Collective
757.3.A-Z	Individual, A-Z
	e.g.
757.3.C37	Cascine
	Streets, bridges, gates, etc.
758	Collective
758.3.A-Z	Individual, A-Z
	Buildings
759	Collective
759.3.A-Z	Individual, A-Z
	Other Tuscan cities see DG975.A+
	Papal States (States of the Church). Holy See. Vatican City
	Cf. BX800+ Catholic Church
791	Periodicals. Societies. Serials
791.2	Sources and documents
	Collected works
791.4	Several authors
791.5	Individual authors
792	Guidebooks
792.5	Monumental and picturesque, etc.
	Description and travel
793	Through 1860
794	1861-
795	Antiquities
795.6	Social life and customs. Civilization
	History
795.7	Biography (Collective)
	Houses, noble families, etc.

Central Italy
Papal States (States of the Church). Holy See. Vatican City
   History
     Houses, noble families, etc. -- Continued

795.75	Collective
795.76.A-Z	Individual, A-Z
	e.g.
795.76.T88	Tuscolo, Counts of
	General works
796	Modern
796.3	Early to 1800
796.5	Military and naval history
796.7.A-Z	Special aspects, A-Z
	Including elements in the population
796.7.B7	British
796.7.F7	French
	Early and medieval
797	General works
797.1	Earliest to Pepin, 756
797.2	756-962. Period of Carolingian emperors
797.3	962-1309. Hohenstaufen, etc.
	"Babylonian captivity," 1309-1377
797.5	General works
797.55.A-Z	Biography, A-Z
	e.g.
797.55.A5	Albornoz, Gil Alvarez Carrillo de, Cardinal
797.6	1377-1499
	For Alexander VI, pope see BX1312
	1499-1870
797.7	General works
	1499-1605
797.8	General works
	Cesare Borgia
797.82	General works
797.825	Charlotte d'Albret, duchesse de Valentinois
797.83	Lucrezia Borgia
	1605-1700
797.9	General works
	Biography and memoirs
797.92	Collective
797.93.A-Z	Individual, A-Z
798	1700-1798
798.2	1798-1799. Roman Republic
	1799-1870. 19th century
798.3	General works
	Biography and memoirs
798.33	Collective

	Central Italy
	Papal States (States of the Church). Holy See. Vatican City
	History
	1499-1870
	1799-1870. 19th century
	Biography and memoirs -- Continued
798.34.A-Z	Individual, A-Z
798.35	1799-1848
	1848-1870
798.4	General works
798.5	1848-1849. Roman Republic
798.6	1859-1870
798.7	1870. End of temporal power
	Cf. DG559 Siege and occupation of Rome, 1870
799	Holy See, 1870-
800	Vatican City, 1929-
	Rome (Modern city)
803	Periodicals. Societies. Serials
803.5	Biography (Collective)
	For individual biography, see the specific period, reign, or place
	Houses, noble families, etc.
803.55	Collective
803.6.A-Z	Individual houses, families, etc., A-Z
	e.g.
803.6.C37	Cardelli family
803.6.P67	Porcari family
804	Guidebooks. Directories. Dictionaries
804.2	General works
804.5	Preservation of historic monuments, landmarks, scenery, etc.
	Description
805	Through 1860
806	1861-1950
806.2	1951-
806.8	Pictorial works
	Antiquities (Medieval, etc.)
	Including description of the city in Medieval and Renaissance times
807	General works
807.4	Catacombs
807.6	Social life and customs. Civilization
	Ethnography
807.7	General works
807.8.A-Z	Individual elements in the population, A-Z
807.8.B75	British

	Central Italy
	Rome (Modern city)
	Ethnography
	Individual elements in the population, A-Z -- Continued
807.8.P65	Poles
807.8.S64	Spaniards
	History
808	General works
809	General special
	Medieval
811	General works
811.6	Rienzo, Cola di
	Modern
812	General works
	15th century. Renaissance
812.1	General works
	Biography and memoirs
812.114	Collective
812.115.A-Z	Individual, A-Z
812.12	1527. Siege
	16th-18th centuries
812.4	General works
812.6.A-Z	Biography, A-Z
	e.g.
812.6.C4	Cenci, Beatrice
812.7	Napoleonic period, 1798-1814
	1815-1870
812.9	General works
	Biography and memoirs
812.92	Collective
812.93.A-Z	Individual, A-Z
	1871-1945
813	General works
	Biography and memoirs
813.12	Collective
813.15.A-Z	Individual, A-Z
	1945-
813.2	General works
	Biography and memoirs
813.22	Collective
813.23.A-Z	Individual, A-Z
814	Other
	Local
	For localities, buildings, or objects possessing archaeological interest see DG61+
	Sections, districts, suburbs, etc.
814.95	Collective

	Central Italy
	Rome (Modern city)
	Local
	Sections, districts, suburbs, etc. -- Continued
815.A-Z	Individual, A-Z
	Monuments, statues, etc.
815.19	Collective
815.2.A-Z	Individual, A-Z
	Cemeteries
815.29	Collective
815.3.A-Z	Individual, A-Z
	Fountains
815.39	Collective
815.4.A-Z	Individual, A-Z
	Parks, squares, etc.
815.49	Collective
815.5.A-Z	Individual, A-Z
815.7	River front (Tiber)
	Streets, bridges, gates, etc.
815.89	Collective
815.9.A-Z	Individual, A-Z
	Buildings
816	General works
	Churches and monasteries
816.29	Collective
816.3.A-Z	Individual, A-Z
	e.g.
816.3.S26	San Giovanni in Laterano
816.3.S33	San Pietro in Vaticano
	Palaces and villas
816.49	Collective
816.5.A-Z	Individual, A-Z
	e.g.
816.5.S3	Castel Sant'Angelo
	Public buildings
816.9	General works
817.A-Z	Individual, A-Z
	e.g.
817.C6	Palazzo della Consulta
817.M3	Palazzo Madama
817.3.A-Z	Other buildings, A-Z
	Suburbs see DG814.95+
	Southern Italy
819	Periodicals. Societies. Serials
820	General works
820.5	Pictorial works
820.8	Historical geography

	Southern Italy -- Continued
821	Description and travel
	Guidebooks see DG416
823	Antiquities
825	Social life and customs. Civilization
	Ethnography
825.4	General works
825.5.A-Z	Individual elements in the population, A-Z
825.5.A44	Albanians
825.5.G73	Greeks
	History
	Cf. DG845.8+ Naples. Kingdom of the Two Sicilies
	Cf. DG865.9+ Sicily
826	General works
	By period
	Early (Southern Italy) see DG53
	Early (Magna Graecia) see DG55.M3
827	Medieval
	Cf. DG847.15+ Hohenstaufen period
	Cf. DG861+ Byzantine, Saracen, and Norman domination
	Modern
828	General works
	By period
828.2	1442-1860
	Cf. DG848+ Kingdom of Naples
	1860-1945
828.3	General works
	Biography and memoirs
828.32	General
828.34.A-Z	Individual, A-Z
828.5	1945-
829	Other
831	Sicily and Malta
	Cf. DG987+ Malta
	Naples. Kingdom of the Two Sicilies
840	Periodicals. Societies. Serials
841	Sources and documents
841.2	Collections, by individual authors
	Biography (Collective)
841.4	General works
841.5	Rulers, kings, queens, etc.
841.55	Public men
	Houses, noble families, etc.
841.6.A1	Collective
841.6.A2-Z	Individual, A-Z
	e.g.

	Southern Italy
	Naples. Kingdom of the Two Sicilies
	Biography (Collective)
	Houses, noble families, etc.
	Individual, A-Z -- Continued
841.6.B68	Bourbon-Two Sicilies, House of
841.6.C3	Carafa family
841.6.P63	Poerio family
842	Guidebooks. Directories. Dictionaries
842.3	General works
842.5	Monumental and picturesque, etc.
842.6	Preservation of historic monuments, etc.
842.7	Historical geography
	Description and travel
	Cf. DG821 Southern Italy
843	Through 1860
844	1861-1950
844.2	1951-
845	Antiquities
	For Magna Graecia see DG55.M3
	For other local Roman and pre-Roman antiquities see DG70.A+
	For pre-Roman and Roman antiquities of Naples see DG70.N35
845.6	Social life and customs. Civilization. Intellectual life
	For specific periods, see the period or reign
	Ethnography
845.65	General works
845.66.A-Z	Individual elements in the population, A-Z
845.66.G47	Germans
	History
	Cf. DG865.9+ Sicily
	Historiography
845.8	General works
	Biography of historians, area studies specialists, archaeologists, etc.
845.83	Collective
845.85.A-Z	Individual, A-Z
	General works
	Including Southern Italy
	Cf. DG826+ Southern Italy
	Cf. DG861+ Sicily
846	Modern
846.3	Early to 1800
846.55	Political history
	For specific periods, see the period
846.6	Sources and documents

	Southern Italy
	Naples. Kingdom of the Two Sicilies
	History
	Political history -- Continued
846.62	General works
	Early and medieval
	General works
847.A2	Through 1800
847.A3-Z	1801-
	Early (Post-Roman) to 1016
	Cf. DG70.N35 Pre-Roman and Roman period
847.1	Sources and documents
847.11	General works
	1016-1268
847.13	General works
	Biography and memoirs
847.135	Collective
847.136.A-Z	Individual, A-Z
847.14	1016-1194. Norman period
	For individual rulers see DG867.24+
	1194-1268. Hohenstaufen period
847.15	General works
847.16	Heinrich VI, 1194-1197
847.162	Friedrich I (Emperor Friedrich II), 1197-1250
847.164	Konrad IV, 1250-1254
847.166	Conradin, 1254-1268
	Cf. D186.5 Latin Orient
	Cf. DD147.5.C64 Biography
847.168	Manfredi, 1258-1266
	1268-1442. Anjou dynasty
847.17	General works
	Biography and memoirs
847.175	Collective
847.18.A-Z	Individual, A-Z
	e.g.
847.18.A33	Acciaiuoli, Niccolo, 1310-1365
847.2	Charles I, 1266-1285
847.3	Charles II, 1285-1309
847.4	Robert, 1309-1343
847.5	Jeanne (Giovanna) I, 1343-1382
847.55	Charles III of Durazzo, 1381-1386
847.58	Louis I, 1381-1382
847.6	Wladislaw, 1386-1414
847.65	Louis II, 1386-1390
847.7	Jeanne (Giovanna) II, 1414-1435

DG

	Southern Italy
	Naples. Kingdom of the Two Sicilies
	History
	Early and medieval
	1268-1442. Anjou dynasty -- Continued
847.8	René I, 1435-1442
	Including Battle of Ponza, 1435
	For biography see DC102.8.R4
	Modern
848	General works
	1442-1707. Spanish rule
848.05	Sources and documents
848.1	General works
848.112.A-Z	Biography and memoirs, A-Z
	e.g.
848.112.A4	Alfonso V, el Magnánimo
	Cf. DP133.1 Spain
848.112.F47	Ferdinando II, d'Aragona, King of Naples, 1467-1496
848.112.P47	Pescara, Alfonso d'Avalos, marchese di, ca. 1450-1495
848.115	1442-1504
848.12	1504-1647
848.13	1647-1648. Masaniello
848.15	1648-1707
	1707-1735. Austrian rule
848.2	General works
	Biography and memoirs
848.23	Collective
848.24.A-Z	Individual, A-Z
	1735-1861. Bourbon dynasty
848.3	General works
	Carlos III, 1735-1759
848.32	Sources and documents
848.33	General works
	Biography and memoirs
848.335	Collective
848.34.A-Z	Individual, A-Z
	1759-1815
848.35	General works
848.37.A-Z	Biography and memoirs, A-Z
848.37.C3	Carolina Maria, Consort of Ferdinand I, King of the Two Sicilies
848.37.C8	Cuoco, Vincenzo
	Maria Carolina, Queen, Consort of Ferdinand I, King of the Two Sicilies, 1752-1814 see DG848.37.C3

DG

Southern Italy
Naples. Kingdom of the Two Sicilies
Local -- Continued
Sections, districts, suburbs, etc.
856	Collective
856.2.A-Z	Individual, A-Z
	Monuments, statues, etc.
856.3	Collective
856.5.A-Z	Individual, A-Z
	Parks, squares, cemeteries, etc.
856.7	Collective
856.8.A-Z	Individual, A-Z
	Streets. Bridges
857	Collective
857.2.A-Z	Individual, A-Z
	Buildings
857.3	Collective
857.5.A-Z	Individual, A-Z
	Other cities of the Kingdom of Naples see DG975.A+
	Sicily
861	Periodicals. Societies. Serials
861.2	Sources and documents
	Collected works
861.4	Several authors
861.5	Individual authors
861.6	Gazetteers. Dictionaries, etc. Place names
	Biography (Collective)
861.7	General works
	Houses, noble families, etc.
861.74	Collective
861.75.A-Z	Individual houses, families, etc., A-Z
861.75.C45	Celestre family
862	Guidebooks
862.4	General works
862.5	Pictorial works
	Historic monuments, landmarks, etc.
862.53	General works
862.55	Preservation
862.57	Historical geography
	Description and travel
863	Through 1860
864	1861-1950
864.2	1951-1980
864.3	1981-
865	Antiquities
865.6	Social life and customs. Civilization
	Ethnography

DG

	Southern Italy
	Sicily
	History
	Early and medieval to 1409 -- Continued
	Sicily under the Hohenstaufen, 1194-1268
867.28	General works
867.29	General special
	For individual rulers see DG847.15+
867.299	1268-1282
867.3	Sicilian Vespers, 1282
	1282-1409
867.33	Sources and documents
867.34	General works
	Biography and memoirs
867.348	Collective
867.349.A-Z	Individual, A-Z
	e.g.
867.349.C67	Costanza, di Svevia, Queen of Aragon and Sicily, 1247?-1302
867.35	Pedro de Aragón, 1282-1285
867.4	Jaime, 1285-1295
867.5	Federico II, 1296-1337
867.6	Pedro II, 1337-1342
867.65	Luis, 1342-1355
867.7	Federico III, 1355-1377
867.8	Maria, etc., 1377-1409
	Modern, 1409-
868	General works
868.2	1409-1504
868.3	1504-1648
	1648-1806
868.35	General works
	Biography and memoirs
868.358	Collective
868.359.A-Z	Individual, A-Z
	19th century
868.4	General works
868.42	1806-1815
868.44	1815-1871
	Expedition of the Thousand, 1860 see DG554.5.E96
868.5	1871-1900
869	20th century
869.2	1900-1945
	1945-
869.3	General works
	Biography and memoirs

DG

Cities (other than metropolitan), provinces, etc., A-Z

Asti -- Continued

975.A86	Other
975.A935	Avesa
975.B25	Bari
975.B27	Barletta
975.B3	Basilicata. Lucania
	Belluno
975.B39	Serials. Collections
975.B4	History and description
975.B41	Other
	Benevento
975.B43	Serials. Collections
975.B44	General works. Description
975.B45	History
975.B46	Other
	Bergamo
975.B48	Serials. Collections
975.B49	General works. Description
975.B5	History
975.B51	Other
975.B54	Biella
	Bologna
975.B57	Serials. Collections
975.B58	Guidebooks
975.B59	Description
	Biography
975.B593A1-.B593A3	Collective
975.B593A4-.B593Z	Individual, A-Z
975.B595	Antiquities
975.B596	Social life and customs. Civilization. Intellectual life
	History
975.B6	General works
975.B61	Medieval
975.B62	Early modern
975.B63	Napoleonic
975.B64	19th-20th centuries
975.B65	Other
975.B68	Bolzano
975.B73	Borromean Islands
	Brescia
975.B77	Serials
975.B78	Sources and documents
975.B785	Gazetteers
975.B79	Description. Guidebooks
975.B8	Biography
975.B81	Antiquities

	Cities (other than metropolitan), provinces, etc., A-Z
	Brescia -- Continued
975.B82	Social life and customs
975.B825	History
975.B83	Through 1796
975.B84	1797-1849
975.B85	1850-
975.B855	Bressanone
975.B86	Brianza
975.B917	Budrio
975.B93	Busseto
975.C115	Cadore
	Cadore (City) see DG975.P55
	Calabria
975.C13	Serials. Collections
975.C14	Gazetteers. Dictionaries. Place names
975.C145	General works
975.C15	Description
	Biography
975.C155A1-.C155A3	Collective
975.C155A4-.C155Z	Individual, A-Z
975.C16	History
975.C17	Campagna di Roma. Pontine Marshes
975.C173	Campania
975.C17448	Canale, Val. Kanal Valley
975.C2	Capri
975.C25	Capua
975.C26	Carpi
975.C2664	Cassino
975.C2673	Castel Bolognese
975.C267462	Castello della Motta Site
975.C267463	Castello di Lagopesole Site
975.C28	Catania
975.C43	Cesena
975.C5	Citta di Castello
975.C54	Civitavecchia
975.C6	Comacchio
975.C64	Comasine
	Como
975.C7	Serials. Collections
975.C71	General works. Description
975.C72	History
975.C7214	Como (Province)
975.C7215	Como, Lake of
975.C735	Corcumello
975.C7384	Corleone (Sicily)
975.C74	Cortina d'Ampezzo

	Cities (other than metropolitan), provinces, etc., A-Z --
	Continued
975.C75	Cortona
	Cremona
975.C79	Serials. Documents. Collections
975.C8	History and description
	Dolomite Alps
975.D66	Periodicals. Societies. Collections
975.D67	General works. History. Description and travel. Pictorial works
975.D68	Special mountains, peaks, trails, etc. (not A-Z)
975.E3	Elba
975.E5	Emilia
975.E53	Emilia-Romagna
975.E8	Euganean Hills
	Ferrara
975.F38	Serials. Collections. Sources and documents
975.F39	Description
975.F395	Biography (Collective)
975.F4	History
975.F42	Medieval
975.F43	16th century
975.F44	19th-20th centuries
	Firenze (Florence) see DG731+
975.F696	Fonte Nuova
	Forlì
975.F71	Serials. Collections. Sources and documents
975.F72	Biography
975.F73	History and description
975.F74	Other
	Frascati. Alban Hills
975.F8	General works. Description
975.F82	History
975.F824	Frassinoro
975.F847	Frignano
975.F85	Friuli
975.F855	Friuli-Venezia Giulia
	Class here works on that part of Venezia Giulia remaining in Italy after 1947
	For Austrian territories prior to 1919 and the Yugoslav territories after 1947 see DR1350.J84
975.G13	Gaeta
975.G18	Gallarate
975.G27	Garda, Lago di
975.G3	Garfagnana
975.G32	Gargano Promontory
975.G35	Genazzano

	Cities (other than metropolitan), provinces, etc., A-Z -- Continued
	Genoa see DG631+
975.G67	Gorizia
	For Görz and Gradiska (General and Slovenia) see DR1475.G67
975.I4	Iesi
975.I5	Imola
	Ionian Sea see DF901.I695
975.I6	Ischia (Island)
	Jesi see DG975.I4
	Kanal Valley see DG975.C17448
975.K38	Kaukana (Extinct city)
975.L2	Lake District. Italian lakes
975.L24	L'Aquila
	Lazio see DG975.L245
975.L245	Latium. Lazio
	Lecce
	Including the city and the province
975.L25	Serials. Sources and documents
	Collected works
975.L26	Several authors
975.L27	Individual authors
975.L3	History and description
975.L33	Lecco
975.L4	Leghorn (Livorno)
975.L68	Liguria
975.L7	Lipari Islands
	Livorno see DG975.L4
	Lucania see DG975.B3
	Lucca
975.L8	Serials. Sources and documents. Collections
975.L81	General works. Description
975.L82	History
975.L825	Luceoli (Extinct city)
975.L89	Luna (Extinct city)
975.M16	Maggiore, Lago
975.M22	Maglie
	Mantua (Mantova)
975.M27	Serials. Collections
975.M28	Sources and documents
	History and description
	General works
975.M29	Early through 1800
975.M3	1801-
975.M31	Medieval
975.M32	16th-18th centuries

DG

Cities (other than metropolitan), provinces, etc., A-Z
Mantua (Mantova)
History and description -- Continued

975.M33	19th-20th centuries
975.M34	Other
975.M4	Marche (Marches)
975.M43	Maremme
975.M52	Merano (Meran)
	Messina
975.M53	Serials. Collections. Sources and documents
975.M532	Description
975.M533	History
975.M534	Other
	Milano (Milan) see DG651+
	Modena
975.M6	Serials. Collections. Sources and documents
975.M61	General works. Description
975.M615	Antiquities
975.M62	History
975.M63	Other
975.M65	Molfetta
975.M67354	Montalcino
975.M67356	Montarrenti Castle Site
	Monte Bianco (Mont Blanc) see DC611.M68
975.M67375	Montebelluna
975.M67378	Montecarlo
975.M675	Montefeltro
975.M68	Montenero
975.M73	Monza
	Napoli (Naples) see DG840+
975.O7	Orvieto
975.O8	Ostia
	Padua
975.P12	Serials. Collections. Sources and documents
975.P13	Description
975.P14	Antiquities
975.P15	History
	Palermo
975.P19	Serials. Collections. Sources and documents
975.P2	General works. Description
975.P21	History
975.P25	Parma
	Including the city, the province, and the duchy of Parma and Piacenza
	Pavia
975.P29	Serials. Collections. Sources and documents
975.P3	General works. History. Description and travel

Cities (other than metropolitan), provinces, etc., A-Z
    Pavia -- Continued

975.P32	Other
975.P37	Pergine Valsugana
975.P375	Pergola (Pesaro e Urbino)
975.P4	Perugia
975.P5	Piacenza
	For the duchy of Parma and Piacenza see DG975.P25
	Piemonte (Piedmont) see DG610+
975.P5443	Pietra Ligure
975.P55	Pieve di Cadore
	Pisa
975.P59	Serials. Collections. Sources and documents
975.P593	Biography
975.P6	General works. History and description
975.P61	Medieval
975.P615	14th-15th centuries
975.P618	16th-18th centuries
975.P62	19th-20th centuries
975.P63	Other
975.P65	Pistoia
	Pontine Marshes see DG975.C17
	Puglia see DG975.A65
975.R25	Ravenna
975.R3	Reggio di Calabria
975.R5	Rimini
975.R6	Riviera
	Romagna
975.R7	Serials. Collections. Sources and documents
975.R71	General works. Description
975.R715	Antiquities
975.R72	History
975.R73	Other
	Rome
	Ancient city see DG61+
	Medieval and modern city see DG803+
975.S17	Salò
975.S19	San Gimignano
975.S1958	San Marco in Boccalama Site
975.S2	San Marino (Republic)
975.S233	San Michele alla Verruca Site
975.S268	Sant'Andrea (Gorizia). Standrež
975.S2757	Santo Niceto Site
	Sardinia
975.S29	Serials. Collections. Sources and documents
975.S3	Description and travel
	Biography

DG

Cities (other than metropolitan), provinces, etc., A-Z
　　Sardinia
　　　Biography -- Continued
975.S304　　　　　　　Collective
975.S306　　　　　　　Individual, A-Z
975.S31　　　　　　　History
　　　　　　　　　Cf. DG618.5+ Kingdom of Sardinia, 1718-1860
975.S33　　　　　　　Other
　　Savoy see DG610+
975.S3724　　　　　　Scrivia Valley
975.S47　　　　　　　Sgonico
　　Siena
975.S49　　　　　　　Serials. Collections. Sources and documents
975.S5　　　　　　　　History and description
975.S54　　　　　　　Soave
975.S7　　　　　　　　Sorrento
　　Standrež see DG975.S268
975.S795　　　　　　Sugana Valley
975.S9　　　　　　　　Syracuse
975.T2　　　　　　　　Taormina
975.T5　　　　　　　　Tiber River and Valley
975.T57　　　　　　　Tiepido Valley
975.T6　　　　　　　　Tivoli
975.T767　　　　　　Trecate
975.T788　　　　　　Trent
975.T792　　　　　　Trentino-Alto Adige
975.T8　　　　　　　　Treviso
975.T825　　　　　　Trieste (City and District)
　　Turin
975.T93　　　　　　　Serials. Collections. Sources and documents
975.T94　　　　　　　Description
975.T95　　　　　　　History
975.T97　　　　　　　Other
975.U3　　　　　　　　Udine
975.U5　　　　　　　　Umbria
　　Urbino
975.U7　　　　　　　　General works. Description
975.U72　　　　　　　History
975.V2　　　　　　　　Vallombrosa
975.V23　　　　　　　Valtellina
975.V267　　　　　　Varazze
975.V3　　　　　　　　Varese
975.V38　　　　　　　Venetia (Veneto)
　　Venezia (Venice) see DG975.T792
　　Venezia Giulia see DG975.F855
　　Venezia Tridentina see DG975.T792
975.V43　　　　　　　Ventimiglia

	Cities (other than metropolitan), provinces, etc., A-Z --
	Continued
	Verona
975.V48	Serials. Collections. Sources and documents
975.V49	Description
975.V495	Antiquities
975.V5	History
975.V51	Medieval
975.V52	Modern
975.V53	Other
975.V6	Vesuvius
	In general, prefer QE523.V5
975.V646	Viadana
975.V7	Vicenza
975.V8	Vincigliata, Castello di
975.V85	Viterbo
	Zgonik see DG975.S47
(980)	Italian colonies (Former)
	Collective see JV2200+
	Individual colonies
	see DS, DT

	History of Malta
987	Periodicals. Societies. Serials
	Museums, exhibitions, etc.
987.2	General works
987.3.A-Z	Individual. By place, A-Z
987.5	Sources and documents
	Collected works (nonserial)
988.2	Several authors
988.3	Individual authors
988.5	Gazetteers. Dictionaries
988.6	Place names (General)
	For etymological studies see PL4731+
988.7	Directories
988.8	Guidebooks
989	General works
989.2	General special
989.25	Pictorial works
	Historic monuments, landmarks, scenery, etc. (General)
	For local see DG999.A+
989.3	General works
989.35	Preservation
989.4	Description and travel
989.5	Antiquities
	For local antiquities see DG999.A+
989.7	Social life and customs. Civilization. Intellectual life
	For specific periods, see the period
	Ethnography
989.74	General works
989.75.A-Z	Individual elements in the population, A-Z
	History
	Periodicals. Societies. Serials see DG987
989.8	Dictionaries. Chronological tables, outlines, etc.
989.83	Biography (Collective)
	For individual biography, see the specific period or place
989.85	Historiography
990	General works
	Ethnography. Race and ethnic relations
990.3	General works
990.35.A-Z	Individual elements in the population, A-Z
990.5	Military history
	For individual campaigns and engagements, see the special period
990.7	Naval history
	For individual campaigns and engagements, see the special period
991	Political history
	For specific periods, see the period

History -- Continued
    Foreign and general relations
        For general works on the diplomatic history of a period, see the
            period
        For works on relations with a specific country regardless
            of period see DG991.6.A+

991.5	General works
991.6.A-Z	Relations with individual regions or countries, A-Z
	By period
	Early to 870. Phoenician, Greek, Roman and Byzantine domination
992	General works
	Biography and memoirs
992.12	Collective
992.13.A-Z	Individual, A-Z
	870-1530. Arabic, Norman, Angevin and Aragonese domination
992.2	General works
	Cf. DG867.299 History of Sicily
	Biography and memoirs
992.26	Collective
992.27.A-Z	Individual, A-Z
992.3	Revolt against Monroy, 1427
	1530-1798. Rule of the Knights of Malta
	Including wars against the Turks and their North African allies, suppression of the Jesuits (1768), and the conquest by Napoleon (1798)
	Cf. DC226.M3 Napoleon's expedition to Egypt and Syria, 1798-1799
992.5	General works
	Biography and memoirs
992.56	Collective
992.57.A-Z	Individual, A-Z
992.6	Siege of Malta, 1565
992.62	Rebellion of the Turkish slaves, 1722
992.65	Rebellion of the priests, 1775
	1798-1964. British colonial rule
992.7	General works
	Biography and memoirs
992.76	Collective
992.77.A-Z	Individual, A-Z
992.8	1798-1802. Interim between Napoleonic conquest and Treaty of Amiens
993	1802-1947. British administration
	Cf. D763.M3 Malta in World War II
993.5	1947-1964. Self-rule under British authority
	1964- . Independent

DG

	History
	By period
	1964- . Independent -- Continued
994	General works
	Biography and memoirs
994.7	Collective
994.8.A-Z	Individual, A-Z
999.A-Z	Local history and description, A-Z
	e.g.
999.G59	Gozo
999.V3	Valletta

History of Low Countries. Benelux Countries
Including Belgium and the Netherlands treated collectively

DH

History
By period
Wars of independence, 1555-1648
Felipe (Philip) II, 1555-1581
Biography and memoirs of contemporaries, A-Z --
Continued

188.O4	Oldenbarnevelt, Joan van
188.W7	Willem I, Prince of Orange
189	Margaretha of Parma, 1559-1567
	Alba (Alva), 1567-1573
191	General works
191.7	Special
	1573-1576
192	General works
192.5	Siege of Leyden, 1573-1574
193	Juan de Austria, 1576-1578
	Alessandro Farnese, 1578-1581
194	General works
195	Union of Utrecht, 1579
	1581-1609
	General works
196	Through 1800
197	1801-
198	Leicester, 1585-1587
199.A-Z	Special events, battles, etc., A-Z
199.C4	Deventer, Surrender of, 1587
199.N4	Nieuport, Battle of, 1600
199.O8	Ostend, Siege of, 1601-1604
200	Pamphlets. By date
201	Armistice, 1609-1621
	1621-1648
204	General works
206.A-Z	Special events, battles, etc., A-Z
206.A55	Antwerp, Siege of, 1584-1585
206.B8	Breda, Siege of, 1624-1625
206.D6	Downs, Battle of, 1639
206.H5	s'Hertogenbosch, Siege of, 1629
207	Pamphlets, 1609-1648. By date

DH

History of Belgium

	History
	Historiography
	Biography of historians -- Continued
506.A-Z	Individual, A-Z
	e.g.
506.K8	Kurth, Godefroid Joseph F.
506.P5	Pirenne, Henri
511	Dictionaries. Chronological tables, outlines, etc.
	Biography (Collective)
	For individual biographies, see the special period, reign, or place
513	General works
514	Rulers, kings, etc.
515	Public men
515.5	Women
516.A-Z	Houses, noble families, etc., A-Z
	e.g.
516.H8	Howarderie, Seigneurs de la
516.L6	Looz, House of
	Study and teaching
516.5	General works
516.6.A-Z	Local, A-Z
	General works
517	Through 1800. Chronicles
521	1801-
523	Compends
525	Topics (not A-Z)
527	Pamphlets, etc.
	General special
531	History of two or more provinces
	Military history
	For individual campaigns and engagements, see the special period
540	General works
541	Biography (Collective)
542	Early and medieval to 1555
543	1555-1815
545	1815-
551	Naval history
	Political and diplomatic history
	Cf. DH571+ Special periods, reigns, etc.
566	General works
569.A-Z	Foreign relations with individual regions or countries, A-Z
	By period
	Early and medieval to 1555
	Cf. DH801.F4+ Flanders
571	General works

DH

DH

	History
	By period
	1794-1909
	1830-
	Leopold II, 1865-1909
	Biography and memoirs of contemporaries --
	Continued
676.A-Z	Individual, A-Z
	e.g.
676.B3	Banning, Emile Théodore J.H.
676.F7	Frère-Orban, Hubert Joseph W.
676.L7	Louise, Princess of Belgium
676.M3	Marie, Countess of Flanders
676.M35	Marie Henriette, Consort of Leopold II
	20th century
677	General works
	Albert, 1909-1934
681	General works on life and reign
681.5	Travels
682	Period of World War I, 1914-1918. Flemish movement
	For the war itself see D501+
683	1920-
	Biography and memoirs of contemporaries
685.A1	Collective
685.A2-Z	Individual, A-Z
	e.g.
685.B6	Borms, August
685.D6	Dorlodot, René de, baron
685.E5	Elizabeth, Consort of Albert I
685.M3	Max, Adolphe
685.R64	Rolin, Henri
	Leopold III, 1934-1951
687	General works on life and reign
	Including his detention in Germany and exile, 1940-1950, and abdication, 1951; regency of Prince Charles, 1944-1950
689.A-Z	Biography and memoirs of contemporaries, A-Z
	e.g.
689.A8	Astrid, Consort of Leopold III
689.C5	Clercq, Gustaaf de
689.H3	Hagemans, John
689.M3	Man, Henri de
	Baudouin I, 1951-1993
690	General works on life and reign
692.A-Z	Biography and memoirs of contemporaries, A-Z
	Albert II, 1993-
693	General works on life and reign

	Local history and description -- Continued
	Brussels
802.A2	Periodicals. Societies. Serials
802.A5-Z	Sources and documents
	Collected works
802.3	Several authors
802.5	Individual authors
802.7.A-Z	Biography, A-Z
803	Directories. Dictionaries
804	Guidebooks
	Description
804.3	Through 1800
804.4	1801-1900
804.5	1901-
804.8	Antiquities
804.9	Social life and customs. Culture
	History
805	General works
805.5	General special
806	Early and medieval
806.5	16th-17th centuries
806.7	18th century
806.9	Napoleonic period
807	19th century
807.5	20th century
	Sections, districts, etc.
809	General works
809.3	Cemeteries
809.4	Churches
809.5	Parks
809.6	Streets. Bridges
	Buildings
809.7	General works
809.8.A-Z	Individual, A-Z
809.9.A-Z	Suburbs, A-Z
809.95	Other special (not A-Z)
	e.g. Mannikin Fountain
811.A-Z	Other cities, towns, etc., A-Z
	Antwerp
811.A55	Periodicals. Societies. Serials
811.A56	Sources and documents
811.A58	General works and description
811.A6	History
811.A63	Early to 1550
811.A64	1550-1600
811.A67	17th-18th centuries
811.A68	19th-20th centuries

Local history and description
  Other cities, towns, etc., a-Z
    Audenarde see DH811.O8
    Bruges

811.B75	Periodicals. Societies. Serials
811.B76	Sources and documents
811.B78	General works and description
811.B79	Antiquities
811.B8	History
811.B82	Early and medieval
811.B83	1550-1660
811.B84	17th-18th centuries
811.B85	19th-20th centuries

    Chimay

811.C5	Periodicals. Societies. Serials
811.C52	Sources and documents
811.C53	General works and description
811.C55	History
811.C8	Courtrai (Kortryk)
811.E6	Enghien

    Ghent

811.G4	Periodicals. Societies. Collections, etc.
811.G43	General works and description
811.G45	History
811.G46	Early and medieval
811.G47	16th century
811.G48	17th-18th centuries
811.G49	19th-20th centuries
811.L5	Liége
811.L7	Louvain
811.M4	Mechlin (Malines, Mechelen)
811.M75	Mons (Bergen)
811.N2	Namur
811.N7	Nieuport
811.O8	Oudenaarde
811.R6	Roeselare
811.S65	Soiron
811.S7	Spa
811.T3	Tervueren

    Tournai (Doornick)

811.T7	Periodicals. Societies. Collections, etc.
811.T73	General works and description
811.T76	History
811.Y8	Ypres

DH

	History of Luxembourg
901	Periodicals. Societies. Serials
902	Sources and documents
903	Gazetteers. Dictionaries, etc.
903.2	Guidebooks
904	Biography (Collective)
905	General works
	Historic monuments, landmarks, scenery, etc. (General)
	For local see DH925.A+
905.4	General works
905.5	Preservation
	Description and travel
906	Through 1945
907	1946-
907.3	Antiquities
907.7	Social life and customs. Civilization
907.9	Ethnography
	History
908	General works
	Political and diplomatic history
908.5	General works
908.6.A-Z	Foreign relations with individual regions or countries, A-Z
	By period
909	Early to 1354 (Countship)
	1354-1815 (Duchy)
910	General works
911	Union with Burgundy, 1444-1477
912	Austria, 1477-1555
913	Spain, 1555-1713 (France, 1684-1697)
914	Austria, 1714-1795
915	France, 1795-1815
	1815- (Grand duchy)
916	General works
	Biography and memoirs
918	Collective
918.5.A-Z	Individual, A-Z
925.A-Z	Local history and description, A-Z
	e.g.
925.L8	Luxembourg

History of Netherlands (Holland)

1	Periodicals. Societies. Serials
3	Sources and documents
	Collected works
4	Several authors
5	Individual authors
14	Gazetteers. Dictionaries, etc.
15	Place names (General)
16	Guidebooks
18	General works
21	Compends
24	Monumental and picturesque
25	Preservation of historic monuments, etc.
27	Dikes, canals, sluices, etc.
30	Historical geography
30.5	Geography
	Description and travel
33	History of travel
34	Through 1500
36	1501-1800
38	1801-1900
39	1901-1945
40	1946-1977
41	1978-
51	Antiquities
	Cf. DJ401+ Local history and description
71	Social life and customs. Civilization. Intellectual life
81	Dutch culture in foreign countries
	Class here general works, or those works in combinations too broad for any one country
	Ethnography
91	General works
91.5	National characteristics
92.A-Z	Individual elements in the population, A-Z
92.A7	Armenians
92.B53	Blacks
92.C5	Chinese
92.E3	East Indians
92.F73	French
92.G45	Germans
92.G73	Greeks
92.H86	Hungarians
92.I53	Indonesians
92.I73	Iranians
92.J35	Japanese
92.K87	Kurds
92.M64	Moluccans

Ethnography
Individual elements in the population, A-Z -- Continued

92.M68	Moroccans
92.M86	Muslims
92.N47	Netherlands Antilleans
92.N67	Norwegians
92.P32	Pakistanis
92.P34	Palestinian Arabs
92.P57	Poles
92.P6	Portuguese
92.S8	Surinamese
92.S95	Swiss
92.T34	Tamil
92.T85	Turks
92.U54	Ukrainians
92.V53	Vietnamese

History
Historiography
95	General works
	Biography of historians
97	Collective
98.A-Z	Individual, A-Z
	e.g.
98.F7	Fruin, Robert Jacobus
101	Dictionaries. Chronological tables, outlines, etc.

Biography (Collective)
For individual biographies, see the special period, reign, or place
103	General works
104	Rulers, kings, etc.
105	Public men
105.5	Women
105.7	Other (not A-Z)
106	Houses, noble families, etc.

Study and teaching
106.5	General works
106.6.A-Z	By region or country, A-Z
	Subarrange by author

General works
107	Through 1800
109	1801-
111	Compends
114	Special aspects
116	Pamphlets, etc.

General special
121	History of two or more provinces

DJ

	History
	By period
	19th-20th centuries -- Continued
226	Kingdom of Holland, 1806-1810
228	Union with France, 1810-1813
236	Kingdom of the Netherlands, 1813-1830
241	Willem I, 1815-1840
251	Willem II, 1840-1849
	Willem III, 1849-1890
261	General works on life and reign
	Biography and memoirs of contemporaries
263.A1	Collective
263.A3	Emma, Consort of William III
263.A4-Z	Other, A-Z
	Wilhelmina, 1890-1948
281	General works on life and reign
	Biography and memoirs of contemporaries
283.A2	Collective
283.A3-Z	Individual, A-Z
	e.g.
283.G4	Geer, Dirk Jan de
283.T7	Troelstra, Pieter Jelles
285	Period of World War I, 1914-1918
286	Period between World War I and World War II, 1918-1939
287	World War II and post-war periods, 1939-1948
	Juliana, 1948-1980
288	General works on life and reign
	Biography and memoirs of contemporaries
289.A1	Collective
	Royal family
289.A2	Collective
289.A3	Bernhard, Leopold, Consort of Juliana
289.A4A-.A4Z	Other royal, A-Z
(289.A4B4)	Beatrix
	see DJ290+
289.A5-Z	Other contemporaries, A-Z
	Beatrix, 1980-
290	General works on life and reign
	Biography and memoirs of contemporaries
291.A1	Collective
	Royal family
291.A2	General works
291.A3	Claus, Consort of Beatrix
291.A4-Z	Other royal, A-Z
292.A-Z	Individual, A-Z
	Local history and description

	Local history and description -- Continued
401.A-Z	Provinces, regions, islands, etc., A-Z
401.A5	Ameland
401.A55	Anna Paulownapolder
401.B7-.B79	Brabant, North (Table D-DR8)
401.D7-.D79	Drenthe (Table D-DR8)
	Flevoland see DJ401.Z784+
401.F5-.F59	Friesland (Table D-DR8)
401.G35	Goeree-en-Overflakee
401.G4-.G49	Groningen (Table D-DR8)
401.G7-.G79	Guelders. Gelderland (Table D-DR8)
	Holland
401.H6-.H69	North and South (Holland and Zealand) (Table D-DR8)
401.H7-.H79	North (Table D-DR8)
401.H8-.H89	South (Table D-DR8)
401.H96	Humsterland
	IJssel Lake see DJ401.Z8
401.L6-.L69	Limburg (Table D-DR8)
	Including works on the duchy
	Early and medieval history
401.L662	General works
	Including Battle of Worringen, 1288
401.M3	Marken
	Markerwaard see DJ401.Z784+
	North Holland see DJ401.H7+
401.O8-.O89	Overijssel (Table D-DR8)
	South Holland see DJ401.H8+
401.T4	Terschelling (Island)
401.T5	Texel Island
401.T9	Twente
401.U7-.U79	Utrecht (Table D-DR8)
401.V4	Veluwe
401.W15	Waddeneilanden. West Frisian Islands
401.W2-.W29	Walcheren (Table D-DR8)
	West Frisian Islands see DJ401.W15
401.Z3	Zaanstreek
401.Z5-.Z59	Zealand (Table D-DR8)
401.Z784-.Z7849	Zuidelijke IJsselmeerpolders (Table D-DR8)
	Including Flevoland and the proposed Markerwaard
401.Z8	Zuyder Zee. IJssel Lake
411.A-Z	Cities, towns, etc., A-Z
	e.g.
411.A45	Amersfoort
	Amsterdam
411.A5	Periodicals. Societies. Serials
411.A52	Directories. Gazetteers, etc.
411.A53	General works and description

Local history and description
    Cities, towns, etc., A-Z
        Amsterdam -- Continued
           Ethnography

411.A54	General works
411.A545A-.A545Z	Individual elements in the population, A-Z
411.A545C55	Chinese
411.A545S95	Surinamese
	History
411.A55	General works
411.A56	Early and medieval
411.A57	17th-18th centuries
411.A58	19th-20th centuries
411.A59	Other
	e.g. K. Paleis
411.A8	Arnhem
411.B4	Bergen-op-Zoom
411.D46	Delft
411.D5	Deventer
411.D6	Dordrecht
411.G6	Gorinchem
411.G7	Groningen
411.H2	Haarlem
411.H33-.H3395	Hague ('s Gravenhage) (Table D-DR4)
411.H5	's Hertogenbosch
411.H7	Hoorn
411.K2	Kampen
411.L4	Leeuwarden
411.L5	Leyden
411.M2	Maastricht
411.M3	Mariënweerd, Gelderland (Abbey)
411.M6	Middelburg
411.N6	Nijmegen
411.R8	Rotterdam
411.T4	Tholen (City and island)
411.U9	Utrecht
411.V66	Voorburg
411.Z35	Zandvoort
411.Z95	Zwolle
(500)	Dutch colonies
	Collective
	see JV2500+
	Individual
	see classes D-F

	History of Eastern Europe (General)
	Cf. DR1+ Balkan Peninsula
1	Periodicals. Societies. Serials
1.5	Congresses
3	Sources and documents
	Collected works (nonserial)
4	Several authors
5	Individual authors
6	Gazetteers. Dictionaries, etc.
7	Place names (General)
7.5	Directories
	Communication of information
7.7	General works
7.75	Electronic information resources
	Including computer network resources, the Internet, digital libraries, etc.
8	Guidebooks
9	General works
10	Pictorial works
	Historic monuments, landmarks, scenery, etc. (General)
10.5	General works
10.6	Preservation
11	Historical geography
12	Geography
	Description and travel
13	History of travel
14	Early through 1500
15	1501-1800
16	1801-1900
17	1901-1950
18	1951-1980
19	1981-
23	Antiquities
	For local antiquities, see individual countries or localities
24	Social life and customs. Civilization. Intellectual life
	For specific periods, see the period
	Ethnography
26	General works
26.5	National characteristics
27	Slavic peoples (General)
	Class here historical studies only
	For ethnological studies see GN549.S6
	Cf. D147 Slavic migrations
	Cf. DR25 Slavs in the Balkan Peninsula
28.A-Z	Other individual elements in the population, A-Z
	Cf. DR27.A+ Balkan Peninsula
28.B84	Bulgarians

Ethnography

Other individual elements in the population, A-Z -- Continued

28.C67	Cossacks
28.F55	Finno-Ugrians (General)
28.G32	Gagauz
28.G4	Germans. Swabians
28.G74	Greeks
	Huculs see DK508.425.H87
28.H86	Hungarians
28.L4	Lemky (General)

                  Cf. DK508.425.L46 Lemky in the Ukraine

28.M32	Macedonians
28.M87	Muslims
28.P64	Poles
28.R85	Russians
28.R87	Ruthenians (General)

                  For Ruthenians in a particular country, see the country

              Scythians see DJK46.7

28.S56	Slovaks
28.S9	Swiss
28.T8	Turks

History

              Periodicals, societies, serials see DJK1

30	Dictionaries. Chronological tables, outlines, etc.
31	Biography (Collective)

                  For individual biography, see the specific period, reign, or place

              Historiography

32	General works
	Biography of historians, area studies specialists, archaeologists, etc.
33	Collective
34.A-Z	Individual, A-Z

              Study and teaching. Slavic studies

35	General works
35.5	Audiovisual materials
36.A-Z	By region or country, A-Z

                  Subarrange by author

              General works

37	Through 1800
38	1801-
39.5	Juvenile works
40	Addresses, essays, lectures. Anecdotes. etc.
40.5	Military history
	Political history
41	Sources and documents
42	General works

DJK

Ethnography -- Continued

34.A-Z	Individual elements in the population, A-Z

Class here works on ethnic groups in the Russian Empire, Soviet Union, or Former Soviet republics collectively

For works on ethnic groups in a specific republic, see the republic

34.A27	Adygei
34.A4	Alani
34.A45	Americans
34.A73	Argentinians
34.A75	Armenians
34.A92	Austrians
34.B25	Balts
34.B3	Bashkir
34.B44	Belgians
34.B53	Blacks
34.B7	British
34.B8	Bulgars
34.C42	Chechens
34.C45	Chinese
34.C54	Chuvash
34.C56	Cimmerians
	For Cimmerians (General) see DJK46.45
34.C57	Circassians
	Cossacks see DK35+
34.D35	Danes
34.D65	Dolgans
34.E77	Estonians
34.E97	Europeans, Western
34.F54	Finno-Ugrians
34.F55	Finns
34.F8	French
34.G3	Germans
34.G74	Greeks
34.I5	Indo-Aryans
34.I53	Ingush
34.I73	Italians
34.J36	Japanese
	Jews see DS134.8+
34.K13	Kabardians
34.K14	Kalmyks
34.K26	Karachay (Turkic people)
34.K29	Karaites
34.K45	Khazars
34.K65	Komi
34.K67	Koreans

Ethnography
  Individual elements in the population, A-Z -- Continued

34.K87	Kurds
34.L34	Latvians
34.M34	Macedonians
34.M37	Mari
34.M39	Mennonites
34.M6	Mordvins
34.M8	Muslims
34.N53	Nigerians
34.N64	Nogai
34.O2	Osimo
34.O79	Ossetes
34.P6	Poles
34.R8	Romanians
34.S17	Sami (European people)
34.S3	Sarmatians
34.S37	Scots
34.S4	Scythians
34.S47	Serbs
34.S63	Spanish
34.S88	Swedes
34.S9	Swiss
34.T37	Tatars
34.T8	Turks
34.U32	Udmurts
34.U35	Ukrainians
34.V4	Veps

Cossacks
35	General works
	Zaporozhians see DK508.55
35.5	Russians in foreign countries (General)
	For Russians in a particular country, see the country

History
36	Dictionaries. Chronological tables, outlines, etc.
	Biography (Collective)
	For individual biography, see the special period, reign, or place
37	General works
37.2	Women
37.4	Statesmen
37.6	Rulers, czars, etc.
	Houses, noble families, etc.
37.7	General works
37.8.A-Z	Special, A-Z
	e.g.
37.8.A3	Aksakov family

DK

History
Biography (Collective)
Houses, noble families, etc.
Special, A-Z -- Continued
37.8.B3   Bakunin family
37.8.R3   Razumovskiĭ family
37.8.R6   Romanov, House of
37.8.S5   Sheremetev family
Historiography
38   General works
Biography of historians, area studies specialists,
archaeologists, etc.
38.5   Collective
38.7.A-Z   Individual, A-Z
e.g.
38.7.K35   Karamzin, Nikolaĭ Mikhaĭlovich
38.7.K6   Kostomarov, Nikolaĭ Ivanovich
Study and teaching
38.8   General works
38.9.A-Z   Individual schools, A-Z
General works
39   Through 1800. Chronicles
40   1801-
41   Elementary textbooks
42   Addresses, essays, lectures. Anecdotes, etc.
43   Special aspects
General special
46   Several parts of the union treated together
49   Philosophy of Russian/Soviet history
Military history
For individual campaigns and engagements, see the special
period
50   Periodicals. Societies. Serials
Biography (Collective)
50.5   General
50.8   Officers
51   General works
51.7   General special
52   Early to 1613
52.5   1613-1801
53   1801-1917
54   1917-
Naval history
For individual campaigns and engagements, see the period
55   Periodicals. Societies. Serials
Biography (Collective)

History
   General special
     Naval history
       Biography (Collective) -- Continued

55.5	General
55.8	Officers
56	General works
56.7	General special
56.9	Addresses, essays, lectures
57	Early to 1689
57.5	1689-1801
58	1801-1917
59	1917-

     Political history
       Class here general works and works on broad periods of
         political history
       For works on a specific period, see the period

60	Sources and documents
61	General works
62	Early to 1462
62.3	1462-1613
62.6	1613-1762
62.9	1762-1917
	1917- see DK266+

     Foreign and general relations
       For works on relations with a specific country regardless of
         period, see DK67.5 DK68.7 DK69.3 DK69.4
       For general works on the diplomatic history of a period, see
         the period

65	Sources and documents
66	General works

       Special
        Europe
         General works see D34.A+; D1065.A+
         Catholic Church see BX1558+
         Balkan Peninsula see DR38.3.A+

67.5.A-Z	Individual countries, A-Z

        Asia
         Class here works on relations of the former Soviet
          republics as a group with Asia
         For works on relations of Russia and the Soviet
          Union with Asia see DS33.4.A+

68	General works
68.5	Middle East
68.7.A-Z	Individual countries, A-Z

DK

DK

	History
	By period
	House of Romanov, 1613-1917
	1689-1801. 18th century -- Continued
	Biography and memoirs
127.4	Collective
127.5.A-Z	Individual, A-Z
	Peter I the Great, 1689-1725
128	Museums, exhibitions, etc.
	Subarrange by author
129	Sources and documents
	Biography and memoirs
130.A1	Collective
130.A2-Z	Individual, A-Z
	e.g.
130.B4	Bergholz, Friedrich Wilhelm von
130.L4	Lefort, François Jacques
	Mazepa, Ivan, Hetman of Ukraine see
	DK508.752.M3
130.S5	Sheremetev, Boris Petrovich, graf
131	General works on life and reign
131.5	Journal
	Personal special
132	General works
132.5	Travels
133	General special. Reforms
	e.g. Revolt of the Streltsy, 1698
	Military history
134	General works
135	Wars with Turkey
	Cf. DR544 Russia in Turkey
136	Wars with Sweden
	Cf. DL738 Invasion of Russia by Sweden
137	Wars with Persia
	Cf. DS293 Afghan wars, etc.
142	Social life and customs. Civilization. Intellectual life
145	Diplomatic history. Foreign and general relations
146	Alexis
147	Eudoxia Lopukhina
148	Testament of Peter the Great
	1725-1762
150	General works
	Biography and memoirs
150.5	Collective
150.8.A-Z	Individual, A-Z
	e.g.

DK

History
By period
House of Romanov, 1613-1917
1689-1801. 18th century
1725-1762
Biography and memoirs
Individual, A-Z -- Continued
150.8.D6 Dolgorukova, Natalīa Borisovna (Sheremeteva), knīaginīa
150.8.M8 Münnich, Burkhard Christoph, graf von
151 Catherine I, 1725-1727
153 Peter II, 1727-1730
156 Anne, Empress of Russia, 1730-1740
157 Biron, Ernst Johann, Duke of Courland
159 Ivan VI and Anna Leopoldovna, 1740-1741
161 Elizabeth, 1741-1762
166 Peter III, 1762
Catherine II, 1762-1796
168 Sources and documents
Biography and memoirs
168.9 Collective
169.A-Z Individual, A-Z
e. g.
169.B3 Bagration, Petr Ivanovich, knīaz'
169.D3 Dashkova, Ekaterina Romanovna (Vorontsova), knīaginīa
169.K8 Kutuzov, Mikhail Illarionovich, svetlēĭshiĭ knīaz' Smolenskiĭ
169.P8 Potemkin, Grigoriĭ Aleksandrovich, knīaz'
169.R8 Rumīantsev, Petr Aleksandrovich, graf
169.S8 Suvorov, Aleksandr Vasil'evich, knīaz' Italiĭskiĭ
169.T3 Tarakanova, Elizaveta knīazhna (i.e. the imposter so styled)
169.U8 Ushakov, Fedor Fedorovich
170 General works on life and reign
170.A2 Personal correspondence
171 Reign only
171.5 General special
171.6 Addresses, essays, lectures
171.7 Military history
172 Social life and customs. Civilization. Intellectual life
Foreign and general relations
173 General works
Individual countries see DK67.5.A+
Political history
180 General works

DK

	History
	By period
	House of Romanov, 1613-1917
	19th century
	Alexander I, 1801-1825 -- Continued
	Collected works (nonserial)
190.8	Several authors
190.9	Individual authors
191	General works on life and reign
192	Personal special
194	General special
195	Addresses, essays, lectures
197	Foreign and general relations
	Cf. D383 Holy alliance
	Cf. DC235+ Russian campaign, 1812
	Cf. DC249 Congress of Vienna
	Cf. DR561 Russo-Turkish War
201	Speranskii. Administrative reforms
	Nicholas I, 1825-1855
209	Sources and documents
	Biography and memoirs
209.3	Collective
209.6.A-Z	Individual, A-Z
	e.g.
209.6.B4	Bestuzhev, Nikolaĭ Aleksandrovich
209.6.H4	Hertzen, Aleksandr Ivanovich
209.6.N3	Nakhimov, Pavel Stepanovich
	Collected works (nonserial)
209.8	Several authors
209.9	Individual authors
210	General works on life and reign
210.4	Coronation
210.7	Alexandra Feodorovna, Consort of Nicholas I
	Reign only
211	General works
212	Insurrection of December 1825 (Decembrists)
213.5	Russo-Khivan Expedition, 1839
	Crimean War, 1853-1856
	Cf. DR567 Turkey during the Crimean War
214	General works
215	General special. Diplomatic history
	Including the Congress of Paris, 1856; Treaty of Paris, etc.
	Special events, battles, etc.
215.1	Alma, September 20, 1854
215.3	Balaklava, October 25, 1854

History
By period
House of Romanov, 1613-1917
19th century
Nicholas I, 1825-1855
Reign only
Crimean War, 1853-1856
Special events, battles, etc. -- Continued

215.5	Inkerman, November 5, 1854
215.7	Sevastopol, 1854-1855
215.8.A-Z	Other, A-Z
215.8.O6	Oltenitza, Battle of, 1853
215.8.P4	Petropavlovsk-Kamchatskiĭ, Battle of, 1854
215.8.S6	Silistria, Siege of, 1854
215.8.S7	Sinope, Battle of 1853
215.9	The war in Asia
215.95	Hospitals, etc.
215.97	Personal narratives
	Russo-Turkish War see DR564
	Alexander II, 1855-1881
219	Sources and documents
	Biography and memoirs
219.3	Collective
219.6.A-Z	Individual, A-Z
	e.g.
219.6.A4	Aleksandr Mikhaĭlovich, Grand Duke of Russia
219.6.C43	Chernyshevskiĭ, Nikolaĭ Gavrilovich
219.6.D6	Dobroliubov, Nikolai Aleksandrovich
219.6.M5	Miliutin, Nikolaĭ Alekseevich
219.6.S35	Samarin, IUriĭ Fedorovich
219.6.S6	Skobelev, Mikhail Dmitrievich
219.6.T54	Tiutcheva, Anna Fedorovna
	Collected works (nonserial)
219.8	Several authors
219.9	Individual authors
220	General works on life and reign
220.7	Personal special
	Reign only. Reforms. Nihilism
221	General works
222	Emancipation of the serfs, 1861
	Cf. HT807+ Serfdom
223	Foreign and general relations
	Alexander III, 1881-1894
234	Sources and documents
	Biography and memoirs
235	Collective

DK

	History
	By period
	House of Romanov, 1613-1917
	20th century
	Nicholas II, 1894-1917
	Revolution of 1905
263.A1	Periodicals. Societies. Serials
263.A2	Sources and documents
	Biography see DK254.A+; DK268.A1+
	Causes, origins see DK262
263.A3-Z	General works
263.13	Pictorial works. Satire, caricature, etc.
263.15	Historiography
263.16	Addresses, essays, lectures
264	Special events
	Personal narratives
264.12	Collective
264.13	Individual
264.2.A-Z	Local revolutionary history. By place, A-Z
	Estonia see DK503.73+
	Latvia see DK504.73+
	Lithuania see DK505.73+
264.3	Prisoners and prisons. Exiles
264.5.A-Z	Other topics, A-Z
264.5.I6	Influence
264.5.I67	Intellectuals
264.5.O36	Officers
264.5.P47	Peasantry
264.5.P8	Public opinion
264.5.R45	Religious aspects
264.5.T7	Transportation
	Including railroad employees
264.7	Celebrations. Memorials. Monuments
264.8	Period of World War I, 1914-1918
	For the war itself see D501+
	Revolution, 1917-1921
265.A1-.A19	Periodicals. Societies. Serials
265.A195A-.A195Z	Museums, exhibitions, etc. By place, A-Z
	Sources and documents
265.A2-.A4	Serials
265.A5-.A55	Nonserials
265.A553	Historiography
265.A556	Study and teaching
	Biography see DK254.A+; DK268.A1+
	Causes, origins, etc. see DK262

History
  By period
    Revolution, 1917-1921 -- Continued

265.A56-Z	General works

        For works by Lenin use:

.L4A1	*Collected works. By date*
.L4A12-.L4A19	*Translations. By language and date*
.L4A2	*Selected works. By date*
.L4A22-.L4A29	*Translations. By language and date*
.L4A3-.L4Z	*Individual works. By title, A-Z*

265.13	Chronology
265.15	Pictorial works. Satire, caricature, etc.
265.17	Addresses, essays, lectures
265.19	February Revolution, 1917. Provisional government (Kerenskii)
	Assassination of Nicholas II see DK258.6
	Military operations
265.2	General works
	Individual campaigns, battles, etc. see DK265.8.A+
265.23.A-Z	Regimental histories, A-Z
	Naval operations
265.3	General works
265.35.A-Z	Individual engagements, ships, etc., A-Z
	Allied intervention, 1918-1920
265.4	General works
265.42.A-Z	By region or country, A-Z
265.5	Prisoners and prisons
265.6	Medical care. Hospitals. Health aspects
	Personal narratives
265.69	Collective
265.7.A-Z	Individual, A-Z
265.8.A-Z	Local revolutionary history. By place, A-Z
	For Ukrainian independence movement, as distinct from Bolshevik activities see DK508.832
265.8.A73	Armenia
265.8.A9	Azerbaijan
265.8.B9	Belarus
265.8.E8	Estonia
265.8.G4	Georgia (Republic). Georgian Sakartvelo
265.8.K39	Kazakhstan
265.8.K57	Kyrgyzstan
265.8.L33	Latvia
265.8.L4	Leningrad
265.8.L58	Lithuania

DK

History
  By period
    Revolution, 1917-1921
      Local revolutionary history. By place, A-Z -- Continued

265.8.M48	Moldova. Bessarabia
265.8.M6	Moscow
265.8.R85	Russia
265.8.S5	Siberia
265.8.S63	Soviet Central Asia
265.8.T27	Tajikistan
265.8.T93	Turkmenistan
265.8.U4	Ukraine
265.8.U9	Uzbekistan
265.9.A-Z	Other topics, A-Z
265.9.A35	Akademiĭa nauk SSSR
265.9.A5	Anarchists. Anarchism
265.9.A6	Armed forces. Army (Political activity)
265.9.A7	Art and the revolution
265.9.A8	Atrocities
265.9.C4	Children
265.9.C5	Civilian relief
265.9.C62	Cossacks
265.9.D45	Democracy and the revolution
265.9.D47	Destruction and pillage
265.9.E2	Economic aspects. Commerce, finance, etc. (General)
265.9.E75	Ethnic relations
265.9.F48	Food supply
265.9.F49	Foreign influences
	Foreign participation
265.9.F5	General works
265.9.F52A-.F52Z	By country, A-Z
265.9.F55	Foreign public opinion
265.9.I5	Influence
265.9.I55	Intellectuals
265.9.J48	Jews
265.9.K73	Krasnaĭa gvardiĭa. Red Guard
265.9.M42	Medals, badges, decorations of honor
265.9.M45	Mensheviks
265.9.P4	Peasantry
265.9.P6	Press
265.9.P74	Protest movements
265.9.P8	Public opinion
265.9.R25	Rabochaĭa oppozĭtsĭa (Political party)
	Red Guard see DK265.9.K73
265.9.R3	Refugees
	Cf. DK269 Emigrés

	History
	By period
	Revolution, 1917-1921
	Other topics, A-Z -- Continued
265.9.R4	Religious aspects
265.9.S4	Secret service, spies, etc.
265.9.S6	Soviets (Councils)
265.9.T48	Theater and the revolution
265.9.T74	Transportation and the revolution
265.9.W57	Women
265.9.W65	Working class
265.95	Celebrations. Memorials. Monuments
	Soviet regime, 1918-1991
266.A2	Periodicals. Societies. Congresses
266.A3	Sources and documents
266.A33	Historiography
266.A4-Z	General works
266.3	General special
	e.g. Espionage and sabotage
266.4	Social life and customs. Civilization. Intellectual life
266.45	Foreign and general relations
266.5	1918-1924. Lenin
	For the biography of Lenin see DK254.L3+
	1925-1953. Stalin
	Periodicals, etc. see DK266.A2
267	General works
267.3	Pamphlets, etc. By date
	Biography and memoirs
268.A1	Collective
268.A2-Z	Individual, A-Z
	e.g.
268.D9	Dzerzhinskiĭ, Feliks Ėdmundovich
268.K3	Kalinin, Mikhail Ivanovich
268.L5	Litvinov, Maksim Maksimovich
268.M64	Molotov, Vi͡acheslav Mikhaĭlovich
268.S8	Stalin, Joseph
268.3	Social life and customs. Civilization. Intellectual life
268.4	Political history
268.5	Foreign and general relations
269	Emigrés
269.5	Public opinion formation. Internal propaganda
	Soviet propaganda in foreign countries
270	General works
272.A-Z	In individual countries, A-Z
	Anti-Soviet propaganda
272.5	General works

	History
	By period
	Soviet regime, 1918-1991
	1925-1953. Stalin
	Anti-Soviet propaganda -- Continued
272.7.A-Z	In individual countries, A-Z
273	Period of World War II, 1939-1945
	For the war itself see D731+
	Cf. DL1095+ Russo-Finnish War, 1939-1940
	1953-1985
274.A2	Periodicals. Societies. Serials
274.A3-Z	General works
274.3	Addresses, essays, lectures
	Biography and memoirs of contemporaries
275.A1	Collective
275.A2-Z	Individual, A-Z
	e.g.
275.A53	Andropov, IU. V.
275.B8	Bulganin, Nikolaĭ Aleksandrovich
275.K5	Khrushchev, Nikita Sergeevich
275.M3	Malenkov, Georgiĭ Maksimilianovich
276	Social life and customs. Civilization. Intellectual life
277	Political history
	Soviet propaganda in foreign countries
278	General works
279.A-Z	Individual countries, A-Z
	Anti-Soviet propaganda
280	General works
281.A-Z	Individual countries, A-Z
282	Foreign and general relations
	1985-1991
285	Periodicals. Societies. Serials
285.5	Sources and documents
286	General works
286.5	Addresses, essays, lectures
287	Social life and customs. Civilization. Intellectual life
288	Political history
289	Foreign and general relations
	Biography and memoirs
290	Collective
290.3.A-Z	Individual, A-Z
	e.g.
(290.3.A53)	Andropov, IU. V.
	see DK275.A53
290.3.G67	Gorbachev, Mikhail Sergeevich, 1931-
292	Attempted coup. 1991

	History
	By period -- Continued
293	1991-
	Class here works on the former Soviet republics treated collectively
	For works on the Commonwealth of Independent States see DK1.5
(401-444)	Poland
	see DK4010+
(445-465)	Finland
	see DL1002+
500.A-Z	Regions not limited to one Republic, A-Z
	e.g.
500.A95	Azov, Sea of, Region
	Baltic States see DK502.3+
500.B55	Black Sea Coast (Soviet Union)
	For Black Sea Coast (Ukraine) and other republics and countries, see the republic and country
	Caucasus see DK509
	Caucasus, Northern (Russia) see DK511.C2
500.C68	Courland Lagoon and Spit (Lithuania and Russia)
500.D65	Dnieper River
	For the Central Dnieper Region (Ukraine) see DK508.9.C46
500.D66	Dniester River (Ukraine and Moldova)
500.D67	Donets Basin (Ukraine and Russia). Donbas
500.F67	Former Polish Eastern Territories
500.K47	Kerch Strait
500.L57	Livonia (Estonia and Latvia)
	Northern Soviet Union see DK501.A2+
	Palesse see DK500.P75
	Polesie see DK500.P75
500.P75	Pripet Marshes
	Siberia see DK751+
	Southern Soviet Union see DK509
	Soviet Asia see DK750
	Soviet Central Asia see DK845+
	Transcaucasia see DK509
500.W48	Western Soviet Union. Western Russia
	Local history and description
	Northern Soviet Union
501.A2	Periodicals. Societies
501.A3	Sources and documents. Serials
501.2	General works
501.3	Antiquities
501.4	Social life and customs. Civilization. Intellectual life

	Local history and description
	Northern Soviet Union -- Continued
501.42	Ethnography
	History
501.5	General works
501.6	Biography (Collective)
	Political history. Foreign and general relations
501.62	General works
(501.622)	By period
	see the specific period
501.63.A-Z	Relations with individual countries, A-Z
	By period
	Early
501.65	General works
	Biography and memoirs
501.66.A2	Collective
501.66.A3-Z	Individual, A-Z
	Colonial
501.7	General works
	Biography and memoirs
501.72.A2	Collective
501.72.A3-Z	Individual, A-Z
	20th century
501.75	General works
	Biography and memoirs
501.76.A2	Collective
501.76.A3-Z	Individual, A-Z
	Independent
501.8	General works
	Biography and memoirs
501.82.A2	Collective
501.82.A3-Z	Individual, A-Z
	Local
	see DK511, DK651, etc.
	Baltic States
	Including Estonia, Latvia, and Lithuania treated collectively
502.3	Periodicals. Societies. Serials
502.35	General works
502.4	Description and travel
502.5	Antiquities
502.6	Social life and customs. Civilization. Intellectual life
	Ethnography
502.63	General works
502.64.A-Z	Individual elements in the population, A-Z
502.64.G47	Germans
502.64.R87	Russians

DK

	Local history and description
	Estonia
	Ethnography -- Continued
503.36	Estonians in foreign countries (General)
	For Estonians in a particular country, see the country
	History
	Periodicals. Societies. Serials see DK503
503.37	Dictionaries. Chronological tables, outlines, etc.
	Biography (Collective)
	For individual biography, see the specific period or place
503.38	General works
503.39	Rulers, kings, etc.
503.4	Queens. Princes and princesses
	Houses, noble families, etc.
503.42	General works
503.43.A-Z	Individual houses, families, etc., A-Z
503.44	Statesmen
503.45	Women
	Cf. CT3490 Biography of women
	Historiography
503.46	General works
	Biography of historians, area studies specialists, archaeologists, etc.
503.47	Collective
503.48.A-Z	Individual, A-Z
	Study and teaching
503.49	General works
503.5.A-Z	By region or country, A-Z
	Subarrange by author
	General works
503.52	Through 1800
503.53	1801-1980
503.54	1981-
503.55	Pictorial works
503.56	Juvenile works
503.57	Addresses, essays, lectures. Anecdotes, etc.
	Military history
	For individual campaigns and engagements, see the special period
503.6	Sources and documents
503.62	General works
	Naval history
	For individual campaigns and engagements, see the special period
503.63	Sources and documents
503.64	General works

Local history and description
  Estonia
    History -- Continued
      Political history
        For specific periods, see the period

503.65	Sources and documents
503.66	General works
	Foreign and general relations
	For works on relations with a specific country regardless of period see DK503.69.A+
503.67	Sources and documents
503.68	General works
503.69.A-Z	Relations with individual countries, A-Z
	By period
503.7	Early to 1200
503.71	1200-1600
503.72	1600-1800
	1800-1918
503.73	General works
	Biography and memoirs
503.735	Collective
503.736.A-Z	Individual, A-Z
	1918-1940
	For works on the Bolshevik Revolution in Estonia see DK265.8.E8
503.74	General works
	Biography and memoirs
503.745	Collective
503.746.A-Z	Individual, A-Z
503.747	War of Independence, 1918-1920
503.748	Communist Coup, 1924
	1940-1991
	For works on World War II as distinct from the time period 1939-1945 see D731+
503.75	General works
	Biography and memoirs
503.76	Collective
503.77.A-Z	Individual, A-Z
	1991-
503.8	General works
503.82	Social life and customs. Civilization. Intellectual life
503.83	Political history
503.835	Foreign and general relations
	Biography and memoirs
503.84	Collective
503.85.A-Z	Individual, A-Z

Local history and description
Estonia -- Continued
Local history and description

503.9.A-Z	Regions, oblasts, etc., A-Z
	Cities and towns
	Tallinn
503.92	Periodicals. Societies. Serials
503.922	Sources and documents
503.923	Directories. Dictionaries. Gazetteers
503.924	Guidebooks
503.925	General works
503.926	Description. Geography
503.927	Pictorial works
503.928	Antiquities
503.929	Social life and customs. Civilization. Intellectual life
	Ethnography
503.93	General works
503.932.A-Z	Individual elements in the population, A-Z
	History
	Biography
503.933	Collective
503.934.A-Z	Individual, A-Z
503.935	General works
	Sections, monuments, parks, streets, buildings, etc.
503.938	Collective
503.939.A-Z	Individual, A-Z
503.95.A-Z	Other cities, towns, etc., A-Z
	e.g.
503.95.T38	Tartu
	Latvia
504	Periodicals. Societies. Serials
	Museums, exhibitions, etc.
504.12	General works
504.13.A-Z	Individual. By place, A-Z
504.14	Congresses
504.15	Sources and documents
	Collected works (nonserial)
504.16	Several authors
504.17	Individual authors
504.18	Gazetteers. Dictionaries, etc.
504.19	Place names (General)
504.2	Directories
504.22	Guidebooks
504.23	General works
504.24	General special
504.25	Pictorial works

	Local history and description
	Latvia -- Continued
	Historic monuments, landmarks, scenery, etc. (General)
	For local see DK504.9+
504.26	General works
504.27	Preservation
504.28	Historical geography
504.29	Description and travel
504.3	Antiquities
	For local antiquities see DK504.9+
504.32	Social life and customs. Civilization. Intellectual life
	For specific periods, see the period
	Ethnography
504.33	General works
504.34	National characteristics
504.35.A-Z	Individual elements in the population, A-Z
504.35.E77	Estonians
504.35.G3	Germans
504.35.P6	Poles
504.35.R86	Russians
504.35.S53	Slavs
504.36	Latvians in foreign countries (General)
	For Latvians in a particular country, see the country
	History
	Periodicals. Societies. Serials see DK504
504.37	Dictionaries. Chronological tables, outlines, etc.
	Biography (Collective)
	For individual biography, see the specific period or place
504.38	General works
504.39	Rulers, kings, etc.
504.4	Queens. Princes and princesses
	Houses, noble families, etc.
504.42	General works
504.43.A-Z	Individual houses, families, etc., A-Z
504.44	Statesmen
504.45	Women
	Cf. CT3490 Biography of women
	Historiography
504.46	General works
	Biography of historians, area studies specialists, archaeologists, etc.
504.47	Collective
504.48.A-Z	Individual, A-Z
	Study and teaching
504.49	General works

DK

Local history and description
Latvia
History
Study and teaching -- Continued
504.5.A-Z   By region or country, A-Z
        Subarrange by author
General works
504.52   Through 1800
504.53   1801-1980
504.54   1981-
504.55   Pictorial works
504.56   Juvenile works
504.57   Addresses, essays, lectures. Anecdotes, etc.
Military history
      For individual campaigns and engagements, see the
        special period
504.6   Sources and documents
504.62   General works
Naval history
      For individual campaigns and engagements, see the
        special period
504.63   Sources and documents
504.64   General works
Political history
      For specific periods, see the period
504.65   Sources and documents
504.66   General works
Foreign and general relations
      For works on relations with a specific country
        regardless of period see DK504.69.A+
504.67   Sources and documents
504.68   General works
504.69.A-Z   Relations with individual countries, A-Z
By period
504.7   Early to 1200
504.71   1200-1600
504.72   1600-1800
1800-1918
504.73   General works
Biography and memoirs
504.735   Collective
504.736.A-Z   Individual, A-Z
504.737   Revolution, 1905-1907
504.738   20th century (General)

	Local history and description
	Latvia
	History
	By period -- Continued
	1918-1940
	For works on the Bolshevik Revolution in Latvia see DK265.8.L33
504.74	General works
504.746	Foreign relations
	Biography and memoirs
504.75	Collective
504.76.A-Z	Individual, A-Z
504.765	War of Independence, 1918-1920
	1940-1991
	For World War II itself as distinct from the time period 1939-1945 see D731+
504.77	General works
504.773	Social life and customs. Civilization. Intellectual life
504.775	Political history
504.777	Foreign and general relations
	Biography and memoirs
504.78	Collective
504.79.A-Z	Individual, A-Z
	1991-
504.8	General works
504.815	Social life and customs. Civilization. Intellectual life
504.82	Political history
504.83	Foreign and general relations
	Biography and memoirs
504.84	Collective
504.85.A-Z	Individual, A-Z
	Local history and description
504.9.A-Z	Regions, oblasts, etc., A-Z
	Cities and towns
	Riga
504.92	Periodicals. Societies. Serials
	Museums, exhibitions, etc.
504.9215	General works
504.9217.A-Z	Individual. By place, A-Z
504.922	Sources and documents
504.923	Directories. Dictionaries. Gazetteers
504.924	Guidebooks
504.925	General works
504.926	Description. Geography
504.927	Pictorial works
504.928	Antiquities

	Local history and description
	Latvia
	Local history and description
	Cities and towns
	Riga -- Continued
504.929	Social life and customs. Civilization. Intellectual life
	Ethnography
504.93	General works
504.932.A-Z	Individual elements in the population, A-Z
	History
	Biography
504.933	Collective
504.934.A-Z	Individual, A-Z
504.935	General works
	Sections, monuments, parks, streets, buildings, etc.
504.938	Collective
504.939.A-Z	Individual, A-Z
504.95.A-Z	Other cities, towns, etc., A-Z
	e.g.
504.95.L48	Liepaja
	Lithuania
505	Periodicals. Societies. Serials
	Museums, exhibitions, etc.
505.12	General works
505.13.A-Z	Individual, A-Z
505.14	Congresses
505.15	Sources and documents
	Collected works (nonserial)
505.16	Several authors
505.17	Individual authors
505.18	Gazetteers. Dictionaries, etc.
505.19	Place names (General)
505.2	Directories
505.22	Guidebooks
505.23	General works
505.24	General special
505.25	Pictorial works
	Historic monuments, landmarks, scenery, etc. (General)
	For local see DK505.9+
505.26	General works
505.27	Preservation
505.28	Historical geography
505.285	Geography
505.29	Description and travel
505.3	Antiquities
	For local antiquities see DK505.9+

Local history and description
Lithuania -- Continued

505.32	Social life and customs. Civilization. Intellectual life
	For specific periods, see the period
	Ethnography
505.33	General works
505.34	National characteristics
505.35.A-Z	Individual elements in the population, A-Z
505.35.B44	Belarusians
505.35.G3	Germans
505.35.K37	Karaims
505.35.P6	Poles
505.35.R87	Russians
505.35.T38	Tatars
505.36	Lithuanians in foreign countries (General)
	For Lithuanians in a particular country, see the country
	History
	Periodicals. Societies. Serials see DK505
505.37	Dictionaries. Chronological tables, outlines, etc.
	Biography (Collective)
	For individual biography, see the specific period or place
505.38	General works
505.39	Rulers, kings, etc.
505.4	Queens. Princes and princesses
	Houses, noble families, etc.
505.42	General works
505.43.A-Z	Individual houses, families, etc., A-Z
505.44	Statesmen
505.45	Women
	Cf. CT3490 Biography of women
	Historiography
505.46	General works
	Biography of historians, area studies specialists, archaeologists, etc.
505.47	Collective
505.48.A-Z	Individual, A-Z
	Study and teaching
505.49	General works
505.5.A-Z	By region or country, A-Z
	Subarrange by author
	General works
505.52	Through 1800
505.53	1801-1980
505.54	1981-
505.55	Pictorial works
505.56	Juvenile works

DK

Local history and description
Lithuania
History -- Continued
505.57   Addresses, essays, lectures. Anecdotes, etc.
Military history
For individual campaigns and engagements, see the
special period
505.6   Sources and documents
505.62   General works
Naval history
For individual campaigns and engagements, see the
special period
505.63   Sources and documents
505.64   General works
Political history
For specific periods, see the period
505.65   Sources and documents
505.66   General works
Foreign and general relations
For works on relations with a specific country
regardless of period see DK505.69.A+
505.67   Sources and documents
505.68   General works
505.69.A-Z   Relations with individual countries, A-Z
By period
Early to 1569
505.695   General works
Early to 1350
505.7   General works
Biography and memoirs
505.705   Collective
505.706.A-Z   Individual, A-Z
1350-1569
505.71   General works
Biography and memoirs
505.713   Collective
505.714.A-Z   Individual, A-Z
e. g.
505.714.K46   Kęstutis, Grand Duke of Lithuania, ca. 1300-
1382
1569-1795
505.72   General works
Biography and memoirs
505.725   Collective
505.726.A-Z   Individual, A-Z
1795-1918

Local history and description
Lithuania
History
By period
1795-1918 -- Continued

505.73	General works
	Biography and memoirs
505.734	Collective
505.735.A-Z	Individual, A-Z
505.736	Revolution, 1830-1832
505.737	Revolution, 1863-1864
505.738	Revolution, 1905-1907
	1918-1940
	For works on the Bolshevik Revolution in Lithuania see DK265.8.L58
505.74	General works
	Biography and memoirs
505.75	Collective
505.76.A-Z	Individual, A-Z
505.765	War of Independence, 1918-1920
	1940-1991
	For works on World War II as distinct from the time period 1939-1945 see D731+
505.77	General works
	Biography and memoirs
505.78	Collective
505.79.A-Z	Individual, A-Z
	1991-
505.8	General works
505.82	Political history
505.83	Foreign and general relations
	Biography and memoirs
505.84	Collective
505.85.A-Z	Individual, A-Z
	Local history and description
505.9.A-Z	Regions, oblasts, etc., A-Z
	Cities and towns
	Vilnius
505.92	Periodicals. Societies. Serials
505.922	Sources and documents
505.923	Directories. Dictionaries. Gazetteers
505.924	Guidebooks
505.925	General works
505.926	Description. Geography
505.927	Pictorial works
505.928	Antiquities

	Local history and description
	Lithuania
	Local history and description
	Cities and towns
	Vilnius -- Continued
505.929	Social life and customs. Civilization. Intellectual life
	Ethnography
505.93	General works
505.932.A-Z	Individual elements in the population, A-Z
505.932.B44	Belarusians
505.932.P64	Poles
	History
	Biography
505.933	Collective
505.934.A-Z	Individual, A-Z
505.935	General works
	Sections, monuments, parks, streets, buildings, etc.
505.938	Collective
505.939.A-Z	Individual, A-Z
505.95.A-Z	Other cities, towns, etc., A-Z
	e.g.
505.95.K125	Kaunas
	Kovno see DK505.95.K125
	Belarus. Byelorussian S.S.R. White Russia
507.A2	Periodicals. Societies. Serials
	Museums, exhibitions, etc.
507.12	General works
507.13.A-Z	Individual, A-Z
507.14	Congresses
507.15	Sources and documents
	Collected works (nonserial)
507.16	Several authors
507.17	Individual authors
507.18	Gazetteers. Dictionaries, etc.
507.19	Place names (General)
507.2	Directories
507.22	Guidebooks
507.23	General works
507.24	General special
507.25	Pictorial works
	Historic monuments, landmarks, scenery, etc. (General)
	For local see DK507.9+
507.26	General works
507.27	Preservation
507.28	Historical geography
507.285	Geography

Local history and description
  Belarus. Byelorussian S.S.R. White Russia -- Continued

507.29	Description and travel
507.3	Antiquities
	For local antiquities see DK507.9+
507.32	Social life and customs. Civilization. Intellectual life
	For specific periods, see the period
	Ethnography
507.33	General works
507.34	National characteristics
507.35.A-Z	Individual elements in the population, A-Z
507.35.D79	Drygavichy
507.35.G3	Germans
507.35.L36	Latvians
507.35.P6	Poles
507.35.T37	Tatars
507.36	Belarusians in foreign countries (General)
	For Belarusians in a particular country, see the country
	History
	Periodicals. Societies. Serials see DK507.A2
507.37	Dictionaries. Chronological tables, outlines, etc.
	Biography (Collective)
	For individual biography, see the specific period or place
507.38	General works
507.39	Rulers, kings, etc.
	Houses, noble families, etc.
507.415	General works
507.4152.A-Z	Indivdual houses, families, etc., A-Z
507.44	Statesmen
507.45	Women
	Cf. CT3490 Biography of women
	Historiography
507.46	General works
	Biography of historians, area studies specialists, archaeologists, etc.
507.47	Collective
507.48.A-Z	Individual, A-Z
	Study and teaching
507.49	General works
507.5.A-Z	By region or country, A-Z
	Subarrange by author
	General works
507.52	Through 1800
507.53	1801-1980
507.54	1981-
507.55	Pictorial works

DK

Local history and description
Belarus. Byelorussian S.S.R. White Russia
History -- Continued

507.56	Juvenile works
507.57	Addresses, essays, lectures. Anecdotes, etc.
	Military history
	For individual campaigns and engagements, see the special period
507.6	Sources and documents
507.62	General works
	Political history
	For specific periods, see the period
507.65	Sources and documents
507.66	General works
	Foreign and general relations
	For works on relations with a specific country regardless of time period see DK507.69.A+
507.67	Sources and documents
507.68	General works
507.69.A-Z	Relations with individual countries, A-Z
	By period
507.7	Early to 1237
	For works on the early history of Rus' see DK70+
507.71	1237-1569
	1569-1795
507.72	General works
	Biography and memoirs
507.725	Collective
507.726.A-Z	Individual, A-Z
	1795-1917
507.727	General works
	Biography and memoirs
507.728	Collective
507.729.A-Z	Individual, A-Z
507.7292	Revolution, 1830-1831
507.7293	Revolution, 1863-1864
	20th century
507.7295	General
507.7296	Revolution, 1905-1907
	1917-1945
	For works on World War II as distinct from the time period 1939-1945 see D731+
	For works on the Bolshevik Revolution in Belorussia see DK265.8.B9
507.73	General works
	Biography and memoirs

Local history and description
  Belarus. Byelorussian S.S.R. White Russia
  History
    By period
      20th century
        1900-1945
          Biography and memoirs -- Continued

507.74	Collective
507.75.A-Z	Individual, A-Z

        1945-1991

507.76	General works
507.762	Social life and customs. Civilization. Intellectual life
507.764	Foreign and general relations

         Biography and memoirs

507.77	Collective
507.78.A-Z	Individual, A-Z

       1991-

507.8	General works
507.815	Social life and customs. Civilization. Intellectual life
507.817	Political history
507.8175	Foreign and general relations

        Biography and memoirs

507.82	Collective
507.822.A-Z	Individual, A-Z

  Local history and description

507.9.A-Z	Regions, oblasts, etc., A-Z

    Cities and towns
      Minsk

507.92	Periodicals. Societies. Serials
507.922	Sources and documents
507.923	Directories. Dictionaries. Gazetteers
507.924	Guidebooks
507.925	General works
507.926	Description. Geography
507.927	Pictorial works
507.928	Antiquities
507.929	Social life and customs. Civilization. Intellectual life

        Ethnography

507.93	General works
507.932.A-Z	Individual elements in the population, A-Z
507.932.P64	Poles

        History
          Biography

507.933	Collective
507.934.A-Z	Individual, A-Z

Local history and description
 Belarus. Byelorussian S.S.R. White Russia
  Local history and description
   Cities and towns
    Minsk
     History -- Continued
507.935   General works
         Sections, monuments, parks, streets, buildings, etc.
507.938   Collective
507.939.A-Z   Individual, A-Z
        Other cities, towns, etc.
507.95.A1   Collective
507.95.A2-Z   Individual, A-Z
507.95.B68   Brest
507.95.G7   Grodno. Hrodna
                 Hrodna see DK507.95.G7
507.95.M58   Mogilev
507.95.V53   Vitebsk
  Ukraine
508.A2   Periodicals. Societies. Serials
         Museums, exhibitions, etc.
508.A22   General works
508.A23A-.A23Z   Individual, A-Z
508.A25 Congresses
508.A3   Sources and documents
         Collected works (nonserial)
508.A32   Several authors
508.A325 Individual authors
508.A4   Gazetteers. Dictionaries, etc.
508.A45 Place names (General)
508.A46 Directories
508.A5-Z Guidebooks
508.12   General works
508.13   General special
508.15   Pictorial works
         Historic monuments, landmarks, scenery, etc. (General)
            For local see DK508.9+
508.154   General works
508.155   Preservation
508.157 Historical geography
508.2   Description and travel
508.3   Antiquities
            For local see DK508.9+
508.4   Social life and customs. Civilization. Intellectual life
            For specific periods, see the period
         Ethnography

498

Local history and description
Ukraine
Ethnography -- Continued

508.42	General works
508.423	National characteristics
508.425.A-Z	Individual elements in the population, A-Z
508.425.A74	Armenians
508.425.B35	Balts
508.425.B84	Bulgarians
508.425.C55	Cimmerians
508.425.G47	Germans
508.425.G74	Greeks
508.425.H87	Hutsuls
508.425.I73	Italians
508.425.K37	Karaims
508.425.K53	Khazars
508.425.L46	Lemky
508.425.M32	Macedonians
508.425.P65	Poles
508.425.P67	Poliany
508.425.R87	Russians
508.425.S39	Scythians
508.425.T37	Tatars
508.425.T87	Turks
508.44	Ukrainians in foreign countries (General)

For Ukrainians in a particular country, see the country

History
Periodicals. Societies. Serials see DK508.A2

508.444	Dictionaries. Chronological tables, outlines, etc.

Biography (Collective)
For individual biography, see the specific period or place

508.45	General works
508.452	Rulers, kings, etc.
508.454	Queens. Princes and princesses

Houses, noble families, etc.

508.456	General works
508.457.A-Z	Individual houses, families, etc., A-Z
508.458	Statesmen
508.459	Women

Cf. CT3490 Biography of women

Historiography

508.46	General works

Biography of historians, area studies specialists,
archaeologists, etc.

508.465	Collective
508.47.A-Z	Individual, A-Z

Local history and description
Ukraine
History -- Continued

508.48	Study and teaching
	General works
508.49	Through 1800
508.5	1801-1985
508.51	1986-
508.515	Juvenile works
508.52	Addresses, essays, lectures. Anecdotes, etc.
508.53	Philosophy of Ukrainian history
508.54	Military history
508.55	Zaporozhians. Zaporiz'ka Sich. Cossacks. Nova Sich, etc.
	For the period 1648-1775, see also DK508.73+
508.554	Political history
	For specific periods, see the period
	Foreign and general relations
508.56	General works
508.57.A-Z	Relations with individual countries, A-Z
(508.6)	Biography
	see the time period
	By period
	For works on early history of Rus' see DK70+
508.66	Early to 1340
	1340-1569. Period of Polish-Lithuanian domination
508.67	General works
	Biography and memoirs
508.674	Collective
508.675.A-Z	Individual, A-Z
	e.g.
508.675.V96	Vyshnevetsʹkyĭ, Dymtro, kni͡azʹ, d. 1563
508.68	1569-1648. Period of Polish rule
	1648-1775
508.73	Sources and documents
508.735	Historiography
508.74	General works
	Biography and memoirs
508.75	Collective
508.752.A-Z	Individual, A-Z
	e.g.
508.752.A6	Apostol, Danylo, Hetman of Ukraine
508.752.K5	Khmelʹnyt͡sʹkyĭ, Bohdan, Hetman of Ukraine
508.752.M3	Mazepa, Ivan, Hetman of Ukraine
508.752.P65	Polubotok, Pavlo, Hetman of Ukraine

Local history and description
Ukraine
History
By period
1648-1775 -- Continued
1648-1657
Including Battle of Berestechko, Treaty of Pereĭaslav, etc.
508.753 General works
Biography and memoirs
508.754 Collective
508.755.A-Z Individual, A-Z
1657-1709
Including Battle of Konotop, etc.
508.756 General works
Biography and memoirs
508.757 Collective
508.758.A-Z Individual, A-Z
1709-1775
Including Uprising of 1768
508.759 General works
Biography and memoirs
508.76 Collective
508.761.A-Z Individual, A-Z
1775-1917
508.77 Sources and documents
508.771 Historiography
508.772 General works
508.773 Social life and customs. Civilization. Intellectual life
Biography and memoirs
508.78 Collective
508.782.A-Z Individual, A-Z
e.g.
508.782.D7 Drahomaniv, Mykhailo
508.782.K3 Karmaliūk, Ustym
20th century
508.788 General works
1917-1945
508.79 Sources and documents
508.8 Historiography
508.812 General works
508.813 Social life and customs. Civilization. Intellectual life
Biography and memoirs
508.82 Collective

Local history and description
Ukraine
History
By period
20th century
1917-1945
Biography and memoirs -- Continued

508.83.A-Z	Individual, A-Z
	e.g.
508.83.D6	Doroshenko, Dmytro
508.83.K6	Konovalets', ÏEvhen
508.83.P4	Petlïūra, Symon
508.83.S55	Skoropads'kyï, Pavlo, Hetman of Ukraine
508.832	1917-1921. Period of independence

Class here works limited to the Ukrainian
independence movement
For Bolshevik Revolution in Ukraine, as distinct
from the independence movement see
DK265.8.U4

1921-1944

508.833	General works
	Biography and memoirs
508.834	Collective
508.835.A-Z	Individual, A-Z
	e.g.
508.835.B3	Bandera, Stepan
	1945-1991
508.84	General works
	Biography and memoirs
508.842	Collective
508.843.A-Z	Individual, A-Z
	1991-
508.845	Sources and documents
508.846	General works
508.847	Social life and customs. Civilization. Intellectual life
508.848	Political history
508.849	Foreign and general relations
	Biography and memoirs
508.850	Collective
508.851.A-Z	Individual, A-Z
	Local history and description
508.9.A-Z	Regions, oblasts, etc., A-Z
	e.g.
508.9.B47	Berezhany Region

Local history and description
Ukraine
Local history and description
Regions, oblasts, etc., A-Z -- Continued

508.9.B48	Bessarabia
	For Bessarabia (General) see DK509.1+
508.9.B56	Black Sea Coast
508.9.B57	Black Sea Lowland
508.9.B65	Boikivshchyna
508.9.B85	Bukovina (Bukovyna)
	For Romanian Bukovina see DR281.S8
508.9.C37	Carpathian Mountains
508.9.C46	Central Dnieper Region
508.9.C47	Chernihivs'ka oblast'
	Crimea see DK508.9.K78
508.9.D64	Dnepropetrovsk (Dnipropetrovske) Region
508.9.D66	Donets'ka oblast'
508.9.D76	Drogobych (Drohobych) Region
	Eastern Galicia see DK508.9.G35
508.9.G35	Galicia, Eastern
	Halychyna Carpathians see DK508.9.G35
508.9.H87	Hutsulshchyna
508.9.I82	Ivano-Frankovskaīa (Ivano-Frankivs'ka) oblast'
	Karpaty see DK508.9.C37
508.9.K53	Khar'kov (Khar'kiv) Region
508.9.K54	Khersonskaīa (Khersons'ka) oblast'
508.9.K55	Khmel'nitskīa (Khmel'nyts'ka) oblast'
508.9.K56	Khortytsīa Island
508.9.K57	Kiev oblast'
508.9.K78	Kryms'ka oblast, Respublika Krym
	Lemberg Region see DK508.9.L85
508.9.L84	Luganskaīa (Luhans'ka) oblast'
508.9.L85	L'vivs'ka oblast'
508.9.N55	Nikolaevskaīa (Nykolaïvs'ka) oblast'
508.9.O33	Odesskaīa oblast'
508.9.P48	Perekop Isthmus
508.9.P64	Podillia
508.9.P65	Poltavskaīa (Poltavs'ka) oblast'
508.9.R67	Ros (Ros') River and Region
508.9.R68	Rovenskaīa (Rivens'ka) oblast'
508.9.S49	Sevastopol'skaīa (Sevastopol's'ka) oblast'
508.9.S59	Sivershchyna
	Stanislavskaīa oblast' see DK508.9.I82
508.9.S96	Sums'ka oblast'
508.9.T38	Taurida
508.9.T48	Ternopil's'ka oblast'

DK

Local history and description
  Ukraine
    Local history and description
      Regions, oblasts, etc., A-Z -- Continued

508.9.U37	Ukraine, Western
	Ukrainian Carpathians see DK508.9.C37
508.9.V47	Verkhovyna Region
508.9.V56	Vinnītskaīa (Vynnyts'ka) oblast'
508.9.V65	Volhynian, Volyns'ka oblast'
508.9.V67	Voroshilovgradskaīa (Voroshylovhrads'ka) oblast'
	Western Ukraine see DK508.9.U37
508.9.Z35	Zakarpatskaīa (Zakarpats'ka) oblast'
508.9.Z36	Zaporozhskaīa (Zaporozhs'ka) oblast'
508.9.Z37	Zbruch Valley
508.9.Z49	ZHytomyrs'ka oblast'

    Cities and towns
      Kiev (Kÿiv)

508.92	Periodicals. Societies. Serials
508.922	Sources and documents
508.923	Directories. Dictionaries. Gazetteers
508.924	Guidebooks
508.925	General works
508.926	Description. Geography
508.927	Pictorial works
508.928	Antiquities
508.929	Social life and customs. Civilization. Intellectual life
	Ethnography
508.93	General works
508.932.A-Z	Individual elements in the population, A-Z
508.932.T36	Tatars
	History
	Biography
508.933	Collective
508.934.A-Z	Individual, A-Z
508.935	General works
	Sections, monuments, parks, streets, buildings, etc.
508.938	Collective
508.939.A-Z	Individual, A-Z
	Other cities, towns, etc.
508.95.A1	Collective
508.95.A2-Z	Individual, A-Z
	e.g.
508.95.B35	Balaklava
508.95.C54	Chernihiv
508.95.C543	Chernivtsi
508.95.C544	Chersonese (City)

Local history and description
  Ukraine
    Local history and description
      Cities and towns
        Other cities, towns, etc.
          Individual, A-Z -- Continued

508.95.D64	Dnipropetrovs'k
508.95.D66	Donets'k
508.95.I24	I͡Alta
508.95.I82	Ivano-Frankivs'k
508.95.K47	Kerch
508.95.K53	Kharkiv
	Kiev see DK508.92+
	Lemberg see DK508.95.L86
508.95.L86	L'viv
508.95.O33	Odesa
508.95.P47	Perei͡aslav-Khmel'nyt͡skyĭ
508.95.S49	Sevastopol'
	Stanislav see DK508.95.I82
508.95.T47	Ternopil'
508.95.U83	Uz͡hhorod
508.95.V56	Vinnyt͡sia
	Yalta see DK508.95.I24
509	Southern Soviet Union

        Including Black Sea, Caucasus, Armenia, Transcaucasia, etc.,
          in various combinations
        For Caucasus, Northern see DK511.C2
    Moldova. Moldavian S.S.R. Bessarabia
        For Ukrainian Bessarabia see DK508.9.B48
        For Romanian Moldavia see DR201+

509.1	Periodicals. Societies. Serials
	Museums, exhibitions, etc.
509.12	General works
509.13.A-Z	Individual, A-Z
509.14	Congresses
509.15	Sources and documents
	Collected works (nonserial)
509.16	Several authors
509.17	Individual authors
509.18	Gazetteers. Dictionaries, etc.
509.19	Place names (General)
509.2	Directories
509.22	Guidebooks
509.23	General works
509.24	General special
509.25	Pictorial works

DK

Local history and description
  Moldova. Moldavian S.S.R. Bessarabia -- Continued
    Historic monuments, landmarks, scenery, etc. (General)
      For local see DK509.9+

509.26	General works
509.27	Preservation
509.28	Historical geography
509.29	Description and travel
509.3	Antiquities

      For local antiquities see DK509.9+

509.32	Social life and customs. Civilization. Intellectual life

      For specific periods, see the period
    Ethnography

509.33	General works
509.34	National characteristics
509.35.A-Z	Individual elements in the population, A-Z
509.35.B84	Bulgarians
509.35.G25	Gagauz
509.35.G3	Germans
509.35.P6	Poles
509.35.R65	Romanians
509.35.R88	Russians
509.35.U38	Ukrainians
509.36	Moldavians in foreign countries (General)

      For Moldavians in a particular country, see the country
    History
      Periodicals. Societies. Serials see DK509.1

509.37	Dictionaries. Chronological tables, outlines, etc.

     Biography (Collective)
      For individual biography, see the specific period or place

509.38	General works
509.39	Rulers, kings, etc.
509.44	Statesmen
509.45	Women

      Cf. CT3490 Biography of women
     Historiography

509.46	General works

     Biography of historians, area studies specialists,
      archaeologists, etc.

509.47	Collective
509.48.A-Z	Individual, A-Z

     Study and teaching

509.49	General works
509.5.A-Z	By region or country, A-Z

     General works

509.52	Through 1800

	Local history and description
	Moldova. Moldavian S.S.R. Bessarabia
	History
	General works -- Continued
509.53	1801-1980
509.54	1981-
509.55	Pictorial works
509.56	Juvenile works
509.57	Addresses, essays, lectures. Anecdotes, etc.
	Military history
	For individual campaigns and engagements, see the special period
509.6	Sources and documents
509.62	General works
	Political history
	For specific periods, see the period
509.65	Sources and documents
509.66	General works
	Foreign and general relations
	For works on relations with a specific country regardless of period see DK509.69.A+
509.67	Sources and documents
509.68	General works
509.69.A-Z	Relations with individual countries, A-Z
	By period
	Early to 1812 see DR238+
	1812-1918
509.7	General works
	Biography and memoirs
509.705	Collective
509.706.A-Z	Individual, A-Z
	1918-1940
	For works on the Bolshevik Revolution in Moldavia see DK265.8.M48
509.71	General works
	Biography and memoirs
509.72	Collective
509.73.A-Z	Individual, A-Z
	1940-1991
	For World War II as distinct from the time period 1939-1945 see D731+
509.74	General works
	Biography and memoirs
509.75	Collective
509.76.A-Z	Individual, A-Z
	1991-

DK

	Local history and description
	Moldova. Moldavian S.S.R. Bessarabia
	History
	By period
	1991- -- Continued
509.772	General works
509.7723	Social life and customs. Civilization. Intellectual life
509.7724	Political history
509.7725	Foreign and general relations
	Biography and memoirs
509.773	Collective
509.774.A-Z	Individual, A-Z
	Local history and description
509.9.A-Z	Regions, oblasts, etc., A-Z
	Cities and towns
	Chisinau. Kishinev
509.92	Periodicals. Societies. Serials
509.922	Sources and documents
509.923	Directories. Dictionaries. Gazetteers
509.924	Guidebooks
509.925	General works
509.926	Description. Geography
509.927	Pictorial works
509.928	Antiquities
509.929	Social life and customs. Civilization. Intellectual life
	Ethnography
509.93	General works
509.932.A-Z	Individual elements in the population, A-Z
	History
	Biography
509.933	Collective
509.934.A-Z	Individual, A-Z
509.935	General works
	Sections, monuments, parks, streets, buildings, etc.
509.938	Collective
509.939.A-Z	Individual, A-Z
509.95.A-Z	Other cities, towns, etc., A-Z
	e.g.
509.95.T57	Tiraspol

Local history and description -- Continued
Russia (Federation). Russian S.F.S.R.
    Class here, DK510-DK510.75, only works that discuss the
        Russian S.F.S.R. since its formation in 1917 by the Soviets
    For works that discuss the same territory for the pre-1917
        period, or the pre-1917 and post-1917 periods
        combined see DK1+
    For local history and description for all periods see
        DK511+
    For local history and description of Siberia for all periods
        see DK751+

510	Periodicals. Societies. Serials
	Museums, exhibitions, etc.
510.12	General works
510.13.A-Z	Individual, A-Z
510.14	Congresses
510.15	Sources and documents
	Collected works (nonserial)
510.16	Several authors
510.17	Individual authors
510.18	Gazetteers. Dictionaries, etc.
510.19	Place names (General)
510.2	Directories
510.22	Guidebooks
510.23	General works
510.24	General special
510.25	Pictorial works
	Historic monuments, landmarks, scenery, etc. (General)
	For local see DK511+
510.26	General works
510.27	Preservation
510.28	Historical geography
510.29	Description and travel
510.3	Antiquities
	For local antiquities see DK511+
510.32	Social life and customs. Civilization. Intellectual life
	For specific periods, see the period
	Ethnography
510.33	General works
510.34	National characteristics
510.35.A-Z	Individual elements in the population, A-Z
510.35.A23	Abaza
510.35.A75	Armenians
510.35.B38	Bashkir
510.35.C45	Chechens
510.35.C5	Chinese

Local history and description
Russia (Federation). Russian S.F.S.R.
Ethnography
Individual elements in the population, A-Z -- Continued

510.35.C55	Chuvash
510.35.C68	Cossacks
510.35.E76	Estonians
510.35.F54	Finno-Ugrians
510.35.F55	Finns
510.35.G28	Georgians (Transcaucasians)
510.35.G3	Germans
510.35.K65	Komi
510.35.K68	Koreans
510.35.L35	Lakhs
510.35.M35	Mari
510.35.M67	Mordvins
510.35.N63	Nogai
510.35.P6	Poles
510.35.S57	Skolts (Sami people)
510.35.T87	Turkic peoples
510.35.U33	Udmurts
510.35.U35	Ukrainians
510.35.U7	Uralic peoples
510.35.V45	Veps
510.36	Russians in foreign countries (General)

            For Russians in a particular country, see the country

History
Periodicals. Societies. Serials see DK510

510.37	Dictionaries. Chronological tables, outlines, etc.

Biography (Collective)
            For individual biography, see the specific period or place

510.38	General works
510.42	Statesmen
510.44	Women

            Cf. CT3490 Biography of women

Historiography

510.46	General works

Biography of historians, area studies specialists,
       archaeologists, etc.

510.47	Collective
510.48.A-Z	Individual, A-Z

Study and teaching

510.49	General works
510.5.A-Z	By region or country, A-Z
510.52	General works
510.55	Pictorial works

Local history and description
Russia (Federation). Russian S.F.S.R.
History -- Continued
510.555   Philosophy of Russian Federation history
510.56   Juvenile works
510.57   Addresses, essays, lectures. Anecdotes, etc.
Military history see DK50+
510.6   Political history
For specific periods, see the period
Foreign and general relations see DK65+
By period
Early to 1917 see DK70+
1917-1945
For World War II as distinct from the time period
1939-1945 see D731+
For works on the Bolshevik Revolution in the
Russian S.F.S.R. see DK265.8.R85
510.7   General works
Biography and memoirs
510.71   Collective
510.72.A-Z   Individual, A-Z
1945-1991
510.73   General works
Biography and memoirs
510.74   Collective
510.75.A-Z   Individual, A-Z
1991-
510.755   Sources and documents
510.76   General works
510.762   Social life and customs. Civilization. Intellectual life
510.763   Political history
510.764   Foreign and general relations
Biography and memoirs
510.765   Collective
510.766.A-Z   Individual, A-Z
Local history and description of European Russian
S.F.S.R.
511.A-Z   Oblasts, regions, etc., A-Z
Cutter numbers listed below are provided as examples
For regions, etc. of Ukraine see DK508.9.A+
511.A28   Adygeĭskaia avtonomnaia oblast'
511.A5   Arkhangel'skaia oblast'
A.S.S.R. Nemtsev Povolsh'ia see DK511.V66
511.A7   Astrakhan'skaia oblast'
511.B33   Bashkirskaia A.S.S.R.
Beloe More see DK511.W53

Local history and description
Russia (Federation). Russian S.F.S.R.
Local history and description of European Russian
S.F.S.R.
Oblasts, regions, etc., A-Z -- Continued

511.C07	Caspian Sea. Caspian Sea Region
511.C2	Caucasus, Northern
511.C5	Chuvashskaĭa A.S.S.R.
511.D8	Don Cossacks (Province)
	East Karelia see DK511.K18
	German Volga A.S.S.R. see DK511.V66
	ĪAroslavskaĭa oblast see DK511.Y2
511.K12	Kabardia
511.K16	Kalmytskaĭa A.S.S.R.
511.K17	Kama River and Valley
511.K18	Karel'skaĭa A.S.S.R.
	Kazan see DK511.T17
	Kazan Region. Khazanskoe khanstvo see DK511.T17
511.K47	Komi A.S.S.R.
511.K475	Komi-Permiatskiĭ natsional'nyĭ okrug
511.K5	Kostromskaĭa oblast'
511.K6	Kubanskaĭa oblast'
511.K8	Kurskaĭa oblast'
	Kuĭbyshevskaĭa oblast' see DK511.S233
511.L13	Ladoga, Lake
511.L195	Leningradskaĭa oblast'
	For city see DK541+
511.M28	Maňskaĭa A.S.S.R.
511.M57	Mordoviia. Mordovskaia (Mordvinian) A.S.S.R.
511.M6	Moscow oblast'
	For city see DK588+
	Nizhni Zemlya see G800
	North Ossetia see DK511.S44
511.N7	Novgorodskaĭa oblast'
511.O45	Olonetskaĭa oblast'
511.O75	Orenburgskaĭa oblast'
511.P17	Pechora River and Valley
511.P2	Permskaĭa oblast'
511.P8	Pskovskaĭa oblast'
511.R9	Rĭazanskaĭa oblast'
511.S233	Samarskaĭa oblast'. Kuĭbyshevskaĭa oblast'
511.S3	Saratovskaĭa oblast'
511.S44	Severo-Ossentiskaia A.S.S.R. North Ossetia
	Siberia see DK751+
	Simbirsk see DK511.U4
511.S7	Smolenskaĭa oblast'

Local history and description
Russia (Federation). Russian S.F.S.R.
Local history and description of European Russian
S.F.S.R.
Oblasts, regions, etc., A-Z -- Continued

511.T1	Tambovskaīa oblast'
511.T17	Tartarstan. Kazan Region. Khazanskoe khanstvo
511.T7	Tverskaīa oblast'
511.U16	Udmurtskaīa A.S.S.R.
511.U2	Ufa Region
511.U4	Ulīanovskaīa oblast'
511.U7	Ural Mountains
511.V6	Vladimirskaīa
511.V65	Volga River and Valley
511.V66	Volga, German (A.S.S.R.)
511.V8	Vologodskaīa oblast'
511.V9	Voronezhskaīa oblast'
511.W53	White Sea
511.Y2	Yaroslavskaīa oblast'

Cities and towns
Saint Petersburg. Leningrad. Petrograd

541	Periodicals. Societies. Serials
542	Museums, exhibitions, etc.
	Subarrange by author
543	Biography
545	Directories. Dictionaries. Gazetteers
549	Guidebooks
	General works. Description
551	Through 1950
552	1951-
553	Pictorial works
555	Antiquities
557	Social life and customs. Civilization. Intellectual life
	Ethnography
559	General works
559.5.A-Z	Individual elements in the population, A-Z
559.5.C94	Czechs
559.5.F54	Finns
559.5.F74	French
559.5.G43	Georgians (Transcaucasians)
559.5.G45	Germans
559.5.P64	Poles
559.5.S54	Swedes
559.5.U56	Ukrainians
	History
561	General works

DK

Local history and description
Russia (Federation). Russian S.F.S.R.
Local history and description
Cities and towns
Saint Petersburg. Leningrad. Petrograd
History -- Continued
By period

565	1703-1800
568	1801-

                    For works on the Bolshevik Revolution in
                          Leningrad see DK265.8.L4
Sections, monuments, parks, streets, etc.

571	Collective
572.A-Z	Individual, A-Z

Buildings

573	Collective
574.A-Z	Individual, A-Z
579	Other

Moscow

588	Periodicals. Societies. Serials
590	Museums, exhibitions, etc.

                          Subarrange by author

591	Sources and documents
593	Biography
595	Directories. Dictionaries. Gazetteers
597	Guidebooks
599	Antiquities
600	Social life and customs. Civilization. Intellectual life

Ethnography

600.2	General works
600.3.A-Z	Individual elements in the population, A-Z
600.3.A35	Africans
600.3.A7	Armenians
600.3.A92	Azerbaijanis
600.3.F74	French
600.3.G46	Georgians (Transcaucasians)
600.3.G5	Germans
600.3.K37	Karaites
600.3.K67	Koreans
600.3.M64	Moldavians
600.3.S84	Swedes

General works. History and description

601	Through 1950

                      Cf. DK265.8.M6 Local revolutionary history,
                          1917-1921

601.2	1951-

	Local history and description
	Russia (Federation). Russian S.F.S.R.
	Local history and description
	Cities and towns
	Moscow -- Continued
601.5	Pictorial works
	Sections, districts, suburbs, etc.
602	Collective
	Individual
602.3	Kreml' (Kremlin)
602.5.A-Z	Other, A-Z
	Streets, squares, parks, etc.
604	Collective
604.3.A-Z	Individual, A-Z
	e.g.
	Krasnai͡a ploshchad' see DK604.3.R4
604.3.R4	Red Square. Krasnai͡a ploshchad'
	Buildings
605	Collective
606.A-Z	Individual, A-Z
	e.g.
606.B64	Bol'shoĭ Kremlevskiĭ dvoret͡s
609	Other
	Other cities, towns, etc.
651.A1	Collective
651.A2-Z	Individual, A-Z
651.A65	Arkhangel'sk
651.A7	Astrakhan
	Ekaterinburg see DK651.S85
651.G6	Gorki. Nizhniĭ Novgorod
651.I28	I͡Aroslavl'
651.K1213	Kaliningrad
651.K2	Kazan'
651.K45	Kirov. Vyatka
651.K6	Kostroma
651.K68	Kronstadt
	Kuĭbyshev see DK651.S36
651.K854	Kuoloi͡arvi. Salla
	Nizhniĭ Novgorod see DK651.G6
651.P23	Pavlovsk
651.P45	Petrodvoret͡s. Peterhof
651.P8	Pskov
651.P93	Pushkin. T͡Sarskoe Selo
651.R7	Rostov
651.S36	Samara. Kuĭbyshev
	Simbirsk see DK651.U4

Local history and description
  Russia (Federation). Russian S.F.S.R.
    Local history and description
      Cities and towns
        Other cities, towns, etc.
          Individual, A-Z

651.S65	Smolensk
651.S7	Stalingrad. Volgograd
651.S85	Sverdlovsk. Ekaterinburg
	TSarkoe Selo see DK651.P93
651.U4	Ulyanovsk. Simbirsk
	Usti͡ug Velikiĭ see DK651.V3
651.V3	Velikiĭ Usti͡ug
651.V55	Vladimir
	Volgograd see DK651.S7
651.V6	Voronezh
651.V93	Vyborg
	Yaroslav see DK651.I28
	Yaroslavl' see DK651.I28

Georgia (Republic). Georgian S.S.R. Georgian Sakartvelo

670	Periodicals. Societies. Serials
	Museums, exhibitions, etc.
671.2	General works
671.3.A-Z	Individual, A-Z
671.4	Congresses
671.5	Sources and documents
	Collected works (nonserial)
671.6	Several authors
671.7	Individual authors
671.8	Gazetteers. Dictionaries, etc.
671.9	Place names (General)
672	Directories
672.2	Guidebooks
672.3	General works
672.4	General special
672.5	Pictorial works
	Historic monuments, landmarks, scenery, etc. (General)
	For local see DK679+
672.6	General works
672.7	Preservation
672.8	Historical geography
672.9	Description and travel
673	Antiquities
	For local antiquities see DK679+
673.2	Social life and customs. Civilization. Intellectual life
	For specific periods, see the period

Local history and description
Georgia (Republic). Georgian S.S.R. Georgian Sakartvelo --
Continued
Ethnography
673.3	General works
673.4	National characteristics
673.5.A-Z	Individual elements in the population, A-Z
673.5.A75	Armenians
673.5.B37	Bats (Transcaucasian people)
673.5.G3	Germans
673.5.G74	Greeks
673.5.K48	Khevzurs
673.5.K52	Khists
673.5.K55	Kipchak
673.5.M47	Meskhetians (Turkic people)
673.5.O75	Ossetes
673.5.P6	Poles
673.6	Georgians in foreign countries (General)
	For Georgians in a particular country, see the country

History
Periodicals. Societies. Serials see DK670
673.7	Dictionaries. Chronological tables, outlines, etc.

Biography (Collective)
For individual biography, see the specific period or place
673.8	General works
673.9	Rulers, kings, etc.
674	Queens. Princes and princesses
	Houses, noble families, etc.
674.2	General works
674.3.A-Z	Individual houses, families, etc., A-Z
674.4	Statesmen
674.5	Women
	Cf. CT3490 Biography of women

Historiography
674.6	General works
	Biography of historians, area studies specialists, archaeologists, etc.
674.7	Collective
674.8.A-Z	Individual, A-Z

Study and teaching
674.9	General works
675.A-Z	By region or country, A-Z
	Subarrange by author

General works
675.2	Through 1800
675.3	1801-1980

Local history and description
   Georgia (Republic). Georgian S.S.R. Georgian Sakartvelo
    History
     General works -- Continued

675.4	1981-
675.5	Pictorial works
675.6	Juvenile works
675.7	Addresses, essays, lectures. Anecdotes, etc.
	Military history
	For individual campaigns and engagements, see the
	special period
676	Sources and documents
676.2	General works
	Political history
	For specific periods, see the period
676.5	Sources and documents
676.6	General works
	Foreign and general relations
	For works on relations with a specific country
	regardless of period see DK676.9.A+
676.7	Sources and documents
676.8	General works
676.9.A-Z	Relations with individual countries, A-Z
	By period
	Early to 330
677.1	General works
	Biography and memoirs
677.13	Collective
677.14.A-Z	Individual, A-Z
677.15	P'arnavaz I, King of the Georgians, fl. 4th - 3rd cent.
	B.C.
	330-1220
677.2	General works
	Biography and memoirs
677.23	Collective
677.24.A-Z	Individual, A-Z
677.25	Vaxtang I, King of the Georgians, d. 502
677.26	Giorgi II, King of Georgia, 1072-1089
677.27	Davit' IV, King of Georgia, 1089-1125
677.275	Demetre I, King of Georgia, 1125-1156
677.28	T'amar, Queen of Georgia, 1184-1213
	1220-1801
677.3	General works
	Biography and memoirs
677.34	Collective
677.35.A-Z	Individual, A-Z

	Local history and description
	Georgia (Republic). Georgian S.S.R. Georgian Sakartvelo
	History
	By period -- Continued
	1801-1921
	For works on the Bolshevik Revolution in Georgia see DK265.8.G4
677.4	General works
	Biography and memoirs
677.5	Collective
677.6.A-Z	Individual, A-Z
	1921-1991
	For World War II as distinct from the time period 1939-1945 see D731+
677.7	General works
	Biography and memoirs
677.8	Collective
677.9.A-Z	Individual, A-Z
677.92	Uprising, 1924
	1991-
678	General works
678.17	Political history
678.18	Foreign and general relations
	Biography and memoirs
678.2	Collective
678.3.A-Z	Individual, A-Z
	Local history and description
679.A-Z	Regions, oblasts, etc., A-Z
	Cities and towns
	Tbilisi. Tiflis
679.2	Periodicals. Societies. Serials
679.22	Sources and documents
679.23	Directories. Dictionaries. Gazetteers
679.24	Guidebooks
679.25	General works
679.26	Description. Geography
679.27	Pictorial works
679.28	Antiquities
679.29	Social life and customs. Civilization. Intellectual life
	Ethnography
679.3	General works
679.32.A-Z	Individual elements in the population, A-Z
	History
	Biography
679.33	Collective
679.34.A-Z	Individual, A-Z

	Local history and description
	Georgia (Republic). Georgian S.S.R. Georgian Sakartvelo
	Local history and description
	Cities and towns
	Tbilisi. Tiflis
	History -- Continued
679.35	General works
	Sections, monuments, parks, streets, buildings, etc.
679.38	Collective
679.39.A-Z	Individual, A-Z
679.5.A-Z	Other cities, towns, etc., A-Z
	Armenia (Republic). Armenian S.S.R.
	For works on the territory of Armenian S.S.R. before
	1920, and/or the historic kingdom and region of
	Armenia as a whole see DS161+
680	Periodicals. Societies. Serials
	Museums, exhibitions, etc.
681.2	General works
681.3.A-Z	Individual, A-Z
681.4	Congresses
681.5	Sources and documents
	Collected works (nonserial)
681.6	Several authors
681.7	Individual authors
681.8	Gazetteers. Dictionaries, etc.
681.9	Place names (General)
682	Directories
682.2	Guidebooks
682.3	General works
682.4	General special
682.5	Pictorial works
	Historic monuments, landmarks, scenery, etc. (General)
	For local see DK689+
682.6	General works
682.7	Preservation
682.8	Historical geography
682.9	Description and travel
683	Antiquities
	For local antiquities see DK689+
683.2	Social life and customs. Civilization. Intellectual life
	For specific periods, see the period
	Ethnography
683.3	General works
683.4	National characteristics
683.5.A-Z	Individual elements in the population, A-Z
683.5.A93	Azerbaijanis

Local history and description
Armenia (Republic). Armenian S.S.R.
Ethnography
Individual elements in the population, A-Z -- Continued

683.5.K87	Kurds
683.5.R9	Russians
683.6	Armenians in foreign countries (General)

For Armenians in a particular country, see the country

History
Periodicals. Societies. Serials see DK680

683.7	Dictionaries. Chronological tables, outlines, etc.

Biography (Collective)
For individual biography, see the specific period or place

683.8	General works
684	Statesmen
684.2	Women

Cf. CT3490 Biography of women

Historiography

684.6	General works

Biography of historians, area studies specialists,
archaeologists, etc.

684.7	Collective
684.8.A-Z	Individual, A-Z

Study and teaching

684.9	General works
685.A-Z	By region or country, A-Z

General works

685.3	1920-1980
685.4	1981-
685.5	Pictorial works
685.6	Juvenile works
685.7	Addresses, essays, lectures. Anecdotes, etc.

By period
Early to 1920 see DS181+
1920-1991
For World War II as distinct from the time period
1939-1945 see D731+
For works on the Bolshevik Revolution in Armenia
see DK265.8.A73

686.9	Sources and documents
687	General works

Biography and memoirs

687.2	Collective
687.3.A-Z	Individual, A-Z

1991-

687.5	General works

Local history and description
   Armenia (Republic). Armenian S.S.R.
     History
      By period
       1991- -- Continued

687.53	Political history
687.54	Foreign and general relations
	Biography and memoirs
687.6	Collective
687.62.A-Z	Individual, A-Z

Local history and description
689.A-Z	Regions, oblasts, etc., A-Z

     Cities and towns
      Yerevan. Erevan

689.2	Periodicals. Societies. Serials
689.22	Sources and documents
689.23	Directories. Dictionaries. Gazetteers
689.24	Guidebooks
689.25	General works
689.26	Description. Geography
689.27	Pictorial works
689.28	Antiquities
689.29	Social life and customs. Civilization. Intellectual life
	Ethnography
689.3	General works
689.32.A-Z	Individual elements in the population, A-Z
	History
	Biography
689.33	Collective
689.34.A-Z	Individual, A-Z
689.35	General works
	Sections, monuments, parks, streets, buildings, etc.
689.38	Collective
689.39.A-Z	Individual, A-Z
689.5.A-Z	Other cities, towns, etc., A-Z
	e.g.
689.5.A77	Artaxata
689.5.K37	Kirovakan

   Azerbaijan. Azerbaijan S.S.R.
690	Periodicals. Societies. Serials
	Museums, exhibitions, etc.
691.2	General works
691.3.A-Z	Individual. By place, A-Z
691.4	Congresses
691.5	Sources and documents
	Collected works (nonserial)

Local history and description
Azerbaijan. Azerbaijan S.S.R.
Collected works (nonserial) -- Continued

691.6	Several authors
691.7	Individual authors
691.8	Gazetteers. Dictionaries, etc.
691.9	Place names (General)
692	Directories
692.2	Guidebooks
692.3	General works
692.4	General special
692.5	Pictorial works

Historic monuments, landmarks, scenery, etc. (General)
For local see DK699+

692.6	General works
692.7	Preservation
692.8	Historical geography
692.85	Geography
692.9	Description and travel
693	Antiquities

For local antiquities see DK699+

693.2	Social life and customs. Civilization. Intellectual life

For specific periods, see the period
Ethnography

693.3	General works
693.4	National characteristics
693.5.A-Z	Individual elements in the population, A-Z
693.5.A75	Armenians
693.5.G46	Georgians (Transcaucasians)
693.5.G47	Germans
693.5.K87	Kurds
693.5.M87	Muslims
693.5.P65	Poles
693.5.R9	Russians
693.5.T38	Tats
693.6	Azerbaijanis in foreign countries (General)

For Azerbaijanis in a particular country, see the country
History
Periodicals. Societies. Serials see DK690

693.7	Dictionaries. Chronological tables, outlines, etc.

Biography (Collective)
For individual biography, see the specific period or place

693.8	General works
693.9	Rulers, kings, etc.
694	Queens. Princes and princesses

Houses, noble families, etc.

Local history and description
   Azerbaijan. Azerbaijan S.S.R.
     History
       Biography (Collective)
         Houses, noble families, etc. -- Continued

694.2	General works
694.3.A-Z	Individual houses, families, etc., A-Z
694.4	Statesmen
694.5	Women
	Cf. CT3490 Biography of women
	Historiography
694.6	General works
	Biography of historians, area studies specialists, archaeologists, etc.
694.7	Collective
694.8.A-Z	Individual, A-Z
	Study and teaching
694.9	General works
695.A-Z	By region or country, A-Z
	Subarrange by author
	General works
695.2	Through 1800
695.3	1801-1980
695.4	1981-
695.5	Pictorial works
695.6	Juvenile works
695.7	Addresses, essays, lectures. Anecdotes, etc.
	Military history
	For individual campaigns and engagements, see the special period
696	Sources and documents
696.2	General works
	Political history
	For specific periods, see the period
696.5	Sources and documents
696.6	General works
	Foreign and general relations
	For works on relations with a specific country regardless of period see DK696.9.A+
696.7	Sources and documents
696.8	General works
696.9.A-Z	Relations with individual countries, A-Z
	By period
697.1	Early to 1813
697.2	1813-1917

Local history and description
Azerbaijan. Azerbaijan S.S.R.
History
By period -- Continued
1917-1991
For works on the Bolshevik Revolution in
Azerbaijan see DK265.8.A9
For works on World War II as distinct from the time
period 1939-1945 see D731+

697.3	General works
	Biography and memoirs
697.4	Collective
697.5.A-Z	Individual, A-Z
	1991-
697.6	General works
697.67	Social life and customs. Civilization. Intellectual life
697.68	Political history
697.69	Foreign and general relations
	Biography and memoirs
697.7	Collective
697.8.A-Z	Individual, A-Z
	Local history and description
699.A-Z	Regions, oblasts, etc., A-Z
	Cities and towns
	Baku
699.2	Periodicals. Societies. Serials
699.22	Sources and documents
699.23	Directories. Dictionaries. Gazetteers
699.24	Guidebooks
699.25	General works
699.26	Description. Geography
699.27	Pictorial works
699.28	Antiquities
699.29	Social life and customs. Civilization. Intellectual life
	Ethnography
699.3	General works
699.32.A-Z	Individual elements in the population, A-Z
	History
	Biography
699.33	Collective
699.34.A-Z	Individual, A-Z
699.35	General works
	Sections, monuments, parks, streets, buildings, etc.
699.38	Collective
699.39.A-Z	Individual, A-Z

Local history and description

  Siberia

    Ethnography

      Individual elements in the population, A-Z -- Continued

(759.G6)	Golds
	see DK759.N34
759.G74	Greeks
759.J37	Japanese
759.K27	Kalmyks
759.K37	Kereks
759.K4	Kets
759.K5	Khakassians
759.K53	Khanty
759.K56	Khirghiz
759.K6	Koryaks
759.L35	Latgals
759.L37	Latvians
759.L58	Lithuanians
759.M33	Mansi
759.M66	Mongols
759.M87	Muslims
759.N34	Nanai. Golds
759.N4	Nganasani
759.O4	Olcha
759.O7	Oroches
759.P6	Poles
759.R9	Russians
759.S3	Samoyeds
759.S4	Selkups
759.S56	Shor
(759.S7)	Soyotes
	see DK759.T93
759.T3	Tatars (General)
	Cf. DK759.C47 Chulyma Tatars
759.T4	Teleut
(759.T9)	Tungus
	see DK759.E83
759.T92	Turkic peoples
759.T93	Tuvinians. Soyotes
759.U3	Udekhe (Asian people)
759.U9	Uzbeks
759.Y2	Yakuts
759.Y8	Yukaghir

    History

761	General works
763	Addresses, essays, lectures. Anecdotes, etc.

	Local history and description
	Siberia
	History -- Continued
	By period
764	Early through 1800
766	19th-20th centuries
	Historiography
767	General works
	Biography of historians, area studies specialists, archaeologists, etc.
768	Collective
768.5.A-Z	Individual, A-Z
	Biography and memoirs
768.7	Collective
769.A-Z	Individual, A-Z
	e.g.
	Ermak, d. 1585 see DK769.Y4
769.K7	Kropotkin, Petr Alekseevich, kníaz'
769.Y4	Yermak
770	Exiles. Political prisoners. Political refugees
	Local history and description
771.A-Z	Regions, oblasts, etc., A-Z
	e.g.
771.A25	Altai Mountains
771.A3	Amur River and Valley, Province, etc.
771.B3	Baikal, Lake
	Bering Sea see F951
771.B5	Biro-Bidjan. Evreĭskaĭa avtonomnaĭa oblast'
771.B8	Buriat-Mongolia
771.C4	Chukotski Peninsula
	Commander Islands see DK771.K7
771.D3	Dal'ne-Vostochnyĭ kraĭ. Soviet Far East. Far Eastern Territory, etc.
	Cf. DS518.7 Far Eastern question
	Eniseĭ River and Valley see DK771.Y4
	Evreĭskaĭa avtonomnaĭa oblast' see DK771.B5
	ĪAkutskaia A.S.S.R. see DK771.Y2
771.K2	Kamchatka
771.K7	Kommander Islands
771.M3	Maritime Province
771.N6	Northeastern Siberia
	Primor'e see DK771.M3
	Primorskiĭ kraĭ see DK771.M3
	Sakha see DK771.Y2
771.S2	Sakhalin
771.T8	Transbaikalia

Local history and description
Siberia
Local history and description
Regions, oblasts, etc., A-Z -- Continued

771.U9	Ussuri
771.W47	Western Siberia
771.Y2	Yakut A.S.S.R. Sakha
771.Y4	Yenisey River and Valley
781.A-Z	Cities and towns, etc., A-Z
	e.g.
781.I7	Irkutsk
781.M3	Magnitogorsk
	Novokuznetsk see DK781.S9
781.S2	Samarovo
781.S9	Stalinsk. Novokuznetsk
781.T6	Tomsk
781.V5	Vladivostok
781.Y4	Yeniseisk

Soviet Central Asia. West Turkestan
Cf. D378+ Central Asian question
Cf. DS327+ Central Asia (General)

845	Periodicals. Societies. Serials
847	Sources and documents
848	Gazetteers. Dictionaries, etc.
851	General works
853	Geography
854	Description and travel
855	Antiquities
855.2	Social life and customs. Civilization. Intellectual life
	Ethnography
855.4	General works
855.5.A-Z	Individual elements in the population, A-Z
855.5.D8	Dungans
855.5.G45	Georgians (Transcaucasians)
855.5.I73	Iranians
855.5.K25	Kara-Kalpaks
855.5.K3	Karluks
855.5.K33	Kazakhs
855.5.K48	Kipchak
855.5.K5	Khirghiz
855.5.K67	Koreans
855.5.M6	Mongols
855.5.M8	Muslims
855.5.O4	Oghuz
855.5.P64	Poles
855.5.R87	Russians

DK

Local history and description
  Soviet Central Asia. West Turkestan
    Ethnography
      Individual elements in the population, A-Z -- Continued

855.5.S2	Sarts
855.5.S55	Shughni
855.5.S64	Sogdians
855.5.T3	Tajiks
855.5.T85	Turkmen
855.5.U35	Uighur (Turkic people)
855.5.U42	Ukrainians
855.5.U9	Uzbeks
855.5.Y34	Yaghnobi
855.7	Biography (Collective)

    History
      Historiography

855.8	General works
	Biography of historians, area studies specialists, archaeologists, etc.
855.82	Collective
855.83.A-Z	Individual, A-Z
856	General works
857	Addresses, essays, lectures. Anecdotes, etc.
857.5	Political history

      Foreign and general relations
        For general works on the diplomatic history of a period, see the period
        For works on relations with a specific country regardless of period, see DK857.75

857.7	General works
857.75.A-Z	Relations with individual countries, A-Z

      By period

858	Early through 1919

        For works on the Bolshevik Revolution in Soviet Central Asia see DK265.8.S5

859	1920-1991

        For works on World War II as distinct from the time period 1939-1945 see D731+
      1991-
        Class here works on states of former Soviet Central Asia treated collectively

859.5	General works
859.56	Political history
859.57	Foreign and general relations
860	Biography (Collective)

  Kazakhstan. Kazakh S.S.R.

DK

Local history and description
Kazakhstan. Kazakh S.S.R.
History -- Continued
Biography (Collective)
For individual biography, see the specific period or place

908.13	General works
908.144	Rulers, kings, statesmen, etc.

Historiography

908.5	General works

Biography of historians, area studies specialists,
archaeologists, etc.

908.52	Collective
908.53.A-Z	Individual, A-Z
908.56	By region or country, A-Z
908.6	General works

Military history
For individual campaigns and engagements, see the
special period

908.65	Sources and documents
908.66	General works

Political history

908.67	Sources and documents
908.68	General works

By period
see the specific period
Foreign and general relations
For general works on the diplomatic history of a period, see
the period
For works on relations with a specific country
regardless of period see DK908.75.A+

908.69	Sources and documents
908.7	General works
908.75.A-Z	Relations with individual countries, A-Z

By period

908.82	Through 500
908.83	500-1400
908.84	1400-1700

1700-1850

908.85	General works

Biography and memoirs

908.855	Collective
908.856.A-Z	Individual, A-Z

1850-1917

908.86	General works

Biography and memoirs

908.8613	Collective

Local history and description
  Kazakhstan. Kazakh S.S.R.
    History
      By period
        1850-1917
          Biography and memoirs -- Continued

908.8614.A-Z	Individual, A-Z
908.8617	Revolt, 1916

        1917-1945
          For works on World War II as distinct from the time
            period 1939-1945 see D731+
          For works on the Bolshevik Revolution in the
            Kazakhstan see DK265.8.K39

908.8618	General works
	Biography and memoirs
908.862	Collective
908.863.A-Z	Individual, A-Z

        1945-1991

908.864	General works
	Biography and memoirs
908.865	Collective
908.866.A-Z	Individual, A-Z

        1991-

908.867	General works
908.8673	Social life and customs. Civilization. Intellectual life
908.8675	Political history
908.8677	Foreign and general relations
	Biography and memoirs
908.868	Collective
908.869.A-Z	Individual, A-Z

    Local history and description

909.A-Z	Regions, oblasts, etc., A-Z
	Cities and towns
	Alma Ata
909.2	Periodicals. Societies. Serials
909.22	Sources and documents
909.23	Directories. Dictionaries. Gazetteers
909.24	Guidebooks
909.25	General works
909.26	Description. Geography
909.27	Pictorial works
909.28	Antiquities
909.29	Social life and customs. Civilization. Intellectual life
	Ethnography
909.3	General works
909.32.A-Z	Individual elements in the population, A-Z

	Local history and description
	Kazakhstan. Kazakh S.S.R.
	Local history and description
	Cities and towns
	Alma Ata -- Continued
	History
	Biography
909.33	Collective
909.34.A-Z	Individual, A-Z
909.35	General works
	Sections, monuments, parks, streets, buildings, etc.
909.38	Collective
909.39.A-Z	Individual, A-Z
909.5.A-Z	Other cities, towns, etc., A-Z
	e.g.
909.5.C55	Chimkent
909.5.K37	Karaganda
909.5.S46	Semipalatinsk
	Kyrgyzstan. Kirghiz S.S.R. Kirghizia
911	Periodicals. Societies. Serials
	Museums, exhibitions, etc.
911.5	General works
911.52.A-Z	Individual. By place, A-Z
911.6	Congresses
912	Sources and documents
	Collected works (nonserial)
912.12	Several authors
912.13	Individual authors
912.14	Gazetteers. Dictionaries, etc.
912.16	Place names (General)
912.17	Directories
912.18	Guidebooks
913	General works
913.12	General special
913.2	Pictorial works
	Historic monuments, landmarks, scenery, etc. (General)
	For local see DK919+
913.3	General works
913.4	Preservation
913.5	Historical geography
914	Description and travel
915	Antiquities
	For local antiquities see DK919+
916	Social life and customs. Civilization. Intellectual life
	Ethnography
917	General works

Local history and description

Kyrgyzstan. Kirghiz S.S.R. Kirghizia

Ethnography -- Continued

917.15.A-Z	Individual elements in the population, A-Z
917.15.A75	Armenians
917.15.B44	Belarusians
917.15.C66	Cossacks
917.15.G47	Germans
917.15.K67	Koreans
917.15.P65	Poles
917.15.R87	Russians
917.15.U38	Uighur (Turkic people)
917.15.U42	Ukrainians
917.2	Kirghiz in foreign countries (General)

For Kirghiz in a particular country, see the country

History

Periodicals. Societies. Serials see DK911

918.12	Dictionaries. Chronological tables, outlines, etc.

Biography (Collective)

For individual biography, see the specific period or place

918.13	General works
918.144	Rulers, kings, statesmen, etc.

Historiography

918.5	General works

Biography of historians, area studies specialists,
       archaeologists, etc.

918.52	Collective
918.53.A-Z	Individual, A-Z
918.6	General works

Foreign and general relations

For general works on the diplomatic history of a period, see
       the period

For works on relations with a specific country regardless of
       period, see DK918.795.A-Z

918.79	General works
918.795.A-Z	Relations with individual countries, A-Z

By period

918.82	Through 500
918.83	500-1700

1700-1917

918.84	General works

Biography and memoirs

918.845	Collective
918.846.A-Z	Individual, A-Z
918.848	Uprising, 1916

	Local history and description
	Kyrgyzstan. Kirghiz S.S.R. Kirghizia
	History
	By period -- Continued
	1917-1945
	For works on World War II as distinct from the time period 1939-1945 see D731+
	For works on the Bolshevik Revolution in the Kirghizistan see DK265.8.K57
918.85	General works
	Biography and memoirs
918.86	Collective
918.87.A-Z	Individual, A-Z
	1945-1991
918.871	General works
	Biography and memoirs
918.872	Collective
918.873.A-Z	Individual, A-Z
	1991-
918.875	General works
918.8757	Political history
	Biography and memoirs
918.876	Collective
918.877.A-Z	Individual, A-Z
	Local history and description
919.A-Z	Regions, oblasts, etc., A-Z
	Cities and towns
	Bishkek. Frunze
919.2	Periodicals. Societies. Serials
919.22	Sources and documents
919.23	Directories. Dictionaries. Gazetteers
919.24	Guidebooks
919.25	General works
919.26	Description. Geography
919.27	Pictorial works
919.28	Antiquities
919.29	Social life and customs. Civilization. Intellectual life
	Ethnography
919.3	General works
919.32.A-Z	Individual elements in the population, A-Z
	History
	Biography
919.33	Collective
919.34.A-Z	Individual, A-Z
919.35	General works
	Sections, monuments, parks, streets, buildings, etc.

Local history and description
Kyrgyzstan. Kirghiz S.S.R. Kirghizia
Local history and description
Cities and towns
Bishkek. Frunze
Sections, monuments, parks, streets, buildings, etc. --
Continued

919.38	Collective
919.39.A-Z	Individual, A-Z
919.5.A-Z	Other cities, towns, etc., A-Z
	e.g.
919.5.D95	Dzhalal-Abad
919.5.O75	Osh
919.5.P79	Przheval'sk

Tajikistan. Tajik S.S.R. Tadzhikistan

921	Periodicals. Societies. Serials
	Museums, exhibitions, etc.
921.5	General works
921.52.A-Z	Individual, A-Z
921.6	Congresses
922	Sources and documents
	Collected works (nonserial)
922.12	Several authors
922.13	Individual authors
922.14	Gazetteers. Dictionaries, etc.
922.16	Place names (General)
922.17	Directories
922.18	Guidebooks
923	General works
923.12	General special
923.2	Pictorial works
	Historic monuments, landmarks, scenery, etc. (General)
	For local see DK929+
923.3	General works
923.4	Preservation
923.5	Historical geography
924	Description and travel
925	Antiquities
	For local antiquities see DK929+
926	Social life and customs. Civilization. Intellectual life
	Ethnography
	For individual elements in the population see
	DK855.5.A+
927	General works
927.2	Tajiks in foreign countries (General)
	For Tajiks in a particular country, see the country

	Local history and description
	Tajikistan. Tajik S.S.R. Tadzhikistan -- Continued
	History
	Periodicals. Societies. Serials see DK921
928.12	Dictionaries. Chronological tables, outlines, etc.
	Biography (Collective)
	For individual biography, see the specific period or place
928.13	General works
928.144	Rulers, kings, etc.
	Historiography
928.5	General works
	Biography of historians, area studies specialists, archaeologists, etc.
928.52	Collective
928.53.A-Z	Individual, A-Z
928.6	General works
	By period
928.82	Through 500
928.83	500-1700
928.84	1850-1917
	1917-1945
	For World War II as distinct from the time period 1939-1945 see D731+
	For works on the Bolshevik Revolution in Tajikistan see DK265.8.T27
928.85	General works
	Biography and memoirs
928.852	Collective
928.853.A-Z	Individual, A-Z
	1945-1991
928.86	General works
	Biography and memoirs
928.862	Collective
928.863.A-Z	Individual, A-Z
	1991-
928.865	General works
928.8657	Political history
928.8658	Foreign and general relations
	Biography and memoirs
928.866	Collective
928.867.A-Z	Individual, A-Z
	Local history and description
929.A-Z	Regions, oblasts, etc., A-Z
	Cities and towns
	Dushanbe
929.2	Periodicals. Societies. Serials

Local history and description
  Tajikistan. Tajik S.S.R. Tadzhikistan
    Local history and description
      Cities and towns
        Dushanbe -- Continued

929.22	Sources and documents
929.23	Directories. Dictionaries. Gazetteers
929.24	Guidebooks
929.25	General works
929.26	Description. Geography
929.27	Pictorial works
929.28	Antiquities
929.29	Social life and customs. Civilization. Intellectual life
	Ethnography
929.3	General works
929.32.A-Z	Individual elements in the population, A-Z
	History
	Biography
929.33	Collective
929.34.A-Z	Individual, A-Z
929.35	General works
	Sections, monuments, parks, streets, buildings, etc.
929.38	Collective
929.39.A-Z	Individual, A-Z
929.5.A-Z	Other cities, towns, etc., A-Z
	e.g.
	Istaravshan see DK929.5.U73
929.5.L46	Leninabad
929.5.U73	Ura Tyube. Istaravshan
	Turkmenistan. Turkmen S.S.R. Turkmenia
931	Periodicals. Societies. Serials
	Museums, exhibitions, etc.
931.5	General works
931.52.A-Z	Individual, A-Z
931.6	Congresses
932	Sources and documents
	Collected works (nonserial)
932.12	Several authors
932.13	Individual authors
932.14	Gazetteers. Dictionaries, etc.
932.16	Place names (General)
932.17	Directories
932.18	Guidebooks
933	General works
933.12	General special
933.2	Pictorial works

DK

Local history and description
Turkmenistan. Turkmen S.S.R. Turkmenia -- Continued
Historic monuments, landmarks, scenery, etc. (General)
For local see DK939+

933.3	General works
933.4	Preservation
933.5	Historical geography
934	Description and travel
935	Antiquities

For local antiquities see DK939+

936	Social life and customs. Civilization. Intellectual life

Ethnography
For individual elements in the population see
DK855.5.A+

937	General works
937.2	Turkmen in foreign countries (General)

For Turkmen in a particular country, see the country

History
Periodicals. Societies. Serials see DK931

938.12	Dictionaries. Chronological tables, outlines, etc.

Biography (Collective)
For individual biography, see the specific period or place

938.13	General works
938.144	Rulers, kings, statesmen, etc.

Historiography

938.5	General works

Biography of historians, area studies specialists,
archaeologists, etc.

938.52	Collective
938.53.A-Z	Individual, A-Z
938.6	General works

By period

938.82	Through 500
938.83	500-1800
938.84	1800-1917
	1917-1945

For works on World War II as distinct from the time
period 1939-1945 see D731+
For works on the Bolshevik Revolution in the
Turkmenistan see DK265.8.T93

938.85	General works

Biography and memoirs

938.852	Collective
938.853.A-Z	Individual, A-Z
	1945-1991
938.86	General works

Local history and description
Turkmenistan. Turkmen S.S.R. Turkmenia
History
By period
1945-1991 -- Continued
Biography and memoirs
938.862 Collective
938.863.A-Z Individual, A-Z
1991-
938.865 General works
938.8657 Political history
938.8658 Foreign and general relations
Biography and memoirs
938.866 Collective
938.867.A-Z Individual, A-Z
Local history and description
939.A-Z Regions, oblasts, etc., A-Z
Cities and towns
Ashkhabad
939.2 Periodicals. Societies. Serials
939.22 Sources and documents
939.23 Directories. Dictionaries. Gazetteers
939.24 Guidebooks
939.25 General works
939.26 Description. Geography
939.27 Pictorial works
939.28 Antiquities
939.29 Social life and customs. Civilization. Intellectual life
Ethnography
939.3 General works
939.32.A-Z Individual elements in the population, A-Z
History
Biography
939.33 Collective
939.34.A-Z Individual, A-Z
939.35 General works
Sections, monuments, parks, streets, buildings, etc.
939.38 Collective
939.39.A-Z Individual, A-Z
Other cities, towns, etc., A-Z
e.g.
939.5.K73 Krasnovodsk
939.5.N43 Nebit-Dag
Uzbekistan. Uzbek S.S.R.
941 Periodicals. Societies. Serials
Museums, exhibitions, etc.

	Local history and description
	Uzbekistan. Uzbek S.S.R.
	Museums, exhibitions, etc. -- Continued
941.5	General works
941.52.A-Z	Individual, A-Z
941.6	Congresses
942	Sources and documents
	Collected works (nonserial)
942.12	Several authors
942.13	Individual authors
942.14	Gazetteers. Dictionaries, etc.
942.16	Place names (General)
942.17	Directories
942.18	Guidebooks
943	General works
943.12	General special
943.2	Pictorial works
	Historic monuments, landmarks, scenery, etc. (General)
	For local see DK949+
943.3	General works
943.4	Preservation
943.5	Historical geography
944	Description and travel
945	Antiquities
	For local antiquities see DK949+
946	Social life and customs. Civilization. Intellectual life
	Ethnography
	For individual elements in the population see
	DK855.5.A+
947	General works
947.15	National characteristics
947.2	Uzbeks in foreign countries (General)
	For Uzbeks in a particular country, see the country
	History
	Periodicals. Societies. Serials see DK941
948.12	Dictionaries. Chronological tables, outlines, etc.
	Biography (Collective)
	For individual biography, see the specific period or place
948.13	General works
948.144	Rulers, kings, statesmen, etc.
	Historiography
948.5	General works
	Biography of historians, area studies specialists,
	archaeologists, etc.
948.52	Collective
948.53.A-Z	Individual, A-Z

	Local history and description
	Uzbekistan. Uzbek S.S.R.
	History -- Continued
	Study and teaching
948.55	General works
948.56.A-Z	By region or country, A-Z
	General works
948.6	Through 1980
948.62	1981-
948.65	Pictorial works
948.66	Juvenile works
948.67	Addresses, essays, lectures. Anecdotes
	Military history
	For individual campaigns and engagements, see the
	specific period
948.7	Sources and documents
948.72	General works
	Political history
	For specific periods, see the period
948.73	Sources and documents
948.75	General works
	Foreign and general relations
948.76	Sources and documents
948.77	General works
948.79.A-Z	Relations with individual countries, A-Z
	By period
948.82	Through 500
948.83	500-1800
948.84	1800-1917
	1917-1945
	For works on World War II as distinct from the time
	period 1939-1945 see D731+
	For works on the Bolshevik Revolution in the
	Uzbekistan see DK265.8.U9
948.85	General works
	Biography and memoirs
948.852	Collective
948.853.A-Z	Individual, A-Z
	1945-1991
948.86	General works
	Biography and memoirs
948.862	Collective
948.863.A-Z	Individual, A-Z
	1991-
948.865	General works
948.8654	Social life and customs. Civilization. Intellectual life

	Local history and description
	Uzbekistan. Uzbek S.S.R.
	History
	By period
	1991- -- Continued
948.8657	Political history
948.8658	Foreign and general relations
	Biography and memoirs
948.866	Collective
948.867.A-Z	Individual, A-Z
	Local history and description
949.A-Z	Regions, oblasts, etc., A-Z
	Cities and towns
	Tashkent
949.2	Periodicals. Societies. Serials
949.22	Sources and documents
949.23	Directories. Dictionaries. Gazetteers
949.24	Guidebooks
949.25	General works
949.26	Description. Geography
949.27	Pictorial works
949.28	Antiquities
949.29	Social life and customs. Civilization. Intellectual life
	Ethnography
949.3	General works
949.32.A-Z	Individual elements in the population, A-Z
949.32.G73	Greeks
	History
	Biography
949.33	Collective
949.34.A-Z	Individual, A-Z
949.35	General works
	Sections, monuments, parks, streets, buildings, etc.
949.38	Collective
949.39.A-Z	Individual, A-Z
949.5.A-Z	Other cities, towns, etc., A-Z
	e.g.
949.5.K65	Kokand
949.5.N35	Namangan
949.5.S35	Samarkand

	History of Poland
4010	Periodicals. Societies. Serials
	Museums, exhibitions, etc.
4015	General works
4016.A-Z	Individual. By place, A-Z
4018	Congresses
4020	Sources and documents
	Collected works
4025	Several authors
4027.A-Z	Individual authors, A-Z
4030	Gazetteers. Dictionaries, etc.
4035	Place names (General)
4036	Directories
4037	Guidebooks
4040	General works
4042	General special
4043	Monumental and picturesque. Pictorial works
	Historic monuments, landmarks, scenery, etc. (General)
4044	General works
4044.5	Preservation
4045	Historical geography
4046	Geography
	Description and travel
4047	History of travel
4050	Early to 1815
4060	1815-1866
4070	1867-1944
4080	1945-1980
4081	1981-
	Antiquities
4088	Periodicals. Societies. Serials
4090	General works
4092	General special
	Local see DK4600+
	Social life and customs. Civilization. Intellectual life
4110	General works
4112	Foreign influences
	Including Latin influence
4115	Intellectual life. Culture
	By period
	see the specific period or reign
	Ethnography
4120	General works
4121	National characteristics. Patriotism. Messianism
4121.5.A-Z	Individual elements in the population, A-Z
4121.5.A7	Armenians
4121.5.B44	Belarusians

	Ethnography
	Individual elements in the population, A-Z -- Continued
4121.5.C9	Czechs
4121.5.E88	Estonians
4121.5.G4	Germans
4121.5.G73	Greeks
4121.5.H85	Hungarians
4121.5.I8	Italians
4121.5.J32	Jaćwież
	Jews see DS134.5+
4121.5.K37	Karaims
4121.5.K87	Kurpie
4121.5.L4	Lemky
4121.5.L56	Lithuanians
4121.5.M33	Macedonians
4121.5.P64	Polanie
4121.5.S35	Scots
4121.5.S55	Slovaks
4121.5.S65	Slovinci
4121.5.T3	Tatars
4121.5.U4	Ukrainians
4121.5.V54	Vietnamese
(4121.5.W5)	White Russians
	see DK4121.5.B44
4122	Poles in foreign countries (General)
	For Poles in a particular country, see that country
	History
	Periodicals, societies, serials see DK4010
4123	Dictionaries. Chronological tables, outlines, etc.
	Biography
	For individual biography, see the specific period, reign, or place
4130	General works
4131	Rulers, kings, etc.
4133	Public men
4135	Women
	Houses, noble families, etc.
4137	General works
4138.A-Z	Individual, A-Z
	e.g.
4138.G6	Górka family
4138.J3	Jagiellons
4138.P5	Piasts
4138.5	Princes and princesses. Queens
	Historiography
4139	General works
	Biography of historians
4139.2	Collective

	History
	Historiography
	Biography of historians -- Continued
4139.25.A-Z	Individual, A-Z
	e.g.
4139.25.B3	Balzer, Oswald Marian
4139.25.D5	Długosz, Jan
4139.25.L4	Lelewel, Joachim
4139.25.N3	Naruszewicz, Adam Stanisław
	Study and teaching
4139.3	General works
4139.4.A-Z	By region or country, A-Z
	Subarrange by author
	General works
	Through 1800 see DK4187; DK4190
4140	1801-
4145	Pictorial works. Albums
4147	Juvenile works
4150	Addresses, essays, lectures
	General special
4155	Philosophy of Polish history
4160	Several parts of Poland treated together
	Military history
4170	General works
4171	General special
4172	Early to 1795
4173	1795-1918
4174	1918-
	Naval history
4177	General works
4178	General special
	Political and diplomatic history. Politics and government
4178.5	Sources and documents
4179	General works
4179.2	General special
	By period
	see the specific period or reign
	Diplomatic history. Foreign and general relations
4179.5	Sources and documents
4180	General works
4182	Polish question
	By period
	see the specific period or reign
4185.A-Z	Relations with individual countries, A-Z
	By period
	To 1795
4186	Sources and documents

DK

History
By period
To 1795 -- Continued
General works

4187	Through 1800
4188	1801-
4188.2	Social life and customs. Civilization. Intellectual life

To 1572

4189	Sources and documents
	General works
4190	Through 1800
4200	1801-
4205	General special
4210	Through 960
4210.5	Goths
4210.7	Romans

960-1386. Piast period

4211	Sources and documents
4212	General works
4212.5	Social life and customs. Civilization. Intellectual life

960-1138. First monarchy

4213	General works
	Biography and memoirs
4214	Collective
4214.5.A-Z	Individual, A-Z
4215	Mieszko I, 960-992
4215.5	Battle of Cedynia, 972
4220	Boleslaus I the Brave, 992-1025
4222	Mieszko II, 1025-1034
4222.5	Interregnum, 1034-1040
4223	Casimir I the Restorer, 1040-1058
4224	Boleslaus II the Bold, 1058-1079
4225	Vladislaus I Herman, 1079-1102
4226	Boleslaus III, the Wrymouth, 1102-1138

1138-1305. Feudal duchies

4227	General works
	Biography and memoirs
4229	Collective
4230.A-Z	Individual, A-Z
	e.g.
4230.B6	Bolesław Pobozny, Prince of Wielkopolska
4230.P78	Przemysł II, Prince of Wielkopolska and King of Poland
4230.W5	Władysław III, Laskonogi, Duke of Wielkopolska and Kraków
4241	Vladislaus II the Exile, 1138-1146
4242	Boleslaus IV the Curly, 1146-1173

	History
	By period
	To 1795
	1572-1763. Elective monarchy -- Continued
4293	Henry III Valois, 1573-1574
4294	Interregnum, 1574-1575
	Stefan Batory, 1575-1586
4295	General works
4297	Livonian War, 1557-1582
4297.4	Battle of Lubieszów, 1577
	Biography and memoirs
4298	Collective
4299.A-Z	Individual, A-Z
	e.g.
4299.A5	Anna Jagiellonka, Consort of Stefan Batory
	Sigismund III, 1587-1632
4300	General works
4301	General special
4301.3	Battle of Byczyna, 1588
4301.4	Battle of Kirchholm, 1605
4301.5	Rebellion of Zebrzydowski, 1606-1609
	Swedish-Polish War, 1617-1629 see DL712+
4301.6	Battle of Cecora, 1620
4301.7	Battle of Chocim (Hotin), 1621
	Biography and memoirs
4301.9	Collective
4302.A-Z	Individual, A-Z
	e.g.
4302.C5	Chodkiewicz, Jan Karol
4302.Z3	Zamojski, Jan
4302.Z6	Zółkiewski, Stanisław
4302.5	17th century (General)
	Wladyslaw IV Zygmunt, 1632-1648
4303	General works
4303.4	Russo-Polish War, 1632-1634
	John II Casimir, 1648-1668
4305	General works
4306	General special
	Polish-Cossack War (Chmielnicki Uprising), 1648-1654 see DK508.755.A+
4306.3	Uprising of Kostka Napierski, 1651
	Swedish-Polish War, 1655-1660 see DL725.6+
4306.33	Russo-Polish War, 1654-1656
4306.35	Polish-Brandenburg War, 1656-1657
4306.36	Russo-Polish War, 1658-1667
	Including the Battle of Chudniv (Cudnów), 1660
4306.4	Rebellion of Lubomirski, 1665-1666

History
  By period
    To 1795
      1572-1763. Elective monarchy
        John II Casimir, 1648-1668 -- Continued
          Biography and memoirs

4307	Collective
4307.5.A-Z	Individual, A-Z
	e.g.
4307.5.C9	Czarniecki, Stefan
4307.5.K6	Kordeki, Augustyn
4307.5.L8	Lubomirski, Jerzy Sebastian
4307.5.M3	Marja Ludwika, Consort of John II Casimir
	Michael Wiśniowiecki, 1669-1673
4308	General works
4309	Gołąbska Konfederacja, 1672
4309.5	Battle of Chocim (Hotin), 1673
	John III Sobieski, 1674-1696
4310	General works
	Turco-Polish Wars, 1683-1699
4311	General works
	Siege of Vienna, 1683 see DR536
4311.5	Battle of Podgaytsy, 1698
	Biography and memoirs
4311.9	Collective
4312.A-Z	Individual, A-Z
	e.g.
4312.L3	Lubomirski, Hieronym Augustyn
4312.M3	Maria Kazimiera, Consort of John III Sobieski
4312.P3	Pasek, Jan Chryzostom
4312.Z3	Załuski, Andrzej Chryzostom
4314	Interregnum, 1696-1697
4314.5	18th century (General)
	Augustus II (Friedrich August I, Elector of Saxony), 1697-1733
	For biography see DD801.S395+
4315	General works on Polish reign
4317	Political and diplomatic history
	Battle of Podgaytsy, 1698 see DK4311.5
	Northern War, 1700-1721 see DL733+
	Biography and memoirs
4318	Collective
4319.A-Z	Individual, A-Z
4320	Stanislaus I Leszczyński, 1704-1709
	Augustus III (Friedrich August II, Elector of Saxony), 1733-1763
	For biography see DD801.S397

History
By period
To 1795
1572-1763. Elective monarchy
Augustus III (Friedrich August II, Elector of Saxony),
1733-1763 -- Continued

4325	General works on Polish reign
4325.5	Social life and customs. Civilization. Intellectual life
4326	Political and diplomatic history
	War of Polish Succession, 1733-1738
4326.5	General works
4327	Treaty of Vienna, 1738
	Biography and memoirs
4327.5	Collective
4328.A-Z	Individual, A-Z
	e.g.
4328.K6	Konarski, Stanisław
	1763-1795. Partition period
4328.9	Sources and documents
4329	General works
4329.5	General special
	Stanislaus II Augustus, 1764-1795
4330	General works
4330.5	Social life and customs. Civilization. Intellectual life
4331	Barska Konfederacja, 1768-1772
4332	First partition, 1772
	Sejm, 1788-1792
4333	General works
4334	Constitution of May, 1791
	Targowicka Konfederacja, 1792-1793
4335	General works
4336	Russo-Polish War, 1792
4337	Second partition, 1793
	Revolution of 1794
4338	Periodicals. Societies. Serials
4339	Sources and documents
	Biography see DK4347+
4340	General works
4341	Pictorial works. Satire, caricature, etc.
4342	General special
4343	Personal narratives
4344.A-Z	Local revolutionary history. By place, A-Z
	e.g.
4344.R3	Battle of Raclawice, 1794
4345.A-Z	Special topics, A-Z
4345.A7	Arms and armament
4345.C37	Catholic Church

DK

	History
	By period
	To 1795
	1763-1795. Partition period
	Stanislaus II Augustus, 1764-1795
	Revolution of 1794
	Special topics, A-Z -- Continued
4345.F67	Foreign public opinion
	Jews see DS134.5+
	Biography and memoirs
4347	Collective
4348.A-Z	Individual, A-Z
	e.g.
4348.K6	Kołłątaj, Hugo
4348.K67	Kościuszko, Tadeusz Andrzej
	Cf. E207.K8 American Revolution
4348.P8	Pułaski, Kazimierz
4348.S8	Staszic, Stanisław
	1795-1918. 19th century (General)
4348.5	Sources and documents
4349	General works
4349.3	General special
4349.4	Social life and customs. Civilization. Intellectual life
4349.5	Biography (Collective)
	For individual biography, see the specific period
	1795-1864
4349.6	Sources and documents
4349.7	General works
4349.8	General special
	1795-1830
4349.9	Sources and documents
4350	General works
4351	General special
4353	Period of Napoleonic Wars, 1795-1815
	Including the Duchy of Warsaw
	For the wars themselves see DC220
	Biography and memoirs
4354	Collective
4355.A-Z	Individual, A-Z
	e.g.
4355.C9	Czartoryski, Adam Jerzy
	Cf. PG7158.C8214+ Polish literature
4355.D3	Dąbrowski, Jan Henryk
4355.P6	Poniatowski, Józef Antoni
4355.W88	Wybicki, Józef
	1830-1864
4356	Sources and documents

History
  By period
    1795-1918. 19th century (General)
      1795-1864
        1830-1864 -- Continued

4357	General works
4358	General special
	Revolution of 1830-1832
4359	Periodicals. Societies. Serials
4359.3	Museums, exhibitions, etc.
	Subarrange by author
4359.5	Sources and documents
	Biography see DK4379+
4360	General works
4361	Pictorial works. Satire, caricature, etc.
4361.3	Addresses, essays, lectures
4361.5	General special
	Military operations
4362	General works
4362.2	Regimental histories
	Subarrange by author
4362.3	Personal narratives
4362.5.A-Z	Local revolutionary history. By place, A-Z
4363.A-Z	Special topics, A-Z
4363.C65	Confiscations
4363.E3	Economic aspects
	Female participation see DK4363.W66
4363.F6	Foreign public opinion
	Health aspects see DK4363.M43
	Hospitals see DK4363.M43
	Jews see DS134.5+
4363.M43	Medical care. Hospitals. Health aspects
4363.P7	Press
4363.R4	Refugees
4363.W66	Women. Female participation
4363.2	Partisan Campaign, 1833
4364	Revolution of 1846
	Revolution of 1848
4365	General works
4365.5.A-Z	Local revolutionary history. By place, A-Z
	Revolution of 1863-1864
4366	Periodicals. Societies. Serials
4367	Museums, exhibitions, etc.
	Subarrange by author
4368	Sources and documents
	Biography see DK4379+
4370	General works

	History
	By period
	1795-1918. 19th century (General)
	1795-1864
	1830-1864
	Revolution of 1863-1864 -- Continued
4372	Pictorial works. Satire, caricature, etc.
4372.2	Addresses, essays, lectures
4372.3	General special
	Military operations
4373	General works
4373.5	Regimental histories
	Subarrange by author
4374	Personal narratives
4376.A-Z	Local revolutionary history. By place, A-Z
4378.A-Z	Special topics, A-Z
4378.C3	Catholic Church
4378.C65	Communications
	Foreign participation
4378.F6	General works
4378.F62A-.F62Z	By country, A-Z
4378.F65	Foreign public opinion
4378.I5	Influence
	Jews see DS134.5+
4378.P7	Press
4378.P75	Prisoners and prisons
4378.R4	Refugees
4378.S4	Secret service. Spies
4378.S6	Social aspects
	Spies see DK4378.S4
4378.T7	Transportation
4378.V46	Veterans
4378.W6	Women
	Biography and memoirs
4379	Collective
4379.5.A-Z	Individual, A-Z
	e.g.
4379.5.D3	Dąbrowski, Jaroslaw
4379.5.D4	Dembowski, Edward
4379.5.M5	Mierosławski, Ludwik
4379.5.T7	Traugutt, Romuald
4379.5.W5	Wielopolski, Aleksander Ignacy
	1864-1918
4379.9	Sources and documents
4380	General works
4381	General special
4381.5	Social life and customs. Civilization. Intellectual life

	History
	By period
	1795-1918. 19th century (General)
	1864-1918 -- Continued
4382	20th century (General)
	Revolution of 1905
4383	Periodicals. Societies. Serials
4384	Sources and documents
	Biography see DK4394+
4385	General works
4385.2	Pictorial works. Satire, caricature, etc.
4385.3	Addresses, essays, lectures
4386	General special
4387	Personal narratives
4388.A-Z	Local revolutionary history. By place, A-Z
4389.A-Z	Special topics, A-Z
4389.A52	Anarchism
4389.P74	Press
4389.S77	Student strikes
	1914-1918. Period of World War I
	Including German occupation, 1914-1918
	For the war itself see D501+
4390	General works
4392	Austrian occupation, 1915-1918
	Biography and memoirs, 1864-1918
4394	Collective
4395.A-Z	Individual, A-Z
	e.g.
4395.B6	Bobrzyński, Michał
4395.K8	Kunicki, Ryszard
	1918-1945
4397	Sources and documents
4400	General works
4401	General special
4401.5	Military history
4401.7	Naval history
4402	Political history
4402.5	Foreign and general relations
4403	Social life and customs. Civilization. Intellectual life
	1918-1926
4403.5	General works
	Wars of 1918-1921
	Including Russo-Polish War, 1919-1920
4404	Periodicals. Societies. Serials
4404.5	Sources and documents
	Biography see DK4419+
4405	General works

DK

History
By period
1918-1945
1918-1926
Wars of 1918-1921 -- Continued
4405.3   Pictorial works. Satire, caricature, etc.
4405.5   General special
4405.7   Diplomatic history
Military operations
4406   General works
4406.2   Cavalry operations
4406.3   Regimental histories
Subarrange by author
4406.4   Aerial operations
4406.45   Naval operations
4406.54   Personal narratives
4407.A-Z   Individual campaigns, battles, etc. By place, A-Z
e.g.
4407.G3   Galicia
4407.L9   Siege of Lvov, 1918-1919
4409.A-Z   Special topics, A-Z
4409.C37   Catholic Church
4409.F54   Flags
4409.F65   Foreign participation
Health aspects see DK4409.M43
Hospitals see DK4409.M43
4409.J68   Journalism
4409.M4   Medals
4409.M43   Medical care. Hospitals. Health aspects
4409.M54   Military intelligence
4409.P64   Police
4409.P75   Prisoners and prisons
4409.P76   Propaganda
4409.T45   Territorial questions
4409.3   Treaty of Riga, 1921
4409.4   Coup d'Etat, 1926
4409.5   1926-1939
1939-1945. Period of World War II
For for the war itself see D731+
4410   General works
Including German occupation, 1939-1945
4415   Russian occupation, 1939-1941
Biography and memoirs, 1918-1945
4419   Collective
4420.A-Z   Individual, A-Z
e.g.
4420.B4   Beck, Józef

History
  By period
    1918-1945
      Biography and memoirs, 1918-1945
        Individual, A-Z -- Continued

4420.P3	Paderewski, Ignacy Jan
4420.P5	Piłsudski, Józef
4420.S5	Sikorski, Władysław

      1945-1989. People's Republic

4429	Sources and documents
4430	General works
4433	General special

        Biography and memoirs, 1945-

4434	Collective
4435.A-Z	Individual, A-Z
	e.g.
4435.B5	Bierut, Bolesław
4435.C88	Cyrankiewicz, Józef
4435.G5	Gierek, Edward
4435.G6	Gomułka, Władysław
4436	Political history
4436.5	Foreign and general relations
4437	Social life and customs. Civilization. Intellectual life

        1945-1956

4438	General works
4439	Uprising, 1956
4440	1956-1980
4442	1980-1989

      1989-

4445	Sources and documents
4446	General works
4448	Social life and customs. Civilization. Intellectual life
4449	Political history
4450	Foreign and general relations

        Biography and memoirs

4451	Collective
4452.A-Z	Individual, A-Z
	e.g.
4452.W34	Wałęsa, Lech

  Local history and description

4600.A-Z	Provinces, counties, historical regions, etc., A-Z

      Jurisdictions of varying size that are named for the same city
        are classed in separate cutter numbers; regions named for
        the same city may be classed with any jurisdiction, as
        appropriate
      e.g.

4600.B37	Beshchady Mountains (Bieszczady)

DK

Local history and description
 Provinces, counties, historical regions, etc., A-Z -- Continued

4600.B4	Beskid Mountains
	For Beskids in Czechoslovakia see DB3000.B4
4600.B52-.B5289	Białystok (Voivodeship) (Table D-DR5)
4600.B88-.B8889	Bydgoszcz (Voivodeship) (Table D-DR5)
4600.C3	Carpathian Mountains
	For Carpathian Mountains (General) see DJK71+
4600.C54-.C5489	Cieszyn (Teschen) Silesia (Table D-DR5)
	For Ceský Těšín region in Czechoslovakia see
	DB2500.C465
4600.C9	Częstochowa
	Dąbrowa Basin see DK4600.S6
4600.G34-.G3489	Galicia (Table D-DR5)
4600.G42-.G4289	Gdańsk (Danzig) (Voivodeship) (Table D-DR5)
4600.G44-.G4489	Gdańsk Pomerania. Pomerelia (Table D-DR5)
	Including Royal Prussia, West Prussia, Polish Pomerania
	(1919-1936), and Danzig-Westpreussen
4600.G54	Głubczyce Plateau
4600.G56	Gniezno
	Grenzmark Posen-Westpreussen see DK4600.M35
4600.I9	Izera Mountains (Jizerské Hory, Isergebirge)
	For Izera Mountains in Czechoslovakia see
	DB2500.J58
4600.K34-.K3489	Kaszuby region (Table D-DR5)
4600.K37-.K3789	Katowice (Voivodeship) (Table D-DR5)
	Cf. DK4600.S48 Silesia (Voivodeship). Województwo
	Slaskie
4600.K43-.K4389	Kielce (Voivodeship) (Table D-DR5)
4600.K53-.K5389	Kłodzko (Glatz) (Table D-DR5)
4600.K6	Kołobrzeg
4600.K67	Kościan
4600.K68-.K6889	Koszalin (Voivodeship) (Table D-DR5)
4600.K72-.K7289	Kraków (Voivodeship). Województwo Małopolskie (Table D-DR5)
4600.K75	Kraków-Czestochowa Highland
4600.K77	Krkonose Mountains (Karkonosze, Riesengebirge)
	For Krkonose Mountains (General and Czechoslovakia)
	see DB2500.K75
4600.K8	Kujawy
4600.L63-.L6389	Łódź (Voivodeship) (Table D-DR5)
4600.L67	Łowicz
4600.L82-.L8289	Lublin (Voivodeship) (Table D-DR5)
4600.L86	Lubusz region
4600.M33	Malopolska. Wojewodztwo Malopolskie (Table D-DR5)
4600.M35	Marchia Graniczna (Grenzmark Posen-Westpreussen)
4600.M36-.M3689	Masovia (Mazowsze) (Table D-DR5)

Local history and description

Provinces, counties, historical regions, etc., A-Z -- Continued

4600.M38-.M3889	Mazury region (Masurenland) (Table D-DR5)
4600.N3	Narew River and Valley
4600.O33-.O3389	Oder-Neisse Line. Western and Northern Territories (Table D-DR5)
	Including Oder River and Valley (General)
4600.O44-.O4489	Olsztyn (Voivodeship) (Table D-DR5)
4600.O66-.O6689	Opole (Oppeln) (Voivodeship) (Table D-DR5)
4600.O8	Oświęcim (Auschwitz)
4600.P54	Pieniny Range
4600.P6	Podhale Highlands
4600.P62	Podkarpackie, Województwo
4600.P64	Podlasie. Województwo Podlaskie
4600.P67-.P6789	Pomerania (Pomorze, Pommern) (Table D-DR5)
	For Pomerelia (Eastern/Gdansk Pomerania) see DK4600.G44+
	For localities of the former province of Pomerania now located in East Germany see DD801.A+
4600.P69-.P6989	Poznań (Posen) (Voivodeship) (Table D-DR5)
	Including Provinz Posen
	Cf. DK4600.W55+ Wielkopolska
4600.P77-.P7789	East Prussia (Prusy Wschodnie, Ostpreussen) (Table D-DR5)
	Including the Teutonic Knights and Ducal Prussia
	For West Prussia see DK4600.G44+
	Royal Prussia (Prusy Królewskie) see DK4600.G44+
4600.R94-.R9489	Rzeszów (Voivodeship) (Table D-DR5)
4600.S42-.S4289	Silesia (Śląsk, Schlesien) (Table D-DR5)
	For Silesia, Czechoslovakia see DB2500.S54
4600.S44-.S4489	Lower Silesia (Dolny Śląsk, Niederschlesien). Województwo dolnośląskie (Table D-DR5)
	For localities of the former province of Lower Silesia now located in East Germany see DD801.A+
4600.S46-.S4689	Upper Silesia (Górny Śląsk, Oberschlesien) (Table D-DR5)
	For Cieszyn Silesia see DK4600.C54+
	For Opole Silesia see DK4600.O66+
4600.S48	Silesia (Voivodeship). Województwo Ślaskie
	Cf. DK4600.K37+ Katowice (Voivodeship)
4600.S6	Zagłębie Śląsko-Dąbrowskie
	Snezka Mountain (Sniezka, Schneekoppe) see DB2500.S65
4600.S656	Spiš (General and Poland)
4600.S7	Sudetes Mountains
	For Sudetes (General and Czechoslovakia) see DB2500.S94
4600.S799	Swietokrzyskie, Wojewodztwo

Local history and description
Provinces, counties, historical regions, etc., A-Z -- Continued

4600.S8	Swiętokrzysz Mountains
4600.S93	Szczecin (Stettin) (Voivodeship). Wojewodztwo Zachodniopomarskie (Table D-DR5)
4600.T3	Tatra Mountains

       For Tatra Mountains (General and Czechoslovakia see DB3000.T37

4600.V5	Vistula (Wisła) River and Valley

       Including Vistula Marsh (Zuławy Wiślane)

4600.W34-.W3489	Warmia (Ermland) (Table D-DR5)
4600.W355	Warmińsko-Mazurskie, Województwo
4600.W37-.W3789	Warsaw (Voivodeship) (Table D-DR5)
4600.W38	Warta River and Valley

       For Wartheland see DK4600.W55+

West Prussia (Prusy Zachodnie, Westpreussen) see DK4600.G44+

Western and Northern Territories see DK4600.O33+

4600.W55-.W5589	Wielkopolska. Województwo Wielkopolskie (Table D-DR5)

       Including Wartheland
       Cf. DK4600.P69+ Poznań (Voivodeship)

Województwo Małopolskie see DK4600.K72+

Wojewodztwo Swietokrzyskie see DK4600.S799

4600.W75-.W7589	Wrocław (Breslau) (Voivodeship) (Table D-DR5)

Zagłębie Śląsko-Dąbrowskie see DK4600.S6

4600.Z55-.Z5589	Zielona Góra (Voivodeship) (Table D-DR5)
	Warsaw (Warszawa)
4610	Periodicals. Societies. Serials
4611	Museums, exhibitions, etc.
4612	Sources and documents
4613	Biography (Collective)

       For individual biography, see the specific period

4614	Directories. Dictionaries. Gazetteers
4616	Guidebooks
	General works. Description
4619	Through 1800
4620	1801-1900
4621	1901-1945
4622	1946-
4624	Monumental and picturesque. Pictorial works
4625	Antiquities
4626	Social life and customs. Civilization. Intellectual life
	Ethnography
4628	General works
4629.A-Z	Individual elements in the population, A-Z
4629.A75	Armenians
	History

Local history and description
Warsaw (Warszawa)
History -- Continued
4630	General works
4631	Early to 1795
4632	1795-1918
	For the Grand Duchy of Warsaw see DK4353
4633	1918-

Sections, districts, suburbs, etc.
4636	Collective
4637.A-Z	Individual, A-Z
	e.g.
4637.S7	Stare Miasto

Monuments. Statues, etc.
4638	Collective
4639.A-Z	Individual, A-Z
	e.g.
4639.P6	Pomnik Kopernika

Parks, Squares. Cemeteries, etc.
4640	Collective
4641.A-Z	Individual, A-Z
	e.g.
4641.R9	Rynek Starego Miasta

Streets. Bridges, etc.
4642	Collective
4643.A-Z	Individual, A-Z

Buildings. Palaces, etc.
4644	Collective
4645.A-Z	Individual, A-Z

Gdansk (Danzig)
4650	Periodicals. Societies. Serials
4651	Museums, exhibitions, etc.
4652	Sources and documents
4653	Biography (Collective)
	For individual biography, see the specific period
4654	Directories. Dictionaries. Gazetteers
4656	Guidebooks

General works. Description
4659	Through 1800
4660	1801-1900
4661	1901-1945
4662	1946-
4664	Monumental and picturesque. Pictorial works
4665	Antiquities
4666	Social life and customs. Civilization. Intellectual life

Ethnography
4668	General works

Local history and description
Gdansk (Danzig)
Ethnography -- Continued

4669.A-Z	Individual elements in the population, A-Z
	History
4670	General works
4671	Early to 1793
4672	1793-1919
4673	1919-1945
	Class here the Free City of Danzig
4674	1945-
	Sections, districts, suburbs, etc.
4676	Collective
4677.A-Z	Individual, A-Z
	Monuments. Statues, etc.
4678	Collective
4679.A-Z	Individual, A-Z
	Parks, Squares. Cemeteries, etc.
4680	Collective
4681.A-Z	Individual, A-Z
	Streets. Bridges, etc.
4682	Collective
4683.A-Z	Individual, A-Z
	Buildings. Palaces, etc.
4684	Collective
4685.A-Z	Individual, A-Z
	e.g.
4685.U6	Uphagenhaus
	Krakow (Cracow)
4700	Periodicals. Societies. Serials
4701	Museums, exhibitions, etc.
4702	Sources and documents
4703	Biography (Collective)
	For individual biography, see the specific period
4704	Directories. Dictionaries. Gazetteers
4706	Guidebooks
	General works. Description
4709	Through 1800
4710	1801-1900
4711	1901-1945
4712	1946-
4714	Monumental and picturesque. Pictorial works
4715	Antiquities
4716	Social life and customs. Civilization. Intellectual life
	Ethnography
4718	General works
4719.A-Z	Individual elements in the population, A-Z

Local history and description
Krakow (Cracow) -- Continued
History

4720	General works
4721	Early to 1795
	1795-1918
4722	General works
4723	1815-1846 (Republic)
4724	1846-1918 (Grand Duchy)
4725	1918-
	Sections, districts, suburbs, etc.
4726	Collective
4727.A-Z	Individual, A-Z
	e.g.
4727.S7	Podgorze
	Monuments. Statues, etc.
4728	Collective
4729.A-Z	Individual, A-Z
	Parks, Squares. Cemeteries, etc.
4730	Collective
4731.A-Z	Individual, A-Z
	e.g.
4731.R9	Rynek
	Streets. Bridges, etc.
4732	Collective
4733.A-Z	Individual, A-Z
	Buildings. Palaces, etc.
4734	Collective
4735.A-Z	Individual, A-Z
	e.g.
4735.W3	Wawel (Castle)
	Zamek Królewski na Wawelu see DK4735.W3
4750	Poznan (Posen) (Table D-DR3)
4780	Wroclaw (Breslau) (Table D-DR3)
	Other cities and towns
4800.A1	Collective
4800.A2-Z	Individual, A-Z
	e.g.
4800.B5	Białystok
4800.B9	Bydgoszcz
4800.C5	Cieszyn (Teschen)
	For Ceský Těšín, Czechoslovakia see DB2650.C467
4800.C9	Częstochowa
4800.D3	Darłowo (Rügenwalde)
4800.E4	Elbląg (Elbing)
4800.F7	Frombork (Frauenburg)
	Gdańsk (Danzig) see DK4650+

DK

Local history and description
Other cities and towns
Individual, A-Z -- Continued

4800.G4	Gdynia
4800.G5	Głogów (Glogau)
4800.G6	Gniezno
4800.G65	Gołdap
4800.G68	Gorzów Wielkopolski (Landesberg)
4800.H4	Hel
4800.J4	Jelenia Góro (Hirschberg)
4800.K3	Kalisz
4800.K32	Kamień Pomorski (Cammin)
4800.K34	Kamienna Góra (Landeshut)
4800.K38	Katowice
4800.K5	Kielce
4800.K6	Kołobrzeg (Kolberg)
4800.K67	Koszalin (Köslin)
	Kraków see DK4700+
4800.K76	Krosno Odrzańskie
4800.L4	Lębork (Lauenburg)
4800.L44	Legnica (Liegnitz)
4800.L48	Leszno
4800.L5	Lidzbark Warmiński
4800.L63-.L6395	Łódź (Table D-DR4)
4800.L78-.L7895	Lublin (Table D-DR4)
4800.M35-.M3595	Malbork (Marienburg) (Table D-DR4)
4800.M5	Miechowice (Mechtal)
4800.M6	Morąg (Mohrungen)
4800.N6	Nowa Huta
4800.N9	Nysa (Neisse)
4800.O4	Olsztyn (Allenstein)
4800.O62-.O6295	Opole (Oppeln) (Table D-DR4)
	Poznań (Posen) see DK4750
4800.P7	Przemyśl
4800.R3	Racibórz (Ratibor)
4800.R34	Radom
4800.R9	Rzeszów
4800.S3	Sandomierz
4800.S4	Słupsk (Stolp)
4800.S8	Swinoujście (Swinemünde)
4800.S93-.S9395	Szczecin (Stettin) (Table D-DR4)
4800.T6	Toruń (Thorn)
4800.W3	Wągrowiec (Wongrowitz)
4800.W34	Wałbrzych (Waldenburg)
	Warsaw see DK4610+
	Wrocław see DK4780
4800.Z3	Zagań (Sagan)

Local history and description
Other cities and towns
Individual, A-Z -- Continued
4800.Z34   Zakopane
4800.Z5   Zielona Góra (Grünberg)

	History of Northern Europe. Scandinavia
1	Periodicals. Societies. Serials
1.5	Congresses
3	Sources and documents
	Collected works
3.5	Several authors
3.6	Pamphlet collections
3.7	Individual authors
4	Gazetteers. Dictionaries. Guidebooks
4.5	Place names (General)
5	General works
5.5	Compends, outlines, etc.
6	Monumental and picturesque
6.5	Historic buildings, castles, churches, etc.
6.7	Historical geography
6.8	Geography
	Description and travel
	For Northern Europe see D965
7	Early through 1500
8	1501-1800
9	1801-1900
10	1901-1950
11	1951-1980
11.5	1981-
	Antiquities
	General works
20	Through 1800
21	1801-
23	Roman
	Social life and customs. Civilization
30	General works
	Old Norse. Earliest Scandinavian
31	General works
33.A-Z	Special, A-Z
33.D8	Dwellings
33.T48	Textile fabrics and clothing
	Ethnography
41	General works
42.A-Z	Individual elements in the population, A-Z
42.B68	Bosnians
42.L36	Lapps. Sami
42.P64	Poles
	Sami see DL42.L36
42.S34	Scots
42.U4	Ukrainians
42.Y84	Yugoslavs

42.5	Scandinavians in foreign regions or countries (General)
	For Scandinavians in a particular region or country, see the
	region or country
	History
43	Dictionaries. Chronological tables, outlines, etc.
	Biography (Collective)
44	General works
44.1	Rulers, kings, etc.
44.2	Princes and princesses
44.3	Houses, noble families, etc.
44.5	Public men
44.7	Women
	Historiography
44.8	General works
	Biography of historians, area studies specialists,
	archaeologists, etc.
44.85	Collective
44.9.A-Z	Individual, A-Z
	e.g.
44.9.M3	Maurer, Konrad von
	Study and teaching
44.95	General works
44.96.A-Z	Local, A-Z
	Subarrange by author
	General works
45	Through 1800. Chronicles
46	1800-
47	Pamphlets, etc.
49	Special aspects
52	Military history
53	Naval history
	Political and diplomatic history
55	General works
57	Scandinavianism
59.A-Z	Relations with individual regions or countries, A-Z
	By period
	Earliest to 1397. Scandinavian Empire
61	General works
	Northmen. Vikings
	For social life and customs see DL31+
	Cf. DL101+ Individual countries
65	General works
66	Juvenile literature
75	1397-1524
78	1523-1814
81	1814-1900
	1900-1945

History
   By period
      1900-1945 -- Continued
83   General works
85   Period of World War I, 1914-1918
87   1945-
   Denmark
101   Periodicals. Societies. Serials
103   Sources and documents
      Collected works
103.5   Several authors
103.6   Pamphlet collections
103.7   Individual authors
105   Gazetteers. Dictionaries, etc.
106   Place names, etc.
107   Guidebooks
109   General works
111   Compends
113   Monumental and picturesque. Pictorial works
      Historic monuments, landmarks, scenery, etc. (General)
        For local see DL271.A+
114   General works
114.5   Preservation
      Description and travel
115   Early through 1500
116   1501-1800
117   1801-1900
118   1901-1950
119   1951-1970
120   1971-
121   Antiquities
        Cf. DL269+ Local history and description
      Social life and customs. Civilization
131   General works
133   Early and medieval
      Ethnography
141   General works
141.5   National characteristics
142.A-Z   Individual elements in the population, A-Z
142.A43   Americans
142.B65   Bosnians
142.C48   Chileans
142.G4   Germans
142.G7   Greenlanders
142.I35   Icelanders
142.L38   Latvians
142.P34   Pakistanis

Denmark
  Ethnography
    Individual elements in the population, A-Z -- Continued

142.P6	Poles
142.R87	Russians
142.5	Danes in foreign regions or countries (General)

  History

143	Dictionaries. Chronological tables, outlines, etc.
143.5	Albums. Pictorial atlases
	Including collections of prints and portraits, etc.

    Biography (Collective)
      For individual biography, see the special period, reign, or
        place

144	General works
144.1	Rulers
144.2	Queens. Princes and princesses
	Houses, noble families, etc.
144.3	Collective
144.32.A-Z	Individual houses, families, etc., A-Z
144.5	Public men
144.7	Women

    Historiography

146	General works
	Biography of historians, area studies specialists,
	archaeologists, etc.
146.5	Collective
146.7.A-Z	Individual, A-Z
	e.g.
146.7.J6	Jørgensen, Adolph Ditlev
146.7.P4	Petersen, Henry

    General works

147	Through 1800. Chronicles
	Including Saxo Grammaticus, etc.
148	1801-
149	Compends
151	Pamphlets, etc.

    General special

153	Several parts of the country treated together
154	Military history
	Naval history
156.A1	Sources and documents
156.A2	Biography (Collective)
156.A3-Z	General works
156.1	Pamphlets, etc.
156.2	Early and medieval
	16th-18th centuries
156.5	General works

	Denmark
	History
	General special
	Naval history
	16th-18th centuries -- Continued
	Biography
156.52	Collective
156.53.A-Z	Individual, A-Z
	19th-20th centuries
156.7	General works
	Biography
156.72	Collective
156.73.A-Z	Individual, A-Z
158	Political history
	Diplomatic history. Foreign and general relations
159	General works
159.5.A-Z	Relations with individual regions or countries, A-Z
	By period
	Early and medieval to 1523
	General works
	Early see DL147+
160	Modern
161	Earliest to 750
	750-1042
162	General works
162.5	Harald Klak, 812-840
163	Gorm den Gamle, d. 936?
163.5	Harald Blaatand, 940-985
164	Svend Tjugeskaeg (Tvesdaeg), 985-1014
	Cf. DA159 Invasion, rule, etc., of England, 1013-1014
165	Knud den Store, 1014-1035
	Cf. DA160 Invasion, rule, etc., of England, 1017-1035
166	Hardeknud, 1035-1042
	Cf. DA162 Invasion, rule, etc., of England, 1040-1042
166.8.A-Z	Biography and memoirs of contemporaries, A-Z
	1042-1241
167	General works
168	Norwegian rule, 1042-1047
169	Svend Estridsøn, 1047-1076
169.5	Harald Hén, 1076-1080
170	Knud IV den Hellige, 1080-1086
170.1	Oluf Hunger, 1086-1095
170.3	Erik Ejegod, 1095-1103
170.5	Niels, 1103-1134

	Denmark
	History
	By period
	Early and medieval to 1523
	1042-1241 -- Continued
170.7	Erik Emune, 1134-1137
170.75	Erik III Lam, 1137-1147
170.8	Svend Grade, 1147-1157
	Including Battle of Gradehede, 1157
171	Valdemar I, 1157-1182
172	Knud VI, 1182-1202
173	Valdemar II, 1202-1241
173.8.A-Z	Biography and memoirs of contemporaries, A-Z
	e.g.
173.8.B3	Berengaria, Consort of Valdemar II
	1241-1387
174	General works
174.1	Erik IV, 1241-1250
174.2	Abel, 1250-1252
174.3	Christoffer I, 1250-1259
174.4	Erik V, 1259-1285
174.5	Erik VI, 1285-1320
	Christoffer II, 1320-1332
174.6	General works
174.7	Valdemar III, 1326-1330
174.8	Interregnum, 1332-1340
175	Valdemar IV, 1340-1375
176	Oluf Haakonssøn, 1375-1387
	Biography and memoirs
176.7	Collective
176.8A.E2	Ebbesen, Niels
176.8.A-Z	Individual, A-Z
	e.g.
	1387-1523
177	General works
	Margrete, 1375/1387-1412
178	General works on life and reign
	Cf. DL483 Reign in Norway
179	Union of Kalmar, 1397
	Cf. DL485 History of Norway
	Cf. DL694 History of Sweden
180	Erik VII, 1412-1439
181	Christoffer III, 1439-1448
181.6.A-Z	Biography and memoirs of contemporaries, 1387-1448, A-Z
	Oldenburg dynasty, 1448-1523
182	General works

DL

Denmark
History
By period
Modern, 1523-
1523-1670
Christian IV, 1588-1648
Biography and memoirs of contemporaries --
Continued

190.5.A2-Z	Individual, A-Z
	e.g.
190.5.B7	Brock, Eske
190.5.S4	Sehested, Christen Thomesen, 1590-1657
190.5.U4	Ulfeldt, Corfitz
	Frederik III, 1648-1670
191	General works on life and reign
191.5	General special
192	Dano-Swedish wars, 1657-1660
	Including Battles of Huen, 1659; the Sound, 1658;
	Siege of Copenhagen, 1658-1660; etc.
	Cf. DL725+ Sweden during wars
192.3	Coup d'etat, 1660
192.8.A-Z	Biography and memoirs of contemporaries, A-Z
	e.g.
192.8.R7	Rosenkrantz, Gunde
192.8.U5	Ulfeldt, Bjørn
192.8.U6	Ulfeldt, Christopher
	1670-1808
193.A2	Sources and documents
193.A3-Z	Biography and memoirs of contemporaries, A-Z
	e.g.
193.B5	Bernstorff, Johan Hartvig E, greve
193.G8	Griffenfeld, Peder, greve af
194	General works
	Christian V, 1670-1699
195	General works on life and reign
195.3	General special
195.8.A-Z	Biography and memoirs of contemporaries, A-Z
195.8.A7	Arenstorff, Frederik von
195.8.G9	Gyldenløve, Ulrik Frederik
	Frederik IV, 1699-1730
196	General works on life and reign
196.3	Denmark during Northern War, 1700-1721
	Cf. DL733+ Northern War
196.8.A-Z	Biography and memoirs, 1699-1746, A-Z
	e.g.
196.8.A5	Anna Sophie, Consort of Frederik IV
196.8.H8	Huitefeldt-Kaas, Henrik Jørgen

Denmark
History
By period
Modern, 1523-
1670-1808
Biography and memoirs, 1699-1746, A-Z --
Continued

196.8.S4	Sehested, Christen Thomesen, 1664-1736
197	Christian VI, 1730-1746
	Frederik V, 1746-1766
198	General works on life and reign
198.3	General special
198.8.A-Z	Biography and memoirs of contemporaries, A-Z
	e.g.
198.8.H6	Holstein, Ulrik Adolf, greve
	Christian VII, 1766-1808
199	General works on life and reign
199.3	General special
199.8.A-Z	Biography and memoirs of contemporaries, A-Z
	e.g.
199.8.B4	Bernstorff, Andreas Peter, greve
199.8.C3	Caroline Mathilde, Consort of Christian VII
199.8.S8	Struensee, Johann Friedrich, greve
	1808-1906. 19th century
201	General works
202	General special
203	Social life and customs. Civilization. Intellectual life
	Biography and memoirs
204.A1	Collective
204.A2-Z	Individual, A-Z
	e.g.
204.E8	Estrup, Jacob Brønnum S.
204.M6	Monrad, Ditlev Gothard, Bp.
	Frederik VI, 1808-1839
205	General works on life and reign
206	War of 1807-1814
207	Other special
	e.g. 1814 (Denmark and Sweden)
208.A-Z	Biography and memoirs of contemporaries, A-Z
	e.g.
208.R5	Rist, Johann Georg
	Christian VIII, 1839-1848
209	General works on life and reign
210	General special
212.A-Z	Biography and memoirs of contemporaries, A-Z
	e.g.
212.H62	Hørup, Viggo Lauritz B.

Denmark
History
By period
Modern, 1523-
1808-1906. 19th century -- Continued
Frederik VII, 1848-1863

213	Sources and documents
214	General works on life and reign
215	General special
216	Pamphlets, etc.
	Schleswig-Holstein War, 1848-1850
217	General works
	For political history (Schleswig-Holstein question, etc.) see DD801.S633+
218	General special
219.A-Z	Special events, battles, etc., A-Z
219.F8	Frederiksstad, Siege of, 1850
223	Treaty of Berlin, 1850
(225)	Constitutional amendments, 1855 see JN7144
228.A-Z	Biography and memoirs of contemporaries, A-Z e.g.
228.A5	Andrae, Carl Christopher G.
228.L4	Lehmann, Orla
	Christian IX, 1863-1906
229	General works on life and reign
	1863-1866
230	Sources and documents
231	General works
232	General special
232.5.A-Z	Pamphlets, A-Z
234	Period of constitutional amendments, 1863
	Schleswig-Holstein War, 1864
	Cf. DD431 Prussia during the war with Denmark
236	General works
239	Political and diplomatic history. Special works on Danish relations
	For general works on the Schleswig-Holstein question see DD801.S633+
	Personal narratives
239.5	Collective
239.6.A-Z	Individual, A-Z
241	The new constitution, 1866
246	1866-1873
248	1873-1906

DL

Denmark
History
By period
Modern, 1523-
1808-1906. 19th century
Christian IX, 1863-1906 -- Continued

249.A-Z	Biography and memoirs of contemporaries, A-Z
	e.g.
249.B27	Bajer, Fredrik
	20th century
250	General works
251	General special
	Biography and memoirs of contemporaries
252.A1	Collective
252.A2-Z	Individual, A-Z
	e.g.
252.S8	Steincke, Karl Kristian V.
	Frederik VIII, 1906-1912
253	General works on life and reign
254.A-Z	Biography and memoirs of contemporaries, A-Z
	Christian X, 1912-1947
255	General works on life and reign
256	Period of World War I, 1914-1918
256.5	1919-1947
	Including period of World War II, 1939-1945
257.A-Z	Biography and memoirs of contemporaries, A-Z
	e.g.
257.A6	Alexandrine, Consort of Christian X
257.C45	Christmas Møller, John
257.H3	Hanssen, Hans Peter
257.K75	Kristensen, Knud
257.S3	Scavenius, Erik Julius C.
257.S8	Stauning, Thorvald
	Frederik IX, 1947-1972
258	General works on life and reign
	Biography and memoirs of contemporaries
260.A1	Collective
260.A2-.A5	Royal family
260.A2	General works
260.A27	Frederik, Prince of Denmark
260.A3	Ingrid, Consort of Frederik IX
260.A6-Z	Other, A-Z
	e.g.
260.P7	Prien, Henri
	Margrethe II, 1972-
261	General works on life and reign
	Biography and memoirs of contemporaries

	Iceland
	History -- Continued
335	Biography (Collective)
	Historiography
335.5	General works
	Biography of historians, area studies specialists, archaeologists, etc.
335.6	Collective
335.7.A-Z	Individual, A-Z
	General works
336	Through 1800. Chronicles
	For sagas, see PT7181+, PT7281+
338	1801-
339	Pamphlets, etc.
	By period
	Early and medieval to 1540
351	General works
	874-1262
352	General works
353	Ulfljotr, 927-929
355	1262-1540
356.A-Z	Biography and memoirs, A-Z
	1540-1800
357	General works
358	Reformation, 1540-1551
360.A-Z	Biography and memoirs, A-Z
	1801-1918
365	General works
367	Althing re-introduced, 1843
369	Troubles with Denmark, 1848
371	New constitution, 1874
373.A-Z	Biography and memoirs, A-Z
	1918-
	Class here works on Iceland as a sovereign state under Danish monarch (1918-1944) and as an independent republic (1944-)
375	General works
380.A-Z	Biography and memoirs, A-Z
	Local history and description
396.A-Z	Districts, regions, etc., A-Z
	e.g.
396.V35	Vatnajökull
398.A-Z	Cities, towns, etc., A-Z
	e.g.
398.R5	Reykjavik
	Norway
401	Periodicals. Societies. Serials

DL

	Norway -- Continued
402	Exhibitions (Historical)
403	Sources and documents
	Collected works
403.5	Several authors
403.7	Individual authors
405	Gazetteers. Dictionaries, etc.
406	Place names, etc.
407	Guidebooks
409	General works
411	Compends
413	Monumental and picturesque
414	Historic buildings, castles, churches, etc.
	Description and travel
415	Early through 1500
416	1501-1800
417	1801-1900
418	1901-1950
419	1951-1980
419.2	1981-
420	Preservation of historic monuments, landmarks, scenery, etc.
421	Antiquities
	Cf. DL576+ Local history and description
	Social life and customs. Civilization
431	General works
433	Early and medieval
	Ethnography
	Including national characteristics
441	General works
442.A-Z	Individual elements in the population, A-Z
442.F5	Finns
442.G73	Greeks
442.L3	Lapps. Sami
442.P34	Pakistanis
	Sami see DL442.L3
442.V53	Vietnamese
442.5	Norwegians in foreign regions or countries (General)
	For Norwegians in a particular region or country, see the region or country
	History
443	Dictionaries. Chronological tables, outlines, etc.
	Biography (Collective)
	For individual biography, see the special period, reign, or place
444	General works
444.1	Rulers, kings, etc.
444.2	Princes and princesses

	Norway
	History
	Biography (Collective) -- Continued
444.3	Houses, noble families, etc.
444.5	Public men
444.7	Women
	Historiography
445	General works
	Biography of historians, area studies specialists, archaeologists, etc.
445.5	Collective
445.7.A-Z	Individual, A-Z
	e.g.
445.7.F7	Friis, Peder Claussøn
445.7.M8	Munch, Peter Andreas
	General works
446	Through 1800. Chronicles
	For sagas (history and criticism) see PT7181+
	For sagas (collections) see PT7261+
	For Heimskringla see PT7276+
448	1801-
449	Compends
451	Pamphlets, etc.
451.5	Comic and satiric works
453	History of two or more provinces
454	Military history
456	Naval history
	Political and diplomatic history. Foreign and general relations
458	General works
459.A-Z	Relations with individual regions or countries, A-Z
	By period
	Early and medieval to 1387
460	General works
461	Early to 872
	872-1035
462	General works
	Harald I, 860-930
463	General works
464	Havsfjord, 872
465	Eirik Blodøks, 930-935
466	Haakon I den Gode, 935-961
467	Olav I Trygvesson, 995-1000
468	Olav II and Christianity, 1015-1030
	Biography and memoirs
468.49	Collective

Norway
 History
  By period
   Early and medieval to 1387
    872-1035
     Biography and memoirs -- Continued

468.5.A-Z	Individual, A-Z
	e.g.
468.5.H34	Hakon Eiriksson, 998-1030

    1035-1319

469	General works
471	Magnus I, 1035-1047
471.1	Harald III, d. 1066
471.2	Magnus III, d. 1103
471.3	Sigurd I Magnusson, d. 1103
471.5	Sverre, 1177-1202
472	Haakon den Gamle, 1217-1263
474	Union of Iceland with Norway, 1262
	Erik II Magnussøn, 1280-1299
475	General works
476	War with Hansa towns
477	Haakon V Hálegyr, 1299-1319
478	1319-1387

    1387-1814

480	General works
482	General special
482.5	Social life and customs. Civilization. Intellectual life
483	Margrete, 1387-1412
	Cf. DL178+ Biography and reign as queen of Denmark
485	Union of Kalmar, 1397
490	Special events. By date
	Prefer DL182+
	Biography and memoirs
495.A2	Collective
495.A3-Z	Individual, A-Z
	e.g.
495.I5	Inger Ottesdatter
495.L6	Lofthus, Christian Jenssøn
495.L8	Lunge, Vincents Vincentssøn
	Napoleonic period
497	Sources and documents
498	General works
499	War of 1807-1814
	1814. Union with Sweden
	Cf. DL805 History of Sweden
500	Sources and documents

DL

	Norway
	History
	By period
	20th century
	Biography and memoirs -- Continued
529.A2-Z	Individual, A-Z
	e.g.
529.C3	Castberg, Johan
529.H3	Hambro, Carl Joachim
529.N8	Nygaardsvold, Johan
529.Q5	Quisling, Vidkun
	Haakon VII, 1905-1957
530	General works on life and reign
530.2	Royal family
(530.3)	Olav, crown prince
	see DL534+
530.4.A-Z	Other royal, A-Z
530.4.A7	Astrid, princess
530.4.M3	Märtha, crown princess
531	Period of World War I, 1914-1918
531.5	Period between the World Wars, 1918-1939
532	Period of World War II, 1939-1945
533	1945-1957
	Olav V, 1957-1991
534	General works on life and reign
	Biography and memoirs of contemporaries
535.A1	Collective
535.A2-.A5	Royal family
535.A2	General works
(535.A3)	Harald, crown prince
	see DL536
535.A6-Z	Other, A-Z
	Harald V, 1991-
536	General works on life and reign
	Biography and memoirs of contemporaries
537.A1	Collective
537.A2-.A5	Royal family
537.A6-Z	Other, A-Z
	Local history and description
576.A-Z	Counties, regions, etc., A-Z
	e.g.
576.B4	Bergen
576.F5	Finmark (Finnmarken)
576.G8	Gudbrandsdal
576.H17	Hålogaland
576.H3	Hardanger
576.H4	Hedmark

Norway
  Local history and description
    Counties, regions, etc., A-Z -- Continued

576.H5	Helgeland
576.H7	Hordaland
576.J2	Jaederen
576.L7	Lofoten
576.N55	Nord-Trøndelag
576.N6	Nordfjord
576.N8	Nordland
576.N95	Norway, Northern
576.O4	Østfold
576.O84	Otterøya
576.R65	Rogaland
576.S57	Søndhordland
576.S63	Solør
576.S7	Spydeberg
576.S8	Stavanger
576.S9	Sunnmøre
576.T4	Telemark
576.T8	Troms
576.T9	Trondheim
576.Y8	Ytre Flekkerøy

    Cities, towns, etc.

581	Oslo (Christiania) (Table D-DR3)
596.A-Z	Other, A-Z
	e.g.
596.A5	Aker
596.A6	Akershus Castle
596.B4	Bergen
596.B9	Bygdøy
596.D3	Dalene
596.D8	Drammen
596.E3	Eidsvold
596.F83	Fredrikstad
596.F84	Fredriksten
596.H22	Halden (Fredrikshald)
596.H25	Hamar
596.H28	Haugesund
596.H75	Hurum (Buskerud)
596.H8	Hvitebjørn
596.K68	Kristiansand
596.K7	Kristiansund
596.K8	Kvinesdal
596.M3	Mandal
596.M7	Moss
596.S3	Sandefjord

Norway
  Local history and description
    Cities, towns, etc.
      Other, A-Z -- Continued

596.S53	Sem
596.S65	Skiringssal
596.S8	Stavanger
596.T7	Tønsberg
596.T8	Tromsø
596.T9	Trondheim
596.V6	Voss

Sweden

601	Periodicals. Societies. Serials
	Museums, exhibitions, etc.
602	General works
602.5.A-Z	Individual. By place, A-Z
603	Sources and documents
	Collected works
604	Several authors
604.5	Individual authors
605	Gazetteers. Dictionaries, etc.
606	Place names (General)
607	Guidebooks
609	General works
611	Compends
613	Monumental and picturesque
	Historic monuments, landmarks, scenery, etc. (General)
	For local see DL971+
614	General works
614.5	Preservation
	Description and travel
614.55	History of travel
615	Early through 1500
616	1501-1800
617	1801-1900
618	1901-1950
619	1951-1980
619.5	1981-
621	Antiquities
	Cf. DL971+ Local history and description
	Social life and customs. Civilization
631	General works
633	Early and medieval
635	Intellectual life
	Ethnography
	Including national characteristics
639	General works

DL

	Sweden
	History
	Historiography -- Continued
	Biography of historians, area studies specialists, archaeologists, etc.
645.5	Collective
645.7.A-Z	Individual, A-Z
	e.g.
645.7.G4	Geijer, Erik Gustaf
645.7.H35	Hildebrand, Hans Olof H.
	Study and teaching
645.9	General works
645.95.A-Z	By region or country, A-Z
	Subarrange by author
	General works
646	Through 1800. Chronicles
	For sagas, see PT7181+, PT7261+
648	1801-
649	Compends
650	Pictorial works
651	Pamphlets, etc.
652	Addresses, essays, lectures. Anecdotes, etc.
653	History of two or more provinces
654	Military history
656	Naval history
	Political and diplomatic history. Foreign and general relations
658.A2	Sources and documents
658.A3-Z	General works
658.2	Early to 1523
	1523-
	General works see DL658.A3+
658.4	1523-1654
658.5	1654-1720
658.6	1720-1818
658.8	1818- . 19th-20th centuries
659.A-Z	Relations with individual regions or countries, A-Z
	By period
660	Early and medieval to 1523
660.5	General special
661	Earliest to 750
	750-1060
662	General works
	Biography and memoirs
663	Collective
663.5.A-Z	Individual, A-Z
664	Olof, 993-1022

Sweden

History

By period

Early and medieval to 1523

750-1060 -- Continued

665	Anund, 1022-1050
666	Emund, 1050-1060
	1060-1134
667	General works
669	Stenkil, 1060-1066
	1134-1234
672	General works
673	Sverker, 1134-1155
675	Erik IX, 1150-1160. Introduction to Christianity
679.A-Z	Biography and memoirs, A-Z
	1234-1523
681	General works
685	Valdemar, 1250-1274
687	Magnus I Ladulås, 1275-1290
688	Birger, 1290-1318
689	Magnus II Eriksson (Smek), 1319-1363
691	Albrecht von Mecklenburg, 1363-1388
692	1389-1397, Regency of Margrete
	Cf. DL178+ Life and reign as queen of Denmark
694	Union of Kalmar, 1397
	Cf. DL179 History of Denmark
695.A-Z	Biography and memoirs of contemporaries, A-Z
	1397-1523
696	Sources and documents
697	General works
698	Other
	1513-1523
699	General works
700	Kristian II, 1520-1521
	Cf. DL183.8+ Life and reign as king of Denmark
700.9.A-Z	Biography and memoirs of contemporaries, A-Z
	e.g.
700.9.G3	Gadh, Hemming, Bp.
700.9.K3	Karl Knutsson, King of Sweden
700.9.S8	Sture, Sten Gustafsson
	Modern, 1523-
	Vasa dynasty, 1523-1654
701	General works
702.A-Z	Biography and memoirs, A-Z
	e.g.
702.A2	Adler Salvius, Johan

DL

	Sweden
	History
	By period
	Modern, 1523-
	Vasa dynasty, 1523-1654
	Biography and memoirs, A-Z -- Continued
702.C4	Cecilia Vasa, Princess of Sweden
702.D3	De Geer, Louis
702.K3	Katarina Jagellonica, Consort of John III
702.S7	Stiernsköld, Nils
703	Gustaf I Vasa, 1523-1560
703.8	Erik XIV, 1560-1568
	Johan III, 1568-1592
704	General works on life and reign
704.2	General special
704.5	Sigismund, 1592-1599
	17th century
704.6	General works
704.7	General special
704.8	Karl IX, 1600/1604-1611
	Gustaf II Adolf, 1611-1632
705.A2	Sources and documents
	Biography and memoirs of contemporaries
705.A3	Collective
705.A4-Z	Individual, A-Z
	e.g.
705.O8	Oxenstierna, Axel Gustafsson, greve
706	General works on life and reign
708	Political and diplomatic history
709	Social life and customs. Civilization
	Military history
	General works see DL706
710	War with Denmark. Kalmar War, 1611-1613
711	War with Russia
	War with Poland, 1617-1629
712	General works
	Special events, battles, etc.
712.3	Hammerstein, Battle of, 1627
712.5	Oliwa, Battle of, 1627
713	Period of Thirty Years' War, 1618-1648
	For the war itself see D251+
715	Personal special
	Kristina, 1632-1654
717	Sources and documents
	Biography and memoirs of contemporaries
717.5	Collective
718.A-Z	Individual, A-Z

	Sweden
	History
	By period
	Modern, 1523-
	1718-1818
	Gustaf III, 1771-1792 -- Continued
770.A-Z	Biography and memoirs of contemporaries, A-Z
	e.g.
770.M8	Munck, Adolf Fredrik, greve, 1749-1831
772	Napoleonic period
	Gustaf IV Adolf, 1792-1809
776	General works on life and reign
780	General special
782	Political and diplomatic history
785	Special events
790	Revolution and loss of Finland, 1809
	Including Russo-Swedish War, 1808-1809
	Karl XIII, 1809-1818
792	General works on life and reign
796	General special
801	Special events
	Including Treaty of Orebro, 1812, etc.
805	Union with Norway, 1814
	Cf. DL500+ History of Norway, 1814
	1814-1907. 19th century
807	Sources and documents
808	General works
809	General special
	Biography and memoirs of contemporaries
810	Collective
811.A-Z	Individual, A-Z
	e.g.
811.G7	Gripenstedt, Johan August, friherre
811.H4	Hedin, Adolf
811.K4	Key, Emil
811.L6	Löwenhielm, Gustaf Carl F., greve
	Karl XIV Johan (Bernadotte), 1818-1844
816	Sources and documents
	Biography and memoirs of contemporaries
818	Collective
819.A-Z	Individual, A-Z
	e.g.
819.D5	Desideria, Consort of Charles XIV
819.H48	Heurlin, Christoffer Isak
820	General works on life and reign
	Cf. DC227+ French Revolution and Napoleonic wars, 1805-1814

	Sweden
	History
	By period
	Modern, 1523-
	20th century
	Gustaf V, 1907-1950 -- Continued
867.5	Political and diplomatic history
868	Period of World War I, 1914-1918
868.5	1919-1950
	Biography and memoirs of contemporaries
869	Collective
870.A-Z	Individual, A-Z
	e.g.
870.B47	Bernadotte af Wisborg, Folke, greve
870.H2	Hamilton, Hugo Erik G., greve
870.H3	Hansson, Per Albin
870.N6	Nothin, Torsten
	Gustaf VI Adolf, 1950-1973
872	General works on life and reign
	Biography and memoirs of contemporaries
875	Collective
875.5	Royal family
876.A-Z	Individual, A-Z
	e.g.
876.A1	Louise, Consort of Gustaf VI
876.A23	Asbrink, Eva
876.B47	Bernadotte, Kerstin
876.B48	Bertil, Prince
	Carl Gustaf, Crown Prince see DL877+
	Karl XVI Gustaf, 1973-
877	General works on life and reign
	Biography and memoirs of contemporaries
878	Collective
878.5	Royal family
879.A-Z	Individual, A-Z
	Local history and description
971.A-Z	Provinces, regions, etc., A-Z
	e.g.
971.A4	Älvsborg
971.B5	Blekinge
	Bohuslän see DL971.G6
971.D2	Dalecarlia (Dalarna)
971.G6	Gothenburg and Bohus
971.G7	Gotland
971.H15	Hälsingland
971.H17	Härjedalen
971.H2	Halland

Sweden
Local history and description
Provinces, regions, etc., A-Z -- Continued

971.I5	Inlands Torpe
971.J3	Jemtland (Jämtland)
971.J5	Jönköping
971.K8	Kronoberg
971.L2	Lapland (General, and Sweden)
971.M15	Mälar Lake and region
971.M4	Medelpad
971.N3	Närke (Närike, Nerike)
971.N6	Norrbotten
971.N65	Norrland
971.O33	Oland
971.O7	Orebro
971.O8	Ostergötland
971.R6	Roslagen
971.S3	Scania (Skåne)
971.S55	Småland
971.S6	Södermanland
971.T5	Tiveden
	Uppland
971.U5	General works
971.U6	Special
971.V2	Värmland
971.V3	Västerbotten
971.V4	Västergötland
971.V5	Västernorrland
971.V6	Västmanland
971.V7	Visingsö (Island)
	Cities, towns, etc.
976	Stockholm (Table D-DR3)
991.A-Z	Other, A-Z
	e.g.
991.A538	Alingsäs
991.A7	Arboga
991.B6	Birka
991.B63	Borås
991.F3	Falun
991.G6-.G695	Göteborg (Table D-DR4)
991.H4	Helsingborg (Hälsingborg)
991.J6	Jönköping
991.K8	Kristianstad
991.L3	Landskrona
991.L9	Lund
991.M2	Malmö
991.M3	Marstrand

Sweden
  Local history and description
    Cities, towns, etc.
      Other, A-Z -- Continued

991.N6	Norrköping
991.P5	Piteå
991.S3	Sala
991.S58	Skellefteå
991.S8	Strängnäs
991.U4	Uddevalla
991.U7	Uppsala
991.V5	Visby

Finland
1002	Periodicals. Societies. Serials
	Museums, exhibitions, etc.
1003	General works
1003.5.A-Z	Individual. By place, A-Z
1004	Congresses
1005	Sources and documents
	Collected works (nonserial)
1006	Several authors
1006.5	Individual authors
1007	Gazetteers. Dictionaries, etc.
1008	Place names (General)
1010	Guidebooks
1012	General works
1013	General special
1014	Pictorial works
1014.5	Historic monuments, landmarks, scenery, etc.
	For local see DL1170+
1014.7	Historical geography
	Description and travel
1015	Through 1900
1015.2	1901-1944
1015.3	1945-1980
1015.4	1981-
1016	Antiquities
	For local antiquities see DL1170+
1017	Social life and customs. Civilization. Intellectual life
	For specific periods, see the period
	Ethnography
1018	General works
1019	National characteristics
1020.A-Z	Individual elements in the population, A-Z
1020.K37	Karelians
1020.L34	Lapps. Sami
1020.P64	Poles

	Finland
	Ethnography
	Individual elements in the population, A-Z -- Continued
1020.R87	Russians
	Sami see DL1020.L34
1020.S93	Swedes
1022	Finns in foreign regions or countries (General)
	For Finns in a particular region or country, see the region or country
	History
	Periodicals. Societies. Serials see DL1002
1024	Biography (Collective)
	For individual biography, see the specific period or place
	Historiography
1025	General works
	Biography of historians, area studies specialists, archaeologists, etc.
1026	Collective
1026.5.A-Z	Individual, A-Z
	Study and teaching
1027	General works
1027.5.A-Z	By region or country, A-Z
	Subarrange by author
1032	General works
1033	Addresses, essays, lectures. Anecdotes, etc.
	Military history
	For individual campaigns and engagements, see the special period
1036	Sources and documents
1037	General works
	Naval history
	For individual campaigns and engagements, see the special period
1040	Sources and documents
1042	General works
	Political history
	For specific periods, see the special period
1043	Sources and documents
1044	General works
	Foreign and general relations
	For general works on the diplomatic history of a period, see the period
	For works on relations with a specific country, regardless of period see DL1048.A+
1045	Sources and documents
1046	General works
1048.A-Z	Relations with individual regions or countries, A-Z

Finland

History -- Continued

By period

Early to 1523

1050	Sources and documents
1052	General works
1052.3	Erik's Crusade, 1157
1052.5	1249-1362
1052.7	1362-1397
1052.9	Danish rule, 1397-1523

Modern, 1523-

1055	Sources and documents
1056	General works

1523-1617

1058	Sources and documents
1058.5	General works

1617-1721

1060	Sources and documents
1060.5	General works

1721-1809

1063	Sources and documents
1063.5	General works
	Biography
1063.7	Collective
1063.8.A-Z	Individual, A-Z
1063.9	Russian conquest, 1808-1809

Russian administration, 1809-1917

1065	Sources and documents
1065.3	General works
	Biography
1065.4	Collective
1065.5.A-Z	Individual, A-Z
1065.6	1809-1899
1065.8	1899-1917

20th century

1066	Sources and documents
1066.5	General works
1066.7	General special
	Biography
1067	Collective
1067.5.A-Z	Individual, A-Z

Revolution, 1917-1918. Civil War

1070	Sources and documents
1072	General works
	Personal narratives
1073	Collective
1073.5	Individual

	Finland
	History
	By period
	Modern, 1523-
	20th century
	1939-1945
	Russo-Finnish War, 1939-1940
	Special topics, A-Z -- Continued
1105.V47	Veterans
	1945-1981
1122	Periodicals. Societies. Serials
1123	Sources and documents
1125	General works
1127	General special
1129	Social life and customs. Civilization. Intellectual life
1132	Political history
1133	Foreign and general relations
	Biography and memoirs
1135	Collective
1135.5.A-Z	Individual, A-Z
	1981-
1140	Periodicals. Societies. Serials
1140.2	Congresses
1140.4	Sources and documents
1140.6	General works
1140.8	Social life and customs. Civilization. Intellectual life
1141	Political history
1141.2	Foreign and general relations
	Biography and memoirs
1141.5	Collective
1141.6.A-Z	Individual, A-Z
	Local history and description
1170.A-Z	Regions, provinces, historical regions, etc., A-Z
	Cities, towns, etc.
	Helsinki (Helsingfors)
1175	Periodicals. Societies. Serials
1175.2	Museums, exhibitions, etc.
	Subarrange by author
1175.24	Directories. Dictionaries. Gazetteers
1175.25	Guidebooks
1175.26	General works
1175.28	Description
1175.3	Antiquities
1175.32	Social life and customs. Intellectual life
	Ethnography

	Finland
	Local history and description
	Cities, towns, etc.
	Helsinki (Helsingfors)
	Ethnography -- Continued
1175.34	General works
1175.36.A-Z	Individual elements in the population, A-Z
	History
1175.4	Biography (Collective)
	For individual biography, see the specific period
1175.42	General works
	By period
1175.44	Through 1800
1175.46	1800-1917
1175.48	1917-
	Sections, districts, suburbs, etc.
1175.5	Collective
1175.55.A-Z	Individual, A-Z
	Streets. Bridges
1175.8	Collective
1175.85.A-Z	Individual, A-Z
	Buildings
1175.9	Collective
1175.95.A-Z	Individual, A-Z
1180.A-Z	Other cities, towns, etc., A-Z
	Salla see DK651.K854

History of Spain
	Periodicals. Societies. Serials
1	Periodicals. Societies. Serials
2	Congresses
3	Sources and documents
	Collected works
4	Several authors
5	Individual authors
11	Directories
12	Gazetteers. Dictionaries, etc.
13	Place names
14	Guidebooks
17	General works
22	Monumental and picturesque
23	Preservation of historic monuments, etc.
26	Compends
27	Historical geography
27.3	Geography
	Description and travel
27.5	History of travel. Old roads, etc.
28	Through 710
32	711-1491
34	1492-1788
38	1789-1813
41	1814-1900
42	1901-1950
43	1951-1980
43.2	1981-
44	Antiquities
	Cf. DP285+ Local history and description
	Social life and customs. Civilization
48	General works
48.9	Spanish culture in foreign countries (General)
	Including general works on Spaniards in foreign countries
	For Spaniards in a particular region or country, see the region or country
	Ethnography
	Including national characteristics
52	General works
53.A-Z	Individual elements in the population, A-Z
53.A35	Africans
53.A43	Americans
53.A9	Autrigones
53.B42	Berbers
53.B45	Blacks
53.C44	Celts
53.C65	Colombians
53.C83	Cubans

	Ethnography
	Individual elements in the population, A-Z -- Continued
53.F54	Finns
53.F74	French
53.I2	Iberians
53.I74	Irish
53.L38	Latin Americans
53.M37	Maragatos
53.M49	Mexicans
	Moriscos see DP104
53.M65	Moroccans
53.M87	Muslims
	Cf. DP104 Mudéjares
53.N67	North Africans
53.P47	Peruvians
53.P63	Poles
53.P65	Portuguese
53.T85	Turmogos
53.V48	Vettones
	Spanish people in foreign countries (General) see DP48.9
	History
56	Dictionaries. Chronological tables, outlines, etc.
	Biography (Collective)
	For individual biography, see the special period, reign, or place
58	General works
59	Rulers, kings, etc.
	Including royal houses
59.2	Aragon
59.4	Castile and Leon
59.6	Leon
59.8	Navarre
59.9	Queens, princesses, etc.
	Houses, noble families, etc.
60.A2	Collective
60.A3-Z	Individual, A-Z
	e.g.
60.A4	Acevedo family
60.L3	Lara family
60.M4	Mendoza family
61	Public men
62	Women
	Historiography
63	General works
	Biography of historians, area studies specialists,
	archaeologists, etc.
63.5	Collective

DP

History
  General special
    Military history -- Continued
78.5   1808- . 19th-20th centuries
    Naval history
      For individual campaigns and engagements, see the special
        period
80   Sources and documents
      Biography and memoirs
80.5   Collective
80.7   Officers
        Individual biography, see the historical period
81   General works
81.2   General special
81.3   Early to 1492
81.5   1492-1700
81.6   1701-1808
81.7   1808- . 19th-20th centuries
    Political and diplomatic history. Foreign and general
      relations
      For special periods, reigns, etc., see the period or reign
83   Sources and documents
84   General works
84.5   Early to 1516
      1516- see DP84
85.3   1516-1700
85.5   1700-1814
85.8   1814-
86.A-Z   Relations with individual regions or countries, A-Z
  By period
    Earliest to 711
91   General works
      General early and medieval see DP98+
92   Pre-Roman period
        For provinces, etc. see DP302.A+
        For cities see DP402.A+
      Roman period, 218 B.C.-414 A.D.
94   General works
95   Celtiberi. Numantia
          Cf. DG59.I15 Iberia (Roman province)
96   Visigoths in Spain, 414-711. Gothic period
      Moorish domination and the Reconquest, 711-1516. Arab
        period
97.3   Congresses
97.4   Sources and documents
97.6   Historiography
      General works

DP

	History
	By period
	Moorish domination and the Reconquest, 711-1516. Arab period
	Aragon (Catalonia) -- Continued
	General works
124.8	Through 1800
125	1801-
126	General special
	Dynasty of Navarre
127	General works
127.2	Ramiro I, 1035-1063
127.4	Sancho I (V of Navarre), 1063-1094
127.5	Pedro I, 1094-1104
	Alfonso I, 1104-1134
127.6	General works on life and reign
127.7.A-Z	Biography and memoirs of contemporaries, A-Z
127.8	Ramiro II, 1134-1137
127.9	Petronilla, 1137-1164
	Dynasty of Barcelona
128	General works
128.3	Ramon-Berenguer, 1131-1162
128.4	Alfonso II, 1162-1196
128.7	Pedro II, 1196-1213
	Jaime I, 1213-1276
129	General works on life and reign
129.4.A-Z	Biography and memoirs of contemporaries, A-Z
130	Pedro III, 1276-1285
130.2	Alfonso III, 1285-1291
	Jaime II, 1291-1327
130.3	General works on life and reign
130.4	General special
130.5	Alfonso IV, 1327-1336
	Pedro IV, 1336-1387
130.7	General works on life and reign
130.8.A-Z	Biography and memoirs of contemporaries, A-Z
131	Juan I, 1387-1395
131.3	Martin, 1395-1410
131.6	Interregnum, 1410-1412
	Dynasty of Castile
132	General works
133	Fernando I, 1412-1416
133.1	Alfonso V, 1416-1458
	Cf. DG848.112.A4 Italy
	Juan II
133.4	General works on life and reign
133.5.A-Z	Biography and memoirs of contemporaries, A-Z

DP

History
  By period
    Moorish domination and the Reconquest, 711-1516. Arab
      period
    Castile and Leon -- Continued
      Juan II, 1406-1454
142.5   General works on life and reign
              Biography and memoirs of contemporaries
142.58   Collective
142.6.A-Z   Individual, A-Z
              Enrique IV, 1454-1474
143   General works on life and reign
              Biography and memoirs of contemporaries
143.18   Collective
143.2.A-Z   Individual, A-Z
                    e.g.
143.2.A34   Alfonso, Infante of Castile, 1453-1468
143.4   Isabel I, 1474-1504
143.6   Juana, 1504-1506
143.7   Felipe I, 1504-1506
143.8   Fernando V, 1507-1516
          León (Asturias)
                Cf. DP302.O8 Oviedo
145   Sources and documents
              General works
145.8   Through 1800. Chronicles
146   1801-
147   General special
              Dynasty of Pelayo
148   General works
148.2   Pelayo, 718-737
148.3   Favila, 737-739
              Dynasty of Alfonso I
148.4   General works
148.5   Alfonso I, 739-757
148.7   Fruela I, 757-768
148.9   Aurelio, 768-774
149   Silo, 774-783
149.2   Mauregato, 783-789
149.4   Bermudo I, 789-792
149.5   Alfonso II, 792-842
150   Ramiro I, 842-850
150.3   Ordoño I, 850-866
150.5   Alfonso III, 866-910
151   Garcia, 910-914
151.2   Ordoño II, 914-923
151.3   Fruela II, 923-925

DP

History
  By period
    Moorish domination and the Reconquest, 711-1516. Arab
      period
      Navarre
        Dynasty of Champagne -- Continued

157.8	Thibaud II, 1253-1270
157.9	Henri I, 1270-1274
	Dynasty of Capetians
158	General works
158.2	Jeanne I, 1274-1305
158.4	Philippe I (IV of France), 1284-1305
158.6	Louis I, 1305-1316
158.7	Philippe II (V of France), 1316-1322
158.8	Charles I, 1322-1328
	Dynasty of Evreux
159	General works
159.3	Jeanne II, 1328-1349
159.5	Philippe III, 1328-1343
159.7	Charles II, 1349-1387
159.9	Charles III, 1387-1425
	Dynasty of Aragon
160	General works
	Juan I, 1425-1479
160.2	General works on life and reign
160.25.C25	Carlos, heir apparent of Aragon, Prince of Viana
160.3	Blanche d'Evreux, 1425-1441
160.4	Leonor, 1479
	1479-1516
160.5	General works
	Dynasty of Foix
160.6	François Phoebus, 1479-1483
	Dynasty of Albret
160.7	Catherine de Foix, 1483-1517
160.8	Jean d'Albret, 1484-1516
	Modern, 1479/1516-
160.9	Periodicals. Societies. Serials
161	General works
	1479-1516. Fernando V and Isabel I
161.5	Sources and documents
	General works on reign
161.8	Through 1800
162	1801-
	Biography
163	Isabel
163.5	Fernando
164	General special

DP

DP

DP

History
  By period
    Modern, 1479/1516-
      20th century. 1886-
        Second Republic, 1931-1939
          Civil War, 1936-1939
            Military operations
              Local history, A-Z -- Continued
                Cantabria see DP269.27.S23

269.27.C3	Catalonia
269.27.C8	Cuenca
269.27.M3	Madrid
	Pais Vasco see DP269.27.B33
269.27.S23	Santander. Cantabria
	Naval operations
269.3	General works
269.35.A-Z	Individual engagements, ships, etc., A-Z
269.4	Aerial operations
269.42	Engineering operations
	Foreign participation
269.45	General works
269.47.A-Z	By nationality, etc., A-Z
	e.g.
269.47.B7	British
269.47.G3	German
269.47.I8	Italian
269.47.R8	Russian
	Atrocities
269.5	General works
269.53	Loyalist
269.55	Insurgent
	Prisoners and prisons
269.6	General works
269.63	Loyalist
269.65	Insurgent
269.67	Concentration camps
269.7	Medical and sanitary services. Hospitals
269.8.A-Z	Other topics, A-Z
	Anniversaries see DP269.8.M4
269.8.A7	Art and the war
	Celebrations see DP269.8.M4
	Charities see DP269.8.R3
269.8.C4	Children
269.8.C7	Crime and criminals
269.8.D47	Desertions
	Displaced persons see DP269.8.R3
269.8.E2	Economic aspects

History
  By period
    Modern, 1479/1516-
      20th century. 1886-
        Second Republic, 1931-1939
          Civil War, 1936-1939
            Other topics, A-Z -- Continued

269.8.E38	Education and the war
269.8.E68	Equipment and supplies
269.8.E93	Evacuation of civilians
269.8.I5	Influence and results
269.8.J68	Journalists
269.8.L42	Libraries
269.8.L5	Literature and the war
	For belles-lettres, see Class P
269.8.M4	Memorials. Monuments. Celebrations
269.8.M6	Motion pictures about the war
269.8.M8	Museums, relics, etc.
269.8.P65	Posters
269.8.P7	Propaganda
269.8.P75	Psychological aspects
269.8.P8	Public opinion
269.8.R3	Refugees
	Cf. DP269.67 Concentration camps
269.8.R4	Religious aspects
269.8.S4	Secret service. Spies, etc.
269.8.S65	Social aspects
269.8.W7	Women
269.9	Personal narratives
	1939-1975
269.97	Sources and documents
270	General works
	Biography and memoirs
271.A2	Collective
271.A3-Z	Individual, A-Z
	1975-
272	General works
272.29	Foreign and general relations
	Biography and memoirs
272.3	Collective
272.4.A-Z	Individual, A-Z
	e.g.
272.4.J8	Juan Carlos I, King of Spain
	Local history and description
285	Northern Spain
291	Northwestern Spain
295	Southern Spain

DP

Local history and description -- Continued

302.A-Z	Provinces, regions, etc., A-Z
	e.g.
302.A0197	Alagón River and Valley
302.A02	Alava
302.A05	Albacete
302.A07	Albarracín Mountains
302.A09	Alboran
302.A11-.A25	Alicante (Table D-DR15)
302.A32	Almanzora River and Valley
302.A33	Almeria
302.A38	Alpujarras
302.A383	Alt Camp Region
302.A3836	Alt Pirineu Region
302.A384	Alt Urgell Region
302.A3844	Alta Ribagorça Region
302.A39	Ampurdán
302.A395	Ancares Mountains
302.A41-.A55	Andalusia (Table D-DR15)
302.A56	Aneo Valley
302.A61-.A75	Aragon (Table D-DR15)
	Cf. DP124+ History of Aragon (Catalonia) to 1516
302.A752	Aragon River and Valley
302.A753	Aramayona Valley
302.A77	Aro Valley
	Asturias see DP302.O8
302.A87	Avila
302.A89	Axarquia Region
302.B05	Baeturia
302.B05	Badajoz
302.B14	Bages Region
302.B15	Baix Camp Region
302.B152	Baix Ebre Region
302.B155	Baix Llobregat Region
302.B157	Baix Penedès Region
302.B1574	Baixa Limia Region
302.B158	Bajo Segura Region
	Balearic Islands
302.B16	Periodicals. Societies. Collections
	Biography
302.B18A1-.B18A29	Collective
302.B18A3-.B18Z	Individual, A-Z
302.B19	Dictionaries. Gazetteers. Directories
302.B2	Guidebooks
302.B21	General works. Description and travel
302.B215	Antiquities
302.B217	Social life and customs. Civilization. Intellectual life

Local history and description
Provinces, regions, etc., A-Z
Balearic Islands -- Continued

302.B22	History
302.B23	General special
302.B24	Cabrera
302.B25	Formentera
302.B255	Guardia
302.B26	Ibiza. Ibiza and Formentera
	Cf. DP302.B25 Formentera
302.B27	Majorca
302.B275	1789-1814
302.B28	Minorca
302.B281	Special
302.B284	Capture by French, 1756
302.B34	Banets Island
302.B35	Barbanza Region
302.B36	Barcelona
302.B37	Barcelonès Region
302.B41-.B55	Basque Provinces (General, and Spain) (Table D-DR15)
	Including Alava, Guipuzcoa, Vizcaya
	Cf. DC611.B31+ France
302.B563	Batuecas River and Valley
302.B567	Baza Region
302.B616	Benasque Valley
302.B64	Bidasoa River and Valley (General, and Spain)
302.B66	Boî Valley
302.B73	Braña Region
302.B81	Burgos
302.C106	Cabrera Region
302.C12	Cáceres
	Cadiz
	For the city see DP402.C215
302.C16	Periodicals. Societies. Collections
	Biography
302.C18A1-.C18A29	Collective
302.C18A3-.C18Z	Individual, A-Z
302.C19	Dictionaries. Gazetteers. Directories
302.C2	Guidebooks
302.C21	General works. Description and travel
302.C215	Antiquities
302.C217	Social life and customs. Civilization. Intellectual life
302.C22	History
302.C23	General special
302.C25	Calamocha Region
302.C258	Calatayud Region
302.C26	Calatrava, Campo de

Local history and description
Provinces, regions, etc., A-Z -- Continued

302.C297	Camp de Tarragona Region
	Campo de Calatrava see DP302.C26
302.C32	Campo de Gibraltar Region
	Canary Islands

           The islands are divided into two provinces: (1) Las Palmas (Fuerteventura, Gran Canaria, and Lanzarote islands) and (2) Santa Cruz de Tenerife (Gomera, Ferro, Palma, and Teneriffe islands)

302.C36	Periodicals. Societies. Collections
302.C365	Congresses
	Biography
302.C37A1-.C37A19	Collective
302.C37A3-.C37Z	Individual, A-Z
302.C38	Dictionaries. Gazetteers. Directories, etc.
302.C385	Guidebooks
302.C39	General works. Description and travel. Geography
302.C395	Antiquities
302.C397	Social life and customs. Civilization. Intellectual life
302.C398	Ethnography
	History
302.C4	General works
	By period
302.C41	Early and medieval
302.C42	Modern
302.C43	Fuerteventura
302.C44	Gomera
302.C447	Graciosa
302.C45	Gran Canaria
302.C46	Ferro (Hierro)
302.C47	Lanzarote
302.C48	Palma
302.C49	Teneriffe
302.C496	Cañete Mountain
302.C54	Cantabrian Mountains

           Class here works on the mountainous region that extends across Northern and Northwestern Spain; For works on the Autonomous region, 1978-   , formerly Santander Province, see DP302.S31+

302.C55	Castellón
302.C553	Castilla-La Mancha
302.C556	Castilla y León

           Class here works on the autonomous region, 1978-
           For works on the Kingdom to 1516 see DP134+

302.C56	Catalan-speaking regions (General and Spain)
	Catalonia

Local history and description
Provinces, regions, etc., A-Z
Catalonia -- Continued

302.C57	Periodicals. Societies. Collections
302.C575	Congresses
	Biography
302.C58A1-.C58A29	Collective
302.C58A3-.C58Z	Individual, A-Z
302.C59	Dictionaries. Gazetteers. Directories, etc.
302.C6	Guidebooks
302.C61	General works. Description and travel
302.C615	Antiquities
302.C616	Social life and customs. Civilization. Intellectual life
302.C617	Ethnography
	History
	Historiography
302.C619	General works
	Biography of historians, area studies specialists, archaeologists, etc.
302.C6195	Collective
302.C6197A-.C6197Z	Individual, A-Z
302.C62	General works
302.C63	General special
	By period
302.C64	Early to 711
302.C65	Medieval
	Cf. DP124+ History of Aragon (Catalonia) to 1516
302.C66	17th-18th centuries
302.C67	1789-1815
302.C68	19th-20th centuries
302.C69	Other
302.C715	Cerdaña
302.C74	Ciudad Real (La Mancha)
302.C743	Ciudad-Rodrigo (Partido Judicial)
302.C745	Collau Zorru Mountains
302.C746	Collsacabra Region
302.C747	Collserola Mountains
302.C75	Columbretes
302.C754	Conca de Barbara Region
302.C76	Córdoba
	For the city see DP402.C7
302.C77	Cornión Peaks
302.C78	Corunna (Coruña)
302.C8	Costa Blanca
302.C95	Cuenca
302.D37	Daroca Region
302.D8	Duero River and Valley

Local history and description
Provinces, regions, etc., A-Z -- Continued

302.D86	Duratón River and Canyon
302.E2	Ebro River and Valley
302.E57	Entença
302.E6	Eo River and Valley
302.E74	Esla River and Valley
302.E83	Estremadura
302.F42	Fenar Valley
302.F56	Finisterre, Cape
302.F59	Flamisell River and Valley
302.F72	Francia Mountain Range
	Galicia
302.G11	Periodicals. Societies. Collections
	Biography
302.G12A1-.G12A29	Collective
302.G12A3-.G12Z	Individual, A-Z
302.G13	Dictionaries. Gazetteers. Directories, etc.
302.G14	Guidebooks
302.G15	General works. Description and travel. Geography
302.G155	Antiquities
302.G157	Social life and customs. Civilization. Intellectual life
302.G158	Ethnography
	History
302.G16	General works
	By period
302.G17	Early and medieval
302.G18	16th-18th centuries
302.G19	19th-20th centuries
302.G2	Other
302.G205	Garraf Region
302.G206	Garrigues Region
302.G208	Gata, Cape
	Gerona
302.G21	Periodicals. Societies. Collections
	Biography
302.G23A1-.G23A29	Collective
302.G23A3-.G23Z	Individual, A-Z
302.G24	Dictionaries. Gazetteers. Directories, etc.
302.G25	Guidebooks
302.G26	General works. Description and travel
302.G265	Antiquities
	History
	By period
302.G27	Early and medieval
302.G28	16th-18th centuries
302.G29	19th-20th centuries

	Local history and description
	Provinces, regions, etc., A-Z
	Gerona -- Continued
302.G3	Other
	Gibraltar
302.G31	Periodicals. Societies. Collections
302.G32	Congresses. Conferences, etc.
	Biography
302.G33A1-.G33A29	Collective
302.G33A3-.G33Z	Individual, A-Z
302.G34	Dictionaries. Gazetteers. Directories, etc.
302.G35	Guidebooks
302.G36	General works. Description and travel
302.G37	Social life and customs. Civilization. Intellectual life
302.G38	History
	By period
302.G39	Early to 1704
302.G4	18th-20th centuries
302.G41	Other
302.G435	Gironès Region
302.G51-.G65	Granada (Province) (Table D-DR15)
302.G66	Granada (Reino)
302.G67	Gredos Mountains
	Guadalajara
302.G71	Periodicals. Societies. Collections
	Biography
302.G73A1-.G73A29	Collective
302.G73A3-.G73Z	Individual, A-Z
302.G74	Dictionaries. Gazetteers. Directories, etc.
302.G75	Guidebooks
302.G76	General works. History and description
302.G765	Antiquities
302.G78	Guadalquiver River and Valley
302.G783	Guadarrama Mountains
302.G785	Guadiama River and Valley
302.G788	Gūdar Mountains
302.G81-.G95	Guipúzcoa (Table D-DR15)
302.H45	Henares River and Valley
302.H7	Huelva
302.H78	Huerna River and Valley
302.H8	Huesca
302.H86	Hurdes Mountains
302.I93	Izaro Island
302.J1	Jaen
302.J16	Jalón River and Valley
302.J22	Jarama River and Valley
302.J355	Jerez de los Caballeros Region

Local history and description
Provinces, regions, etc., A-Z -- Continued

302.J37	Jerte River and Valley
302.J84	Júcar River and Valley
	La Coruña see DP302.C78
	La Mancha see DP302.C74
302.L18	La Rioja
	Las Palmas see DP302.C36
302.L21-.L35	León (Table D-DR15)
302.L46	Lérida
302.L48	Levante Coast. Maresme
302.L56	Llanada Alavesa Region
302.L59	Llobregat River and Valley
302.L595	Lluçanés
302.L65	Loma y Las Villas Region
302.L68	Lozoya River and Valley
	Los Vélez Region see DP302.V35
302.L75	Luiñas Region
302.M1	Madrid
302.M13	Maestrazgo
302.M15	Mágina Mountains
	Majorca see DP302.B27
302.M21-.M35	Malaga (Table D-DR15)
	Mancha see DP302.C74
302.M356	Manzanares River and Valley
302.M36	Maragatería Region
	Maresme see DP302.L48
302.M39	Mastia
302.M44	Mena Valley
302.M52	Miño River and Valley
	Minorca see DP302.B28
302.M57	Molina de Aragón Region
302.M576	Moncayo Mountains
302.M579	Monfragüe Region
302.M582	Montaña Alavesa
302.M64	Montsià
302.M8	Murcia
302.N21-.N35	Navarre (Table D-DR15)
302.N58	Noguera Region
302.N6	Noguera Ribagorzana River and Valley
302.N8	Nuria River and Valley
302.O59	Ordás Region
302.O6	Orense
302.O75	Oscos Region
302.O77	Osona Region
302.O78	Oteros Region
302.O8	Oviedo. Asturias

Local history and description

Provinces, regions, etc., A-Z -- Continued

302.O9	Oyarzún River and Valley
	Paîs Vasco see DP302.B41+
	Päisos Catalans see DP302.C56
302.P1	Palencia
302.P25	Pallars
	Including the regions of Pallars Jussà and Pallars Sobirà
302.P365	Parque Nacional de Las Tablas de Daimiel
302.P367	Parque Natural de Sant Llorenç del Munt i l'Obac
302.P38	Pedroches Region
302.P395	Peñalara
302.P47	Picos de Europa
302.P58	Pla D'Urgell
302.P6	Pontevedra
302.P62	Pontevedra Estuary
302.P75	Puenteáreas (Partido Judicial)
302.P8	Pyrenees
	For works treating both French and Spanish Pyrenees see DC611.P98+
302.R47	Ribagorza Region
	Including the condado of Ribagorza
302.R475	Ribera Baixa Region
302.R477	Ribera D'Ebre Region
302.R48	Ribera de Xúquer Region
302.R49	Rincón de Ademuz Region
302.R5	Ripollès Region
302.S11-.S25	Salamanca (Table D-DR15)
	For the city see DP402.S1
302.S27	Sanabria Region
	Santa Cruz de Tenerife see DP302.C36+
	Santander. Cantabria (Autonomous region)
302.S31	Periodicals. Societies. Collections
	Biography
302.S33A1-.S33A29	Collective
302.S33A3-.S33Z	Individual, A-Z
302.S34	Dictionaries. Gazetteers. Directories, etc.
302.S35	Guidebooks
302.S36	General works. History and description
302.S365	Antiquities
302.S38	Social life and customs. Civilization. Intellectual life
	Saragossa
302.S41	Periodicals. Societies. Collections
	Biography
302.S43A1-.S43A29	Collective
302.S43A3-.S43Z	Individual, A-Z
302.S44	Dictionaries. Gazetteers. Directories, etc.

Local history and description
   Provinces, regions, etc., A-Z
      Saragossa -- Continued

302.S45	Guidebooks
302.S46	General works. History and description
302.S465	Antiquities
302.S48	Segovia
302.S52	Segrià Region
302.S55	Selva Region
	Seville
	For the city see DP402.S36+
302.S56	Periodicals. Societies. Collections
	Biography
302.S563A1- .S563A29	Collective
302.S563A3-.S563Z	Individual, A-Z
302.S57	Dictionaries. Gazetteers. Directories, etc.
302.S58	General works. Description and travel. Guidebooks
302.S585	Antiquities
302.S59	History
302.S6	Other
302.S634	Sierra del Rincón
302.S64	Sierra Morena
302.S65	Sierra Nevada
302.S68	Solsonès Region
	Soria
302.S71	Periodicals. Societies. Collections
302.S72	Dictionaries. Gazetteers. Directories, etc.
302.S725	Guidebooks
302.S73	General works. Description and travel
302.S735	Antiquities
302.S74	History
302.S75	Other
302.S89	Sueve Mountains
302.T06	Tagus River and Valley (General, and Spain)
302.T07	Tajuña River and Valley
302.T08	Talarn (Corregimiento)
	Tarragona
302.T11	Periodicals. Societies. Collections
302.T13	General works. Description and travel
302.T135	Antiquities
302.T14	History
302.T15	Other
302.T29	Terra Alta Region
302.T295	Terra de Trives Region
	Teruel
302.T31	Periodicals. Societies. Collections

	Local history and description
	Provinces, regions, etc., A-Z
	Teruel -- Continued
302.T32	Dictionaries. Gazetteers. Directories, etc.
302.T325	Guidebooks
302.T33	General works. Description and travel
302.T335	Antiquities
302.T34	History
302.T35	Other
302.T42	Tierra de Barros Region
302.T46	Tiétar River and Valley
302.T51	Toledo
	For the city see DP402.T7
302.T83	Tudmīr
302.U73	Urgell Region
302.V105	Valcueva Valley
302.V107	Valdejalón Region
302.V109	Valdeorras Region
	Valencia
302.V11	Periodicals. Societies. Collections
	Biography
302.V13A1-.V13A29	Collective
302.V13A3-.V13Z	Individual, A-Z
302.V14	Dictionaries. Gazetteers. Directories, etc.
302.V15	Guidebooks
302.V16	General works. Description and travel. Pictorial works
302.V165	Antiquities
302.V167	Social life and customs. Civilization
302.V17	History
302.V18	General special
	By period
302.V2	Early and medieval to 1516
302.V201	Earliest to 715
302.V203	Moors, 715-1238
302.V205	1238-1516
302.V21	1516-1789
302.V22	16th century
302.V225	Expulsion of Moors, 1609
302.V23	1789-1815
302.V24	19th-20th centuries
302.V25	Other
302.V29	Vall d'Albaida Region
302.V31	Valladolid
302.V33	Vallès Occidental Region
302.V334	Vallès Oriental Region
302.V35	Vélez Region
	Vizcaya

DP

Local history and description
Provinces, regions, etc., A-Z
Vizcaya -- Continued

302.V41	Periodicals. Societies. Collections
	Biography
302.V42A1-.V42A29	Collective
302.V42A3-.V42Z	Individual, A-Z
302.V43	Dictionaries. Gazetteers. Directories, etc.
302.V44	Guidebooks
302.V45	General works. Description and travel. Geography
302.V455	Antiquities
302.V457	Social life and customs. Civilization. Intellectual life
302.V458	Ethnography
	History
302.V46	General works
	By period
302.V47	Early and medieval
302.V48	16th-18th centuries
302.V49	19th-20th centuries
302.V5	Other
302.Z1	Zamora
	Zaragoza see DP302.S41+
302.Z65	Zona Centro Region
	Madrid
350	Periodicals. Societies. Collections
352	Directories. Dictionaries
353	Biography (Collective)
	For individual biography, see the period
354	General works. Description and travel
355	Guidebooks
356	Antiquities
357	Social life and customs. Culture
	Ethnography
358	General works
358.3.A-Z	Individual elements in the population, A-Z
358.3.A36	Africans
	History and description
	General works see DP354
	By period
359	Through 1500
360	1501-1800
361	1801-1950
362	1951-
364.A-Z	Sections, districts, etc., A-Z
	Monuments, statues, etc.
365	Collective
365.5.A-Z	Individual, A-Z

	Local history and description
	Madrid -- Continued
	Streets, suburbs, etc.
367.A3	Collective
367.A4-Z	Individual, A-Z
	e.g.
367.A5	Alcalá
367.C5	Ciudad Lineal
367.P84	Puerta del Sol
367.T7	Toledo
	Buildings
370	General works
371.A-Z	Special. Churches, theaters, etc., A-Z
371.P3	Palacio nacional
374	Other special
402.A-Z	Other cities, towns, etc., A-Z
	e.g.
402.A173	Ajofrín
402.A3	Alcalá de Henares
402.A4	Alhambra
	Cf. NA387 Moorish architecture
402.A42	Alicante
402.A47	Ampurias
402.A85	Avila
	Barcelona
402.B2	Periodicals. Societies. Collections
402.B22	Directories. Dictionaries
402.B23	Biography (Collective)
402.B24	Guidebooks
402.B25	General works. Description and travel. Geography
402.B26	Antiquities
402.B265	Social life and customs. Civilization. Intellectual life
402.B267	Ethnography
	Including individual elements in the population
	History
402.B27	General works
402.B28	Early and medieval
402.B29	Modern
	Sections, districts, suburbs, etc.
402.B2912	General works
402.B292A-.B292Z	Individual, A-Z
	Buildings
402.B295	General works
402.B296A-.B296Z	Individual, A-Z
402.B3	Other
402.B5	Bilbao
402.B8	Burgos

DP

Local history and description
Other cities, towns, etc., A-Z -- Continued

402.C15	Cáceres
402.C2	Cadaques
	Cadiz
402.C215	Periodicals. Societies. Collections
402.C217	Directories. Dictionaries, etc.
402.C22	Biography (Collective)
402.C23	Guidebooks
402.C24	General works. Description
402.C25	Social life and customs. Culture
402.C26	Antiquities
402.C27	History
402.C28	Early and medieval
402.C29	Modern
402.C3	Other
402.C4	Cartagena
(402.C544)	Ceuta (Spain)
	see DT329.C5
402.C6	Ciudadela (Minorca)
402.C7	Córdoba
402.C795	Cudillero
402.C8	Cuenca
402.E8	Escorial
402.G4	Gerona
402.G6	Granada
402.G9	Guadalupe
402.J3	Játiva
402.J4	Jerez de la Frontera
402.L3	León
402.L33	Lérida
	Madrid see DP350+
402.M2	Malaga
	Melilla (Spain) see DT329.M4
402.M9	Murcia
402.N64	Noja
402.P33	Palma (Majorca)
402.P35	Pamplona
402.P382	Paterna
402.R6	Roncesvalles
402.S1	Salamanca
402.S145	Sanlúcar de Barrameda
402.S17	Social life and customs. Civilization. Intellectual life
402.S2	San Sebastian
402.S214	Santa Eulalia
402.S23	Santiago de Compostela
402.S3-.S32	Saragossa

                       Local history and description
                         Other cities, towns, etc., A-Z
                           Saragossa -- Continued

402.S3	Periodicals. Societies. Collections. Documents
402.S31	General works. Description and travel. Guidebooks
402.S317	Social life and customs. Civilization. Intellectual life
402.S32	History
402.S35	Segovia
402.S36-.S48	Seville
402.S36	Periodicals. Societies. Collections. Sources and documents
402.S37	Directories. Dictionaries, etc.
402.S373	Biography (Collective)
402.S38	Guidebooks
402.S4	General works. Description and travel
402.S41	Antiquities
402.S415	Social life and customs. Intellectual life
402.S42	History
	By period
402.S43	Early history
402.S44	Arab period, 711-1492
402.S45	16th-18th centuries
402.S46	19th-20th centuries
	Buildings
402.S469	Collective
	Individual
402.S47	Alcázar
402.S48A-.S48Z	Other, A-Z
402.T25	Tarazona
402.T3	Tarragona
	Tarshish (Kingdom) see DP402.T36
402.T36	Tartessos (Kingdom)
402.T7-.T746	Toledo
402.T7	General works. Description and travel. Guidebooks
402.T71	Social life and customs. Intellectual life
402.T72	History
	By period
402.T73	Early and medieval
402.T74	Modern
	Buildings
402.T745	Collective
402.T746A-.T746Z	Individual, A-Z
402.T85	Tossa
402.V15-.V25	Valencia
402.V15	Periodicals. Societies. Sources and documents
402.V16	Directories. Dictionaries, etc.
	Biography

Local history and description
Other cities, towns, etc., A-Z
Valencia
Biography -- Continued

402.V17	Collective
402.V172A-.V172Z	Individual, A-Z
402.V18	Guidebooks
402.V19	General works. Description
402.V195	Antiquities
402.V2	History
	By period
402.V22	Early and medieval
402.V23	Modern
	Buildings
402.V235	Collective
402.V236A-.V236Z	Individual, A-Z
402.V25	Pamphlets, etc.
402.V3	Valladolid
402.V5	Vigo
402.V5138	Vilalba
402.V56	Vitoria
	Zaragoza see DP402.S3

History
    Biography (Collective) -- Continued
      Houses, noble families, etc.

536.3.A1	Collective
536.3.A2-Z	Individual, A-Z
	e.g.
536.3.A6	Albuquerque family
536.5	Public men
536.7	Women
	Historiography
536.8	General works
	Biography of historians and antiquarians
536.9.A2	Collective
536.9.A3-Z	Individual, A-Z
	e.g.
536.9.L6	Lopes, Fernão
536.9.O6	Oliveira Martins, Joaquim Pedro
	Study and teaching
536.95	General works
536.96.A-Z	By region or country, A-Z
	Subarrange by author
	General works
537	Through 1800. Chronicles
538	1801-
539	Compends
540	Anecdotes, etc.
542	Pamphlets, etc.
543.A-Z	Special topics, A-Z
543.B7	British in Portugal
543.I8	Italians in Portugal
546	Philosophy of Portuguese history
547	Military history
	Naval history
	Biography and memoirs
550	Collective
550.5	Officers
	Individual biography, see the historical period
551	General works
	Political and diplomatic history. Foreign and general
	relations
	Cf. DP558+ Special periods, reigns, etc.
555	Sources and documents
556	General works
556.1	General special
556.2	Early to 1580
	1580-
556.4	General works

DP

DP

History
By period
1580-
1640-1816. House of Braganza
Jose I, 1750-1777 -- Continued

639	General works on life and reign
640	Tavora plot, 1758
641	Marquis de Pombal, 1699-1782
641.7	Pamphlets, etc.
641.9.A-Z	Biography and memoirs of contemporaries, A-Z
	e.g.
641.9.M3	Marianna Victoria, Consort of Joseph I
642	Maria I and Pedro III, 1777-1816
	Including biography of Maria I
642.7	Biography of Pedro III, Consort of Maria I
643	Regency of João, 1792-1816
	For works on his life and reign see DP650+
644	Period of Peninsular War, 1805-1814
	For the war itself see DC231+
644.9.A-Z	Biography and memoirs of contemporaries, A-Z
	e.g.
644.9.C6	Costa e Almeida, Francisco Bernardo da
644.9.M27	Manique, Diogo Ignacio de Pina
644.9.N5	Nisa, Domingos Zavier de Lima, marques de

1816-1853/1908

645.A1	Sources and documents
	Biography and memoirs
645.A2	Collective
645.A3-Z	Individual, A-Z
	e.g.
645.L6	Lobo, Francisco Alexandre, Bp.
645.S2	Saldanha, João Carlos de Saldanha de Oliveira e Daun, 1. duque de
645.S25	Santarem, Manuel Francisco de Barros, 2. visconde de
645.S3	Saraiva, Francisco de São Luiz, cardinal
645.S6	Sousa-Holstein, Pedro de, duque de Palmella
646	General works
647	Social life and customs. Civilization. Intellectual life

João VI, 1816-1826. Revolution of 1820

650	General works on life and reign
651.A-Z	Biography and memoirs of contemporaries, A-Z
653	Pedro IV (I of Brazil), 1826
654	Maria II, 1826-1828

Miguel I, 1828-1834

655	General works on life and reign
	Biography and memoirs

	History
	By period
	1580-
	1816-1853/1908
	Miguel I, 1828-1834
	Biography and memoirs -- Continued
656	Collective
656.2.A-Z	Individual, A-Z
657	Wars of succession, 1826-1840
659	Maria II (restored), 1834-1853
660.A-Z	Biography and memoirs of contemporaries, A-Z
	e.g.
660.F4	Fernando II, Consort of Maria II
	1853-1908
661.A1	Sources and documents
	Biography and memoirs
661.A2	Collective
661.A3-Z	Individual, A-Z
	e.g.
661.M5	Miguel, Duke of Bragança
661.Q8	Quillinan, Luiz de
662	General works
	Pedro V, 1853-1861
664	General works on life and reign
664.5	Estephania, Consort of Peter V
666	Luiz I, 1861-1889
667.A-Z	Biography and memoirs of contemporaries, A-Z
	e.g.
667.A6	Affonso Henriques, Crown Prince
667.Q6	Oliveira Martins, Joaquim Pedro
	Carlos I, 1889-1908
668	General works on life and reign
	Biography and memoirs of contemporaries
669.A2	Collective
669.A3-Z	Individual, A-Z
	e.g.
669.A6	Amelia, Consort of Charles I
	20th century
670	Sources and documents
670.5	Social life and customs. Civilization. Intellectual life
	Biography and memoirs
671.A2	Collective
671.A3-Z	Individual
	e.g.
671.B7	Bragança, Duarte Nuno de Bragança, duque de
671.P3	Paiva Couceiro, Henrique de
672	General works

DP

	Local history and description
	Provinces, regions, etc., A-Z
	Algarve. Faro (District)
	History
	By period -- Continued
702.A33	19th-20th centuries
702.A34	Other
702.A42	Arrábida Mountain Range
702.A45	Atlantic Coast
702.A51-.A60	Aveiro (Table D-DR9)
	Azores
702.A81	Periodicals. Societies. Collections
702.A83	Biography (Collective)
702.A84	Dictionaries. Gazetteers. Directories, etc.
702.A85	Guidebooks
702.A86	General works. Description and travel. Pictorial works
702.A865	Social life and customs. Civilization
	History
702.A87	General works
702.A88	Early and medieval
702.A89	16th-18th centuries
702.A9	19th-20th centuries
	Individual islands
702.A91	Corvo
702.A92	Fayal (Faial)
702.A93	Flores
702.A94	Graciosa
702.A95	Pico
702.A96	Santa Maria
702.A97	São Jorge
702.A98	São Miguel (Saint Michael)
702.A99	Terceira
702.B05	Bairrada (Region)
702.B11-.B20	Beira region (Table D-DR9)
	Including Beira province before 1936
	Individual provinces, 1936-
702.B22	Beira Alta
702.B23	Beira Baixa
702.B24	Beira Litoral
	Beja
702.B26	Periodicals. Societies. Collections
702.B3	General works. Description and travel
702.B31	History
702.B35	Other
	Braga
702.B46	Periodicals. Societies. Collections
702.B5	Description and travel

	Local history and description
	Provinces, regions, etc., A-Z
	Braga -- Continued
702.B51	History
702.B61-.B70	Bragança (Table D-DR9)
702.C11-.C20	Castello Branco (Table D-DR9)
	Coimbra
702.C41	Periodicals. Societies. Collections
702.C412	Biography (Collective)
702.C413	Dictionaries. Gazetteers. Directories, etc.
702.C414	Guidebooks
702.C42	General works. Description and travel. Pictorial works
	History
702.C43	General works
702.C44	Early and medieval
702.C45	Modern
702.C49	Coura River and Valley
702.D6	Douro-Litoral
702.E21-.E30	Entre-Minho-e-Douro (Table D-DR9)
702.E34	Estoril Coast
702.E35	Estrella (Estrêla), Serra da
	Estremadura
702.E46	Periodicals. Societies. Collections
702.E49	Guidebooks
702.E5	General works
702.E52	History
702.E55	Other
702.E71-.E80	Evora (Table D-DR9)
	Faro (District) see DP702.A25+
702.G3	Gafanha
702.G8	Guarda
702.L2	Leiria
702.L25	Lima River and Valley
702.L3	Lisbon (Lisboa)
	Madeira
702.M11	Periodicals. Societies. Collections
702.M12	Biography
702.M13	Dictionaries. Gazetteers. Directories, etc.
702.M15	Guidebooks
702.M16	General works. Description and travel. Pictorial works
702.M165	Social life and customs. Civilization. Intellectual life
702.M17	History
702.M18	General special
	By period
702.M19	Early and medieval
702.M2	16th-18th centuries
702.M21	19th-20th centuries

	Local history and description
	Lisbon -- Continued
	Streets, suburbs, etc.
769.A1	Collective
769.A2-Z	Individual, A-Z
	e.g.
769.B4	Belem
769.C26	Calçada da Ajuda
769.C3	Rua das Canastras
	Buildings
772	General works
	Special. Churches, theaters, etc.
773.A1	Collective
773.A2-Z	Individual, A-Z
	e.g.
773.C6	Conceição Velha (Church)
773.P3	Palacio da Ajuda
776	Other special
802.A-Z	Other cities, towns, etc., A-Z
	e.g.
802.A517	Alcobaça
802.B3	Barcellos
802.B7	Braga
802.B8	Bussaco
802.C45	Chaves
802.C5	Cintra
802.C6	Coimbra
802.C65	Corvilhao
802.E9	Evora
802.F4	Feira
802.F8	Fundâo
802.G8	Guimarães
802.M25	Mafra
802.O6	Oporto
802.P38	Penamacor
	Porto see DP802.O6
802.S2	Santarém
	Sintra see DP802.C5
802.S7	Soure
802.T5	Tomar (Thomar)
802.V5	Vianna do Castello (Viana do Castelo)
802.V7	Villa Nova de Gaia
802.V73	Villa Viçosa
	Portuguese colonies
	Collective see JV4200+
	Individual colonies
	see classes D-F

	Ethnography
	Individual elements in the population, A-Z -- Continued
49.I9	Italians
49.M87	Muslims
49.P6	Poles
49.R65	Romanians
49.S47	Serbs
49.S56	Slovaks
49.S65	Spaniards
49.S68	Sri Lankans
49.T5	Tibetans
49.T87	Turks
49.V54	Vietnamese
49.Z35	Zairians
49.5	Swiss in foreign regions or countries (General)
	For Swiss in a particular region or country, see the region or country
	History
51	Dictionaries. Chronological tables, outlines, etc.
	Biography (Collective)
	For individual biography, see the special period, reign, or place
52	General works
52.1	Rulers, presidents, etc.
52.5.A-Z	Houses, noble families, etc., A-Z
	e.g.
52.5.B4	Benzinger family
52.6	Public men
52.7	Women
	Historiography
52.8	General works
	Biography of historians, area studies specialists, archaeologists, etc.
52.9.A2	Collective
52.9.A3-Z	Individual, A-Z
	e.g.
52.9.T7	Tschudi, Aegidius
52.95	Study and teaching
	General works
53	Through 1800. Chronicles
54	1801-
55	Compends
55.5	Pictorial works
56	Pamphlets, etc.
57	History of several cantons or cities
	Including French-speaking Switzerland, etc.

DQ

History
By period
Federation and Independence, 1291-1516 -- Continued

100	Wars of Mülhausen and of Waldshut, 1468
	Wars of Burgundy, 1474-1477
101	General works
103	Battle of Grandson, 1476
104	Battle of Morat, 1476
	Wars against Swabian League, 1499
106	General works
107.A-Z	By canton, A-Z
	e.g.
107.S8	Solothurn
	Including Battle of Dornach, 1499
109	Swiss in Italy. Battle of Marignano, 1515
110.A-Z	Biography and memoirs, A-Z
	e.g.
110.S3	Schinner, Mathaus, cardinal
	1516-1798
111	General works
	1516-1648
113	Sources and documents
114	General works
116	General special
117	Pamphlets, etc.
118.A-Z	Biography and memoirs, A-Z
	e.g.
118.P6	Platter, Thomas
118.R65	Roll, Walter
	Peasants' War, 1641 see DQ421+
	1648-1712
121	General works
121.8.A-Z	Biography and memoirs, A-Z
	e.g.
121.8.T6	Thurn, Fidel von
	1712-1798
122	General works
	Biography and memoirs
123.A2	Collective
123.A3-Z	Individual, A-Z
	e.g.
123.L4	Lentulus, Robert Scipio, freiherr von
123.S3	Schinz, Johann Heinrich
123.Z4	Zellweger, Laurenz
	19th century
124	General works
	Biography

	History
	By period
	19th century
	1848-1900
	Biography and memoirs
	Individual, A-Z -- Continued
178.E8	Escher, Johann H. Alfred
178.F87	Furrer, Jonas
178.S35	Schenk, Karl
178.S36	Scherer-Boccard, Theodor
178.S75	Steiger, Edmund von
178.T8	Tschudi, Friedrich von
181	1848-1871
	For the Neuchatel question see DQ539.4
191	1871-1900
	20th century
201	General works
203	General special
	1900-1945
205	General works
	Biography and memoirs
206	Collective
207.A-Z	Individual, A-Z
	e.g.
207.S35	Schmid, Jacques
	1945-
208	General works
	Biography and memoirs
209	Collective
210.A-Z	Individual, A-Z
	Local history and description
	Cantons (and cantonal capitals)
301-320.35	Aargau (Argovie) (Table D-DR10)
321-340.35	Appenzell (Table D-DR10)
	Including Ausserrhoden (Outer Rhodes) and Innerrhoden (Inner Rhodes)
341-360.35	Jura (Table D-DR10)
361-380.35	Basel-Land (Bâle-Campagne) (Table D-DR10)
381-400.35	Basel-Stadt (Bâle-Ville) (Table D-DR10)
	Including Basel Canton before 1832
389	Basel (City)
401-420.35	Bern (Berne) (Table D-DR10)
421-440.35	Fribourg (Freiburg) (Table D-DR10)
441-460.35	Geneva (Geneve, Genf) (Table D-DR10)
461-480.35	Glarus (Glaris) (Table D-DR10)
481-500.35	Grisons (Graubünden, Grigioni, Grischun) (Table D-DR10)
	Jura see DQ341+

Local history and description

Cantons (and cantonal capitals) -- Continued

501-520.35	Lucerne (Luzern) (Table D-DR10)
521-540.35	Neuchatel (Neuenburg) (Table D-DR10 modified)
539.3	19th century
539.4	Neuchatel question
541-560.35	Saint Gall (Saint Gallen, Sankt Gallen) (Table D-DR10)
561-580.35	Schaffhausen (Schaffhouse) (Table D-DR10)
581-600.35	Schwyz (Schwiz) (Table D-DR10)
601-620.35	Solothurn (Soleure) (Table D-DR10)
621-640.35	Thurgau (Thurgovie) (Table D-DR10)
641-660.35	Ticino (Tessin) (Table D-DR10)
661-680.35	Unterwalden (Table D-DR10)
	Including Unterwalden nid dem Wald (Lower Walden) and Unterwalden ob dem Wald (Upper Walden)
681-700.35	Uri (Table D-DR10)
701-720.35	Valais (Wallis) (Table D-DR10)
721-740.35	Vaud (Waadt) (Table D-DR10)
741-760.35	Zug (Zoug) (Table D-DR10)
781-800.35	Zurich (Zurich) (Table D-DR10)
	Alps
	For individual mountains, peaks, etc., see the specific country
	Cf. DB101+ Austrian Alps
	Cf. DB761+ Tyrol
	Cf. DC611.A553+ French Alps
	Cf. DD801.A28 Allgäu Alps
	Cf. DG975.D66+ Dolomite Alps
820	Periodicals. Collections
821	Societies
	Cf. GV199.8+ Mountaineering clubs and societies
822	Congresses
	General works
823	Through 1960
823.5	1961-
824	General special
825	Western Alps (Italian and French Alps)
826	Pennine Alps
827	Central Alps (Bernese Oberland)
828	Eastern Alps
829	Ticino Alps
841.A-Z	Regions, peaks, etc., A-Z
	Including Alps other than in DQ820+
	e.g.
841.A35	Aiguille du Dru
841.A4	Aletach Glacier
841.B4	Bernina Alps

DQ

Local history and description
Regions, peaks, etc., A-Z -- Continued

841.B6	Biel (Lake). Lac de Bienne
	Including Saint-Pierre Island
841.B8	Bregaglia
841.D5	Disentis
841.E47	Eiger
841.E5	Engadine
841.F47	Ferret Valley
841.F7	Freiamt
841.G2	Gaster
841.G4	Geneva (Lake)
841.G6	Gornergrat
841.G77	Grimselpass
841.G8	Grindelwald
841.G9	Gruyère (County)
841.J8	Jungfrau
841.J9	Jura Mountains
841.K6	Klettgau
841.L8	Lucerne (Lake)
841.M4	Matterhorn
	Mont Blanc see DC611.M68
841.M8	Monte Viso
841.O4	Ofenberg. Ofenpass
841.P6	Pilatus, Mount
841.R5	Rigi
841.S12	Saastal
841.S15	Saint Bernard, Great (Pass)
841.S2	Saint Gotthard
	Saint-Pierre Island see DQ841.B6
841.S4	Sense River and Valley
841.S45	Sihl River and Valley
841.S8	Susten Pass
841.T5	Thun (Lake). Thunersee
	Cities, towns, etc.
851.A1	Collective
851.A2-Z	Individual, A-Z
	e.g.
	For cantonal capitals see DQ301+
851.A8	Avenches
851.B13	Baden
851.B6	Bex
851.B625	Biel
851.C4	Chillon
851.D3	Davos
851.D5	Diessenhofen
851.E3	Einsiedeln

Local history and description
Cities, towns, etc.
Individual, A-Z -- Continued

851.E4	Elm
851.H65	Horgen
851.I76	Ittigen
851.K45	Kirchberg
851.L3	Laufen
851.M8	Montreux
851.P6	Pontresina
851.R7	Rorschach
	Including the castle
851.S24	Saint Moritz
851.T5	Thun
851.V4	Vevey
851.W3	Wallisellen
851.W5	Widen (Castle)
851.W62	Windisch (Vindonissa)
851.W63	Winterthur
851.Y8	Yverdon

DQ

	History of Balkan Peninsula
	Cf. DJK1+ Eastern Europe
	Cf. DJK61+ Black Sea region
1	Periodicals. Societies. Serials
1.5	Congresses. Conferences, etc.
1.7	Sources and documents
	Collected works
2	Several authors
3	Individual authors
5	Gazetteers. Dictionaries, etc.
6	Place names (General)
7	Guidebooks
	General works
9	Through 1800
10	1801-
10.5	Pictorial works
11	Historical geography
	Description and travel
11.5	History of travel
12	Early through 1600
13	1601-1800
14	1801-1900
15	1901-1950
16	1951-
20	Antiquities
23	Social life and customs. Civilization. Intellectual life
	Ethnography
24	General works
24.5	National characteristics
25	Slavic peoples in the Balkan Peninsula
27.A-Z	Other individual elements in the population, A-Z
	For individual Balkan regions and countries see DR49+
	Cf. DJK28.A+ Eastern Europe
27.A4	Albanians
27.A8	Aromanians
27.G34	Gagauz
27.G4	Germans. Swabians
27.G8	Greeks
27.K55	Kipchak
27.M87	Muslims
27.P47	Pechenegs
27.P49	Pelasgi
27.R6	Romance-language-speaking peoples. Latins
27.R64	Romanians
27.S58	Slovaks
	Swabians see DR27.G4
27.T8	Turks

	Ethnography
	Other individual elements in the population, A-Z -- Continued
27.Y87	Yuruks
	History
32	Dictionaries
33	Biography (Collective)
	Historiography
34	General works
	Biography of historians
34.6	Collective
34.7.A-Z	Individual, A-Z
	Study and teaching. Balkan studies
34.8	General works
34.9.A-Z	By region or country, A-Z
	General works
35	Through 1800
36	1801-
37	General special
38	Pamphlets, etc.
38.15	Military history
38.2	Political and diplomatic history
	Cf. D371+ Eastern question
	Cf. D461+ Eastern question (20th century)
38.3.A-Z	Balkan relations with individual regions or countries, A-Z
	By period
	Early and medieval to 1500
39	General works
39.3	Celts
39.5	Illyrians
	Cf. DG59.I2 Roman Illyria (Illyricum)
39.6	Romans
41	1500-1800
43	1800-1900
	20th century (General)
45	General works
	1900-1913
45.5	General works
	Balkan War, 1912-1913
46.A2	Sources and documents
46.A3	Historiography
46.A4-Z	General works
46.05	Pictorial works. Satire, caricature, etc.
46.1	Pamphlets, etc.
46.2	Naval history
46.3	Diplomatic history
	Cf. D461+ Eastern question
	Special campaigns

DR

History
 By period
  20th century (General)
   1900-1913
    Balkan War, 1912-1913
     Special campaigns -- Continued
46.4   Turkish
46.5   Bulgarian
46.6   Serbian
46.7   Montenegrin
46.8   Greek
46.9.A-Z   Local events, battles, etc., A-Z
              e.g.
46.9.E3   Edirne (Turkey), Siege of, 1912-1913
46.93.A-Z   Special topics, A-Z
46.93.A87   Atrocities
46.93.J68   Journalism, Military
46.95   Bucharest, Treaty of, 1913
46.97   Personal narratives
47   1913-1919
            Cf. D501+ World War I, 1914-1918
48   1919-1945
48.5   1945-1989
            Cf. D847.2 Warsaw pact, 1955
48.6   1989-
      Local history and description
       Lower Danube Valley
          For the Danube Valley of individual countries, see the specific
            country
49   General works
49.2   General special
49.23   Description and travel
49.24   Antiquities
49.25   Ethnography (General)
            For individual elements of the Lower Danube Valley
              see DR25
49.26   History
49.7   Rumelia. Rumeli (General)
            For Eastern Rumelia (Bulgaria) see DR95.R8
       Thrace
          Class here general works on Thrace and the ancient Thracians.
          For ancient Thrace in relation to Greek civilization see
            DF261.T6
          For modern Greek Thrace see DF901.T75
          For modern Bulgarian Thrace see DR95.T45
          For Turkish Thrace see DR701.T5
50   Periodicals. Societies. Serials

	Bulgaria
	Collected works -- Continued
52.7	Individual authors
53	Gazetteers
53.3	Place names (General)
53.7	Directories
54	Guidebooks
55	General works
56	Monuments and picturesque. Views
	Historic monuments, landmarks, scenery, etc. (General)
	For local see DR95+
56.5	General works
56.7	Preservation
	Description and travel
57	Through 1400
58	1401-1800
59	1801-1878
60	1879-1950
60.2	1951-
61	Historical geography
61.5	Geography
62	Antiquities
	Cf. DR95+ Local history and description
63	Social life and customs. Civilization
	Ethnography
64	General works
64.15	National characteristics
64.2.A-Z	Individual elements in the population, A-Z
64.2.A44	Aliani. Kŭzŭlbashi
64.2.A74	Armenians
64.2.A76	Aromanians
64.2.C9	Czechs
64.2.G73	Greeks
64.2.H84	Hungarians
64.2.I74	Irish
64.2.K37	Kapant͡si
64.2.K39	Kariots
	Kŭzŭlbashi see DR64.2.A44
64.2.M33	Macedonians
64.2.M8	Muslims
64.2.P64	Poles
64.2.P66	Pomaks
64.2.R65	Romanians
64.2.R84	Russians
64.2.S27	Sarakatsans
64.2.S56	Slovaks
64.2.T87	Turks

Bulgaria

    Ethnology

64.5   Bulgarians in foreign regions or countries (General)

          For Bulgarians in a particular region or country, see the
            region or country

    History

65   Dictionaries. Chronological tables, outlines, etc.

       Biography (Collective)

          For individual biography, see the special period, reign, or
            place

66   General works

66.2   Rulers, kings, etc.

66.5   Statesmen

66.6   Women

       Historiography

66.7   General works

          Biography of historians, area studies specialists,
            archaeologists, etc.

66.8   Collective

66.9.A-Z   Individual, A-Z

       Study and teaching

66.95   General works

66.97.A-Z   By region or country, A-Z

            Subarrange by author

67   General works

67.5   Pictorial works

67.7   Juvenile works

68   Addresses, essays, lectures. Anecdotes, etc.

69   Philosophy of Bulgarian history

69.5   History of several parts of Bulgaria treated together

70   Military history

       Political and diplomatic history. Foreign and general
         relations

72   General works

          Cf. D371+ Eastern question

          Cf. D461+ Eastern question (20th century)

73.A-Z   Relations with individual regions or countries, A-Z

       By period

         Early to 1396

73.7   Sources and documents

74   General works

74.2   Social life and customs. Civilization. Intellectual life

74.25   Military history

74.3   Early to 681

         First Bulgarian Empire, 681-1018

74.5   General works

           681-893

DR

Bulgaria
  History
    By period
      Turkish rule, 1396-1878 -- Continued
        1396-1762

82	General works
82.15	Social life and customs. Civilization. Intellectual life

Biography and memoirs

82.2	Collective
82.25.A-Z	Individual, A-Z
82.3	Uprising of 1403
82.5	Uprising of 1598

1762-1878. National revival

82.9	Sources and documents
83	General works
83.15	Social life and customs. Civilization. Intellectual life

Biography and memoirs

83.2.A1	Collective
83.2.A2-Z	Individual, A-Z

e.g.

83.2.B6	Botev, Khristo
83.2.L4	Levski, Vasil Ivanov
83.2.R3	Rakovski, Georgi Stoikov
83.2.S8	Stoĭanov, Zakhari
83.3	Uprising of 1849
83.4	Uprising of 1850
83.5	Uprising of 1857

April Uprising, 1876

83.7	General works
83.72	Pictorial works
83.73	Regimental histories

Subarrange by author

83.74	Personal narratives
83.75.A-Z	Local revolutionary history. By place, A-Z

e.g.

83.75.D74	Drianovski manastir
83.76.A-Z	Special topics, A-Z
83.76.B85	Bulgarian Orthodox Eastern Church

Health aspects see DR83.76.M44
Hospitals see DR83.76.M44

83.76.M44	Medical care. Hospitals. Health aspects
83.76.P73	Press
83.76.P75	Propaganda
83.76.P83	Public opinion
83.76.W65	Women
83.8	Celebrations. Memorials. Monuments

DR

Bulgaria
    History
        By period
            Turkish rule, 1396-1878
                1762-1878. National revival -- Continued
84   Period of Russo-Turkish War, 1877-1878
                        For the war itself see DR573
                    1878-1944
84.9   Sources and documents
85   General works
85.2   Social life and customs. Civilization. Intellectual life
85.3   Military history
85.4   Foreign and general relations
                        Biography and memoirs
85.5.A1   Collective
85.5.A2-Z   Individual, A-Z
                                e.g.
                                    Dimitrov, Georgi see DR88.D5
85.5.G4   Geshov, Ivan Evstratiev
85.5.K5   Kiñakov, Petko, 1844-1900
                                Petko, voivoda, 1844-1900 see DR85.5.K5
85.5.S7   Stambulov, Stefan
                        Alexander, 1879-1886
85.9   Sources and documents
86   General works on life and reign
                        Biography and memoirs of contemporaries
86.2   Collective
86.22.A-Z   Individual, A-Z
86.3   Coup d'état, 1881
                        Serbo-Bulgarian War see DR2027
86.5   Interregnum, 1886-1887
                    Ferdinand, 1887-1918
87   General works on life and reign
87.3   General special
87.5   Pamphlets, etc.
87.7   Period of Balkan War, 1912-1913
                            For the war itself see DR46+
87.8   Period of World War I, 1914-1918
                            For the war itself see D501+
87.9   Vladaya Uprising, 1918
                        Biography and memoirs of contemporaries
88.A1   Collective
88.A2-Z   Individual, A-Z
                                e.g.
88.B6   Blagoev, Dimitŭr
88.D5   Dimitrov, Georgi
88.S77   Stamboliĭski, Aleksandŭr S.

	Bulgaria
	History
	By period
	1878-1944 -- Continued
88.5	20th century
	1918-1944. Boris III, 1918-1943
88.9	Sources and documents
89	General works on life and reign
89.15	Social life and customs. Civilization. Intellectual life
	Biography and memoirs of contemporaries
89.2.A1	Collective
89.2.A2-Z	Individual, A-Z
89.22	June Uprising, 1923
	September Uprising, 1923
89.3	General works
89.32	Pictorial works
89.34	Personal narratives
89.35.A-Z	Local revolutionary history. By place, A-Z
89.36.A-Z	Special topics, A-Z
89.36.C65	Communications
89.36.I53	Influence
89.36.P73	Press
89.36.W65	Women
89.36.Y68	Youth
89.5	April events, 1925
89.8	1939-1944. Period of World War II
	For the war itself see D731+
	1944-1990
	Including regency of Simeon II, 1943-1946 and the People's Republic, 1946-
89.9	Sources and documents
90	General works
90.3	Addresses, essays, lectures
91	Social life and customs. Civilization
92	Foreign and general relations
	Biography and memoirs
93.A1	Collective
93.A2-Z	Individual, A-Z
	e.g.
	Dimitrov, Georgi see DR88.D5
93.Z48	Zhivkov, Todor
	September Uprising, 1944
93.3	General works
93.32	Pictorial works
93.34	Personal narratives
	1990-
93.4	Sources and documents

DR

Bulgaria
  History
    By period
      1990- -- Continued
93.42   General works
93.43   Social life and customs. Civilization. Intellectual life
93.44   Political history
93.45   Foreign and general relations
                        Biography and memoirs
93.46   Collective
93.47.A-Z   Individual, A-Z
                    Local history and description
95.A-Z   Provinces, regions, etc., A-Z
                        e.g.
95.B54   Black Sea region
95.B55   Blagoevgrad (Okrug). Pirin Macedonia
                          For ancient Greek Macedonia see DF261.M2
                          For modern Greek Macedonia see DF901.M3
                          For Macedonia (General, and Yugoslavia) see
                              DR2152+
                          Cf. DR95.P46 Pirin Mountains Region
95.D6   Dobruja
                          For Dobruja (General, and Romania) see DR281.D5
                        Istranca Mountains Region see DR95.S8
                        Pirin Macedonia see DR95.B55
95.P46   Pirin Mountains Region
95.R8   Rumelia (Eastern)
                          For Rumelia (General) see DR49.7
95.S8   Strandzha Mountains Region
95.S87   Struma River and Valley
95.T45   Thrace
                          For ancient Greek Thrace see DF261.T6
                          For modern Greek Thrace see DF901.T75
                          For general works on Thrace see DR50+
                          For Turkish Thrace see DR701.T5
                      Cities, towns, etc.
97   Sofia (Table D-DR3)
98.A-Z   Other
98.A1   Collective
98.A2-Z   Individual, A-Z
98.B6   Boboshevo
98.D7   Dragalevtsi
98.P55   Plovdiv
98.T5   Tirnovo, Tŭrnovo (Veliko Tŭrnovo)
98.T7   Troyan (Lovech)
                          Tŭrnovo (Veliko Tŭrnovo) see DR98.T5
                          Veliko Tŭrnovo see DR98.T5

(101-196)	Montenegro
	see DR1802+
	Romania
	Including Moldavia and Wallachia
201	Periodicals. Societies. Serials
201.2	Congresses. Conferences, etc.
	Museums, exhibitions, etc.
201.3	General works
201.32.A-Z	Individual. By place, A-Z
203	Sources and documents
	Collected works
203.5	Several authors
203.7	Individual authors
204	Gazetteers. Dictionaries, etc.
204.3	Place names
204.5	Guidebooks
205	General works
206	Monumental and picturesque. Pictorial works
206.5	Historical geography
206.8	Geography
	Description and travel
207	Through 1800
208	1801-1865
209	1866-1950
210	1951-
211	Antiquities
	Cf. DR279+ Local history and description
212	Social life and customs. Civilization. Intellectual life
	Ethnography
213	General works
214.A-Z	Individual elements in the population, A-Z
214.A43	Albanians
214.A75	Armenians
214.B8	Bulgarians
	Carpi see DR239.22
214.C69	Croats
214.C73	Csangos
214.C94	Czechs
	Dacians see DR239.2
214.G4	Germans
214.G73	Greeks
214.H9	Hungarians
214.M68	Moti
214.M87	Muslims
214.P64	Poles
214.S47	Serbs
214.S55	Slovaks

	Romania
	Ethnography
	Individual elements in the population, A-Z -- Continued
214.U47	Ukrainians
214.2	Romanians in foreign regions or countries (General)
	For Romanians in a particular region or country, see the region or country
	History
215	Dictionaries. Chronological tables, outlines, etc.
216	Biography (Collective)
	For individual biography, see the special period, reign, or place
	Historiography
216.7	General works
	Biography of historians, area studies specialists, archaeologists, etc.
216.8	Collective
216.9.A-Z	Individual, A-Z
	e.g.
216.9.B3	Bâlcescu, Nicolae
216.9.I5	Iorga, Nicolae
	For literary works see PC839.I58
216.92	Study and teaching
217	General works
218	Pamphlets, etc.
219	Military history
225	Naval history
	Political and diplomatic history. Foreign and general relations
	For general works on the political and the diplomatic history of a period, see the period
	For works on relations with a specific region or country, regardless of period see DR229.A+
	Cf. D371+ Eastern question (19th century)
	Cf. D461+ Eastern question (20th century)
226	General works
229.A-Z	Relations with individual regions or countries, A-Z
	By period
	Early and medieval to 1601
238	General works
	Earliest and Roman period
239	General works
239.2	Dacians. Getae
	Cf. DG59.D3 Dacia
239.22	Carpi
	Medieval period
240	General works

Romania
　History
　　By period
　　　Early and medieval to 1601
　　　　Medieval period -- Continued
　　　　　Biography and memoirs
240.5.A2　　　　　　Collective
240.5.A3-Z　　　　　Individual, A-Z
　　　　　　　　e. g.
240.5.M5　　　　　　　Michael, voivode of Wallachia, 1558-1601
240.5.N4　　　　　　　Neagoe Basarab, voivode of Wallachia
240.5.S7　　　　　　　Stephen, Voivode of Moldavia, d. 1504
240.5.V55　　　　　　Vlad II, Dracul, Prince of Wallachia
240.5.V553　　　　　Vlad III, Prince of Wallachia (Vlad Țepeș)
　　　　Phanariote regime, 1601-1822
241　　　　　General works
　　　　　Biography and memoirs
241.5.A2　　　　　　Collective
241.5.A3-Z　　　　　Individual, A-Z
　　　　　　　　e.g.
241.5.V55　　　　　　Vladimirescu, Tudor
　　　　1822-1881. 19th century
242　　　　　General works
244　　　　　　1822-1866
246　　　　　　1866-1876
　　　　　1876-1881
248　　　　　　General works
　　　　　　Biography and memoirs
249.A1　　　　　　　Collective
249.A2-Z　　　　　　Individual, A-Z
　　　　　　　　e.g.
249.S7　　　　　　　Soutsos, Nikolaos, Prince
　　　　1866/1881-1944
250　　　　　General works
　　　　　Carol I, 1881-1914
252　　　　　　Sources and documents
　　　　　　Collected works
252.3　　　　　　　Several authors
252.6　　　　　　　Individual authors
253.A-Z　　　　　　Biography and memoirs of contemporaries, A-Z
254　　　　　　Elizabeth, Consort of Charles I (Carmen Sylva)
255　　　　　　General works on life and reign
256　　　　　　Reign only
257　　　　　　General special
258　　　　　　Period of the Balkan War, 1912-1913
　　　　　　　For the war itself see DR46+
　　　　　Ferdinand, 1914-1927

Romania
  History
    By period
      1866/1881-1944
        Ferdinand, 1914-1927 -- Continued

260	Sources and documents
261	General works on life and reign
	Biography and memoirs of contemporaries
262.A1	Collective
	Royal family
262.A2	Maria (Marie), Consort of Ferdinand I
262.A3-.A4	Other members of the royal family
262.A5-Z	Other, A-Z
	e.g.
262.A5	Antonescu, Ion
262.C6	Codreanu, Corneliu
263	Period of World War I, 1914-1918
	For the war itself see D501+
	1918-1944
264	General works
265	Michael
	Class here works on regency of 1927-1930 and as king, 1940-1947
	Carol II, 1930-1940
266	General works on life and reign
	Biography and memoirs of contemporaries
266.2	Collective
266.3.A-Z	Individual, A-Z
266.5	Period of World War II, 1940-1944
	For the war itself see D731+
	1944-1989
267	General works
	Biography and memoirs
267.5.A1	Collective
267.5.A2-Z	Individual, A-Z
	e.g.
267.5.C4	Ceauşescu, Nicolae
	1989-
268	General works
	Biography and memoirs
268.8	Collective
268.82.A-Z	Individual, A-Z
	Revolution, 1989
269.5	General works
269.6	Personal narratives
	Local history and description
	Transylvania

Romania
  Local history and description
    Transylvania -- Continued

279	Periodicals. Societies. Serials
279.2	Sources and documents
279.3	Gazetteers. Dictionaries, etc. Guidebooks
279.5	General works
	Description and travel
279.6	Earliest through 1800
279.62	1801-1950
279.64	1951-
279.68	Antiquities
279.7	Social life and customs. Civilization
	Ethnography
279.8	General works
279.9	Romanians
279.92.A-Z	Other individual elements in the population, A-Z
279.92.B8	Bulgarians
279.92.G4	Germans
	Including the so-called "Saxons"
279.92.G74	Greeks
279.92.H8	Hungarians
	Saxons see DR279.92.G4
279.92.S9	Szeklers
279.92.T87	Turks
279.95	Biography (Collective)
	For individual biography, see period
	History
280	General works
	By period
	Earliest to 1526
280.2	General works
	Biography and memoirs
280.24	Collective
280.26.A-Z	Individual, A-Z
	1526-1918
280.4	General works
	Biography and memoirs
280.42	Collective
280.44.A-Z	Individual, A-Z
	e.g.
280.44.B4	Bethlen, Gábor, Prince of Transylvania, 1580-1629
	1918-
280.7	General works
	Biography and memoirs
280.72	Collective

Romania
  Local history and description
    Transylvania
      History
        By period
          1919-
            Biography and memoirs -- Continued

280.74.A-Z	Individual, A-Z
	Regions, cities, towns, etc. see DR281.A+
281.A-Z	Other provinces, regions, etc., A-Z
	e.g.
281.B25	Banat
	For Hungarian Banat see DB975.B2
281.C6	Constanţa
281.D5	Dobruja
	For Dobruja (Bulgaria) see DR95.D6
281.S8	Suceava. Romanian Bukovina
	For Bukovina (General, and Ukraine) see DK508.9.B85
	Cities, towns, etc.
286	Bucharest (Table D-DR3)
296.A-Z	Other, A-Z
	e.g.
296.B74	Braşov. Brasso. Kronstadt. Stalin
296.B784	Buridava
296.C45	Cetatea Şcheia
296.D7	Drăguş
	Kronstadt see DR296.B74
296.R658	Romula
296.S26	Sarmizegetusa (Ancient city)
	Şcheia Fortress see DR296.C45
296.S6	Sinaĩa
	Stalin see DR296.B74
296.S92	Sucidava
296.T47	Tibiscum (Extinct city)
296.T86	Turnu Roşu
296.Z57	Ziridava
(301-396)	Yugoslavia
	see DR1202+
	Turkey
	For ancient Asia Minor to 1453 see DS155+
401	Periodicals. Societies. Serials
401.2	Congresses
403	Sources and documents
	Collected works
404	Several authors
405	Individual authors

	Turkey -- Continued
413	Directories
414	Gazetteers. Dictionaries, etc.
415	Place names (General)
416	Guidebooks
417	General works
417.2	Pictorial works
417.4	Juvenile works
418	Compends
418.5	Historical geography
419	Geography
	Description and travel
	For guidebooks regardless of the historical period see DR416
421	To 1453
423	1453-1565
424	1566-1700
425	1701-1829
427	1830-1900
428	1901-1950
429	1951-1980
429.4	1981-
431	Antiquities
	Cf. DR701+ Local history and description
432	Social life and customs. Civilization
	Ethnography
	Cf. DS26+ Turks
434	General works
435.A-Z	Individual elements in the population, A-Z
435.A43	Albanians
435.A66	Arabs
435.A7	Armenians
435.A95	Azerbaijanis
435.B35	Balkan Muslims
435.B44	Belgians
435.B74	British
435.B84	Bulgarians
435.C57	Circassians
435.E87	Europeans
435.G38	Georgians (Transcaucasians)
435.G4	Germans
435.G8	Greeks. Phanariots
435.H44	Hemshin
435.K35	Karachay (Turkic people)
435.K87	Kurds
435.L39	Laz
435.L49	Lezgians

DR

	Turkey
	Ethnography
	Individual elements in the population, A-Z -- Continued
435.N67	Nosairians
	Phanariots see DR435.G8
435.P6	Poles
435.R65	Romanians
435.S95	Syriac Christians
435.Y8	Yuruks
	History
	Including Ottoman Empire, 1288-1918
436	Dictionaries. Chronological tables, outlines, etc.
	Biography (Collective)
	For individual biography, see the special period, reign, or place
438	General works
438.1	Rulers, etc.
438.3	Houses, noble families, etc.
438.5	Public men
438.7	Women
	Historiography
438.8	General works
	Biography of historians and antiquarians
438.9.A2	Collective
438.9.A3-Z	Individual, A-Z
	e.g.
438.9.A5	Akçura, Yusuf
	Study and teaching
438.94	General works
438.95.A-Z	By region or country, A-Z
	General works
439	Through 1800
440	1801-
441	Compends
442	Pamphlets, etc.
	Several parts of the empire treated together
445	European or European-Asiatic-African
	For combinations within Slavic provinces see DR1+
446	Asiatic-African
	Including Egypt and Syria under Turkish dominion
	For description and travel, see individual countries
448	Military history
	For individual campaigns and engagements, see the special period
451	Naval history
	Political and diplomatic history
	Cf. DR481+ Special periods, reigns, etc.

DR

	Turkey
	History
	By period
	1281/1453-1918
	Solyman I the Magnificent, 15200-1566
508	Pamphlets, etc.
509.A-Z	Biography and memoirs of contemporaries, A-Z
	e.g.
509.S6	Sokolli Mehmet, pasha
	1566-1640. Period of decline
511	General works
	Selim II, 1566-1574
513	General works on life and reign
	Cyprian War, 1570-1571. Holy League, 1571
515	General works
515.5	Pamphlets, etc.
516	Battle of Lepanto, 1571
	Murad III, 1574-1595
519	General works on life and reign
521	Border wars with Hungary, 1575-1606
523	Wars with Persia, 1576-1639
525	Mohammed III, 1595-1603
526	Ahmed I, 1603-1617
	Mustafa I, 1617-1623
527	General works on life and reign
528	Osman II, 1618-1622
529	Murad IV, 1623-1640
	1640-1789
531	General works
533	Ibrahim, 1640-1648
	Mohammed IV, 1648-1687
	Cf. DG678.33+ Venice
534	General works on life and reign
	War of Candia, 1644-1669
534.2	General works
534.25	Pamphlets, etc.
	Siege of Candia, 1667-1669
534.3	General works
534.4	Pamphlets, etc.
534.5.A-Z	Other special events, A-Z
534.5.C55	Chios, Battle of, 1657
534.5.D3	Dardanelles, Battle of, 1656
536	Siege of Vienna, 1683. Holy League against the Turks, 1684
	Cf. DB853 Vienna (17th-18th centuries)
536.5	Siege of Buda, 1686
537	Solyman III, 1687-1691

Turkey
  History
    By period
      1281/1453-1918
        Tanzimat (Reorganization) 1839-1876 -- Continued

565	General works
	Abdul Mejid, 1839-1861
566	General works on life and reign
567	Period of Crimean War
	For the war itself see DK214+
	1861-1909
568	General works
568.8.A-Z	Biography and memoirs, A-Z
	e.g.
568.8.A46	Ahmet Muhtar Paşa, 1839-1918
568.8.C4	Cevdet, Ahmet, pasha
	Gazi Ahmet Muhtar Paşa see DR568.8.A46
568.8.I7	Ismail Kemal Bey
568.8.M6	Midhat, pasha
569	Abdul-Aziz, 1861-1876
570	Murad V, 1876
	Abdul-Hamid II, 1876-1909. Constitutional movement
571	General works on life and reign
571.5	Personal special
572	General special
572.5	Committee of Union and Progress (Young Turks)
	(İttihat ve Terakki Cemiyeti), 1889-1908
	Cf. DR584.5 Committee of Union and Progress
	(Young Turks), 1908-1918
	War with Russia, 1877-1878
572.9	Museums, exhibitions, etc.
	Subarrange by author
573	General works
573.3	General special
	Military operations
	General works see DR573
573.35	Regimental histories
	Subarrange by author
573.4	Personal narratives
573.5.A-Z	Special events, battles, etc., A-Z
	e.g.
573.5.P6	Pleven, Bulgaria (City), Siege of, 1877
573.5.P76	Prokhod Shipchenski, Battle of, 1877
573.7	Treaty of San Stefano, 1878
	Cf. D375.3 Eastern question (19th century)
573.8.A-Z	Special topics, A-Z
	Hospitals see DR573.8.M44

Turkey
History
By period
1281/1453-1918
1861-1909
Abdul-Hamid II, 1876-1909. Constitutional movement
War with Russia, 1877-1878
Special topics, A-Z

573.8.M44	Medical and sanitary affairs. Hospitals
573.8.O78	Orthodox Eastern Church
573.8.R44	Refugees
573.8.T47	Territorial questions
573.8.W6	Women
574	Shaykh ʻUbayd Allāh Rebellion, 1880
575	Period of war with Greece, 1897
	For the war itself see DF827

20th century

576	General works
	Mohammed V, 1909-1918
583	General works on life and reign
584	General special
584.5	Committee of Union and Progress (Young Turks) (Ittihat ve Terakki Cemiyeti), 1908-1918
	Cf. DR572.5 Committee of Union and Progress (Young Turks), 1889-1908
586	Period of Turco-Italian War, 1911-1912
	For the war itself see DT234
587	Period of Balkan War, 1912-1913
	For the war itself see DR46+
588	Period of World War I, 1914-1918
	For the war itself see D501+
	1918-
589	Mohammed VI, 1918-1922
	Including Turkish Revolution, 1918-1923
	Cf. DF845.5+ War with Greece, 1921-1922
590	First Republic, 1923-1960. Kemalism
	Biography and memoirs
592.A1	Collective
592.A2-Z	Individual, A-Z
	e.g.
592.A4	Adivar, Halide Edib
	Atatürk, Kemal see DR592.K4
592.E55	Enver, pasha
592.I5	Inönü, Ismet
592.K4	Kemal, Mustafa (Kemal Atatürk)
592.N8	Nur, Riza, 1879-1942 or 3
	Riza Nur, 1879-1942 or 3 see DR592.N8

DR

Turkey
  History
    By period
      20th century
        1918- -- Continued
          Second Republic, 1960-1980

593	General works
594	Coup d'etat, 1960
600	Coup d'etat, 1971
601	Coup d'etat, 1980
	Third Republic, 1980-
603	General works
	Biography and memoirs
605.A1	Collective
605.A2-Z	Individual, A-Z
605.O35	Ocalan, Abdullah
	Local history and description (European Turkey)
701.A-Z	Provinces, regions, etc., A-Z
	e.g.
701.A2	Aegean Sea
	For Aegean Sea region see DF895
	For Turkish islands in the Aegean Sea see DS51.A+
	Albania see DR901+
701.D2	Dardanelles
701.G3	Gallipoli Peninsula
	Janina see DF951.I5
	Kosovo see DR2075+
	Macedonia see DR2152+
	Monastir see DR2275.B58
	Rumelia (Rumeli) see DR49.7
	Saloniki (Thessalonike) see DF951.T45
701.T5	Thrace, Eastern (European Turkey)
	For ancient Greek Thrace see DF261.T6
	For modern Greek Thrace see DF901.T75
	For general works on Thrace see DR50+
	For Bulgarian Thrace see DR95.T45
	Istanbul (Constantinople)
716	Sources and documents
	Cf. DR403 Sources and documents of Turkey
717	Gazetteers
718	Guidebooks
719	General works
	Description
720	Early through 1800
	For history of Istanbul (early to 1800) see DR729+
721	1801-1900
722	1901-1950

Turkey
    Local history and description (European Turkey) -- Continued
741.A-Z   Other cities, towns, etc., A-Z
          e.g.
          Athos, Mount see DF901.A77
741.B7   Bosporus (Strait)
741.E4   Edirne (Adrianople)
(741.T5)   Tirana, Albania
            see DR997
    Ancient Asia Minor to 1453 see DS155+
    Turkey in Asia after 1453 see DS47+
Albania
901   Periodicals. Societies. Serials
        Museums, exhibitions, etc.
902   General works
903.A-Z   Individual. By place, A-Z
903.5   Congresses
904   Sources and documents
        Collected works
905   Several authors
906   Individual authors
907   Gazetteers. Dictionaries, etc.
908   Place names (General)
909   Guidebooks
910   General works
911   General special
912   Pictorial works
        Historic monuments, landmarks, etc. (General)
          For local see DR996+
913   General works
913.5   Preservation
914   Historical geography
914.5   Geography
        Description and travel
915   History of travel
916   Through 1900
917   1901-1970
918   1971-
921   Antiquities
          For local see DR996+
922   Social life and customs. Civilization. Intellectual life
          For specific periods, see the period or reign
        Ethnography
923   General works
924   National characteristics
925.A-Z   Individual elements in the population, A-Z
925.B84   Bulgarians

	Albania
	Ethnography
	Individual elements in the population, A-Z -- Continued
925.G35	Germans
925.G48	Ghegs
925.G7	Greeks
925.M33	Macedonians
925.S47	Serbs
925.S53	Slavs, Southern
925.T65	Tosks
925.Y84	Yugoslavs
926	Albanians in foreign regions or countries (General)
	For Albanians in a particular region or country, see the region or country
	History
	Periodicals. Societies. Serials see DR901+
927	Dictionaries. Chronological tables, outlines, etc
	Biography (Collective)
	For individual biography, see the specific period, reign, or place
928	General works
929	Rulers, kings, etc.
930	Queens. Princes and princesses
	Houses, noble families, etc.
931	Collective
932	Individual houses, families, etc.
933	Statesmen
934	Women
	Historiography
935	General works
	Biography of historians
936	Collective
937.A-Z	Individual, A-Z
	Study and teaching
938	General works
939.A-Z	By region or country, A-Z
	Subarrange by author
	General works
939.5	Through 1800
940	1801-1975
941	1976-
942	Pictorial works
943	Juvenile works
944	Addresses, essays, lectures
945	Philosophy of Albanian history
946	History of several parts of Albania treated together
947	Military history

Albania

History -- Continued

948	Naval history
	Political history
	For specific periods, see the period or reign
949	Sources and documents
950	General works
	Foreign and general relations
	For general works on the diplomatic history of a period, see the period
	For works on relations with a specific region or country regardless of period see DR953.A+
951	Sources and documents
952	General works
953.A-Z	Relations with individual regions or countries, A-Z
	By period
	To 1501
954	Sources and documents
955	General works
956	Through 600
	Cf. DG59.I2 Illyricum
	Cf. DR39.5 Illyrians
957	600-1190
	1190-1389. Feudal principalities
958	General works
	Biography and memoirs
958.2	Collective
958.25.A-Z	Individual, A-Z
	1389-1501. Turkish Wars
958.9	Sources and documents
959	General works
	Biography and memoirs
959.2	Collective
959.25.A-Z	Individual, A-Z
	Scanderbeg, 1443-1468
960	General works on life and reign
960.3	Kotodeshi Plain, Battle of, 1444
960.5	Albanian-Venetian War, 1447-1448
	Including Battle of the Drin, Battle of Orovnik, etc.
	1501-1912. Turkish rule
961	Sources and documents
962	General works
	1501-1840
962.9	Sources and documents
963	General works
	Biography and memoirs
963.2	Collective

Albania

History

By period

1501-1912. Turkish rule

1501-1840

Biography and memoirs -- Continued

963.25.A-Z	Individual, A-Z
	e.g.
963.25.V47	Veqilharxhi, Naum, b. 1797

Bushati family. Pashallek of Shkodër, 1757-1831

964	General works
	Biography and memoirs
964.2	Collective
964.25.A-Z	Individual, A-Z
965	Ali Paşa, Tepedelinli (Pasha of Janina), 1744?-1822

1840-1912. National renaissance. Independence movement

965.9	Sources and documents
966	General works
966.14	Social life and customs. Civilization. Intellectual life
966.18	Foreign and general relations
	Biography and memoirs
966.2	Collective
966.25.A-Z	Individual, A-Z
	e.g.
966.25.F7	Frashëri, Naum, 1846-1900
966.25.F72	Frashëri, Sami, 1850-1904
966.25.I84	Ismail Kemal Bey, 1844-1919
967	League of Prizren, 1878-1881
968	Congress of Monastir (Bitola), 1908
969	Uprisings, 1910-1912

20th century

969.8	General works
	1912-1944
970	Sources and documents
971	General works
971.18	Foreign and general relations
	Biography and memoirs
971.2	Collective
971.25.A-Z	Individual, A-Z
	e. g.
971.25.V45	Vlora, Ekrem, 1885-1964
971.25.W54	William, Prince of Wied, b. 1876
972	1912-1918. Period of Balkan War and World War I

For World War I itself see D501+

For the Balkan War, 1912-1913, itself see DR46+

1918-1925

DR

Albania
  History
    By period
      20th century
        1912-1944
          1918-1925 -- Continued

973	General works
973.5	June Revolution, 1924
	Zog I, 1925-1939
974	General works
974.5	Fier Uprising, 1935
975	1939-1944. Period of World War II
	For the war itself see D731+
	1944-1990
976	Sources and documents
977	General works
977.14	Social life and customs. Civilization. Intellectual life
977.18	Foreign and general relations
	Biography and memoirs
977.2	Collective
977.25.A-Z	Individual, A-Z
	e.g.
977.25.H67	Hoxha, Enver, 1908-
	1990-
977.9	Sources and documents
978	General works
978.2	Social life and customs. Civilization. Intellectual life
978.3	Political history
978.4	Foreign and general relations
	Biography and memoirs
978.5	Collective
978.52.A-Z	Individual, A-Z
	Local history and description
996.A-Z	Provinces, regions, etc., A-Z
996.E64	Epirus, Northern
	For ancient Epirus see DF261.E65
	For modern Epirus see DF901.E6
	Cities, towns, etc.
997	Tiranë (Table D-DR3)
998.A-Z	Other, A-Z
998.B88	Butrint
998.D85	Durrës (Durazzo, Drač)
998.H555	Himarë
998.K65	Korçë (Koritsa, Coriza)
998.S48	Shkodër (Scutari, Skadar)
998.V44	Vlorë (Valona, Vlonë)

Yugoslavia
    For works limited to specific republics, see the individual republic

1202	Periodicals. Societies. Serials
	Museums, exhibitions, etc.
1203	General works
1204.A-Z	Individual. By place, A-Z
1205	Congresses
1206	Sources and documents
	Collected works
1207	Several authors
1208	Individual authors
1209	Gazetteers. Dictionaries, etc.
1210	Place names (General)
1212	Directories
1213	Guidebooks
1214	General works
1215	General special
1216	Pictorial works
	Historic monuments, landmarks, scenery, etc. (General)
	For local see DR1350+
1217	General works
1217.5	Preservation
1218	Historical geography
	Description and travel
1220	Early through 1900
1221	1901-1944
1223	1945-1970
1224	1971-
1227	Antiquities
	For local antiquities see DR1350+
1228	Social life and customs. Civilization. Intellectual life
	For specific periods, see the period or reign
	Ethnography
1229	General works
1230.A-Z	Individual elements in the population, A-Z
	For individual elements in specific republics, see the republic
1230.A4	Albanians
1230.A75	Aromanians
1230.C75	Croats
1230.C93	Czechs
1230.G47	Germans
	Gypsies see DX271
1230.H85	Hungarians
1230.I8	Italians
1230.M3	Macedonians
1230.M65	Montenegrins
1230.M87	Muslims

DR

Yugoslavia
  Ethnography
    Individual elements in the population, A-Z -- Continued

1230.P64	Poles
1230.R65	Romanians
	Romanies see DX271
1230.R85	Russians
1230.R87	Ruthenians
1230.S46	Serbs
1230.S55	Slovaks
1230.S56	Slovenes
1230.T87	Turks
1231	Yugoslavs in foreign regions or countries (General)

        For Yugoslavs in a particular region or country, see the region
          or country
  History
    Periodicals. Societies. Serials see DR1202

1232	Dictionaries. Chronological tables, outlines, etc.

    Biography (Collective)
        For individual biography, see the specific period, reign or
          place

1233	General works
1234	Rulers, kings, etc.
1235	Statesmen

    Historiography

1239	General works

      Biography of historians, area studies specialists,
        archaeologists, etc.

1240	Collective
1241.A-Z	Individual, A-Z

    Study and teaching

1242	General works
1243.A-Z	By region or country, A-Z

      Subarrange by author
    General works

1244	Through 1800
1245	1801-1980
1246	1981-
1246.5	Pictorial works
1246.6	Juvenile works
1247	Addresses, essays, lectures. Anecdotes, etc.
1248	Philosophy of Yugoslav history
1249	History of several parts of Yugoslavia treated together

    Military history
        For specific periods, including individual campaigns and
          engagements, see the special period or reign

1250	Sources and documents

Yugoslavia

History

Military history -- Continued

1251   General works

Naval history

For specific periods, including individual campaigns and engagements, see the special period or reign

1252   Sources and documents

1253   General works

Political history

For specific periods, see the period or reign

1254   Sources and documents

1255   General works

Foreign and general relations

For general works on the diplomatic history of a period, see the period

For works on relations with a specific region or country regardless of period see DR1258.A+

1256   Sources and documents

1257   General works

1258.A-Z   Relations with individual regions or countries, A-Z

By period

Early and medieval to 1500

1259   Sources and documents

1260   General works

Biography and memoirs

1264   Collective

1265.A-Z   Individual, A-Z

1500-1800

1266   Sources and documents

1267   General works

Biography and memoirs

1271   Collective

1272.A-Z   Individual, A-Z

1800-1918

1273   Sources and documents

1274   General works

Biography and memoirs

1278   Collective

1279.A-Z   Individual, A-Z

1280   1914-1918. Period of World War I

For the war itself see D501+

1918-

1281   Sources and documents

1282   General works

1283   Biography and memoirs (Collective)

For individual biography, see the specific period

Yugoslavia
History
By period
1918- -- Continued
1918-1945. Kingdom of the Serbs, Croats, and
Slovenes (1918-1929) and Kingdom of Yugoslavia
(1929-1945)

1288	Sources and documents
1289	General works
1290	Social life and customs. Civilization. Intellectual life
1291	Political history
1292	Foreign and general relations
	Biography and memoirs
1293	Collective
1294.A-Z	Individual, A-Z
	e.g.
1294.M54	Mihailović, Draža, 1893-1946
1294.P39	Pavle, Prince of Yugoslavia, 1893-
1294.T78	Trumbić, Ante, 1864-1938
1295	Peter I, 1918-1921

For general works on Peter's life and reign, as
well as his reign as King of Serbia see
DR2030

1296	Alexander I, 1921-1934
	Peter II, 1934-1945

Including the Regency, 1934-1945

1297	General works on life and reign
1298	1941-1945. Axis occupation

For World War II see D731+

1945-1980. Tito regime

1299	Sources and documents
1300	General works on life and administration
1301	Social life and customs. Civilization. Intellectual life
1302	Political history
1303	Foreign and general relations
	Biography and memoirs
1304	Collective
1305.A-Z	Individual, A-Z
	e.g.
1305.D56	Djilas, Milovan, 1911-

1980-1992

1306	Sources and documents
1307	General works
1308	Social life and customs. Civilization. Intellectual life
1309	Political history
1310	Foreign and general relations
	Biography and memoirs

Yugoslavia
History
By period
1918-
1980-
Biography and memoirs -- Continued

1311	Collective
1312.A-Z	Individual, A-Z

Yugoslav War, 1991-1995

1313.A2	Sources and documents
1313.A4-Z	General works
1313.11	Chronology
1313.12	Pictorial works
1313.125	Study and teaching
1313.15	Juvenile literature

Military operations

1313.2	General works

By region or country
Class here works on military operations occurring
in specific places

Bosnia and Hercegovina

1313.3	General works
1313.32.A-Z	Local, A-Z

Croatia

1313.4	General works
1313.42.A-Z	Local, A-Z

Serbia/Montenegro (Yugoslavia)

1313.5	General works
1313.52.A-Z	Local, A-Z

Slovenia

1313.6	General works
1313.62.A-Z	Local, A-Z
1313.7.A-Z	Special topics, A-Z
1313.7.A47	Aerial operations
1313.7.A85	Atrocities
1313.7.B56	Blockades
1313.7.C37	Casualties
1313.7.C56	Children
1313.7.C58	Civilian relief
1313.7.C63	Commando operations
1313.7.C65	Communications
1313.7.C67	Conscientious objectors. War resisters. Draft resisters
	Concentration camps see DR1313.7.P74
1313.7.D48	Destruction and pillage
1313.7.D58	Diplomatic history
	Draft resisters see DR1313.7.C67

Yugoslavia -- Continued
Local history and description
For individual regions, geographic features, cities, etc., see the
local provisions under specific republics
1350.A-Z   Regions not limited to specific republics, A-Z
For areas of the following regions totally within particular
republics, see the local provisions under specific
republics
1350.A35   Adriatic coastal regions
1350.D35   Danube River and Valley
For the Danube River (General) see DJK76.2+
1350.D55   Dinaric Alps
Including the Karst region
1350.D7   Drava River and Valley
1350.D74   Drina River and Valley
1350.I45   Illyrian Provinces. Illyria (Kingdom)
1350.I78   Istria
1350.J84   Julian March (Venezia Giulia) (General and Yugoslavia)
Including the Littoral (Küstenland)
For Friuli Venezia Giulia (Italy) see DG975.F855
1350.L56   Lim River and Valley
1350.M54   Military Frontier (Vojna Krajina)
1350.M64   Mokra Mountains
1350.N47   Neretva River and Valley
1350.S25   Sandžak
1350.S27   Sar Mountains
1350.S29   Sava River and Valley
1350.S56   Skopska Crna Gora Mountains
Slovenia
Including Carniola
1352   Periodicals. Societies. Serials
1354   Congresses
1355   Sources and documents
Collected works
1356   Several authors
1357   Individual authors
1357.5   Gazetteers. Dictionaries, etc.
1358   Place names (General)
1358.5   Directories
1359   Guidebooks
1360   General works
1362   Pictorial works
Historic monuments, landmarks, scenery, etc. (General)
For local see DR1475+
1363   General works
1363.5   Preservation
1367   Description and travel

DR

	Yugoslavia
	Local history and description
	Slovenia -- Continued
1369	Geography
1371	Antiquities
	For local antiquities see DR1475+
1372	Social life and customs. Civilization. Intellectual life
	For specific periods, see the period or reign
	Ethnography
1373	General works
1373.5	National characteristics
1374.A-Z	Individual elements in the population, A-Z
1374.C76	Croats
1374.G47	Germans
1374.H84	Hungarians
1374.I8	Italians
1375	Slovenes in foreign regions or countries (General)
	For Slovenes in a particular region or country, see the region or country
	History
	Periodicals. Societies. Serials see DR1352
1375.5	Dictionaries. Chronological tables, outlines, etc.
	Biography (Collective)
	For individual biography, see the specific period, reign, or place
1376	General works
	Houses, noble families, etc.
1378	Collective
1378.5.A-Z	Individual houses, families, etc., A-Z
	e.g.
1378.5.C44	Celje, Counts of
	Historiography
1381	General works
	Biography of historians, area studies specialists, archaeologists, etc.
1382	Collective
1382.5.A-Z	Individual, A-Z
	Study and teaching
1383	General works
1384.A-Z	By region or country, A-Z
	Subarrange by author
1385	General works
1390	Military history
	For specific periods, including individual campaigns and engagements, see the special period or reign

Yugoslavia
Local history and description
Slovenia
History -- Continued
1391 Naval history
For specific periods, including individual campaigns and
engagements, see the special period or reign
1392 Political history
For specific periods, see the period or reign
Foreign and general relations
For general works on the diplomatic history of a period,
see the period
For works on relations with a specific region or
country regardless of period see DR1396.A+
1395 General works
1396.A-Z Relations with individual regions or countries, A-Z
By period
Early and medieval to 1456
1397 Sources and documents
1398 General works
Biography and memoirs
1402 Collective
1402.5.A-Z Individual, A-Z
1456-1814. Slovenia under Habsburg rule
1405 Sources and documents
1406 General works
1407 Social life and customs. Civilization. Intellectual
life
Biography and memoirs
1410 Collective
1410.5.A-Z Individual, A-Z
1411 Peasant Uprising, 1573
Cf. DR1573 Croatian uprising
1411.5 Peasant Uprising, 1635
1809-1814. Slovenia as part of the Illyrian
Provinces
1414 Sources and documents
1415 General works
Biography and memoirs
1419 Collective
1419.5.A-Z Individual, A-Z
1814-1918
1422 Sources and documents
1423 General works
1424 Social life and customs. Civilization. Intellectual
life
1425 Political history

DR

Yugoslavia
  Local history and description
    Slovenia
      History
        By period
          1814-1918 -- Continued
            Biography and memoirs
1427   Collective
1428.A-Z   Individual, A-Z
1430   Revolutionary events, 1848-1849
              1849-1918. Awakening of national consciousness
1431   General works
1434   1914-1918. Period of World War I
                For World War I see D501+
              1918-1945. Slovenia as part of Yugoslavia
                Including the Dravska banovina, 1929-1941
1435   Sources and documents
1436   General works
1437   Social life and customs. Civilization. Intellectual
                life
1438   Political history
              Biography and memoirs
1440   Collective
1441.A-Z   Individual, A-Z
1443   1941-1945. Axis occupation
                For World War II see D731+
              1945-1990. Federal People's Republic
1444   Sources and documents
1445   General works
1446   Social life and customs. Civilization. Intellectual
                life
1447   Political history
              Biography and memoirs
1449   Collective
1450.A-Z   Individual, A-Z
              1990-
1452   Sources and documents
1453   General works
1454   Social life and customs. Civilization. Intellectual
                life
1455   Political history
1456   Foreign and general relations
              Biography and memoirs
1457   Collective
1457.5.A-Z   Individual, A-Z
          Local history and description

Yugoslavia
  Local history and description
    Slovenia
      Local history and description -- Continued

1475.A-Z	Provinces, regions, geographic features, etc., A-Z
	e.g.
1475.C37	Carinthia
	For Carinthia (General and Austria) see DB281+
	Carniola see DR1352
1475.G67	Görz and Gradiska (Goriška) (General and Slovenia)
	For the Gorizia region (Italy) see DG975.G67
1475.J67	Julian Alps
1475.K37	Karavanke (Karawanken) Mountains
1475.M87	Mur River and Valley
1475.S56	Slovensko Primorje
1475.S89	Styria, Lower
	For Styria (General and Austria) see DB681+
	Cities and towns
1475.9	Collective
1476	Ljubljana (Table D-DR3)
1485.A-Z	Other cities, towns, etc., A-Z
	e.g.
1485.C44	Celje
	Croatia
1502	Periodicals. Societies. Serials
	Museums, exhibitions, etc.
1503	General works
1503.5.A-Z	Individual. By place, A-Z
1504	Congresses
1505	Sources and documents
	Collected works
1506	Several authors
1507	Individual authors
1507.5	Gazetteers. Dictionaries, etc.
1508	Place names (General)
1508.5	Directories
1509	Guidebooks
1510	General works
1512	Pictorial works
1513	Historic monuments, landmarks, scenery, etc. (General)
	For local see DR1620+
1515	Historical geography
1517	Description and travel
1521	Antiquities
	For local antiquities see DR1620+
1522	Social life and customs. Civilization. Intellectual life
	For specific periods, see the period or reign

DR

Yugoslavia
Local history and description
Croatia -- Continued
Ethnography

1523	General works
1523.5	National characteristics
1524.A-Z	Individual elements in the population, A-Z
1524.C94	Czechs
1524.G47	Germans
1524.H85	Hungarians
1524.R88	Russians
1524.S47	Serbs
1524.S49	Slovenes
1525	Croats in foreign regions or countries (General)

For Croats in a particular region or country, see the
region or country

History
Periodicals. Societies. Serials see DR1502+

1525.5	Dictionaries. Chronological tables, outlines, etc.

Biography (Collective)
For individual biography, see the specific period, reign or
place

1526	General works

Houses, noble families, etc.

1527	Collective
1528.A-Z	Individual houses, families, etc., A-Z
	e.g.
1528.F7	Frankopan family

Historiography

1531	General works

Biography of historians, area studies specialists,
archaeologists, etc.

1532	Collective
1532.5.A-Z	Individual, A-Z

Study and teaching

1533	General works
1534.A-Z	By region or country, A-Z
	Subarrange by author
1535	General works
1537	Pictorial works
1539	Philosophy of Croatian history
1540	Military history

For specific periods, including individual campaigns and
engagements, see the special period or reign

1541	Naval history

For specific periods, including individual campaigns and
engagements, see the special period or reign

Yugoslavia
　　Local history and description
　　　Croatia
　　　　History -- Continued
1542　　　　　　Political history
　　　　　　　　For specific periods, see the period or reign
　　　　　　Foreign and general relations
　　　　　　　　For general works on the diplomatic history of a period,
　　　　　　　　　see the period
　　　　　　　　For works on relations with a specific region or
　　　　　　　　　country, regardless of period see DR1546.A+
1545　　　　　　General works
1546.A-Z　　　　Relations with individual regions or countries, A-Z
　　　　　　By period
　　　　　　　Early to 1102. Independent kingdom
1547　　　　　　　Sources and documents
1548　　　　　　　General works
　　　　　　　　Biography and memoirs
1552　　　　　　　　Collective
1552.5.A-Z　　　　　Individual, A-Z
1554　　　　　　　　Tomislav, 910-928
1555　　　　　　　　Stjepan Drzislav, 969-997
1556　　　　　　　　Peter Krešimir, 1058-1074
1557　　　　　　　　Dimitrije Zvonimir, 1075-1089
　　　　　　　1102-1527. Arpad and Angevin dynasties
1559　　　　　　　Sources and documents
1560　　　　　　　General works
　　　　　　　　Biography and memoirs
1564　　　　　　　　Collective
1564.5.A-Z　　　　　Individual, A-Z
1566　　　　　　　　1463-1526. Turkish invasions
　　　　　　　　　　For the Battle of Mohács see DR507
　　　　　　　1527-1918. Croatia under Habsburg rule
1567　　　　　　　Sources and documents
1568　　　　　　　General works
1569　　　　　　　Social life and customs. Civilization. Intellectual
　　　　　　　　　life
1570　　　　　　　Political history
　　　　　　　　Biography and memoirs
1572　　　　　　　　Collective
1572.5.A-Z　　　　　Individual, A-Z
1573　　　　　　　Peasant Uprising, 1573
　　　　　　　　　Cf. DR1411 Slovenian uprising
1574　　　　　　　Zrinski-Frankopan Conspiracy, 1664-1671
　　　　　　　　1800-1849
1576　　　　　　　　General works
　　　　　　　　　Biography and memoirs

DR

	Yugoslavia
	Local history and description
	Croatia
	History
	By period
	1527-1918. Croatia under Habsburg rule
	1800-1849
	Biography and memoirs -- Continued
1577	Collective
1578.A-Z	Individual, A-Z
	e.g.
1578.G34	Gaj, Ljudevit, 1809-1872
1578.J44	Jelačić, Josip, 1801-1859
1578.8	Revolutionary events, 1848-1849
	1849-1918
1579	General works
	Biography and memoirs
1580	Collective
1580.5.A-Z	Individual, A-Z
	e.g.
1580.5.S8	Starčević, Ante, 1823-1896
1581	Nagodba of 1868
1581.5	Rakovica Rebellion, 1871
1582	1914-1918. Period of World War I
	For World War I see D501+
	1918-1945. Croatia as part of Yugoslavia
	Including the Savska and Primorska banovinas, 1929-1939, and Banovina Hrvatska, 1939-1941
1583	Sources and documents
1584	General works
1585	Social life and customs. Civilization. Intellectual life
1586	Political history
	Biography and memoirs
1588	Collective
1589.A-Z	Individual, A-Z
	e.g.
1589.P38	Pavelić, Ante, 1889-1959
1589.R33	Radić, Stjepan, 1871-1928
1591	1941-1945. Period of World War II. Independent state
	For World War II see D731+
	1945-1990. Federal People's Republic
1592	Sources and documents
1593	General works
1594	Social life and customs. Civilization. Intellectual life

Yugoslavia
  Local history and description
    Croatia
      History
        By period
          1945-1990. Federal People's Republic -- Continued
1595   Political history
                  Biography and memoirs
1597   Collective
1598.A-Z   Individual, A-Z
                  1990-
1600   Sources and documents
1601   General works
1602   Social life and customs. Civilization. Intellectual
                      life
1603   Political history
1604   Foreign and general relations
                    Biography and memoirs
1605   Collective
1605.2.A-Z   Individual, A-Z
                         e.g.
1605.2.T83   Tuđman, Franjo
      Local history and description
        Provinces, regions, geographic features, etc.
          Dalmatia
1620   Periodicals. Societies. Serials
1620.3   Sources and documents
1620.9   Guidebooks
1621   General works
1621.5   Pictorial works
1622   Description and travel
1623   Antiquities
                    For local antiquities see DR1637.A+
1624   Social life and customs. Civilization. Intellectual
                  life
                    For specific periods, see the period
                Ethnography
1625   General works
1625.5.A-Z   Individual elements in the population, A-Z
1625.5.G74   Greeks
1625.5.I8   Italians
1625.5.S47   Serbs
                History
1625.7   Biography (Collective)
                      For individual biography, see the specific period
1626   General works
                  By period

Yugoslavia
  Local history and description
    Croatia
      Local history and description
        Provinces, regions, geographic features, etc.
          Dalmatia
          History
            By period -- Continued

1627	Early to 1420
1628	1420-1797. Venetian rule
	1797-1918. Austrian rule
1629	General works
	Biography and memoirs
1629.4	Collective
1629.5.A-Z	Individual, A-Z
1629.6	French occupation, 1797-1814
	1918-
1630	General works
	Biography and memoirs
1630.4	Collective
1630.5.A-Z	Individual, A-Z
	Slavonia
1633	Periodicals. Societies. Serials
1633.3	Sources and documents
1633.9	Guidebooks
1634	General works
1634.5	Pictorial works
1635	Description and travel
1635.5	Antiquities
1635.6	Social life and customs. Civilization. Intellectual life
	For specific period, see the period
	Ethnography
1635.7	General works
1635.75.A-Z	Individual elements in the population, A-Z
1635.75.G47	Germans
1635.75.S565	Slovaks
	History
1635.8	Biography (Collective)
	For individual biography, see the specific period
1636	General works
1636.2	General special
	By period
1636.3	Early to 1526
1636.4	1526-1918
1636.5	1918-

	Yugoslavia
	Local history and description
	Croatia
	Local history and description
	Provinces, regions, geographic features, etc. -- Continued
1637.A-Z	Other regions, etc., A-Z
	e.g.
1637.B37	Baranja
	For Baranya (General and Hungary) see DB975.B3
1637.H78	Hrvatsko Zagorje
1637.H85	Hvar
1637.M43	Medjimurje
1637.M55	Military Frontier (Militärgrenze)
	Cities and towns
1638	Zagreb (Table D-DR3)
1645.A-Z	Other cities and towns, etc., A-Z
	e.g.
1645.D8	Dubrovnik
	Bosnia and Hercegovina
	Class here works on Bosnia alone or Bosnia and Hercegovina together
	For Hercegovina alone see DR1775.H47
1652	Periodicals. Societies. Serials
	Museums, exhibitions, etc.
1653	General works
1653.5.A-Z	Individual. By place, A-Z
1654	Congresses
1655	Sources and documents
	Collected works
1656	Several authors
1657	Individual authors
1657.5	Gazetteers. Dictionaries, etc.
1658	Place names (General)
1659	Guidebooks
1660	General works
1662	Pictorial works
1663	Historic monuments, landmarks, scenery, etc. (General)
	For local see DR1775+
1665	Historical geography
1667	Description and travel
1671	Antiquities
	For local antiquities see DR1775+
1672	Social life and customs. Civilization. Intellectual life
	For specific periods, see the period or reign
	Ethnography

DR

	Yugoslavia
	Local history and description
	Bosnia and Hercegovina
	Ethnography -- Continued
1673	General works
1674.A-Z	Individual elements in the population, A-Z
1674.A76	Aromanians
1674.C76	Croats
1674.G47	Germans
1674.M87	Muslims
1674.R65	Romanians
1674.S47	Serbs
1674.U47	Ukrainians
	History
	Periodicals. Societies. Serials see DR1652+
1675.5	Dictionaries. Chronological tables, outlines, etc.
	Biography (Collective)
	For individual biography, see the specific period, reign, or place
1676	General works
	Houses, noble families, etc.
1677	Collective
1678.A-Z	Individual houses, families, etc., A-Z
	Historiography
1681	General works
	Biography of historians, area studies specialists, archaeologists, etc.
1682	Collective
1682.5.A-Z	Individual, A-Z
	Study and teaching
1683	General works
1684.A-Z	By region or country, A-Z
	Subarrange by author
1685	General works
1690	Military history
	For specific periods, including individual campaigns and engagements, see the special period or reign
1692	Political history
	For specific periods, see the special period or reign
	Foreign and general relations
	For general works on the diplomatic history of a period, see the period
	For works on relations with a specific region or country regardless of period see DR1696.A+
1695	General works
1696.A-Z	Relations with individual regions or countries, A-Z
	By period

Yugoslavia
Local history and description
Bosnia and Hercegovina
History
By period -- Continued
Early to 1463
1697   Sources and documents
1698   General works
1699   Social life and customs. Civilization. Intellectual
               life
           Biography and memoirs
1702   Collective
1702.5.A-Z   Individual, A-Z
           Early to 1254
1703   General works
1705   Kulin, 1180-1204
           1254-1463. Kotromanić dynasty
1706   General works
1707   Stefan Kotromanić, 1322-1353
1708   Tvrtko I, 1353-1391
1710   Tomaš, 1443-1461
           1463-1878. Turkish rule
1711   Sources and documents
1712   General works
1713   Social life and customs. Civilization. Intellectual
               life
           Biography and memoirs
1716   Collective
1717.A-Z   Individual, A-Z
           Rebellion of 1875
1720   General works
1720.5   Personal narratives
1721.A-Z   Local history. By place, A-Z
           1878-1918. Austrian administration
1722   Sources and documents
1723   General works
1724   Social life and customs. Civilization. Intellectual
               life
1725   Political history
           Biography and memoirs
1727   Collective
1728.A-Z   Individual, A-Z
1731   Annexation to Austria, 1908. Bosnian crisis
1732   1914-1918. Period of World War I
               For World War I see D501+

Yugoslavia
  Local history and description
    Bosnia and Hercegovina
      History
        By period -- Continued
          1918-1945. Bosnia and Hercegovina as part of
            Yugoslavia
              Including the Drinska and Vrbaska banovinas, 1929-
                1944

1733	Sources and documents
1734	General works
1735	Social life and customs. Civilization. Intellectual life
1736	Political history
	Biography and memoirs
1738	Collective
1739.5.A-Z	Individual, A-Z
1741	1941-1945. Axis occupation
	For World War II see D731+
	1945-1992. Federal People's Republic. Socialist Republic
1742	Sources and documents
1743	General works
1744	Social life and customs. Civilization. Intellectual life
1745	Political history
	Biography and memoirs
1747	Collective
1748.A-Z	Individual, A-Z
	1992- . Independent State
1749	Sources and documents
1750	General works
1751	Social life and customs. Civilization. Intellectual life
1752	Political history
1753	Foreign and general relations
	Biography and memoirs
1754	Collective
1755.A-Z	Individual, A-Z
1756	Partition, 1995
	Local history and description
1775.A-Z	Provinces, regions, geographic features, etc., A-Z
	e.g.
1775.H47	Hercegovina (Hum)
1775.K7	Krajina
1775.M34	Majevica Mountains
	Cities and towns

Yugoslavia
Local history and description
Bosnia and Hercegovina
Local history and description
Cities and towns -- Continued

1776	Sarajevo (Table D-DR3)
1785.A-Z	Other cities and towns, etc., A-Z
	e.g.
1785.B35	Banja Luka

Montenegro

1802	Periodicals. Societies. Serials
1804	Congresses
1805	Sources and documents

Collected works

1806	Several authors
1807	Individual authors
1807.5	Gazetteers. Dictionaries, etc.
1808	Place names (General)
1809	Guidebooks
1810	General works
1812	Pictorial works
1813	Historic monuments, landmarks, scenery, etc. (General)
	For local see DR1925+
1817	Description and travel
1821	Antiquities
	For local antiquities see DR1925+
1822	Social life and customs. Civilization. Intellectual life
	For specific periods, see the period or reign

Ethnography

1823	General works
1824.A-Z	Individual elements in the population, A-Z
1824.A4	Albanians
1825	Montenegrins in foreign regions or countries

History
Periodicals. Societies. Serials see DR1802+
Biography (Collective)
For individual biography, see the specific period, reign, or place

1827	General works
1827.5	Rulers, kings, etc.
1827.7	Queens. Princes and princesses

Houses, noble families, etc.

1828	Collective
1829.A-Z	Individual houses, families, etc., A-Z
	e.g.
1829.P48	Petrović-Njegosh, House of

Historiography

Yugoslavia
 Local history and description
  Montenegro
   History
    Historiography -- Continued
1832   General works
                         Biography of historians, area studies specialists,
                          archaeologists, etc.
1833   Collective
1833.5.A-Z   Individual, A-Z
                         Study and teaching
1834   General works
1834.5.A-Z   By region or country, A-Z
                           Subarrange by author
1835   General works
1840   Military history
                         For special periods, including individual campaigns and
                          engagements, see the special period or reign
1841   Naval history
                         For special periods, including individual campaigns and
                          engagements, see the period or reign
1842   Political history
                         For special periods, see the period or reign
                        Foreign and general relations
                         For general works on the diplomatic history of a period,
                          see the period
                         For works on relations with a specific region or
                          country regardless of period see DR1846.A+
1845   General works
1846.A-Z   Relations with individual regions or countries, A-Z
                        By period
                         Early to 1516
                           Including the province of Zeta (Duklja)
1847   Sources and documents
1848   General works
                          Biography and memoirs
1852   Collective
1852.5.A-Z   Individual, A-Z
                         1516-1782. Vladike
1855   Sources and documents
1856   General works
                           Biography and memoirs
1860   Collective
1860.5.A-Z   Individual, A-Z
1863   Danilo I, 1697-1735
                            Sava, 1735-1782
1864   General works on life and reign

Yugoslavia
  Local history and description
    Montenegro
      History
        By period
          1516-1782. Vladike
            Sava, 1735-1782 -- Continued

1865	Vasilije, 1740-1766
1866	Stephan Mali, 1768-1774

          1782-1918. Expansion and secularization

1867	Sources and documents
1868	General works
1869	Social life and customs. Civilization. Intellectual life

            Biography and memoirs

1872	Collective
1873.A-Z	Individual, A-Z
1874	Peter I, 1782-1830
1875	Peter II, 1830-1851

            Danilo II, 1851-1860

1876	General works on life and reign

              Biography and memoirs

1877	Collective
1877.5.A-Z	Individual, A-Z
	e.g.
1877.5.D37	Darinka, Queen Consort of Danilo, 1836-1892

            Nicholas I, 1860-1918

1878	General works on life and reign

              Biography and memoirs

1879	Collective
1879.5.A-Z	Individual, A-Z
	e.g.
1879.5.R33	Radović, Andrija, 1872-
1881	Turco-Montenegrin War, 1876-1878
1883	1912-1918. Period of the Balkan Wars and World War I

For World War I see D501+
For the Balkan Wars see DR46+

          1918-1945. Montenegro as part of Yugoslavia
            Including the Zetska banovina, 1929-1941

1884	Sources and documents
1885	General works
1886	Social life and customs. Civilization. Intellectual life
1887	Political history

            Biography and memoirs

1890	Collective

Yugoslavia
  Local history and description
    Montenegro
      History
        By period
          1918-1945. Montenegro as part of Yugoslavia
            Biography and memoirs -- Continued

1891.A-Z	Individual, A-Z
1892	Christmas Uprising, 1918
1893	1941-1945. Period of World War II

                  For World War II see D731+

              1945-1992. Federal People's Republic. Socialist Republic

1894	Sources and documents
1895	General works
1896	Social life and customs. Civilization. Intellectual life
1897	Political history

              Biography and memoirs

1899	Collective
1900.A-Z	Individual, A-Z

             1992-

1901	Sources and documents
1902	General works
1903	Social life and customs. Civilization. Intellectual life
1904	Political history
1905	Foreign and general relations

             Biography and memoirs

1906	Collective
1907.A-Z	Individual, A-Z

          Local history and description

1925.A-Z	Provinces, regions, geographic features, etc., A-Z

              e.g.

1925.K38	Kotorska Boka
1925.N67	North Albanian Alps
1925.S56	Skadarsko jezero (Scutari Lake)

           Cities and towns

1927	Podgorica (Titograd) (Table D-DR3)
1928.A-Z	Other cities, towns, etc., A-Z

              e.g.

1928.C48	Cetinje

        Serbia

1932	Periodicals. Societies. Serials
1934	Congresses
1935	Sources and documents

          Collected works

	Yugoslavia
	Local history and description
	Serbia
	Collected works -- Continued
1936	Several authors
1937	Individual authors
1937.5	Gazetteers. Dictionaries, etc.
1938	Place names (General)
1938.5	Directories
1939	Guidebooks
1940	General works
1942	Pictorial works
1943	Historic monuments, landmarks, scenery, etc. (General)
	For local see DR2075+
1945	Historical geography
1947	Description and travel
1951	Antiquities
	For local antiquities see DR2075+
1952	Social life and customs. Civilization. Intellectual life
	For specific periods, see the period or reign
	Ethnography
1953	General works
1953.5	National characteristics
1954.A-Z	Individual elements in the population, A-Z
	For individual elements in Kosovo see DR2080.5.A+
	For individual elements in Vojvodina see DR2095.5.A+
1954.A43	Albanians
1954.B84	Bulgarians
1954.G74	Greeks
1954.K34	Kalmyks
1954.M34	Macedonians
1954.M87	Muslims
1954.P64	Polabian Slavs
1954.R65	Romanians
1954.R87	Russians
1955	Serbs in foreign regions or countries (General)
	For Serbs in a particular region or country, see the region or country
	History
	Periodicals. Societies. Serials see DR1932+
	Biography (Collective)
	For individual biography, see the specific period, reign, or place
1956	General works
1956.5	Rulers, kings, etc.

	Yugoslavia
	Local history and description
	Serbia
	History
	Biography (Collective) -- Continued
1956.7	Queens. Princes and princesses
	Houses, noble families, etc.
1957	Collective
1958.A-Z	Individual houses, families, etc., A-Z
	e.g.
1958.O26	Obrenović, House of
	Historiography
1961	General works
	Biography of historians, area studies specialists,
	archaeologists, etc.
1962	Collective
1962.5.A-Z	Individual, A-Z
	Study and teaching
1963	General works
1964.A-Z	By region or country, A-Z
	Subarrange by author
1965	General works
1970	Military history
	For specific periods, including individual campaigns and
	engagements, see the period or reign
1972	Political history
	For specific periods, see the period or reign
	Foreign and general relations
	For general works on the diplomatic history of a period,
	see the period
	For works on relations with a specific region or
	country regardless of period see DR1976.A+
1975	General works
1976.A-Z	Relations with individual regions or countries, A-Z
	By period
	Early to 1459
1977	Sources and documents
1978	General works
	Biography and memoirs
1982	Collective
1982.5.A-Z	Individual, A-Z
1983	Early to 1167. House of Višeslav. Rise of Raška
	For Zeta see DR1847+
1985	1167-1389. Nemanja dynasty
1986	Stefan Nemanja, 1167-1196
1987	Stefan Prvovenčani, 1196-1228
1989	Stefan Uros I, 1243-1276

Yugoslavia
　Local history and description
　　Serbia
　　　History
　　　　By period
　　　　　Early to 1459
　　　　　　1167-1389. Nemanja dynasty -- Continued
1990　　　　　　　Milutin (Stefan Uroš II), 1282-1321
1991　　　　　　　Stefan Uroš III, Dečanski, 1322-1331
1992　　　　　　　Stefan Dušan, 1331-1355
1993　　　　　　　Uros, 1355-1371
　　　　　　　　Lazar, 1371-1389
1994　　　　　　　　General works on life and reign
　　　　　　　　　Biography and memoirs
1995　　　　　　　　　Collective
1995.5.A-Z　　　　　　Individual, A-Z
　　　　　　　　　　　e.g.
1995.5.M37　　　　　　　Marko, Prince of Serbia, 1335-1394
　　　　　　　　　Battle of Kosovo, 1389 see DR495
　　　　　　　1389-1459. Despotate
1996　　　　　　　General works
1997　　　　　　　Stefan Lazarevič, 1389-1427
　　　　　　　　Đurađ Branković, 1427-1456
1998　　　　　　　　General works on life and reign
　　　　　　　　　Biography and memoirs
1999　　　　　　　　　Collective
1999.5　　　　　　　　Individual, A-Z
　　　　　　　　　　　e.g.
1999.5.M5　　　　　　　Micha¿owicz, Konstanty, b. ca. 1435
　　　　　　　　　Battle of Varna, 1444 see DR498
　　　　　　　　　Battle of Kosovo, 1448 see DR498
　　　　　　　1459-1804. Turkish rule
2000　　　　　　　Sources and documents
2001　　　　　　　General works
2002　　　　　　　Social life and customs. Civilization. Intellectual
　　　　　　　　　life
2003　　　　　　　Political history
　　　　　　　　Biography and memoirs
2004　　　　　　　　Collective
2004.5.A-Z　　　　　　Individual, A-Z
　　　　　　　　　　e.g.
2004.5.B7　　　　　　　Branković, Đorđe, grof, 1645-1711
2004.8　　　　　　Great Emigration, 1690
2005　　　　　　Insurrection, 1788
　　　　　　　1804-1918. Autonomy and independence
2006　　　　　　　Sources and documents
2007　　　　　　　General works

DR

Yugoslavia
  Local history and description
    Serbia
      History
        By period
          1804-1918. Autonomy and independence --
            Continued

2008	Social life and customs. Civilization. Intellectual life
2009	Political history
2010	Foreign and general relations
	Biography and memoirs
2012	Collective
2012.5.A-Z	Individual, A-Z
	e.g.
2012.5.G37	Garašanin, Ilija, 1812-1874
2012.5.P37	Pašić, Nikola, 1845-1926
2012.5.R57	Ristić, Jovan, 1831-1899
	Insurrections, 1804-1813
2013	Sources and documents
2014	General works
	Biography and memoirs
2015	Collective
2015.5.A-Z	Individual, A-Z
	e.g.
2015.5.K37	Karađorđe, 1768?-1817
2015.7	Ivankovac, Battle of, 1805
	Miloš Obrenović I, 1814-1839
2016	General works on life and reign
	Biography and memoirs
2017	Collective
2017.5.A-Z	Individual, A-Z
2017.6	Insurrection, 1815-1817
2017.8	Milan II, 1839
2018	Mihail Obrenović III, 1839-1842
	Alexander Karađorđević, 1842-1858
2019	General works on life and reign
	Biography and memoirs
2020	Collective
2020.5.A-Z	Individual, A-Z
2021	Miloš I, 1858-1860
	Mihail III, 1860-1868
2022	General works on life and reign
	Biography and memoirs
2023	Collective
2023.5.A-Z	Individual, A-Z

Yugoslavia
  Local history and description
    Serbia
      History
        By period
          1804-1918. Autonomy and independence --
            Continued
            Milan Obrenović IV, 1868-1889
              Including the Regency, 1868-1872
2024   General works on life and reign
                  Biography and memoirs
2025   Collective
2025.5.A-Z   Individual, A-Z
2025.8   Serbo-Turkish War, 1876
2026   Serbo-Turkish War, 1877-1878
2026.8   Revolt, 1883
2027   Serbo-Bulgarian War, 1885
            Aleksandar Obrenović, 1889-1903
              Including the Regency, 1889-1893
2028   General works on life and reign
                  Biography and memoirs
2029   Collective
2029.5.A-Z   Individual, A-Z
                      e.g.
2029.5.D7   Draga, Queen Consort of Aleksandar, 1867-
                        1903
            Peter I Karađorđević, 1903-1918
              For Peter's reign as King of the Kingdom of the
                Serbs, Croats and Slovenes (1918-1921)
                see DR1295
2029.9   Sources and documents
2030   General works on life and reign
                  Biography and memoirs
2031   Collective
2031.5.A-Z   Individual, A-Z
2032   1912-1918. Period of the Balkan Wars and World
                    War I
                    For World War I see D501+
                    For the Balkan Wars see DR46+
2032.5   20th century (General)
                1918-1945. Serbia as part of Yugoslavia
                  Including the Dunavska and Moravska banovinas,
                    1929-1941
2033   Sources and documents
2034   General works
2035   Social life and customs. Civilization. Intellectual
                    life

DR

Yugoslavia
 Local history and description
  Serbia
   Local history and description
    Provinces, regions, geographic features, etc.
     Kosovo -- Continued

2078	Antiquities
	For local antiquities see DR2105.A+
2079	Social life and customs. Civilization. Intellectual life
	For specific periods, see the period or reign
	Ethnography
2080	General works
2080.5.A-Z	Individual elements in the population, A-Z
2080.5.A4	Albanians
2080.5.S47	Serbs
	History
2081	Biography (Collective)
	For individual biography, see the specific period, reign, or place
2081.3	Historiography
2082	General works
	By period
2083	Early to 1389
	Battle of Kosovo, 1389 see DR495
	1389-1913. Turkish rule
	Including the Kosovo vilayet
2084	General works
	Biography and memoirs
2084.4	Collective
2084.5.A-Z	Individual, A-Z
	1913-1945. Kosovo as part of Serbia and Yugoslavia
2085	General works
	Biography and memoirs
2085.4	Collective
2085.5.A-Z	Individual, A-Z
	e.g.
2085.5.P74	Prishtina, Hasan, 1873-1933
	1945- . Autonomous region
2086	General works
	Biography and memoirs
2086.4	Collective
2086.5.A-Z	Individual, A-Z
	Civil War, 1998-1999
2087	General works
2087.12	Pictorial works

Yugoslavia
  Local history and description
    Serbia
      Local history and description
        Provinces, regions, geographic features, etc.
          Kosovo
           History
             By period
               1945- . Autonomous region
                 Civil War, 1998-1999 -- Continued

2087.2.A-Z	Local events, battles, etc. By place, A-Z
2087.5	Operation Allied Force, 1999
2087.6.A-Z	Special topics, A-Z
2087.6.A76	Atrocities
2087.6.C37	Casualties
2087.6.C54	Children
2087.6.C59	Civilian relief
2087.6.D46	Destruction and pillage
2087.6.D54	Diplomatic history
2087.6.E45	Environmental aspects
	Foreign participation
2087.6.F65	General works
2087.6.F652.A-Z	By region or country, A-Z
2087.6.F67	Foreign public opinion
2087.6.H46	Health aspects
2087.6.M37	Mass media
2087.6.M67	Moral and ethical aspects
2087.6.P33	Pacifism
2087.6.P43	Peace
2087.6.P72	Press coverage
2087.6.P74	Protest movements
2087.6.R34	Radio broadcasting
2087.6.R43	Refugees
2087.6.R45	Religious aspects
2087.6.T44	Technology
2087.7	Personal narratives

          Vojvodina

2090	Periodicals. Societies. Serials
2090.3	Sources and documents
2090.9	Guidebooks
2091	General works
2091.5	Pictorial works
2092	Description and travel
2093	Antiquities
	For local antiquities see DR2105.A+

Yugoslavia
  Local history and description
    Serbia
      Local history and description
        Provinces, regions, geographic features, etc.
          Vojvodina -- Continued
2094   Social life and customs. Civilization. Intellectual
                  life
                  For specific periods, see the period or reign
                Ethnography
2095   General works
2095.5.A-Z   Individual elements in the population, A-Z
2095.5.C75   Croats
2095.5.G47   Germans
2095.5.H85   Hungarians
2095.5.R65   Romanians
2095.5.R87   Ruthenians
2095.5.S47   Serbs
2095.5.S56   Slovaks
                History
2096   Biography (Collective)
                    For individual biography, see the specific period,
                      reign, or place
2097   General works
                By period
2098   Early to 1526
                  1526-1918. Turkish rule and Austro-Hungarian
                    rule
2099   General works
                   Biography and memoirs
2099.4   Collective
2099.5.A-Z   Individual, A-Z
2099.7   Revolutionary events, 1848-1849
                  1918-1945. Vojvodina as part of Yugoslavia
2100   General works
                   Biography and memoirs
2100.4   Collective
2100.5.A-Z   Individual, A-Z
                  1945-   . Autonomous region
2101   General works
                   Biography and memoirs
2101.4   Collective
2101.5.A-Z   Individual, A-Z
2105.A-Z   Other regions, etc., A-Z
                  e.g.

Yugoslavia
Local history and description
Serbia
Local history and description
Provinces, regions, geographic features, etc.
Other regions, etc., A-Z -- Continued

2105.B32	Bačka (General and Serbia)
	Including works on Bács-Bodrog
	For Bácska (Hungary) see DB975.B15
2105.B35	Banat
	For Banat (General, and Romania) see DR281.B25
2105.I75	Iron Gates region (Đerdap) (General and Serbia)
2105.K67	Kosovo Polje
2105.M48	Metohija
2105.R84	Ruĭ Mountains
	For the Ruĭ Mountains (General and Bulgaria) see DR95.R8
2105.T57	Tisa (Tisza) River and Valley
	Cities and towns
	Belgrade
2106	Periodicals. Societies. Serials
2107	Museums, exhibitions, etc.
	Subarrange by author
2108	Sources and documents
	Collected works
2108.4	Several authors
2108.5	Individual authors
2108.6	Directories. Dictionaries. Gazetteers
2109	Guidebooks
2110	General works
2111	Description
2113	Pictorial works
2114	Antiquities
2115	Social life and customs. Intellectual life
	Ethnography
2116	General works
2116.5.A-Z	Individual elements in the population, A-Z
	History
2117	Biography (Collective)
	For individual biography, see the specific period
2118	General works
	By period
2119	Early and medieval
2119.2	1500-1918
2119.3	1918-
	Sections, districts, suburbs, etc.

	Yugoslavia
	Local history and description
	Serbia
	Local history and description
	Cities and towns
	Belgrade
	Sections, districts, suburbs, etc. -- Continued
2120	Collective
2120.5.A-Z	Individual, A-Z
	Monuments, statues, etc.
2121	Collective
2121.5.A-Z	Individual, A-Z
	Parks, squares, cemeteries, etc.
2122	Collective
2122.5.A-Z	Individual, A-Z
	Streets. Bridges
2123	Collective
2123.5.A-Z	Individual, A-Z
	Buildings
2124	Collective
2124.5.A-Z	Individual, A-Z
2125.A-Z	Other cities, towns, etc., A-Z
	e.g.
2125.N57	Niš
	Macedonia
	Class here works on medieval and modern Macedonia and the Socialist Republic of Macedonia
	For Macedonian period and King Philip see DF232.5+
	For ancient Greek Macedonia see DF261.M2
	For Aegean Macedonia (Greece) see DF901.M3
	For Pirin Macedonia (Bulgaria) see DR95.B55
2152	Periodicals. Societies. Serials
2154	Congresses
2155	Sources and documents
	Collected works
2156	Several authors
2157	Individual authors
2157.5	Gazetteers. Dictionaries, etc.
2158	Place names (General)
2159	Guidebooks
2160	General works
2162	Pictorial works
2163	Historic monuments, landmarks, scenery, etc. (General)
	For local see DR2275+
2165	Historical geography
2167	Description and travel

Yugoslavia
Local history and description
Macedonia -- Continued

2171	Antiquities
	For local antiquities see DR2275+
2172	Social life and customs. Civilization. Intellectual life
	For specific periods, see the period or reign
	Ethnography
2173	General works
2173.5	National characteristics
2174.A-Z	Individual elements in the population, A-Z
2174.A52	Albanians
2174.A75	Aromanians
2174.B84	Bulgarians
2174.E36	Egyptians
2174.G73	Greeks
2174.M87	Muslims
2174.S47	Serbs
2174.S55	Slavs
2174.T87	Turks
2175	Macedonians in foreign countries (General)
	History
	Periodicals. Societies. Serials see DR2152+
2175.5	Dictionaries. Chronological tables, outlines, etc.
2176	Biography (Collective)
	For individual biography, see the specific period, reign, or place
	Historiography
2181	General works
	Biography of historians, area studies specialists, archaeologists, etc.
2182	Collective
2182.5.A-Z	Individual, A-Z
	Study and teaching
2183	General works
2184.A-Z	By region or country, A-Z
	Subarrange by author
2185	General works
2187	Philosophy of Macedonian history
2188	History of several parts of Macedonia treated together
2190	Military history
	For specific periods, including individual campaigns and engagements, see the special period or reign
2192	Political history
	For specific periods, see the period or reign

Yugoslavia
  Local history and description
    Macedonia
      History -- Continued
        Foreign and general relations
            For general works on the diplomatic history of a period,
              see the period
            For works on relations with a specific country
              regardless of period see DR2196
2195   General works
2196   Relations with individual regions or countries, A-Z
          By period
            Early to 1389
2197   Sources and documents
2198   General works
              Biography and memoirs
2202   Collective
2202.5.A-Z   Individual, A-Z
              Battle of Kosovo see DR495
            1389-1912. Turkish rule
2205   Sources and documents
2206   General works
2207   Social life and customs. Civilization. Intellectual
                  life
              Biography and memoirs
2210   Collective
2210.5.A-Z   Individual, A-Z
2211   Karpos Uprising, 1689
2212   19th century (General)
              1878-1912. Independence movement
2213   Sources and documents
2214   General works
2215   Political history
2216   Foreign and general relations
                Biography and memoirs
2217   Collective
2218.A-Z   Individual, A-Z
                      e.g.
2218.D14   Delcev, Goce, 1872-1903
2218.G78   Gruev, Damian Ivanov, 1871-1906
2218.S25   Sandanski, Jane, 1875-1915
2219   Kresna Uprising, 1878
                Ilinden Uprising, 1903
2221   Sources and documents
2223   General works
2225   Personal narratives
2226.A-Z   Local history. By place, A-Z

	Yugoslavia
	Local history and description
	Macedonia
	History
	By period
	1992- . Independent state -- Continued
2253	Political history
2254	Foreign and general relations
	Biography and memoirs
2255	Collective
2256.A-Z	Individual, A-Z
	Local history and description
2275.A-Z	Provinces, regions, geographic features, etc., A-Z
	e.g.
2275.B58	Bitola
	Including the Monastir vilayet
2275.D64	Dojransko ezero
2275.O64	Ohridsko ezero
2275.P44	Pelagonia
2275.P73	Prespansko ezero
2275.V3	Vardar River and Valley
	Cities and towns
2276	Skopje (Table D-DR3)
2285.A-Z	Other cities and towns, etc., A-Z
	e.g.
2285.A1	Collective
2285.P74	Prilep

.A2	Periodicals. Societies
.A3	Sources and documents. Serials
.A5-.Z	General works
.2	Description and travel. Guidebooks. Gazetteers
.3	Antiquities
.4	Social life and customs. Civilization. Intellectual life
.42	Ethnography
	History
.5	General works
.6	Biography (Collective)
	Political history. Foreign and general relations
.62	General works
(.622)	By period
	see the specific period
.63.A-Z	Relations with individual countries, A-Z
	By period
	Early
.65	General works
	Biography and memoirs
.66.A2	Collective
.66.A3-Z	Individual, A-Z
	Colonial
.7	General works
	Biography and memoirs
.72.A2	Collective
.72.A3-Z	Individual, A-Z
	20th century
.75	General works
	Biography and memoirs
.76.A2	Collective
.76.A3-Z	Individual, A-Z
	Independent
.8	General works
	Biography and memoirs
.82.A2	Collective
.82.A3-Z	Individual, A-Z
.9.A-Z	Local, A-Z

.xA2-.xA29	Periodicals. Societies
.xA3-.xA39	Sources and documents. Serials
.xA5-.xZ	General works
.x2	Description and travel. Guidebooks. Gazetteers
.x3	Antiquities
.x4	Social life and customs. Civilization. Intellectual life
.x42	Ethnography
	History
.x5	General works
.x6	Biography (Collective)
	Political history. Foreign and general relations
.x62	General works
(.x622)	By period
	see the specific period
.x63A-.x63Z	Relations with individual countries, A-Z
	By period
	Early
.x65	General works
	Biography and memoirs
.x66A2-.x66A29	Collective
.x66A3-.x66Z	Individual, A-Z
	Colonial
.x7	General works
	Biography and memoirs
.x72A2-.x72A29	Collective
.x72A3-.x72Z	Individual, A-Z
	20th century
.x75	General works
	Biography and memoirs
.x76A2-.x76A29	Collective
.x76A3-.x76Z	Individual, A-Z
	Independent
.x8	General works
	Biography and memoirs
.x82A2-.x82A29	Collective
.x82A3-.x82Z	Individual, A-Z
.x9A-.x9Z	Local, A-Z

TABLES

	To be used only where indicated in schedule
.A2	Periodicals. Societies. Serials
.A3	Museums, exhibitions, etc.
	Subarrange by author
.A4	Guidebooks. Gazetteers. Directories
.A5-.Z	General works. Description
.1	Pictorial works
.13	Addresses, essays, lectures. Anecdotes, etc.
.15	Antiquities
.2	Social life and customs. Civilization. Intellectual life
	History
	Biography
.23.A2	Collective
.23.A3-Z	Individual, A-Z
.25	Historiography. Study and teaching
.3	General works
	Sections, districts, suburbs, etc.
.4.A2	Collective
.4.A3-Z	Individual, A-Z
	Monuments, statues, etc.
.5.A2	Collective
.5.A3-Z	Individual, A-Z
	Parks, squares, cemeteries, etc.
.6.A2	Collective
.6.A3-Z	Individual, A-Z
	Streets, bridges, etc.
.7.A2	Collective
.7.A3-Z	Individual, A-Z
	Buildings
.8.A2	Collective
.8.A3-Z	Individual, A-Z
	Elements in the population
.9.A2	Collective
.9.A3-Z	Individual, A-Z
	Natural features such as mountains, rivers, etc.
.95.A2	Collective
.95.A3-Z	Individual, A-Z

	To be used only where indicated in schedule
	The x in this table represents the cutter number for the city
.x	Periodicals. Societies. Serials
.x2	Museums, exhibitions, etc.
	Subarrange by author
.x3	Guidebooks. Gazetteers. Directories
.x4	General works. Description
.x43	Pictorial works
.x45	Addresses, essays, lectures. Anecdotes, etc.
.x47	Antiquities
.x5	Social life and customs. Civilization. Intellectual life
	History
	Biography
.x53A2-.x53A29	Collective
.x53A3-.x53Z	Individual, A-Z
.x55	Historiography. Study and teaching
.x57	General works
	Sections, districts, suburbs, etc.
.x6A2-.x6A29	Collective
.x6A3-.x6Z	Individual, A-Z
	Monuments, statues, etc.
.x65A2-.x65A29	Collective
.x65A3-.x65Z	Individual, A-Z
	Parks, squares, cemeteries, etc.
.x7A2-.x7A29	Collective
.x7A3-.x7Z	Individual, A-Z
	Streets, bridges, etc.
.x75A2-.x75A29	Collective
.x75A3-.x75Z	Individual, A-Z
	Buildings
.x8A2-.x8A29	Collective
.x8A3-.x8Z	Individual, A-Z
	Elements in the population
.x9A2-.x9A29	Collective
.x9A3-.x9Z	Individual, A-Z
	Natural features such as mountains, rivers, etc.
.x95A2-.x95A29	Collective
.x95A3-.x95Z	Individual, A-Z

TABLES

.xA2-.xA29	Periodicals. Societies. Serials
.xA3-.xA39	Sources and documents
.xA5-.xZ	General works
.x2	Description and travel. Guidebooks. Gazetteers
.x3	Antiquities
.x4	Social life and customs. Civilization. Intellectual life
.x42	Ethnography
	History
.x5	General works
.x6	Biography (Collective)
	Political history. Foreign and general relations
.x62	General works
	By period
	see the specific period
.x63A-.x63Z	Relations with individual countries, A-Z
	By period
	Early and medieval to 1526
.x65	General works
	Biography and memoirs
.x66A2-.x66A29	Collective
.x66A3-.x66Z	Individual, A-Z
	1526-1815
.x7	General works
	Biography and memoirs
.x72A2-.x72A29	Collective
.x72A3-.x72Z	Individual, A-Z
	1815-1918
.x75	General works
	Biography and memoirs
.x76A2-.x76A29	Collective
.x76A3-.x76Z	Individual, A-Z
	1918-1945
.x8	General works
	Biography and memoirs
.x82A2-.x82A29	Collective
.x82A3-.x82Z	Individual, A-Z
	1945-1989
.x85	General works
	Biography and memoirs
.x86A2-.x86A29	Collective
.x86A3-.x86Z	Individual, A-Z
	1989-
.x88	General works
	Biography and memoirs
.x89A2-.x89A29	Collective
.x89A3-.x89Z	Individual, A-Z

History -- Continued

(.x9)   Local, A-Z

see separate Cutter numbers in DK4600, DK4800

TABLES

1	Periodicals. Societies. Serials
2	Congresses
3	Sources and documents. Collections
4	Gazetteers
4.5	Place names
4.7	Directories
5	Guidebooks
6	Description and history (General)
	Description and travel
7	Early and medieval
8	1601-1800
9	1801-1945
9.2	1945-
10	Antiquities
10.5	Social life and customs. Civilization. Intellectual life
10.7	Ethnography
	History
11	Dictionaries, tables, etc.
	Biography
12.A2	Collective
12.A3-Z	Individual, A-Z
12.5	Historiography
	General works
14	Through 1800
15	1801-
15.1	Compends
16	General special
	By period
17	Early and medieval to 1800
18	19th century
19	20th century

.x	Periodicals. Societies. Collections. Sources and documents
.x1	Minor collections
.x3	General works. Description and travel
.x4	Antiquities
.x45	Ethnography
.x47	Social life and customs. Civilization. Culture
.x5	History
	Early and medieval
.x6	Works through 1800
.x62	Works, 1801-
.x7	17th-18th centuries
.x8	19th-20th centuries
.x9	Special topics

TABLES

.x	Periodicals. Societies. Collections
	May include "Sources and documents"
.x1	Sources and documents
	If preferred, may class with "Periodicals. Societies. Collections"
.x3	General works. Description and travel
.x35	Antiquities
.x4	Biography
	In general, class individual biography with the period
.x5	History
	By period
	Early and medieval
	General works
.x6	Through 1800
.x62	1801-
.x64	15th-16th centuries
.x7	17th-18th centuries
.x8	19th-20th centuries
.x9	Other

	Instructions for constructing Cutter numbers using this table: Delete the final digit from the first Cutter number of the span to which this table applies, and substitute the resulting Cutter for .x1 in this table. Delete the final digit from the last Cutter number of the span to which the table applies, and substitute the resulting Cutter for .x2 in this table. Example: For the span DP702.B61-B70, delete the digit "1" from the Cutter "B61" and substitute the resulting Cutter (B6) for .x1 in the table, yielding the Cutters .B61, .B62, .B63, .B64, .B65, .B655, .B67, .B68, and .B69. Delete the digit "0" from the Cutter "B70" and substitute the resulting Cutter (B7) for .x2 in the table, yielding the Cutter .B7.
.x11	Periodicals. Societies. Collections
.x12	Biography
.x13	Dictionaries. Gazetteers. Directories, etc.
.x14	Guidebooks
.x15	General works. Description and travel
.x155	Social life and customs. Civilization. Intellectual life
	History
	By period
.x17	Early and medieval
.x18	16th-18th centuries
.x19	19th-20th centuries
.x2	Other

TABLES

1	Periodicals. Societies. Serials
2	Museums, exhibitions, etc.
3	Sources and documents. Collections
4	Gazetteers
4.5	Directories
5	Guidebooks
6	General works
6.5	Monumental and picturesque
	Including castles, cathedrals, monuments, etc.
	Description and travel
7	Early through 1500
7.2	1501-1800
7.6	1801-1900
8	1901-1950
8.2	1951-
	Cantonal capital
	Including guidebooks, etc.
9	General works
9.2	Directories
	Biography
	see 12, 19.3, etc.
9.3	Earliest history and description (Roman and Celtic)
9.4	Middle ages to 1477
9.5	1477-1802
9.6	19th-20th centuries
9.8	Streets. Buildings. Institutions
9.9	Other special
	Antiquities
10	General works
10.3	Roman period
10.5	Medieval
10.7	Social life and customs. Civilization. Intellectual life
	Ethnography
10.8	General works
10.82.A-Z	Individual elements in the population, A-Z
10.82.C46	Chileans
10.82.P64	Poles
10.82.W47	West Africans
	History
11	Dictionaries, tables, etc.
12	Biography and memoirs (Collective)
	Historiography
13	General works
	Biography of historians and antiquarians
13.3	Collective
13.5.A-Z	Individual, A-Z

	History -- Continued
	General works
14	Through 1800
15	1801-
16	General special
	By period
17	Early and medieval
	15th century
17.5	General works
	Biography and memoirs
17.53	Collective
17.54.A-Z	Individual, A-Z
	16th-17th centuries
18	General works
	Biography and memoirs
18.53	Collective
18.54.A-Z	Individual, A-Z
	18th century
19	General works
	Biography and memoirs
19.3	Collective
19.35.A-Z	Individual, A-Z
19.5	1789-1815
	1789-1800
	see DQ140
	19th century
19.6	General works
	Biography and memoirs
19.7	Collective
19.75.A-Z	Individual, A-Z
	20th century
20	General works
	Biography and memoirs
20.3	Collective
20.35.A-Z	Individual, A-Z

TABLES

.x	This number not used
.x1	Periodicals. Societies. Serials
.x13	Museums, exhibitions, etc.
	Subarrange by author
.x15	Congresses
.x2	Sources and documents
.x23	Gazetteers, directories, dictionaries, etc.
.x25	Biography (Collective)
.x3	General works. Description and travel. Guidebooks
.x4	Antiquities
.x45	Social life and customs. Civilization
.x46	Ethnography
.x5	History (General)
	By period
	Including history and description and travel
.x6	Early
.x7	Medieval and early modern
.x8	Modern
	Biography and memoirs
.x82	Collective
.x83A-.x83Z	Individual, A-Z
.x9	Special topics (not A-Z)

1	Periodicals. Societies. Sources and documents
2	Description and travel. Guidebooks
	Including biography, antiquities, social life and customs, civilization
3	History

.x	This number not used
.x1	Periodicals. Societies. Serials
.x13	Museums, exhibitions, etc.
	Subarrange by author
.x15	Congresses
.x2	Sources and documents
.x3	Gazetteers, directories, dictionaries, etc.
.x35	Biography (Collective)
.x4	General works. Description and travel. Guidebooks.
	Geography
.x45	Antiquities
.x47	Social life and customs. Civilization. Intellectual life
.x48	Ethnography
	History
.x5	General works
	By period
.x6	Early and medieval
.x7	16th-18th centuries
.x8	19th-20th centuries
.x9	Special topics (not A-Z)

1	Periodicals. Societies. Serials
2	General works. Description and travel. History

        Including antiquities, social life and customs, civilization, biography

Instructions for constructing Cutter numbers using this table: Delete the final digit from the first Cutter number of the span to which this table applies, and substitute the resulting Cutter for .x1 in this table. Delete the final digit from the last Cutter number of the span to which the table applies, and substitute the resulting Cutter for .x2 in this table. Example: For the span DP302.G81-G95, delete the digit "1" from the Cutter "G81" and substitute the resulting Cutter (G8) for .x1 in the table, yielding the Cutters .G81, .G82, .G83A1-.G83A29, .G83A3-.G83Z, .G84, .G85, .G86, .G865, .G867, .G868, .G869, .G87, .G88, and .G89. Delete the digit "5" from the Cutter "G95" and substitute the resulting Cutter (G9) for .x2 in the table, yielding the Cutters .G9, .G91 .G92, .G93, and .G95.

.x11	Periodicals. Societies. Collections
.x12	Congresses. Conferences, etc.
	Biography
.x13A1-.x13A29	Collective
.x13A3-.x13Z	Individual, A-Z
.x14	Dictionaries. Gazetteers. Directories, etc.
.x15	Guidebooks
.x16	General works. Description and travel. Views. Geography
.x165	Antiquities
.x167	Social life and customs. Civilization
.x168	Ethnography
	History
.x169	Study and teaching
.x17	General works
.x18	General special
	By period
.x19	Earliest (Roman and Gothic)
.x2	Moorish, 750-1492
.x21	1492-1789
.x22	1789-1815
.x23	19th-20th centuries
.x25	Other

A

American press
  World War I: D632
Americans in Denmark: DL142.A43
Americans in England: DA125.A6
Americans in France: DC34.5.A44
  Paris: DC718.A44
Americans in Germany: DD78.A52
  Berlin: DD867.5.A42
Americans in Greece: DF747.A5
Americans in Italy: DG457.A75
Americans in Russia: DK34.A45
Americans in Soviet Union: DK34.A45
Americans in Spain: DP53.A43
Americans in Sweden: DL641.A49
Americans of Japanese descent
  World War II: D769.8.A6
Americas
  World War II: D768+
Amerina, Via: DG29.A4
Amersfoort (Netherlands): DJ411.A45
Amiata, Monte (Italy): DG55.A53
Amiens, Battle of, 1870: DC309.A5
Amiens (France): DC801.A51
  Treaty of, 1802: DC222.5
Amiternum (Italy): DG70.A576
Ammersee (Germany): DD801.A47
Amphibious operations
  World War II: D784.5+
Amphicthyonic Council, 336 B.C.:
  DF234.31
Amphipolis (Greece): DF261.A47
Amphissian War, 339-338 B.C.:
  DF233.55
Amphitheaters
  Roman antiquities: DG135.5
Amphoras
  Greek and Roman antiquities:
    DE61.A55
  Roman antiquities: DG97.2
Ampurdán (Spain): DP302.A39
Ampurias (Spain): DP402.A47
Amrum (Germany): DD801.A48
Amsterdam (Netherlands): DJ411.A5+
Anagni (Italy): DG70.A578
Anarchism
  Polish Revolution, 1905: DK4389.A52
  Russian Revolution: DK265.9.A5

Anarchism
  World War I: D639.A64
  World War II: D810.A6
Anarchists
  Russian Revolution: DK265.9.A5
  World War I: D639.A64
  World War II: D810.A6
Anastasius, Emperor of the East
  I: DF567
  II: DF578.5
Ancares Mountains (Spain):
  DP302.A395
Ancient Greece: DF10+
Ancient history: D51+
Ancient Italy: DG11+
Ancient nations: D78+
Ancona (Italy)
  Ancient: DG70.A58
  Modern: DG975.A48+
Ancus Marcius, King of Rome:
  DG233.6
Andalusia (Spain): DP302.A41+
Andersen, Jens, called Beldenak:
  DL183.9.A6
Andorra: DC921+
Andrae, Carl Christopher G.: DL228.A5
András (Endre) II: DB929.6+
Andräs III: DB929.8
Andrássy, Gyula, gróf: DB941.A6
Andreĭ Bogoliūbskiĭ, Grand Duke of
  Vladimir-Suzdal': DK83
Andronicus, Emperor of the East
  I Comnenus: DF608.3
  II Palaeologus: DF636+
  III Palaeologus: DF637
  IV (Rival emperor): DF638
Andros Island (Greece)
  Ancient: DF261.A5
  Modern: DF901.A6
Aneo Valley (Spain): DP302.A56
Angeln (Germany): DD801.A53
Angera (Italy): DG70.A583
Angers (France): DC801.A55
Angevin dynasty: DA200+
  Croatia: DR1559+
Anglesey (Wales): DA740.A5
Anglo-Dutch War, 1672-1674: DJ193

Boyen, Hermann von: DD418.6.B7
Boyne, Battle of the: DA945
Brabant (Belgium): DH801.B7+
Brabant, North (Netherlands): DJ401.B7+
Bradford, Yorkshire (England): DA690.B7
Braga (Portugal)
  City: DP802.B7
  District: DP702.B46+
Bragança, Duarte Nuno de Bragança, duque de: DP671.B7
Bragança (Portugal): DP702.B61+
Braganza, House of: DP632
Bramstedt (Germany): DD901.B63
Braña Region (Spain): DP302.B73
Brandenburg (Germany)
  City: DD901.B65
  Province: DD801.B68+
Brandt, Willy: DD260.8+
Branković, Đorđe, grof: DR2004.5.B7
Branting, Hjalmar: DL865.B7
Braşov (Romania): DR296.B74
Brasso (Romania): DR296.B74
Bratislava (Slovakia): DB3100+
Braunau (Czechoslovakia): DB879.B49
Braunschweig (Germany): DD901.B95
Brauron (Greece): DF261.B77
Brazil
  World War II: D768.3
Breadalbane (Scotland): DA880.B76
Brecknockshire (Wales): DA740.B8
Breda, Peace of, 1667: D274.6
Breda, Siege of, 1624-1625: DH206.B8
Bregaglia (Switzerland): DQ841.B8
Bregenz (Austria): DB879.B5
Breisgau (Germany): DD801.B7+
Bremen (Germany)
  City: DD901.B7+
  Province: DD801.B793
Bremerhavn (Germany): DD901.B82
Brescia (Italy)
  Ancient: DG70.B8
  Modern: DG975.B77+
Brescia, Ten Days, 1849: DG553.5.B74
Bressanone (Italy)
  Ancient: DG70.B82

Bressanone (Italy)
  Modern: DG975.B855
Brest (France): DC801.B83+
Bretigny, Peace of, 1360: DC99.5.B7
Bretons in France
  Paris: DC718.B72
Briand, Aristide: DC373.B7
Brianza (Italy): DG975.B86
Bricks
  Roman antiquities: DG97.3
Bridges
  Ancient Rome: DG28+
  Ancient Rome (City): DG67
  London: DA689.B8
Bridges of the Rhine (World War I): D650.B7
Brie (France): DC611.B92
Bright, John: DA565.B8
Brighton (England): DA690.B78
Brindisi (Italy)
  City: DG70.B83
  Province: DG55.B74
Bristol (England): DA690.B8
  World War II: D760.8.B7
Bristow (England): DA690.B84
British Empire: DA10+
British in France: DC34.5.B75
  Paris: DC718.B74
British in Italy
  Rome: DG807.8.B75
  Sicily: DG865.8.B7
British in Papal States: DG796.7.B7
British in Portugal: DP543.B7
British in Russia: DK34.B7
British in Soviet Union: DK34.B7
British in Spanish Civil War: DP269.47.B7
British in Turkey: DR435.B74
British Islands: DA668
Brittany (Bretagne): DC611.B841+
Britton, John: DA93.B7
Brivadois (France): DC611.B923
Brno (Czechoslovakia)
  City: DB2650.B75
  Region: DB2500.B75
Brock, Eske: DL190.5.B7
Brömsebro, Treaty of, 1645: DL190

E

East Africa
  World War II: D766.84
East Anglia (England): DA670.E13+
  World War I: D547.8.E3
East Asia
  World War II
    Reconstruction: D829.E2
East Downing (England)
  World War II: D760.8.E3
East End (London): DA685.E1
East Europeans in Germany:
  DD281.2.E27
East Friesland (Germany): DD801.E23
East Frisian Islands (Germany):
  DD801.E23
East Indians in Netherlands: DJ92.E3
East London: DA685.E1
East Lothian (Scotland): DA880.E2
Easter Rising, 1916 (Ireland): DA962
Eastern Europe: DJK1+
Eastern Hemisphere: D890+
Eastern Mediterranean
  World War II: D766+
Eastern military operations
  World War I: D550+
Eastern question
  19th century: D371+
  20th century: D461+
Eating
  Greek antiquities: DF100
  Roman antiquities: DG101
Ebbesen, Niels: DL176.8A.E2
Ebert, Friedrich: DD247.E2
  Administration: DD249
Eboli, Ana de Mendoza y la Cerda,
  princesa de: DP181.E2
Ebro River and Valley (Spain):
  DP302.E2
Eckardstein, Hermann, freiherr von:
  DD231.E25
Eckmühl, Battle of, 1809: DC234.3
Ecology
  Greek and Roman antiquities:
    DE61.E25

Economic aspects
  Holocaust, Jewish (1939-1945):
    D804.7.E26
  Poland
    Revolution, 1830-1832: DK4363.E3
  Russian Revolution: DK265.9.E2
  Spanish Civil War: DP269.8.E2
  World War I: D635
  World War II: D800
  Yugoslav War, 1991-1995:
    DR1313.7.E36
Economics
  Ancient Rome: DG85
Eden, Anthony: DA566.9.E28
Edessa (Latin Kingdom of Jerusalem):
  D190
Edgar, King of England: DA154.5
Edgar, King of Scotland: DA781.5
Edinburgh Castle: DA890.E4C3
Edinburgh (Scotland): DA890.E2+
Edinburghshire (Scotland): DA880.M6
Edirne (Istanbul): DR741.E4
Edirne (Turkey), Siege, 1912-1913:
  DR46.9.E3
Edmund, King of England
  I: DA154.2
  II Ironside: DA154.75
Edmund, Saint, King of East Anglia:
  DA152.5.E2
Edred, King of England: DA154.3
Education
  Greek antiquities: DF95
  Roman antiquities: DF95
Education and the Spanish Civil War:
  DP269.8.E38
Education and the war
  Yugoslav War, 1991-1995:
    DR1313.7.E38
Education and World War I: D639.E2+
Education and World War II: D810.E2+
Edward Augustus, Duke of Kent:
  DA506.A6
Edward, King of England
  I: DA229
  II: DA230
  III: DA233
  IV: DA258

Edward, King of England
 the Confessor: DA154.8
 the Elder: DA154
 the Martyr: DA154.6
 V: DA259
 VI: DA345+
 VII, King of Great Britain: DA567+
 VIII: DA580+
Edwy, King of England: DA154.4
Eger River and Valley (Czechoslovakia):
 DB2500.O57
Egerland (Czechoslovakia):
 DB2500.C54
Eggmühl, Battle of, 1809: DC234.3
Egmont, Lamoral, comte d': DH188.E3
Egnatia (Italy): DG70.G57
Egnatia, Via: DG29.E34
Egypt
 Athenian expedition to: DF227.77
 Conquest by Alexander: DF234.45
 World War I: D568.2
 World War II: D766.9
Egypt and Syria, Expedition to, 1798-
 1799: DC225+
Egyptians in France: DC34.5.E35
Egyptians in Italy: DG225.E43
Egyptians in Macedonia: DR2174.E36
Egyptians in West Germany:
 DD258.55.E35
Eichstätt (Germany): DD901.E25
Eider River and Valley (Germany):
 DD801.E25
Eiderstedt (Germany): DD801.E26
Eidsvold (Norway): DL596.E3
Eifel (Germany): DD801.E272
Eiger (Switzerland): DQ841.E47
Einaudi, Luigi: DG579.E4
Einsiedeln (Switzerland): DQ851.E3
Eion, Capture of: DF227.6
Eire, 1937-1949: DA963
El-Arish, Convention of, 1800:
 DC226.E4
Elagabalus, Emperor of Rome: DG303
Elatea (Greece): DF261.E3
Elba (Italy)
 Ancient: DG55.E45
 Modern: DG975.E3

Elba (Italy)
 Napoleon: DC211
Elbe River: DD801.E3
Elbe River (Czechoslovakia):
 DB2500.L33
Elbe River (Germany): DD801.E3
Elbe Sandstone Rocks
 (Czechoslovakia): DB2500.E53
Elchingen, Battle of, 1805: DC227.5.E6
Eleanor of Aquitaine, Consort of Henry
 II: DA209.E6
Electronic information resources
 Eastern Europe: DJK7.75
Eleia (Greece)
 Ancient: DF261.P94
 Modern: DF901.E44
Elena, Consort of Victor Emanuel III:
 DG575.A2
Elephants
 Greek and Roman antiquities:
 DE61.E5
Eleusis (Greece): DF261.E4
Eleutherna (Greece): DF261.E413
Elgin, James Bruce, 8th Earl of:
 DA17.E4
Elginshire (Scotland): DA880.M8
Elis (Greece): DF261.E42
Elisa (Bonaparte family): DC216.83
Elisabeth Christine, Consort of Frederick
 II, King of Prussia: DD404.5
Elisabeth, Consort of Christian II, King
 of Denmark: DL183.9.E38
Elisabeth, Consort of Francis Joseph I:
 DB88
Elisabeth, Princess of France: DC137.4
Elizabeth, Consort of Albert I:
 DH685.E5
Elizabeth, Consort of Charles I, King of
 Romania (Carmen Sylva): DR254
Elizabeth, Consort of George VI:
 DA585.A2
Elizabeth, Empress of Russia, 1741-
 1762: DK161
Elizabeth I, Queen of England: DA350+
Elizabeth II, Queen of Great Britain:
 DA590+

Italians in Australia
  Internment
    World War II: D767.83.A98
Italians in Austria: DB34.I8
Italians in Belgium: DH492.I8
Italians in Dalmatia: DR1625.5.I8
Italians in England: DA125.I85
Italians in Europe: D1056.2.I82
Italians in France: DC34.5.I8
  Paris: DC718.I73
Italians in Germany: DD78.I77
Italians in Poland: DK4121.5.I8
Italians in Portugal: DP534.I73,
  DP543.I8
Italians in Russia: DK34.I73
Italians in Scotland: DA774.4.I732
Italians in Slovenia: DR1374.I8
Italians in Soviet Union: DK34.I73
Italians in Sweden: DL641.I8
Italians in Switzerland: DQ49.I9
Italians in Turkey
  Istanbul: DR727.I75
Italians in Ukraine: DK508.425.I73
Italians in Yugoslavia: DR1230.I8
Italic peoples (General): DG221+
Italy: DG11+
  World War I: D520.I7, D617
  World War II: D763.I8+
Italy, Pre-Roman: DG221+
Ithaca Island (Greece): DF221.I84
  Ancient: DF261.I87
  Modern: DF901.I8
Itineraria: DG28+
Ittigen (Switzerland): DQ851.I76
Ittireddu (Italy): DG70.I87
I͡Uriĭ II: DK86
I͡Urii III: DK94
Ivailo, Tsar of Bulgaria: DR80.65
Ivan
  I Kalita: DK96
  II: DK98
  III: DK101+
  IV (The Terrible): DK106+
  VI: DK159
Ivan Alexander, Tsar of Bulgaria:
  DR80.7
Ivan Asen I, Tsar of Bulgaria: DR80.3

Ivan Asen II, Tsar of Bulgaria: DR80.6
Ivan Shishman, Tsar of Bulgaria:
  DR80.8
Ivan Vladislav: DR77.8
Ivankovac, Battle of: DR2015.7
Iwo Jima
  World War II: D767.99.I9
Izaro Island (Spain): DP302.I93
Izmir (Turkey)
  Greek war with Turkey, 1921-1922:
    DF845.53.I94

J

Jacobins: DC178
Jacoby, Johann: DD211.J2
Jaćwież in Poland: DK4121.5.J32
Jadwiga: DK4249.5
Jaederen (Norway): DL576.J2
Jaegersborg (Denmark): DL291.J28
Jaén, Occupation of, 1808-1813:
  DC233.J34
Jaen (Spain): DP302.J1
Jagiellons: DK4249.7+
Jahn, Friedrich Ludwig: DD205.J3
Jaime, King of Aragon
  I: DP129+
  II: DP130.3+
Jalón River and Valley (Spain):
  DP302.J16
Jamaica
  World War I: D547.J3
James, King of England
  I: DA391+
  II: DA450+
James, King of Scotland
  I: DA783.6
  II: DA783.7
  III: DA783.8
  IV: DA784.5+, DA784.5
  V: DA784.7
James, Prince of Wales, the Old
  Pretender: DA814.A3
Jämtland (Sweden): DL971.J3
Jan Lucemburský, King of Bohemia:
  DB2102
Janina (Greece): DF951.I5

Monuments
  Greek and Roman antiquities:
    DE61.M65
  Russian Revolution: DK265.95
  Russian Revolution, 1905: DK264.7
  Spanish Civil War: DP269.8.M4
  World War II: D830+
Monza (Italy): DG975.M73
Monzani, Cirillo: DG556.M65
Moordorf (Germany): DD901.M62513
Moore, Sir John: DA68.12.M8
Moorish domination and reconquest
  (Spain): DP97.3+
Moors in Spain: DP100+
  Valencia: DP302.V203
    Expulsion, 1609: DP302.V225
Moral and ethical aspects
  Holocaust, Jewish (1939-1945):
    D804.7.M67
  Kosovo Civil War, 1998-1999:
    DR2087.6.M67
Morat, Battle of, 1476: DQ104
Morata, Olympia Fulvia: DG540.8.M7
Moravia: DB2300+
Moray (Scotland): DA880.M8
Morbihan (France): DC611.M831+
Mordvins in Russia: DK34.M6
Mordvins in Russia (Federation):
  DK510.35.M67
Mordvins in Soviet Union: DK34.M6
More, Thomas, Saint: DA334.M8
Morea (Greece): DF261.P3
Moreau, Jean Victor M.: DC146.M8
Moresenet (Belgium): DH801.M6
Morgantina (Sicily): DG70.M66
Morgarten, Battle of, November 15:
  DQ94
Morini (Celtic people) in France:
  DC62.2.M67
Morinie (Brittany): DC611.M859
Moriscos after 1516: DP104
Morley, John Morley, Viscount:
  DA565.M78
Mornay, Philippe de, seigneur du
  Plessis-Marley: DC112.M9
Morny, Charles Auguste, L.J., duc de:
  DC280.5.M7

Moroccans: DP53.M65
Moroccans in Belgium: DH492.M65
Moroccans in France: DC34.5.M7
Moroccans in Germany: DD78.M67
Moroccans in Italy: DG457.M67
Moroccans in Netherlands: DJ92.M68
Moroccans in Portugal: DP534.M67
Morocco, Expedition to, 1578: DP614
Morvan (France): DC611.M891+
Mosaic pavements
  Roman antiquities: DG141
Moscow (Russia): DK588+
  Burning of, 1812: DC235.5.M8
Moselle (France): DC611.M897+
Moselle River and Valley (Germany):
  DD801.M7
  Roman period: DG59.M74
Möser, Justus: DD192.M6
Moslem civilization (Spain): DP103
Mosley, Sir Oswald, Bart: DA574.M6
Moss (Norway): DL596.M7
Moti in Romania: DR214.M68
Motion pictures
  World War I: D522.23
  World War II: D743.23
Motion pictures about the Spanish Civil
  War: DP269.8.M6
Motorcycle troops
  World War II
    Germany: D757.64
Motya (Mozia), San Pantaleo Island
  (Sicily): DG70.M67
Mountain troops
  World War II (Germany): D757.39+,
    D757.39
Moura, Christovão de, marquez de
  Castello Rodrigo: DP629.M7
Mouthier-en-Bresse (France):
  DC611.M925
Mouthpieces (Grave goods)
  Greek antiquities: DF101.2
Mowbray, Vale of (England): DA670.M9
Möwe (Steamship)
  World War I: D582.M6
Mozambicans in Germany:
  DD281.2.M68
Møen (Denmark): DL271.M7

Public men
Netherlands: DJ105
Public opinion
April Uprising, 1876 (Bulgaria):
DR83.76.P83
Franco-Prussian War: DC326.5.P82
Hungarian Revolution, 1848-1849:
DB938+
Russian Revolution: DK265.9.P8
Russian Revolution, 1905:
DK264.5.P8
Spanish Civil War: DP269.8.P8
Stalin era: DK269.5
World War I: D639.P87+
World War II: D810.P8+
Yugoslav War, 1991-1995:
DR1313.7.P83
Public opinion, Foreign
Russian Revolution: DK265.9.F55
Publicity
World War I: D631+
World War II: D798+
Pückler-Muskau, Hermann, fürst:
D352.8.P3
Puenteáreas (Spain)
Partido Judicial: DP302.P75
Puerta del Sol (Madrid): DP367.P84
Puglia (Italy): DG55.A65
Modern: DG975.A65
Pulcheria, Co-Empress and sister of
Theodosius II: DF562.5
Pultusk, Battle of, 1807: DC230.P6
Punakaarti: DL1075.P86
Punic War, First: DG243+
Punic War, Second: DG247+
Punic War, Third: DG252.6
Punic Wars: DG242
Purbeck, Isle of (England): DA670.P98
Puteoli (Italy): DG70.P9
Puy-de-Dôme (France): DC611.P9798
Pylona (Greece): DF221.P94
Pylos (Greece): DF261.P94
Battle of, 1827: DF810.N3
Pym, John: DA396.P9
Pyrenees-Atlantiques (France):
DC611.P98+

Pyrenees (General, and French):
DC611.P98+
Pyrenees, Peace of the, 1659:
DC124.45
Pyrenees (Spain): DP302.P8
Pyrgi (Italy): DG70.P95
Pyrrhus, King of Epirus: DF235.48.P9

Q

Quadrado José Maria: DP63.7.Q3
Quadruple Alliance
1718: D287.5
1815: D383
Quakers in England: DA125.Q34
Quantock Hills (England): DA670.Q2
Quartermaster base depots (World War
II): D769.753
Quartermaster Corps (U.S. Army)
World War I: D570.75
Quartier Barbette (Paris): DC752.Q2
Quartier Latin (Paris): DC752.L38
Quartier Saint-Georges (Paris):
DC752.Q67
Quartier Saint Victor (Paris): DC752.Q8
Queens: D107.3
Queen's County (Ireland): DA990.L6
Queen's Own Oxfordshire Hussars
World War I: D547.Q18
Queen's Own Royal West Kent
Regiment
World War I: D547.Q2
Queen's Westminster and Civil Service
Rifles
World War I: D547.Q3
Quercy (France): DC611.Q4
Quiberon Expedition, 1795:
DC218.3.Q5
Quillinan, Luiz de: DP661.Q8
Quisling, Vidkun: DL529.Q5

R

Rabochaia oppozītsīa
Russian Revolution: DK265.9.R25
Race problems
World War I: D639.A7

INDEX

Race problems
World War II: D810.R3
Rachis, King of Lombardy: DG514.3
Radar
World War II: D810.R33
Radetzky von Radetz, Johann Joseph
W.A.F.K, graf: DB90.R2
Radić, Stjepan: DR1589.R33
Radio
World War II: D798+
Radio broadcasting
Kosovo Civil War, 1998-1999:
DR2087.6.R34
Radio, radar, etc
World War I: D639.T35
World War II: D810.R33
Radnorshire (Wales): DA740.R3
Radović, Andrija: DR1879.5.R33
Radziwill, Elise, Polish princess:
DD223.9
Radziwill, Luise, ksiezna: DD416.R2
Raginbert, King of Lombardy: DG513.6
Ragusa (Italy): DG70.R34
Railroad employees
Russian Revolution, 1905:
DK264.5.T7
Rainier III, Prince of Monaco:
DC943.R3
Rais, Gilles de Laval, seigneur de:
DC102.8.R2
Räkóczi Uprising (Hungary): DB932.4
Rákosi, Mátyás: DB956.6.R34
Rakovica Rebellion, 1871 (Croatia):
DR1581.5
Rakovski, Georgi Stoikov: DR83.2.R3
Raleigh, Sir Walter: DA86.22.R2
Rambervillers, Battle of, October 9,
1870: DC309.R2
Rambouillet (France): DC801.R16
Ramiro, King of Aragon
II: DP127.2, DP127.8
Ramiro, King of Asturias
I: DP150
II: DP151.7
III: DP152.3
Ramon-Berenguer, King of Aragon:
DP128.3

Rance River (Côtes-du-Nord) France:
DC611.R237
Randers (Denmark): DL271.R2
Ranke, Leopold von: D15.R3
Rantzau, Daniel: DL188.8.R3
Rantzau, Henrik: DL188.8.R32
Raoul (Rodolphe), King of France:
DC79.7
Rappoltstein (Germany): DD801.R12
Raška, Rise of: DR1983
Rasputin, Grigorii Efimovich: DK254.R3
Rastatt, Congress of, 1797-1799:
DC222.R3
Rathenau, Walther: DD231.R3
Ratisbon, Electoral Assembly of, 1630:
D267.R3
Ratisbon (Germany): DD901.R4
Ratzeburg (Germany): DD801.R15
Ravanusa (Italy): DG70.R36
Ravenna (Italy)
Ancient: DG70.R37
Modern: DG975.R25
Ravensberg (Germany): DD901.R42
Razumovskii family (Biography):
DK37.8.R3
Re Island (France): DC611.R281+
Reading (England): DA690.R28
Reading, Rufus Daniel Isaacs, 1st
Marquis of: DA566.9.R3
Reate (Italy): DG70.R4
Rebecca Riots, 1839-1844: DA722+
Rebellion of 1703 (Turkey): DR541.3
Rebellion of 1798 (Ireland): DA949+
Rebellion of 1875 (Bosnia and
Hercegovina): DR1720+
Rebellion of the priests, 1775 (Malta):
DG992.65
Rebellion of the Turkish slaves, 1722
(Maltal): DG992.62
Récamier, Jeanne Françoise J.A.
(Bernard): DC255.R3
Rechberg, Hans von: DD171.5.R2
Recklinghausen (Germany):
DD901.R425
Reconnaissance battalions
World War II (United States):
D769.3058

GPO U.S. GOVERNMENT PRINTING OFFICE: 2007–330–111/60006